Money, Morality and Law

International Banking and Finance Law Series

VOLUME 36

Series Editors

Professor Joseph Norton, Professor Ross Buckley and Professor Douglas Arner.

Subjects

Topical issues in international banking and financial services law, such as regulatory responses to the global financial crisis or regulation of alternative investment funds.

Objective & Readership

To provide authoritative analysis of trends and complex subjects for academics, regulators and practitioners involved in international banking and financial services law.

The titles published in this series are listed at the end of this volume.

Money, Morality and Law

A Case for Financial Crisis Accountability

Gerald Nels Olson

Wolters Kluwer

Published by:
Kluwer Law International B.V.
PO Box 316
2400 AH Alphen aan den Rijn
The Netherlands
E-mail: international-sales@wolterskluwer.com
Website: lrus.wolterskluwer.com

Sold and distributed in North, Central and South America by:
Wolters Kluwer Legal & Regulatory U.S.
7201 McKinney Circle
Frederick, MD 21704
United States of America
Email: customer.service@wolterskluwer.com

Sold and distributed in all other countries by:
Air Business Subscriptions
Rockwood House
Haywards Heath
West Sussex
RH16 3DH
United Kingdom
Email: international-customerservice@wolterskluwer.com

Printed on acid-free paper.

Printed and bound by CPI Group (UK) Ltd, Croydon, CR0 4YY

ISBN 978-94-035-0941-9

e-Book: ISBN 978-94-035-0980-8
web-PDF: ISBN 978-94-035-1024-8

About the Author

Dr. Gerald Nels (Jerry) Olson is President, G N Olson & Company, LLC, Advisory Services, and Adjunct Professor, Banking Law and Regulation and Global Financial Markets Regulation, Southern Methodist University, Dedman School of Law, Dallas, Texas (2009–). Jerry served as Senior Visiting Fellow at the Centre for Commercial Law Studies, Queen Mary College, University of London (1994–1999). Is the author of *Banks in Distress, Lessons from the American Experience of the 1980s (2000); Subprime Meltdown—It's all About Money (Implications for Commercial Property Investment) (2008); as well as* Bachelor of Arts Degree University of North Texas. Juris Doctor Degree Southern Methodist University. Doctor of Philosophy Degree from Queen Mary College, University of London. Jerry has written and lectured extensively on legal and business aspects of banking and finance in the US and internationally in England, Europe and South America. He is also the author of more than 30 professional papers and 13 book chapters. He has made more than 20 personal presentations at prestigious international conferences. Author of more than 30 Confidential White Papers addressing clients' interests and issues of business, operations, legal, accounting, regulatory, and valuation issues affecting commercial real estate, banking, finance, investment and capital markets. Written and lectured extensively on legal and business aspects of banking and finance in the United States, internationally in England, Europe and South America.

Over the past two thousand years, kings, queens and noblemen of every station have lost their heads and empires have fallen at the hands of outraged citizens impoverished and devastated by the ravages of money debasement.

Money debasement by the state and its instruments is systemic, intentional fraud. It constitutes lying cheating and stealing, at the most fundamental and vulnerable level of society.

The American Revolution was informed by the public's demand for fair treatment by their government and protection of their civil rights by the rule of law. From the time of *Magna Charta* the English common law protected its citizens' civil right to sound money without debasement under the penalty of death. Article I. Section 8, Clause 5 of the United States Constitution requires that the United States Congress create and regulate the value of American sovereign money.

The United States Congress' first exercise of its power and duty to coin money and regulate its value, the *Coinage Act of 1792*, established the penalty for currency debasement - death - a capital crime.

Money debasement is now the foundation of Washington's and Wall Street's promise of the American Dream; the foundation for the American economy; and for the monetary policy of the Federal Reserve System.

Dishonesty and abuse of power have become a central theme of business models, business plans, an accepted code of conduct, and measure for success in Washington and on Wall Street. Lying, cheating and stealing have become a way of life in Washington and on Wall Street. Washington has lost all credibility, but not wealth and not power. Wall Street has fully exploited the state of affairs. That conclusion is no news to most Americans. The fact that the people have a strong legal case for Washington and Wall Street financial crisis accountability is news. As we face the prospect of the next financial crisis, ordinary Americans must take the initiative, take action, legal action, to restore the our country's moral foundation and primacy of the American rule of law

America's six largest Wall Street banks, the American government, specifically Congress, the Executive Branch and its financial regulatory agencies and related government sponsored entities, including the Federal Reserve system, Fannie Mae and Freddie Mac and their respective federal regulators, securities regulatory agencies and securities rating agencies caused the financial crisis resulting in more than $20 trillion in financial damages to the American public.

These parties are responsible for the financial stability and integrity of the American financial system. They collectively represent the financial and economic elite of our country. The American public is entitled to reasonably rely on these entities and the individual who control them to perform their respective legal obligations in accordance with their respective applicable legal standard of care.

The group, acting individually and in concert with one another and their respective professional service providers, have intentionally breached their specific legal obligations under the United States Constitution, common law, federal and state statutory law. The American public is entitled to damages caused by these breaches, penalties to deter future illegal activity and equitable relief imposed by the judicial system to assure future legal compliance.

Congress has failed to regulate the value of the sovereign money of the United States. Financial institutions have capitalized on that failure to intentionally manipulate and to misrepresent the dollar value of their assets, debase the value, and to corrupt and misrepresent the value and liquidity of credit created through this system.

They have abused their monopoly power over the financial system to concentrate wealth and power amongst themselves, robbing the American public of the value of the fruits of their labor and savings and destroying to a great extent the functioning of the American economy.

They have systematically misappropriated the income and wealth of the American public. The case made in this work is based on the existing American rule of law. The legal case is the only civilized relief available to ordinary Americans. The United States Department of Justice has ignored its duty to the American public. The United States Attorneys General have been and remain creatures of Wall Street. Their failure to make the case described here and impose legal, financial and economic accountability upon Washington and Wall Street will likely lead to civil disobedience, resulting ultimately in violence. That result is an all too common historic response to crimes of the type for which the case made here. The legal case made in this work is the only viable and civilized alternative available to ordinary Americans to enforce financial crisis accountability.

Commentators on the financial crisis have uniformly reached common agreement on the facts of and moral foundation for these cases. None have heretofore made a legal case for Washington and Wall Street accountability for the financial crisis under the rule of law. This book makes a case.

Table of Contents

About the Author v

Dedication and Acknowledgments xxi

Notes and Disclaimers xxiii

Preface xxv

List of Figures lv

Chapter 1
Introduction 1
§1.01 Context 1
§1.02 True Scope of the Financial Crisis Affecting Ordinary Americans 5
§1.03 Ordinary Americans Have Been Injured in Fact 8
[A] Ordinary American Household Damages 9
[B] How Have Washington and Wall Street Wrought These Damages on Ordinary American Households? 9
§1.04 Money Debasement Constitutes an Intentional Misrepresentation of Money and Assets Denominated in That Money 10
[A] Debasement of American Money and the American Rule of Law 10
[B] Ordinary American's Damages from the Washington's and Wall Street's Money Debasement Constitute Real Injuries in Fact 11
[C] Money Debasement Is an Ancient Crime: An Ancient Tort—It Is Not a New Phenomenon 13
§1.05 The Emperor Has No Clothes 14
[A] American Tolerance of Lying, Cheating and Stealing 16
[B] Why Have Washington and Wall Street Gotten a Free Pass? 20
[C] The Available Heuristic: Staying on Message 20

§1.06 The Washington and Wall Street Enterprise's Message Constitutes a Web of Intentionally False Narratives 22
§1.07 Existing Literature Skirts Legal Accountability for Money Debasement Driven Financial Crises 25
§1.08 Risky Money Manipulation 28
§1.09 Washington and Wall Street Money Manipulation Is Money Debasement 30
[A] Washington and Wall Street Manage Money and Systemic Risk for Their Own Benefit at Public Expense 30
[B] The American Ponzi Scheme 33
[C] In Economics, Debt Is Also a Figment of Language Rather than a Fundamental Concept 33
§1.10 Three Structural Failures 35
[A] Transparency 35
[B] Money as a Tool of Measurement of Liquid Value Is Not Regulated 36
[C] The Washington Wall Street Enterprise Intentionally Manipulates the Value and Liquidity of Money for Its Own Benefit at Public Expense 36
§1.11 The Washington and Wall Street Enterprise 37
[A] The Washington Wall Street Enterprise's Accountability for Financial Crises 37
[B] The Washington Wall Street Enterprise Intentionally Exploits Shadow Banking and Shadow Money to Effect Money Debasement 39
[C] Washington Wall Street Enterprise's Moral and Legal Standards for Accountability 41
§1.12 The Flow of This Work 43

Chapter 2
Money 47
§2.01 The Nature of Money 47
§2.02 Banks and Money Are Inseparable 52
§2.03 Intervention by the State in Money and Banking 53
[A] Regulation of Money and Banks 53
[B] The Principle of Sound Money 54
[C] Importance of Credit Money as Honest, Safe, and Sound Money 56
[D] Honest, Safe, and Sound Money Is Based on Shared Trust and Confidence 57
[E] Literacy, Law, Numeracy, and Accounting 60
[F] Control over Money 63
[G] Fiduciary Issue of Money 64
§2.04 Money in an Ideal System 65
§2.05 Concentration of Money and Power 67
[A] The Banker of Lyon 70

[B] The Sovereign Versus the Bankers 72
[C] Calling the Sovereign to Account 74
[D] Seeds of an Iniquitous Partnership 75
§2.06 The Necessity of a Standard of Value for Sovereign Money and the Final Settlement Medium Asset 76
[A] John Locke's Troublesome Legacy of the Necessity of Commodity Money as Sovereign Money 78
§2.07 The Ancient Understanding of Money and the Foundation of the United States 82
§2.08 A New Understanding of Money Following the Founding of the United States 82
§2.09 Money Is a Basic and Crucial Social Mechanism Based on Moral Principles 84
[A] Fairness Is Crucial to Social Relationships, Especially, Economic, Monetary and Financial Social Relationships 86
[B] The Great Underlying Social, Moral, Political and Economic Conflicts That Plague Modern Day Money and Banking 89
§2.10 Concluding Observations 89

CHAPTER 3
Shadow Money and Shadow Banking 91
§3.01 Credit Money and Shadow Money 91
§3.02 Risk and Uncertainty Are Inherent in Credit Money 95
[A] Risk 95
[B] Uncertainty 95
§3.03 Structured Finance or Structured Credit 96
[A] Sovereign Money and Shadow Money 97
[B] Risk Versus Uncertainty 104
[C] Outside of the Box and Inside the Box 105
§3.04 Moral and Legal Evolution of Shadow Banking 108
[A] The "Real Bills Doctrine" 110
[B] Acceptance Finance 111
[C] Origin of Fiat Money 113
[D] Liquidity and Economic Growth 113
[E] Central Bank Support of Bank Notes 115
[F] Wrapping Shadow Money: Alignment of Liability and Accountability 116
[G] The Trusted Bank and the Trusted Banker 117
[H] Structured Insulation from Liability and Accountability: The Oxymoron of Monetized Long-Term Illiquid Assets 117
§3.05 Sacrifice of Traditional Principles of Commercial Banking Law in Shadow Banking 118
[A] Securities Law as a Poor Substitute for the Law of Money, Commerce and Banking 119
[B] Shadow Banking with No Effective Shadow Banking Law 120

[C] Transfer Payments, Regulatory Manipulation and Failure of Transparency 124
[D] Outside of the Box: The Shadow Banking System 127
[E] Inside the Box: Traditional Banking System 127
[1] Where Does Liquidity Go in a Liquidity Crisis? 127
[2] Shadow Banking Money Acting as Liquid Sovereign Money at Par 132
[3] Repo Markets Create "Fake" Over-Valued Shadow Banking Money on a Massive Scale: Illiquid at Precisely the Time Liquidity Is Required 134
[4] Intentional Misrepresentation of the Value and Liquidity of Shadow Money Through Shadow Banking 136
§3.06 The Fed and Shadow Banking 137
[A] The Conceptual Abuse of Money Derivatives 139
[B] The Federal Reserve System Must Accommodate and Constrain the Shadow Banking System 140
§3.07 Concluding Observations 143

Chapter 4
Money Debasement 145
§4.01 Ancient Crime 145
§4.02 Debasement of the Dollar Is a Matter of Fact 150
[A] Offshore Derivative Trading Has Escaped *Dodd Frank* 153
[B] Dark Pools and High-Speed Trading 154
[C] Washington Wall Street Enterprise Profiteering from US Money Debasement 155
§4.03 Money Debasement and Law 157
[A] Perverse Incentives 158
[B] Circumscribed, Managed and Minimized Financial Crisis Related Legal Accountability 160
[C] Money Debasement Causes Financial Crises Suffered Predominately by Ordinary American Households 164
[D] *Ignorantia Affectata* 166
[E] Money Debasement and The Supreme Court's Announced Monetary Law of the Land 169
[1] Legal Tender Cases 169
[2] Gold Clause Cases 170
§4.04 A Legal Claim Based on the Intentional Tort of Money Debasement Goes to the Heart of Americas Moral and Legal Foundations 170
§4.05 Civil and Criminal Accountability for Money Debasement 171
[A] Surreptitious Insulation from Government Liability and Accountability 173
[B] Creation and Direction of Money from Nothing to Disguise Money Debasement and Wealth Creation 176
[C] A New Risk-Free Economy 179

[D] Risk and Uncertainty 180
§4.06 Money Debasement Redistributes Wealth and Income 184
§4.07 Ordinary Americans Are the American Sovereign 188
§4.08 Concluding Observations 192

CHAPTER 5
Money and Morality 193
§5.01 The Prime Washington Wall Street False Narrative 193
§5.02 Honesty Versus the Ends Justifying the Means 193
[A] The Moral Foundation for Sovereign Money 194
[B] Honor and Honesty Are Integral to American Sovereign and Shadow Money 197
[C] The Twisted Tension of Honor, Honesty, Truth and Justice Surrounding Money in America 198
[1] Debasement of American Money 198
[2] Debasement of Honest Money Drives Debasement of Honesty Throughout American Society 200
§5.03 Failure of Honest Money as a Moral Social Covenant 202
§5.04 False Narrative That Monetary Morality Is Separate from the Law of Money 203
[A] Coincidence of American Morality and the American Law of Money 205
[B] Connections, Identity and Inclusiveness of American Moral Law, Constitutional Law and Civil and Criminal Tort Law Relating to Honest Money 209
[C] Tort of Fraud Versus Fraud as Breach of Contract 214
[1] Honesty 215
[2] Lying 215
[3] Cheating and Stealing 215
[4] Common Law Torts of Deceit, Misrepresentation and Fraud 216
§5.05 Universal or Natural Law, Morality, and Ethics as a Jurisprudential Foundation for the American Rule of the Law of Money 219
[A] Legal Positivism Versus Natural Law: An Echo of Consequentialism Versus Universal Natural Law 219
§5.06 The Moral Foundation of Enforcement of the American Law of Money 224
[A] Washington's and Wall Street's Monetary Duties 224
[B] Weak, Ineffective and Unenforced Duties Comprising American Banking Law and Regulation 227
§5.07 Concluding Observations 228

CHAPTER 6
Degradation of the American Law of Money 233
§6.01 The Tortured Path of the Law of Monetary Duties and Accountability 233
§6.02 The Constitutional Framework for the American Law of Money 235

[A] Constitutional Principles and the American Rule of the Law of Money 238
[B] Money Debasement as a Capital Crime 240
§6.03 American Borrowing Versus Money Debasement to Finance Existential War 244
[A] Constitutional Powers and Duties 244
[B] The Constitutional Convention of 1787 247
§6.04 Greenbacks, the Legal Tender Acts and National Banks as Partners with Washington in the Creation of Money 249
[A] E.G. Spaulding: Civil War Existential Demand for War Exception to Permit Debasement 251
[B] The *Legal Tender Cases* and Paper Money 256
[C] Financial Crisis of 1907: Establishment of the Federal Reserve System and Money Debasement—The *Pujo Report* 258
[1] Tension Between Sovereign Banking and Shadow Banking 258
[2] The *Pujo Report* 260
[3] Jekyll Island, the Aldrich Plan and the Federal Reserve Act 261
[a] The Plan Devised on Jekyll Island 262
[b] The Objectives Discussed in the 1910 Meeting 263
[c] Passing the Federal Reserve Act 263
[d] So What Is the Fed? 264
[e] The Creature from Jekyll Island 265
[4] The Federal Reserve System 266
[5] Reserves Redeemable in Gold under the Federal Reserve Act 269
[6] Reserves Redeemable in Gold Reduced to a “Fraction” of Deposits 269
[7] Reserves No Longer Redeemable in Gold 269
[8] Reserves No Longer Established by Law and Effectively Reduced to Zero 269
[9] The Federal Reserve Act: Too Vague and Nebulous to Enforce 270
[10] What the Fed Does Not Do 273
§6.05 Financial Crisis in 1929: End of the Domestic Gold Standard In 1933—*The Pecora Report* - *Glass Steagall* - The SEC, the FDIC, and Money 275
[A] Another Financial Crisis: Another Report 275
[B] The *Pecora Report* 276
[C] Congress’ 1933 Repudiation of the Exercise of Its Constitutional Power and Duty to Coin Money and Regulate Its Value 277
[D] The Great Depression and World War II 279
[E] The *Gold Clause Cases* 280
§6.06 The Nixon Shock and the Oil Crisis 285
[A] Nixon and OPEC 285

[B] Nixon's Opinion That His Critics Claim That the US Has a Problem of Too Much Liquidity, Is Just Bullshit! 288
[C] US Monetary Policy Became Officially "Money from Nothing" 289
[D] Unconstrained American Money Debasement Created the American Banking and Financial System Crisis of the 1980s and 1990s 290
[E] The Great Financial Crisis in 2008 and Ongoing Money Debasement 293
§6.07 Concluding Observations 295

CHAPTER 7
The Washington Wall Street Enterprise Web of False Narratives 297
§7.01 False Narrative: Ordinary Americans Excess Borrowing Caused the Financial Crisis 297
§7.02 False Narrative: American Economic and Monetary Policy Are Not Constrained by Law 304
§7.03 Although Congress Has the Power It Does Not Necessarily Have the Duty to Regulate the Value of Money 306
§7.04 False Narrative: Tradition Regulation of the Value of Money by a Standard Such as the Gold Standard Is an Anachronism 307
§7.05 False Narrative: Constitutional Money, the Value of Which Is Regulated by Congress Is Obsolete: It Has Been Lawfully—Constitutionally—Superseded by Fiat Money 311
§7.06 False Narrative: The Constraints of Traditional Commercial Law Can Be Replaced Through Conversion of Debt Instruments into Securities Protected only Disclosure Requirement of Securities Laws 313
§7.07 False Narrative: Congress Has Lawfully Delegated to the Fed and the Fed Has Lawfully Delegated to Wall Street the Power and Duty to Create, Emit and Regulate the Value of the Dollar 322
§7.08 Legal Requirements for Congressional Delegation of Powers and Duties 327
[A] False Narrative of Congressional Delegation to the Fed 327
[B] False Narrative: Fed Delegation to the Wall Street Banks 340
[C] False Narrative: The Greenspan Doctrine of Self-Regulating Wall Street Banks 340
§7.09 False Narrative: The Federal Safety Net Protects Ordinary Americans from the Ravages of Money Debasement by Protecting Bank Depositors and Banks too Big to Fail 349
§7.10 False Narrative: Sovereign Money and Shadow Money Can Safely Dwell in Separate Regulatory Spheres 350
§7.11 False Narrative: The Regulated Monetary System Is Separate and Insulated from the Shadow Banking System 354
§7.12 False Narrative: Shadow Money Does Not Act as Sovereign Money 356
§7.13 False Narrative: Dodd Frank Held Washington and Wall Street Accountable for the Financial Crisis 360

[A] Dodd Frank Preceded and Did Not Respond to the Conclusions in the Report 360
[B] The Financial Crisis Inquiry Report 360
§7.14 Concluding Observations 364

CHAPTER 8
False Narrative of Asset Liquidity and Value 367
§8.01 American Economic, Fiscal, Monetary Theory Policy and Action Are Subject and Subordinate to the American Rule of Law 376
§8.02 Deregulation, Liquidity and Asset Values 378
[A] Deregulation: Again 381
[B] Regulation of Money and Banks 381
[C] Safety and Soundness Means Asset Values and Liquidity Are Measured Against Independent Standards and Recorded Honestly 382
[D] Limitations of Banking Law and Regulation 386
§8.03 An Independent Regulated Constitutional Standard of Value Is Essential for the Creation and Circulation of Constitutional, Trusted, Honest, Safe and Sound Sovereign Money in America 387
[A] Creation and Regulation of the Value of Money 387
[B] The Meaning of Safety and Soundness 389
[C] The Degradation of Bank Safety and Soundness to a Euphemism 389
[D] The Bank Regulatory Policy of Extend and Pretend 393
§8.04 Bank Asset Valuation, Liquidity, Safety and Soundness and the Flawed Certainty of Generally Accepted Accounting Principles 397
§8.05 Banks and Bankers Duty and Standard of Care 401
[A] The Reasonable and Prudent Banker 401
[B] Bank Duties and Standards of Care 403
[C] External and Internal Costs of Breach of Duty to Honestly Regulate the Value of Money 405
[D] Shadow Banks Duties and Standards of Care 406
§8.06 Systemic Risk, Banking and Financial Crises 411
§8.07 Chairman Alan Greenspan and the Failure of Bank Regulation 413
§8.08 Concluding Observations 415

CHAPTER 9
Enforcement of Financial Crisis Accountability 419
§9.01 Nature of Claims for Financial Crisis Accountability 419
§9.02 The Tortured Path of the Law of Monetary Duty and Accountability 422
§9.03 Denial of Due Process under and Equal Protection of the Law 424
§9.04 Abuse of Power: Anti-trust, Anti-monopoly and Anti-tying Law 426
§9.05 Bank Fraud and RICO 429
[A] Origin of the Washington Wall Street RICO Enterprise 432

[B] Application of Common Law and the *Restatement (Second) of Torts* § 874A 432
[C] Moral and Legal Character of Honest, Safe, and Sound United States Money 437
[D] The Washington Wall Street Enterprise Has Denied to the American People Due Process and Equal Protection of the Law 440
§9.06 Public Policy and Common Law Precedent for the Case for Financial Crisis Accountability 442
[A] Common Law Evolution into Statutory Laws Regarding Securities Fraud and Crime as a Public Policy Precedent 442
[B] Common Law Evolution into Statutory Consumer Protection Law as a Public Policy Precedent 443
§9.07 Class Action in *Pares Patriae* by One or More States Attorneys General 444
§9.08 Definition of a Class of Plaintiffs in a Case for Financial Crisis Accountability 445
§9.09 Ordinary Americans Have Suffered Discrete, Palpable Injuries in Fact Caused by the Washington Wall Street Enterprise 447
[A] The Wall Street Defendants 447
[B] The Rating Agency Defendants 447
[C] The Washington Defendants 447
§9.10 Practical, Technical and Procedural Issues 448
[A] Immunity Issues 448
[B] Statutes of Limitation 449
[1] Limitations: Abuse of Power—Anti-tying 449
[2] Limitations: RICO Bank Fraud 449
[3] Tolling 449
[C] Standing and Class Certification 450
[1] Threshold Issues Regarding Standing 451
[2] Standing Generally 452
[3] Not a Citizen Suit 453
[4] Justiciability 456
[5] Case or Controversy 459
[6] Advisory Opinions 463
[7] Mootness and Ripeness 464
[8] Judicial Restraint 465
[9] Political Question Doctrine 466
[D] Will the Case Involve a Decision That Has Been Constitutionally Committed to Another Branch? 467
[E] Does the Suit Involve a Lack of Judicially Discoverable and Manageable Standards? 468
[F] Other Baker Factors 468
§9.11 Concluding Observations 471

CHAPTER 10
Concluding Observations 477
§10.01 Washington and Wall Street Are Accountable for the Financial Crisis 477
§10.02 Washington and Wall Street Have Accomplished Their Concentration of Income, Wealth, and Power Through Ancient Crime of Money Debasement 479
§10.03 Enforcement of Financial Crisis Accountability Does Not Pose an Existential Threat to America 484
§10.04 Weak, Ineffective and Unenforced Banking Law and Regulation Proves No Substitute to the Recognition and Enforcement of Washington and Wall Street Fiduciary Monetary Powers and Duties 498
§10.05 First Principles of Moral and Legal Accountability for Abuse of Power and Intentional False Misrepresentation of Asset Value Through Money Debasement 499
§10.06 The Essence of Civil and Criminal Accountability for Financial Crises 502
§10.07 The False Promise of Committee and Regulatory Investigations and Reports 507
§10.08 Financial Crisis Accountability Can Be Found in Our Existing American Law, Accounting and Our Judicial System 508
[A] Equitable Justice and Equitable Relief 508
[B] Award of Compensatory Monetary Damages as Retributive Justice 509
[C] Calculation of Money Damages and Penalties as Retributive Justice 509
[D] The False Dread Specter of a Wall Street Financial Death Sentence 511
§10.09 Restorative Justice 512
§10.10 This Case Is a Civil Rights Case 512
§10.11 Structure Payment of Monetary Damages and Restorative Justice 514
§10.12 Practical Recommendations for Ordinary Americans to Initiate Legal Action for Financial Crises 514
§10.13 Concluding Thoughts and Recommendations 515

End Notes 520

Dedication and Acknowledgments

This book is dedicated to my friend and colleague of many years, Professor Joe Norton, LLB (Hons, Edinburgh); Diplome (Hague); SJD (Michigan), Dphil (Oxford), LLD (London), LLD(hc)(Stockholm), LLD(hc)(Edinburgh); James L Walsh Distinguished Faculty Fellow and Professor of Financial Institutions Law (SMU); formerly Sir John Lubbock Professor of Banking Law (London) (1993-2004); Honorary Professor of CCLS (Queen Mary-London); Nomura Distinguished Visiting Professor of Law in Financial Systems, Harvard Law School (spring 2006); Vice Chancellor's Distinguished Visiting Professor of Law, Hong Kong University (1999-2001); and Distinguished Visiting Professor, Peking University Faculty of Law (present).

This publication would not have been possible without Professor Norton's many years of constant engagement, challenge and discussion of the subject matter, for all of which I am most grateful.

I am also grateful to Professor Douglas W. Arner and Professor Ross Bukley for their support in publication of this work. Professor Arner is Kerry Holdings Professor in Law, BA(Drury), JD(SMU), LLM, PhD (London). He is the Kerry Holdings Professor in Law at the University of Hong Kong. In addition, he is Director of the HKU LLM in Compliance and Regulation, and a Senior Visiting Fellow of Melbourne Law School, University of Melbourne.

Professor Buckley is Professor of Law, UNSW, BEcon, LLB (Hons) (Queenslandd); PhD (UNSW), LLD (Melbourne), FASSA, FAAL. He is Scientia Professor, King & Wood Mallesons Chair of International Finance Law.

I am grateful to Cynthia Murphy and to my children Elisa and Chip for their good natured patience with my obsession of the subject matter of this work for these many years.

Notes and Disclaimers

This book is published for educational purposes only, as well as to give readers general information and a general understanding of the law, not to provide specific legal advice. By using this work, readers understand that this work does not establish any attorney client relationship between the reader and the author. This work should not be relied upon for specific legal action and should not be used as a substitute for competent legal advice from a licensed professional attorney in the reader's state.

This work is not legal advice. The author is a licensed (inactive) attorney. The foregoing work and the Supplement, Volume II of this work, do not create or constitute an attorney client relationship and do not constitute any legal advice or opinion with respect to the subject matter thereof. The Author is not an actively practicing attorney and the copyright holder of this work is not a law firm. Any person, firm or entity taking an interest in the legal analysis presented, the legal case advocated in this work, or any strategies or tactics relating thereto is hereby advised to retain independent legal counsel with respect to such matters.

Ownership of work product. All work product of the author produced pursuant to the creation of this work, including specifically, but without limitation, all mental impressions, conclusions, reports, opinions and legal or business theories, and all memoranda, notes, statements, correspondence, interviews and all records of any kind relating to such work product is proprietary to and shall constitute the property of G N Olson & Company, a limited liability company.

Assumptions and limiting conditions. The legal documents, financial information and all other documentation and information consulted or referenced in this work are assumed to be correct, and neither the author nor the copyright holder assumes any responsibility or liability whatsoever for errors or inaccuracies therein or for the incompleteness thereof.

The author's conclusions and recommendations are based upon good faith interpretation of information readily available in light of present circumstances, but any changes in information or in such circumstances may affect the author's conclusions and recommendations. The author cannot provide assurance to any recipient or reader of this work that it has examined or taken into consideration every influence or factor which could affect his conclusions or recommendations nor that his interpretation or understanding of present circumstances is correct.

No portion of this work may be used out of context nor for any purpose other than that for general information and education. The author shall not be responsible to any person, firm or entity for any action taken in reliance upon or as a result of or in response to all or any portion of this work.

Except as required by law, neither all nor any part of this work may be conveyed to the public through advertising, public relations, news releases, sales materials or any other media or reproduction process without the express prior written consent of the author and the copyright holder. The author shall not be required to give testimony in any hearing or deposition with respect to the subject matter of this work unless prior arrangements have been made with the author and its affected personnel, including arrangements for the payment of reasonable compensation and expenses and the provision of reasonable time to prepare for such hearing or deposition.

Disclaimer: Any legal case filed based on the case made in this book is subject to careful further consideration, identifying fact specifics to support the case and detailed briefing to support the specific case filed. Consideration of state laws that might be applicable to the case made here is advisable, but beyond the scope of this work.

While every effort has been made to ensure the accuracy of the foregoing book and its supplement, it is not intended to provide legal advice, as individual situations will differ and should be discussed with an independent expert and legal counsel.

Preface

Washington and Wall Street have violated fundamental legal principles relating to money, credit, honesty, trust and confidence in banking that are 4,000 years old. Washington and Wall Street have breached the legal duties and standards of care governing money and banking that are nearly 2,000 years old. These violations caused the financial crisis.

These same legal principles, duties, standards of care and laws exist today and may be enforced by the United States Department of Justice. They care are so important, they are firmly enshrined in ancient Anglo-American common law, the Magna Carta, the United States Constitution, Bill of Rights and in United States federal statutory civil and criminal law. The Department of Justice has so far refused to enforce the American rule of law in a case of financial crisis accountability.

These legal principles, duties and standards of care are so important, however, that they may be enforced by the private legal action of the American people.

They are so important that federal law provides for the recovery of treble damages by the American people.

According to government publications and published reports of respected commentators, Americans' financial damages approach $20 trillion. Globally, financial damages exceed $60 trillion. Human suffering is inestimable and untold.

One individual, acting alone, cannot bear the burden of American's collective obligation to protect the people's constitutional civil right to honest, safe and sound sovereign money through legal enforcement of these fundamental principles and laws.

This book is offered as documentation of these dynamics and in aid of public efforts to mobilize ordinary Americans to take on the entrenched interests in Washington and Wall Street in a case for financial crisis accountability.

It is also offered to enable others to assess the viability of the claims advanced here and to encourage ordinary Americans to add their efforts and resources to, and to attract to well-informed and dedicated professional leadership, to enable the American people to take action under the American rule of law to recover their damages; penalize wrongdoing by Washington and Wall Street; provide incentives to changed conduct;

and deter further wrongdoing and damage to the American public by Washington and Wall Street.

By taking action based on this work, informed members of the American public can exponentially increase grass roots public, social media and organizational power and influence in service of their objectives; harness the energy and talent of the American public's activist base; and allow the public to break free of Washington and Wall Street dogma.

The American public can and must demonstrate its commitment to not only effect change. It can actually contribute to the accountability and justice for the American people, the imposition of which is a condition to meaningful change in Washington and on Wall Street.

American public leadership can and must contribute directly to the re-establishment of America's fundamental values and help repair the shredded American social, economic and monetary fabric. Chapter 1, the Introduction to this book, elaborates on the background to this work.

American Money

Money is the most basic and essential tool of modern society. Its utility allows free markets for goods and services to be exchanged fairly and efficiently. It allows us to provide for our own economic security, the sustenance of our families. Money has taken numerous and varied forms through the years. These are briefly chronicled in Chapter 2. Growth of societies and cultures into forms of government; tribes, polis, kingdoms and nation states. Governments, whether established by force or consensually, provided for the growth and cohesiveness and as a part of that cohesion, for the provision of modes of social protection and preservation. The first among government purposes has been demonstrated purposes has proven to be preservation of its existence; provision for the common defense against aggression, war and its devastating consequences. It is that prime purpose that has served as cover for abuse of government power, and specifically the power of government to create sovereign money and the regulation of its value for the common good, the first of which was the common collective defense of its existence, since governments were first formed. That is the case in America. America's form of government is established under our Constitution for that purpose as well other important purposes and most importantly to establish the fundamental rights of the people. Our Declaration of Independence recites the basis for our government and our structure and mode of government established under our Constitution:

We hold these truths to be self-evident, all Men are created equal, that they are endowed by their Creator with certain unalienable Rights, that among these are Life, Liberty, and the Pursuit of Happiness—That to secure these Rights, Governments are instituted among Men, deriving their just Powers from the Consent of the Governed, that whenever any form of Government becomes destructive of these Ends, it is the Right of the People to alter or to abolish it, and to institute new Government, laying its Foundation on such Principles, and organizing its Powers in such form, as to them shall seem most likely to effect their Safety and Happiness.

We recall that our form of government includes provision for the provision of economic stability and security and the common hallmarks of civil society, including the growth and prosperity of society and the most vulnerable among us; the sick and disabled, the elderly, children and the families, communities, cities and states that comprise our union. This book is based on the widespread conviction amongst international legal scholars that our system of global finance and its regulation is not working. Central bankers, bankers and academics have been challenged to re-conceptualize; to re-think the global financial system and it's regulation to identify actions and processes of change to the system and it's regulation that will minimize financial crises and provide the financial, systemic and regulatory features that will assure future global financial resilience and stability. In furtherance of our declaration and establishment of our constitution, we confirm the primacy of the people's natural civil rights and for the limited delegation by the people to our government stated of powers and duties to be exercised by government for the benefit of the sovereign people. Our founding documents; the *Declaration of Independence* and the *Constitution* illustrate both wrongs inflicted on the people inducing them to form our government, and for establishment of our new government to remedy those wrongs and to delineate the governmental structure under which the government was, and is entrusted with the protection and promotion of the public good. The government is the servant of the people. Governments service is enabled by the public trust and confidence that the government recognize and meet its and fiduciary duties that reciprocate such trust and confidence. The fiduciary nature of the government with its constituents, the American people, now observe more in the breach than its honor. It is useful to remember with clarity the nature and definition of that fiduciary relationship:

> The term [fiduciary] is derived from the Roman law, and means (as a noun) a person holding the character of a trustee, or a character analogous to that of a trustee, in respect to the trust and confidence involved in it and the scrupulous good faith and candor which it requires.[1]

Congress' limited, delegated power and duty to create and regulate the value of American sovereign money is Congress prime fiduciary to the people. Safe, sound and honest constitutional money is essential to the honest and honorable exercise of all other powers and duties delegated to Congress and effected through all three branches of American government. Honest, safe and sound money provides the mechanism by which the people communicate American values to the government and is it essential for the social, economic, financial and legal relationships amongst our people and the people in other countries around the world. Fiduciary duty is the highest duty provided for under the American rule of law. Upon the ratification of the *Constitution* on June 21, 1788, pursuant to and in exercise of its monetary power and fiduciary duty to American citizens under Article I, §8, Clause 5 thereof, on April 2, 1792, Congress passed the *Coinage Act of 1792*[2], creating the United States dollar as the country's standard unit of money, established the United States Mint, and regulated the coinage of the United States. The long title of the legislation is *An act establishing a mint, and regulating the Coins of the United States*. This act established the silver dollar as the unit of money in the United States, declared it to be lawful tender, and created a decimal system for U.S. currency.

In addition and very important in consideration of the current monetary system in America addressed especially in the first four chapters of this work, Section 19 of the *Coinage Act of 1792*, entitled "Penalty on Debasing the Coins," the law provided that money debasement constituted a felony, and a capital offense, punishable by death.

So, the American people delegated to Congress the power and fiduciary duty to create honest, safe and sound money, and by prompt legislation, Congress did so, and provided for the penalty of death for the debasement of money. The highest duty under the law, fiduciary duty, governed defined and delineated Congress' monetary powers. By its legislation provided the ultimate penalty for its debasement: death. American law established by the American people in the *Constitution* and the resultant will of Congress pursuant to its high duty thereunder met its charge to create honest, safe and sound money under penalty of death for its debasement.

The founding American preeminent moral and legal principles relating to the creation and regulation of the value of the dollar as honest, safe and sound sovereign American money could not have been made clearer.

How is it then, that in the light of this moral and legal clarity, the American monetary system has devolved to the point that money is created in a manner wholly inconsistent with its moral and legal foundation and that the value of American is indeterminate and the policy of the only governmental instrumentality, the Federal Reserve System and its constituents, the Wall Street banks for a monetary policy based on manipulation of the value of money and assets denominated in that money, ostensibly in the public interest but demonstrably, factually, and solely in the institutional interests of our government in Washington, financial powers on Wall Street and in the individual political, financial and bureaucratic interest of our political and financial elite?

The 180° shift in and departure from our founding moral and legal principles governing American sovereign money in the opposed interests of Washington and Wall Street manufacturing of pseudo income, wealth and the mythical American dream is the very cause of every incident of financial distress and crises in American history, including the great financial crisis of 2008 and the most divisive polarization of the interests of "haves" and "have nots" in American history. This, on top of the $20 trillion in damages imposed on ordinary American households, while Washington and Wall Street continue of prosper and concentrate their profits, wealth and power.

The story of Washington's failure to meet its obligation and the breach of its fiduciary duty to the American people to create, maintain and regulate the value of American money has enabled the most egregious monetary, economic and financial fraud in world history. That fraud has been enabled and conducted by the joint enterprise of Washington and the Wall Street banks, incrementally and perniciously, beginning at the time our government was founded by the people and culminating in the financial crises, social, and economic distortions that have been visited upon us in the past forty years; since the Nixon shock, which destroyed what remained of the integrity of our monetary system, our economy and society. The Washington and Wall

Street enterprise in fraudulent monetary manipulation and debasement has corrupted our society to its very core.

Financial crises over the past 40 years specifically following the Nixon shock have been caused by the United States government's dominance of global finance in league with the developed world's other global economies' and their combined intentional and wrongful departure from the first principles of money, banking and finance: the maintenance of American economic integrity based on honest, safe and sound sovereign money, the value of which is assured by the active transparent exercise by Congress of its power in furtherance of its fiduciary duty to do so.

Wealthy powerful constituents of the status quo have entrenched, vested interests in and benefit directly from the dysfunction of national and global finance and its regulation which depends on global practice of debasement of money, in a futile attempt to meet fiscal and monetary policy promises that are demonstrably unachievable, except by unabashed employment of the ancient crime of money debasement. This has been perpetrated without a whisper of the basis for enforcement of the accountability of the Washington Wall Street enterprise of fraud that underlies America's financial crises leading to unprecedented economic in equality and enormous damage to ordinary Americans. "The top 20% of US households own more than 84% of the wealth, and the bottom 40% combine for a paltry 0.3%."[3]

Scientific American cited a study published in 2014 by Norton and Sorapop Kiatpongsan, assessing perceptions of income inequality: "The median American estimated that the CEO-to-worker pay-ratio was 30-to-1, and that ideally, it'd be 7-to-1. The reality? 354-to-1. Fifty years ago, it was 20-to-1. Again, the patterns were the same for all subgroups, regardless of age, education, political affiliation, or opinion on inequality and pay. "In sum," the researchers concluded, "respondents underestimate actual pay gaps, and their ideal pay gaps are even further from reality than those underestimates.[4]"

The fundamental first principles that are the foundation of safe, sound, resilient and stable national and global financial systems are embedded in and protected by the rule of law; specifically the Anglo-American rule of law. The wealthy and powerful parties with vested interests in the status quo have deliberately abandoned the moral foundation and the first principles and laws of money, banking and finance, domestically and globally.

The press has characterized the self-serving treatment of those parties; individual persons and institutions, as too big to manage, fail, prosecute or be rendered subject to civil and criminal accountability and justice under the rule of law; in other words, they have become, in effect, "too big to fail and too big to jail."

Politicians and the American justice system have warned the public that initiating any process of holding Washington, Wall Street, including individual personal and institutional parties, accountable and bringing them to justice as the persons and institutions culpable for causing financial crises through actions that they have acknowledged as "immoral" but "not illegal," would, in and of itself, precipitate another deeper and more destructive financial crisis. Washington and Wall Street insist that they are the experts in all matters of money banking finance and economic systems; they are the best and brightest we have; and that they are appropriately and responsibly in charge; meeting their responsibilities and protecting the American public and the global communities' interests. Their actions may have been irresponsible and wrong, but they were not illegal.

Efforts in the public interest in the years following the financial crisis to impose accountability on those responsible for the financial and human devastation wrought by the crisis have largely been expressions of public frustration and anger that do not intelligently or strategically advance the process. Washington and Wall Street have the power and resources to divide, minimize, marginalize and co-opt private, public as well as legislative and regulatory action to impose accountability on those responsible for the crisis. So far, Washington and Wall Street have successfully wielded their power and resources. There has been a lot of talk by frustrated Americans demanding accountability without really understanding what it means or how to get it. Simply complaining and petitioning the government demanding results has gone nowhere. Politics, political and social activism and moral suasion have proved to be empty threats.

A look at the effective options available to impose accountability on Washington and Wall Street under the rule of law clearly reveals that the American public must directly confront the most powerful individuals and institutions in the country. That means economic claims against and recovery of damages, in compensation and as punishment, from Wall Street, and indirectly, Washington, for their specific legal wrongdoing, and for deterrence of their ongoing and likely future wrongdoing.

Legal action designed to hold Washington and Wall Street accountable under the rule of law can only succeed within a context of public grass roots support. That means public education through a sophisticated, experienced public relations, public media, social media and grass roots organizational operation to form, fund a "war chest" commensurate with the resources available to the defendants and manage a powerful, large-scale public campaign to focus attention on the American public's demand for legal accountability.

The overall campaign must place the legal action in the context of a widespread apolitical public demand for Americans' civil right to honest money, banking and a real economy for the American public who have been damaged by the financial crisis.

Broken Connections: Money, Morality and Law

As we will see in the detailed chronicle of American financial crises in this work, the immorality of the damages caused by each financial crises has been apparent at the time and chronicled in crisis reports followed by legal and regulatory action and reform in each case. The legal and regulatory action and reform have been reactive in each case and has been conducted without connection of first, the moral principles of honesty and fiduciary duty so flagrantly violated with, second, the American rule of law tied to those moral principles. Beginning with the most recent financial crises in the late 1980s and 1990s, the broken connection between well and long established moral principles and legal principles is readily apparent.

The Real Estate, S&L and Banking Crisis of 1980s and 1990s

Large numbers of surviving institutions still operating as the crisis of the late 80s and early 90s wound down had allegedly been defrauded. Insider fraud was allegedly present in approximately 25% of all bank failures in 1989 and in 33% of thrift failures. 64% of RTC (Resolution Trust Company) controlled thrifts had allegedly suspect criminal conduct referred to the American Department of Justice (DOJ).

More than 1,000 additional banks were slated for closure at the end of 1991, but, mysteriously, after a firestorm in the press and in the banking community, that horrible prospect simply dropped off the radar screen—what happened? Well, the Fed knew that manipulation of interest rates can be used as a method to subsidize losses for banks that are "too big to fail," and as a method to subsidize what would otherwise be deposit insurance funds necessary to "resolve" distressed banks."

Presto, the specter of the failure of an additional 1,071 banks was hidden away. There was no general disclosure of this process—the unlucky banks closed before this sleight of hand was administered were simply wiped out. Their officers, directors and borrowers hounded by prosecutors having no understanding of the vast shell game of perceived value creation followed by vanishing values and losses measured in money with no backing by any proper congressionally established standard of value. The value that "vanished" was thought to have been literally stolen. The non-transparent policy of hidden "bailouts" that took up where wrongheaded prosecutorial zeal left off, was accompanied by the intentional deliberate but wholly nontransparent regulatory policy of "extend and pretend," "delay and pray" and "deny and lie" that hid the ultimate effects of the crisis and did nothing to remediate damages to the

American public. The clear meanings of these colloquial phrases plainly refer to an open public policy of officially sanctioned lying, cheating and stealing. These dishonest, immoral and illegal policies continue today. The following is excerpted from *Subprime Meltdown—It's All about Money*, G N Olson (2008) pp 180-182 and from *Banks in Distress*, G N Olson (2000) pp 215-218:[5]

> As it happened, bank fraud and crime on a micro basis at individual financial institutions (inside of the box) played an almost minuscule role in the crisis of the late 1980, and early 1990s.

According to the response of Justice to the GAO Report (the Justice Response) in October, 1992, the near collapse of the thrift industry was the result of a "series of complex factors." "Regardless of whose numbers one looks at, fraud has not been shown to be a major factor in the industry's failures." Also, according to Justice, "the prevalent view that the collapse is primarily a law enforcement issue is untrue. Blaming all of the S&L losses on criminals may be politically convenient, but it is not responsible and it is not accurate."

Responding to the GAO Report assessing the government's efforts to investigate and prosecute financial institution fraud, Justice stated that "while fraud and real estate related fraud in particular were certainly factors in some failures, it cannot fairly be said that they were major factors in all or even a majority of the failures. Economic factors in the real estate and other markets seem to have played a far larger role than fraud (what does this mean, "economic factors"?). Notwithstanding the unsupported findings of the Report, the extent of fraud as a factor in S&L failures is simply not known at this time, and indeed may never be known. Moreover, it cannot be reasonably inferred without empirical and anecdotal study of the reasons for all of the failures."

Justice advised the GAO that "professional prosecutors simply will not indict someone because they are named in a criminal referral as a part of a misplaced search for scapegoats: nor should they. The U.S. criminal justice system must not become a tool of partisan politics or cater in any way to a lynch-mob mentality." The legislative legacy of the late 1980s and early 1990s, notably, FIRREA, the *Crime Control Act* and FDICIA represents a significant departure from what one might consider "appropriate and usual" law pertaining to financial fraud and crime.

Also, according to the U.S. General Accounting Office (GAO), fraud and insider abuse were major factors in a significant portion of American financial institution failures in the 1980s. Real estate projects were common vehicles for financial institution fraud—real estate projects were considered the "perfect device for fraud and insider abuse" and were very effective in destroying financial institutions.

In December, 1989, American Attorney General Richard Thornburg set Justice's goal as being to "bring to justice all those who have sought to capitalize on the American dream....by destroying the financial solvency of institutions designed to serve them. "In June, 1990, American President Bush pledged to "put the cheats ... chiselers, and ... charlatans behind bars."

FIRREA was enacted in 1989 to address financial institution fraud by strengthening civil and criminal penalties for defrauding or otherwise damaging financial institutions and depositors. *The Crime Control Act*, enacted in 1990, built upon *FIRREA* to provide additional tools to combat financial institution fraud, including: new financial institution related offenses, increased fines and prison terms, expanded restitution, and measures to protect assets from wrongful disposition—so-called "asset-freezes."

Following enactment of *FIRREA*, the American Attorney General designated criminal fraud in financial institutions as a top enforcement priority. The Dallas Bank Fraud Task Force was established to prosecute criminal fraud in financial institutions. The Crime Control Act authorized a doubling of resources directed to "the enormous and unprecedented challenge," and created a new Justice Office of Financial Institution Fraud. Using the Dallas Bank Fraud Task Force as a model, Justice planned to combine resources of financial institution regulators, Justice's Criminal Division, the FBI, IRS, U.S. Secret Service and other investigative agencies to create Bank Fraud Task Forces in 26 American cities where criminal bank and thrift fraud was considered to be most prevalent.

Only two additional task forces were established based upon the Dallas model. 3,500 defendants were charged and 2,603 defendants were convicted, involving losses estimated at $11.5 billion, during the period between October 1, 1988 and June 30, 1992. Of the 2,603 convicted, 1700 were sentenced to prison, most for terms of less than two years. Fewer than 2% of those convicted received sentences of more than 10 years. Restitution and fines ordered in these cases totaled $846 million. At July 31, 1992, approximately 4.5% of the total restitution ordered was collected. For various reasons,

Justice believed that the "money had disappeared" How could it disappear? Could it be that the institution's asset values were misrepresented in monetary terms because the tool of measurement had been systemically corrupted and therefore misrepresented?), and that there was little or nothing to recover at the conclusion of the criminal case. The GAO determined that the extent and impact of fraud was difficult to ascertain, because one must first determine when and if suspect activity crossed the line between poor business judgment and fraud. The GAO also found that putting a dollar value on losses caused by fraud was difficult.

According to the Justice Response in October, 1992, the near collapse of the thrift industry was the result of a "series of complex factors." "Regardless of whose numbers one looks at, fraud has not been shown to be a major factor in the industry's failures." Also, according to Justice, "the prevalent view that the collapse is primarily a law enforcement issue is untrue. Blaming all of the S&L losses on criminals may be politically convenient, but it is not responsible and it is not accurate."

With respect to the role of banking fraud and financial misconduct in the American bank and thrift crisis, the *FDIC Report* on the crises, published in December 1997 dissembles, briefly, in a page and a half note in the Report's Summary and Implications section, weakly regurgitating the GAO statistics. The FDIC acknowledges that "a number of factors make it difficult to measure the effect of fraud and abuse," but concludes, nevertheless, that "it seems reasonable to infer that fraud and abuse not only were present in a large number of bank and thrift failures in the 1980-94 period but also contributed to some of them."

The subjects "crime," "fraud" and "financial misconduct," however, are not even listed in the Index to the FDIC Report. President Bush's pledge to "put the cheats, chiselers and charlatans behind bars" and Justice's pledge to "bring to justice all those who have sought to capitalize on the American dream by destroying the financial solvency of institutions designed to serve them," began with a bang and died with barely a whimper, leaving untold financial and personal carnage in their wake.

The FDIC Report concludes, in essence, that the FDIC did a swell job, conclusively demonstrating that they need an expanded role and additional funding and resources to deal with future crises. It goes on to observe that the fundamental systemic issues were outside its mandate, and that if new systemic problems "... are allowed to develop in the future, bank regulations alone will not be able to prevent a major increase in the number of bank failures."

What was wrong? What was wrong in every American financial crisis can be tied directly to intentional Washington public policy and Wall Street private bank controlled action in the creation of systemic financial risk through unregulated creation of money, including credit, with no firm relation to a reliable outside standard of market value, to achieve short terms objectives of political expedience. That continued and ever increasing incidence of policy and action was, and remains, wrong. It was and remains irresponsible. But was it criminal? If so, who is responsible? The FDIC came nowhere near identifying the actual culpable parties and their conduct. How can the culpable parties be identified and held to account under the American rule of civil and criminal law? Although it is clear that systemic financial crises are grounded in wrongful and irresponsible conduct, neither the FDIC nor the U.S. Justice Department have ever investigated the obvious, apparent publicly sanctions crimes of institutional abuse of power and intentional misrepresentation of asset values and liquidity that not only took place as asset bubbles boomed, but also, most importantly, after their busts. They have likewise refused to address the obvious moral and legal failures that are the clear causation of crises throughout American history as well as the current crisis. The misdirected focus of Washington and Wall Street with respect to the great financial crisis has been evident in public pronouncements from both Washington and Wall Street. Consider the following:

The Great Financial Crisis

Old Testament Justice

The positions of Washington and Wall Street are poignantly - actually ridiculously - represented by the following statements of the President of the United States and the former Treasury Secretary of the United States The statement of former United Stated Treasury Secretary William Geithner: "Old Testament vengeance appeals to the populist fury of the moment, but the truly moral thing to do during a raging financial inferno is to put it out. The goal should be to protect the innocent, even if some of the arsonists escape their full measure of justice." … "Geithner's more sustained attack, however, is on the kind of populism [United States Senator Elizabeth] Warren has come to represent on the left, which he describes as "the Old Testament view" that "[t]he venal should be punished. The irresponsible shouldn't be bailed out." He cites the appetite for "Old Testament vengeance," "Old Testament justice," "Old Testament impulses," "Old Testament populism," "Old Testament cravings," and so forth, no fewer than 18 times.[6]"

Morality Versus Law

United States President Barack Obama addressed the great financial crisis of 2008 in his State of the Union Address in 2012 as follows:

In 2008, the house of cards collapsed. We learned that mortgages had been sold to people who couldn't afford or understand them. Banks had made huge bets and bonuses with other people's money. Regulators had looked the other way, or didn't have the authority to stop the bad behavior.

It was wrong. It was irresponsible.

And it plunged our economy into a crisis that put millions out of work, saddled us with more debt, and left innocent, hard-working Americans holding the bag. …

We'll also establish a Financial Crimes Unit of highly trained investigators to crack down on large-scale fraud and protect people's investments. Some financial firms violate major antifraud laws because there's no real penalty for being a repeat offender. That's bad for consumers, and it's bad for the vast majority of bankers and financial service professionals who do the right thing. So pass legislation that makes the penalties for fraud count.

And tonight, I'm asking my attorney general to create a special unit of federal prosecutors and leading state attorneys general to expand our investigations into the abusive lending and packaging of risky mortgages that led to the housing crisis. This new unit will hold accountable those who broke the law, speed assistance to homeowners, and help turn the page on an era of recklessness that hurt so many Americans.

President Obama's statements reflect the views commonly held by his administration, Congress, federal financial regulators and Wall Street bankers: that the symptoms of systemic financial crises, borrower and lender fraud, lender abusive practices and Wall Street bankers' greed constitute the systemic financial crisis. Bad conduct by these parties is indeed wrong and irresponsible—they are in most cases illegal; but these wrong and irresponsible—yes illegal actions are symptoms of systemic financial crises—not the causes.

In fact, the remedial actions taken by Washington and Wall Street in the face of the great financial crisis protected only the Washington and Wall Street criminal enterprise described in this work and abandoned the innocent American public to its fate; a fate that included monetary damages approaching of $20 trillion and untold personal suffering. The Fed's enormous discount lending programs designed to promote artificially high asset prices and liquidity; Quantitative Easing Programs; artificial maintenance of record low interest rates from the inception of the crisis in 2008 through today combined with regulatory forbearance across the board created the most massive consequent coordinated intentional continuous misrepresentation of asset values on the books of the Fed, the federal regulatory agencies, the Wall Street banks and our entire economy, in history. The intentional coordinated program of "extend and pretend," "delay and pray" and "deny and lie" is pervasive globally from the individual asset basis through sovereign accounts in global finance—in effect a world-wide Ponzi scheme. This Ponzi scheme is irresponsible, immoral and yes illegal. Notwithstanding the fact that it has been institutionalized by our government and financial system.

The Convergence of Morality and Law of Money

The Old Testament as well as American common law, the *Constitution* and federal statutes condemn lying, cheating and stealing by all who commit those crimes, specifically including the likes of former Treasury Secretary Geithner and his co-conspirators who have accomplished their crimes and civil wrongdoing through the intentional misrepresentation of the value of money in their accounts, their financial records and reports and those of their public and private banking customers, and through intentional abuse of the powers legally entrusted to them by the American public.

While innovation in global financial regulation is necessary and laudable; in order to achieve a safe, sound, resilient and stable global financial system, compliance with the indispensable foundation of fundamental moral and legal principles, the existing rule of law, regulations and regulatory principles must be applied and enforced. Violations of law must be prosecuted under civil law; criminal law; punishments assessed and the culpable parties must be subjected to appropriate lawful provision of disincentives to future wrongful conduct. Moral and legal accountability is the first and primary condition to our country's enjoyment of the benefits of the re-conceptualizing and re-thinking of the global financial system and its regulation.

Morality is the foundation for and common denominator of conduct in a civil society. Money is the primary indispensable economic connector amongst people in a civil society. Honest, safe sound money, trusted money, in which society has confidence, is the thread that weaves the economic fabric of civil society. Money is integral to every aspect of each persons' ability to work, create and preserve the fruits of their labor, whether represented by production of goods and services, and to make fair and honest exchanges of value to sustain each person, each family, the society's form of government and integrity of civil society as a whole. American law related to money rests on a clear, indisputable foundation of morality. The moral imperative and admonition that one shall not lie, cheat or steal seems clear enough. This moral imperative is indisputably embodied in the American rule of law. The characterization of Washington and Wall Street actions in abuse of power and systemic misrepresentation of the value and liquidity of assets through manipulation of our nation's money as "immoral but not illegal" is intentionally, demonstrably false and rings ever so hollow, in the understanding of American households so damaged by repeated financial crises; specifically the great financial crisis, and likely to be repeated in future financial crisis. This manipulation and misrepresentation are much, much more flagrant than can be justified as merely a political spin. Failure of the American public and their government to act decisively as suggested in this work will, sooner or later, and most likely soon, result in the next American and global financial crisis.

This book provides an historical, factual and legal analysis supporting both public and private enforcement of the rule of law that, if followed, will lead to a level playing field for the actualization of the ongoing re-thinking and re-conceptualization of global finance and its regulation by other interested scholars.

Personal Interest and Experience

I have personally experienced every banking and financial crisis since the Nixon shock in 1971. I have studied, lectured and written about financial crises for more than 25 years. I have published two books on financial crises including my doctoral thesis at the Centre for Commercial Law Studies, Queen Mary College University of London. I have deep profound personal interest in advancing the proposed legal case and achieving some measure of accountability and justice for the American people.

The issues raised and to be resolved by the proposed case are the most important issues facing the American public. Unless and until the proposed legal case is made, the power of vested interests in money and banking will continue to erode the social fabric and economic foundation for America's government and the reality of the American Dream, if any remnant of that reality, in fact, remains.

All of my individual efforts to advance this effort have been met with the frustrating combination of initial enthusiasm followed by fear of intimidation and retribution by government and the Wall Street banks.

Occupy Wall Street failed to meet its potential due to lack of: a sound intellectual foundation; a clearly articulated objective; a well-articulated plan to meet that objective; the organizational structure and strength to focus and discipline human and financial resources to achieve its objective; and well-informed, professional leadership.

I have provided here the first three of the missing ingredients. I ask readers of this book to aid the effort by helping provide the last two missing ingredients necessary to the successful prosecution of a direct, well-defined effort to achieve accountability and justice for the $20 trillion of economic damages and untold personal suffering inflicted by Washington and Wall Street on the American people.

Ordinary Americans Are Not Powerless

The seemingly unlikely, even impossible, idea of American legal action by ordinary Americans to enforce legal accountability of Washington and Wall Street for the financial crisis, and to effect meaningful change short of violent action, is in fact feasible and necessary.

Efforts in the public interest in the years following the financial crisis to impose accountability on those responsible for the financial and human devastation wrought by the crisis have largely been expressions of public frustration and anger that do not intelligently or strategically advance the process. Washington and Wall Street have the power and resources to divide, minimize, marginalize and co-opt private, public as well as legislative and regulatory action to impose accountability on those responsible for the crisis. So far, Washington and Wall Street have successfully wielded their power and resources. Honest, honorable performance of fiduciary duties inherent in government and banking has been turned on its head. Washington and Wall Street have become global standards for corruption through money debasement to fulfill personal and institutional concentrations of wealth and power. There has been a lot of talk by frustrated Americans demanding accountability without really understanding what it means or how to get it. Simply complaining and petitioning the government demanding results has gone nowhere. Politics, political and social activism and moral suasion have proved to be empty threats.

A look at the effective options available to impose accountability on Washington and Wall Street under the rule of law clearly reveals that the American public must directly confront the most powerful individuals and institutions in the country.

That means financial claims against and recovery of damages, in compensation and as punishment, from Wall Street, and indirectly, Washington, for their specific legal wrongdoing, and for deterrence of their ongoing and likely future wrongdoing. Legal action designed to hold Washington and Wall Street accountable under the rule of law can only succeed within a context of public grass roots support and involvement. That means public education through sophisticated, experienced public relations, public media, social media and grass roots organizational operation to form, fund a "war chest" commensurate with the resources available to the defendants and manage a powerful, large-scale public campaign to focus attention on the American public's demand for legal accountability.

The overall campaign must place the legal action in the context of a widespread apolitical public demand for Americans' civil right to honest money, banking and a real economy for the American public.

Re-thinking and Re-conceptualizing Money, Morality and Law in America

The premise of this book is that what we have now is not working. Re-thinking and re-conceptualization of global finance and regulation requires a return to first principles. Effective global finance and regulation requires effective domestic finance and regulation: specifically in the United States, the home of the world's reserve currency and the current model for the world's other domestic economies that have had to conform to the U.S. financial system in order to function globally. Effective American domestic finance is now dependent on the integrity and effectiveness of American money. American money consists almost entirely of credit denominated in United States Dollar Federal Reserve Notes. For credit to function effectively as money it must meet certain conceptual requirements.

These requirements are as valid today as they have been for four millennia. Felix Martin, in his excellent work examining the nature of money, *Money: The Unauthorized Biography*[7] (Martin) provides an excellent foundation for understanding the history of the use and misuse of credit as money over the past 4,000 years. Martin observes that, historically, money in the form of credit consisted of trade accounts, the creditworthiness of which was supported by close-knit communities with personal knowledge of parties and counterparties. The history of ancient use of credit as money lacks the overwhelming evidence of the use of precious metal tokens or coins in daily transaction because, after all this time, the record represented by coins largely remains intact. The ancient history of credit as money has been largely lost to the historical record. Martin does, however, amply document the pervasive dominance of credit as money, most specifically credit supporting large, cross border (now global) finance. "Currency is ephemeral and cosmetic: it is the underlying mechanism of credit accounts and clearing that is the essence of money."[8] Money is not a commodity medium of exchange, but a social technology composed of three fundamental elements.

The first is an abstract unit of value in which money is denominated. The second is a system of accounts, which keeps track of the individuals' or the institutions' credit or debt balances as they engage in trade with one another. The third is the possibility that the original creditor in a relationship can freely transfer their debtor's obligation to a third party in settlement of some unrelated debt.[9]

This book examines the failures of these fundamental elements and the principles they represent that have led to the great financial crisis. This book identifies the existing and necessary needs and mechanisms for driving effective conformity of our global financial system to these fundamental elements or principles under the rule of law and supplemental regulation that are essential to a stable effective global financial system.

The fundamental responsibility of those in control of the financial system, specifically government and their partners in finance, financial intermediaries, known generally as banks but including all credit and money creators and intermediators, is, and has always been, to assure the safety and soundness of money, in the public interest, as fiduciaries whose duty is to do just that. When traditional, classic conditions for creation of effective money and credit can no longer be functionally met in the market place, the state has historically stepped in to provide for the safety and soundness of money through banking law and regulation through the rule of law.

Due to the enormous expansion of global finance in amount, complexity and velocity over the past forty years the need for government and their partners in banking to maintain safe and sound money is critical. In 1933 domestic regulation of the value of money by reference to an effective external standard was abandoned. The Nixon shock in 1971 severed the last thread of external discipline on the value of U.S. money internationally under the *Breton Woods Accords*. The U.S. dollar and credit denominated in dollars, as well as counterparty transactions globally and traded through the U.S. domestic and globally dominated global financial system has since been drastically debased and corrupted by Wall Street, under the authority of the Federal Reserve System, federal regulators of financial institutions and the United States Congress.

Following the abandonment of the constitutional mandate for regulation of the value of the dollar, the reaction of the American government has been a vacillating reactive process of regulation and deregulation of banking and finance in a failed attempt to regulate domestic and global finance in a safe and sound manner. The extensive body of banking law and regulation developed over the past forty years has largely been a failure. Its enactment has been reactive. Closing the barn door after the animals have all left the scene, so to speak. The tools of banking law, regulation, guidance, opinions have been corrupted through the woven threads of largely unmitigated and unaccountable discretion wielded by bureaucrats. Each American financial crisis has been followed by commission reports and finding that, in each case, regulatory failure constituted a fundament cause of financial crisis. These failures have been well-documented. Proof is largely a matter of public record. This work builds on and connects that proof with the application and enforcement of the American rule of law.

One may not rationally conclude that banking law and regulation are an effective substitute for accountability for the breach of the established foundation of honest, safe and sound money and banking; the fiduciary duties of Washington and Wall Street to protect the public interest, imposed by the prompt enforcement the rights of ordinary American people under the American rule of law. It has failed for two fundamental reasons.

First, the government and the financial industry have failed to acknowledge the first and fundamental moral and legal requirements (including the recognition of the fundamental legal status of Washington and Wall Street as fiduciaries to the trusting American public and beneficiaries of those fiduciaries in monetary matters) for effective, safe and sound money actively regulated in accordance with an effective, flexible standard of value grounded in the real economy and, therefore domestic and global finance.

Second, existing banking law and regulation have not been systematically, consistently or effectively enforced. Without enforcement of the rule of law the global financial system cannot function effectively. Without enforcement of the rule of law, financial and economic accountability, and justice have failed.

The rule of law that has traditionally and historically supported the effective functioning of both domestic and global finance exists. They define the action required to enforce the rule of law; and to enforce accountability for financial crises by punishing violators of the law, compensating victims and deterring future violations of law. The demonstrable failure of government, legislative and regulatory institutions, aided and abetted by the failure of law enforcement action by the United States Department of Justice (DOJ), presents a vain and misguided attempt to maintain the false appearance of systemic financial stability through an intentional cover-up of their collective abandonment of critical fundamental principles that must underlie any sound, safe and stable financial system.

This failure, combined with bankers' unabashed capitalization on and abuse of this institutional and personal government failure through profit taking across the board, has resulted in up to $20 trillion in damage to the American people and approximately $60 trillion globally, accompanied by massive wealth and income re-distribution from the working public to banks and government. The American public are required to use the American dollar or accounts denominated by the American dollar in payment of all debts public and private and intermediated through the American banking and financial system. When Washington and Wall Street combine to violate the American rule of law by exploiting the consistent and ongoing diminishment and debasement of the dollar's value as represented by Federal Reserve Notes, the American people are entitled to be protected by the DOJ from Washington's and Wall Street's criminal conduct; breach of their fiduciary duties to the American public and as well as recovery through the federal judicial system of actual damages to recover their losses as well as exemplary damages imposed in punishment for their past wrongdoing and to deter their future and foreseeable wrongdoing through private legal action from the ravages of lying, cheating and theft accomplished through the massive American money debasement and financial crisis directly caused thereby.

Existing Literature Fails to Address the Moral and Legal Imperative of Enforcement of Accountability for the Financial Crisis and a Return to Honest, Safe, and Sound Money

The massive body of popular and scholarly writing on the subject of the great financial crisis is distinguished by the truly comprehensive extent documentation (proof), analysis and commentary; and, on the one hand, leading to a common conclusion that each respective author hopes that something will eventually be done about the terrible menace of financial crisis; while, on the other hand, at the same time, the same sources acknowledging that financial reform has been slow coming, and of mainly peripheral effects. Calls for meaningful action are met by hollow echoes.

This book explores the causes of the existing systemic failure of American moral standards and the American rule of law, leading directly to the financial crisis and lays out a case for public and private enforcement of the American rule of law which, if successful, would re-establish the importance and effectiveness of the rule of law as the moral and legal foundation for an effective and functional system of global finance and regulation.

The case is based on Washington's and Wall Street's intentional abuse of power and dishonesty: intentional bank fraud. It is a case based on Washington's and Wall Street's systemic, intentional program of lying to, and cheating and stealing from ordinary Americans. Washington and Wall Street have convinced us that the case is impossible to make, but it is actually quite simple and realistic. The successful dissemination of that message to ordinary Americans is dependent on generation of a widespread recognition that the case is not only possible, but it is vital to our way of life.

Any complexity in the book is necessitated by detailed refutation of the range of false narratives spawned by Washington and Wall Street as well as anticipated push back from Washington and Wall Street.

Washington and Wall Street will likely first seek to minimize and discredit the work until they are forced by the American public to join the battle. Washington and Wall Street will use their power and wealth to wreak intimidation and retribution on the messenger. A well-planned strategy of exciting public awareness, of and support for the work is crucial to establishing and enforcing accountability for financial crises.

Under the case presented, Wall Street could expect a judicial mandate, at the Supreme Court level, that Congress and the Executive, including federal financial regulators, must meet their legal obligations. Washington is liable for the damages. Under the case I present, damages would be tripled to $60 trillion; an enormous sum, triple the amount of the national debt. Public acceptance of the foundation and proof of the case will generate global attention.

The monetary damages are separate and apart from the massive bailouts, subsidies, benefits from quantitative easing, fines and damages awarded in securities fraud cases. Washington and Wall Street are more wealthy and powerful than ever. They control the dominant public narratives: false narratives. Washington and Wall Street have conceded wrongdoing; but not illegality. Washington and Wall Street have all but convinced us that we are powerless to protect ourselves. We are angry and frustrated. The effects of existing and increasing violence, and existing and increasing income, wealth and power polarization and disparity are palpable.

Washington's and Wall Street's false narratives rely on oversimplification of lies, repetition of the lies, and on surrounding the lies with a complex web of "expert" justification of their actions to defend and protect them from challenge. False narratives in cases such as those at issue here are most effective when propounded by the wealthy and powerful, in whom the public have confidently entrusted monopoly power over monetary affairs, based on the accompanying duty to exercise that power to protect the public interest under the rule of law that embodies the balance of trust, power and duty. The false narrative are not therefore easily susceptible to contradiction by public polarizing rants of conflicting, oversimplified angry narrative, grounded in unfocused outrage.

America's status as a developed economy is now openly challenged. In a new *book, The Vanishing Middle Class: Prejudice and Power in a Dual Economy*, Peter Temin, Professor Emeritus of economics at MIT, finds that "the US is no longer one country, but divided into two separate economic and political words." Lynn Parramore, Senior Research Analyst at the Institute for New Economic Thinking, begins her review of Professor Temin's book with the assertion that "*America is Regressing into a Developing Nation for Most People.*" Temin's trenchant observations and conclusions however do not extend to advocacy of any plan of action to ameliorate the situation. He foresees America not only reverting to developing country status; but he also contends that America is "increasingly ripe for serious social turmoil that has not been seen in generations." Emmanuel Saez Professor of Economics at U.C. Berkeley, who has researched the phenomenon of cyclical growth of income and wealth inequality in depth, from the beginning of the use of money as a social and cultural tool form ancient Mesopotamia to the present, has shown pertinently that income and wealth inequality in America have reached the highest level since 1928.

The progression in this pernicious cycle of growing disparity of income and wealth in America has increased dramatically since the 1970s. Stanford Professor Walter Scheidel, in his recent book *The Great Leveler*, argues that income and wealth inequality are essentially an inevitable byproduct of civilization, the only remedy to which appears to be societal upheaval, produced by war, disease, state collapse or revolution. "Inasmuch as policy measures have worked, they were usually rooted meaningfully in one or more of these violent shocks." On a more optimistic note, Scheidel notes that although policy alone is unlikely to curb the widening gap, in the U.S. there are still plenty of policies that can be implemented successfully. Scheidel argues that the reduction of inequality achieved by welfare states, communist revolutions and confiscatory taxes required by world wars were one-offs. Paul Mason, in a review of Scheidel's book, commented that:

> Social democracy wishes to suppress inequality in a controlled, consensual way, using the very state the elite has fashioned to entrench it; heading off pestilence, state failure and violent revolution. The vast wealth being generated in the highly technologically efficient society of the 21st century must, contrary to Scheidel, offer the possibility of an even greater redistributional space in which social democracy can operate.
>
> The only problem is, for 30 years, social democracy lost the will to redistribute (other than upwards to its allies in the yachting and mafia fraternities). Since around 2011, with the mass revolts of technologically empowered and educated people, the world has been offered the possibility of a break from the cycle of relentless inequality. In effect it turned the offer down—and in saying no to a future of social justice it has, for now, opened the door to the past: to kleptocrats, mafiosi, politicians whose imaginations are trapped in that tight space between the golden tower and the golden shower."

America is on the verge of a new financial crisis. The bases for the next crisis are already in place. The divisions in and polarization of American society are readily apparent, as well as nascent, if not obvious, in every other developed nation. America's example has been exported the global financial and monetary system with disastrous effects. All of the destructive developments described by Professor Temin, Thomas Picketty, Saez, Scheidel and other authorities on finance and economic matters, have ignored the fact that the modern era of social dysfunction and polarization can be traced in their origin to the collapse of any modern political interest in honest, safe and sound money that followed the Nixon shock in 1971. Money in America is created and controlled by the "haves": Washington, Wall Street, and the largest finance, technology and electronics industries. The "have nots" are all of the rest of us; you, your family, friends, neighbors; the 99% of Americans not among or beholden in some way to the "haves."

The response of ordinary Americans to the current state of affairs, particularly in the years immediately following the great financial crisis of 2008, has been righteous anger based on the betrayal of their interests by those to whom they entrusted political and economic power. A "change in policy" is neither required nor sufficient to redress Washington's and Wall Street's intentional violation of ordinary American's civil right to honest, safe and sound money. Legal action, based on existing law, to enforce that civil right is the only available and viable alternative to the specter presented by Professor Scheidel:

> Only specific types of violence have consistently forced down inequality," Scheidel writes. War has to be total; revolution has to be ultraviolent and socially pervasive; state failure has to lead to violence so intense that "it wipes the slate clean." Ditto the social effects of pandemics.

This account of the emergence of systemic inequality follows the classic materialist schema: only with the emergence of a durable economic surplus in early societies do you get archaeological evidence of inequality—that is where social status begins to map on to economic status. States, defensible and transferable forms of wealth, hereditary elites and the rituals to endow them with status emerge together, Scheidel's review of the evidence shows, to create the "original 1%"—from ..." ancient Mesopotamia to the present day.

There is, however, no readily apparent forum through which ordinary Americans can seek fairness, redress, recompense and justice. Congress has been gerrymandered into paralysis. The federal financial regulators have been corrupted and serve almost exclusively the interests of the regulated, and the preservation of the revolving door admitting so-called public servants to the comfort of waiting positions in the industries they have so assiduously served and protected. The public; ordinary Americans, have been left out. The FBI and the Department of Justice have simply left the building.

Despite the failure of America's governmental and financial elites to protect ordinary Americans' civil right to honest, safe and sound money as required by law, the last and most often ignored focus for Americans' imposition on Washington and Wall Street of moral, legal, financial and equitable accountability for financial crises damage to ordinary Americans, remains our civil right as American's to initiate direct action based on the rule of law and our system of justice. The Department of Justice has refused to act based on purely political considerations; this despite their self-proclaimed responsibility for the redress of government, finance and business "lying, cheating and stealing." Recent financial crises are the greatest and most profound incidence of institutional and individual conduct of intentional lying, cheating and steal in history.

The people, however, have direct private rights of legal action available to them. Moral and legal accountability is the necessary predicate for any shift in the *status quo* that can make practical reform feasible and establish proper incentives to meaningful monetary, and therefore social, economic, and political reform a reality. Failing that, we will be facing the serious social turmoil anticipated by Professor Temin. History informs us that that such turmoil most often means violence and war.

Without a tether of credit to the discipline of honest, safe and sound sovereign money restraining credit excess and unsupported credit creation, ordinary Americans have no shelter from Washington's and Wall Street's, as well as other institutional and corporate "haves'," economic, social, cultural and political predations.

Washington and Well Street Web of False Narratives

The following narratives propounded by Washington and Wall Street are demonstrably false but have dominated America's understanding of accountability for financial crises:

- *Ordinary Americans are responsible—they borrowed too much money—they should have known better.*

It is impossible for ordinary Americans to responsibly and critically assess future income and expenses or asset values when Washington and Wall Street corrupt and debase American money, which is the foundation for that decision making. Washington and Wall Street capitalize on the circumstances they have intentionally through "pumping and dumping" money in the form of housing finance, student loans and other consumer credit as structured money equivalents.

- *Washington and Wall Street; America's experts in money and banking, could not have foreseen, anticipated or prepared for the financial crisis.*

The academic literature is replete with description of the methods and consequences of money debasement. As banking experts Washington and Wall Street are obligated to be fully informed in these disciplines and the laws that relate to them, specifically including the Constitution, E. G. Spaulding on Legal Tender and the Civil War, the Legal Tender Cases, the Gold Clause Cases and the series of congressionally commissions and reports following each American financial crisis.

- *The financial crisis was unavoidable and without the concerted actions of Washington and Wall Street, the effects of the financial crisis on ordinary Americans would have been far worse.*

The Financial Crisis Inquiry Committee found that the crisis was avoidable. The literature preceding and following the crisis confirm that finding. On one hand, the mergers, bailouts, forbearances and subsidies enacted by Washington and Wall Street kept them from experiencing the consequences they deserve, and did little to nothing to benefit ordinary Americans.

- *Ordinary Americans are unable to assign culpability for damages caused to them by the financial crisis and are powerless to enforce accountability for the financial crisis.*

This work is the detailed and scholarly refutation of this false narrative.

- *The causes of America's financial crises are immoral but not illegal.*

Money debasement is both immoral and illegal. This book makes the case.

- *The truly moral thing to do during a raging financial inferno is to put it out and to protect the innocent, even if some of the arsonists escape their full measure of justice.*

Ordinary Americans are entitled to and must demand not only the protection of the innocent but also the punishment of the culpable and prevention of the perpetuation of the perverted system that lies at the heart of the crime.

- *The Old Testament view that the venal should be punished is impossible to accomplish. Old Testament vengeance, Old Testament justice, Old Testament impulses, Old Testament populism, Old Testament cravings for heads on stakes, are archaic and unproductive.*

Old Testament justice and the American rule of law provide the foundation for justice for ordinary Americans—today's equivalent to capital punishment, the ancient remedy for money debasement. Even the Vatican recently acknowledged the immoral, illegal, criminal and civil fraud and wrongdoing that lie at the heart of global financial crises[10].

- *Washington, Wall Street and ordinary Americans' interests are best served by moving on, recovering, and rebuilding America's financial system and economy. "Washington and Wall Street had an over-riding obligation to protect the integrity of the American banking and financial system centered in Washington and on Wall Street, as opposed to the public interest in honesty, safety and soundness in money, banking, and finance as the foundation for our legal, political, social and economic compact.*

Washington and Wall Street are indeed obligated to protect the integrity of the American banking and financial system. To purport to do so through money manipulation and debasement is unalterably antithetical to an honest, safe and sound system of money, banking, and finance.

- *Although the public has constitutionally delegated, granted to and empowered Congress to exercise the exclusive fiduciary power and duty to create and regulate the value of America's sovereign money, the constitutional imperative has become archaic and is rightly ignored.*

Congressional power and duty to regulate the value of American money is as real and immediate in its effect as it ever has been. The American rule of law is very clear on this subject.

- *The evolution of Washington, Wall Street and the great prosperity created by the American economic, banking and financial system has outgrown Wall Street as well as the outmoded and impractical historical concepts of the imposition of legal and fiduciary powers and duties to constrain the supply of American sovereign money.*

The American rule of law defies this self-serving web of false narratives.

- *The Supreme Court decisions in the Legal Tender Cases and the Gold Clause Cases permit the creation by the American banking system of fiat "legal tender" sovereign money intentionally bereft of the constitutionally required Congressional regulation of its value.*

In fact, although these cases confirm Congress' ability to create paper legal tender. These cases each confirm the necessary Constitutional congressional power and duty to regulate the value of that legal tender money.

- *The monetary demands of existential war such as the Revolutionary War, the War of 1812, the American Civil War and World Wars I and II and the near continuous state of war, primarily undeclared war, maintained following World War II, constituted legally justifiable exceptions to the proper exercise of Congress' fiduciary monetary powers and duties to the American public to maintain honest, safe and sound sovereign money.*

The existential demand exception to Congress duty to regulate the value of money is unconstitutional. The exceptions made during the Revolutionary War, the War of 1812 and the Civil War were justified on the governments necessity to pay costs of war in the absence of a fully developed and functioning system of national banking and finance, both public and private. Those circumstances no longer obtain. The existential threat to our national existence is the very device, money debasement that Washington and Wall Street then turned to and now will lead to what will become the next national and global financial crises. If this is not addressed by us now, in a civil manner under the American rule of law, it will likely be accompanied by conflict, war and violence so intense that it would "wipe the slate clean."

- *The limited and temporary suspension by Congress of the exercise of its constitutional fiduciary monetary powers and duties when the country faces annihilation by war, can be lawfully and perpetually and permanently extended by Washington and Wall Street for purposes of intentional, unrestrained manipulation of the value of American sovereign money in service of the Washington's and Wall Street's political, economic and financial advantages and self-interested objectives accomplished under cover of Washington's and Wall Street's continuous debasement of American sovereign money in an era of hyped and perpetual, continuous, but undeclared and non-existential American wars.*

False narratives continuously repeated cannot deprive ordinary Americans of their human, constitutional, legal and civil right to honest, safe and sound sovereign money.

- *Concentration of wealth and power in Washington and on Wall Street through money debasement is a laudable and desirable objective of a free, capitalist economy.*

Money debasement by Washington and Wall Street violates the Constitution, federal statutory law and the common law. It is criminal. It is intentionally manipulative and biased in favor of Washington and Wall Street who control our money supply. It is no surprise that our economy is no longer a free economy. Income, expense and the values of assets and services in our economy are driven—not by the free market—but by Congressional manipulation of fiscal and regulatory policy capture by the Washington /Wall Street corrupt criminal racketeering enterprise, as well as by distortions in credit creation and direction as in a command economy, not a free market economy. To assert otherwise is an obvious, intentional adoption of abject ignorance about the subject.

- *Although money debasement has historically constituted a capital crime, punishable by death, and notwithstanding the public's constitutionally protected civil right to honest, safe and sound sovereign money and Congress' constitutional fiduciary power and duty to provide it to the American public, Washington and Wall Street can now lawfully debase American sovereign money for their own self-serving interests: money debasement is no longer illegal; it is obsolete legal doctrine, an archaic phenomenon; and it no longer matters.*

It is not outmoded, obsolete or archaic. It is needed now more than ever. The stakes for enforcement of the value of money and cessation of money debasement have never been higher.

- *Money debasement is no longer illegal, but in fact, can lawfully form the foundation for American monetary policy conducted by the Fed, primarily through its shareholders and partners in the American monetary and banking system, the Wall Street banks, as well as the American economic and financial system.*

When the Fed was formed, the value of money was regulated under the *Currency Act of 1792*, as amended, which also provided that money debasement was a federal capital crime, punished by death. Congress has never lawfully delegated its limited constitutional money powers and duties. It has simply abandoned both the power and accompanying duties and, in a criminally corrupt racketeering enterprise with their associates in Washington and on Wall Street, have exploited the absence.

- *The Federal Reserve has unfettered power and unbridled discretion over all matters relating to American sovereign money.*

The Federal Reserve's power and discretion may only be exercised for the purposes set forth in its enabling legislation. Those purposes do not include creation or regulation of the value of money. The Federal Reserve System is bound by the Constitution and its purposes and policies are subordinate to the Constitutional congressional power and duty to regulate the value of money in accordance with and limited by an appropriate external standard of value that curbs and constrains the possibility of American money debasement.

- *Congress has lawfully and effectively delegated its monetary powers and duties to the Fed.*

Congress has not delegated that power and could only delegate that power in accordance with a Congressional, constitutionally and legally established standard of value that protects the public interest in and civil right to honest, safe and sound money.

- *The Fed has lawfully and effectively delegated its monetary powers and duties to Wall Street.*

Congressional constitutional monetary duties have not been lawfully delegated to the Fed and cannot be, and have not been lawfully delegated to Wall Street.

- *Neither Washington nor Wall Street have a legal, fiduciary duty to the American public to maintain honest, safe and sound money that is legally enforceable by the American people.*

Those who occupy public office are fiduciaries to the public in the scope of their delegated powers and duties. Monetary and banking powers have historically been and remain fiduciary by their nature.

- *Intentional money debasement is essential to the exercise by the Fed of American monetary policy.*

American monetary policy is subject and subordinate and may only be exercise with the Constitutional congressional mandate of the power and duty to regulate the value of money and therefore to maintain an honest, safe and sound banking, financial and monetary systems and monetary policy.

- *Federal bank and financial regulatory policies and processes provide a legally honest, safe, sound and effective substitute for the proper exercise by Congress of its fiduciary duty to the American public to create honest, safe and sound constitutional sovereign money, and to adequately protect the public interest in, and civil right to honest, safe and sound sovereign money.*

That narrative is demonstrably false based upon the facts publicly known and documented by the Financial Crisis Inquiry Committee, the balance of the public record, and the literature published prior to and following the crisis.

- *The commonly accepted narratives of "extend and pretend," "kick the can down the road," "deny and lie," "too big to fail," "too big to jail," bailouts, subsidies, Quantitative Easing, interest rate and asset valuation manipulation, cumulatively constitute systemic lying to, cheating and stealing from ordinary Americans, but yet are legitimate monetary and regulatory policies necessary to assure an honest, safe and sound American sovereign money, financial system and economy.*

This narrative is absolutely false on its face. This narrative of Washington and Wall Street "memes" is inherently false. The meanings of the words used in these false narratives confirm the deceit, dishonesty and intentional misleading and fraudulent inherent in the narratives.

- *There exists no legal foundation for the judicial system to protect the interests of the American public's civil right to honest, safe and sound sovereign money.*

This narrative is demonstrably false. The legal foundation is grounded in the Congressional delegated powers and duties to ordinary Americans under Article I, § 8, Clause 5 of the Constitution, in its context, as well as in ordinary Americans' fundamental civil right to protection of their property rights in the face of deprivation of the value of their property through Washington's and Wall Street's violations of their civil right to due process of the law under the Fifth and Fourteenth Amendments to the Constitution and to equal protection of the law under the 5th and 14th *Amendments to the United States Constitution*, bank fraud, RICO, anti-monopoly, anti-trust and anti-tying statutes.

Washington's and Wall Street's actions are illegal. Americans have legal recourse. Individually, with limited resources, we are powerless. Together we can take meaningful action. The book establishes that prospect.

American society is based on the common belief that honesty, truth and justice will, somehow eventually prevail. That can only be assured if asserted in the last available forum designed to protect honesty truth and justice under the American rule of law: the judicial system. Congress has failed us. The executive has failed us. The judicial system is ordinary American's last stop before anger, outrage and violence overrun informed dialogue.

Ordinary Americans do not now see how they can get relief. We have been force fed the false narratives, and now believe that our path to justice through the American legal system is too complicated. It is not too complicated. The legal issues are simple and clear. The factual proof exists in the public record. Connection of the facts to existing law is simple. The legal wrongdoing at issue is the systematic abuse of power by Washington and Wall Street to conduct a massive program of misrepresentation of the value of money and, therefore, the value of assets denominated in that money. The moral principles are simple and clear. Ordinary Americans' quest for honesty and justice through our legal system can prevail over Washington's and Wall Street's abuse of monetary power and monetary fraud through enforcement of due process and equal protection of the American people under the American rule of law. Washington and Wall Street perpetuation of their complex web of false narratives covering up their course of lying cheating and stealing through money debasement cannot be permitted to prevail.

Understanding the simplicity of the case and acting on it are two different things. Not only must we take our legal rights in hand, but we must be equipped to weather Washington's and Wall Street's justifications, defenses and threats of retribution and retaliation that undoubtedly will meet our well-articulated public legal demands for justice.

The detail of my work enforces the reality of the prevailing false narratives, picks them apart and confirms that the American rule of law, enforced by the people through a judiciary free from corruption, can provide financial crisis accountability, retribution, and a foundation upon which honesty, truth and justice once again serve the interests or ordinary Americans.

So, my book acknowledges and builds on the vast body of knowledge and expert analysis that have been developed over long history and continued in the wake of the great financial crisis and connect it to meaningful action. The published work to date is powerful and consistent, but fails to advocate a course or meaningful action to protect the interests of the American public under the American rule of law.

The extensive existing literature has stopped short of demanding simple basic legal accountability. To take meaningful action, Americans must appreciate the legal simplicity of the necessary action, but also they must be convinced that the legal action can be proved out and accountability enforced in the face of the predominant false narratives and the complexities they present. This book advocates a specific meaningful course of action that can, and must be pursued in protection of our nation, our security and our way of life.

Big Data, Abuse of Power and Fraud

America, led by financial, economic and monetary experts in Washington and on Wall Street, have driven headlong into dominant use of the tools of big data accumulation feeding back through high tech systems and mathematical algorithms as unworthy substitutes for wisdom and value judgments. The old canard that the numbers do not lie is a profound falsehood. The numbers are highly manipulated and that manipulation goes to the heart of the intentional financial misrepresentations that reverberate through our society resulting directly in financial fraud and financial crises. No less a luminary than Henry Kissinger recently commented on the implications of that fact on matters of fundamental, thoughtful, wise, moral, legal and thoughtful decision making.[11]

As Kissinger notes: "Truth becomes relative. Information threatens to overwhelm wisdom." As a matter of fact, it has repeatedly overwhelmed wisdom. The supporting facts are replete throughout the literature and, specifically, in the *Financial Crisis Inquiry Report*. Kissinger notes that the purpose of financial data systems:

> ... is to ratify knowledge through the accumulation and manipulation of ever-expanding data. Human cognition *loses its personal character*. Individuals turn into data and data becomes regnant.

Users of the internet emphasize retrieving and manipulating information over contextualizing or conceptualizing its meaning. They rarely interrogate history or philosophy; as a rule, they demand information relevant to their immediate practical needs.[12]

Political leaders, and their partners on Wall Street, are ostensibly serving their own interests as well as the public interest, in a manifestly dangerous and damaging manner, through The *National Bank Acts*, the *National Currency Act* and the *Federal Reserve Act*, all as amended, who are charged with the primary constitutional duty to regulate the value of the dollar so it may serve as an honest, safe and sound currency binding our society and culture, have all abjectly failed in their overriding constitutional duty to Americans. Kissinger further notes:

The ability [of Washington and Wall Street] to target micro-groups has broken up the previous consensus on priorities by permitting a focus on specialized purposes or grievances. Political leaders, overwhelmed by niche pressures, are deprived of time to think or reflect on context, contracting the space available for them to develop vision.

The digital world's emphasis on speed inhibits reflection; its incentive empowers the radical over the thoughtful; its values are shaped by subgroup consensus, not by introspection. For all its achievements, it runs the risk of turning on itself as its impositions overwhelm its conveniences.[13]

We must all come to understand that our economic and monetary systems have mutated from its intended purpose to a game of numbers manipulation that is rigged favor of Washington and Wall Street. The game embraces a subversive and damaging illegal policy and practice of deliberate, intentional abuse of power and fraud that have led to financial crises and a crisis of income and wealth diversion and concentration that threatens our national existence.

Ordinary Americans do not have to labor through each technical issue that stands between them and justice. A work of the power, depth and breadth of my book is indispensable to support public confidence and incentive to band together and take meaningful legal action. The now embedded systemic tragedy of pervasive abuse of power to entrench systemic economic oppression is known in the hearts of most Americans, and will inevitably come to an end. History and the existing literature confirm that it will end upon either the enforcement of accountability under the American rule of law, or as the grisly product of violence. That has been the case since the invention of money and government.

Dishonesty and abuse of power have perversely become business models, business plans and an accepted code of conduct and measure for success in Washington and on Wall Street. Washington has lost all credibility, but not wealth and not power. Wall Street has fully exploited the state of affairs. That conclusion is no news to most Americans.

Kissinger sums up the crises we face in his own terms:

> By treating a mathematical process as if it were a thought process, and either trying to mimic that process ourselves or merely accepting the results, we are in danger of losing the capacity that has been the essence of human cognition.[14]

Every American has a legal civil right to honest, safe and sound money. We are entitled to be protected from the almost unfathomable harm we have already suffered. Every American must contribute to our shared mission to dispel the false narratives that divide us and block mobilization of action to bring Washington and Wall Street to justice and restore honesty in financial and governmental relationships. Ordinary Americans can and must, as an existential matter of survival, enforce and re-establish the sovereignty of ordinary Americans through enforcement of due process of and equal protection under the existing American rule of the law of money.

Imposition of the legal and financial accountability of Washington and Wall Street for the financial crisis will enable Americans to enforce the reestablishment of money on the basis of honesty, stability, safety and soundness. Honest money is the glue that binds our society.

Washington and Wall Street will engage with the public in rebalancing of the scales of justice only when faced with the financial death penalty of $60 trillion in liability, a judicial mandate for compliance with the American law of money, and recognition of the limited powers and fiduciary duties of Washington and Wall Street with respect to sovereign money, and their ongoing responsibility to serve the public interest in creating, emitting and regulating the value of honest, safe and sound money. America's judicial system can provide the proper forum for:

- The open, transparent and measured allocation of losses from the financial crisis.
- Enforcement of the constitutional, common law and statutory protection of the honesty, safety, and soundness of American money.

Enable the people to achieve some measure of compensation in damages and deterrence to ongoing money debasement, while:

- enabling Washington and Wall Street to shed their practices of abuse of power and lying to, cheating and stealing from the public, that have led to a seemingly unbridgeable gap of income and wealth disparity, and
- enabling Washington to finance itself by means other than money debasement while eliminating Wall Street's ability to debase sovereign money.

Ordinary Americans' legal case is no less significant and constitutionally based civil rights case than the landmark civil rights case of *Brown v. Board of Education*[15]. Following the precedent of *Brown II*[16], which provided the road map for protection of ordinary Americans from unlawful discrimination, the American people must take judicial action to enforce their claims for losses, damages, deterrence and costs suffered in the Great Financial Crisis as well as to formulate and enforce a judicial mandated and supervised return to honest, safe and sound money in a reasonable and practical manner that enforces, protects and preserves ordinary American's civil rights and that reins in the criminal, corrupt fraudulent manipulation and corruption of American money for the benefit of the Washington Wall Street corrupt racketeering enterprise. The surreptitious abuse of power and bank fraud by America's government and financial elite has proven, ultimately, historically, to be fatal to societies that fail to take initiative through legal action to protect and preserve honest, safe and sound money as the foundation on which the societies' economic, financial and legal relationships are grounded.

Clear Objectives

The success of any civil legal proceedings for accountability and justice would also establish a clear foundation for the public to:

- Hold Wall Street banks accountable for their actions by subjecting them to liability for damages, for punishment and for deterrence from future illegal conduct;
- Compel the United States Congress and the Fed to meet their obligation to regulate the value of money in accordance with the United States Constitution and the existing decisions of the United States Supreme Court; and
- Strip from the United Stated Department of Justice (DOJ) their ability to continue to obstruct the public's right to justice through systematic denial, dissembling, delay and by deliberately ignoring its responsibilities to the American people under the American rule of law; and it would compel the public's servants at the DOJ to provide due process and equal treatment to the American public under the American rule of law, including specifically the enforcement of applicable state and federal criminal laws.

Reform of the American banking, financial and monetary system to conform to and embody the fundamental moral principles and the rule of law is possible. It is feasible. What we lack is political will. Historically and even prospectively as urged by recent commentators hold that money and banking has been and will likely only ever be accomplished by violent revolution.

I believe that the necessary reform can be achieved and the incentives to reform—personal and political will—can be asserted by the American people through a legal action for financial crisis accountability as explored in this book.

Gerald Nels Olson
1 March 2019
Dallas, Texas

List of Figures

Figure 1.1	Holdings of Family Wealth, by Wealth Groups
Figure 1.2	Share of Families in Debt and Average Indebtedness for Those Families
Figure 1.3	How Money Is Created
Figure 1.4	Money Supply Versus Dollar Buying Power
Figure 3.1	Fed Balance Sheet
Figure 4.1	US Dollar Purchasing Power / 1774-2012 (Log Scale)
Figure 4.2	Average Income per Family
Figure 4.3	Household: Average and Change
Figure 4.4	Wealth Distribution
Figure 4.5	Average Incomes United States: 1913-2012
Figure 4.6	Mortgage and Credit Crisis-Related Litigation and Settlement
Figure 4.7	Credit Crisis and Mortgage-Related Settlements for Selected Bank Holding Companies
Figure 4.8	$Billions Paid in Settlements
Figure 4.9	Cumulative Inflation by Decade Since 1913
Figure 4.10	US Purchasing Power as Measured by Gold
Figure 4.11	US Purchasing Power During the 20th Century
Figure 4.12	US Household Income (2011 $s)
Figure 4.13	Income Distribution in the US
Figure 4.14	Balance Sheet Policy as the Exact Analog of Interest Rate Policy
Figure 5.1	Heads on Pikes
Figure 6.1	Required Reserves Minus Vault Cash (As Adjusted for Inflation)
Figure 8.1	NCREIF Property Index
Figure 8.2	NCREIF Annual NPI Return History
Figure 10.1	US BLS Consumer Price Index NSA (CPUSAM) Versus Switzerland Franks per Dollar (USDCHF)

Figure 10.2 Concentration of Wealth United States and Political Division and Dysfunction in the United States
Figure 10.3 Average Household Income—Change of Share in Income

CHAPTER 1
Introduction

§1.01 CONTEXT

Money debasement, by definition, is the intentional misrepresentation of the underlying value, supposedly represented by that money. Historically money debasement has been a capital crime, punishable by death. The most severe punishment under law.

In America, ordinary Americans, constitutionally delegated to Congress, as a fiduciary, the power and duty to maintain honest, safe, and sound money. Fiduciary duty is the highest duty under law. By definition, one who has been entrusted with fiduciary power and duty must place the interest of the grantor of that power and duty ahead of the fiduciary holder of that power and duty.

It is clear that the fiduciary power duty to maintain honest, safe, and sound money, without debasement; a power and duty that represents the highest duty under law, is assured by the correlative sanction; the most severe punishment under the law applicable to its violation—the death penalty.

Historically, a society's government and wealthy elite have sought to debase money—an intentional fraud upon the society who use and depend on the integrity of that money. In the modern era, money debasement has only rarely been constrained by enforcement of any form of accountability under law. The historic cycle of enforced accountability for money debasement has been accomplished through bloody revolution and war. The historical record of these cycles of intentional fraud followed by society's remedies of bloody violence and death confirms the high importance of honest, safe and sound money. Bloody violence and death, often leading to societal collapse, can, and must be avoided by the enforcement of the American rule of law.

Americans established the fiduciary power and duty of the American law of money in our *Constitution*. The death penalty for debasement of money was established in America's first legislation relating to the law of money. It is not at all clear whether the death penalty for money debasement has been repealed, although other aspects of that legislation have been repealed or superseded over time. It is indisputable that fiduciary duty incorporated in America's constitutional law of money.

These simple statements, as incredible as it may seem, are true. Most politicians, financial regulators and bankers would deny the existence of America's basic and fundamental law of money. American history details the progressive, persistent and unceasing efforts of our governmental and financial elite to obscure public perception of the nature of money debasement and the definitional existence of the fiduciary standard applicable to their powers and duties in our monetary system, to the point that our monetary system has been so manipulated by Washington and Wall Street to have been literally stood on its head.

It cannot reasonable or accurate to deny that Congress has the constitutionally established fiduciary duty to create and emit money and to regulate its value. Bank depositor used to own their own money, whether in hand or deposited with a bank. The bank was obligated, as a fiduciary, to keep the depositor's money safe and sound, and to return it to the depositor without diminution in kind, quality or quantity; that is to say, without debasement.

Depositors no longer own their money on deposit; they loan it to the bank to use as it will; free subject it to future risk and uncertainty of repayment, for the banks own profit and benefit. That relationship is the polar opposite of the fiduciary standard. Depositors are now simply consumers of bank financial services. Protection of bank customers interests have been fully subordinated to the interests of bankers, financial regulators and government officials who trade their policies and actions for lobbyists contributions and a shot at their turn in the highly profitable world of Wall Street banking. Wall Street bankers now take the position that as opposed to a fiduciary standard, the pubic, customers, should know, expect and anticipate that the banks will lie to them about their legal duties and standards of care and should not expect the banks should be truthful. A recent pleading filed by Wells Fargo & Company and certain of its officers to that effect.[17] There have even been cases holding, in effect, that government has no duty to tell truth to the public.

We, the American public have stood back and watched our value system, most conspicuously represented by our monetary system eviscerated? The status quo does not respect the American civil constitutional right to honest safe and sound money it does not respect the fiduciary duty upon which money and banking are based. In fact, one might argue that the death penalty for its violation may still apply and be enforced.

Life is not that simple. We are tasked with our own duty to pick apart the insidious stripping away of American rights and endorse our rights under the American rule of law. No matter the outrageous results of the long history of the apparent degradation of the American civil right to money free of debasement, and the incalculable damage to our society, times have changed. The perpetrators of the current regime of money debasement to now assume that a civilized hanging or beheading of the actors in Washington and on Wall Street are not likely where we will find justice. But unless we enforce the rule of law and protect our rights, history instructs us that the eventual alternatives will be bloody and violent.

We cannot expect voluntary acknowledgment by Washington and Wall Street of their fiduciary duty and any meaningful action to provide justice and accountability.

Their object is to postpone the certain day of reckoning, and our current President expressed his attitude toward fiscal irresponsibility—just do not care because he would not be around for the day of reckoning.

It is time for action. It is past time for action. But what can we do? Will it work? How can we act effectively to avoid to the specter of bloody war and revolution that has ever been the unavoidable consequence of money debasement? This book is my contribution to the dialogue that can lead directly to effective action.

Before we jump the gun and demand the abolition of the Fed—and imposition of a death penalty of a sort on the Fed and the Wall Street banks, please remember that the Fed is a creature of Congress, which, in cahoots with the other financial regulators and their partners, the Wall Street banks, are the masters of money debasement and are not entirely or absolutely dispensable. The relief sought in the case for financial crisis accountability must serve the interests of justice and protect ordinary Americans rights and interests without triggering a financial Armageddon. Simply adopting ridiculous policies of too big to fail or too big to jail, without any supporting evidence or public debate and consent makes a mockery of the law of money and principles of justice.[18]

We all look to the Fed for honesty safety, soundness, and stability in monetary, financial and economic affairs. You must know however, despite all rhetoric to the contrary, the Feds legislative mandate is to produce social and economic outcomes through money manipulation and debasement. There is, however, no credible evidence that it has been successful in meeting its mandate. It may have the capability to play an important role in ending money debasement and aiding in prevention of financial crises. In fact, its existing mandate is expressly subject to the constitutional mandate for Congress to create and regulate the value of our sovereign money. That mandate could be but has not been delegated to the Fed in accordance with law applicable to such a delegation, that would preserve the prime constitutional imperative of honest, safe, and sound sovereign money. Any reformed mandate for the continuation of the Fed as America's central bank and the keeper of our monetary policy must also include provision for, or rather restoration of the commercial legal principles that constrain the creation and attempted monetization of shadow banking credit and derivatives. That means legal imposition of direct accountability of the issuers and transferors of those instruments of financial liability as endorsers, whose combined financial strength represents the ultimate source of repayment of the underlying credit in sovereign money, the value of which has been regulated by Congress.

Any remedial legislative mandate arising from ordinary Americans' legal case for financial crisis accountability, may preserve the Feds statutory objectives for monetary policy—maximum employment, stable prices, and moderate long-term interest rates; provided there exists sufficient evidence that the Fed can successfully do so; and provided further that such mandate must be subject and subordinate to and constrained by Congress proper exercise of its fiduciary power and duty under the *Constitution* to create, emit and maintain a monetary system based on honest safe and sound money.

It is time to directly address the matter of moral and legal accountability for the financial crisis. It is time for ordinary Americans to invoke the enforcement of the

American rule of law. Disinformation and outright misrepresentation have become the standard for government and institutional communication. Washington and Wall Street, acting together as a corrupt racketeering enterprise (Washington Wall Street enterprise) have made it very difficult for Americans to come to grips with what they instinctively know but, individually, do not possess the resources to define and counter.

Immorality is the defining character of ordinary Americans understanding of financial crises. They know they have been lied to, cheated and stolen from. They know who did it. They have been told that nothing can be done about it. They have been assured that the appropriate response to the crisis should be for all Americans to just move on and put the past behind. While Washington and Wall Street may have done so, and in fact have profited enormously by doing so, regular Americans remain oppressed by Washington's and Wall Street's unprecedented abuse of the enormous powers entrusted to them by American public over the matter of money. That abuse of powers has been realized in the intentional misrepresentation to all Americans of the value and liquidity of assets that course through our monetary, economic, banking and financial systems.

The class warfare that has been building between the "haves" and the "have-nots" in America can lead to civil strife that has the potential to dwarf the economic, racial, and political strife experienced in America in the 1960s and 1970s, expressed in protest, riots, demonstrations and repression.

All branches of the American government now appear to have been suborned or coopted by the concentrated power of the Wall Street banks. Congress has abdicated its responsibilities. The Executive branch acting through the federal financial regulators and The DOJ has literally been asleep at the wheel, when not outright subverting ordinary Americans' right to an honest monetary, economic and financial system. These public servants remain obsessed with their potential for power and riches as they await their turn through the revolving golden door of Wall Street. The judiciary has developed a history of kowtowing to the "political nature" and "political imperative" of the monetary, economic and financial wrongs wrought on society by the American political and moneyed elite; seemingly impervious to their constitutional mandate to serve as a check on and balance of the massive abuse of power by Congress and the Executive to the demonstrable damage and injury to ordinary Americans.

Washington and Wall Street have developed false narratives to justify their behavior. That behavior mocks the clear and unequivocal American moral and legal standards that bind them. The public record of their joint conduct conclusively shows that their conduct in control over money and banking directly conflicts with and violates their constitutional, statutory and common law duties to the American polity. The narratives they offer to ordinary Americans in support of their conduct are in direct opposition to the legitimate exercise of their special monopoly powers and fiduciary duties in service to ordinary Americans, as the trusted experts and specialists in money, economy, and finance. The battle lines being drawn are not new. The current wave of abuse of power by Washington and Wall Street to deceive the American public and literally steal Americans' wealth to line their own pockets has occurred episodically throughout American and world history. The abuse of power, misrepresentation and theft of the fruits of ordinary citizens' labor and capital through intentional money debasement by partnerships of government and powerful banks throughout history follows an oft bloody arc.

The financial crisis that exploded in 2008 however is in many ways more destructive, widespread and pervasive than any that have preceded it, not only in America but globally. The tragic plight of America's working households, for the most part, has not been meaningfully addressed by either Washington or Wall Street. The questions on the one hand are whether and how the American public can enforce moral and legal accountability for the injury, damage and destruction they have suffered, directly caused by the financial crisis perpetrated by Washington and Wall Street; and whether ordinary Americans can re-secure economic change, financial safety, soundness and stability consistent with American ideals and principles under the rule of law; or whether, on the other hand, the economic divisions in America are so entrenched that civil strife and violence become the only apparently viable action alternatives; as has more often than not been the case historically since the invention of money, banking and government, as so ably chronicled in existing literature. The willingness of both banking and government to abuse their powers to levels that have become unsupportable and unsustainable by our society and thus to their very limits of toleration, have left our nation fully exposed to the portents of another, the next, oncoming financial disaster and the specter of violence among the 99 percent of society who have borne the personal, social and economic carnage directly attributable to the financial crisis.

§1.02 TRUE SCOPE OF THE FINANCIAL CRISIS AFFECTING ORDINARY AMERICANS

The Associate Press reported on Monday, June 11, 2012, that according to the Fed: *"US Wealth Fell Nearly 40% in 2007-2010 on Housing Losses."* Referring to the AP report on the Fed study, John Carville asked in a CNN blog the next day: "What if the rich lost 40% of their wealth?

Let's imagine that yesterday there was a front-page story in The New York Times that:

> The recent economic crisis left the top 1% of Americans in 2010 with no more wealth than in the early 1990s, erasing almost two decades of accumulated prosperity.
>
> A hypothetical family richer than the median net worth of the top 1% of the nation's families had a net worth of $77.3 million in 2010, compared with $126.4 million in 2007, the Fed said. The crash of the stock market, in addition to the collapse of housing prices in Greenwich, Connecticut, the Upper East Side of New York City, Beverly Hills, Highland Park in Dallas and the North Shore of Chicago, directly accounted for three-quarters of the loss.

What do you think the reaction would be to that?

The elite would call for the suspension of habeas corpus, the government would call out the National Guard, invade Honduras and the Supreme Court would announce that it is in session 24/7 to take any action deemed necessary to help their friends.

> *The Wall Street Journal* would have a black border on the newspaper. *The Financial Times* would go from pink to gray. CNBC would play funeral music for nine months. Steve Schwarzman would compare it to the H-word. Cable networks would roadblock all coverage.
>
> Minimum wage laws would be suspended, the 40-hour work week would be thrown out, perhaps they would even do away with child labor laws to get productivity up so profits could increase to make up for lost revenue.
>
> OK, we know that story did not appear in Wednesday's *New York Times*, and we would certainly agree that a massive loss of wealth in the top 1% would wreak economic havoc on the country. But there was, if anything, a worse story on that front page with only minor variations from our hypothetical scenario.
>
> The story said that the recent economic crisis left the average American family in 2010 with no more wealth than in the early 1990s, erasing almost two decades of accumulated prosperity, reducing their net worth by almost 40% ....
>
> To put it bluntly, the middle class in this country has been screwed, blued and tattooed.
>
> > It is a depressing state of affairs when about two-thirds of our fellow citizens are caught in an economic trap that is wrecking their lives financially and emotionally.

The American government's reaction to all of this has been tepid, at best. Americans losses have been characterized as just "housing losses".

Stacy Curtin, recently observed in a *Yahoo News* post that *Better Markets*, a pro-financial reform Wall Street watchdog, has released what it is calling the "first-ever" report totaling the loss of American wealth since Lehman filed for bankruptcy on September 15, 2008:

> The Washington Post recently reported that: "[t]he Great Recession and the subsequent recovery from it have deepened the wedge between the very wealthy and everyone else in America, plunging the poor deeper into debt and wiping out two-fifths of the wealth held by families in the heart of the middle class. The wealthiest Americans, meanwhile, appear close to regaining all their losses over the same period, according to a new analysis released Thursday by the Congressional Budget Office (CBO)."
>
> The analysis shows the wealthiest 10 percent of Americans now hold three-quarters of the nation's wealth, up from two-thirds in 1989, and a three percentage-point increase from the start of the recession. Most Americans found themselves with less wealth in 2013 than Americans of a similar age had in 1989; the only age group doing better than its counterparts from a quarter-century ago was senior citizens.
>
> The report was commissioned at the request of Senator Bernie Sanders of Vermont, who made inequality a central theme of his run for the Democratic presidential nomination this year. In a statement, he said the analysis "makes clear that since the 1980s there has been an enormous transfer of wealth from the middle class and the poor to the wealthiest people in this country.

Figure 1.1 Holdings of Family Wealth, by Wealth Groups

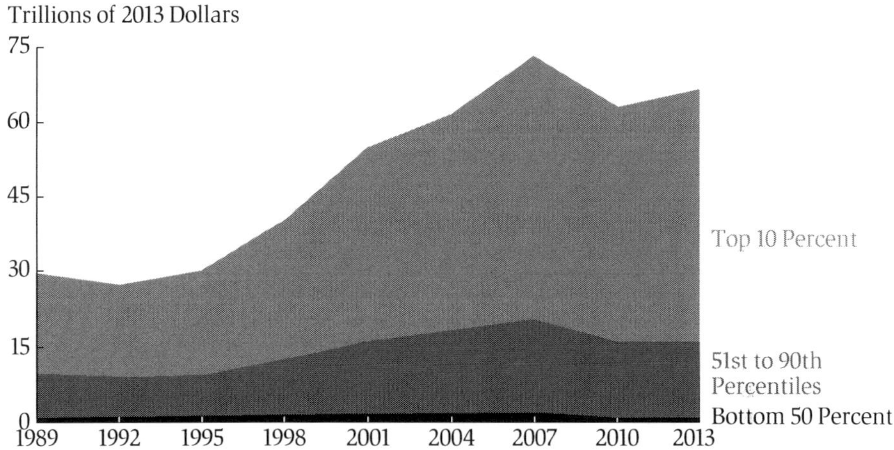

Source: Congressional Budget Office, using data from the Survey of Consumer Finances, supplemented with data from Forber magazine's list of the nation's 400 wealthiest people.
The Survey of Consumer Finances is conducted every three years.

CBO shows that the median family had about the same amount of wealth — roughly $80,000 — in 2013 as it did in 1989, after adjusting for inflation. The average family in the top 10 percent had $4.1 million in wealth, up from $2.15 million in 1989. Both groups had substantially more wealth before the recession hit, but those at the top have seen theirs bounce back at a much faster rate than those in the middle.

The story at the very bottom is much worse. Americans who live in poverty, or even at the lower end of the middle class, have never had much wealth. They do not tend to play the stock market much, or even own their own houses. From 1989 to 2007, the average family in the bottom 25 percent of the wealth distribution found itself with around $1,000 in debt. After the recession that average debt ballooned to $13,000 per family.

More than half of the homeowners at that bottom end of the wealth distribution were underwater on their mortgages in 2013, the CBO reported, meaning they owe more than their homes are worth. That's up from 10 percent underwater before the recession.

Those families have also borrowed heavily for education, the report notes: "Over that period," CBO says, "the share of families with student debt increased from 25 percent to 36 percent, and the average amount increased from $24,000 to $36,000." By contrast, the share of those low-wealth families with credit card debt actually declined.

CBO also blames underwater mortgages and increased student borrowing for a broader trend in the recovery: a 50 percent increase in the share of American homes in debt.

Figure 1.2 Share of Families in Debt and Average Indebtedness for Those Families

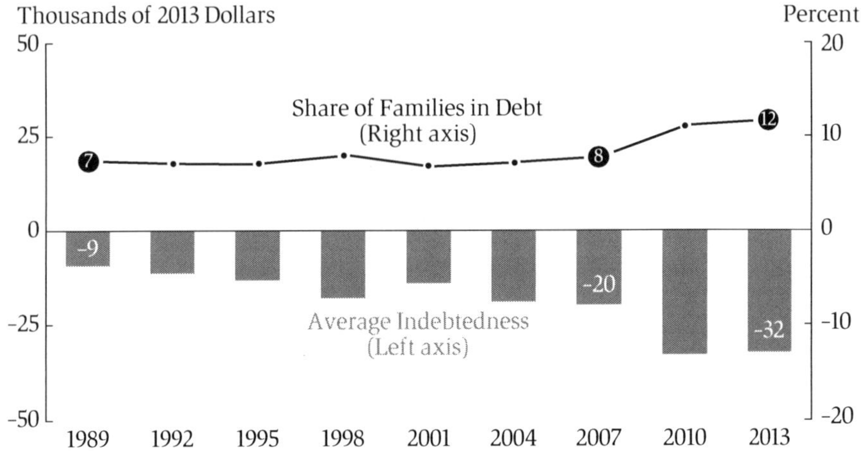

Source: Congressional Budget Office, using data from the Survey of Consumer Finances. The Survey of Consumer Finances is conducted every three years.

In 2007, the report notes, 8 percent of American families were in debt, at an average debt level of $20,000 each. By 2013, 12 percent of families were in debt — and the average level had grown to $32,000."[19]

The injuries and damages we have suffered are massive. They have not been redressed. Ordinary Americans remain the losers from the crisis while Washington and Wall Street have successfully protected and improved their own interests in income, wealth and power. Ordinary Americans' incomes remain at 1974 levels, inflation adjusted. The gap in wealth and power in America between ordinary Americans and America's wealth and power elite in Washington and on Wall Street are greater now than at the time of the Great Depression.

§1.03 ORDINARY AMERICANS HAVE BEEN INJURED IN FACT

The great body of ordinary American's has, and continues to suffer the damages inflicted upon us by the Washington and Wall Street corrupt criminal racketeering enterprise, consists specifically of:

- the innocent American individuals or households; all American individual depositors, customers and counterparties of federally insured or regulated financial institutions; and all American individuals or households whose credit or loan accounts at federally regulated depository financial institutions whose accounts and banking activities are denominated in United States official sovereign money, United Stated Federal Reserve Notes, within the ten year period preceding the publication of the Commission Report; and

- who have suffered one or more of the actual or threatened injuries in fact objectively itemized by the government and expert reports as having been suffered by ordinary Americans in common with one another, to a greater of lesser degree, and for which we must demand redress under the American rule of law.

Estimates of the number of members of public, who constitute the affected households, range from 155,559,000 to 159,068,557 ordinary people.

According to the US Bureau of Labor Statistics, there are 11,742,000 working age Americans that are officially unemployed. In addition, the US Bureau of Labor Statistics says that there are 89,967,000 working age Americans that are "not in the labor force". That is a new all-time record, and that number increased by a whopping 663,000 during the month of March alone. When you add 11,742,000 working age Americans that are officially unemployed to the 89,967,000 working age Americans that are "not in the labor force", you come up with a grand total of 101,709,000 working age Americans that do not have a job.[20]

[A] Ordinary American Household Damages

The Federal Reserve Bank of Dallas in 2013 estimated damages ranging from $50,000 to $120,000 per household, for a range of total damages of $6 trillion to $14 trillion based on their assumption of 120 million households. The United States Census, 2010—2014, prepared by the United States Department of Commerce estimates American households of 116,211,092.[21]

The Federal Reserve Bank of Dallas,[22] The US Department of the Treasury[23] estimates $19.2 trillion in lost household wealth, or $160,000 per household based upon 120 million households, and the Feds *Survey of Consumer Finances* estimate of damage in the form of lost median household net worth of $49,000 per household, between 2007 and 2010) have all calculated loss, cost or damage by reference to American households. In addition, *Better Markets* in its reports on the cost of the crisis, dated, September 15, 2012 and July 2014, estimate, loss, cost or damage by house hold and on a gross basis, more than $12.8 trillion ($106,667 per household) in 2012, and more than $20 trillion ($166,667, per household) in 2015, respectively. Accordingly, Washington and Wall Street could conceivably face a class composed of approximately 120 million American households, suffering damages of $83,334 per household, identified and calculated by the criteria set forth above.

[B] How Have Washington and Wall Street Wrought These Damages on Ordinary American Households?

Washington and Wall Street have acted in concert to usurp and abuse the power to create sovereign money; the value of which is not regulated in accordance with the requirements of the *United States Constitution*; is emitted through the Federal Reserve System (the Fed) and national banking systems, based upon the United States dollar as the medium for the discharge of all debts, public and private. The American dollar is the exclusive defined unit in use to denominate accounts, serve as a medium of exchange, a store of value and as a standard for deferred payments.

Washington and Wall Street have acted in concert to wield the power they have illegally seized in their economic and financial assault on their targeted victims, ordinary Americans and their households. Their collective and concerted action constitutes the ancient tort of money debasement.

§1.04 MONEY DEBASEMENT CONSTITUTES AN INTENTIONAL MISREPRESENTATION OF MONEY AND ASSETS DENOMINATED IN THAT MONEY

Washington's and Wall Street's money debasement is realized by dilution and diminishment the value of the dollar as it used in all its capacities, and specifically by the ordinary people and households of America.

Americans have looked to the powerful, privileged governmental, economic and financial institutions of America to protect their interests in accordance with the law of the land, but who instead combined as a corrupt racketeering enterprise to loot the value of the dollar through the weapon of fraudulent debasement, to profit and benefit the enterprise from that fraud and to beat the accompanying losses and damages onto unsuspecting ordinary working American households. A beating with an economic and financial cudgel money debasement leaving losses and damages as the wounds, broken bones, cuts bruises and ruined lives of the ordinary working American households—the fruits of their labor appropriated by the Washington Wall Street corrupt criminal racketeering enterprise.

[A] Debasement of American Money and the American Rule of Law

American money debasement and the entirely predictable damages it causes is in fact is fairly traceable to the conduct of the Washington Wall Street corrupt enterprise and can be redressed in an adversary legal context capable of judicial resolution.

Americans have been devastated by the financial crisis. Each American individual household member has sufficient personal stake in the outcome of the case to ensure the court that each is a "proper party to present the claim in a legally adversary context and in a form historically viewed as capable of judicial resolution." Personal stake is established when the damaged party or parties allege having suffered a "discrete", "palpable", "injury-in-fact" fairly traceable to the conduct of the Washington / Wall Street enterprise and likely to be redressed by the requested relief. Ordinary Americans as a class have suffered and been damaged, "injured in fact", in a myriad of individual ways and to a greater or lesser degree, by the financial crisis.

[B] Ordinary American's Damages from the Washington's and Wall Street's Money Debasement Constitute Real Injuries in Fact

According to the Federal Reserve Bank of Dallas, *Staff Report No. 20,* July 2013, the *General Accounting Office Report to Congressional Requesters* (GAO), GAO - 13 - 180, January 2013, and other official sources, the symptoms of the injury in fact suffered by each American household in fact are the following, appearing in different varieties and to greater of lesser degrees. Each and all of the injuries are a manifestation, or symptom, of the injury in fact suffered and constituting for each them as a household and as aggregated, caused by Washington's and Wall Street's commission of the tort of intentional misrepresentation of the value of their money and assets through money debasement. The debasement of American money is violation of the common law, the *United States Constitution* and federal statutes. The GAO has described Americans' injuries in fact as:

- Erosion of savings home equity and fair return on savings, sacrificed to support profits and bonuses for bankers and banker support of politicians and bureaucrats through the revolving door between Washington power and Wall Street riches resulting in lost consumption for the public.
- National trauma.
- Unemployment and underemployment—extended bouts of forced unemployment resulting in exit from the labor force permanently.
- Non-pecuniary costs such as stress, shame and feelings of loss of control.
- Costs of joblessness beyond lost income.
- Decreases of job security and anxiety about job prospects.
- Loss of place and prospects in work force loss of familiarity with technical aspects of occupation.
- Reduced opportunities associated with severe job cuts.
- Stigma of being outside productive labor force.
- Deterioration of existing skill sets in changing marketplace.
- Psychological consequences.
- Destruction of the idea of earned success.
- Worse physical and psychological health, stress related diseases, depression heart attacks, strokes, suicide—all worsen as unemployment and income and wealth disparities increase and savings are depleted.
- Less likely to be rehired even if extended unemployment is due only to weak economic conditions.
- Cut off of access to credit for people least able to afford it.
- Lowering rate of household formation.
- Decline in labor market participation rate.
- Loss of trust in government institutions and capitalistic economic system and democratic representative government due to preference shown to rich and powerful to protect them from consequences of the direct actions; privatizing profits and socializing losses violating a basic tenet of American democracy and capitalism.

- Bailouts and subsidies that are economically and politically offensive and a perversion of the principles of capitalism, crippling public trust.
- Less secure property rights.
- Bigger government's increased regulation of business while bankers and politicians get a free pass from the same treatment.
- Favoritism to special interest groups.

The scourge of money debasement includes demonstrable higher rates of incidence of crime and violence. The bloodstained headlines of the news have not appeared from nowhere, *sua sponte*, so to speak. They are part and parcel of the injury in fact complained of in this case.

Increasing violence and crime is a caused and exacerbated by and is a direct response to dramatic increases and distortions of unjustified economic inequality which are inherent in the intentional fraudulent debasement of money perpetrated by the corrupt racketeering enterprise as confirmed by the evidence in this case.[24]

Increasing violence and crime is a caused and exacerbated by and is a direct response to dramatic increases and distortions of unjustified economic inequality which are inherent in the intentional fraudulent debasement of money perpetrated by the defendant corrupt racketeering enterprise as confirmed by the evidence in this case. See, *e.g.*, "Jealous of the Joneses: conspicuous consumption, inequality, and crime," Oxf. Econ. Pap. (2014) 66 (4): 1090-1120 first published online June 20, 2014; Pablo Fajnzylber, University of Minas Gerais Daniel Lederman, World Bank and Norman Loayza, World Bank Inequality and Violent Crime*, *Journal of Law and Economics*, vol. XLV (April 2002), The University of Chicago; and Walter Scheidel, "*The Great Leveler: Violence and the Global History of Inequality from the Stone Age to the Present*", Princeton University Press (2014, 2015); and see Mark Buchanan and Mark Whitehouse, "Want to Fight Crime? Address Economic Inequality," *Bloomberg*, January 6, 2013. http://www.bloombergview.com/articles/2013-01-06/want-to-fight-crime-address-economic-inequality.

A new study published in June 2014 in the *British Journal of Psychiatry*, by researchers at Oxford and the London School of Hygiene and Tropical Medicine, has found that suicide rates increased in North America and Europe during the recent economic recession, resulting in at least 10,000 additional deaths between 2008 and 2010.[25]

The foregoing described symptoms are manifestations of Americans' injuries in fact of which they complain and for which they can seek redress under the American rule of law. These injuries bear the same relationship to the injury in fact, by comparison, as the relationship of the bloody wounds, broken bones, bruises and trauma that are the proof of the tort of assault committed on unwitting victims, bears on a physical brutal beating.

The well documented phenomenon of today's increasing levels of violence and crime is caused and exacerbated by, and is a direct response to dramatic increases and distortions of unjustified economic inequality which are inherent in the intentional fraudulent debasement of money perpetrated by the Washington Wall Street corrupt racketeering enterprise, has been chronicled in my books. This is not a new phenomenon. It has occurred regularly throughout history. The cause is always the same. The response can be conducted in accordance with the rule of law, or it will eventually out in crime and violence to the point of increasing repression, violent and bloody war, revolution and the upheaval and chaotic transformation of society; wiping the slate clean, so to speak and forcing a levelling of the economic playing field.

[C] Money Debasement Is an Ancient Crime: An Ancient Tort—It Is Not a New Phenomenon

Money debasement through the distortions of unsupportable credit creation, as in today's shadow banking system, undisciplined by a constant standard of money valuation and the application of ancient restraints on credit creation and its monetization are recognized to lie at the heart of financial crises going back at least 800 years. *This Time is Different* by Carmen M. Rhinehart and Kenneth S. Rogoff is an excellent recent work often cited with approval by former American Treasury Secretary Geitner. It is one of several recent books published by highly credible and respected authors focusing on systemic risk of money debasement through unrestrained credit creation and monetization as the fundamental cause of systemic banking and financial crises. Other recent contributions to the literature on systemic financial risk and crises include *Exorbitant Privilege* by Barry Eichengreen, *Hall of Mirrors: The Great Depression, the Great Recession, and the Uses—and Misuses—of History,* also by Barry Eichengreen, *Inflated,* by R. Christopher Whalen, *Financial Stability; Fraud, Confidence, and the Wealth of Nations,* by Frederick L Feldkamp and R. Christopher Whalen, the Second Edition of *New Monetarism,* and now *Sovereign Discredit,* both by David Roche and Bob McKee and *The Ascent of Money,* by Niall Ferguson The classic starting point for knowledge of this subject is *Manias, Panics, and Crashes; a History of Financial Manias, Panics, and Crashes; a History of Financial Crises,* first published in 1978, the Fourth Edition published in 2000, Charles Kindleberger. The classic of work of history confirming the recurring nature of crises of money debasement such as the current great financial crisis is Yale Professor Paul Kennedy's monumental work *The Rise and Fall of Great Powers.*

The American revolutionary war was fought over much more diminutive grounds of abuse of power than the U.S. government and its partner banks on Wall Street have displayed in this financial crisis.

The financial crisis is wrong and irresponsible; but is it criminal? In order to get to the bottom of accountability the financial crisis, we have to answer some fundamental questions:

- What is the American financial system comprised of; what are its components?
- What laws, if any have been broken by the Washington and Wall Street?
- Who in Washington and on Wall Street are morally and legally responsible for the integrity of the American financial system and its components, including specifically, money, under the American rule of law and who have failed to meet those responsibilities?

- Who, if anyone, can be held accountable under the American rule of law for the failures of the American financial system that brought on this crisis?
- Should we, the American people, punish those persons and institutions that are responsible and accountable for the bad behavior that caused the crises, and if so, how can we do this under the rule of American law?
- How can we deter the continuation or repetition of the wrong, irresponsible, and illegal conduct in the future?
- What action can be taken, if any, to avoid the likelihood of future crises?

This book is my third on the subject of financial crises and builds on the ground covered in the first two.

§1.05 THE EMPEROR HAS NO CLOTHES

In this work, I shine a spotlight on the "elephant in the room" that few acknowledge. Hans Christian Andersen made the point in *"The Emperor's New Clothes*[26]", a short tale about two weavers who promise an Emperor a new suit of clothes that is invisible to those unfit for their positions, stupid, or incompetent. When the Emperor parades before his subjects in his new clothes, a child cries out, "But he isn't wearing anything at all!" This ancient fairy tale expression reflects a timeless wisdom that applies today. We are assured that our legal, accounting, financial, fiscal, monetary and regulatory systems are the world's best and most effective; and that failures leading to financial crises come from somewhere and someone outside of our system.

Someone needs to demonstrate that it just isn't so. Apparently, that is the responsibility of the intellectual "Hans Christian Anderson" children amongst us. The courtiers in Washington seem to think that their ineffective to non-existent legal, accounting, financial, fiscal, monetary and regulatory clothes are well suited to the Emperors represented by Washington and Wall Street. The rest of us are intellectual children, apparently unfit to question congressional, federal regulatory and Wall Street motives and actions. We are by their definition stupid, or incompetent to judge. The rest of us, intellectual children, must, however, forcibly demonstrate definitively and at once that it just isn't so.

The reader may know, and by now should not be surprised to discover, that there is considerable obfuscation in the description of the various components of the American financial system. The components that our government legally defines as the components of our financial system do not include all the components of the financial system at work in the real marketplace. There appears to be some level of accepted wisdom (one of the web of false monetary narratives) amongst the experts that this situation is to be expected, since the accepted wisdom is also that we can also expect that the private sector is somehow smarter than the government and will always be able to cook up some financial structure not anticipated by the American and global "official" financial system. In the words of Charles Kindleberger "the process (of creating new forms of money and credit) is endless: 'Fix any 'M' and the market will create new forms of money in periods of boom to get around the limit and create the necessity to fix a new variable M1." That was true at the time. Today the lines between government and banking have blurred even further. Money has moved largely out of the banking system and into the shadow banking system. The "M"s are no longer even defined or calculated; much less regulated as to value.

This failure does not mean, however, that is acceptable for us to simply pretend that it isn't worth the effort or that it is somehow not feasible or practical to regulate the value and amount of money in our financial system on an ongoing basis, rather than to naively pretend we have an effective and responsible financial system, and that the systemic financial crises we continue to experience arise exogenously—outside of our system in the shadow banking system. Because the financial imbalances have supposedly developed outside of our banking system, congress, the federal financial regulators and the Wall Street banks consider themselves absolved from responsibility or accountability for the ongoing series of financial crises since 1971, and specifically, the current 2008 financial crisis. We cannot define away the problem. Congress, the federal financial regulators and their tools, the Wall Street banks, deliberately and intentionally created these financial imbalances largely outside of the regulated banking system.

Our system does include many factors considered to be irretrievably outside the system, i.e., exogenous. It is time for responsible Americans to point out that the Emperor has no clothes. The assumption that the systemic financial crisis arose outside of our system and is therefore outside the scope of responsibility of Congress, the federal financial regulators and the Wall Street banks, must be shown to be false. These parties are culpable in the systemic financial crisis. The assumption that they can continue business as usual must be stripped away. They cannot seek protection in the invisible clothes of presumed innocence and immunity from the consequences of their policies and actions.

Leadership of the government financial sector is loaded with former senior management experts from the firms they are supposed to regulate. Many of these firms, including specifically the systemically important Wall Street banks, whose former officers were at the controls of government when this crisis began, contributed directly to the divergence of the economic components of the markets and the use of money for its broad purpose of serving as a unit of measurement of value, medium of exchange of relative value in the marketplace, as a store of value over time and as a standard for deferred payments, through the legally segregated and limited sectors of the banking financial system, subject to formal regulation, examination and supervision.

The creation and evolution of the shadow banking system outside of traditional legal and regulatory constraints was not a secret. It was not unanticipated. It was not a surprise. The shadow banking system was in fact deliberately promoted and directly supported and facilitated by the very people who had the responsibility for ensuring that the shadow banking system was in fact brought under the financial regulatory, supervision, examination and enforcement mechanisms that have long been in place.

In this work I describe the formal culpability of specific institutions and individual persons responsible for our systemic financial crisis and preceding systemic financial crises, occurring from the beginning of the development of money and banking globally and domestically, and for directly relevant purposes of this book, from the tumultuous 1970s; as a direct consequence of intentional currency debasement. Financial crime and punishment have heretofore been relegated to the street level players in the story. These culprits are the individual, greedy and unprincipled lending institutions run amuck, as well as unscrupulous, devious and speculative borrowers, all of whom have misrepresented their financial position and the value of assets available to pay debt they have created and incurred on an unprecedented scale; all without any understanding of the role of money debasement as the primary structural cause of the collapse of the asset value booms and busts.

[A] American Tolerance of Lying, Cheating and Stealing

Americans have a history of tolerance, indeed, an expectation of lies and deceit from government. Tolerance and expectations are often expressed in a humorous way that belies the seriousness of the current state of affairs. Some well-known and oft-quoted examples:

- "When they call the roll in the Senate, the Senators do not know whether to answer 'Present' or 'Not guilty.'" Theodore Roosevelt
- "A government which robs Peter to pay Paul can always depend on the support of Paul." George Bernard Shaw
- "I don't make jokes. I just watch the government and report the facts." Will Rogers
- "No man's life, liberty, or property is safe while the legislature is in session." Mark Twain
- "The government is like a baby's alimentary canal, with a happy appetite at one end and no responsibility at the other." Ronald Reagan
- "There is no distinctly Native American criminal class ... save Congress." Mark Twain
- "We hang the petty thieves and appoint the great ones to public office." Aesop
- "In politics, an absurdity is not a handicap." Napoleon Bonaparte

More seriously:

- "We are easily shocked by crimes which appear at once in their full magnitude, but the gradual growth of our own wickedness, endeared by interest, and palliated by all the artifices of self-deceit, gives us time to form distinctions in our own favor," Samuel Johnson
- "When a well-packaged web of lies has been sold gradually to the masses over generations, the truth will seem utterly preposterous and its speaker a raving lunatic." Dresden James
- "We have now sunk to a depth at which the restatement of the obvious is the first duty of intelligent men." George Orwell
- "During times of universal deceit, telling the truth becomes a revolutionary act" George Orwell
- "No man is justified in doing evil on the ground of expediency." Theodore Roosevelt
- "Repetition does not transform a lie into a truth." Franklin D. Roosevelt

- "A long habit of not thinking a thing wrong gives it a superficial appearance of being right." Thomas Paine
- "As an individual, who undertakes to live by borrowing, soon finds his original means devoured by interest, and next no one left to borrow from—so must it be with a government." Abraham Lincoln

The humor has now gone from our current experience and American tolerance has evaporated

There is then, of course, the time-honored tradition of the public figure to explain how he or she should rightly expect to just look the other way. Jerry Jones, owner of the Dallas Cowboys football team, in an interview seeking to sidestep his earlier stated position on a sports related matter, quoted a former governor of the State of Arkansas—"Just because I said it doesn't make it so." And so it is today in the political and bureaucratic world of money, banking and finance. Just because the Congressman, Treasury Secretary, Chairman of the Fed, Comptroller of the Currency, Chairman of the FDIC, Attorney General and the Wall Street bank scions say they are acting in the public interest and preserving the American and global financial system, does not make it so.

The phenomenon of political "lies" is rising in the level of public's attention. CNN reported June 1, 2012, that "It's very complicated, the way we process information," said Ron Riggio, an organizational psychology professor at Claremont McKenna College speaking broadly about the nature of lying. "It's the politics of audacity. The more outrageous and audacious the lie is, the more people say, 'that's got to be true because why would someone make something like that up?'" "While many politicians are truthful, honest public servants, too many politicians and their surrogates often lie, and voters often let them get away with it, Riggio contends. In the world of politics, lies are treated as that relative no one really likes, but everyone reluctantly invites to Thanksgiving dinner."

From Richard Nixon—"I'm not a crook"—to Bill Clinton—"I did not have sexual relations with that woman, Miss Lewinsky"—to Marion Barry—"It's all made up... I don't know what happened"—to John Edwards—"The story is false... It's completely untrue, ridiculous"—and to Donald Trump—Mexico will pay for the wall—and—I have nothing to do with Russia, American politicians have had a history of political deception, or at least stretching the truth." CNN provided a number of additional current public examples. "I think voters are well aware that politicians stretch the truth—sometimes to the breaking point," said Bill Adair, editor of *PolitiFact* and Washington bureau chief of the *Tampa Bay Times*. "And I think voters are also savvy enough to realize there are shades of gray that turn a seemingly accurate statement into a half truth." However, unlike the days when webs of political deception were tougher to untangle, savvy voters now have more tools on hand.

What's different today is that there is so much information available to help people make sense of the political discourse and discern the difference between an exaggeration and a pants-on-fire lie," Adair said. Sound bites from members of congress, federal financial regulators and Wall Street bank spokesmen are often expressed as" dodges", "evasions", half-thoughts and half-truths, and most recently, a "short circuited" explanation [Hillary Clinton], "alternative facts" [Kellyanne Conway] "abbreviated language" [Rudy Giuliani]: new euphemisms for prevarication—for intentional misrepresentation.

These casual and fundamental intentionally dishonest communications have now segued into formal legal action involving Well Fargo Bank. The bank contends that third parties are not entitled to rely on its public statements—which they should have expected and known to be meaningless—to the effect that the banks efforts at "transparency", "rebuilding trust", and general statements "about reputation, integrity and compliance with ethical norms ... are simply inactionable 'puffery,'" that the third parties should not have believed or relied on the statements, and that the bank had reasonably relied on its "policies, procedures and internal controls."[27]

Each successive set of parties responsible for each successive systemic financial crisis tell us that the crisis came at them from outside of the system; an unpredictable exogenous event, and that, without the dramatic action they have taken in the interest of the American public, we would have faced an even greater financial crisis; that it is in the interest of the American public that we preserve our financial system at all cost through acts of political expedience irrespective of law and regulation already on the books; and that, in fact, it is only because of their respective expertise in such matters and their sacrifice, hard work and new reactive legislation in the public interest—closing the barn door after the cows are out and gone, so to speak—that the system has been saved and the American public protected from these ominous specters of dark, destructive "exogenous" forces. Each of such statements is true, in some part, and in some part, it is a dodge, an evasion, a cover-up of collective irresponsibility, and failure to maintain an honest, safe and sound financial system in the first instance. It begs the question, what could and should have been done in the first instance, and by whom, to mitigate or avoid the systemic financial crises entirely? What would happen if Americans insisted on the application of the laws and regulations already on the books for public protection from and moral and legal accountability for financial crises?

Each time these public figures state something, intending that we rely on it, and it isn't so, another little slice of the American Dream evaporates. Such statements are, in fact, intentional lies and misrepresentations. They are deceitful. They are fraudulent. Intentional lies, deceits and misrepresentations are irresponsible and immoral. They are the wrongs that underlie the fraud visited upon us by the financial crisis. They are illegal.

Intentional misrepresentations are wrong; they constitute torts committed against those to whom the fraud is addressed and all who honestly rely on what they are told and suffer from that reliance. These misrepresentations are forced on Americans by Washington and Wall Street's persistent abuse of the power they wield in the world of money, economics and finance. The abuses of power and the body of intentional misrepresentations at the heart of the financial crisis are set out in detail in this work. The intentional misrepresentations inflicted on ordinary Americans by Washington's and Wall Street's abuse of power in this financial crisis echo similar abuses of power and fraudulent conduct by societies' power elite since the development of central government, money and banking. They have all eventually come to an end: either an end through violence, war and revolution, or through decisive political change and dramatic and consistent enforcement of the ancient moral and legal principles upon which civil societies are based. The fraud perpetrated by Washington and Wall Street through their abuse of power constitutes crimes against the American civil society of ordinary Americans and their households. The lies add up. Intentional fraud committed by politicians and bankers who once again wield and abuse unprecedented power in America, cheat the American public out of an honest shot at achieving the American Dream. When the days of reckoning arrive in the form of financial crises, the false prosperity that has been intentionally and fraudulently created by Washington and Wall Street then evaporates. It is literally stolen away. Losses are borne by the public whose interests have been betrayed by Washington and Wall Street. The public economic system bears the losses. Washington and Wall Street, however, continue to prosper under a mutual closed economic and financial system. Ari Melber of MSNBC recently noted Jamie Dimon's acknowledgment of a two-tiered economic system in America (a "bifurcated economy"): one system on Wall Street and in Washington operated by and for the one percent; and the largely separate subordinate system for the rest of us, the ninety-nine percent on Main Street. The members of this closed and privileged economy have been protected from the losses they have created. Citing their independent and collective importance to America's economy, and their necessary immunity to accountability as a matter of existential expedience, Washington and Wall Street have managed to consolidate power and profits and further entrench their financial cabal.

America is a nation based on the rule of law. That rule of law is grounded in ancient and fundamental moral principles upon which all civil societies are based. We have rules of law that apply to the conduct of public figures, the violation of which has led us to the current financial crises. Contrary to what these public figures would have us believe, they are not exempt from accountability for intentional lies, deceit, misrepresentation and fraud. It is high time for the DOJ to enforce America's laws. We must not be diverted by the impotent diversions that appear as the creation of "special units'" conducting misdirected efforts to remedy systemic crises through individual cases of micro-economic accountability and adjustment; generally targeting the wrong parties; the most vulnerable and least culpable amongst us, as examples; mere tokens of accountability. In recent years the blatant refusal of the DOJ to act responsibly is an embarrassment to and betrayal of our system of justice based on the rule of law. The historical reluctance of the judicial system, specifically the United States Supreme Court, to hear cases based on the constitutional, federal statutory and common law principles that exist to protect the ordinary people of the United States is reprehensible. All excuses for avoidance of moral and accountability through the federal judiciary and the Supreme Court is a disgrace to the legal profession and the Judicial Branch of United States government. The dramatic degradation of professional responsibilities that bear on maintaining such accountability can be laid directly on Washington and Wall Street, as the accounting and legal professions, which have intentionally ignored the moral and legal foundations that form the foundation for the American social, economic, financial and financial system. It is time for Americans to exercise the tradition of self-reliance and take direct legal action to enforce financial crisis accountability.

[B] Why Have Washington and Wall Street Gotten a Free Pass?

The invisible kingpins in the wrongful, irresponsible and illegal combination leading to and covering up the true scale of this systemic financial crisis have been considered "out of bounds." The kingpins in this story are the keepers of the keys to our national and personal vaults. They have hidden behind the invisible fabric and demonstrably false narrative of institutional prestige and a protected network of unprecedented, unfettered control over the economic and financial lives or ordinary Americans.

Every one of these persons and the organizations they represent in Washington and on Wall Street has gotten a free pass for three reasons:

- One, they control the financial information disseminated to the American public and the global financial community.
- Two, they claim they have been acting in the best interest of the American citizens and without their expertise; we would all be worse off—the system might collapse.
- Three, holding Washington and Wall Street accountable would trigger another crisis; to be avoided only by the public standing down and accepting their fate as the price to be paid for America's global dominance in trade and finance.

The response to these reasons is actually quite simple and fundamental. The moral principles upon which our civilization exist, and the laws based on those principles exist. They must be enforced. The day of reckoning is now upon us.

Washington and Wall Street have not provided transparent, accurate and timely information to us. They have consistently acted in their own personal and organizational interests; deliberately ignoring the constitutional and other legal, regulatory and accounting standards that apply to them that are designed to protect the public interest. Washington and Wall Street act as if they are above the rule of law; that they have an unfettered and unlimited mandate to do as they will. They occupy lofty positions towering over the interest of ordinary Americans. After all, they are the recognized experts on the economy, the leading lights on government economic and fiscal policy, monetary policy and financial regulatory supervisory and enforcement standards both in America, and as the dominant players in the global economy. Trust us and look the other way. As President Reagan famously said, "The nine most terrifying words in the English language are, 'I'm from the government and I'm here to help.'" We have here arrogant paternalism of America's power elite at its worst and most destructive.

[C] The Available Heuristic: Staying on Message

According to Daniel Khaneman, Professor Emeritus of Psychology and Public Affairs at Princeton University's Woodrow Wilson School and Nobel Prize winner, and Amos Tversky, his long-time colleague and collaborator in the work that led to Khaneman's Nobel Prize (Tversky died before the prize was awarded) and Davis Brack Professor of Behavioral Sciences at Stanford University, people often assess the probability of an event or its consequences by asking themselves whether relevant examples are "cognitively available"—that is—they can be easily remembered. They cling to the response and assessment that is most readily available to their memories, even though reflection would show that what might be immediately cognitively available could not possibly be true.

This is what politicians and bureaucrats call "controlling the narrative," "staying on message;" sticking to the established position. Khaneman and Tversky call it the "available heuristic."[28] It may be the best immediately available guide they possess to answer a question or make a decision, without time or effort for careful consideration. It may be their best guide. It is the guide, however, that deliberately avoids examination of difficult conscientious consideration of the facts. Khaneman observed that "reliable statistical evidence will outperform the available heuristic every time." Washington and Wall Street are clothed in the armor of twitter feed, slogans and sound bites; spun by lobbyists and media players who are well-rewarded by Washington and Wall Street for their contributions to creating the "available heuristic"—a tangled web of false narratives—despite the demonstrable facts—appearing in the public record—that as created, they coalesce and are reflected in the intentional misrepresentation of the nation's and the banks' financial condition; the ongoing debasement of the United States Dollar; and the financial evisceration of 99 percent of the American public. There has been no sincere admission by Washington or Wall Street of their mutual culpability; no regret or remorse expressed for their actions. In fact, their immoral and illegal conduct continues unabated and has strengthened. It is time to follow the lead of Professor Khaneman and present first, individually, through federal statutes that provide for private action by those Americans damages by the crisis; and second, through the DOJ the evidence; the known facts and the existing laws, that will "outperform" the intentionally dishonest, immoral and illegal "available heuristic" propagated, nurtured and dealt out as intentional misrepresentations by Washington and Wall Street through the abuse of their power and control over our economic and financial system. Yes. Now it is time to do just that.

Politicians and bureaucrats find that by adopting simple, limited judgmental options, sticking to the party line, staying on message and by avoiding the assembly and honest assessment of critical, relevant data they can hide in plain sight; away from meaningful focused criticism and away from the often difficult task of making a proper, conscious, information-based and law-based decisions or actions. Use of the available heuristic can and, in this context, emphatically has led to severe and systematic errors. Phil Graham, co-author of *Graham-Leach-Bliley*,[29] is emblematic of most politicians and has provided an excellent example of his exploitation of available heuristic or intentionally false narrative. The legislation he sponsored led directly to the explosive growth of the shadow banking system and its exploitation by the Wall Street Banks. Among the general population, the available heuristic, in a casual way, may often be useful, as a part of making daily life decisions. When the available heuristic is adopted as a reckless convenience by politicians and bureaucrats to deliberately present biased or incomplete and inaccurate data; intentional deceit and misrepresentation—it becomes the medium of deliberate lies; a deliberate program of intentional financial misrepresentation, by those we should hold to a higher standard of conduct as protectors of America's economic and political stability and our model of civil society.[30]

§1.06 THE WASHINGTON AND WALL STREET ENTERPRISE'S MESSAGE CONSTITUTES A WEB OF INTENTIONALLY FALSE NARRATIVES

This book answers the question left hanging by the literature regarding financial crises. The bases for the crises are well documented. The barriers—the available heuristics—the messages shielding the Washington Wall Street enterprise are not well identified. This book dissects the web of false narrative shielding Washington and Wall Street from legal accountability and identifies the path to enforcement of the Washington Wall Street Enterprise's legal accountability for financial crises, damages from the illegal conduct, deterrence to future wrongdoing and equitable remedies available to Americans interest in justice, transparency in monetary matters and to restore monetary affairs to honest, safe and sound conduct.

Most readers, including recognized experts in law, economics, monetary, and banking disciplines have largely accepted the explanations and rationalizations advanced in support of the apparent status quo, which specifically relies on a series of false narratives propounded by Washington and Wall Street intended to obfuscate legal accountability. Readers should question the veracity and power of these false narratives. This book provides responses that dispel or refute the truth and validity of the false narratives, which are repeated here and addressed throughout the balance of this work:

Ordinary Americans are responsible—they borrowed too much money—they should have known better.

- Washington and Wall Street; America's experts in money and banking, could not have foreseen, anticipated or prepared for the financial crisis.
- The financial crisis was unavoidable and without the concerted actions of Washington and Wall Street, the effects of the financial crisis on ordinary Americans would have been far worse.
- Ordinary Americans are unable to assign culpability for damages caused to them by the financial crisis and are powerless to enforce accountability for the financial crisis.
- The causes of America's financial crises are immoral but not illegal.
- The truly moral thing to do during a raging financial inferno is to put it out and to protect the innocent, even if some of the arsonists escape their full measure of justice.
- The Old Testament view that the venal should be punished is impossible to accomplish. Old Testament vengeance, Old Testament justice, Old Testament impulses, Old Testament populism, Old Testament cravings for heads on stakes, are archaic and unproductive.
- Washington, Wall Street and ordinary Americans' interests are best served by moving on, recovering, and rebuilding America's financial system and

economy. "Washington and Wall Street had an over-riding obligation to protect the integrity of the American banking and financial system concentrated in Washington and on Wall Street, as opposed to the public interest in honesty, safety and soundness in money, banking, and finance as the foundation for our legal, political, social and economic compact.

- Although the public has constitutionally delegated, granted to and empowered Congress to exercise the exclusive fiduciary power and duty to create and regulate the value of America's sovereign money, the constitutional imperative has become archaic and is rightly ignored.
- The evolution of Washington, Wall Street and the great prosperity created by the American economic, banking and financial system has outgrown Wall Street as well as the outmoded and impractical historical concepts of the imposition of legal and fiduciary powers and duties to constrain the supply of American sovereign money, including credit.
- The Supreme Court decisions in the Legal Tender Cases and the Gold Clause Cases permit the creation by the American banking system of fiat "legal tender" sovereign money intentionally bereft of the constitutionally required congressional regulation of its value.
- The monetary demands of existential war such as the Revolutionary War, the War of 1812, the American Civil War and World Wars I and II and the near continuous state of war, primarily undeclared war, maintained following World War II, constituted and now constitute legally justifiable exceptions to the proper exercise of Congress' fiduciary monetary powers and duties to the American public to maintain honest, safe and sound sovereign money.
- Concentration of wealth and power in Washington and on Wall Street through money debasement is a laudable and desirable objective of a free, capitalist economy.
- Although money debasement has historically constituted a capital crime, punishable by death, and notwithstanding the public's constitutionally protected civil right to honest, safe and sound sovereign money and Congress' constitutional fiduciary power and duty to provide it to the American public, Washington and Wall Street have, can now continue to lawfully debase American sovereign money for their own self-serving interests: money debasement is no longer illegal; it is an obsolete legal doctrine, an archaic phenomenon; and it no longer matters.
- Money debasement is no longer illegal, but in fact, can lawfully form the foundation for American monetary policy conducted by the Fed, primarily through its shareholders and partners in the American monetary and banking system, the Wall Street banks, as well as the American economic and financial system.
- The Federal Reserve has unfettered power and unbridled discretion over all matters relating to American sovereign money.
- Congress has lawfully and effectively delegated its monetary powers and duties to the Fed.

- The Fed has lawfully and effectively delegated its monetary powers and duties to Wall Street.
- Neither Washington nor Wall Street have a legal, fiduciary duty to the American public to maintain honest, safe and sound money that is legally enforceable by the American people.
- Intentional money debasement is essential to the exercise by the Fed of American monetary policy.
- Federal bank and financial regulatory policies and processes provide a legally honest, safe, sound and effective substitute for the proper exercise by Congress of its fiduciary duty to the American public to create honest, safe and sound constitutional sovereign money, and to adequately protect the public interest in, and civil right to honest, safe and sound sovereign money.
- The commonly accepted narratives of "extend and pretend", "kick the can down the road", "deny and lie", "too big to fail", "too big to jail", bailouts, subsidies, Quantitative Easing, interest rate and asset valuation manipulation, cumulatively constitute systemic lying to, cheating and stealing from ordinary Americans, but yet somehow constitute legitimate monetary and regulatory policies necessary to assure an honest, safe and sound American sovereign money, financial system and economy.
- There exists no legal foundation for the judicial system to protect the interests of the American public's civil right to honest, safe and sound sovereign money.

Enforced accountability of Washington and Wall Street for financial crises, including financial consequences to Wall Street banks and the financial consequences to the economy will be manifest and implicit in a return to the financial constraints of honest, safe and sound money, the liquid value of which is transparently regulated by Congress. Washington and Wall Street will cry out that the subjection of shadow banking instruments of structured finance, including securitizations and derivatives, to the constraints of historical commercial law limiting the transferability and preserving the liability for repayment of those instruments by makers and endorsers, would destroy America's banking and financial sector and lead to the a disastrous, ruinous financial crises that America could not survive. This fearmongering is not without a grain of truth. American legal remedies can account for fairness and equity as a component of the remedies they may seek.

The barriers of interrelated false narratives erected to shield the Washington Wall Street enterprise from moral and legal accountability for financial crisis is formidable. This book systematically breaks down each of these barriers and makes a case for Washington and Wall Street accountability, including damages from the illegal conduct, deterrence to future wrongdoing and equitable remedies available to Americans interest in justice, transparency in monetary matters and to restore monetary affairs to honest, safe and sound conduct.

§1.07 EXISTING LITERATURE SKIRTS LEGAL ACCOUNTABILITY FOR MONEY DEBASEMENT DRIVEN FINANCIAL CRISES

My first published book, *Banks in Distress*,[31] was grounded in the recognition that significant government action: legislative, regulatory and accounting rules governing and implementing banking, monetary and fiscal policy were the cause of the financial crisis of the late 1980s and early 1990s in the US. The book traced those factors and outlined lessons to be learned from the systemic nature of the crisis. When I thought to expand my analysis and additionally concentrate on the role of proliferation of new money-like instruments and unprecedented currency debasement through the devices of undisciplined fiscal, trade and current account deficits, as contributing causes to the systemic crisis, I was advised to stay away from that subject; as there are many recognized experts in this area who truly understand it. The subject was outside of my primary area of expertise. As I noted in *Banks in Distress*, however, the experts who created the federal regulatory response to that systemic financial crisis, as expressed by the Federal Deposit Insurance Corporation (FDIC) in its two volume report on the crisis, issued on behalf of all of the contributing federal regulatory agencies, at page 84 and as noted below, concluded that in as much as the crisis was systemic in its nature, and to the extent any future crisis was systemic in nature, there was nothing the FDIC could do about it then or in the future.

For years, the FDIC has conducted a series of seminars in conjunction with the *Journal of Financial Services Research (JFSR)* to address banking crises. The focus of the FDIC and the JFSR was, and continues to be on micro-economic, micro-supervisory and micro-regulatory and enforcement factors. Not until 2011, after the passage of *Dodd Frank*,[32] did these seminars include any presentation on the role of systemic risk in banking and financial crises. The FDIC holds itself out as a "recognized leader in promoting sound public policies, addressing risks in the nation's financial system," The current mantra out of Washington now focuses heavily on the systemic nature of the current 2008 crisis; but without getting to the fundamental underlying causes, or to institutional and individual responsibility and accountability for the crisis: Money Debasement. Clear focus on the systemic causes of systemic financial crises should lead to recognition of relative responsibilities and then proceed to enforced accountability, setting the stage for productive action and a positive change in policy direction and action. Tragically, that has not occurred.

President Obama's *State of the Union Address* and the *FDIC/ Journal of Financial Services Research Seminar* and related papers beg the question: what are the first principles of the American financial system and their erosion to do with the components of the systemic risk upon which the Journal editors, the FDIC and their colleagues in federal financial regulation have now, belatedly, focused?

It seems clear that systemic risk and systemic crises arise from systemic failure: the pervasive abandonment of first principles relating to money and the laws grounded in the principles that underlie our financial system; not from failing to address or from addressing ineffectively the perceived individual micro-components; merely symptoms of systemic risk. For example, considering whether centralizing "counterparties for OTC derivatives" will reduce systemic risk. This topic is indeed relevant, but not fundamental. *Dodd Frank*, the much heralded recent financial reform legislation passed by Congress in 2010 does recognize systemic risk as a fundamental cause of systemic crises,[33] but still does not recognize and come to terms with the abandonment of first principles that create the systemic risks presented by the use of structured financial products such as securitized debt and derivatives that led to this financial crisis.

My second book, *Subprime Meltdown*[34] published in April 2008, focused on the systemic nature of the past crises as well the forthcoming crisis that I anticipated, beginning in 1999; was hinted at in the markets in 2007; and was visited in its full wrath in September 2008, a few months after the book's publication. Systemic risk in the financial markets and banking system, including the so-called "shadow banking system", is now recognized to lie at the heart of financial crises going back at least 800 years. *This Time is Different*[35] by Carmen M. Rhinehart and Kenneth S. Rogoff is an excellent recent work often cited with approval by former American Treasury Secretary Geithner. It is one of several recent books published by highly credible and respected authors focusing on systemic risk as the fundamental cause of systemic banking and financial crises. Other recent contributions to the literature on systemic financial risk and crises include *Exorbitant Privilege*[36] by Barry Eichengreen, *Hall of Mirrors: The Great Depression, the Great Recession, and the Uses—and Misuses—of History,*[37] also by Barry Eichengreen, *Inflated,*[38] by R. Christopher Whalen, *Financial Stability; Fraud, Confidence, and the Wealth of Nations,*[39] by Frederick L Feldkamp and R. Christopher Whalen, the Second Edition of *New Monetarism,* and now *Sovereign Discredit,* both by David Roche and Bob McKee, *The Power and Independence of the Federal Reserve,*[40] by Peter Conti Brown, *Between Debt and the Devil, Money, Credit and Fixing Global Finance,* by Adair Turner,[41] *Currency Wars—The Making of the Next Global Crisis, The Death of Money—The Coming Collapse of the International Monetary system,* and *The new Case for Gold,* all by James Rickards,[42] *Bailout,*[43] by Neal Barofsky, *The End of Alchemy—Money, Banking, and the Global Economy,*[44] by Mervin King, and *The Ascent of Money,*[45] by Niall Ferguson The classic starting point for knowledge of this subject is *Manias, Panics, and Crashes; a History of Financial Crises,*[46] first published in 1978, the Fourth Edition published in 2000, Charles Kindleberger. The classic source of reference to money and the law is *The Legal Aspect of Money,*[47] by F. A. Mann, in its Fourth Edition. The defining work on money today is *Money—the Unauthorized Biography,*[48] by Felix Martin. I will refer to these excellent works often. These references are, of course, not exclusive.

David Kotok, Chairman and Chief Investment Officer of Cumberland Advisors, in an essay recently circulated by John Maudlin in his *Outside the Box* newsletter, April 8, 2012, stated that "When I get worried, I read and re-read in my library. I can honestly say that I have had my nose in a thousand of those books. The library holds many texts by giants. They wrote about history, economics, and finance. They took the strategic view. George Akerlof, Jared Diamond, Niall Ferguson, Carmen Reinhart & Ken Rogoff, Robert Shiller, and Nassim Taleb are among the modern writers. Milton Friedman, Martin Gilbert, Friedrich Hayek and his [supposed] polar opposite John Maynard Keynes, Ludwig von Mises, R.R. Palmer, and Adam Smith are among the classics." Kotok's collection includes as well one of his favorites, Yale Professor Paul Kennedy's monumental work *The Rise and Fall of Great Powers*.[49] Professor Kennedy's book put me on the trail leading to this writing more than twenty-five years ago.

Recognition of the systemic risk of intentional money debasement as the cause of systemic financial crises is one thing. Defining it, doing something about it; rooting out who has done what that was wrong and irresponsible in creating systemic money debasement financial risk and resultant financial crises; and, most importantly, holding them to account under the rule of law, is another thing entirely.

We cannot move to long term solutions to our structural financial instability without a change in perspective brought about by an American public demonstration and display of responsibility, accountability and disincentive to further bad acts such as those at the bottom of this crisis, grounded in an intentional policy of ongoing money debasement.

How do we get to the root causes of systemic financial crises? We must identify Washington's and Wall Street's duties to the American public to create and emit honest, safe and sound money, the value of which has been transparently regulated by Congress, the breach of which has led to the enormous damages documented by the General Accounting Office and the Federal Reserve Bank of Dallas as well as numerous other studies and assessments prepared by well-respected and credible sources. It seems reasonable to expect that the root causes of systemic financial crises may be found in an excess of unregulated, undisclosed and uncontrolled systemic financial risk. Congress, the federal financial regulators and the Wall Street banks that control the American financial system, and the specific institutions and the individuals who control those institutions, have the responsibility to American society for maintaining a safe and sound American financial system. These people and institutions are not special—they are not exempt from accountability to the American public for violating public trust, natural law principles of morality and justice as embodied in the American *Constitution* and in America's civil and criminal law.

In fact, as I will later explore, those members of a society empower to control a nation's money, in our case Washington and Wall Street, have a special duty, accurately classified as a fiduciary duty to their constituents including all of America's ordinary working households, to maintain the integrity, safety and soundness of that nation's money and monetary system. That duty is the highest duty known to the law.

As a result of this financial crisis the American public has and will experience an estimated systemic loss of ranging from $12.8 trillion up to $20 trillion—ruined careers and personal lives—creating financial and personal stress beyond endurance, with nowhere to turn.

"Better Markets, a pro-financial reform Wall Street watchdog, has released what it is calling the "first-ever" report totalling the loss of American wealth since Lehman filed for bankruptcy on September 15, 2008.

According to the report, entitled *"Cost of the Crisis"*, the financial and economic crisis cost Americans $12.8 trillion, including:

> Estimated actual gross domestic product ("GDP") loss from 2008 to 2018, of $7.6 trillion. This is the cumulative difference between potential GDP — what GDP

> would have been but for the financial and economic crises — and actual and forecast GDP during the period.
>
> Estimated avoided GDP loss from 2008 to 2012 of $5.2 trillion. This figure is the estimated additional amount of GDP loss that was prevented only by extraordinary fiscal and monetary policy actions.

But $12.8 trillion is a conservative estimate, says *Better Markets* (Better Markets) President & CEO Dennis Kelleher, The report also highlights the current impact to the US economy, including:

- 23.1 million Americans, or 15 percent of the public, are out of work or unable to find full-time jobs using the broadest measure of unemployment, or U-6.
- 9.3 million Americans have lost their health insurance.
- 11 million homeowners, almost 1 in 4, are saddled with mortgages higher than the value of their homes."

The Better Markets July 2015 revision of their report details damages to ordinary Americans at $20 trillion and counting. What do we expect the individuals who comprise and control Washington and Wall Street to experience as a result of the financial crisis? What they have experienced so far is job security, hefty compensation and bonuses, golden parachutes, the best retirement plans and medical insurance money can buy, political and personal power without accountability, and lucrative off the books relationships amongst one another to assure the continuation of their good life despite the effect of the financial crisis on the American public.

§1.08 RISKY MONEY MANIPULATION

Reasonable minds may differ on how we might identify, regulate and limit systemic financial risk to mitigate or avoid systemic financial crises. Many participants in the American financial system believe that the financial markets for financial products are essentially self-correcting and that the government should not interfere with the workings of the "invisible hand" of a free financial marketplace in an unregulated free market financial system. There are essentially two ways to regulate our financial system to mitigate or avoid systemic financial risk. Our American culture and those who oppose governmental intervention in "free markets" would have us enjoy a "self-regulated" financial system based on transparency of information and the discipline of the invisible free hand of the market based on complete information. Although America does strive to achieve market transparency, and does the best job of providing such transparency of any of the developed economies in the free world; that does not suffice in the American "financial" market place, or financial system whose central bank is based on the mission of market manipulation to achieve political objectives as opposed to open an honest transparent financial system based upon money the value of which has been transparently and lawfully regulated by Congress as required by the *United States Constitution*.

We do know that the neither the American nor the global financial system are really free markets. We know that we have a regulated banking system combined with a system of central banks, such as the Fed, supposedly charged with responsibility to perform certain circumscribed, but non-transparent actions to control the amount and "quality" of money, including the amount of credit and the structure of credit as money in the economy. The Fed's organizational mission (as opposed to the broader publicly stated mission as set forth in its organizational legislation, its written material as well as on its public web site) is "to promote effectively the goals of maximum employment, stable prices and moderate long-term interest rates." They purport do this by a combination of the following, from time to time: increasing or lowering government spending; increasing or lowering government borrowing; changing the rate at which the government loans or borrows money; manipulation of exchange rates; taxation on or tax breaks for imports or exports of capital into a country; raising or lowering bank reserve requirements; and regulation or prohibition of private currencies.

As one can readily discern, none of these actions is consistent with a transparent, free market financial system. The tools of the Fed's trade then, are non-transparent actions of purely discretionary "quasi" government intervention and manipulation, albeit ostensibly to serve legitimate social and political objectives; but in reality, creating massive political risk threatening, by its very definition, to a strong foundation for systemic financial stability and safety and soundness of that system. Congress and the Fed's efforts to promote and achieve the *Federal Reserve Act's*[50] stated purposes have been a failure, as a matter of fact. A failure that is thoroughly documented.

The Fed's failed organizational mission then, is not as expressed in its public statements—its intentionally false narrative. It is fundamentally circumscribed. As the Fed constantly reminds us and as we have seen in the 2008 crisis, the Fed does not appear to have any specific organizationally founded tools to combat an excess of systemic financial risk. It does however claim the mandate, confirmed by legislation subsequent to its organization, that it can fulfill only by the introduction of broadly disseminated financial transparency, reporting the factual information necessary for market participants to understand the effects of its actions and actions of Congress, the federal financial regulatory agencies and the Wall Street banks on the publics' reasonable expectation of a system of money that provides a safe, sound and stable medium of exchange, unit of account, store of value and standard for deferred payment. In fact, although control of systemic financial risk is not an organizational mission of the Fed, it does publicly represent that to be a material component of its mission on its official web site as: "supervising and regulating banking institutions to ensure the safety and soundness of the nation's banking and financial system and to protect the credit rights of consumers; maintaining the stability of the financial system and containing systemic risk that may arise in financial markets." Washington's and Wall Street's failure to meet this mission is a matter of fact; a failure that is thoroughly documented but hidden in the seemingly mysterious Fed deliberations, pronouncements and actions which are opaque at best, but more often deliberation misrepresentations of intent and action that are weaved together as a false narrative of public policy, completely divorced from the fundamental morality and law of the land.

§1.09 WASHINGTON AND WALL STREET MONEY MANIPULATION IS MONEY DEBASEMENT

As the front line of operational responsibility for our financial system—our central bank—the Fed is the first among all other culpable parties, apart from Congress, creator of the Fed. Contrary to periodic calls to abolish the Fed—apparently Congress has not seen fit to abolish the Fed or, alternatively, to clarify the Fed's mission so that it cannot pretend it does not have the tools to do the job. Congress pretends it has dumped responsibility for systemic risk on the Fed. The Fed pretends that it does not have authority to meet that responsibility; but at the same time says it does. Furthermore, although it bastardized the use of Fed discount window borrowing to secretly lend more than $7 trillion to the Wall Street banks and other banks and financial institutions as well as private businesses, in America and globally, in response to the 2008 crisis, dwarfing the amount of the formal financial institution bailout authorized by Congress, the Fed continues to complain of its limited tools. The Fed has not been held back by its limited tools when intervening in the markets for asset-backed securities, supposedly to encourage borrowing by business and by home buyers, thereby, hopefully, creating jobs (the perverse incentives for which played a huge role in the current crisis through creation of unsustainable levels of public and private debt in the first instance). This, despite considerable evidence that this policy of 'Quantitative Easing" and "Twisting" has not and by all informed accounts, will not, meet the Fed's expressed objectives. And at what cost of failure?

The Fed does not call Congress out on the question because, theoretically, it is responsible to Congress. Both parties seem to find useful cover in the opacity and conflict. Neither institution has credibly proposed to clarify the lines of authority, responsibility and accountability: from Congress to its committees to the Fed; and from the Fed to the federal financial regulators, and the concentration of their respective conduct on the protection of America's public interest; not just protection of the interests of the most wealthy 1 percent of Americans, shielded by Washington and Wall Street from the predictable effects of the their failed policies and actions.

[A] Washington and Wall Street Manage Money and Systemic Risk for Their Own Benefit at Public Expense

The Washington and Wall Street enterprise described later in this work is a fraudulent Ponzi scheme. The public receives current benefits intended to be paid for in the future by tax contributions from a subsequent generation (until inevitable collapse of the scheme when the level of deferred payment deficits becomes unsustainable). The ultimate price paid for the current benefit exceeds the current intrinsic value of the benefit as represented by Congress, when it is ultimately paid, with interest by subsequent generations of Americans. This Ponzi scheme is funded with money created out of thin air—the value of which is not only unregulated, it is hidden and misrepresented at every level of use. Consequently, the value of assets denominated in US dollars on the books of the Fed, the Wall Street banks and on the books of every holder of US dollars has been intentionally, willfully misrepresented by those who create the dollars, whether Federal Reserve Notes, bank credit or shadow bank credit instruments, including derivatives.

Lawrence Kotlikoff, Professor of Economics at Boston University, provides a succinct description of how the American Ponzi scheme is funded:[51]

> The new money created is created out of debt, i.e. the Central Bank created the 10 billion with the expectation that it will all be paid back. So essentially, MONEY = DEBT. [In fact, under our current system, one cannot exist without the other. If everyone paid off all their debt, there would be no money for the economy to function. The crazy thing is, the world does not even have enough money to pay off all the debt that exists (Figure 1.3 will answer why this is so).]

Figure 1.3 How Money Is Created

Once the Federal Government receives the new money, it places it into a bank account to become legal tender money, adding 10 billion to the money supply.
And that's how money is created, though today it's done electronically and within a few seconds. But it doesn't end there.

Once the 10 billion is deposited into a bank, that bank can then lend out that money. The only limit being said bank needs to keep a percentage of the original deposit on hold as a "reserve" (usually around 10%); e.g. out of the 10 billion deposited, the bank can now lend out 9 billion. [This process is referred to as "Fractional Reserve Banking."]

However, while logic would have you think that banks lend out that 9 billion from the original 10 billion, the truth is that 9 billion is lent ON TOP of that original 10 billion. That's right, 9 billion in brand new money is created into the economy simply because there is a demand for this loan and there is enough money in the bank to fulfil the reserve requirements. So basically, after the bank asks you for assets (e.g. your car) to back up your mortgage, the bank in turn creates and lends you money from nothing, money that's backed up by nothing except a hypothetical liability: money that you're expected to pay back and then some.

The implications of this are huge, as this process will happen all over again in the bank where that 9 billion is next deposited (minus the 10% reserve) and again in the next bank and the next, etc.

If this process runs its course, that initial 10 billion the Federal government called into existence has the potential to add another 90 billion into the economic system. All of this is money created out of nothing.

But if the money came from nothing, where does it get its value? The only place it can: from the existing money supply. The new money steals value from the existing money supply, expanding the money supply irrespective of the demand, thus reducing its worth and creating inflation. This means that our Fractional Reserve System is inherently inflationary, thus reducing the buying power of our money (see chart).

Figure 1.4 Money Supply Versus Dollar Buying Power

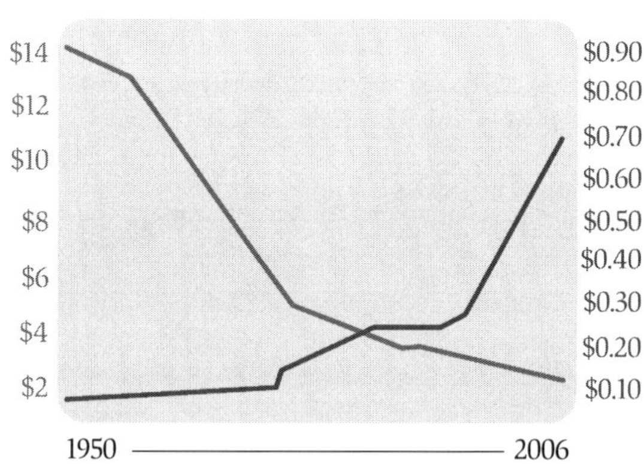

This inflation acts as a built in non-transparent unconstitutional tax upon society and is a built-in trait of our financial system.

[B] The American Ponzi Scheme

Professor Kotlikoff clarifies the true state of American fiscal and monetary policy in stark terms:[52]

> The fiscal gap tells us whether our government's long-term finances are in balance—whether its assets can cover its liabilities. Unfortunately, the answer is no. In fact, our country's fiscal gap, calculated based on the Congressional Budget Office's June 22, 2011 long-term forecast (known as the Alternative Fiscal Scenario) is simply enormous. It is $211 trillion- or 14-times GDP!
>
> The fiscal gap is our nation's credit card bill. If we do not pay it or at least interest on it, it will get bigger. And it is getting bigger. It rose by $6 trillion between this year and last. Closing the fiscal gap by raising taxes alone requires an immediate and permanent 64 percent increase in the personal income tax, the corporate income tax, the FICA payroll tax, the estate and gift tax, and all federal excise taxes. Closing the fiscal gap by cutting spending, other than interest on official debt, requires an immediate and permanent 40 percent cut in all mandatory and non-mandatory expenditures.
>
> Measured relative to GDP, the U.S. may actually have the largest fiscal gap of any developed country. By comparison, Greece's fiscal gap is about 12 times GDP, and Germany's is about 3 times GDP. This is true notwithstanding our more favorable demographics.
>
> Why is our real fiscal gap so large? About 60 percent of the gap reflects faster projected future growth in federal healthcare spending than is projected for GDP. The CBO projects spending on Medicare, Medicaid, Child Health and Infant Protection, and the new Health Exchanges to rise over the next seventy-five years, from 5.6 to 19.4 percent of GDP. Hence, one painless way to cut the fiscal gap is to keep federal healthcare spending even with the size of the economy.
>
> Why hasn't the fiscal gap shown up in the official debt figures? Our politicians have been very careful to keep most of the promises they have made us off the books. They have done this by taking "taxes" from young workers and promising them large benefits in retirement in return. Had they called the monies so taken "borrowing," our official debt would be vastly larger than is now reported, an estimated $211 trillion. Yes, trillion!

[C] In Economics, Debt Is Also a Figment of Language Rather than a Fundamental Concept

Unfortunately, nothing in economics pins down how the government should label its receipts and payments. This is called the economics labeling problem. As in physics, where time, distance, and mass all depend on the frame of reference or language of the observer, in economics, the debt is also a figment of language rather than a fundamental concept. The infinite horizon fiscal gap, in contrast, is a fundamental concept. Its size is invariant to the government's fiscal labeling conventions.

All Ponzi schemes rely on fraudulent accounting, and postwar generational policy is a Ponzi scheme, plain and simple. This is not to deny the enormous benefits provided to those on the receiving end of the scheme, many of whom are highly deserving and would otherwise have languished in poverty with little or no healthcare...

The standard metric of long-term fiscal imbalance is official government debt (Reinhart and Rogoff 2009). But, as shown in Green and Kotlikoff (2009), official debt, like time and distance in physics, is not a well-defined economic concept.

> In physics, the measurement of time and distance depends on one's frame of reference, which can be viewed as one's language. Measurement of debt is also language dependent.
>
> Unfortunately, language is highly flexible. And there is an infinite number of ways to label an economy's fiscal policy in neoclassical economies with rational agents, no matter how well or how poorly such economies function. Each labelling convention results in a different history and projected future time path of official debt. The same holds true of taxes, transfer payments, disposable income, personal saving, private saving, government saving, private wealth, and government wealth. Each of these measures is devoid of economic content.
>
> With the right labels, unsustainable fiscal policies are compatible with huge and exponentially growing reported surpluses. Likewise, sustainable policies are compatible with huge and exponentially growing deficits.
>
> The timing of policy is also up for grabs. There is no use saying our fiscal problems lie in the future. They do with one set of words (our short-run cash flows look great) and do not with another (our short-run cash flows look terrible). On the contrary, our fiscal problems lie in the state-contingent policy path being followed, and its analysis defies truncation.

The manipulation of by Washington and Wall Street in our Ponzi scheme analysis of language and numbers is at the bottom of the acts of willful misrepresentation and fraud complained of in this work.

Is looking the other way and declining to act in fulfillment of their organizational mission by the responsible Federal financial regulatory agencies and the responsible Congressional Committees wrong or irresponsible? Of course. If they would have consistently looked the right way, could they have made a difference? No doubt. Were they "willfully blind" to the consequences of their failure to look, see and act? The answer is yes. They were willfully blind to the risk and expressly cognizant of their mutual benefit derived from their conduct.

As noted above, the federal financial regulators and congressional committees have been fully aware, at least since January 16, 1997, the date of the symposium conducted by the FDIC and resulting in its published two volume report, *History of the Eighties——Lessons for the Future*,[53] that systemic risk was at the heart of the crisis of the late 1980s and early 1990s; it was not simply criminal conduct by failed financial institutions and their customers. The FDIC Report stated that "fundamental systemic issues were outside its mandate." How can this statement be reconciled with its acknowledged jurisdiction, mission and vision laid out on its own web site and in the laws under which it was created? Did the FDIC and its sister regulatory agencies simply find the truth inconvenient? Was deliberate disregard of the facts and the truth in the best individual personal regulators' and respective regulatory agencies' interests? How can any of the federal financial regulatory agencies, individual regulators or responsible congressional committees or members of congress contend with a straight face that they "didn't have the authority to stop the bad behavior; that their damaging conduct was outside their mandate?" To the contrary, it was and is their expressed mandate.

§1.10 THREE STRUCTURAL FAILURES

[A] Transparency

The first structural failure is that the financial system is not transparent. There are two fundamental components of the lack of transparency in the American financial system.

The first component of this failure of transparency is the failure to regulate the value of our money. The value of our money is no longer determined by reference to any outside component or components of our markets for goods and services. Without the regulation of the value of our money, we have an indeterminate and constantly variable measure of value, unit of account, store of value and standard for deferred payments. We do not know what our money is worth on any disciplined basis; now or in the future.

The second failure of transparency is our failure to accurately define and measure the amount and quality of American credit creation as the dominant method of the creation of money. For most of history, the creation of credit on any large scale was the province of sovereign nations. When the private creation of credit began to develop on a large scale, the amount, quality and cost of credit was created and regulated through banking systems whose purpose was to hold short terms deposits and create credit to facilitate the intermediation of money and facilitate commerce. With the development and proliferation of government intervention in the creation and regulation of credit through a public policy of "deficits that don't matter" to fund and to serve social and political objectives; the accounting for all of which became based on a unit of measurement, store of value and exchange, and standard of deferred payment that was infinitely variable, and the vast majority of which has been hidden "off balance sheet," any pretense of transparency has been lost.

After the systemic financial crisis of the late 1980s and early 1990s, the re-regulation of the financial system choked off the poorly regulated growth of available so-called regulated credit through the banking system, drove and facilitated the transfer of the continued explosion of credit growth to what became known as the securitization and derivatives based "shadow banking system", where any pretense of transparency in the creation, direction and velocity of money based on credit creation was lost. The financial system escaped from the feeble and ineffective regulatory box clumsily constructed by primarily by Wall Street itself, and acquiesced in and adopted by Washington, comprised of competing and self-serving regulatory fiefdoms that purported to define and contain it. All semblance of regulatory control has been thereby dashed.

[B] Money as a Tool of Measurement of Liquid Value Is Not Regulated

The second structural failure of our financial system is that, because our financial system is not transparent, the market is unable to properly measure the value of goods and services in the marketplace. Values are distorted by the amount and quality of money available in the marketplace and the proliferation of perverse incentives in the amount, direction and velocity of use of money in the marketplace, to fulfill and magnify artificial political and social objectives concocted together by Washington and Wall Street. In other countries where the official financial system is state controlled, this process is called "directed credit" and the risk of changes in the direction of credit based on political decisions and actions is well known as political risk. Just because we do not purport to have a" state controlled economy and financial system", through the years, with the growth, size, reach and power of Wall Street acting jointly with our central government, we have grown much, much closer to a centrally planned economy rife with political risk than we have dared to admit.

[C] The Washington Wall Street Enterprise Intentionally Manipulates the Value and Liquidity of Money for Its Own Benefit at Public Expense

The third structural failure of our financial system is the failure to recognize, anticipate and expect that an excess of systemic financial risk might be caused by decisions and actions that drive the working of the financial system. This structural failure is the failure of the system to provide any clear process to address the two fundamental failures of transparency described above, and the many and diverse distortions imposed on our economy through intervention to achieve social and political objectives. This failure is compounded through the manipulation of the value of money, including credit, rather than through the constitutionally prescribed mandate for debate, determination of identified sources for funding of those objectives and publicly legislatively appropriating such funding in the cleansing light of day. The opacity of American fiscal budgeting and fiscal policy driven by favoritism to special interests, however, in reality provides another source of the destruction of financial and monetary transparency. Thus Wall Street and Washington intentions and conduct cannot readily be brought into the light of day and those responsible for the destructive aspects of money debasement that constitute the fraudulent Washington Wall Street enterprise, Ponzi scheme, and the resulting systemic financial crises, cannot readily be identified and the perpetrators held to account under the American rule of law.

We know that congress, the federal financial regulatory agencies and the systemically important Wall Street banks constitute the infrastructure of our financial system; they have failed; their failure represents the failure of these doyennes of our financial system have who have acted cooperatively, each for their own and their mutual respective individual and institutional interests, as a cabal, but ostensibly for the interest of their respective constituents. Their individual and mutual interests are best served by a lack of transparency in the financial system. As we will see in later in this work, in times of crisis——war essentially—the public has turned a blind eye to systemic money debasement and high levels of public debt as a matter of survival of the nation. The rationale is that if we do not increase the money supply through money debasement, we cannot win the war, our nation will be destroyed and the strictures of the constitutional will no longer matter. Over time, one so-called existential crisis has led to another. Crises of war have segued into oil crises, social crises and finally the never-ending crises of expectations from our government that we simply don't want to pay for through current taxation, in the hope that, in the end, someone else will pay later for what we demand now.

The tax system, the constitutionally defined mechanism through which government is required to fund the financial requirements of its legislation, is rife with protection of special interests and political and social incentives that are non-transparent, and in the vast majority of situations, undiscoverable by any well intentioned and interested citizen not an expert in the special subject matter. The further manipulation of our economy by Washington and Wall Street compounds the disparity between the wealth of special interests and the American public.

§1.11 THE WASHINGTON AND WALL STREET ENTERPRISE

Washington and Wall Street are the parties who claim authority over our financial system but decline to admit responsibility for systemic financial crises. For illustrative purposes, we will paint an overview of this portrait of wrongdoing and irresponsible conduct with a broad brush. We will examine what these actors have had to say about their respective roles and responsibilities. In addition, we must acknowledge that the press is warming up to the colossal fraud led by Wall Street banks, federal housing agencies, in collusion with rating agencies and the Federal financial regulators and by Congress, serving their respective interests at the expense of their constituents, in the years leading up to and now covering up the scope of this crisis.

[A] The Washington Wall Street Enterprise's Accountability for Financial Crises

The actions of individual Americans are subject to the rigorous standards and sanctions imposed in cases of banking, securities and consumer fraud and crime. Politicians and the power elite throughout history have a well justified general reputation of duplicity and mendacity accompanied by the continued ability to get away with it, time after time. Thus, the low regard in which they are held by the public. These "power elite" as well as the American public seem to think that, no matter how outrageous the behavior of the power elite and no matter the level of outrage expressed by the American public, the power elite are somehow exempt from the standards, laws and sanctions imposed on the rest of the American public in cases of banking, securities and consumer fraud and crime.

The closer one gets to the responsible individuals comprising the power elite, the more difficult it is for those who have suffered by deceit, misrepresentation or fraud by the power elite to successfully seek justice. They risk running afoul of the pervasive power held by the powerful public figures and the institutions they represent. The customary and official method of dealing with the public figures and holding them accountable is for voters and shareholders to "throw the bums out." Unfortunately, the new participants who follow those thrown out, tend to fall into the age-old patterns of active pursuit of self-interest held by their predecessors, in derogation of their formal individual and institutional responsibilities under the American rule of law.

We are familiar with the generally held, some might say, cynical, view of those American citizens and company shareholders who find themselves at the end of what the power elite view as acceptable levels of "tail end losses" caused by their policies and actions. There really is not anything we can do about it. It is just the nature of the system. From each side of the political spectrum, the briefly popular, but so far largely ineffective, "Occupy Wall Street" movement and the more coherent and focused but largely intellectually bankrupt activity of the "tea party" movement, express public frustration with our collective inability to enforce responsibility and accountability for the immeasurable harm caused by the financial crises. Professor Paul Kennedy has thoroughly documented the historic consequences of successive societies' failure to enforce responsibility and accountability of the governing power elite through the mechanisms of civil society. When the gap between action and rhetoric becomes too great, the mobs in fact do form, violence and war coalesce and heads do actually roll.

When you get down to the essence of the issue, however, despite the widespread anger and frustration with the "tail end loss" allocation process in the ongoing American and global financial crises, we must be reminded that Congressmen, federal financial regulators and their systemic tools, the Wall Street banks and bankers are not exempt from the legal standards and sanctions already provided for in our legal system. Their apparent insulation from the consequences of their actions is purely an illegitimate claim of perverse public policy not supported by the rule of law and constitutes an act of raw unconstitutional usurpation of the sovereignty of the people of the United States and the irresponsible——and as we will indeed see—criminal exercise of unlawful political power by the American congressional, bureaucratic and Wall Street power elite. How can this happen?

Consider the juxtaposition of the views of James Madison, father of the American *Constitution* and author of the pertinent Federal papers, with the views of former Senator Phil Gramm, an economist——one of the experts and power elite——and co-author and co-sponsor of the *Graham-Leach-Bliley Act* which unleashed the explosive growth of the shadow banking system and then, predictably, topped the cake in corruption of our currency, economy and financial system, resulting in visible systemic financial disaster within sixty days after his remarks were made:

In *Federalist No. 48*[54] James Madison warned that in a representative system, the people must be most wary of the legislature. Its actions are masked by complexity, and its access to the "pockets of the people" makes it especially dangerous. In "Vices of the Political System" he attributed to legislators three motives for seeking office: ambition, interest, and the public good, of which the latter is least and the second is most often in play. When self-interest is the motive, the legislator is especially energetic in gaining and keeping office. When a majority of legislators with like interests can form a majority, they can "join in a perfidious sacrifice" of the interest of their constituents so as better to serve their own. Elections might be thought to enable the public to rid themselves of this menace. But "base and selfish measures" are often "masked by pretexts of public good and apparent expediency." Other more "honest but unenlightened representatives" are then taken in by this masquerade and become its unwitting supporters."

On the other hand: "Senator Phil Gramm, R-Texas, former member of the Senate Budget Committee, former Chairman of the US Senate Committee on Banking, Housing and Urban Affairs, author of the *Gramm-Leach-Bliley Act,* which repealed the *Glass-Steagall Act of 1933,* recipient of more than $1 million in campaign contributions from the securities industry and now vice chair of Swiss banking giant UBS, told the *Washington Times* that[55]:

> The US economy is being weighed down by the belief by Americans that the economy is bad." You've heard of mental depression; this is a mental recession," Gramm told the Washington Times, adding that despite all the bad news out there US economic growth continues at a rate of approximately 1 percent. "We may have a recession; we haven't had one yet."
>
> Added Gramm: "We have sort of become a nation of whiners. You just hear this constant whining, complaining about a loss of competitiveness, America in decline...We've never been more dominant; we've never had more natural advantages than we have today...Misery sells newspapers. Thank God the economy is not as bad as you read in the newspaper every day."

[B] The Washington Wall Street Enterprise Intentionally Exploits Shadow Banking and Shadow Money to Effect Money Debasement

The examination of the role of the shadow banking system provides an extensive analysis of the factors giving rise to the civil torts and statutory crimes of abuse of power, deceit, intentional misrepresentation and fraud that are the cause of the financial crisis. These factors were not, and are not now hidden, secret or irrelevant, except to the bad actors themselves. These same factors, in one guise or another, have led to systemic financial crisis after crises through the years. In virtually every case, responsibility devolves on those in positions of power who, under the guise of protecting vital national sovereignty, in fact have preserved and used that power to create money to be awarded for short-term political and personal gain, based upon the reckless assumption that others following after will have to deal with the consequences of what Barry Eichengreen calls America's *"Exorbitant Privilege."*[56]

Professor Eichengreen's assessment, however, begs the questions: what is the constitutional basis for this privilege, if any, and if not a legitimate privilege, what is the nature of the so-called privileged conduct? Whatever it is, we know it is wrong and irresponsible. It is illegal. The foundation for this conclusion is grounded in the early history of America's financial system, the evolution of the departure from a constitutionally mandated policy of sound money as the cornerstone of our economic and political stability, and the increasing level of public tolerance of the fundamental process of government lying, cheating and stealing from the American public through ill-considered acts expediency, initially justified at the time as existential necessity, and now conveniently adopted by the bad actors as a policy foundation of "exorbitant privilege."

This work builds on my earlier work by briefly examining the effects of the *Graham Leach Bliley Act*, passed in November 1999, unleashing rapid and dramatic expansion of the shadow banking system; as well as the evolution of the *Basle Accords (I, II and III*——now possibly *IV*[57]*)* in a largely ineffective attempt to establish international norms for financial capital requirements adequate to address the ever higher risk of uncertainty in the global financial system; to an examination of *Dodd Frank*, a well -intentioned but inordinately complex program of financial system reform that circles but fails to address the fundamental drivers of financial crisis in America and globally. The examination of certain provisions of the *Dodd Frank Act*, confirms the continuation of the ongoing underlying misrepresentation of our nation's and our citizens financial position through the failure to regulate the value of the US Dollar, leading to an explosion of unsustainable levels of national debt, trade and current account deficits. These unsustainable financial imbalances create systemic financial crises after crises, through largely empty gestures to address the specter of systemic financial risk, combined with distracting and misdirected detailed micro-prudential and micro-regulatory and supervisory responses, rules and regulations.

I refer you to the recent books cited above as well as to the sources cited and in my earlier works, to confirm the long history of systemic financial crises resulting from the patterns of misrepresentation of the value of currencies (through deficit spending, increases in public and private debt and inflation) and therefore of the values of the assets and liabilities denominated in such currencies. Failure to take at least these observations and recommendations to heart in substance will surely result in an ongoing continuation and deterioration of the financial crisis as its underlying facts inevitably bubble to the level of public consciousness.

Regulation of the value of currency and debt denominated in that currency is a difficult proposition, but it is not impossible. Wholesale abandonment of any effort to regulate the value of the US dollar undermines every act of the American government that is dependent on a considered and budgeted expense by taxation and authorized transparent, transfer payments to serve each branch of government's constitutional responsibilities. The difficulties inherent in, and the willful blindness to the constitutional requirement of regulating the value of American money, combined with the highly touted flexible benefits of political expedience consisting of abandonment of any pretense of regulation, and finally, the actual consequential failure to regulate the value of American money, has resulted in the patterns of deceit, misrepresentation, fraud and systemic financial crises that I and others have long identified.

[C] Washington Wall Street Enterprise's Moral and Legal Standards for Accountability

Much has been written and discussed about this subject; mostly consisting of partial slivers of inquiry and inconclusive cases for partial slivers of accountability. This result is no surprise. The financial crisis is about the individuals and institutions who have been protected or benefited by this crisis—those powerful parties' objective—is to frustrate, confuse and to avoid accountability for their actions. These circumstances aren't without precedent. There is short collective memory and a remarkable ability to rationalize prior periodic financial crises; their causes; and the efforts mounted by the responsible power elite to avoid accountability for the damage wrought by financial crises.

While America has been historically a relatively prosperous country, with a dynamic economy grounded on the rule of law; when it comes to matters of money, notwithstanding the very clear interests and objectives of the founding fathers, it did not take long for before the most wealthy and powerful in American to emerge and begin what has been the continuation of a long and consistent history of government and powerful bankers and financiers efforts to bend money and banking to their will in their self-interest. The history of money and banking throughout world history and throughout American history has been the same old story of persistent incremental concentration and exploitation of power and wealth. The same rationalizations by Washington and Wall Street have been consistently and repeated trotted out and displayed for public consumption.

The Fed, federal financial regulators and the Wall Street banks have made much of the fact that emergency funding under TARP,[58] and the plethora of additional government programs, accompanied by unprecedented disguise of Wall Street bank insolvency through unrestrained advances at the Fed discount window to the domestic and global banking, business and financial community of more than $7.7 trillion, have been or will be repaid with no losses incurred and that thereby the American financial system has been preserved. This ignores the fact that approximately $3.9 trillion in asset purchases by the Fed under Quantitative Easing remain on the Fed's balance sheet—the value of those asset being booked at their purchase prices——not at market value.[59] This despite Fed statements that the purchases were made through competitive bids in an environment where there was no price competition and the prices were set to serve as an additional Wall Street bank bailout. The value of securities purchased is problematic at best. Both securities and Treasury bills purchase by the Fed are subject of significant risk of forthcoming higher interest rates and corresponding reduction of values.

First, the emergency loans and investments have in many cases——not been repaid——but refinanced under other government relief programs, through interest rate and inflated asset purchase price subsidies and accounting manipulation.

Second, the assertion that the financial system allegedly successfully protected the American public at no cost through decisive government and Wall Street Bank action is in fact, largely limited to the parties in the closed Washington-Wall Street financial system: the self-serving iniquitous circle of wealth and power that has emerged from the financial crisis larger, wealthier and more powerful than ever. The policies and actions of Washington and Wall Street have largely excluding the American public from this circle of strength and prosperity. Amazingly, temporarily included within the protected circle, for purposes of capturing the necessary political support, as noted above, the bailout program included many foreign borrowers and many borrowers not a part of the American banking system at all!

The members of the Washington and Wall Street money cartel system have lied about their motives and actions, cheated the American public and stolen from them the hard-earned fruits of labor and wealth worked for and accumulated over lifetimes. The American public's financial and personal losses have been characterized by the self-satisfied and paternalistic experts in Washington and on Wall Street as "acceptable levels of tail losses" necessary to be borne by the public for the supposed greater good of the country produced by the dominance of Washington and Wall Street in the global political and financial world. This intentional corruption of the American dream as a backdrop to the insatiable grasp by Washington and Wall Street of wealth and power would be sad, perhaps tragic, if it were not so clearly offensive to American ideals and outrageous in its effects.

The public has relied on the integrity of their money for capital accumulation for business formation and conduct, investment and for hard-earned and well-earned protection for retirement, disability and against the myriad vicissitudes of life. The protection by the Washington Wall Street criminal enterprise of their members' self-interest has left the American public, impoverished, played for fools and scrambling to salvage their personal and financial affairs in the shadow of the now ongoing greatest growth and prosperity amongst the Washington and Wall Street cabal ever experienced. The actions of the Washington Wall Street criminal enterprise are unlawful, un-American and must be brought to account by the American public.

The ability and record of success of popular efforts for restoration of integrity in public and private finance is not encouraging. The fact that the developed nations in the global economy have followed Americas leadership, adopting a monetary structure that is inherently and obviously unsound, has led to public acceptance of the narrative peddled by the power elite that America's (and the global) financial and economic system and structure is credit based; not asset based; and that promote and leverage economic growth in pursuit of a—literal—dream—the American dream, promoted and expanded beyond any reasonable or sustainable level; with the assurance of our nations experts—coincidentally the power elite who benefit most from this dream; that adverse economic consequences are minimal—acceptable levels of "tail losses." The economic consequences of the financial crisis have proved to be minimal only to those in political and financial power. The Washington Wall Street narrative induces many Americans to accept this state of affairs because the threat of the consequences of the leveraged ideal of the American Dream is distant and remote; and not intended to be borne by the majority of us in current times.

History is replete with examples of monetary and political systems; entire civilizations, that have fallen upon the practice of debasement of money to maintain a grip on concentrations of wealth and power amongst a relatively small elite (today's 1 percent) and justified by protestations of political necessity, expedience or simply because, at present Washington and Wall street can do it and get away with it. Failure to establish and maintain a safe, sound, honest and transparent monetary and banking system has consistently, historically, led to violent civil strife, conflict, disorder, violence and very often war.

According to Washington and Wall Street, notwithstanding the effects of money debasement driven financial crises, the existing American financial system works. To the extent that their efforts continue, unabated and without consequence, the system will continue to work, more or less, at the expense of the American public, until the inevitable day, when it simply does not work; when the forced public recognition of the damage done is inescapable, in the face of claims by Washington and Wall Street that the coming of that inevitable day is unexpected, unexplainable and for which these powerful individuals and institutions are not responsible or accountable. When that day comes, as it always does, government and bankers' focus shifts immediately from accountability to minimizing any threat to the system they have created, abused and that benefited from, causing the crisis to begin with. At the same time, Washington and Wall Street use the crisis to promote and effect further concentration of power and wealth in the guise of "moving on and putting the crisis behind us."

The only hope and prospect for imposing accountability on Washington and Wall Street is to return to public enforcement of first principles, either pursuant to the rule of law which this work advocates; or outside the legal process by the peoples' enforcement of their basic human civil right to honest money, an honest economy and honest government, by any means necessary, including revolution as contemplated by our founding fathers. The American Revolution was fought not all that long ago, relatively speaking, to achieve that very same objective.

Accountability for the most recent 2008 crisis requires that society and government alike turn to the clarity and discipline of the first principles of social and political economy and the American rule of law. Accountability for Washington and Wall Street requires public action, not complaints and passive acceptance of the status quo.

§1.12 THE FLOW OF THIS WORK

This book first examines the attributes of sovereign money, shadow money and shadow banking and money debasement. With this information before us, the book treats both the moral and then the legal attributes of money. It identifies the first principles and the basis for application of the American rule of law that can return these first principles to their proper place in defining our economic relationships in a fair open and transparent manner, enforceable by each American citizen under the American rule of law. The American public and American ideals and first principles must not be held hostage to the power insidiously and unabashedly grabbed by the American power elite. It is wrong and it is un-American. Each American public is entitled to a clean, clear shot at honestly achieving the American Dream.

This book identifies the primary false narratives propounded by the Washington Wall Street enterprise that appear to confound any attempt to hold them morally and legally accountable for financial crises.

This book revisits the foundational concepts of bank fraud and crime and their grounding in the fundamental moral principles upon which our civil society is based; principles specifically applicable to the use of credit as money under our current financial regime. This work presents a re-evaluation of the role of accountability for bank fraud and crime as an aspect of new thinking in global finance and its regulation. This work challenges and condemns the current institutionally accepted false narratives and assumptions that financial reform should focus on the potential for systemic institutional harm government and financial institutions have suffered; and the corollary narrative and assumption that their suffering has been due to fraud inflicted upon them.

Washington and Wall Street have proudly proclaimed that taxpayers have been repaid and suffered no loss from massive government bailouts. The fact is that Wall Street has simply appeared to repay the publicly identified bailouts through some obvious, but primarily through hidden, government subsidies circling through the monetary system referred to as Fed "monetary policy" and "open market operations," in response to a crisis. This official sounding narrative offered to the public in the interest of "financial stability," has uncritically passed by without scrutiny associated with the basis for establishing accountability. Washington and Wall Street have simply cooked the books. Any suggestion that taxpayers have been repaid for the cost and protected from the damage caused by the financial crisis is farcical when examined in the shadow of a Federal Reserve balance sheet that has ballooned to nearly $4.5 trillion at week end July 2, 2014, and specter of domestic damages to the American people estimated by the government at in excess of $12.8 trillion, up to as much as $20 trillion, and damages to people outside of America estimated by the Fed at in excess of $40 trillion. Recent analysis by Frederic Feldkamp and Christopher Whalen[60] place the damage estimate domestically at $30 trillion and globally at $67 trillion. These analyses confirm damages to the American public in amounts almost too large to imagine. According to the World Bank, the Gross Domestic Product (GDP) in the United States was worth 16,800 billion US dollars in 2013. The GDP value of the United States represents 27.10 percent of the world economy.

Before you dismiss this book as the random musings of a modern day financial, monetary and legal Luddite, I urge you to take a moment to examine the historical and current factual context; and the actual, evolved moral, economic and legal theories and first principles that bear on the issue of accountability for crises, as opposed to emergency objectives and emergency action to relieve human suffering (in fact, to protect Washington and Wall Street and not designed to protect the public interest). These policies and principles have been well and thoroughly documented and debated.

The factual foundation for assessing Washington's and Wall Street's legal accountability for the financial crisis has been extensively documented by Washington itself. Informed by *The Financial Crisis Inquiry Report*[61] (Report) issued by the National Commission on the Causes of the Financial and Economic Crisis in the United States (Commission) in January, 2011, I urge the reader to consider the application of the common law foundation for the establishment and enforcement of accountability for financial crises, as well as the American *Constitutions*, state law and federal statutory law that can and should be brought to bear to provide a meaningful context for legal action that can lead to a level and stable field for effective implementation of the thoughts and ideas for financial and legal reform advanced by scholars to date.

American law pertaining to money is exhaustively detailed in Edwin Vieira, Jr.'s massive 1,700 pages, two volume work *Pieces of Eight, The Monetary Powers and Disabilities of the United States Constitution.*[62] Dr Vieira provides much needed clarity with respect to the relationship of the present global financial crisis to the abandoned strictures America's founding fathers designed to prevent money debasement and related financial crises through the crafting of *United States Constitution.*

Recognition of systemic risk of money debasement as the cause of systemic financial crises is one thing. Defining it, doing something about it by rooting out who has done what that was wrong and who is irresponsible in creating systemic financial risk and systemic financial crises; and most importantly, by holding them to account under the rule of law, is another thing entirely. We cannot move to long term solutions to our structural financial instability without a change in perspective brought about by public action to impose responsibility, accountability on Washington and Wall Street, and establish legal disincentives to further bad acts, such as those at the bottom of the financial crisis.

The sustainability of global finance as a useful and honest tool will ultimately be determined by whether governments and financial institutions can be held accountable under the rule of law for the pervasive course of the bank fraud and crime of abuse of power and discretion in effecting money debasement that has directly caused financial crisis after crisis. There is no issue more important or necessary to Americans than the recognition of and legal redress for the crisis through the imposition of accountability by the American public through the American judicial system and the American rule of law.

As a component of new thinking about financial crises, the grounding of our analysis in the fundamental moral principles embodied in the laws at the center of the case for Washington and Wall Street accountability for the financial crisis through application of the *United States Constitution* and the federal statutory law and common law of civil and criminal financial fraud and crime is not outside of the square. The thinking is not new. The naming of names of the institutions and individuals that caused the financial crisis and the specification of violations of American law that have worked such fraud and crime upon the American public, however, has been scrupulously avoided. This book presents a current recognition of the existence and validity of moral and legal standards for accountability and justice that apply to Washington and Wall Street; provide for and sustain the American, and global standards of integrity, trust and confidence necessary to money and banking as fundamental components of domestic and global commerce and civil society. These moral and legal standards are as old as money and banking. One simply cannot deny that integrity, honesty and confidence in money and banking are the essence of public interest. These factors apply to every member of every civilized society every day.

Today's rhetoric, from former President Obama to former president of the Federal Reserve Bank of New York and Treasury Secretary Geithner, is that the crisis was wrong, it was irresponsible, but not illegal. Old Testament style revenge would ruin the global economy. We just need to move on. What is called Keynesian style monetary stimulus is the order of the day. As we will note later, neither Keynes nor Hayek, both distinguished economists, did countenance in their writing, nor would they countenance today, the establishment of a foundation of civil and criminal fraud as support for national and global monetary and fiscal policy. But civil and criminal fraud is in fact the policies that now obtain in America, and through American example and leadership, globally. Upon reflection, this situation should be no surprise to any reader of this work. The surprise, the rethinking and the new thinking presented here is surprising only because it has been simply ignored in the ongoing dialogue amongst experts on financial crises and reform.

New thinking with respect to bank fraud and crime effected through money debasement in today's context is driven by a return to and appreciation of an historical understanding of the first moral and legal principles of finance. Finance, of course, is the structuring of credit. Credit is now, and with very few exceptions, has always constituted the bulk of money. Felix Martin observed that "[t]he vast majority of our national money—around 90 per cent in the US, for example, and 97 per cent in the UK—has no physical existence at all. It consists merely of our account balances at our banks."[63] Martin could have gone on to note that the value of the money in our accounts is supported primarily by the loans and investments made by those banks as well as loans and investments made by all other banks in the system denominated in the same currency, as well as by, in the US, the full faith and credit of the US government—meaning of course, the American tax payers.

Banks or bank-like institutions have historically evolved as the creators and inter-mediators of credit serving as money through societies and their economies and importantly, acting hand in hand, as partners with government in pursuit of political objectives, including war. To get to the heart of bank and financial fraud and crime we will take a look at the basic components and the associated attributes of those components and the respective rights, powers, duties and responsibilities of the constituent parties involved in money and banking; how these parties have historically been held morally and legally accountable for their respective actions; how accountability has failed during relatively recent times and what must be done and by whom to protect and preserve our global financial system against the destructive forces of financial crises spawned by bank and financial fraud and crime perpetrated by Washington and Wall Street.

As I write this, the political environment has gone all in for dishonesty and intentional misrepresentation as the accepted basis for public policy. In the monetary arena, cyber coins reign supreme. A form of money deliberately designed to be separate from any commercial reality, apart from raw speculation. Money and political power are based on dishonesty. Both are the instruments of abuse of power and discretion by Washington and Wall Street to enable them to lie to, cheat and steal from ordinary Americans. This cannot be the new American Dream.

CHAPTER 2
Money

§2.01 THE NATURE OF MONEY

Walter Bagehot, an oft quoted 19th century English banker and commentator—who understood our current and the longtime conundrum in the world of banking and finance, wrote in 1857 that:

> "[M]en of business in England do not like the currency question. They are perplexed to define accurately what money is: how to count they know, but what to count they do not know."[64]

John Maynard Keynes:

> The whole object of the accumulation of wealth is to produce results, or potential results, at a comparatively distant, and sometimes at an indefinitely distant, date. Thus, the fact that our knowledge of the future is fluctuating, vague and uncertain renders wealth a peculiarly unsuitable subject for the methods of classical economic theory.[65]

In other words, investment depends heavily on conventional judgments and the existing state of opinion, but ultimately, investment sits on an insecure foundation. Money originated as the most reliable and liquid goods—evaluated by kind, quality and quantity to serve as a unit of account, medium of exchange and store of value. Precious metals—gold, silver and copper pre-dominated the selection of goods useful as money.

Increased production of goods and services over current needs permitted savings—stockpiles of goods at home—then with brokers and merchants—and later, stockpiles of money—precious metals with specialized brokers—banks—which kept account of deposits and held them safe and sound.

Ludwig von Mises, in *The Theory of Money and Credit*,[66] explains that money only becomes necessary in a society when its economic order entails production based upon a division of labor and in which private property consists not only of consumption goods but also production goods. What is produced and how it is produced is decided in each instance by the owners of the means of production who produce not only for their own needs but also for the needs of others. Producers attach use value to their products and other members of the community attach an estimated use value to the products. The balance of production and consumption takes place in the market through the process of bargaining with one another.

A single product to be exchanged by its producer for a second product produced by another can be accomplished directly through barter as a result of bargaining over the relative consumption value of each product to the others' product in the marketplace, without need for money as a medium of exchange. When the number of producers and consumers multiply and supply and demand do not coincide quantitatively; and where the instances of division of labor increases and the wants of consumption become more refined, money as a medium of exchange becomes more useful:

> In order to successfully exchange the less marketable products for products that are for consumption or are more useful as marketable in further exchanges in the market place, the producer seeks to continually exchange the products he receives in exchange for other products that are increasingly more marketable.
>
> "In this way, the goods that are originally the most marketable become most useful as a common medium of exchange. The function of money is to facilitate the business of the market by acting as a common medium of exchange."[67]
>
> Through the years, "the requirements of the market have gradually led to the selection of certain commodities as common media of exchange. The various commodities used as a common medium of exchange have varied highly and differed from country to country and industry to industry. The development and expansion of trade led inexorably, by stages, where the parties to exchange rejected the least marketable commodity as a medium of exchange in favor of the most marketable and available, "until at last only a single commodity remained, which was universally employed as a medium of exchange; in a word, money.
>
> This stage of development in the use of media of exchange, the exclusive employment of a single economic good, is not yet completely attained. In quite early times, sooner in some places than others, the extension of indirect exchange led to the employment of the two precious metals gold and silver as common media of exchange." The use of gold and silver as media of exchange, or money, has been widespread for thousands of years, up to the relatively near present.
>
> Economic history is the story of the gradual extension of the economic community beyond its original limits of the single household to embrace the nation and then the world. But every increase has led to a fresh duality of the medium of exchange whenever the two amalgamating communities have not had the same sort of money.[68]

The governing fundamental principle supporting the successful use of money was and remains trust and confidence by market participants of the quality, weight and measure of the respective media of exchange; in early time consisting at the highest level of trust and confidence of silver and gold. According to von Mises, the duality of gold and silver then evolved to three primary types of money:[69]

> Commodity money.
>
> Commodity money is a general-purpose medium of exchange and a tradable commodity in its own right. An example is coin made of precious metal. Commodity money is often viewed as more stable, although that is not always the case. Its supply is supply relative to other goods and services; subject to regular and

sometimes extraordinary fluctuations in purchasing power, i.e. the prices of goods rise, because the supply of goods did not keep pace with the increased supply of money; price never goes to zero as fiat currencies may (in theory). The advantage of gold and silver, unlike fiat paper currency, the supply cannot be increased arbitrarily by a central bank. Trading value of commodity money may be greater than its value as a medium of exchange when governments attempt to fix exchange rates between different commodity moneys. People then start melting down coins and reselling the metal used to make them. Commodity money's ability to function as a store of value is also limited by its nature. For example, copper and tin risk rust and corrosion, and gold and silver are soft metals that can lose weight through scratches and abrasions; it may have a tendency to restrain growth in a very active economy in order to maintain the price of goods and services produced. Total production can easily outstrip the supply of those commodities, which leads to price deflation. Production within commodity-based economies tends to be limited by the supply of the commodity currency. This problem is compounded by the fact that money also serves as a store of value. This encourages hoarding (in other circumstances known as "saving") and takes the commodity money out of circulation, reducing the supply. The supply of circulating commodity currency is further reduced by the fact that commodity moneys also have competing non-monetary uses. For example, gold and silver are used in jewelry, and nickel and copper have important industrial uses. Use of commodity money may limit the geographic extent of the trading market. To make large purchases either a large volume or a high weight or both of the commodities must be transported to the seller. The cost of transportation of the currency raises the transaction cost and makes long distance sales less attractive.

Representative money.

Representative money consists of token coins, other physical tokens such as certificates, and even non-physical "digital certificates" (now including authenticated digital transactions) that can be reliably exchanged for a fixed quantity of a commodity such as gold, silver or potentially water, oil or food. Representative money stands in direct and fixed relation to the commodity which backs it, while not itself being composed of that commodity.

Credit money.

Credit Money consists of any claim against a physical or legal person that can be used for the purchase of goods and services. Credit money differs from commodity and fiat money in that it is not payable on demand (although in the case of fiat money, "demand payment" is a purely symbolic act since all that can be demanded is other types of fiat currency) and there is some element of risk that the real value upon fulfillment of the claim will not be equal to real value expected at the time of purchase. This risk comes about in two ways and affects both buyer and seller. First it is a claim and the claimant may default (not pay). High levels of default have destructive supply side effects. If manufacturers and service providers do not receive payment for the goods they produce, they will not have the resources to buy the labor and materials needed to produce new goods and services. This reduces supply, increases prices and raises unemployment, possibly triggering a period of stagflation:

In extreme cases, widespread defaults can cause a lack of confidence in lending institutions and lead to economic depression. Abuse of credit arrangements is a fundamental cause of the Great Depression of the 1930s, the crises of the 70s, 80s, 90s, 2000, and of 2008. The second source of risk is time. Credit money is a promise of future payment. If the interest rate on the claim fails to compensate for the combined impact of the inflation (or deflation) rate and the time value of money, the seller will receive less real value than anticipated. If the interest rate on the claim overcompensates, the buyer will pay more than expected.

Over the last two centuries, following the American and French Revolutions, credit money has once again steadily risen as the main source of money creation, progressively replacing first commodity and then representative money. In many cases, credit money has been converted to fiat money (see below), as governments have backed certain private credit instruments (first banknotes from central banks, then later certain types of deposits to banks as well as securities of government sponsored enterprises backed by credit instruments), thus converting central banknotes to legal tender, and other types of notes (deposit certificates of less than a certain value) to a status not very different from fiat money, since they are backed by the power of the central government to redeem eventually with tax collection.

According to Von Mises:

> A particular problem with credit money is that its supply moves in line with credit/business cycles (colloquially: "booms" and "busts"). When lenders are optimistic (notably when the debt level is low), they increase their lending activity, thus creating new money. This may also trigger inflation and bull markets. When creditors are pessimistic (for instance, when debt level is perceived as too high, or unwise lending activity in the past has resulted in situations where defaults are expected to follow), then creditors reduce their lending activity and money becomes "tight" or "illiquid." Bankruptcies and market recessions (so-called bear markets) then follow.

Credit money depends for its effectiveness on the application of commercial law to purchase, sales and credit transactions, including the evolution of the law of bills and notes into the *Uniform Commercial Code*, the law of secured transactions, creditors rights and bankruptcy law and securities law and laws governing financial fraud.[70] These laws plus prudent banking practices based upon the establishment of relationships of mutual trust and confidence between and amongst the parties; development of legal documentation identifying and allocating transactional risks accompanied by studied; and prudent discounting for credit quality and liquidity of the credit instruments serving as money enabled increased commercial activity and supported a more productive and prosperous society:

> Fiat money.
>
> Fiat Money is any money whose value is determined by legal means, rather than the by strict availability of goods and services which are named on the representative note. Fiat money is created when a type of credit money (typically notes from a central bank, such as the Federal Reserve System in the US) is declared by a government act (fiat) to be acceptable and officially recognized payment for all debts, both public and private. Fiat money may thus be symbolic of a commodity or a government promise, though not a completely specified amount of either of these. Fiat money is thus not technically fungible or tradable directly for fixed quantities of anything, except more of the same government's fiat money. Fiat moneys usually trade against each other in value in an international market, as with other goods. An exception to this is when currencies are locked to each other.

Many but not all fiat moneys are accepted on the international market as having value. Those that are, trade indirectly against any internationally available goods and services. Thus the numbers of US dollars or Japanese yen which are equivalent to each other, or to a gram of gold metal, are all market decisions which change from moment to moment on a daily basis. Occasionally, a country will peg the value of its fiat money to that of the fiat money of a larger economy, so there is no floating value ratio of the two currencies.

Representative, credit, and fiat money all provide solutions to several limitations of commodity money. Depending on the laws, there may be little or no need to physically transport the money — an electronic exchange may be sufficient. Other types of moneys have as their sole use to be medium of exchange, so their supply is not limited by competing alternate uses. Credit and fiat monies can be created without limit in theory, so there is no limit on trade volumes.

Some of the benefits of fiat money can present a double-edged sword. For example, if the amount of money in active circulation outstrips the available goods and services for sale, the effect can be inflationary. This can easily happen if governments print money without attention to the level of economic activity. This has been a consistent problem for the US since the abandonment of the Bretton Woods Accord tie to the gold standard in 1971.

The criticism of credit and fiat moneys relates to the fact that their stabilities are highly dependent on the stability of the legal system backing the currency; should the legal system fail, so will the value of any type of money that depends on it. The US legal system appears to have no understanding of the sanctity of the first principle and constitutional promise of "sound money" underlying the legal contract of the US fiat dollar with its holders. If the creation of money or wealth is by means of any legal promise to provide goods or services in the future (as is the case with both credit and fiat type money), then any failure of a legal system to back up the rights of the debt-holder to collect on the promise will act to jeopardize the value of future promises.

Part of the confusion surrounding money derives from the difference between money in an economic sense versus money as a legal concept. From an economic perspective, money is primarily and medium of exchange and a unit of account in consummating an exchange of goods or services. Von Mises reminds us that, "from a legal point of view, money is not the common medium of exchange, but the common medium of payment or debt settlement. But Money only becomes a medium of payment by virtue of being a medium of exchange. And it is only because it is a medium of exchange that the law also makes it the medium for fulfilling obligations not contracted in terms of money, but whose fulfillment is for some reason or other impossible.

The fact that the law regards money only as a means of cancelling outstanding obligations has important consequences for the legal definition of money. What the law understands by money is in fact not the common medium of exchange but the legal medium of payment. It does not come within the scope of the legislator or jurist to define the economic concepts of money "In determining how monetary debts may be effectively paid off there is no reason for being too exclusive. It is customary in business to tender and accept in payment certain money substitutes instead of money itself. If the law refused to recognize the validity of money substitutes that are sanctioned by commercial usage, it would only open the door to all sorts of fraud and deceit."

According to von Mises:

"The law may declare anything it likes to be a medium of payment.... [b]ut bestowing the property of legal tender on a thing does not suffice to make it money in the economic sense. Goods can become common media of exchange only through the practice of those who take part in commercial transactions; and it is the valuations of these persons alone that determine the exchange ratios of the market. Quite possibly, commerce may take into use those things to which the state has ascribed the power of payment; but it need not do so. It may, if it likes, reject them."

When the state declares an object to be a legal means of fulfilling an obligation, three situations are possible: first, the legal means of payment may be identical with the medium of exchange contemplated by the parties or, if not identical, it may be of equal value with contemplated medium at the time of payment; second, if the state mandated medium of payment is something with a higher value than the contemplated medium at the time of payment (sufficiently rare as to be disregarded), the payee would receive a windfall; in the more likely case where the state mandated medium of payment is something with a lower value than the contemplated medium at the time of payment—acceptance of the state mandated payment amounts to a state mandated legal relief or discount of the payer's obligation to the extent of the reduction in value of the state mandated medium of payment from the value of the originally contemplated medium."

Unfortunately, the third situation has dominated the US economy and monetary system since the original abandonment of our constitutional requirement of sound money at the time of the Civil War, the Great Depression and most recently with the breakdown of the *Bretton Woods Accords,*[71] and the explosion of an enormous class of money substitutes constituting market "liquidity". The dramatic development in past decades of "structured finance" instruments as money substitutes has resulted in a dramatic separation from the historic legal, accounting and banking practices attendant to the prudent use of credit instruments as money substitutes. Conversion of credit money substitutes to homogenized securities and derivatives of those securities on enormous scale, readily transferred in enormous markets where values are based upon "disclosures" mandated by securities laws lost in a world of anonymous electronic high speed trading, as opposed to credit money substitutes created based on the carefully constructed credit money substitutes created based on traditional and conservative legal and accounting principles, accompanied by the mutual trust and confidence between and amongst parties and well considered discounts to the value of the credit money substitutes for credit quality and liquidity, has provided a fertile field for fraud on an institutional scale and resulted in a perversion of the legal, accounting and banking principles that historically facilitated credit as a money substitute in an honest, transparent and productive basis.

§2.02 BANKS AND MONEY ARE INSEPARABLE

Banks' existence is based on the public's need for money. Banks were initially organized to hold customers' money in the form of precious metals. The banks duties were simply to maintain transparent and accurate accounts, provide receipts for deposit and withdrawal of money; and to hold that money in safety—so that it would not be lost or stolen; and to maintain the soundness the commodity money held on deposit, promising that the depositor get would get back from the bank upon withdrawal what he had deposited—the same, if not the identical commodity—in kind, amount and quality.

For convenience, businessmen began to issue discounted bills of exchange and bills of credit redeemable in stated specie (commodity money) by a stated bank in lieu of the necessity of hauling about heavy and unwieldy amounts of precious metals; thus the beginning of money based a representation of commodity money due from the bank upon withdrawal. These bills representing the debt of the bank and credit to the depositor were traded at a discount reflecting the risk of safety and soundness of the bank and its ability to safely and soundly hold the money as specie of a commodity in the form of precious metal and return it to the holder of the bill who was entitled to withdrawal previous held by the original depositor.

§2.03 INTERVENTION BY THE STATE IN MONEY AND BANKING

With political and societal evolution, states intervened in markets for goods and services based on right of conquest and sustained by threat of force. The purpose of the intervention was to enable the state to calculate and collect revenue to support the state's administration and protection, primarily through wars.

Money facilitated state assessment and collection of taxes. Control over money as exercise of sovereignty provided an additional revenue source as well as an opportunity to increase revenue though debasement of the quality and amount of specie—causing inflation, lack of confidence in safety and soundness of money and constriction of trade due to uncertainty of values of money, goods and services and their connection to one another.

[A] Regulation of Money and Banks

The essence of regulation of money and banks is the public's need for safety and soundness of money held in the hands of banks—not strictly safety and soundness of banks themselves. Regulation of bank safety and soundness is a corollary only of safety and soundness of money: banks must protect depositors against loss or theft of their money or its debasement as to kind, quality and quantity. Herein lays the rub.

In order for banks to facilitate the use of specie by bills of credit and bills of exchange redeemable in specie, it became necessary to establish uniformity of units of specie as to kind, quality and amount, as a clear representation of value transferable in the marketplace, where the market value of goods and services might fluctuate in relationship to the relative consistency of the amount and value of the money. This arrangement worked well enough, subject to occasional theft, dishonesty of bankers and bankers' debasement of specie or issuance of fraudulent bills of credit or exchange, often resulting in bank failure.

The growth of the importance and amount of money in circulation created a constant and growing tension between depositors of money with banks and the states' perceived need for ever increasing revenue to finances wars, excesses of state consumption of resources and the state power that wielding large amounts of wealth represented by money can bring. As a matter of political expediency and the exercise of power backed by force, the interest of the state in money and banking was first and foremost to exploit the nature and limitations of specie as money in support of the representation and projection of state power won by conquest and maintained under threat of force. State interest in banks, banking and money, previously purely a market-based convenience; then necessarily grew apace. Currency counterfeiting and debasement became a political way of life in authoritarian state societies.

Development of widespread use of specie as money and credit based on specie as money historically has been limited by the owners' requirement that their money be safe and sound. F.A. Mann, author of the definitive treatise on the legal aspects of money, observed that the primary functions of a commodity based money such as the gold standard was to first, constitute, emit and then regulate and stabilize value, and second, to regulate and limit the volume of money, based on reserve requirements.[72] Rather than elaborate on the questionable constitutionality, legal efficacy or propriety of the demise of the gold standard following the collapse of the *Bretton Woods Accords*, Mann simply acknowledged that this tectonic shift away from; this literal abandonment of the fundamental protection for regulation and stabilization of the quality and quantity of sovereign money became simply a matter of historical interest.[73] The greatest ongoing threat to the safety and soundness of money became acts of government intervention and manipulation of money value and amount, through weakening law and regulation; diffusion and vitiation of accountability through a web of opacity, unbounded regulatory discretion and forbearance of accountability for duty to create and maintain sound money through regulation of its value and quantity; and through ceding of Washington's ultimate power over sound money to Wall Street, where that power has and continues to be abused for private gain in derogation of the public interest with impunity.

[B] The Principle of Sound Money

Ludwig von Mises wrote a Part Four to his *The Theory of Money and Credit* in 1952 that first appeared in the 1953 American edition published by Yale University Press:[74]

> The principle of sound money that guided the nineteenth-century monetary doctrines and policies was a product of classical political economy. It was an essential part of the liberal program as developed by eighteenth century social philosophy and propagated in the following century by the most influential political parties of Europe and America.
>
> The liberal doctrine sees in the market economy the best, even the only possible, system of economic organization of society. Private ownership of the means of production tends to shift control of production to the hands of those best fitted for this job and thus to secure for all members of society the fullest possible satisfaction of their needs. It assigns to consumers the power to choose those purveyors who supply them in the cheapest way with those articles they are most urgently asking for and thus subjects the entrepreneurs and owners of the means of production, namely, the capitalists and the landowners, to the sovereignty of the buying public. It makes nations and their citizens free and provides ample sustenance for a steadily increasing population.

It is impossible to grasp the meaning of the concept of sound money if one does not realize that it was devised as an instrument for the protection of civil liberties against the despotic inroads on the part of government. Ideologically, it belongs in the same class with political constitutions and bills of rights. ... "The postulate of sound money was first brought up as a response to the princely practice of debasing the coinage. It was later carefully elaborated and perfected in the age which—through the experience of the American continental currency, the paper money of the French Revolution and the British restriction period—had learned what a government can do to a nation's currency system.

The Sound Money Principle has two aspects: first, it is affirmative in approving the markets choice of a commonly used medium of exchange; and second, it is negative in obstructing the government's propensity to meddle with the currency system.

America's currency was founded on the basis of sound money. At that time, sound money meant a metallic standard. Then followed the battle of standards: gold versus silver versus fiat money. The debate among experts trended towards money and banking amongst "routinists" unfamiliar with economics or with the essential tie between the market-based determination of relative value through the integrity of the medium of exchange. The arguments about money, its supply and the effects of inflation and deflation are as old as the concept of money.

For the naïve mind there is something miraculous in the issuance of fiat money. A magic word spoken by the government creates out of nothing a thing which can be exchanged against any merchandise a man would like to get. How pale is the art of sorcerers, witches, and conjurors when compared to that of the government's Treasury Department! The government, professors tell us "can raise all of the money it needs by printing it." Taxes for revenue, announced a chairman of the Federal Reserve Bank of New York, are "obsolete."

These enthusiasts do not see that the working of inflation is conditioned by the ignorance of the public, and that inflation ceases to work as soon as the many become aware of its affects upon the monetary unit's purchasing power. In normal times, that is, in periods in which the government does not tamper with the monetary standard, people do not bother about monetary problems. Quite naively they take it that the monetary unit's purchasing power is 'stable'. They pay attention to changes occurring in the money prices of the various commodities. They know very well that the exchange ratios between various commodities vary. But they are not conscious of the fact that the exchange ratio between money on the one side, and all commodities and services is variable too. When the inevitable consequences of inflation appear and prices soar, they think that commodities are becoming dearer and fail to see that money is getting cheaper.

This ignorance of the public is the indispensable basis of the inflationary policy..." "It is a display of considerable naivety to recommend openly a monetary system that can work only if its essential features are ignored by the public."

First, there is a need to remember that the gold standard did not collapse. Governments abolished it in order to pave the way for inflation. The whole grim apparatus of oppression and coercion—policemen, custom guards, penal courts, prisons, in some countries, even executioners—had to be put into action in order to destroy the gold standard, solemn pledges were broken, retroactive laws were promulgated, provisions of *Constitutions* and bills of rights were openly defied, and hosts of servile writers praised what the governments had done and hailed the dawn of the fiat-money-millennium.

The emergency that brings about inflation is this: the people or the majority of the people, are not prepared to defray the costs incurred by their ruler's policies. They support these policies only to the extent that they believe that their conduct

> does not burden themselves." The mission of the government is then to convince the people that someone else—perhaps the "rich", will have to pay. Such practices take advantage of the masses' ignorance to cheat the voters instead of trying to convince them. "It is not just an accident that in our age, inflation has become the accepted method of money management. Inflation is the fiscal complement of statism and arbitrary government." It is the particular tool of a massive bureaucracy composed of competing regulatory agencies seeking to maximize budgets and minimize responsibilities by defining them away.[75]

The respective vested interests and myopic views of US economists and financial institutions have blinded them to the necessity of understanding and their mutual culpability in abandoning, responsibility for and continually debasing and manipulating one of the most important foundations for our economy and our individual financial wellbeing—our money, the US dollar, our United States currency. Congress and the institutions it has created have the power, and with it constitutional responsibility, to maintain a sound, uniform and stable currency and to regulate its value (*United States Constitution,* Article I, § 8, Clause 5: "The Congress shall have power to coin money, regulate the value thereof, and of foreign coin, and fix the standard of weights and measures").

The constitutional requirement that our Congress maintain a sound, uniform and stable currency is a fundamental responsibility of our government that it has abrogated at our peril.

[C] Importance of Credit Money as Honest, Safe, and Sound Money

Felix Martin provides a very useful context for understanding the central role of credit and credit systems as money, beginning nearly four thousand years ago. Martin identifies the overriding concern of our founding fathers to establish and preserve a system of commodity money—silver and then gold—as a central response to contemporaneous widespread currency and banking abuses deemed to constitute a threat to the establishment and conduct of democratic government. These concerns were the fundamental focus of John Locke, the foremost philosophical advocate for the establishment of democracy and the curbing of monetary abuses by sovereign monarchies throughout Europe. A deep understanding of the historical development of money, as a social, economic, political and legal instrument, is necessary to clarify the ancient sources of conflict in recognizing the fundamental role of money in maintaining social and political order as well as standards of justice, both social and legal; and the necessary methods and primacy of the rule of law and its enforcement as the fundamental social and political purpose of a democratic government; a purpose presently unfulfilled. The failure of Washington to provide sound money combined with Washington's pact with Wall Street to exploit that failure has predictably spawned a polarized and unjust redistribution of power and wealth from society as a whole to those few who are able to corrupt the fundamentally democratic and constitutionally based process for successful definition of money, its emission as a legal instrument, the regulation of its value in accordance with democratically established standard(s) of value essential to the successful, fair, just and honest use of sound money in today's society.

[D] Honest, Safe, and Sound Money Is Based on Shared Trust and Confidence

Felix Martin carefully clarifies the relative role of tangible commodity money, such a gold and silver preferred by John Locke and others throughout the history of money, and more dramatically in the use enormous stone *fei* used by the residents of Yap in Micronesia and the "Cod Money" used in Early Newfoundland, as contrasted with "the underlying system of credit accounts and clearing of accounts which, they helped to track. In these societies, as in early American society, the commodities operated as tokens by which accounts were kept. The users of the tokens could accumulate credits and debts in the course of their trading in various commodities to be offset against one another in order to periodically settle balances of payments. Outstanding balances of account denominated in these units of commodities could be carried forward "at the end of a single exchange, or a day, or week, might, if the counterparties so wished, be settled by the exchange of currency—*fei* [in Yap]—to the appropriate value; this being a tangible and visible record of the outstanding credit that the seller enjoyed with the rest of Yap [in the case of the use of *fei*].[76]

"Coins and currency, in other words, are useful tokens to record the underlying system of credit accounts and to implement the underlying process of clearing."[77]... "But currency is not itself money. Money is the system of credit accounts and their clearing that currency represents."[78]

Martin observes that the role of commodities as money was intuitive when the tokens could be readily exchanged for the denominated units of the underlying agreed commodity standard. He also correctly observes that in today's world, "[m]odern banknotes are quite transparently nothing but tokens. What is more, most of the currency in our contemporary economies does not enjoy even the precarious physical existence of a banknote. The vast majority of our national money—around 90 per cent in the US, for example, and 97% per cent in the UK—has no physical existence at all. It consists merely of our account balances at our banks. The only tangible apparatus employed in most monetary payments today is a plastic card and a keypad. It would be a brave theorist indeed who would try to maintain that a pair of microchips and a Wi-Fi connection are a commodity medium of exchange."[79]

While Martin's explanation of money as a system and a process rather than a commodity appears early in the work, Martin does not hone in on the substantive shift in in the system and process of money away from one based on a discipline—a regulation of the value and quantity of money— through the indispensable component of redemption—the ability at any time to convert the carried account balances to something real and tangible, a commodity that is an agreed standard of value by type, measured unit and number of units.

The fundamental principles that are the foundation for modern money—and historical money going back to the first uses of written systems of account in Uruk, ancient Mesopotamia around 3100 BC, center on the relationship of money tokens to outside standards of valuation based on commodities of some type, establishing the fundamental trust and confidence in the value of the money represented by the social phenomenon of the use of system and process to implement money.[80] The first step was to use a token representing a commodity, pressing it into a clay tablet to make a record, and ultimately to dispense with the token and simply mark the tablet with a representative image with a reed pen (cuneiform script), and to dispense with repetitive images with newly created symbols for numbers, giving rise to the possibility of development of mathematics.[81]

The ongoing development of systems and processes for accounting in terms of money from the time of Ur to the present has been a story of the devising of ever more efficient and flexible techniques.[82] Such efficiency and flexibility also led to increasing complexity and to the periodic abuse by the account keepers and their masters to manipulate the processes and systems to distance the accounts from the discipline of redemption in order debase the money in the system for their own advantage. That abuse of the monetary systems and processes was politically based and politically justified; then, as now.

Martin correctly observes that today "currency is ephemeral and cosmetic: it is the underlying mechanism of credit accounts and clearing that is the essence of money." This social technological concept is laid on the foundation of:[83]

- An abstract unit of value in which money is denominated;
- A system of accounts which keeps track of the individuals' or institutions' credit or debt balances as they engage in trade with one another; and
- The possibility that the original creditor in a relationship can transfer their debtor's obligation to a third party in settlement of some unrelated debt.

A bilateral credit relationship is simply a loan. "It is credit, but it is not money."[84] It is when that credit—loan—can be passed on to a third party through "negotiation" and "endorsement" that the credit becomes money. Money is not just credit, but rather readily transferable credit.[85] Quoting nineteenth-century economist and lawyer Henry Dunning Macleod, Martin observes that:

> If we were asked—Who made the discovery which has most deeply affected the fortunes of the human race? We think, after full consideration, we might safely answer—the man who first discovered that a Debt is a Saleable Commodity.[86]

For a seller to accept a buyer's credit instrument in payment, however, the seller must be convinced that:

- the debtor whose payment obligation they are about to accept will, if it comes to it, be able to satisfy their claim—that the money's issuer is creditworthy; and
- the seller must also trust that third parties will be willing to accept the debtors credit obligation in payment as well—that it is and remain indefinitely, transferable—that the market for it is liquid.

Such convictions can be based only on and consist of trust and confidence. According to Martin, then, "[d]epending on how powerful are the reasons to believe these two things, it will be easier or harder for an issuer's [debt] to circulate as money."[87] Martin refers to the process of negotiation and endorsement of a credit instrument through the system of processes of accounting and clearing a "financial jargon."[88] These two words represent more than jargon. The concept of "negotiation" describes the process of the seller and buyer reaching mutual agreement with respect to the value of the credit evidence to be transferred as money at the time of transfer. The negotiation and mutual determination of the value of the credit item at the time of transfer, through "endorsement" requires that the buyer have both trust and confidence in the ability of the underlying issuer to repay his debt, and creditable independent evidence supporting that establishment of trust and confidence in the market value of the credit item. A monetary system based on well-founded trust and confidence will yield sound money

In the absence of any other factors, that necessary evidence is found by the buyer in an examination and confirmation of the issuer's assets and liabilities and the issuer's ability to readily liquidate its assets in amounts and at values sufficient to repay his debt in accordance with its terms. Because that present determination must take into account the future risks and uncertainties that may adversely affect the issuer's future ability to so perform. The buyer must take into account the perceived risk and uncertainty of future performance by the issuer in determining the present value at which he will accept the transfer of the credit item through endorsement.

The negotiated value of the item presented is generally less that the face amount of the item, due to the corresponding assessment by the buyer of the present value of the item adjusted -discounted—to reflect his assessment of the degree to which the items current liquidity is affected by future risk and uncertainty of payment off the item in full at maturity in accordance with its terms. The assessment and negotiation of present liquid value of the item is a precondition to its transfer to the buyer and his evaluation of his ability to transfer it on to unrelated third parties through the systems and process that constitute the socially acceptable monetary scheme at the time.

The challenge of conducting such transfer through negotiation and endorsement of credit items as money through the prevailing systems of valuation, accounting and decentralized transferability—that is repeated transferability of the item to successive, unknown third parties in an expeditious and efficient manner requires that the socially acceptable monetary system establish some governing concept or principle of confirmation of trust and confidence in a transferable credit item's present liquid value without the necessity of continued repetitive revaluation of the item at the time of each transfer of each item. The more confidence and trustworthy value and its homogeneity, the greater with be the efficiency, utility and reliability of the monetary system comprise of such credit items.

During the dark ages, when "there was no money," there was considerable disorder in the conduct of commercial transactions. Households were, in general self-sufficient, and trade by barter was the norm. The role of monetary systems had largely been lost to history. How did society "function without any markets or money at all? What did the job before money and markets existed?" Martin introduces the Dark

Age principles evidenced by the "three social institutions that played important roles in organized the community." These institutions were social, but also political. The first principle related specifically to the conduct of war. The principle activity of the Dark Ages that required collective action and financing. Not too much different today, except by order of magnitude. The institution that governed the participants' dedication the activity of was the social and political mechanism of sharing of booty following the defeat of enemies. This mechanism effected various systems for the distribution of income derived from war. These systems were varied and not uniform by any means. As an alternative to war and the collection and distribution of booty, to assure a visible and tangible bond between social equals and cement the relationships between and among group members of the social infrastructure, tribal or group leaders exchanged reciprocal gifts. Within groups or tribes, the leaders conducted ritual sacrifices of animals, such as oxen, sheep and the like and, important particularly in Greek culture, the sharing of the sacrificed to the gods and cooked animals and "the distribution of its meat in equal parts to the aggregation of the tribe." This ritual represented the most basic principle of Greek society— "the fact that every male member of the tribe was of equal social worth, and by the same token, owed an equal obligation to the community as a whole."[89]

These "interlocking institutions of booty distribution, reciprocal gift exchange, and the distribution of the sacrifice" are "typical of the practices of small-scale, tribal societies." As these institutions were adopted by different peoples, Martin, citing anthropologists Maurice Bloch and Jonathan Perry, finds a pattern of "two related but separate transactional orders: on the one hand transactions concerned with the reproduction of the long-term social or cosmic order; on the other, a 'sphere' of short-term transactions concerned with the arena of individual competition." So Martin finds on the one hand the societal foundational principle of egalitarian distribution and communal consumption; and on the other, reciprocal gift-exchange and booty distribution that was not concerned with social order and class harmony, but rather with "the more mundane matter of ensuring that the everyday business of primitive society—drinking and hunting when at peace; rape and pillage when at war—did not dissolve into violent disorder."[90]

The social conventions that held primitive Dark Age society together have continued to evolve and now form the nucleus of confusion over the bifurcated social function of money, its creation and distribution in social organization as they have evolved into separate and distinct, but inter-related social, commercial and political societies

[E] Literacy, Law, Numeracy, and Accounting

According to Martin:

> "The invention of writing and abstract number set the stage for the development of the third technology at the heart of Mesopotamian society: accounting. The hierarchical control of economic activity by clerical bureaucracies required a management information system: a technique for quantifying stocks and flows of

> raw materials and finished goods, for using these quantities in forward planning, and for checking that the plan was being correctly carried out on the ground."[91] This process sounds remarkably similar in a fundamental sense to the capital and liquidity planning processes now being emphasized in banking and financial services companies in the wake of the recent financial crises. The technology of these processes enable policy making decisions to be translated into "practical instructions—and for the fulfillment of those instruction to be verified, by that most familiar, most forbidding, and as it transpires, most ancient of professional figures: the accountant.[92]

Martin writes that despite the development of these important social technologies, neither the ancient Mesopotamians nor the primitive Dark Age Greeks had any use for money. Why not? They had not developed any consistency in the methodology of measurement. These peoples did indeed measure things, but only according to widely varying standards specific to individual commodities and individual societies. The provision of the *United States Constitution* that establishes the congressional power and duty for the creation and regulation of the value of money also grants to Congress the power and duty to establish uniform weights and measures. The combination of these separate but integral congressional powers and duties is no accident. Martin notes that it was not until October 14,1960 that the "quadrennial General Conference on Weights and measures was convened to consider a set of proposals made by the International Committee for Weights and Measures, received by them from the international Bureau of Weights and Measures.... [It was] at this meeting [it] was agreed, for the first time in history, [upon] a simple and universal system of units of measurement based on internationally agreed standards—the *Système International d'Unités,* or SI for short":[93]

> If the dollar is a unit of measurement, what does it measure? The answer on the face of it, is simple: value—or more precisely, economic value. "What is the standard for economic value? Martin observes that the bureaucrats in Paris would discover that the determination of that standard would be faced with a great variety of notions of value contending for our attention in decision-making.[94] Martin finds the notion of value applicable to historic value, aesthetic value, moral value, religious value and sentimental value, as examples: all limited purpose concepts of value ... "[95]

In contrast to this rabble of limited purpose concepts of value, "economic value can be applied not just to things that have a particular physical property—temperature, length, or mass for example—but, at least in principle, to absolutely anything at all. Goods have economic value; but so do services. The three physical dimensions are no constrain: time is money, after all. Abstract notions are no strangers to monetary evaluation: what price success? Even a solely spiritual existence was no obstacle in the days when people cared about such things: the wages of sin could readily be offset by clerical indulgences whose value was measured, and paid for in pounds, shillings and pence. In fact, there seems to be no intrinsic limit to the parts that the concept of economic value can reach. Even human life itself is regularly assigned an economic value by government economists in the cost-benefit analysis that they use to weigh up new laws.... Economic Value has attained the last word in universality—without any input from the bureaucrats whatsoever."[96]

Although the concept of economic value is uniquely universal, its standards are still national. According to Martin, the development of a single, universal, international standard—defined in terms of universal standards found in nature would be ideal. "The problem is that there is a fundamental difference between the concept of economic value and the concepts measured by the SI. Economic value is a property of the social reality; whereas linear extension, mass, temperature and so on are properties of physical reality. The choice of standard for the measurement of physical concepts is a question of technical efficiency. But the uses to which measurement of the social property of economic value are put are qualitatively quite different; and so the choice of its standard is quite different as well. The choice of standard for the measurement of economic value—the choice of the standard for the monetary unit, in other words—affects not how easy it is to build bridges, but how wealth and income are distributed and who bears the economic risks. It is, therefore, not just a technical, but also an ethical question; and the criterion for choosing it is not only what standard is efficient, but which is fair. Of course, the determination of what is fair is nothing but politics."[97] Perhaps unfortunately, America's founders and the American people delegated the assurance of ethics and fairness in the regulation of the value to Congress, an unlikely arbiter of ethics and fairness in the regulation of the value of money. Congress has made a mockery of their fiduciary duty to regulate the value of money at all, and even more emphatically, to assure the ethics and fairness of active honest and transparent regulation of the value of money.

In ancient societies, the communality of the tribe and the equality of its members established the concept of social value were every member counted equally. [T]he idea of the equal worth of every member of the tribe was a social constant: a standard against which social value could be measured." Here then, was a "nascent concept of universal value and a standard against which to measure it, *prêt-à-porter*. Here was an answer to the question begged by the new perspective on society and the economy. Where the new understanding of physical reality had man, the observer of an objective universe, the new understanding of social reality had the idea of the self, separate from society—an objective entity consisting of relationships measurable in a standard unit universal scale of economic value. It was a critical conceptual development—the missing link, on the intellectual level, in the invention of money."[98]

Mesopotamia had a system of accounting based on writing and numeracy. "It required and perfected a variety of limited-purpose concepts of value, each with its respective standard. It therefore did not develop the first component of money: a unit of abstract, universally applicable economic value."[99]

Dark Age Greece "had a primitive concept of universal value and a standard by which to measure it; but had neither literacy nor numeracy—let alone a system of accounting."[100]... "They had, in nascent form, the first component of money, but lacked the second."[101]

When these essential concepts were united, "the conceptual preconditions for money were at last in place."[102] The use of measured precious commodity units as universally applicable units of value accompanies by the more widespread practice of keeping accounts based on such usage dramatically increased the use of money. Development of the principle of decentralized negotiability reinforced the increasing role of money in commerce. "The new idea of a universal economic value made possible the offsetting of obligations without reference to a centralized authority."[103] In order to transact commerce, however, negotiations between buyers and sellers required "a common language—a shared idea of what words mean. For markets to function there therefore needs to be a shared concept of value and standardized units in which to measure it. Not a shared idea of what particular goods or services are worth—that is where the haggling comes in—but a shared unit of economic value so that the haggling can take place at all."[104]

Once traditional social obligations could be valued on a universal scale and transferred from one party to another on a decentralized basis, the combination led to what we now know as financial markets. The invention and development of the concept of coinage in Lydia and Ionia, in present day Turkey in the early sixth century BC; spreading to the city-states of Greece and the Aegean, presented an ideal means of representing the new concept of economic value. "By around 480 BC there were nearly a hundred mints operating in the Greek world."[105] Increased monetization of traditional social obligations transformed those obligations into financial relationships. Sharecroppers became contractual tenants paying rent. "The traditional 'so-called 'liturgies'—the ancient, civic obligations of the thousand wealthiest inhabitants of the city to provide public services ranging from Choruses for the theatre to ships for the navy—were now assessed in financial terms."[106]

The increasingly widespread use of money promised both social mobility and political stability. Rigid social systems gave way to ambition, entrepreneurship and social mobility. "[M]oney, the concept of universal value and the idea of an objective economic space were founded upon the ancient institution of communal sacrifice; and as such upon the invisible but irresistible community of mankind. And money made its miraculous promise to combine apparent opposites on the personal level as well. It catered to two fundamental aspects of human psychology: the desire for freedom and the desire for stability. The ethics of the traditional society has sacrificed the former on the altar of the latter. The new world of monetary society promised both."[107] Monetary society also provided for an effective way to manage social obligations as well a mechanism to "fuse together both the short-term and the long-term 'transactional orders'—to govern both the minutia of getting and spending in the everyday and the profundities of social harmony for the ages."[108]

[F] Control over Money

> [B]eneath the relentless spread of the market mentality and the overweening dominance of the idea of universal economic value lies something much older, and much more deeply ingrained in the way our societies work: the social technology of money. And the tensions and dissonances that we feel today are not new at all: they have flexed and echoed down the centuries ever since money's first invention, more than two and a half thousand years ago, on the shores of the Greek Aegean.

If money was such a powerful invention—such a revolutionary force for the transformation of society and the economy—the next question is obvious. It is one posed with brilliant clarity by the father of English political philosophy John Locke, in his *First Treatise of Government*:

> "The great question which in all ages has disturbed mankind, and brought on them the greatest part of those mischiefs which have ruined cities, depopulated countries, and disordered the peace of the world, has been, not whether there be power in the world, nor whence it came, but who should have it."[109]

According to Martin:

> [o]ne of the most provocative acts of the British Crown's jurisdiction over its American possessions was to outlaw the colonies' printing of their own monies-and one of the first acts of the First Continental Congress was to authorize the printing of a new currency with which to finance the War of Independence.... Not for nothing does the very first article of the *Constitution* of the United States give Congress the exclusive power to mint money. In the mind of the conservative politician, with good historical reason, it is but a short step from the *Crédito* (a mutual credit money issued by local exchange clubs on their own, independent standard, in Argentina in 2002) to the Continental Dollar—from cocking a picturesque snook at globalization to monetary insurrection; and from monetary insurrection to political revolt.[110]

The *United States Constitution* notwithstanding, Martin observes that there are now thousands of private monies in circulation all over America, generally treated as harmless sideshows, but always with the potential of destabilizing the states franchise over the institution of money.[111] Bitcoin is a current example.

[G] Fiduciary Issue of Money

We will discover as this work progresses that, in fact, the destabilization of the American dollar and other currencies world-wide, constituting the present day financial crisis, has not occurred through a proliferation of private monies but by the states' abandonment—intentional ceding—of their control over the regulation of the value of their state sponsored currencies to private creators of credit money and other money substitutes such as credit asset backed securities and derivatives, denominated in state sponsored currencies—ostensible state money, to the Wall Street banks in America as well as other large global financial institutions, world-wide. The financial crisis is the direct result of the failure of the United States to manage its sovereign duty to the American public to regulate the economic value of the dollar as delegated to it by the American public specifically under the *United States Constitution*. Congress, the federal financial regulators and their tools, the Wall Street banks have broken the social compact represented by America's system of money and credit. That social compact is also a moral compact and it's a legal compact. It is not a contract. It is a public delegation of power and duty and it establishes a legal standard of care and conduct that must be observed, and for which Congress, as the holder of the power and duty, and Wall Street, Congress' chosen partner in this course of conduct, must be held accountable. Mann goes so far as to characterize the state monetary issue of sovereign money to constitute a "fiduciary issue."[112] This characterization became even more significant with the abandonment of *The Bretton Woods Accords,* following which the sovereign money, the dollar, and currencies backed by the dollar are no longer backed by gold or silver.

Mann does observe, as he often does, despite his stated objective of sticking strictly to matters of money specific only to law, that "experience shows that in most [such as in America], if not all modern cases, a unit of account can in fact be linked by a rate of conversion to an antecedent unit, and Knapp's doctrine [...that the unit of account could be defined historically only, and that its received its meaning by nothing but by its 'recurrent linking' to the previous currency[113]] can therefore be adopted as a useful working principle.[114] Knapp's doctrine is particularly relevant to any assessment of the linking of the current and progressively debased value of the dollar in reference and linking to the value of the dollar under to previous dollar currencies tied to ever-diminishing quantity and quality of gold and silver and ever-diminishing reserve requirements, until they vanished entirely, as the dominant factor in periodic financial crises throughout American history, and specifically since the Nixon shock in 1971.

§2.04 MONEY IN AN IDEAL SYSTEM

The essential foundation for the operation of a credit based monetary system are two essential principles:[115]

- First, every member must maintain his creditworthiness. Only then can society be confident in the value of his money.
- Second, all members must know one another, if not at first hand, then at second; or have some other grounds, by convention or compulsion, to accept society's word for an unknown member's credit.

In a small community these principles can be observed and enforced. In modern society these principles are threatened by the depth and breadth of the members of a large national, and global society. These fundamental principles are honesty, trust and confidence. They are moral principles, and as such, are the foundations for and are incorporated in American law relating to money.

James Madison, the chief architect of the *United States Constitution* wrote in the *Federalist Papers*, "[i]f men were angels, no government would be necessary. And if men were angels—if there was never any question of overspending, or defaulting, or simply skipping town, and if they trusted one another implicitly—no government money would be necessary.... But men are no more angels in economics than in politics. In a utopian community, money can consist of credit accumulated against the abstract notion of society—because every member has actively opted into that community. But in the real world, the hard-nosed creditor is bound to herself facing not the noble ideal of the community but the altogether less fanciful prospect of the individual issuer. And the problem with the individual issuer is that he may default on his liabilities—and that other people might believe he will default. Money on any significant scale can therefore never consist of liquid credit accumulated against "society". The alternative is obvious—and was so at money's birth. Money will naturally consist of liquid credit accumulated against society's more concrete manifestation: the sovereign.[116]

The sovereign has unique advantages. "Above all, it enjoys by definition and unlike any private agent, political authority. The sovereign's creditworthiness therefore rests not on our assessment of its ability to earn credit in the marketplace, but on the strength of this authority and on the sovereign's willingness to deploy it to accumulate credit from its subjects via taxation.... So long as the state is held to be legitimate, its money enjoys trust not only on commercial or legal, but on ideological and even spiritual grounds."[117]

Although the sovereign may be the closest thing to society itself, it is not the society. "What if the interests of the two diverge? What if the sovereign were to use its near monopoly on money for its own gain—for example by overissuing money in order to fund spending simply to secure its popularity or re-election? What if it were to manipulate the system so that it produced not the marvelous combination of freedom and stability promised by money, but something else altogether? Hard-nosed realism may dictate that sovereigns issue money—but as the First Continental Congress demonstrated, that only begs the question of who one would want to be sovereign. Or even—to side with the Monetary Maquis—whether one wouldn't be better off without any of the available sovereign at all."[118]

While Aristotle and the Greeks seized upon the conventional Western theory of money that held that "for the purposes of barter men made a mutual compact to give and accept some substance of such a sort as, being itself, a useful commodity, was useful to handle in use for everyday life, iron for instance, silver and other metals..." the Chinese, during the same time period took a very different view. "Money, they wrote, is a tool of the sovereign—part of his machinery of government: "[t]he former kings used money to preserve wealth and goods and thereby regulate the productive activities of the people, whereupon they brought peace and order to the Subcelestial Realm."[119] For the Chinese, the value of money was unrelated to the intrinsic value of money. The tokens used in their society, "offer no warmth to the naked, nor can they fill the bellies of the hungry."[120] For their society, "money's value was directly proportional to how much of it was in circulation compared to the quantity of goods available. The role of the sovereign, therefore, was to modulate the quantity of money available in order to vary the value of the monetary standard in terms of those goods:[121]

> Varying the monetary standard in this way could serve two purposes. First, it would provide a powerful means of redistributing wealth and income amongst the sovereign's subjects, as inflation eroded the claims of creditors and eased the burdens of debtors, shifting wealth from the former to the latter—or deflation did the opposite. Moreover, the most important redistribution, if new money were minted, would be to the sovereign from his subjects as he spent new money into circulation at essentially no cost—the miraculous power that economists in the Western tradition later come to call "seigniorage." Second, it would regulate economic activity by making the primary instrument for the organization and settlement of trade more or less readily available. The goal of government should

> be a harmonious society and monetary policy was a powerful tool with which to achieve it.[122]

For the Chinese system to be effective, however, the sovereign must retain exclusive control over the supply of money. Issuance by any other party would serve to usurp the power of the sovereign.

§2.05 CONCENTRATION OF MONEY AND POWER

Martin recounts:

> "Within a few centuries of its birth in the Aegean, money was everywhere in Rome. The financial structure was vast and complex."[123] Rome produced a trusted coinage for use in small transactions, but the bulk of money creation was through the use of credit—promissory notes and checks. The history of Rome's experience with a credit based monetary system dramatically illustrates the deficiencies in that structure, then as well as in the present day in America and globally.
>
> In AD 33, the Emperor Tiberias' financial officials were persuaded that the recent boom in private lending had become excessive. It was decided that regulation must be tightened in order to extinguish this irrational exuberance. After a brief review of the statutes, it was discovered that none other than the father of the dynasty, Julius Caesar, had in his wisdom instituted a law many decades before specifying strict limits on how much of their patrimony wealthy aristocrats could farm out in loans. He had, in other words, introduced a rigorous capital adequacy requirement for lenders. The law was clear enough; but not for the first time in history, industrious lenders had proved remarkably skilled at circumventing it. Their ingenious evasions, the historian Tacitus reported 'though continually put down by new regulations, still, through strange artifices, reappeared."[124]

The Emperor decreed that the law be enforced and "[t]he consequences were chaotic. As soon as the ruling was made, it was realized with some embarrassment that most of the Senate was in breach of it. All of the familiar features of a modern banking crisis followed":[125]

- Loans were called
- Authorities tried to soften the impact by granting forbearances and providing for transitional periods, but too late
- The property market collapsed
- Land was sold in "fire sales" to fund loan repayments
- Mass bankruptcies threated the entire financial system
- In the grip of a "credit crunch" the Emperor was forced to implement a massive bailout
- The Imperial treasury refinanced overextended lenders with a three-year, interest free program of loans against the security of deliberately overvalued real estate
- Credit was gradually restored
- Private lending resumed.

In the late third century AD as Roman civilization collapsed, there was serious monetary disorder, including inflation in AD 274-5 when prices rose by 1,000 per cent in a single year. "After AD 300, bankers disappear from the records—the social and political stability required to underpin professional finance had, it seems, disintegrated."[126]

The concept of universal economic value did not vanish completely during the Dark Ages. With the consolidation of the Frankish Empire under Charlemagne in the late eighth century, a system of monetary units of pounds, shillings and pence was established on a fairly consistent basis throughout Europe. It was not until the last quarter of the twelfth century that feudal obligations in the Low Countries traditionally payable in kind began to be transformed to rents payable in money. Vassal servitude to overlords began to be replaced by paid labor. Civil official began to be paid salaries and direct taxation was reintroduced for the first time since the Roman Era.[127]

The renewal of the phenomenon of monetization jolted static social relations, giving rise to new prospects for social mobility through ambition and avarice and the accumulation of money as wealth. Although money was denominated by a variety of issuers in constant terminology, the value of each unit issue, however, "depended on the particular standard maintained by the individual feudal issuer."[128] Further, since the structure for taxation and its collection failed to keep pace with the explosion of monetization, political authority increasingly relied on the "manipulation of the monetary standard as a source of revenue. The practice of successive debasement of various issues of metal coinage as a "one-off wealth tax" on each occasion, on the holders of coined money became prevalent. This practice of debasement was "a constant game of cat and mouse between the coin-issuer and the coin-user, with even a coin's precious metal content, which served as collateral for the creditworthiness of its issuer, always vulnerable to erosion by the predations of the sovereign."[129]

Martin continues the historical record:

> In 1299, for example, the total revenues of the French crown amounted to just under £2 million: of this, fully one half had come from the seigniorage profits of the Mint following a debasement and general recoining. Two generations later, the recoinage of 1349 generated nearly three-quarters of all revenues collected that year by the king. When such large sums could be raised, it is hardly surprising that there were no fewer than 123 debasements in France alone between 1285 and 1490.[130]

The re-monetization of society during this period gave rise to the same two dominant conflicting interests in the wealth that could be accumulated through the creation of money, and through the exercise of power that the monetized wealth enabled:[131]

- The first dominating interest was comprised of the individuals and institutions who transacted in money and therefore was able to accumulate it as wealth.
- The second dominating interest was the addiction of the sovereigns who were able to generate far more income and wealth through the seigniorage leveled on the creation of new money and through the grater facilitation of the

collection of taxes as well as the increased base of taxation created by increased monetary activities.

The limits of the sovereigns' avarice and excesses was political. To address the assertion by the monied interests and the general populace of limits on sovereign power accumulation and consolidation of wealth, and thus power, in the mid-fourteenth century, "the first work [was produced] in the Western canon on a topic that was thereafter to receive considerably more attention but become considerably more obscure: monetary policy."[132]

The damages in excess seigniorage in France during that period culminated in the preparation by Nicolas Oresme, Grand Master of the College of Navarre, of a tract addressed to the Dauphine Charles entitled, in English, *A Treatise on the Origin, Nature, Law, and Alterations of Money* (Around 1360). "Oresme stated clearly the two disputes it sought to untangle at its outset: was it right that the sovereign should manipulate the monetary standard? And if it was, then in whose interest should he do so?"[133] Money, and its manipulation during the feudal period had been thought to be the exclusive domain of the sovereign. "Oresme introduced a radically different perspective. Money, he said, is not the property of the sovereign but of the entire community that uses it."[134] In "a world in which private transactions were extensively conducted, and private wealth widely held, in monetary form—the issuance of money constituted an essential public service and should therefore be operated in the interest of the public at large."[135] Oresme's position was not necessarily a populist position. His views were advanced largely on behalf of the monied interests, the interests then considered by Orisme to "suffer the most from the scourge of redistributed seigniorage—and in whose interest the sovereign should manage his money....The sovereign, Oresme pronounced '[i]s not the lord or owner of the money current in his principality. For money is a balancing instrument for the exchange of natural wealth ... [i]t is therefore the property of those who possess such wealth."[136]

"Can any words be too strong" he asked, "to express how unjust, how detestable it is, especially in a prince, to reduce the weight without altering the mark?" Both social justice and economic efficiency required a more reasonable and predictable monetary system.[137]

Orisme did conclude, however that "[i]n extreme cases, debasement might be necessary—but only in order to insure that the supply of coined money was sufficient to meet the needs of the community: 'if [the community] trusts the Prince with the [debasement of money], within a reasonable limit ... the Prince would not undertake it as main author, but as the executor of a public ordinance'":[138]

> Orisme had uncovered a genuine and profound paradox that would, as we shall see, haunt monetary thought over subsequent centuries. There had to be a means of restraining the sovereign's inveterate impulse to fund his innate profligacy for free via seigniorage. There needed, that is, to be a rule governing the issuance of money: the standard should not be infinitely flexible. But if such rule resulted in periodic dearths of money, it would impose an undesirable constraint on commerce. This would seem to call for someone to have the discretion to adjust the supply of money in response: the standard should not be immutably fixed, either.... [I]n considering monetary policy's ability to redistribute wealth and

incomes and its ability to stimulate or stifle trade, it was not the sovereign's fiscal needs that should take priority, but the wider community's commercial well-being.[139]

As Martin observed:

> Orisme's "*Treatise's* conclusion could not have been more blunt: "the community alone has the right to decide if, when and how, and to what extent [money] is to be altered, and the prince may not in any way usurp it. What is more, it clearly implied more general limits on the sovereign's power, and was not afraid to acknowledge these as well: 'he is greater and more powerful than any of his subjects, but of less power or wealth than the whole community and so stands in the middle.[140]

Despite the power of Orisme's analysis, the sovereign did not eagerly follow it. Enforcement of fairness and economic justice through the power of Orisme's analysis could not compel the sovereign to act. The subsequent development that addressed the issue of enforcement through concentration lay outside the traditional feudal bastions of power, the sovereign and the church. The mercantile class, the commercial monied interest "did not need scholastic logic to justify their activities. They were busily discovering a new invention that would turn monetary society on its head in a way in which Orisme's brilliantly argued tract never could. That invention was the bank."[141]

[A] The Banker of Lyon

By the mid fifteen hundreds, Lyon, in France had become a commercial mecca. A clearing house for global trade. The merchants of Lyon become more and more interest in the "legal and financial aspects of international trade—the change of title to goods, and to the money received in return; and the calculus of balancing revenues in one currency with expenses incurred in another. The tedious business of getting goods from one place to another was farmed out to a lesser class of businessman."[142] Whereas Lyon developed as a commercial trading center with built on local trade at the base, wholesalers and international traders in the middle and the netting out of accounts accumulated in these transactions as a facilitation. "By 1555, the primary role of the fair of Lyons was as a clearing house for the credit and debit balances accrued by the merchant houses of Europe against one another in issuing these bills of exchange to finance trade. It had become the most important market in Europe not for goods, but for money."[143]

"Nothing real changed hands except bundles of bills. Commerce had become a branch of mathematics. The standard textbook on the subject, published in Venice in 1494 by the Franciscan friar, Luca Pacioli, was called *Arithmetica*—on 'Arithmatic.'"[144] According to Martin, five hundred years later, a fictional practitioner of the alchemy of mathematics and finance was described, in what today remains a familiar caricature:

> Her English husband Ossie, now he is rich-for-life, but he works in money, in pure money. His job has nothing to do with anything except money, the stuff itself. No fucking around with stocks, shares, commodities, futures. Just money. Sitting in his spectral towers on Sixth Avenue and Cheapside, blond Ossie uses money to

> buy and sell money. Equipped only with a telephone, he buys money with money, sells money with money. He works in the cracks and vents of currencies, buying and selling on the margin, riding the daily tides of exchange. For these services he is rewarded with money. Lots of it.[145]

Today, the only difference in this tale is that, having learned of the profits gained in the trade of money, clever bankers have now turned stocks, shares, derivatives, commodities and futures into money as well!

How and why did the Ossie's business, and the business of the developing cadre of merchant bankers mange to get so rich, "How did the emergence of these powerful and unaccountable parliaments of merchants relate to the established political powers of the day—the sovereign, the nobility, and the church?"[146] The answer was, intentionally unclear. In other words, how was "tens of millions of pounds' worth of business [...] being done, with the sovereign's money almost nowhere to be seen. The great merchant houses of Europe had rediscovered the art of banking—how to produce and manage private money on an industrial scale."[147]

How did the development of these vast private networks of mutual credit correlate to the traditional bastions of power? The early answer to this inquiry was the acknowledged recognition of their respective divergent interests and the rebellion of the merchant bankers against the controls of the traditional powers and the separation of money creation from sovereignty. Martin then points out, however, that there are "natural limits to commercial and personal familiarity and the fragility of confidence [that] impose[s] constraints on scale. They cannot function as a mechanism to organize a whole economy: in the real world, only the money of the sovereign enjoys sufficient currency for that."[148]

Merchant bankers responded to the challenge by creating a hierarchical organization of credit. Local tradesmen's personal promises would suffice in a local market for credit-based money. But [I]f a great merchant substituted his word for that of a local tradesman, an IOU that might previously circulated at most within the local economy could be transformed into one that could circulate anywhere where the great merchant's prestige was acknowledged. A pyramid of credit could be constructed, with the obligations of local tradesmen (and now largely, consumers) as the base, larger wholesalers in the in the middle, and the most exclusive, well known, and tight-knit circle of international merchants at the top."[149] Thus local bi-lateral credit was transformed in to liquid liabilities that could reliably be traded to unknown third parties, based on the foundation of the Great merchant banking houses credit, even though the original issuer of the credit instrument and his business were entirely unknown to the subsequent counterparties.

According to Martin: "It was here—in the creation of a private payments system—that the invention of modern banking originated."[150] "[T]heir ability to finance and settle payments is the more fundamental activity. This is banks' specifically monetary role, and what makes them special. A bank is in essence an institution which writes IOUs on the one hand—these are its deposits, its bonds, its notes; generically, its liabilities—and accumulates IOUs on the other—its loans and its securities portfolio; generically its assets.... A banks real assets are always negligible....

The reason that a bank can do so is that almost all of its assets are nothing but promises to pay, and almost all of its liabilities, likewise.

As we discovered, any IOU has two fundamental characteristics:

- Its credit worthiness—how likely it is that it will be paid when it comes due—and
- Its liquidity—how quickly it can be realized, either by sale to a third party or simply by coming due if no sale is sought. The risks associated with any promise to pay depends upon these two characteristics.[151]

Once a bank has examined and underwritten the credit supporting and liquidity of the IOU on its asset side of the balance sheet, its function, Felix martin refers to it as an art re-discovered by the international merchants and bankers of the Middle Ages, was their ability to synchronize, "in the aggregate, of incoming and outgoing payments due on his assets and liabilities—which are themselves, of course, the aggregated liabilities of all of his borrowers and creditors."[152]

This process of re-discovery began in earnest as early as the twelfth century and by the end of that century had taken hold in Genoa, Tuscany and Barcelona. By the fourteenth century there were as many and eighty banks operating in Florence alone. These merchant bankers had "facilitated fully decentralized clearing just as the sovereign's coinage did."[153]

[B] The Sovereign Versus the Bankers

The re-discovery of the ancient banking processes once again threatened the control and domination by the sovereigns of the Middle Ages over the creation and movement of money. "Then there were the ominous lessons of the potential microeconomic risks associated with large-scale banking contained in the ancient texts like Tacitus' account of the Tiberian financial crisis. Above all, there was the sovereign's interest in ensuring the continuing priority of their money, and hence their seigniorage. As a result, the new invention of money was subject to draconian regulation."[154]

In 1341 Venice authorities discovered that the merchants were practicing "fractional reserve" banking; holding on hand only a very small proportion of assets in coin of the sovereign. The authorities "specified that banks must be able to meet all requests for withdrawal of coin in three days."[155] At the same time, Catalonian officials "revised their 1300 order that failed bankers be forced to live on bread and water alone until all of their clients were reimbursed. Henceforth, any banker who failed to meet his clients' demands was to be publicly denounced—and then summarily beheaded in front of his bank. It was not idle threat, as the hapless Barcelona banker Francesch Castello discovered in 1360."[156]

Over time the merchant bankers developed a reliable process of periodic clearing of accounts maintained through their own mutual protocols, consistent with Pacioli's De *"Arithametica,"* represented primarily by bills of exchange using their own units of account such as the *écu du marc*. Abstract imaginary units such as the *écu du marc*, enabled the merchants engaged in a specific network of exchange bankers to use a mutually acceptable private monetary standard of abstract value so that they could "haggle with one another over the value of the various sovereign moneys of the continent."[157] Each bilateral "international" transaction then involved a minimum of two exchanges, one from the denominated sovereign money into the common artificial standard and again from that standard into one or more different sovereign moneys. The build-up bills of exchange balances on a large scale necessitated periodic clearings offsetting and verification balances within the private systems. All these transactions, naturally, were conducted for fees payable to the large merchant/banking houses that held, accounted for, cleared and verified participants' offsetting balances. "The system of exchange by bills had become nothing other than a supranational private money interacting with domestic public monies. By crowning a pan-European hierarchy of credit with the self-regulating network of their cosmopolitan but close-knit cabal, the exchange bankers had succeeded in building a Utopia. With their perfection of the system of exchange by bills, they had constructed a viable private money on a continent-wide scale."[158]

This Utopian financial structure was based on several factors that were indispensable to its successful operation:

- a tight knit cosmopolitan elite of controlling participants;
- a highly structured hierarchy of credit networks; and
- that eliminated the need of precious metal to serve as collateral for its promises to pay.

This networks private "money was invisible, intangible, consisting only of the confidence of the small group of exchange bankers at the tip of the pyramid in one another's abilities to assess risks, to be able to meet payments as they become due and to limit the issuance of credit."[159] The power of these merchant bankers' cabals became so powerful that they could threaten to abandon the use of a sovereign's money if it was not managed in accordance with cabals' interests.[160]

In the final years of the profligate rein of Henry VIII, the English pound depreciated more than 50% against Flemish shillings in just seven years, from 1544 to 1551. Naturally the English crown cast blame on the low-country and Italian bankers for exaggerating their low opinion of English creditworthiness as a scam "to earn them unjustified profits."[161]

In response to the bankers expression of their low opinion of sovereign money in the exchange markets, at the urging of the crown, young Edward VI's Regency council, pressed by Minister William Cecil, Sir Thomas Gresham, devised a program for an exchange stabilization fund, one of the first efforts by sovereign powers to intervene in currency exchanges, "to neutralize the bankers' power to sell sterling whenever they disapproved of the English crown's policies."[162] Although this modern tool of government monetary policy was short-lived, ahead of its time, in the face of market skepticism, the program was cancelled. It was replaced with a new plan: "The foreign currency reserves of the English merchants at Antwerp were to be commandeered as a forced loan to the crown. The crown's foreign currency debts due to the slippery exchange-bankers would be refinanced into a sterling loan from its own subjects. It was ingenious and effective—but it was an admission of defeat. The exchange bankers could not be beaten at their own game. The only remedy was for the sovereign to exert its power of coercion over its subjects."[163]

[C] Calling the Sovereign to Account

It took two centuries of sovereign abuse of the monetary system and oppression of the citizenry for "the furnace of the French enlightenment to fuse together previously separate strands of economic and political thought. France in the mid-eighteenth century was ripe for such a catalytic role."[164] Although the French *Ancien Régime* "- an unreconstructed feudal monarchy in a continent long since disturbed by the winds of constitutional change...[f]inancially, France was one of the most backward states in Western Europe." (Id.) The dramatic contract between its "dazzling republic of letters and its moribund bodies politic and financial meant that it was the thinkers of the French Enlightenment who first articulated the link between money, banking and politics."[165]

Charles-Louis de Secondat, Baron de la Brède et de Montesquieu, the greatest constitutional thinker of the age, "gave special attention and praise to the role of commerce as a beneficial force in political development, and reserved his greatest admiration for international finance."[166]

Montesquieu's recognition and articulation of the counter-productive effects of the sovereign's attempts to manipulate currency for its own ends, in lieu of honest taxation accompanied by political and legal accountability, "could not take place in our time....The foreign exchanges have enabled bankers to compare all of the monies of the world and to evaluate what they are really worth ... They have eliminated the great and sudden arbitrary actions of the sovereign—or at least the effectiveness of such actions."[167]

The Enlightenment vision of money was a vision of a force that could discipline even the mightiest sovereign. The Scotsman James Steuart, in his 1787 *Inquiry into the Principles of Political Economy*, one of the first works of economics in the English language observed that "[m]onetary society... was nothing other than the 'most effective bridle ever was invented against the folly of despotism.'"[168]

The "most effective bridle against the folly of despotism" described by Steuart, however, came burdened by the same risks and limitations as sovereign money:

> On the one hand, it was essential that banking remain the exclusive preserve of a narrow elite. Only a self-regulating clique could incubate the interpersonal trust necessary to operate a private monetary network, and the barrier to new entrants were negligible once its principles were understood. Unlike the sovereign, the bankers had not power of coercion to enforce their franchise. As a result, bankers guarded its secrets jealously and started a proud tradition of "shroud[ing] their practices in a finicky formalism which lent itself to preserving their monopoly'. But these very same conditions also imposed obvious limits to its expansion. The credit notes of the international bankers could circulate amongst themselves, but outside that magic circle, they were bound to be a conundrum. The very features

that made the bankers' private money work were the ones which meant it could not actually displace sovereign money.

The result was a chronically unstable monetary disequilibrium—a long running guerrilla war between sovereign and the private money interest which neither side could win.[169]

[D] Seeds of an Iniquitous Partnership

In the seventeenth century, England was wracked by civil war, the Cromwellian experiment with republican government. The foundation of this cauldron of conflict was nothing new. "[T]he fiscal incontinence of the sovereign that had been the immediate cause of the civil war had deteriorated further. So decrepit were the restored King Charles II's finances (following the overthrow of Cromwell) by 1672 that he was forced to default on his debts, announcing a 'Stop to the Exchequer'. The predictable result was a collapse in the crown's credit."[170]

Charles II was deposed and executed. He was followed by William of Orange, who continued the depredations by the crown of the English monetary system; continuing and expanding the war with the French to defend Holland against the continued predatory aggression of the French under Louis IV. The English political and economic thinkers of the time struggled to contrive some method to fund the ongoing and growing deficits. "Almost all boiled down to the same basic idea of finding a mechanism for borrowing against future tax revenue. The trick was to discover a formula which satisfied creditor's desire for better security and more control, and yet preserved the dignity of the sovereign."[171]

These demanding circumstances resulted in the proposal by William Patterson of the formation of a bank that:

> would fundamentally reorganize the funding of the king's debts. Investors would subscribe capital to the banks, and the bank would lend money to the government. The establishment of a bank to raise money for the sovereign was certainly not an innovation in itself. There had been public banks in the city states of the Mediterranean on and off since the Middle Ages. Holland had had a public bank at Amsterdam since 1609; Sweden, one in Stockholm since 1656. What was new about the Projector William Patterson's (one of many who submitted proposals to finance the English deficit) proposal was that this Bank of England would in effect be a public-private partnership. The Bank's primary role would undoubtedly be to put the sovereign's credit and finances on a surer footing. Indeed, its design, governance and management were to be delegated to the mercantile classes precisely in order to ensure confidence in its operations and credit control. But in return the sovereign was to grant important privileges. Above all, the Bank was to enjoy the right to issue banknotes—a license to put into circulation paper currency representing its own liabilities, which could circulate as money. There was to quite literally, a quid pro quo.[172]

The English moneyed class immediately recognized that "[t]o be granted the privilege of note issue by the crown, which would anoint the liabilities of a private bank with the authority of the sovereign—this, they realized was the Philosopher's Stone of money. It was the endorsement that could liberate private bank money from its parochial bounds. They would lend their credit to the sovereign—he would lend their authority to their bank. What they would sow by agreeing to lend, they would reap a hundredfold in being allowed to create private money with the sovereign's endorsement. Henceforth, the seigniorage would be shared."[173]

Thereafter, according to the analysis of Adam Smith, in 1776: [t]he stability of the Bank of England is equal to that of the British government." A virtuous circle. "Without the state, the Bank would have lacked authority; without the bank, the state would have lacked credit."[174]

The Bank of England public private partnership established the foundation for the modern monetary world. The creation and management of money was almost completely delegated by the sovereign to private banks. Sovereign money however remained the final settlement asset.[175]

Under America's current monetary scheme, this critical function has been intentionally abandoned. The results have been a moral, social, economic and legal catastrophe.

Under the original Bank of England structure, sovereign credit constituted the only credit balance with which the banks on the penultimate tier of the pyramid could be certain of settling payments to one or another or to the state. The intended resolution of the conflict and uncertainty remaining in this system; the rights and interests of the state versus the rights and interests of banks; originally designed to impose James Steuart's "most effective bridle" on the folly of state despotism, purportedly shifted the balance of economic and monetary policy and power from the state to the banks.

Money had thereby undergone a radical transformation. The new theory of monetary society became the "social science of economics."[176] Under this transformation, "money would no longer be understood either as a tool of the sovereign, or a tool against the sovereign: it would cease to be understood as something political at all. Until now, money had been understood as a powerful social technology; its central idea of economic value as an ingenious shared concept for the coordination of social activity; and the monetary standard as a potent tool for the redistribution of wealth and the stimulation of commerce, whose manipulation was therefore the deserving object of heated contention. But money was about to become an inert lump of metal, value an innocuous property of the natural world, and monetary policy, let alone any debate over it, a contradiction in terms."[177]

§2.06 THE NECESSITY OF A STANDARD OF VALUE FOR SOVEREIGN MONEY AND THE FINAL SETTLEMENT MEDIUM ASSET

The most vital unanswered question presented by the Bank of England central public-private partnership bank and economic structure: "What was to be the standard on which the Bank of England was to issue its new public-private money?"[178]

The objective of the Bank of England central bank structure was to mediate the interests of the sovereign and the commercial classes. How could the structure bridge the gaps between competing objectives? In 1696 Parliament was forced to deal with the problem of the old form of money—coinage. [T]he use of precious-metal coinage involves an automatic technical challenge."[179] If the value of the metal exceed the value of the coin it would be melted and converted to bullion. In 1666, the English Parliament passed the *Act for the Encouraging of Coinage*. The act abolished the seigniorage levy on coinage and raised the price paid for bullion by the same amount in an attempt to bring the price of silver to be coined in line with the market price for silver. This attempt and other attempts to regulate the price of silver for coinage in order to keep silver coinage circulating presented many opportunities for coinage holders to "game the system", as we say today. The persistent problem of removal of silver coinage from circulation due to market price differentials for silver, was compounded by "a merciless assault of clipping, filing and shearing, as unscrupulous users scavenged as much bullion as they could without actually rendering the coins unrecognizable. Since the increasing general shortage meant that only the most monstrous mutilation could prevent coins from passing at their legal value. This was a racket that could be seriously profitable."[180]

William Lowndes, then Secretary of the English Treasury, prepared a report on the situation. Lowndes concluded that "precisely the same difficulties had occurred on several occasions in the later Middle Ages."[181] Lowndes recognized that the then ongoing policy of continually raising the face value of coinage in response to increases in the bullion price of silver, "from time to time, as Exigence or Occasion required", was inevitable. "It was the only reasonable policy response. The fall in value of money must be acknowledged by raising the price paid for silver by the mint—or by reducing the quantity of silver in an official, full-weight coin. The monetary standard had shifted—a pound was worth less than before. The mint policy had to accommodate itself to this fact: there was no point in fighting the market."[182]

This supposedly "eminently sensible and realistic solution, based on sound historical precedent", however, was implacably opposed by the "most highly respected public intellectual of the age: the philosopher John Locke." Locke was the "leading theorist of the new system of constitutional government, and the chief intellectual guardian of its principles."[183] According to Locke, "Lowndes fanciful justification that there was some metaphysical plane on which a coin would retain its 'value' despite losing 20 percent of its silver was therefore as bare-faced and ridiculous a deceit as claiming 'to lengthen a foot by dividing it into Fifteen parts, instead of 'Twelve' while still 'calling them 'inches'" ... Lowndes' conceptual errors meant that his policy recommendation was dangerously deluded, if not positively treasonous":[184]

> What had really happened was that there had been an outbreak of mass criminal deviance unparalleled in English History. The coinage had been clipped, sheared and melted down on a previously undreamt-of scale. Since money was worth just the silver it was made of, this amounted to nothing other than the robbing of unfortunate coin-users in broad daylight."[185] According to Locke, Lowndes proposal constituted "nothing short of conniving with the coin clippers." (Locke agreed that a recoinage was in order, as proposed by Lowndes, "[b]ut it should not be one that meekly acquiesced in a criminal debasement of the coinage. It should

> be one that restored the current, mutilated coin issues their full, official weight of silver."[186]

As it happened, the recoinage was affected. The result was a dramatic official recognition of the dramatic depreciation. The well informed rapidly exchanged their old coins for new, often on a preferential basis accommodated by bribed corrupt Revenue officials. The less well informed were left holding the old debased coinage. "There were riots in Yorkshire, Staffordshire and Derbyshire, and in July the government was even forced into a partial concession, offering to exchange the silver in light coins for a special government bond issue at sixpence per ounce more than the mint would pay."[187] The overall economic consequences of the recoinage and official recognition of the debasement included an immediate wealth redistribution from the less well informed to those better informed, a reduction in coinage in circulation upon reminting, export of new coins as bullion all leading to a shortage of coins, deflation, a collapse of business confidence, and an accompanying trade contraction.[188]

Martin quotes a pamphleteer who hinted at the human cost of this self-inflicted economic trauma when he reported from Norwich in July 1696 that:

> No trade is managed but by trust, out tenants can pay no rent. Our corn factors can pay for nothing for what they have had and will trade no more, so all is at a stand. And the people are discontented to the utmost; many self-murders happen in small families for want, and all things look very black ... [189]

[A] John Locke's Troublesome Legacy of the Necessity of Commodity Money as Sovereign Money

Locke's opponents pointed out the obvious facts that flowed from his policies as implemented in the recoinage: "- starting with the self-evident truth that there was no intrinsic link between the silver content of the coins and their nominal value, nor had there ever been, the monetary standard had always been flexible: Indeed, that was precisely what the perennial struggle between the sovereign and his mercantile subjects had always been about. The value of money depended not on the stuff that the coinage was made of but on the credit-worthiness and authority of the sovereign who stood behind the tariff that specified the nominal value of the coin."[190]

Historically, [a]mongst the ancients, the understanding was that economic value was quite obviously a property of the social world, and that money was an archetypal social phenomenon. The very term the Greeks used for money was *nomisma*, 'something sanctioned by current usage or custom. In the *Republic*, Plato called it a symbol that exists for the sake of exchange.' His pupil Aristotle held the same view, arguing that it exists not by nature but by convention, and it is in our power to change it and make it useless.'"[191] "Money was a technology built on the basis of the revolutionary notion of economic value—an invisible substance that was both everywhere and nowhere, and which had a presence in the physical world only via the symbolism of coinage. As such it came naturally to the Greeks."[192]

Monetary exchange, Aquinas said, "was invented by reason, not by nature.' It was the 'one thing by which everything could be measured ... not by its nature but because it has been made a measure by men. As such it served at the pleasure of the relevant authorities, and if the king or the community so decides, it loses its value.'"[193] Thus, money constitutes a property of the social world rather than of physical reality.

Even as Locke continued to propound his unorthodox conception of money, coinage was rapidly losing its franchise as money. With the creation of the Bank of England and the first issuance of its paper currency (a step away from bills of exchange circulated as money), the disabilities and the advantages of coinage was finally made clear. In addition to a purely social convention, money was of distinct and critical political importance. Locke's position was grounded in his efforts, as a constitutionalist, "to demolish the intellectual credentials of absolute monarchy and secure the claims of political Liberalism and constitutional government. At the center of his philosophical system was the axiom that the property rights of the individual exist by nature—not by dint of sovereign approval. This principle was the foundation on which Locke's defence of civil liberties against the infringement of absolute power had been constructed and the ideological basis of the new regime of constitutional government. There was no question that money—self-evidently one of the most important of all classes of property—could be exempted from this reasoning."[194]

The revolution in thought presented by Locke was not a revolutionary view of money as such; its role in the natural world of tangible property of the then existing social order dominated by the absolute authority of the sovereign monarch. *Locke's revolutionary thinking was political.* Locke believed that the "existence of such absolute power of the sovereign over his people was not just unjust but unnatural."[195]

The financial revolution that proceed apace with the political revolution presented by the rising cry for constitutional government grounded in the will of the people as opposed to a sovereign absolute monarchy, "had already demonstrated as never before that the bankers' mysterious art of credit creation was a source of great political power":[196]

> With the correct understanding of money, the Bank [of England] might be the dream instrument for coordinating the balance of power between the sovereign and his subjects—a financial counterpart to the ingenious political concept of King-in-parliament. If however, [according to Locke] the delusions of men like Lowndes and Barbon were allowed to convince people that the value of money was nothing but what the sovereign—and now his bankers—said it was, financial and political tyranny surely lay in wait. The only way for the monetary system promulgated by the Bank of England "safe for constitutional government was by committing unswervingly to a fixed monetary standard, impervious to interference from the sovereign, the bankers or anyone else. The possibility of a free monetary order had to be sacrificed to ensure that a free political order could be guaranteed victory."[197]

Once again, the dialogue concerning the nature of money, its role in the real world and its foundations, both social and political, sunk beneath turbulent waters. The disastrous consequences of the forced recoinage of silver yielded the rise of the increased use of gold to augment and fulfill the role of silver coinage.

It is within the social and political controversy of the wars, social and political conflict and controversy of the late seventeenth and early eighteenth centuries that the ambiguities and dichotomies of modern monetary thought became entrenched. Money was just a precious metal. Since nature demanded that its standard be fixed—just like weights and measures or time, the predatory policies of the sovereign and the nobility during medieval times were justifiable viewed as "exercises in daylight robbery whereby they had stolen their subjects' property by abusing their uncivil authority. Money was precious metal: the standard simply a shorthand for weight."[198]

Critically, the function that went largely without comment during this time was the necessary connection between the coinage of precious metals as money, regulated by weight and quality that satisfied Locke's constitutional concerns, and the new public private money promulgated by the sovereign and the bankers through the Bank of England. That connection was required convertibility of the new paper money into coinage, the value of which had been regulated by the new constitutional parliament by type, quantity and quality, on demand. The feature of convertibility served as a brake on excessive emission and circulation of Bank of England, public-private paper money as well as credit repayable ultimately on money that value of which was regulated by reference to the standard of precious metal type, weight and quality. Without that discipline, that brake on credit creation, greed and abuse of power that would otherwise continue to lead to abuse and depreciation of the value of the paper money.

Martin chronicles the role of money during this period as a:

> [V]igorous and pervasive social change on an undreamt of scale—to say nothing of the political revolution that its chief accomplice, banking, had fomented.[199]
>
> Social fluidity was only half of the bargain. The other half was the paradoxical promise of continued stability. Monetary society did not promise anarchy—that would never have caught on. Instead it promised a rule for anarchy: both mobility and stability, both freedom and certainty. And the feature of money that delivered the second part of its promise was the fundamental axiom of the fixed nominal value of credit and debt. Whatever social obligations were destroyed, financial obligations—debts—were heaped in their place. And the whole point of debts was that unlike the obsolete social obligations they had just replaced they were not going to be "swept away." [Adam] Smith and his school had constructed a theory that purported to show how both parts of money's promise could hold—how objective laws governing monetary society would so choreograph things that the fixed financial obligations would not themselves fall foul of money's indefatigable promotion of social change. But the reality of monetary society is—and has always been—strikingly at odds with this idea.[200]

Martin connects this inherent conflict with today's financial crises:

> [T]he unsustainable accumulation of debt can present not just incidental but existential challenges to monetary society. Money's intrinsic tendency to create instability, in other words, is a danger not only to the victims of crashes and recessions—but ultimately to money itself. When a financial crisis results in half of the youth population being out of work, or civil servants facing the sack to free up funds to pay foreign bondholders, then conventional remedies available within the current economic system can begin to look unappealing. Central bankers and

> finance ministers work on the assumption that monetary society itself works fine. Its rules must be respected, they counsel, and any injustices that result should be remedied by more progressive taxation or transfusions from wealthy benefactors abroad. But the mood of those at the sharp end of the debt crisis is less business-as-usual.[201]

The conflict as presented by Martin does not fully address two important corollaries. First, the United States Congress and US monetary authorities gradually, beginning with the American Civil War have continuously and progressively stretched and finally broken the fundamental foundation for monetary, social and political equilibrium. American and now the global social, political and monetary world has intentionally abandoned the indispensable feature of money that delivered the second part of its promise, social stability, was the fundamental axiom of the fixed nominal value of credit and debt. The historic record of this abandonment, primarily in America constitutes much of the foundation for the public's current case for the enforcement of the rule of law, which if not intentionally set aside, could have formed the foundation for active attention to the prospect of financial instability and ongoing responsible actions by government to approximate, and maximize the overall objective and promise of both monetary and social stability.

As we will see, powerful vested interests in Washington and Wall Street have perverted the established legal mechanisms to address social and monetary and social stability with the now obvious attempt to accomplish just what Locke, Adam smith and America's founding fathers feared.

John Maynard Keynes, having resigned from the British delegation to the Versailles peace negotiations the wake of World War I, trenchantly, and presciently observed that:

> It is not just craven politicians at peace negotiations who create unsustainable debts ... the problem is intrinsic to monetary society: "The powers of uninterrupted usury are great. If the accretions of vested interest were to grow without mitigation for many generations, half of the population would be no better that slaves to the other half." So those who set up respect for contact as an idol while forgetting the higher law that all financial contracts must be fair to be sustainable ... by overlooking one of the greatest of all social principles, namely the fundamental distinction between the right of the individual to repudiate contract and right of the state to control vested interest, are the worst enemies of what they seek to preserve. For nothing can preserve the integrity of contract between individuals except a discretionary authority in the State to revise what has become intolerable.[202]
>
> Money promises to organize society in a manner that combines freedom and stability. This it will achieve first by transforming social obligations—traditional rights and duties that are fundamentally incommensurable with one another—into financial obligations—assets and liabilities all measured in the same units of economic value; and then by making these financial obligations liquid—allowing them to be transferred from one person to another. The trouble is that the world is an uncertain place. Liquidity evaporates, solvency is reassessed; the network of indebtedness that a moment ago was sustainable is suddenly not. The network

must adapt—but there's the rub. Money has created interests vested in the network as it stands.[203]

Martin points out that from the time of Oresme to the present, "monetary thought, and indeed economics more broadly, is simply a corrupt discipline.... Modern finance theorists ... were no the impartial scientists they made themselves out to be. They were just cheerleaders for the banking lobby, handsomely remunerated to produce an elaborate intellectual justification for an immoral commercial enterprise. The debt crisis was an *Inside Job* (referring to Charles Ferguson's Oscar winning documentary of the role of economics in this financial crisis, of that name)."

Martin suggests that alternatively, that may likely be the "consequent of a mistake on the level ideas." Specifically, that the "real culprit for the gargantuan blind spot in the theory of [Adam] Smith and his school is not a set of vested interests, but an idea—none other than the conventional understanding of money promulgated by John Locke."[204]

§2.07 THE ANCIENT UNDERSTANDING OF MONEY AND THE FOUNDATION OF THE UNITED STATES

The ancient traditional understanding had been that money as credit is useful in commerce especially, and coinage a physical representation of it. The integrity of the coinage and requirement for settlement through payment or redemption of credit by coinage served as a brake on excess credit creation. The curb on credit creation established by sovereign coinage of precious metals augmented the discipline on credit creation imposed by the relatively small circulation, or liquidity, of credit amongst known and trusted counterparties, and the sovereign.[205] The other curb on credit creation lay in the application of the commercial law of relating to credit, its creation, evidence and negotiability.

"The important social and political nature of money was known, respected, and hotly debated on an ongoing basis. It was well known and understood that the monetary standard was the fulcrum on which the scales weighing the competing claims of the sovereign and his subjects were balanced, and where that fulcrum should sit was the quintessential question of political (and social) justice."[206]

§2.08 A NEW UNDERSTANDING OF MONEY FOLLOWING THE FOUNDING OF THE UNITED STATES

John Locke's departure and the "new traditional" understanding became that money was a thing, value was a natural property, and the monetary standard therefore became an objective fact. The operating standard for regulating the value of money than became a matter of specificity in identification of the "thing", and then accuracy and consistency in the mechanics of application of agreed or state specified standards of weights and measures to the thing. "Far from being a natural property of the physical world, there was a time, as we have seen, when the concept of economic value simply didn't exist—because money had not yet been invented."[207]

What is now apparently a dim and faint memory for today's monetary experts, "[f]ar from being any true objectively true standard against which economic value must be measured, the choice of a monetary standard is always a political one—because the standard itself represents nothing but a decision as to what is a fair distribution of wealth, income and the risks of economic uncertainty."[208]

What we are left with today is our short national history apparently grounded, "not in a new age of objectivity in economic affairs", as propounded by John Locke in support of the new experiment in democratic and constitutional governance, of which the United States was the first and arguable they best example. Perversely, Locke's attempt to achieve economic objectivity and defeat intentional economic manipulation of the public interest by the state, failed to acknowledge and accommodate the fundament function of money in civil society. Instead, "[i]t opened the way to the dominance of particular, quite arbitrary prejudices—and even worse, it covered their tracks with a veil of apparent scientific objectivity":[209]

> For the new understanding did not mean that there was no ethical debate to be had about money; not a bit of it. It was that the ethics of money now meant something completely different. The old dilemmas disappeared. If money was a thing and value a physical property, to discuss either in ethical terms no longer even made sense: to call the monetary standard unjust made about as much sense as calling the weather unfair.[210]
>
> It may seem awkward and disingenuous in today's political, economic and financial environment to state, as has Martin that, "the Liberal shibboleths of the free pursuit of self-interest and respect for contract became the overriding focus of moralizing attention. Morality in monetary society now meant whether you submitted unquestioningly to the philosophy of laissez fair, and whether or not you paid your debts. Money's commandments, like those of the law, had to be obeyed; it was disobedience that constituted unethical behavior:[211]

The disastrous paradoxical corollary to John Locke's laudable effort to curb abuse of the monetary system by the usual suspects, politicians, bankers and powerful vested interest by subjecting them to the inexorable discipline and "morality" of a *laissez faire* system, has, in fact, failed abjectly to make money safe for democracy. It has served only to provide the cover of a "license" to the politicians, economists, financial authorities and bankers to unquestioningly, one might say, and as I have said, in a commonly accepted aura of *ignorantia affectata,* that they are entitle to, and indeed must, "treat respect for the unimpeded action of the market as the moral duty of every rational person that was in the end its most baleful consequence."[212]

According to Martin, the traditional ethical dilemmas over monetary society, and the ever-ongoing open debate over the extent to which money should be the coordinating mechanism for human social life, had been banished by the impartial discipline of things as money. The new supposedly impartial and objective view of money, however depended upon a simultaneous formal acknowledgement by the revolutionary new republic of the United States of America, a country founded upon the fundamental principle of the sovereignty of its people, established through the relatively rapid trend of Anglo-American common law, and the careful construction of the *United States Constitution* based on common law principles, of the necessity of a connection between the kind of purely physical money advocated by John Locke with the ancient, powerful and pervasive role of credit, and banking, in a monetary society disciplined by constant and unending social, political, governmental, bureaucratic, and yes the public-private institution of banking discipline over money, in the sole sovereign interests of society: the sovereign people of the United States of America.

As we will see, the *United States Constitution*, in fact, establishes and delegates specifically to the United States Congress the specific power, duty and mechanism for the constant and ongoing balancing and coordination of the emission and regulation of the value of money, through transparent and lawful means, by making ongoing decisions, on behalf of and solely in the interest of the sovereign American people, as to what is a fair distribution of wealth, income and the risks of economic uncertainty that is effected by American money, both through credit and through discipline of credit serving as money to ensure that the credit meets the ancient criterion and attributes for just what credit as money must possess, including a mechanism for repayment and redemption that constantly and publicly tests the responsiveness of America's money to the social, ethical, moral and functional utility thereof to the sovereign American people.

That means the interest of American people, not congress, not the executive branch of government, not powerful vested economic and political interest, and especially not to the self-serving public-private partnership of the American financial services monopoly, now effecting a cabal of criminal racketeering enterprise of conspirators and actors who have exploited the crack in monetary discipline offered by Locke, notwithstanding clear constitutional and legal foundation for the maintenance of such discipline as, arguably the most important feature of American society's organizational document and compact, the *United States Constitution*. Without the monetary discipline mandated by law; mandated by the *Constitution*, all other governmental powers and activities delegated to the American government by the sovereign American citizens under the *Constitution*, and respecting the broad social contract these limited powers represent, their constitutional effects are fundamentally corrupted.

Those limited powers are conducted with a conclusive presumption of a full and complete understanding by those wielding such powers, of their social, political, and legal purposes and limitations, and of their respective accountability in all areas, including legal accountability for those powers as exercised and corrupted in their ultimate effects.

§2.09 MONEY IS A BASIC AND CRUCIAL SOCIAL MECHANISM BASED ON MORAL PRINCIPLES

The Greeks recognized that: "the lack of any intrinsic limit to consumption, accumulation and quest for status..." might, as we now know, has led to weak, or non-existent limits to the individuals' "imperative to get money may lead [and has now led] to a lack of limits to what people will do to get it."[213] The success of money as an economic mater in the first instance, carries the corollary described by Martin, following British thinkers Robert and Edward Skidelsky and their book entitled *How Much is Enough?*, who argued "that only a substantive ethical conception of what a good life consists of can answer that eternal question: hoping that the market mechanism will impose limits on itself is a pipedream. What we need is to be specific about what we think is good and bad, and then have the moral fibre to stick to our judgment."[214]

According to Martin, the Greeks understood that life in a monetary society inextricably involves a commitment to:

- the idea of universal economic value;
- conventions of calculating that value; and
- the possibility of its decentralized transfer from one person to another.

Economic value is a social contrivance. Not a natural property. Wealth in money is not an abundance of real useful physical things—it has value only—and can exist only—in society. One may have an abundance of money and yet starve, as Martin reminds us quoting the legend of Midas. Money and its value rely on other people; but it is that necessary social relationship and its "social technology which isolates us from other people, by transforming the rich and varied ecology of human relationships into the mechanical and monotonous clockwork of financial relationships."[215]

According to Martin, John Law, the now discredited Controller-General of the Finances of France during the 1720s, accurately observed that: "All income and wealth flows in the end from the productive economy—and it is claims on this income alone that money ultimately represents. That income is, however, uncertain, because the world is an uncertain place—so the value of those claims is in reality uncertain too."[216] Law's solution was to convert all debt to equity, essentially the value of each monetary unit would then become variable depending upon its relationship to the overall income of the country, centralized through the state.

"Law's System was ingenious, innovative, and centuries ahead of its time. It was even to prove prophetic two hundred and fifty years later, when the international gold exchange standard finally disintegrated in 1973 and fiat monetary standards became the worldwide norm. Yet it failed spectacularly."[217] Law underestimated his own abilities. He underestimated the vested interests that his System would disenfranchise. He attempted too much in too short a period of time it would take to implement his system.

If money is simply transferable credit, Law reasoned, then the debate between Locke and Lowndes had really been missing the point. They had not, in fact been, arguing about the nature of money itself, but about what the standard of abstract economic value should be. This, Law believed, was the single most important question in all economic policy, for two reasons:

- The first was that for an economy to prosper, the choice of a standard such as to ensure a sufficient supply of money—an objective that had been acknowledged as important monetary pamphleteers all of the way back to Nicholas Oresme.

- The second was that the choice of standard also determines the distribution of wealth and income.

The most important defect in Law's system was a replay of the original iteration of it in ancient Greece, as money evolved to replace the system of overlords with social responsibilities and peasants who shared crops. "[F]inancial obligations cannot fulfil every role that social obligations can; and left unchecked, the exhilarating independence that money promises becomes destructive isolation. The leaders of the people ... are ripe to suffer many griefs for their great arrogance ... for they know not how to restrain their greed."[218]

[A] Fairness Is Crucial to Social Relationships, Especially, Economic, Monetary and Financial Social Relationships

As it happened, just as the precedent for the French crisis was the Greek crisis; the precedent for the Greek Crisis, was the Mesopotamian crisis. Although the Mesopotamian society was not fully monetized, the disparities of the monetary system they used created the same income and wealth redistributions and disparities to which John Law addressed his system, and eventually the French Revolution, the "Great Terror", the Committee of Public Safety, and the Guillotine ground to a bloody halt. "In ancient Mesopotamia, it was the responsibility of the king, who was heaven's divine representative on earth, to restore social balance by cancelling some or all of the debts. The earliest known examples pf this Mesopotamian practice of proclaiming a clean slate when the burden of debt became socially unsupportable are almost as old as the earliest evidence for interest-bearing debt relief itself—dating from the reign of Enmetana of Lagash in around 2,400 B.C. It was that tradition that survived in the Ancient Near East into biblical times, in the form of the instrument of the jubilee, which the Book of Leviticus enjoined the Hebrews to declare every fifty years."[219] By the time of the Greek crisis, however "[t]the religious cosmology of traditional society no longer cut the mustard as the definitive guide for the distribution of power on earth. 'Man controls his destiny' was the spirit of the age.' So, man himself must determine the fair distribution of wealth and power."[220]

The Greeks recognized that in a democratic society, and in the particular political culture it fostered, "[a]n ulterior ideal of social order would indeed be imposed upon the uncontrolled excesses of monetary society. But this ideal would not be a simulacrum of the divine order of heaven. It would be a human notion of fairness in society hammered out by man. It would be determined, in short, through politics."[221] The *Constitution* demands that Congress shall so determine by fairly and continually regulating the value of American money.

Solon, the elected Greek chief magistrate of his city, in 594 B.C., enacted "a series of social reforms known from then on as the "Shaking-off of Burdens", Chief amongst these was the cancellation of debts—but one which differed fundamentally from the oriental practice of the jubilee. For the central decision of any debt relief—who should gain and who should lose—was a matter of political compromise."[222]

According to Solon, the immutable boundaries of social obligation that had governed society in the interest of social justice—the system "would have to be adaptable to the social changes that money by its nature brings. And in the world in which mankind controlled its destiny, there could only be one source of legitimacy for that new standard of fairness: democratic politics."[223]

Solon's reforms did not stop with the debt cancellations enforced through the Shaking-off of Burdens, but included:

- abolition of sharecropping;
- taxation by economic category rather than by class; and
- guarantee of the right to trial by jury

More than two centuries later, Aristotle argued that this last reform was:

> said to have been the chief basis of the powers of the multitude ... for the people, having control over the courts, thereby have control over the government. But another aspect of Solon's reforms was more important than any single measure. For the critical role to be played in future by political decisions regarding what was and was not economically fair called for a new and more formal system of recording such decisions and assessing compliance with them. What was required—and what Solon therefore supplied, inscribed on a famous set of rotating wooden tablets—was a comprehensive body of law. *With Solon's achievement of a democratic state under the rule of law, the formula for making money work was complete.*[224] (Author's emphasis added in italics)
>
> It was Solon who had seen how the strategy might work, all of the way back at the beginning. *Only the compromises of democratic politics can durably decide what is fair; and only the promises of the democratic government can reliably last.* This was the secret of the recalibration of the standard—the secret of harnessing money's benefits while avoiding its flaws.[225] (Authors' emphasis added in italics)

Martin documents the ongoing historical necessity of society continually grappling with the "contradictions inherent in money's promise to combine freedom and stability..."[226]

According to Martin and Solon:

> The original standard of economic value—the standard that had allowed money to serve, not only as a device for organizing one line of trade or one part of the bureaucracy, but the entire economy and the whole of society—expressed a political ideal; the equal social value of the individual member of the tribe. But by its nature, money permits social mobility and the accumulation of wealth and power over others. Any fixed standard of monetary value will therefore necessarily become obsolete—and that obsolescence spells mortal danger, for it is at the root of civil strife. Instead, the state must always be vigilant to ensure that the architecture of financial obligations reflects what society believes to be fair. *Only politics—democratic politics, in constant activity—can furnish such an evolving standard. And only law its debate, codification and rule—can enact it.*

It is a strategy for harnessing money's potential as relevant today as it was two and a half millennia ago.[227] (Authors' emphasis added in italics)

Fortunately, in America the constitutional methodology for following Solon's methodology has been politically determined. The *United States Constitution* provides the expressed legal foundation for the democratically based, active management of the identification of money, its emission and the regulation of its value. Congress has failed to meet its obligations to do so. It has failed to enforce the rule of law. The Executive branch of the United States government has failed to enforce the existing rule of law. The sole remaining recourse for American society for redress of the wrongful action by Washington and Wall Street through their deliberate, intentional manipulation of the value of American money is resort by ordinary Americans to the American judicial system and the judicial compulsion of the enforcement of the rule of law.

The great failure of modern American and global society is in perversion and now intentional misrepresentation of the existence, manner and effects of what Washington and Wall Street present as "conventions of defining and calculating the value of money." Washington and Wall Street have unilaterally declared themselves free to trumpet the ideal of the universal unit of economic value as denominated as the American dollar, and have become wizards at its decentralized transfer on money in a whirl of purely financial activity (the "mechanical and monotonous clockwork of financial relationships") having ever diminishing relevance to the decentralized transfer of economic value in the interest of the society as a whole, but providing instead a furnace of contrived purely financial—meaning purely monetary—activity from whence enormous profits can be extracted through the intentional misrepresentation by Washington and Wall Street, and thereby the public appearance of monetization of universal units of economic value; but which, in fact, are units diminished in value through each transfer in which the standard of calculating that value is automatically diminished. The result is the ongoing intentional depreciation, debasement and misrepresentation of the value of each dollar unit on each transfer, every second of every minute, hour, day, month and year. This process is immoral. It is illegal.

The questions for our society are whether the existing actual process of creating and circulating money without a standard for its value and a convention for the establishment of its honest use as a transfer mechanism of units of universal economic value a good thing or a bad thing, a right thing or a wrong thing, a fair thing or and unfair thing for American society? The current process appears to benefit almost exclusively Washington and Wall Street; and to the detriment of the interests of our society as a whole. If the American legal system that embodies our social and moral compact and defines the process as it has evolved to the present day, defines this process as fundamentally a bad thing, a wrong thing and an unfair thing; as it demonstrably does; does it provide also specifically provide for a societal; a moral, a legal, redress for the wrong, enforceable by those who have suffered the wrong? The answers to those questions are uniformly, yes. Articulation and clarification of these questions and answers is the fundamental role of this work.

[B] The Great Underlying Social, Moral, Political and Economic Conflicts That Plague Modern Day Money and Banking

I submit that, in the broad context of Martin's book and the additional range of information available to the world's leading experts on money, banking, finance and economics addressed in this work, financial crises are indeed grounded in the conflict between Locke's political philosophical concept of money developed as a foundation for the social and political development of democratic ideals, and the indisputable fact that every form of global money consists virtually entirely of credit. But I further submit, and Martin's observations and arguments confirm, that while Locke's then revolutionary, and now considered conventional, understanding of money presents a seemingly intractable conflict with the historical dominance of credit as the foundation for monetary society that is, now in America and globally, a fundament conflict that threatens the very foundations of modern civilization. American and global politicians, financial regulators, examiners and supervisors, bankers and financiers; all with a vested interest in the status quo, are, or should, responsibly, have been fully aware of this fundamental conflict. They should have been working unceasingly, transparently, as our trusted experts in these matters, in meeting their respective fiduciary duty to American society to do so.

§2.10 CONCLUDING OBSERVATIONS

Some say money is the root of all evil.[228] Money is a tool. Its utility is based on trust and confidence. If money's relationship has a transparent, honest, trusted, fair and reliable relationship to value and relative values of assets goods and services in an open market, it will be the cornerstone of a prosperous civil society. If money's connection to value is manipulated, deliberately misrepresented to its users for the preferred benefit of those who define, create and control it, the value represented is a lie; its promulgation and circulation is deceitful and constitutes a persistent systemic course of intentional misrepresentation by which those in control, Washington and Wall Street, abuse their power to steal the value of the fruits of labor, goods and services, savings and investment of ordinary Americans. Money so created and used is evil. While the damage inflicted on society is diffused by dissembling, lying and delaying the truth of the circumstances, it can, in fact, be as lethal to ordinary Americans as a gunshot wound, a bomb or a beating with a cudgel. The breadth, depth and scale of damage intentionally inflicted by Washington and Wall Street on innocent members of society, ordinary American households, is unprecedented in the history of civilization. Washington and Wall Street conduct their damaging exploitation largely through what has come to be known as shadow banking. Martin has recorded the development of shadow banking. Mann has confirmed the necessity of a fiduciary correlation of the units of value of shadow money to its corresponding units of sovereign money, the value of which is honestly, transparently and fairly regulated. We turn now to an examination of the impact of modern-day credit money arising outside of the formal banking system, cleverly re-denominated as shadow money and shadow banking.

CHAPTER 3

Shadow Money and Shadow Banking

§3.01 CREDIT MONEY AND SHADOW MONEY

The Economist Paul McCulley coined the modern term "shadow banking" in 2007, but credit has existed outside the banking system for centuries. As banks became the backbone of finance, governments introduced rules to safeguard people's savings and rein in risk-taking by banks. Yet mechanisms to take advantage of being outside that regulation always found a way in.[229] Until relatively recently, credit money was largely created directly incident to the purchase and sale of goods in trade between businesses and through small trade accounts. The predominant use of larger credit arrangements was sovereign lending and borrowing to finance war—or simply state centered financial profligacy for political gain.

As balances on account at banks grew, money not required to be liquid and available for immediate use or redemption in specie also grew. Bankers increased the practice of lending money held on deposit for short periods of time and charging interest to compensate for the risk and uncertainty that the loans would not be repaid in time to meet requirements for redemption by depositors in safe and sound sovereign money in the ordinary course of business. Banks also became acceptors of real bills of exchange through the practice of endorsement by the payee, discount and transfer. Banks thereby became participants in the world of commerce; serving as arbiters of the credit represented by the real bills of exchange arising out of sale of goods. "Bills that were written in the absence of a real exchange were described as 'fictitious' or 'accommodation' paper. Any tradesman who was caught issuing fictitious bills was considered a fraud and excluded from the financial network."[230]

Shadow money and shadow banking is not a new phenomenon. The evolution of trade in real bills as money substitutes is as old as the use of transferable credit instruments. Recent commentators, members of the Shadow Banking Colloquium, a project of the Financial Stability Research Program of the Institute for New Economic Thinking, have harkened back to the commentary of Walter Bagehot in 1873:[231]

> The modern shadow banking system, at its core, bears a surprising resemblance to the 19th century world that Walter Bagehot helped us to understand in his magisterial book *Lombard Street: A Description of the [London] Money Market* (1873). At the heart of both worlds is the wholesale money market and operating as crucial liquidity backstop in both worlds is the central bank. At the time Bagehot was writing, this backstop function was not yet fully understood, much less accepted; and much the same could be said of the central bank's backstop of the shadow banking system today.
>
> We are living today in a Bagehot moment, when the outlines of the new are just emerging from the ashes of the old. During crisis, the central banks of Bagehot's time and our own both dutifully employed their own balance sheets to stem the downturn. But they did so without any overarching theory of why it worked, much less any thought about implications for their role in more normal times. The time for all of that would come later, after the crisis had died down. Bagehot's book started the process of necessary rethinking for his own time by bringing out into the open how the Bank of England had acted during previous crises. We start our own process of necessary rethinking, for our own time, by using Bagehot as an entry point into understanding the modern shadow banking system, and the global financial crisis of our own time.[232]

The creation of credit through bank lending presented an expansion of the opportunity for bank profit through the assumption of greater risk and uncertainty over time. The utilization of fractional reserve banking developed to enable banks to hold less sovereign money in reserve to meet depositor demand for withdrawal. So long as demands for liquidity could be predicted, the bank would then be free to put the sovereign money to loans and investments earning higher returns than the cost of holding funds in reserve.

Mehrling et.al., succinctly describe the shadow banking system of Bagehot's time as:

> ... a world where government securities are not yet the focal point of trading and prices, as they came to be in the 20th century. Instead, the focal point was the private bill market, which domestic manufacturers tapped as a source of working capital, and which traders worldwide tapped to finance the movement of tradable goods. It was a market in short-term private debt, typically collateralized by tradable goods, quite different from the 20th century market in long-term public debt, which is typically unsecured.
>
> Supplying funds to the bill market were, among others, banks that purchased bills at discount from face value using their own deposit liabilities, typically planning to hold to maturity and redeem at par. The institution of "acceptance", by which a bank or some other party guaranteed payment of a bill at maturity, was the way non-prime bills became prime. Backstopping the whole thing was the Bank of England, whose posted "Bank Rate" in effect put a floor on the price of prime bills; bank rate was usually somewhat higher than the market rate of discount. Banks whose immediate cash outflow (from deposit withdrawals) outran their immediate cash inflow (from maturing bills) could always take their prime bill assets to the Bank of England for rediscount, and get cash for them. Normally, though, they were able to get a somewhat higher price by tapping the lively secondary market in bills to find a private buyer. In normal times, the central

> bank backstop operated only to support the market; in crisis times, the central bank backstop became the market.[233]

In Baghot's time, the central bank backstop consisted of providing ready availability of sovereign money (then backed by gold) to provide the ready liquidity necessary to calm the market and meet the liquidity needs necessary to return to market stability. At first blush, the shadow money and banking system of Bagehot's time and the present appear to function in essentially the same manner and call for the same response from the central bank in times of liquidity crisis. Mehrling, *et.al.* however, posit that:

> ... [o]n the surface, the modern system looks quite different. The closest we have to the institution of "acceptance" is the credit default swap, but that does not so much guarantee eventual par payment as current market value: price of "risk free" security = price of risky security + price of risk insurance (Mehrling 2010). Further, ours is fundamentally a world of long-term debt which connects to the world of short-term bills through the institution of the interest rate swap: price of short term security = price of long term security + price of interest rate swap. And finally, since the gold standard is long gone, in our world securities contain currency risk so we have the institution of the FX swap: price of dollar security = price of foreign currency security + price of FX swap.
>
> These differences from the world of Bagehot are significant but should not distract us from seeing that at the heart of both worlds is the money market and operating as crucial backstop in both worlds is the central bank. Indeed, it could be said that the whole point of the various swaps is to manufacture prime bills from diverse raw materials. Price of "risk-free" prime bills = price of risky security + price of risk insurance + price of interest rate swap + price of FX swap. When we look at shadow banking through the eyes of Bagehot, the crucial difference between his world and ours is not so much the weird and wonderful world of financial derivatives but rather the fact that Bagehot's world was organized as a network of promises to pay in the event that someone else doesn't pay (i.e. "acceptances"), whereas our own is organized as a network of promises to buy in the event that someone else doesn't buy.[234]

The desire for greater profits, in the absence imposition of the highest level of duty and care to the depositors—fiduciary duty, and in the absence of requirements to demonstrably tie valuation and liquidity requirements of loans and investments to demands for liquidity of deposits at face value denominated in units of sovereign money, the value of which has been regulated by Congress in accordance with the their constitutional mandate, led inexorably to progressively lower reserve requirements, dilution of the bankers duty of care through creation of a personal discretion-based bank regulatory structure. This as opposed to a strict rule of law-based structure of the commercial law of negotiable instruments, greater risk taking in investment environments of greater uncertainty accompanied by greater profitability and wealth creation for the larger, politically well-connected banks with strong webs of interconnection with government and its very profitable deposit and financing market offerings, has left a ragged fringe of risk and uncertainty undertaken by smaller banks imbedded in their portfolios, rendering them most susceptible to realization of the losses inexorably and periodically experienced in loans and investments in the corresponding fringe of greater loan and investment risk and uncertainty. This phenomenon has continued and grown through US history leading to a growing and ever more visible disparities in market and regulatory treatment between large banks tied to Washington through webs of interlocking mutual financial and political benefits, with the rest of the pack living outside that compact and locked into banking's Main Street commerce and finance; while Main Street remains buffeted and damaged by the economic and financial cycles driven by the Washington Wall Street enterprise.

The reduction of the money, banking, legal and accounting protections and constraints on credit excess inherent in shadow money and shadow banking in Bagehot's era, cannot be replicated by the structured, formulaic modelling process described by Mehrling and his colleagues, backed by a "dealer of last resort" in addition to a "lender of last resort" central bank: the Bank of England in Bagehot's day, and for our purposes, the Federal Reserve System in the present day. The fundamental principles driving the honesty, safety, soundness, and the integrity of sovereign money on the one hand, and shadow money on the other have been lost. The necessary condition to learning and applying lessons from periodic but infrequent liquidity crises in Bagehot's time compares favorably to our present ongoing and ever more destructive crises of asset value and liquidity booms and collapses, and resultant economic and market value crises, posing in simplicity as liquidity crises.

The fundamental purpose of banking systems in modern times is to intermediate between long-term illiquid credit assets and short-term liquid money instruments, essentially liquid on demand. The challenge of this intermediation process, of which bankers are thought to be the masters, are risk of loss of value or liquidity of assets in the market and uncertainty of market conditions over time—the distance between current asset liquidity and liquidity at a distant time in the future. The clarity and importance of moral and legal principles that historically supported social and economic stability, and a legal, commercial and economic financial and monetary system that readily, predictably and effectively, enforced accountably for adherence to the moral and legal foundations for social, commercial and economic welfare have been eroded to the point that they no longer can said to be functioning at a tolerable or sustainable level.

American sovereign money has been stripped of its essential legal and economic attributes. Credit or shadow money has been stripped of its primary commercial function and its related legal and economic attributes under commercial law of credit and its negotiability. The American central bank established in the Federal Reserve System has as its central feature, not the fairness, equity, honesty, safety, soundness and integrity of American sovereign money and the American monetary system as the foundation for American social and economic welfare but, to the contrary, serves primarily as a promoter of deceit and a manipulator of the value of money and asset values and liquidity that serves the essentially diametrically opposed political, speculative greed and elitist purposes and interests of the Washington Wall Street enterprise. As noted in the Introduction, we now can see and say that the emperors of Washington and Wall Street truly have no clothes.

§3.02 RISK AND UNCERTAINTY ARE INHERENT IN CREDIT MONEY

Today's regulated depository banking system is inextricably intertwined with the workings, assets and liabilities, income and liquidity that resides in the system of shadow money and shadow banking. Shadow money and the shadow banking system are not a parallel system, whose effects and interaction with the regulated depository state and federally regulated banking system in American and globally are formal, much less readily identifiable and transparent. The systems are fully integrated and interdependent. To pretend otherwise is simply a ruse perpetuated by Washington and Wall Street to manipulate risk and uncertainty inherent in both sovereign and shadow money, money creation and asset values as tools of economic and financial exploitation by the intentional misrepresentation of immediate liquid value of the without recognizing any discount or ongoing payment liability for the stated values of illiquid assets. In studying shadow money and shadow banking we must return to the economic and commercial challenges of risk and uncertainty and the respective and complementary roles serves by sovereign money and shadow money in a cohesive system that requires a return to the first moral and legal principles that support that system and to the vital function of enforcement of moral and legal accountability for participants' failure to adhere to those principles.

[A] Risk

The risk is that the attributes and the valuation of collateral and other borrower resources for the repayment of the credit may deteriorate.

Risk is recognized, allocated and protected against through the establishment of documented loan to asset value ratios reflecting discounts due to perceived market illiquidity during the credit term, debt service coverage ratios, operating income ratios, asset operational requirements and accountability and borrower and guarantor net worth maintenance requirements, established to provides protection in the event of unanticipated reductions in income of the borrower or of the collateral, if any, and additional structured cushions—hedges against the failure to pay or perform condition to payment when due, through guarantees of payment and performance of action necessary to assure payment, insurance and calls for additional collateral or assurance of repayment under certain condition and constant reporting with respect to the status of conditions affecting repayment. This is a fertile field for regulators and lawyers.

[B] Uncertainty

In addition to risks to loan repayment that can reasonably be anticipated, evaluated and protected against, there is always uncertainty regarding the occurrence of events outside the strict lender/borrower/source of repayment relationship that can affect the timely and full repayment of a credit.

The uncertainty of credit repayment is most often presented by political risk—changes in government incentives and inducements to the extension of credit, labor or other market disputes and conflicts, war, physical or weather calamities and other unforeseen events which present additional and uncertain—unpredictable—risk of loss. The protection banks maintain against uncertainty is bank capital and reserves. If losses in expected credit repayments are incurred, the banks' capital serves as a reserve fund against which the loss can be charged, and bank reserves provide the necessary liquidity to support deposit withdrawals without impairing the banks' ability to redeem bank borrower deposits when due, with honest, safe and sound money, at par.

As noted above, regulators and banks in America, from the close of the Civil War, have continuously reduced capital and reserve requirement in a quest for higher profits.

§3.03 STRUCTURED FINANCE OR STRUCTURED CREDIT

Attempts at allocation or mitigation of the growing proportion of risk and uncertainty not covered through adequate bank capital, reserves or loan and investment underwriting and documentation, through hedging of risk through derivatives, essential credit support insurance instruments, has been in large part, self-defeating and, by creating a false and opaque sense of security and stability of asset values and liquidity created on unprecedented enormous scale through the originate and distribute structured finance model, has created and imbedded enormous unexamined risk and uncertainty in a mountain of shadow money that serves primarily as chits in a grand scheme of speculative trading that bears little relationship to the shadow money and shadow banking system of Bagehot's day that served as the foundation of the dramatic growth of commercial and global trade that ushered in an era of stable and growing prosperity through banking. Government and banking progressive compromise and discard of the moral and legal protections that cradled and nurtured the successful growth of the developing economies of the western world has led us inexorably to a stated where a "shadow system" of artificially structured assets have been created on a massive scale to serve primarily as chits in a vast scheme of speculation—shadow money denominated in units of Federal Reserve Notes, is the direct cause of the financial crisis and to continuing, ongoing money and capital market dysfunction. That dysfunction courses through official regulated depository banking institutions and shadow institutions such as investment banks, hedge funds, private equity funds and every other enterprise that is able to originate and distribute sovereign dollar denominated credit and credit asset-based securities and derivatives, supported by long terms illiquid assets posing as liquid instruments monetized and tradable at par and immune from the ravages of risk and uncertainty over time, into the monetary system as components of our financial and economic system.

[A] Sovereign Money and Shadow Money

Bagehot:

> (M)en of business in England do not like the currency question. They are perplexed to define accurately what money is: how to count they know, but what to count they do not know.[235]

John Maynard Keynes:

> The whole object of the accumulation of wealth is to produce results, or potential results, at a comparatively distant, and sometimes at an indefinitely distant, date. Thus, the fact that our knowledge of the future is fluctuating, vague and uncertain renders wealth a peculiarly unsuitable subject for the methods of classical economic theory.[236]

In other words, investment depends heavily on conventional judgments and the existing state of opinion, but ultimately, investment sits on an insecure foundation. The process of deciphering what to count as money, how to protect and preserve the wealth it represents as it moves in and out of the marketplace over time is a perpetual conundrum. The struggle for answers and maintenance of a safe and sound monetary system requires constant attention, debate, and above all the protection of interests of society as opposed to the manipulative and solely self-interested motives now exhibited by Washington and Wall Street.

As discussed in Chapter 2, sovereign money, such as that mandated by the *United States Constitution*, serves as the most stable common denominator of value and liquidity for all other forms of money and assets whose value is denominated in units of sovereign money in American society. The bulk of money not held in actual units of sovereign money but whose liquidity and value is measured in terms of units of sovereign money must be constantly revalued in those same units to reflect the markets effects on those money forms and related assets, as affected by shifting risk and uncertainty. This requires constant evaluation and it is Congress' responsibility to conduct the assessment and adjustments in value feedback from the market and its effect on the regulation of the value of sovereign money required to maintain an equitable, fair, honest, safe and sound monetary system and to provide the elasticity in the sovereign money supply necessary to maintain the financial stability, safety and soundness that is the bedrock of a free market economy, including the shadow banking system

F. A. Mann, the author of what has been to date the defining text on the legal aspects of money, *The Legal Aspect of Money, 4th Ed.*1982, quoting the George Canning's[237] ridicule of his rival Lord Castlereagh's definition of the pound sterling in 1811, "as 'a sense of value in reference to currency as compared with commodities,' and the inventors and champions of 'abstract currency,' those who, after exhausting in vain every attempt to find an earthly substitute for the legal and ancient standard of our money, have divested the pound sterling of all of the properties of matter and pursued it under the name of the 'ideal unit' into the regions of nonentity and nonsense."[238] According to Mann, one of the principle legal concerns with money is whether it is merely a measure or whether it is measured by something else. Mann's view, "whether the currency system is independent of any other system of measurement or there exists a connecting link or tie between its unit and another substance, and whether in the latter event the organization of the monetary system produces consequences in the sphere of private law."[239]

Mann emphasizes the importance of the gold standard as the link to state sovereign that served to regulate the value of state money but also served to "regulate and limit the volume of money by the requirement of the note issue being backed by a quantity of gold held in reserve as security. The gold standard in this sense has also disappeared [as a sovereign matter in America and England, but also internationally after the abandonment of the *Bretton Woods Accords*], and is, therefore, again of historical interest only."[240]

Mann goes on to concentrate on considerations of comparative and private international law, consigning what is undoubtedly the central issue of law and money to a lengthy consideration of the legal role of money as a principle of nominalism. That is, money is viewed simply as a number. Consideration of disparities in relative value at various times is addressed in some detail but without tying his discussion to the moral and legal principles that underlie any real meaning behind the legal nominalism, which he simply assumes away. Mann does note in several instances that, in minor ways, the principle of state money, sovereign money, that provides for its significance, is now totally absent from considerations of money, morality and the law. On considering the demise of role of gold reserves in supporting the value and liquidity of sovereign money, Mann observed that "since 1939, the gold reserve has played no role in the note issue which has become purely fiduciary."[241] While the value of sovereign money was backed by gold and regulated in value sovereign money was also fiduciary money. The duty of the issuer with respect to the integrity and stability of value was the highest duty known to the law. Thus, the concept of constraints on money creation and valuation created by the concept of moral hazard (and necessarily to s system of laws, legal hazard) implicit in the creation and emission of sovereign American money is a constant and ingrained concept; much discussed but seldom enforced. Originally, under the uniform commercial code, money was defined as "a medium of exchange authorized or adopted" by government "as a part of its currency."[242] Today it means a "medium of exchange authorized or adopted by a domestic or foreign government and includes a monetary account established by an intergovernmental organization or by agreement between two or more nations."[243] This definition is hardly a guiding model of clarity in today's state of dominance of shadow banking over the state and federally chartered and regulated banking institutions.

Although Mann does not elaborate on the characterization of a sovereign note issue as fiduciary in nature, and although he does note that the state may alter value and liquidity of sovereign money, even to the point of enacting gold abrogation clauses and establishing purely fiat money, the characterization of sovereign money as possessing a fiduciary character does inform the theme of this work. Bagehot, aware of the characterization of "fiduciary money" based on securities, by the Germans that urged that the Bank of England note be backed solely by gold. In this view then shadow banking world of "cheque currency" [modern era checks and checking accounts] posed sufficient risk and flexibility to the banking and monetary system and the law that the gold-backed sovereign Bank of England note backed by gold was the "only law which seriously restricts the banker in the conduct of his business ... ."[244] Insofar as the law of money is considered, the most highly regarded authorities in Germany and England, Mann and Bagehot, recognized the necessity of sovereign fiduciary money as indispensable to the constraint of the shadow money of checks and other forms of transferable credit, and they emphasized the fiduciary character sovereign money as emblematic of the state issuer's fiduciary duty to its society to equitably, fairly and honestly create and maintain the regulated value of the sovereign money. The overarching fiduciary duty of the state to its society to regulate the value of sovereign money is the primary function of legal necessity for a properly functioning banking and monetary system that serves the society and the economy it supports. A point that is wholly lost to today's monetary authorities as well as the legal and accounting professions that serve them.

For money to properly and effectively serve its social, economic and political functions, its character must be grounded in moral principles of honesty, integrity and be free of deceit, misrepresentation or serve as a tool of fraud. Those moral principles must be, and are in America, grounded in the rule of law, including the *United States Constitution* and federal statutory law and common law. There lies the foundation for the concept of moral hazard posed by the creation and emission of sovereign money, the liquid value of which is not regulated by Congress as required by the *United States Constitution* as the final settlement asset for settlement of accounts, including credit shadow money substitutes created in the shadow banking system. Legal hazard and legal accountability must be the bottom-line grounding and subsuming moral hazard. Moral hazard to safety and soundness has a hollow ring. By violating their fiduciary standards, Washington and Wall Street have rolled right over moral hazard and legal hazard manifest by legal action for accountability for the fraud perpetrated on ordinary Americans is the final and last resort for equity, fairness and justice.

Sovereign or state money is the basic; the ultimate, final and most highly trusted grounding settlement mechanism for all monetary purposes. Credit money and other money substitutes which flow through the shadow banking system, but which can, and must always be disciplined in value and liquidity to the stability, safety, soundness and integrity of state money. In the US, that money is defined by the standard of value of which is required to be regulated by Congress to meet those moral and legal requirements. The standard for the exercise by Congress of such power and duty, and the standard for the exercise by the executive and the judicial branches of American government of their respective powers and duties to enforce these laws and confirm their underlying moral and legal significance, is so fundamental to the public interest that, to Mann's credit, whether he realized it or not, he along with Bagehot, confirmed that standard as a fiduciary standard.

As a matter of interest, while Mann identifies what surely is the primary legal concern with money and upon which all other questions of the laws of money depend, he proceeds through the bulk of his book to concentrate on money simply as a numbers that are affected by law, without connecting the moral and legal implications of that approach. Virtually all lawyers now simply consider money as a number or numbers, without emphasis on the deeper significance those numbers carry. That is the concept of nominalism.[245] Mann explores the conflicts that arise due to the change in the relative value of money versus its nominal stated value over time, particularly with respect to sovereign fiat money. But he does not connect this issue to the history of sovereign money and the imperative for the sovereign to regulate its value in accordance with an outside standard, such as gold or silver, or the American constitutional requirement for such regulation of value. The credit and other shadow money substitutes created in the shadow banking system depend on the law of sovereign money. Credit and collateral backing the shadow money must be ultimately constrained by the value of the denominating sovereign money that defines it. The honest service of shadow money depends on the discipline required for ultimate payment of the obligation when due in units of sovereign money, the value of which is regulated, in the case of America, by Congress. Money begins with sovereign money possessing stable, safe and sound value in which the public can safely repose their trust and confidence.

When sovereign money cannot be used with trust and confidence because its value is unregulated and its liquidity therefor is questioned and the values of money substitutes, shadow money, is corrupted in its valuation relationship to the sovereign money, whose value and ultimate liquidity provide the common and singular denominator in the calculation and expression of discounts rates reflecting the risk and uncertainty in the ultimate collection of those substitutes. In the final analysis, the vast body of liquid shadow money that has historically provided the engine for society's growth and prosperity can be and has been fatally compromised. Financial crises are the direct result.

Discounts in the value of shadow money substitutes for sovereign money and denominated in units of sovereign money must be a constant, informed process. This process requires thought and deliberation that cannot be found in even the most complex financial models and "quant" analytics that have proved to provide a dangerous and false sense of certainty and predictability, and which, due to the very nature of future risk and uncertainty will always manifest unforeseen components distorting financial models and programs that are based on data from the past in a closed model system, or on an assumed foreseeable future that is subject to risk and uncertainty unfamiliar to financial quants.

These necessary, ever changing discounts and shifting valuations are not susceptible to representations as programmed certainty. The lower the true and realistic discount in valuation of a money substitute, driven by honest assessment of risk and uncertainty, the more useful and reliable that substitute becomes.

Congress failure: (i) to regulate the value of our sovereign monetary unit—the dollar—as required by the *Constitution*; (ii) to effectively discipline the use of credit money substitutes through required valuation disciplined by the constant requirement for redemption in terms of discount to the present value of constitutional sovereign denominated money units; and (iii) to maintain unquestionable trust and confidence in the credit quality of the credit money substitutes, are the cause of the financial crisis. Credit money substitutes for sovereign money have historically been subject to structural, legal restriction on their use. Bills, notes and other negotiable credit instruments were, and remain governed by a well-defined framework of legal and accounting principles and simple commercial structures that protect the value and liquidity of shadow money by incorporation of multiple levels of liability for non-payment together with other legal constraints, and protected in the last analysis by the establishment of a lender of last resort conforming to Bagehot's definition of such a lender of last resort. The US has not only abandoned the constraints on terms of lending by lenders of last resort, but has extended the role to incorporate a function of asset purchaser of last resort of bank assets at par, or book value, without discount marking the assets to market value or imposing any other constraints that should be designed to constrain values in respect of the moral [and legal] hazard that has enabled creation of money substitutes incorporating high levels of undiscounted and unconstrained asset values' risk and uncertainty. Moral hazard has run amok and is now the accepted model for our economic, financial and monetary systems. Legal hazard must now be imposed. Failing that, history informs us that the final hazard to be faced will be violence, war and bloodshed.

Intentional abuse of the devices of structured finance to separate securitized and derivative instruments from the legal, accounting and commercial discipline otherwise governing the underlying credit assets—historically "real bills" the later "accommodation paper" to today: residential and commercial mortgages, credit card balances, student loans, automobile financing; and every form of credit that can, and has been mass-produced securitized and matched with webs of derivatives. The legal, accounting and commercial discipline applicable to the valuation and liquidity of the credit assets underlying the shadow banking domain of credit assets viewed as sovereign money equivalents have been confused, obfuscated and ultimately ignored by Washington and Wall Street, flaunting moral hazard and underlying legal constraints in their creation, in their quest for wealth and power at public expense.

The legal, accounting and commercial disciplines sacrificed in service to the homogeneity of asset liquidity and value misrepresented by structured, securitized credit and derivatives that constitute the overwhelming bulk of today's shadow banking system, have infected a sovereign monetary and banking system lacking the constitutionally mandated anchor for measuring liquidity and value. The anchor must be re-established. The discipline of legal, accounting and commercial mechanisms that historically provided that anchor must be grounded in the active priority of moral principle and fiduciary duty as opposed to a constant quest to pervert those principles and duties through structures and practices whose primary purposes are to create a caricatured and contrived misrepresentation of historically well-functioning shadow money, while avoiding the application to these new structured securitized products and derivatives of substance of the fiduciary and moral imperative essential to their integrity in of value and liquidity. This re-establishment of the anchor of professional moral, legal, accounting and commercial discipline cannot be achieved without the prior re-establishment of legal and financial incentives to Washington and Wall Street to embrace and support it accompanied by the enforcement of legal accountability for their failure to meet their obligations.

If you are still with me dear reader, you will surely have guessed that the systemic nature of the current financial crisis in America and globally derives from the nature and structure of our financial system. There is a clear difference of understanding when we refer to systemic financial crises. Washington and Wall Street have appeared to view the financial crisis in the American system exclusively within their current closed legislative and regulatory arena. Money and monetary assets through the years evolved from assets and liabilities arising almost exclusively in the market place for the exchange of goods and services and for the preservation of wealth over time, recorded on the books and records of banks—excluding for the moment sovereign debt which historically has arisen outside the purview of day to day commerce, at least up until the last 100 years or so. The weakness of money lies in the challenge of maintenance of value and liquidity over time, which presents risk, uncertainty and threatens wealth preservation.

The necessity of preservation of wealth over time and the exigencies of increasing domestic and international trade gave rise over time to the development of central banks as lenders of last resort and more formalized monetary systems, centered on banking institutions. The monetary and financial system developed over the past 100 years; certainly, from the time of formation of the Federal Reserve System, to facilitate exchange of bills of exchange and trade acceptances as negotiable instruments. Capital and reserve requirements were met by holding sovereign money in cash in the form of United States dollars created and emitted by Congress, the value of which had been regulated by Congress as required of it by the *United States Constitution.*

The development of American and international financial markets and the nature of banking and sovereign debt crises has recently been brought up to date by Rheinhart and Rogoff, Barry Eichengreen, James Rickards, and Christopher Whalen, as well as other well-recognized experts in banking and finance as well as history, whose works are referred to in the Introduction and are cited throughout this work. I have provided references to this history of development throughout this work generally, but my concentration is on the fundamental principles that were designed to govern our financial system as well as any other safe and sound financial system. A cumulative progression of departures from these principles have led our recent financial crises. The importance of recognizing and understanding the scope of the complete financial system is essential to the enforcement of accountability for the financial crisis. The system includes the traditional notion of America's banking and financial system, including traditional global banking and finance, but more importantly for purposes of America's response to the ongoing financial crisis; the nature and extent of the so-called shadow banking system.

The shadow banking system developed in earnest out of the massive American balance of payments deficits, fiscal deficits and national debt that resulted directly from the Nixon shock and the final abandonment of any vestige of an attempt to tie the value of the dollar to any external source of reference by the abandonment of the *Bretton Woods Accords.* The explosion of undisciplined creation of money both in the banking system leading to the banking crisis of the late 1980s and early 1990s [asset value bubbles inflated and burst, high interest rates and high reported rates of inflation followed by bank and S&L failures, mitigated by regulatory forbearance and Fed interest rate subsidies to offset charges to bank capital] and then in both the regulated banking system through affiliates, complex counterparty arrangements and credit created to appear as true sales at artificially inflated values to avoid balance sheet disclosure, yielded the shadow banking system in which both Washington and Wall Street played primary roles. This process resulted in a financial crisis from which they emerged largely unscathed due to unprecedented Fed discount window lending to all comers, but particularly Wall Street banks, without adequate collateral and due to Fed purchases of shadow banking assets backed onto Wall Street bank balance sheets at artificially inflated values, while ordinary American households suffered damages estimated up to $20 trillion, approximately double the current gross assets of the primary Wall Street banks.

The explosion of public and private debt and dollars exported throughout the world through abandonment of any tie of the currency to a standard of value supported an American policy structure that established as a priority the principle that somehow the political expediency of spending and consuming more than we produce, as a conscious public policy, and the creation of huge portfolios of long terms assets, many of which at overstated and illiquid values, structured and misrepresented as short-term, high-quality liquid cash equivalent securities, could continue without end and without disastrous consequences. These policy principles and financial practices are the result of the power of accumulated wealth accompanying repeated decisive victories in world wars represent American national political hubris at its worst and most destructive. It also resulted in damages to ordinary citizens globally of up to at least $60 trillion.

F. A. Mann observed that:

> [i]t follows from the state theory of money that, generally, extrinsic alterations of currency can only be effected by legislative measures [in America, legislative measures taken in compliance with Article I, § 8, Clause 5 of the *United States Constitution*—not mentioned by Mann]. As regards the question under what circumstances intrinsic alterations may destroy the identity of the currency, a hard-and-fast rule cannot be laid down. With respect to depreciation of money, the working principle will probably have to be adopted that a "collapse," a catastrophic depreciation is required, or that the money must have become "worthless" or fantastically depreciated or was, as said in an American case, so depreciated as to "shock the conscience and produce an exclamation."

Mann leaves the issue there. Surely creation of an asset boom and bust causing up to at least $60 trillion globally, while Washington and Wall Street have made a mockery of fundamental moral principles of moral hazard and fiduciary legal duty through intentional corruption of the principles applicable to lenders of last resort to make of the central banks' "asset purchasers of last resort" through successive and continuing global practices of quantitative easing, which have served only as euphemistic bailouts for the Wall Street banks and political cover for Washington, is sufficient to "shock the conscience and produce an exclamation." Unfortunately, Mann has little to say about moral or legal protection of ordinary people from such crises or the accompanying perversion of the fundamental mission of central banks, in order to protect the interests of Washington and Wall Street.

As a matter of interest, note that Mann refers to what commentators call financial crises as resulting from money depreciation. Depreciation commonly refers to a decrease in the monetary value of an asset over time due to use, wear and tear or obsolescence. This decrease is measured as depreciation. Depreciation of an assets value over its useful life is an expected and anticipated occurrence. Debasement, on the other hand, is the practice of surreptitious lowering—debauching,[246] of the value of sovereign money created in the current circumstances by Washington and Wall Street through the existing Federal Reserve System, in relation to the corresponding value of assets in the market place, so that the actual value of the denominated money unit is reduced. Money debasement is illegal, a tort and a crime: an intentional misrepresentation of values represented in the banking system held by ordinary Americans. This distinction is clarified in detail in subsequent chapters of this work.

In order to enforce accountability for the current crisis, we need to understand the nature of the shadow banking system that has subsumed, distorted and corrupted our traditional banking system. Developing this understanding presents a number of difficulties. To continue the public policy charade that deficits, composed of public and private indebtedness do not matter, it has been necessary for Washington and Wall Street to deliberately ignore the actual size, composition and effects of the enormous amount of debt created through their banking credit originate and distribute model, securitized and moved off of bank records into public securities markets outside the strictures and control mechanisms of the closed world of regulated banking institutions, as it works its way through the shadow banking system as money of uncertain value yet denominated as United States dollars, and feeds back into the traditional banking sector, with disastrous effects all around.

To develop our understanding of what is generally viewed as inside the banking system as viewed by Washington and Wall Street we must define and evaluate the forces at play in the evolution and then the explosion in size and effect of the shadow banking system. This will drive confirm the fraudulent misrepresentations—bank fraud—conducted though Washington and Wall Street abuse of power. What is inside of the traditional box and what has been outside of that box—in the shadow banking system?

[B] Risk Versus Uncertainty

Risk is predictable and can be specifically and legally allocated. This has been the traditional business of bankers in performing their traditional banking role. This allocation of risk contractually in the form of loan documentation constitutes the bread and butter of most American banking attorneys' law practice.

Uncertainty due to the passage of time, political risk, and development of new forms of money in the "shadow banking system", changes in money supply and changes in velocity of money circulation is not predictable.

- Money is messy more now than ever.
- Money is not a given assumption inside the box—either in amount, value, velocity of use or liquidity.

Bank assets are valued and exchanged in monetary terms and those monetary accounts express the continued value of the assets in monetary terms over time as determined by banking law and regulation and by Generally Accepted Accounting Principles, consistently applied.

- High revealed levels of monetary uncertainty →
- High levels of value uncertainty →
- High discounts rates in asset valuation →
- Capital market dysfunction →
- Charges to bank capital and income →
- Greater illiquidity →
- Liquidity crisis →
- Solvency crisis.

[C] Outside of the Box and Inside the Box

Outside the Box v. Inside the Box. High revealed levels of monetary uncertainty equate to high levels of value uncertainty; which equate to high discounts rates in asset valuation; which equate to capital market dysfunction; Which, in the absence of regulatory enforcement forbearance and/or wide open Federal Reserve discount window lending, bailout legislation and Quantitative Easing shadow banking financial asset purchases by the Fed from Wall Street banks at inflated values supported by artificially low interest rates, leads to write downs of asset values, recognition of non-performing assets and charges to bank capital and income; which results in a liquidity crisis; which ultimately produces a solvency crisis and systemic financial and economic crisis.

Outside of the Box	vs	Inside the Box
Economic shadow money	vs	Sovereign legal money
Unregulated credit money		Fiat money Regulated credit money
Unrestrained creation of credit money, including securities, derivative, fiscal deficits, and global financial imbalances	vs	Bad acts, regulatory pressure fear of institutional contagion
External	vs	Internal
Macroeconomic	vs	Microeconomic
Macroprudential supervision and regulation	vs	Microprudential supervision and regulation
Exogenous	vs	Endogenous
Outside sovereign legal monetary financial box	vs	Inside sovereign legal monetary financial box

Money denominated in US dollars created outside the box is fungible and thus moves inside, betwixt and between the boxes, debasing the value of all money denominated in US dollars. In an attempt to soak up excess liquidity unsupported by corresponding value the Fed has simply removed the overvalued illiquid assets from the market place in exchange for substituted newly created units of sovereign money denominated in Federal Reserve Notes backed by no standard of value regulated in accordance with the *United States Constitution*. The losses are now hidden by holding them at par on the Fed's balance sheet while artificially supporting values by such purchases and by artificially suppressing interest rates through Fed policy and purchases of government bonds by the Fed. Any semblance of regulation of the value of the dollar or of the securitized shadow banking assets imported onto the Fed's balance sheet has been abandoned.

Figure 3.1 Fed Balance Sheet

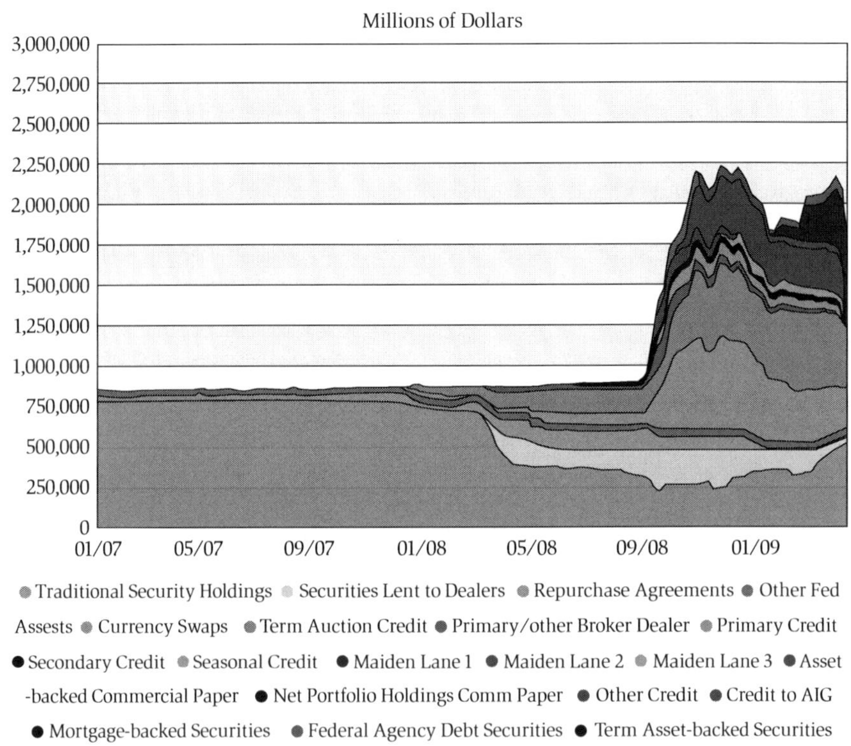

The massive investment by the Fed illustrated in the chart above has left it incredibly over-leveraged by any reasonable standard. According to William F. Ford, former president of the Federal Reserve Bank of Atlanta, holder of the Weatherford Chair of Finance at Middle Tennessee State University and visiting research fellow at the American Institute for Economic Research, in a *Forbes* article May 6, 2011: "At year-end 2007, the Fed had capital equal to about 4% of its total assets, or 25:1 leverage. By year-end 2010, the Fed had only 2.2% capital (now 1.95%), which implies leverage of 45:1 (now over 51:1). The Federal Reserve Bank of New York also now has an astounding 98:1 leverage ratio."

Also, according to Ford, "At year-end 2010 the Federal Reserve Banks held $2.224 trillion (now $2.464 trillion) of U.S. Treasury securities and long-term mortgage-backed securities. Currently, only about $18 billion of the Fed's holdings are short-term Treasury bills.

The Fed has said that it will sell some of the medium and long-term securities when it decides to shrink its balance sheet toward its pre-recession 2007 level (about $915 billion). Under GAAP and banking regulations, such "available-for-sale securities" should be marked to market value in financial reports. But the Fed does not do this. Also, the public does not know the actual market value of those assets—many of which the Fed took off the hands of deeply troubled financial institutions." Of course, this mark to market value has not been done. In fact, as described later in this chapter, the Fed has sporadically continued its purchases using principal payments on its portfolio to continue to maintain its portfolio and as good assets pay off, concentrate its portfolio in an ever-growing percentage of toxic assets. These so-called open market purchases has but a pale pretense of market discipline through a bidding process that is in fact largely limited to the same institutions continuing to play footsie with the Fed. Quantitative Tightening, much heralded as a Fed effort to return the banking system to some semblance, has faced the same fate as planned and announced increases in the Fed benchmark interest rate to what the Fed considered more appropriate levels. The Fed's waffling positions on quantitative tightening and a higher interest rate policy constitute a continuing policy of "delay and pray" with the aspiration that the prospects for financial crisis accountability will continue to be delayed and ultimately avoided.

Many of these same deeply troubled financial institutions also served as the Fed's agents in effecting the so-called open market bid purchases, but which were in substance simply creating dollars to replace the losses that should have been booked on the respective banks records, but having moved to the Fed's books, were not disclosed. They have not been disclosed yet. Maintenance by the Fed of artificially low interest rates, thereby artificially supporting the values of these types of securities, whether on the Fed's books or on the books of other financial institutions. It all boils down to deliberate, planned, intentional, manipulation and misrepresentation of the value of supposedly money equivalent securities and thus also the values of derivatives based on those securities that constituted the flood of money in the shadow banking system.

The Fed's massive asset purchases have not served to force market pricing and clearing of financial assets; they have not added new money to the financial system—they have merely publicly monetized what had previously been privately monetized in the shadow banking system at ever increasing inflated values. This binge has served only to buy time, extending and pretending—kicking the can down the road—to use a few of the popular idiomatic catch phrases of the day, producing an illusion of stability, liquidity and value sustainability in the current state of American economic affairs. Little to none of the money created by the Fed as a part of this program has benefitted the economy or created jobs. It has simply misrepresented asset and money values in the Washington/Wall Street financial economy to sustain Wall Street and effect the policy of Washington and Wall Street as privileged players, too big to fail, too big to jail, too big to hold accountable. That constitutes Washington's and Wall Street's mutually beneficial compact of self-protection and self-dealing through fraud, abuse of power, and deprivation of all other participants in the financial markets of their constitutional right to due process under and equal protection of the American rule of law; leaving a $20 trillion trail of damages to the American public in their wake. The Washington Wall Street enterprise constitutes a fraudulent scheme that purports to resolve the financial crisis, while at the same time continuing and increasingly benefiting Washington and Wall Street.

Shadow banking was at one time a well-defined commercial process that fed the engines of commerce and increased economic prosperity. At that time, financial probity, mutual knowledge and respect, trust and confidence were the prevailing characteristics of the merchants and the bankers, taken as a group. Shadow banking grew out of the practice of discounting and trading bills of exchange, acceptances and notes arising out of commercial transactions and bearing the personal liability of the maker, dealer, acceptor and endorser; and the liquidity of the market for these high quality financial assets being backed, in England, by the central bank, the Bank of England. A review of the origins of what we now refer to as shadow banking; that is banking outside of the regulated depository financial institution model, is in order. It clarifies the dominant role of moral and legal principles and personal and institutional accountability for adherence to those principles as the defining characteristics of 19th century shadow banking. This can be contrasted with the dominant role of avoidance of and insulation from and disregard of moral and legal principles and personal and institutional accountability for adherence to those principles as the defining characteristics of 21st century shadow banking.

§3.04 MORAL AND LEGAL EVOLUTION OF SHADOW BANKING

Carolyn Sissoke of the USC Gould School of Law, Center for Law and Social Science has provided and excellent comparison and contrast of shadow banking's origins in 19th century English commerce and contrasting its moral and legal foundation and structured accountability for performance with that of the 21st century American and global show banking system that led directly to the financial crisis.[247] The current shadow banking system is fatally flawed from a both a moral and legal prospective. Without fundamental reform. This system is poised for a continuation of the ongoing crisis and a dramatic forced rebalancing of our financial and monetary systems through potentially catastrophic social, financial, economic, moral and legal upheaval.

Ms. Sissoko observes that:

> Financial institutional development matured in the 19th c. and I argue that it set off a wave of economic growth in what are now known as the "developed" countries that has continued more or less up through the present day. The foundational institutional structure that made it possible for 19th c. economies to overcome the

> financial constraints that had restrained economic growth for millennia provides very important lessons about economic incentives and the means by which institutions can be used to align them. The lessons of 19th c. finance are important, in my view, first, because we in the 21st century have inherited an institutional structure the key components of which we have yet to study and understand, and second, because changes that have been made to this structure in recent decades may well be undermining its integrity. If I am correct, then structural damage to the financial system, if it continues, has the potential to lead to a complete collapse of the financial system—and a return to the growth rates that were experienced before the modern era.[248]

Although Ms. Sissoko's primary goal in her paper is to examine the use of short term collateralized money market instruments to finance the banking system, her response to the case made by Mehrling, et.al., for the continued use of the now omnipresent structured finance model, backed by a new "dealer of last resort" that would provide asset price support for investment bank dealers, just as the Fed as the lender of last resort for bankers is intended to provide liquidity support to the banks is important. Ms. Sissoko makes her case for the lack of an appropriate foundation for the creation and use of a dealer of last resort structure to support shadow bank financing of banking through the pervasive use of short term collateralized money market instruments that serve to monetize, on a basis that is represented to be liquid at par, ultimately backed by a web of structural devices, including securitization and derivatives based thereon, by financial models, opinions and ratings, repurchase agreements, re-hypothecation transactions, booking loans as true sales for accounting purposes and other devices designed to reduce capital requirements and reserves and increase leverage, and ultimately backed by information-intensive long term illiquid credit secured by illiquid assets, aggregated in pools and sliced into tranches that are virtually impossible to unwind in the event of a default. For our purposes, Ms. Sisokko's secondary goal is most compelling: to "... interpret the history of banking, and more particularly to demonstrate how utterly unfounded are many commonplace assertions about that history," as that history relates to the current state of shadow money and shadow banking:

> I find that in 19th c. Britain, the unsecured money market instruments that circulated were of extremely high quality and there was virtually no risk of creditor losses. How was it possible to establish such a safe system of unsecured credit? First, the instruments that circulated bore at least two promises to pay, that of the issuer and that of the acceptor, and in order to sell the instrument the seller had to promise to pay it too. This legal structure had the effect of aligning the incentives of everyone who circulated the debt. Second, bank owners, even joint share owners, were subject to capital calls in the event that creditors were losing money in the liquidation of a bank. Once again, the legal structure aligned the incentives of the market participants. Third, the assets that were financed were short-term, limiting their price volatility and exposure to unexpected events. Finally, whenever there was a crisis of confidence in the system, the Bank of England as lender of last resort stood ready to expand the money supply and prevent the panic and general withdrawal of access to credit from causing needless defaults. Because the bankers had to guarantee all the debt they circulated, the lender of last resort protected not only the economy, but also the bankers from having to liquidate their personal assets in order to make good on all the defaults that would have taken

place in a general collapse of credit. In short, the lender of last resort made the continued offering of banking services incentive compatible despite the bankers' liability for bad debts … .

It is remarkable that none of these lessons about the incentives faced by bankers that can be drawn from the 19th c. British experience are recognized in the current literature on banking. On the contrary, the process of securitization employed a complex sequence of transactions in order circumvent the traditional bank guarantee on the assets sold—only to meet with the surprised discovery that the traditional rule was designed to align incentives. Instead of recognizing that the foundations of modern banking were laid in an environment where bankers were liable for the debts they circulated and where the existence of a lender of last resort was necessary to reduce the risks faced by bankers sufficiently that banking services could be provided throughout the economy, it is commonly argued that banks are "always" bailed out in crises. Instead of analyzing why the finance of long-term assets on money markets creates extraordinary risks for the economy, the modern literature assumes that this is what a money market does. In short, until we make the effort to understand the value of the institutions that we have inherited, we are in danger of destroying them out of ignorance.[249]

It is in the 19th century shadow banking environment that we begin to discover the well-defined separate functions of:

- sovereign money, the value of which was regulated by reference to specified quantities and qualities of gold and silver, produced by the central bank on behalf of the sovereign;
- depository banking system, holding and lending sovereign money backed by gold or silver;
- dealers in real bills; and
- merchants that exchanged goods and services for real bills.

This structure substantively accomplished the birth of modern banking:

[It] was a revolution in unsecured lending that fostered modern economic growth by overcoming the liquidity constraints that are ubiquitous in an unbanked economy. The key elements of the revolution are, first, private banks that (i) are trusted not to default, and that (ii) use their own ability to borrow to make it possible for the other members of the economy to borrow by offering them overdraft accounts and monitoring their behavior, and, second, a central bank that can provide liquidity to protect this credit system from collapsing at the first hint of trouble.[250]

[A] The "Real Bills Doctrine"

As the middle ages were ending Europe developed a financial instrument called the bill of exchange that was managed by a network of wealthy merchant bankers. In its initial form the bill of exchange was used to finance international trade between Europe's leading cities. The bill was a short-term debt contract that was payable in a foreign country. Clearing mechanisms enabled trade in these bills to minimize the transport of gold and silver across Europe.

Starting in the sixteenth century the bill of exchange evolved into a very different instrument. Endorsement allowed bills to circulate from hand to hand before being redeemed, and domestic bills became the norm in highly developed commercial economies. Local bankers managed local networks and stood ready to discount bills before they were due. Thus, a tradesman with a local bank account could write a bill in the name of a supplier, who could then choose to hold the bill, endorse the bill over to a creditor of his own, or cash it—less a discount—at the bank. The bill was a form of commercial paper that was endorsable and effectively allowed banks to underwrite a system of trade credit for the local community. The result was that trade in urban economies began to take place on the basis of a paper monetary system that was supported by a network of banks.

In order for the system to work, standards had to be put into place to prevent the local tradesmen from writing too many bills. In practice a single principle was used to regulate this credit system: A bill was valid only if it was issued in exchange for goods. Bills that were written in the absence of a real exchange were described as "fictitious" or "accommodation paper." Any tradesman who was caught issuing fictitious bills was considered a fraud and excluded from the financial network. Suspicion of such fraud could also derail a tradesman's career.

The principle that bills were valid only when they were issued in exchange for real goods—or when they were "real bills"—was the standard our early modern ancestors put in place to ensure that finance served the needs of trade. It had the advantage of being applied at the individual level, creating a completely decentralized means by which the issue of financial paper could be controlled. Nowadays the term real bills is used only in the context of "the real bills doctrine," which played an important part in the debate over monetary policy that took place in England in the early 19th century, and is associated with Adam Smith. The Currency School argued that the Bank of England should be constrained to issue bank notes in an amount that did not exceed the amount of gold it held in its vaults, while the Banking School argued that, since the bills circulating were real, this fact was sufficient to control the money supply and that the Bank needed to have the flexibility to issue an indeterminate quantity of bank notes when discounting real bills. It's worth noting that the idea that the only valid bills were real bills was so fundamental to the 18th and early 19th century concept of financial stability, that no one questioned it. The issue in the debate was whether limiting the circulating money supply to real bills was alone sufficient to ensure financial stability.[251]

[B] Acceptance Finance

In the meanwhile, the British economy was steadily outgrowing the restriction to circulating only real bills. By the start of the 19th century in England the system of domestic bills had evolved into acceptance finance. A country tradesman who regularly shipped his wares to a London middleman for sale would draw on his account with the middleman when making purchases in his own local community. The tradesman would write a bill drawn on the London middleman to pay his local supplier. The supplier would go ahead and circulate the bill through endorsement. However, until the bill was discounted at the local bank, sent by the banker off to his London correspondent for settlement and formally accepted by the London middleman as an obligation, there was no certainty under the law that the middleman would pay:

> In short, acceptance finance was a prototype for the checking account system that would develop decades later—just like a checking account system it required that (i) bad bills or checks be passed infrequently and (ii) middlemen or bankers could be relied on to honor their obligations. When one recognizes the sophistication of the financial system in Britain at the turn of the 19th century, one begins to understand why Henry Thornton considered the "science" of credit to be the fundamental source of British growth at the time. ...
>
> It was probably inevitable that the practice of acceptance finance broke down the cultural barriers that had supported the restriction to the circulation of real bills only. Henry Thornton's *Paper Credit* makes it clear that by the early years of the 19th century, some British bankers were beginning to realize that a "good bill" could be backed by nothing more than an individual's personal credit.
>
> Legal cases demonstrate that the use of accommodation paper was growing—and becoming more acceptable—through the first decades of the 19th century. The Banking Act of 1844 started a different trend: banks that were no longer allowed to issue bank notes found another way to create money, the checking account. These two trends combined to create a new financial system centered around banks as the arbiters of credit.
>
> The 19th century witnessed a transition from a decentralized system of paper money that was controlled by the principle that only real bills were valid to a more complex system in which short-term monetized credit was allocated by banks. A new approach had to be found to control the growth of the new monetary system based on checking accounts. The Banking Act of 1844 had been a first effort at direct control of the money supply. It was unsuccessful in many ways: In the first quarter century after it was passed, it had to be suspended three times in order to protect the economy from the ravages of liquidity crises. And the growth of checking accounts effectively neutered the Act.
>
> In the meanwhile, however, the Bank of England had a discovered a new tool for controlling the money supply. In the 18th century the Bank's discount rate had remained fixed at 5%. As a consequence, in normal times competing banks took most of the trade, and the Bank's discount business was relatively small. In a liquidity crisis, however, the Bank's discounts would increase astronomically for a few days or even weeks only to fall back to normal when the panic had eased.
>
> In the first half of the 19th century a major concern of the Bank was the maintenance of its gold reserves. Thus, the outflow of gold that was associated with crises and strong demand for discounts at the Bank caused concern. It didn't take long for the Directors of the Bank to realize that by raising the discount rate, they could moderate the outflow of gold. In the 1820s Bank Rate, or the discount rate of the Bank of England, started to be used as a policy tool. By the middle of the century Bank Rate was the principal policy tool that the Bank used to control the flows of gold to and from the Bank and to moderate the growth of credit and of the money supply.[252]

[C] Origin of Fiat Money

The finance of the Napoleonic wars in the late 1700s put any enormous train of the English banking system, particularly on the Bank of England, which risked running out of gold. The bulk of daily monetary transactions had come to be settled primarily through local bank notes. Large transactions were conducted with Bank of England notes. In 1797 the Bank of England suspended convertibility to conserve gold reserves. At the same time, the Bank of England discovered that it could conserve gold by raising its discount rate. Thus began the policy of central bank use of tits discount rate as a toll to moderated the outflow of gold and by the Bank of England management of its discount rate became the principal policy tool the bank used to control the flow of gold to and from the bank and to moderate the growth of credit and the growth of the money supply.[253]

During the period of suspension of convertibility of bank notes in gold, the Bank of England converted to a system of redemption of bank notes by Bank of England notes that came to be considered to be as good as gold. Thus the English monetary system shifted to a fiat system where the dominant money shifted to bank notes redeemable by notes of the Bank of England When the Bank of England resumed convertibility of the Bank of England notes into gold after 25 years after its experience with fiat money, it reverted to the original conversion. The same mistake made by the Federal Reserve following the Great Depression. The fiat money experience led to an increase in the money supply that could not then be supported by the conversion rate attendant to the smaller money supply. In both cases, the return to the pre-crisis conversion ratio led to a damaging reduction in the money supply that led to recession and depression.[254] When the Bank of England resumed convertibility of its notes into gold, Bank of England notes had displaced gold as a mode of settling trades because the notes had become accepted as a gold substitute in the final settlement of debt:[255]

> Thus, the foundations of a modern banking system were laid in 19th century Britain. Paper bank notes were universally accepted in final settlement of debt. The banking system offered checking accounts to the general public and short-term credit to those that met the criteria of the bankers. And finally the whole system was moderated by the Bank of England's control over the short term interest rate on bills discounted at the Bank, and, as will be discussed in detail below, supported by the Bank of England's practice of acting as a source of liquidity for the whole banking system during a financial crisis.[256]

[D] Liquidity and Economic Growth

The discipline of the English monetary system and its ability to expand in alignment with the increase in trade was the foundation for the growth and prosperity of English trade, commerce and industry. The foundation for the growth and prosperity was that:[257]

- English banks were trusted not to default on their unsecured obligations.
- This trust supported broad lending on an unsecured basis within the local community.
- Banks monitored the borrowers.
- Banks could rely on the Bank of England to support the system of unsecured credit at times of crisis.

The notes that circulated in England originated largely as bills of exchange with their origins in trade credit, supported by the personal liability "wrapping structure" and backed by the Bank of England discount in exchange for Bank of England notes that were redeemable in specie. This process permitted expansion of the money supply grounded in knowledge, origin in real market exchanges—real bills—backed by the Bank of England that were as good as the gold in which they could be redeemed. Although the bills that traded on a daily basis were unsecured, the banking system structure was grounded in the real market, the wrapping of liability to support and provide accountability for payment, and gold and silver redemption at the central bank level.[258] This system inspired and supported trust in the monetary system; trust and confidence being the fundamental drivers of liquidity. And liquidity being driven by alignment of the parties in the integrity of the "wrapped liability" supporting the real transactions where the credit originated and the backing of the central bank reserves in specie and willingness to lend to support liquidity as a lender of last resort. Sissoko summarizes the features of this structure as follows:[259]

- Public trust and confidence in the fortune, probity and prudence of a particular banker.
- Belief that the banker is always ready to pay upon demand such of his notes as are likely to be at any time presented to him.
- Those notes then come to have the same currency as gold and silver money, based on the trust and confidence that such money can at any time be had for them.

Henry Thornton, a London banker at the turn of the century, emphasized that "the local commercial community supported the circulation of a banker's liabilities, because they were the ones who benefited from the banker's loans. Thus, the key function of banks was to provide credit to commerce that would not have been available in the absence of the circulation of bankers' liabilities. Of course, as lenders, bankers were also monitors of those who borrowed. For Thornton, the key to the economic growth that he was witnessing in Britain was the fact that Britain had bankers in most country towns monitoring the unsecured credit that was being extended within the local community. He writes:

> Through the creation of banks, the appreciation of the credit of numberless persons engaged in commerce has become a science; and to the height to which this science is now carried in Great Britain we are in no small degree indebted for the flourishing state of our internal commerce, for the general reputation of our merchants abroad, and for the preference which in that respect they enjoy over the traders of all other nations. It is certainly the interest, and, I believe, it is also the

> general practice, of banks to limit not only the loan which anyone trader shall obtain from themselves, but the total amount also, as far as they are able, of the sum which the same person shall borrow in different places; at the same time, reciprocally to communicate intelligence for their mutual assistance; and, above all, to discourage bills of accommodation.[260]

[E] Central Bank Support of Bank Notes

Adam Smith and Henry Thornton both recognized that the foundation for the monetary structure based on unsecured credit was the existence of a central bank ready at all time to provide liquidity. Central bank willingness to provide liquidity in times of liquidity crises was based upon the "clear connection between the system of unsecured credit that was underwritten by the banking system and economic growth. The essential elements of this system of unsecured credit were."[261]

- First, private banks that: (i) were trusted by the members of the local community; and that (ii) used their own ability to borrow to make it possible for the other members of the economy to borrow by lending to them and monitoring their behavior, and,
- Second, a central bank that provides liquidity to protect this unsecured credit system from collapsing when the trust on which the system is based is thrown temporarily into doubt.

The entire system of shadow money in 19th century England was based on the integrity of unsecured credit that was virtually risk free. The combination of factors that gave rise to this risk-free character of the circulating bank notes detailed above meant that any monetary crisis that occurred was purely a liquidity crisis—not a solvency crisis.

The role of the bank of England, as a lender of last resort then, was circumscribed and aligned with the monetary foundation for which it served as a base.

> This system of trusted bankers who underwrote the debt of the broader economy and were supported by the central bank was able to generate assets that were effectively risk-free. Because of the high quality of the assets, the crises that took place in 19th c. Britain were pure liquidity crisis, and, when the Bank of England acted as a lender of last resort, almost all losses on the assets were borne by market participants, not the Bank. There were no central bank bailouts of banks in 19th c. Britain.
>
> The Bank of England, which was a publicly listed company and had no formal obligation to support the banking system, was willing to provide liquidity to the banking system, because it did so by purchasing assets that were virtually risk-free even though they were unsecured. After explaining the costs associated with managing collateral, Thornton concludes that these costs clearly exceeded any benefits from taking collateral, given the quality of the assets the bank purchased: "the bills which the bank discounts, are, generally speaking, so safe, that the security either of goods, or stocks, or land, none of which are received in pledge by the directors, may be considered as nearly superfluous." Seventy years later, Walter Bagehot explained that the lender of last resort could reject dubious assets—because there are so few of them in a "commercial country":

> No advances indeed need be made by which the Bank will ultimately lose. The amount of bad business in commercial countries is an infinitesimally small fraction of the whole business. That in a panic the bank, or banks, holding the ultimate reserve should refuse bad bills or bad securities will not make the panic really worse; the 'unsound' people are a feeble minority, and they are afraid even to look frightened for fear their unsoundness may be detected.
>
> And after careful analysis of the data economic historians have found that these contemporary authors were indeed correct: "The Bank of England operated in an almost perfectly risk-free market, whereby losses were entirely transferred to market participants."[262]

The characteristics made it possible for the 19th century English banking system to create risk free assets were:

- "wrapping" of the debt by every party who sold it;
- the requirement that even stockholders in a failed joint stock bank protect creditors by contributing to the liquidation of the failed bank;
- the limitation of the money market to short-term debt; and
- the presence of a lender of last resort which made it possible for the money market to survive a financial panic without collapsing.[263]

[F] Wrapping Shadow Money: Alignment of Liability and Accountability

Notes circulating in the shadow banking system of 19th Century England, provided what the 21st Century Americana and global shadow banking system specifically lacks:[264]

- Each bill or note issuer was liable for its payment.
- Each bill or note endorser was liable for its payment.
- Each banker who discounted the bill or note and endorsed it over to another party was liable for its payment.
- The Bank of England only discounted bills or notes that had been accepted by a merchant bank which thereby put its own guarantee to pay on the bill.
- Once a bill or note had been accepted, it circulated as a liquid money market instrument in London because it could be discounted by any of several eligible discounters.
- The liquidity of each money market bill or note derived from the combination of bank guarantees and the availability of the central bank as a backstop.

As a result of this system, every bill discounted by the Bank of England carried with it three independent promises of payment: that of the issuer, that of the acceptor, and that of the discounter. Observe that the legal structure of such guarantees was designed to align every party's interest in the quality of the underlying debt. Because the discounter was fully liable for the debt, debt was likely discounted only if the discounter had reason to believe that it was good. Similarly, the acceptor would only accept the bill if the issuer of the bill either had funds (or more accurately goods) deposited with the acceptor or the acceptor was confident that value of the bill would soon be available. Thus, a bank-based monetary system developed in an environment where all of the parties transacting in debt were liable and none had any interest in circulating debt that was not of high quality.[265]

There bills and notes were virtually risk free.

As we will later see, shadow money in the 21st century is structured to create not multiple of liability and accountability for payment, but rather to begin with information and underwriting collateral, to mix and bundle similar credits, to do so through multiple layers of special purpose entities that serve to shield liability at each level and separate payment priorities into tranches, issue the trading assets as securities requiring disclosures only that do a very poor job of preserving liability and accountability, but in fact substituting at each level complex structures of derivatives, swaps, repurchase agreement interspersed with rating agency opinions and other forms of credit enhancements that rather that supporting payment liability and account and accountability, instead diffuse it, confuse it and render these structural instruments virtually and practically unenforceable in the event of a liquidity crisis. Traditional shadow banking has now been turned on its head and now magnifies risk and uncertainty and defeats accountability.

[G] The Trusted Bank and the Trusted Banker

The trusted banker that was the arbiter of credit supporting the high-quality unsecured debt that constituted the 19th century English shadow banking monetary system were highly regarded. The trust and confidence they inspired was not limited to purely assessments of character. "The fact that issuers and bankers faced unlimited liability—or capital calls if they were stockholders—on their obligations also played an important role in the risk-free nature of 19th century money market assets. While the unlimited liability of partners in an unincorporated bank is well-understood, many do not realize that the joint-stock banks that proliferated over the course of the 19th century in Britain were also structured so that the owners would face a capital call in the event that there were unpaid debts in bankruptcy:

> Joint stock investors in 19th c. Britain typically paid only a fraction of the par value of the shares. For this reason, the corporation—or in the case of bankruptcy the liquidator—retained the right to call the remaining value of the shares until par was fully paid up. Given this liability structure, in 19th c. Britain one of the reasons for confidence in the guarantees provided by the banking system was the visible personal wealth of the bankers themselves and the knowledge that this wealth was at stake.[266]

[H] Structured Insulation from Liability and Accountability: The Oxymoron of Monetized Long-Term Illiquid Assets

Bills and notes negotiated and exchanges in the 19th century shadow banking system were all of short term and the highest quality. The short term of the instruments mitigated against elements of risk and uncertainty of payment that likelihood of which increases in over time. Shadow money in the 20th century is plagued with the high levels of risk and uncertainty inherent in the long term assets backing them, the rapid deterioration of information relating to collateral and credit of the underlying issuers, and diffusion of responsibility for underwriting and incentives to originators to mix higher quality assets with lower quality assets in pools and to render confirmation and reconfirmation of credit and asset quality through the employment of algorithmic models and assumed homogeneity of data bases and relevance of past data to future performance and long term asset valuation and liquidity. Where 19th century shadow money benefited from trust and confidence in liability and accountability for payment, value, and liquidity, 21st century shadow money suffers from long term illiquid assets, may of low quality, or "subprime" not called "toxic", posing as short term, high quality, liquid assets, with risk, uncertainty, liability and accountability for payment presented as diversified and stabilized when in fact these negative asset characteristics are in fact concentrated and compounded and represent artificially created value attributable to credit concentrations driven by profitability of structure and represent purely short term financial assets suitable primarily for speculative trading and which do not drive trade and economic growth. All in all, 21st century shadow money is the diametric opposite in terms of clarity and predictability of structure, alignment of liability and accountability, applications of traditional banking skills to credit and underwriting and the avoidance of presentation as the highest quality short term liquid assets—money substitutes—that possess none of the qualities that supported the success of shadow money substitutes in the 19th century shadow banking world and the economic growth and social stability for which it was the fundamental driver.

It is no surprise that creation of shadow money by financial engineers and securities dealers through structured securitized finance is constructed upon layer after layer of ever more diffused levels of ownership without a structural component of continuity of direct liability and accountability for payment, and where the manufacturers of these instruments of speculation are compensated currently at each level creation of the money instruments without retaining liability for the value and liquidity of the monetized product will ultimately result in ever diminishing asset quality. That is the story of the financial crisis.

§3.05 SACRIFICE OF TRADITIONAL PRINCIPLES OF COMMERCIAL BANKING LAW IN SHADOW BANKING

The "monetary assets" purchased by the Fed should either have been denied the public expectations of liquidity and value sustainability through regulation of the value of currency in the first instance; or if these short term derivatives of long term assets were contemplated to be treated as monetary assets, their liquidity and value sustainability should have been regulated through rights of redemption supported by regulation of the value of money by Congress in accordance with the requirements of the *Constitution* and through the protections offered by the fundamental principles of commercial law relating to the credit instruments underlying the securities and corresponding derivatives, and the values discounted to reflect the inherent long term illiquid nature of the underlying assets. The applicable commercial law protections are based on and incorporated in the *Uniform Commercial Code* (UCC). When the code was adopted, it expressed the first principles of "good faith" meaning "honesty in fact in the conduct or transaction concerned ((UCC 1—201 (19))[267] that affect the members of the general public. Even amongst merchants, the standard under UCC 2—104[268] meant "honesty in fact and the observance of the reasonable commercial standards of fair dealing in the trade", a requirement that applied to every step of "performance or enforcement." Further, a related provision that applies to the disparity in bargaining power between the American public on the one hand and the Washington Wall Street combination on the other, was UCC 2—302[269] which deals with "unconscionable" or "one-sided" contracts and clauses. The principle at work here is the prevention of oppression and unfair surprise for the unsuspecting public through a device that unfairly or deceptively distorts the allocation of risk and uncertainty inherent in the long term assets underlying the short term derivative money substitutes based thereon, through the exploitation of superior bargaining power and the perpetuation of misleading commercial, legal and accounting structures.

The UCC also incorporated extensive provisions designed to protect parties to financial transactions relating to confirmation of asset quality, title, warranties, and duties of care in conduct of transactions, liability of transferors or endorsers, sureties for performance or payment of negotiable instruments. The power and ability to enforce these commercial law protections is diffused and diminished through the complexity of securitization (which substitutes meaningless disclosures for substantive rights) and structured finance and absolutely and completely lost through the creation of derivatives based on the securities, based upon the platform of supposedly homogenized credit instruments. Washington and Wall Street have combined to violate these first principles of commercial law on all counts through their exploitation of the shadow banking system.

[A] Securities Law as a Poor Substitute for the Law of Money, Commerce and Banking

Even so, the attempt to separate the protections afforded by commercial law to the public from the defects of shadow money created through securitizations and derivatives, has still failed to thwart all claims for liability for securities fraud committed by the originators and distributors of shadow money instruments. Wall Street accountability for securities fraud on an occasional basis does not address the intentionally fraudulent combinations beginning at the individual credit asset level and magnified through the structured finance process through the creation of shadow money and its further leverage through diffusion through the formal banking and monetary system. There has been massive widespread fraud through each level of creation of the shadow banking and shadow money monster, but the base level of intentional fraud and misrepresentation, and ultimate accountability for it lies in the ultimate corruption and debasement of American sovereign money by Washington and Wall Street through the abuse of their combined power for self-interest.

[B] Shadow Banking with No Effective Shadow Banking Law

The Fed has now become the central bank of the world, without any debate on the floor of the Senate or the Congress and without the knowledge or understanding of the American people.[270]

Its stock in trade and power has been expanded throughout the shadow banking world without acknowledgement or respect of the duties and obligations attendant to expansion of its power and influence.

The adequacy of the collateralization of the enormous amount of shadow banking credit assets purchased by the Fed is unclear and represents considerable risk, particularly in contemplation of Fed interest rate increases. As rates go up, securities' values determined irrespective of collateral and underwriting quality, based solely on yield measurement in the capital and financial markets, will decrease and thus will losses imbedded in the structure of those assets also increase. The Committee on Financial Market Regulation has recommended that any Fed holdings of credit to the private sector which are uncollateralized or insufficiently collateralized should be transferred in an orderly fashion to the federal government—the Treasury. Any losses suffered by the Fed or Treasury are ultimately losses for the US taxpayers and should be directly and transparently accounted for as a part of the federal budget.[271]

Instead, *Reuters* reported that at December 31, 2015 the Fed "buys $4.1 billion of mortgage bonds, sells none. The Federal Reserve bought $4.138 billion of agency mortgage-backed securities in the week from Nov. 26 to Dec. 2, compared with $5.974 billion purchased the previous week, the New York Federal Reserve Bank said on Thursday. In a move to help the housing market begun in October 2011, the US central bank has been using funds from principal payments on the agency debt and agency mortgage-backed securities, or MBS, it holds to reinvest in agency MBS. The New York Fed said on its website the Fed sold no mortgage securities guaranteed by Fannie Mae, Freddie Mac or the Government National Mortgage Association, or Ginnie Mae, in the latest week. It sold none the prior week."[272]

Although the Fed announced a policy of gradual increases in the Fed funds rate accompanied by a reduction in its securities holding, The Fed quickly walked back those policy decisions in response to pressure from the financial markets. The protests were predictable in any event. The maintenance of an ultra-low Fed funds rate accompanied by curtailment of the announced quantitative tightening suits their interests, but not necessarily the public interest. On September 26, 2008, just before the Great Financial Crisis, the Fed's holdings of securities totaled just under $780 billion. As of this writing, the Fed's securities totaled just under $3.9 trillion.[273] So much for quantitative tightening and honest market pricing of shadow money.

There is no credible evidence that these open market activities by the Fed achieve any purpose other than to maintain the existence of the originate and distribute model favored by Washington and the government sponsored financial institutions, and enable them to hedge against the predictable effects of pending interest rate increases on the securities purchased by the Fed and moved off of the Washington and Wall Street insiders books at par while they maintain their fee and trading income franchises.

Reinhart and Rogoff, discussing the concept of contagion, have observed that "[c]ommon shocks need not be all external. Countries may share common "domestic" macroeconomic fundamentals, such as housing bubbles, capital inflow bonanzas, increasing private and (or) public leveraging, and so on."[274] This goes with the concept that system is global and that global phenomena such as proliferation of fiat currency, credit securitization and supporting derivatives, when revealed as unsustainable, provide system wide shocks. "The most significant hurdle in establishing and effective and credible early warning system, however, is not the design of a systemic framework that is capable of producing relatively reliable signals of distress from the various indicators in a timely manner. The greatest barrier to success is the well-entrenched tendency of policy makers and market participants to treat the signals as irrelevant archaic residuals of an outdated framework [including the commercial law protections and conventions that support valid and honest valuation and accounting for credit assets], assuming that the old rules of valuation no longer apply. If the past we have studied in this book is any guide, these signals will be dismissed more often than not. That is why we also need to think about improving institutions.[275]

Reinhart & Rogoff further observed that "[f]or governments, the International Monetary fund (IMF) could provide a public good by having an extremely rigorous standard for government debt accounting that included implicit guarantees and off-balance sheet items." The IMF's 1996 initiative, the Special Data Dissemination Standard, provides a major first step, but much more can be done in this regard. One has only to look at how opaque the United States government's books have become during the 2007 financial crisis to see how helpful an outside standard would be. (The Federal Reserve alone has taken trillions of dollars of difficult-to-price private assets onto its books, but during the depths of the crisis it refused to disclose the composition of some of these assets even to the US Congress. This assumption of assets was admittedly an extraordinarily delicate and sensitive operation, yet over the long run systemic transparency has to be the right approach.) The task of enforcing transparency is far more easily said than done, for governments have many incentives to obfuscate their books."[276]

> We have come full circle to the concept of financial fragility in economies with massive indebtedness. All too often, periods of heavy borrowing can take place in a bubble and last for a surprisingly long time. But highly leveraged economies, particularly those in which continual rollover of short-term debt is sustained only by confidence in relatively illiquid underlying assets, seldom survive forever, particularly if leverage continues to grow unchecked. This time may seem different, but all too often a deeper look shows it is not. Encouragingly, history does point to warning signs that policy makers can look at to assess risk—if only

they do not become too drunk with their credit bubble-fueled success and say, as their predecessors have for centuries, "This time is different."[277]

Current evidence of this recurring theme is again on the front pages of the financial press. Indeed, Reinhart and Rogoff must agree that this time is in fact no different. In addition to the Fed's continuing folly, *Reuters* reported that at December 3, 2015, "[t]he European Central Bank adjusted its asset purchase program known as quantitative easing on Thursday, extending the scheme's duration into 2017 and agreeing to buy euro-denominated municipal and regional bonds, ECB President Mario Draghi said. Purchases of mainly government bonds—at 60 billion euros a month—are now seen running until at least March 2017 instead of next September. He also said that proceeds from the various assets bought would be reinvested back into the scheme.... [C]ritics have said QE has done little for inflation so far, the ECB's biggest worry, with headline figures hovering near zero and core inflation around 1 percent, well short of the central bank's target of nearly 2 percent."[278]

And once again, reported by *Reuters* the same day, the flip side of the QE refrain "[a]n expansive monetary policy is the right way to support growth but one must watch for negative side effects such as property bubbles, European Central Bank Governing Council member Ewald Nowotny said in a television interview on Thursday. "We must of course be careful that this healthy medicine does not have negative side effects," Nowotny told Austrian broadcaster ORF. "It could be, for example, that there is a development of bubbles in property markets."[279]

There appears to be a total disconnect in the minds of central bankers between the intentional policies of deliberate manipulation of asset prices through interference in the real market for those assets in service of the supposed prudent exercise of monetary policy will, in fact, inexorably result in asset price distortions as a direct result of their actions. These are not unintended and unexpected consequences. These results are entirely predictable in their effect. What is also predictable, and provable, is that the central bankers persist in market interference in asset pricing and values and there continues to be no credible evidence that such policies in America, or in Europe, or at any time or place during history has resulted in any defined degree of permanent job creation or sustainable economic growth.

The fundamental drivers of capital market dysfunction and bank concerns today are outside the box. As the scope and power of Fed monetary policy has waned through transfer of money creation into the shadow banking system—outside the box—the Fed has increasingly looked to Wall Street banks and other systemically important financial institutions that are deeply invested in the shadow banking system as the only available option through which to exercise monetary policy. Further, Congress has turned to the Wall Street banks and other systemically important financial institutions to intermediate its political, social and fiscal policies, off-budget and without adequate public hearings or debate and without regulation of the value of newly imagined and created monetary assets through the shadow banking system.

All that can really be said about the effectiveness of the Fed in this crisis is its willingness to publicly purchase and pile on its balance sheet the supposedly liquid and value sustainable shadow banking system financial assets that have floated Outside the

Box, without which purchases the capital markets would have remained frozen and values collapsed. Providing liquidity to these assets may help keep the financial system operating at a tolerable level of liquidity, but more importantly, it discourages and confuses any meaningful attempt to call for the regulation of the value of money, and specifically these same "structured" monetary assets that serve as money. We may now know what the Fed has purchased, but we do not know the volume and value of those assets or of similar monetary assets still in the shadow banking system and off the Fed's balance sheet and outside any semblance of regulation of their value.

For purposes of this work, the corollary of the fact that these parties, these bad actors, have no incentive to change their conduct, is, stated in another way, so far, they have no disincentive to continuation of their conduct.

It was wrong; it was irresponsible; but in addition, in a position not heretofore asserted in any meaningful way by any federal financial regulator or enforcement agency; the conduct of the Washington Wall Street enterprise as presented in this work violates the *United States Constitution*, including the *Bill of Rights* protection of the American public's right to equal protection of their civil right to the dollar denominated value of their income and savings under the American rule of law, as well as their civil, statutory and common law right to insist that the value of their income and savings not be stripped away through money debasement and sucked up by the Washington Wall Street enterprise, without due process and equal protection under the rule of law. Vigorous enforcement of Washington and Wall Street legal accountability under the *Constitution*, fundamental American common law and state and federal statutory civil and criminal law, appears to be the only appropriate disincentive to their active and intentional process of American money debasement, and to provide incentives to compliance with the American rule of law.

The DOJ has been bought off through the payoffs of the revolving door between Washington and Wall Street, leaving the public to their own devices, individually, privately, seeking their own protection under the existing American rule of law.

In a nation built upon the rule of law, the financial crises we have suffered calls out for a catalyst to compel Washington and Wall Street compliance with the laws of the United Stated of America. Additional financial reform, such as Dodd-Frank, may be marginally helpful, in spite of its pernicious weakening through interpretive regulation drafted by Wall Street and adopted willingly by Washington, but the plight or ordinary American public can be remedied only through judicially enforced compliance by Washington and by Wall Street with the American rule of law, driven by the imposition of damages, penalties and equitable enforcement by the Judicial branch of government of the *Constitution* and other legal obligations of Congress and the Executive branch, specifically the federal financial regulators and federal law enforcement agencies.

Systemic conduct that has been labelled by President Obama and accepted by the public as merely wrong and irresponsible, but without consequences of legal accountability.

The Committee Report, the GAO Report, the Report of the Dallas Fed and the Better Market Reports put into context and perspective the claims by Washington and Wall Street that the system has suffered no losses from the "too big to fail" Wall Street bailout, subsidy and preferences solution to the financial crisis. Does anyone really think the Special Financial Crimes Unit put together by the US Attorney General is investigating the $20 trillion dollar systemic losses suffered by ordinary Americans as a part of the financial crisis?

Again, as stated in the Introduction, the American revolutionary war was fought over much more diminutive grounds of abuse of power than the US government has displayed in this systemic financial crisis.

[C] Transfer Payments, Regulatory Manipulation and Failure of Transparency

Every act of government represents, by definition, the implementation of a transfer payment. Citizens pay taxes to enable the government to undertake collective action on their behalf that they could not successfully or practically take on their own. The government is constitutionally enabled to borrow money, if necessary, to its lawful actions and with transparent budgetary support. The US government's failure to maintain a sound and stable currency has severed our ability as citizens to hold our government to account for its policies and actions. This ongoing failure has repeatedly subjected our economy to the law of perhaps so-called unintended, but certainly foreseeable and predictable, consequences.

Minsky took the position that "the creation of new economic institutions which constrain the impact of uncertainty is necessary," arguing that the "aim of policy is to assure that the economic prerequisites for sustaining the civil and civilized standards of an open liberal society exist. If amplified uncertainty and extremes in income mal-distribution and social inequalities attenuate the economic underpinnings of democracy, then the market behavior that creates these conditions has to be constrained."[280]

We are in a world where relative use-values of assets are constantly evolving and developing, just as our domestic and the global economy have evolved and developed. Our tool for accounting for and storing value is not working. The apparently mysterious connection between money and asset use-value is vital to our national interest; it is vital to our national security. It must keep pace with the market.

We must connect money as a unit of account, tool of measurement, store of value over time and standard for deferred payment to changing concepts of use-value, as new goods and services are introduced into the marketplace that have to find their use-value in the heart of the real, as opposed to the strictly financial, marketplace.

To the extent our government is able to separate money creation from any underlying disciplined connection to asset market values, the government is free to manipulate all of its activities as represented by money used as a store of value, medium of exchange and unit of account, and standard for deferred payment. The public transparency of and accountability for its essential publicly constitutionally enabled and mandated transfer payment activities are hidden, distorted and misrepresented; and manipulate through money debasement to insure that the Washington Wall Street enterprise is protected at all cost, and enabled to flourish following financial crises, while ordinary Americans are left to manage their $20 trillion in damages on their own.

This opaque and devious development is characterized most often as "political expediency" and "existential necessity" but is perpetrated almost solely in the interests of politicians, bankers and bureaucrats and, in fact, has departed from the transparent use of regulatory incentives to specific conduct, including creation of money through credit or creation of other monetary equivalents, for political and social purposes. It constitutes a deliberate program of institutional fraud by politicians, bankers and bureaucrats on US taxpayers. Our founding fathers feared this development and now we have it.

The fundamental drivers of capital market dysfunction and bank concerns today are outside the box. As the scope and power of Fed monetary policy has waned through abandonment of money creation into the shadow banking system—outside the box of the congressional mandate. The Fed has increasingly looked to Wall Street banks and other systemically important financial institutions that are deeply invested in the shadow banking system as the only available option through which to exercise monetary policy. Further, Congress has turned to the Wall Street banks and other systemically important financial institutions to intermediate its political, social and fiscal policies, all too often off-budget and without adequate public hearings or debate and without regulation of the value of newly imagined and created monetary assets through the shadow banking system.

Until World War II, economic cycles defined financial markets. Today financial markets define the economic cycle. Newly created forms of structured money substitutes offering traditional liquidity and constituting the shadow banking system now dwarf traditionally defined money, as shown below. These illusions of liquidity and value lie at the heart of the last great financial crisis and portend the next.

The following analysis has been provided by Roche and McKee and illustrated by an inverted "liquidity pyramid, with the largest segment of liquidity with the highest associated degree of risk as the top and decreasing as the categories move down the structure.[281]

Roche and McKee compare and contrast US liquidity in 1990 and 2007:

Liquidity	*1990*	*2000*	*% of World GDP*	*% of Liquidity*
Derivatives:	$17 trillion	$125 trillion	1012%	89%
Securitized Debt:	$13.7 trillion	$49 trillion	129%	10%
Broad Money:	$3.9 trillion	$10 trillion	115%	9%
Power Money:	$0.3 trillion	0.9 trillion	8%	1%

Derivatives are financial contracts whose prices are determined by, or are "derived from" the value of some underlying asset, rate, index or event. They are not used for capital formation or investment; rather they are instruments for hedging against risk or for speculating on changes in prices, interest rates, likelihood of events occurring or not occurring.[282]

With the rise of asset securitization; most importantly mortgage backed securities (MBS), Collateralized debt obligations (CDO) constructed by bundling pools of MBS and splitting and pricing underlying of CDOs into tranches or bundles presenting theoretically, different profiles of risk (largely interest rate risk and default rate risk); followed by "synthetic" CDOs consisting of artificial financial instruments consisting only of "probabilities" of change in risk rate and allocation based only on indexed references to unrelated actual MBS and CDOs; each instrument or book entry of item and ownership by counterparties representing a "valuation" "created" by the securities ratings agencies based on complex financial models far, far removed from the actual financial transactions, characteristics and values of the underlying actual current incomes of homeowners, home values, mortgages payments and willing home buyers prepared to payment the present value of "rental" as a purchase price on purchases and sales of homes.

Roche and McKee view the US current account deficit as, in effect, a global ATM:[283]

- Liquidity causes asset/price wealth gains →
- Excessive consumption—an illusion of the American Dream →
- U.S. current account widens →
- Pumps cheap dollars into the global financial system, producing →
  - → Offshore multiplier—dollars are lent and borrowed abroad
  - → Domestic multiplier—dollars flow unsterilized[284] into local currencies
  - → Recycling multiplier—feeding back into U.S. liquiditykeeping capital costs down

Roche and McKee contrast the old relationship banking model with what they describe as the new transaction-oriented model.

Under the old relationship banking model, savers and depositors interacted with banks who interacted with borrowers. Lines of rights and obligations and the rules of law applicable to these relationships were well-settled.

Under the new transaction oriented model, banks occupy a central position intermediating with savers and depositor and borrowers but also with special purpose investment vehicles and wholesale money markets, with which savers and depositors also deal directly, along with Wall Street banks and governments depositories and government sponsored enterprises who deal to rapid massive trading, including massively leveraged and re-hypothecation transactions in overnight trading markets, introducing to bankers, savers and depositors, as well as borrowers, a degree of leverage, opacity and unrestrained risk-taking heretofore segregated from the old relationship model of banking.[285]

[D] Outside of the Box: The Shadow Banking System

The large top the inverted pyramid of liquidity described by Roche and McKee consists of derivatives and other exotic purely financial assets that comprise nearly 75 percent of global liquidity. Derivatives, the biggest, fastest growing component of liquidity, are destined for buying financial assets, not for shopping for goods and services. The price of the former has soared. The price of the latter has collapsed—that is pending market recognition of the amount of empty dollars included in the overall pile of debt.[286]

The next component of the liquidity pyramid consists of securitized debt, where much traditional bank lending is securitized and sold off as bonds.[287]

You can buy a house and use credit cards with broad money. With derivatives, you can only invest in financial asset and commodities. Between 1990 and 2005, liquidity expanded by 300 percent. GDP grew only 80 percent. Securitized debt grew by 200 percent. The liquidity to buy financial assets grew twice as fast as liquidity for consumer use.[288]

Power money sits in your pocket or bank account and pays bills.[289]

[E] Inside the Box: Traditional Banking System

According to Roche and McKee, global liquidity represents nearly twelve years of GDP. In the years leading up to the financial crisis, global liquidity grew at least five times faster than GDP. Liquidity is shown above as an inverted pyramid with a tiny triangle of central bank power money at the bottom. This supports and expands into broad money (bank accounts, loans and credit accounts). Power money, together with broad money has been, fundamentally, the total sum of liquidity as we have understood it historically.

[1] Where Does Liquidity Go in a Liquidity Crisis?

As liquidity explodes, asset prices rise and "wealth" is created. What happens to it? Some of it turns into consumer spending (through selling assets, home equity withdrawals or increased borrowing, e.g., credit card debt). Also, consumers save less because their assets are theoretically saving for them simply by increasing in value. This "wealth effect" makes consumers more confident in their economic position and therefore they spend more. Since in the US consumers spend more than they produce, the excess creates a current account deficit equal to the savings shortfall. A current account deficit means that dollars created by the liquidity pyramid, which get spent on excess consumption, get sent abroad to pay for imports and are left in the hands of foreigners. Some of these dollars never return home and end up in foreign monetary systems and in offshore banks. There they can be lent and borrowed many times over so that each dollar can get multiplied into more than one. Some dollars get changed into local currency in countries running an external surplus with the US. Those dollars, converted into local currency, are deposited into local banks. If the local currency equivalent of the dollar inflow is not borrowed by the central bank (i.e., sterilized), once again the credit multiplier applies. Dollars that are changed into local currency end up in the foreign central bank. The foreign central bank (or finance ministry in some Asian countries) recycles them back to the US where they are invested in fixed income securities, so sustaining or adding to, the US credit pyramid.[290]

Liquidity has historically been set by the reserve ratios of the central banks and the size of their power money. Liquidity equalled power money multiplied by the inverse of the reserve ratio. The supply and velocity of money movement is now governed by forces that were limited or non-existent in prior cycles.[291] Neither our Congress, its creature the Fed, our central bank, nor its tools, the Wall Street banks, control the quantity and price of money.

We ordinary American citizens and Congress, our representatives of and fiduciaries to American society, constitutionally charged with the responsibility to "coin money, regulate the value thereof, and foreign coin, and fix the standards of weights and measures," have all been totally asleep at the wheel. We have trusted Washington and their partners on Wall Street. They have responded by lying to, cheating and stealing from us. Final responsibility for holding the Washington Wall Street enterprise legally accountable for this disaster rest now with ordinary American families, acting together.

The fog of liquidity consisting of securitized debt, derivatives and other purely financial assets has blocked financial transparency and our ability to make sound economic and financial decisions. Central bank-dictated reserves no longer set the credit multiplier. Raising (Fed benchmark policy) interest rates does little to nothing to affect the cost of capital in the liquidity pyramid. The Fed reduction of the benchmark "policy" rates, on top of earlier reductions in response to our liquidity crisis, and now follow on modest increase in the policy rates has not, nor will it likely have any meaningful effect on the cost of capital in the shadow banking system.

Once the cost of long term capital rises above the natural interest rate, we should expect the liquidity pyramid to contract sharply if the expansion and contraction phases are to remain symmetrical.[292] The Fed is now doing its upmost to avoid that contraction, but to little ultimate avail.

When the asset bubbles start to collapse, central banks, being unable to bear the economic costs (guilt) will act asymmetrically. The collapse of the asset bubble has been largely limited to home prices, and securities and derivatives based on housing stock. Central bank and regulatory policy in the US have disguised, delayed and extended the day of reckoning in the form of broad-based precipitous asset price deflation. Keeping the flow of money moving has not led to an economic recovery, it has simply "covered up" the inevitable consequences of creation of the asset bubble. Central banks have been and are now considering raising rates either to normalize them from post-9.11 easy monetary policy or to combat inflation. But at the first sign of asset price deflation, they have eased, and will again will ease precipitously (since 2008 they have also accomplished the same effect through various non-transparent policy maneuvers, including quantitative easing—acquiring securitized asset and treasury bills, suppressing the Fed benchmark policy rates and supporting asset values). Thus, any pain of being invested in an asset bubble would be of short duration.

This reinforces the markets' conviction that global monetary policy is asymmetric and biased in favor of investors and speculators.

The currency accelerator, illustrated by Roche and McKee, showing how currencies in circulation concentrate through trade into the major reserve currencies, primarily the US dollar, has helped maintain dollar supremacy, although that is now being openly questioned. In Roche and McKee's Figure 21, at the top of the currency accelerator is global GDP, split among the various global currencies. The next level down illustrates the composition of world trade, split among global currencies. The third level down illustrates the composition of payments for imports, split among global currencies. The amounts paid for imports end up in the exporting country. In current account surplus countries, this generally means the currency earned ends up in the exporters' central banks. The bottom level of the Roche and McKee currency accelerator chart illustrates the composition of central bank international reserves, split among global currencies.[293]

As currency moves through this system, at each successive stage, the proportion of currency, primarily in dollars and euros, grows. The "real" economy of global GDP and international trade cascades over a series of narrowing weirs increasingly focusing transaction demand for currency into two or three of the world's most important currencies, including a small component of yen. Minor currencies of countries accounting for roughly half of global output and trade are filtered out in the process. The dominance of the dollar and euro in international trade favors strength and low volatility in those currencies.[294] The "real" economy progressively channels currency demand into the major currencies that drive global liquidity and central banks act to insure that this pattern is preserved in the store of assets they control.

Thus, the global liquidity pyramid is being inflated by the mechanism of world trade. Liquidity is boosted by global imbalances such as the US current account deficits and Japan's massive exports of savings (through the carry trade), both of which can be traced to under-priced capital. For the dollar, these weak fundamentals are suppressed by "real" economy demand for dollar as a medium of transaction in international trade and as the predominant reserve currency. This lends the dollar some stability, which in turn means that it can be used as the major currency in the liquidity pyramid. That generates further dollar demand and, in turn, creates even more liquidity.[295]

Because the dollar remains the global "reserve currency", the dollar's ongoing weakening, any perceived "dumping" of dollars as central bank reserves would likely collapse the liquidity pyramid, despite the fact that central bank reserves are only a modest part of the total available liquidity in the pyramid. In addition to the financial world's requirement of the dollar to serve as the world's reserve currency, US financial imbalances are also supported by global demand for the dollar as a medium to meet investment demand and transaction demand from the real economy.[296]

Roche and McKee's two primary conclusions:

- Demand for the dollar extends the day of reckoning for US financial imbalances; and

- Currency turmoil surrounding the dollar will likely be a cause or effect of widespread liquidity contraction, as global trade and asset markets recognize and begin to reject the weakest dominant currency—the dollar.

Mitigating this recognition and rejection of the dollar is the fact that derivatives have been used to freeze approximately $50 trillion of capital, the equivalent of five years of US GDP as measured by the notional value of the credits represented by interest rate swaps, at historically low interest rates. This derivative currency "lock-up" delays the impact of Fed Rate hikes. Increases in central bank interest rates remain stuck in the small, narrow apex of the pyramid occupied by central bank and short-term money. That is why liquidity continues to grow.[297]

The final straw that broke the camel's back in the securitization boom precipitating the great financial crisis was the dramatic increase of the use of the credit default swap to permit the Wall Street banks and other systemically important financial institutions globally to continue to hold the most junior tranches of collateralized debt obligations on their balance sheets at par:[298]

> Investment banks presumably did not anticipate the size of the hole that CDOs could blow in their balance sheets. But they probably did anticipate earning low returns on this part of their portfolios. Their response was to attempt to boost the return on capital by expanding their balance sheets. In other words, they used more borrowed money—in some cases, much more borrowed money—to maintain the now customary profit margin. From this flowed the explosive growth of leverage—the ratio of borrowed funds to own capital—of bank and non-bank financial institutions.
>
> This was not a phenomenon limited to investment banks at the center of the crisis. Other financial institutions not so deeply invested in residential mortgage-backed securities, CDOs, and other "sophisticated financial instruments also levered up. Behind this was the growth of a wholesale money market on which financial institutions could borrow large sums for periods as short as overnight. There was also the willingness of regulators to look the other way. In particular, investment banks, which once only gambled only their partners' money, now gambled the money of others, and their conduits and special purpose vehicles remained largely outside the regulatory net."[299]

Note that the regulatory net did encompass these activities, the regulators, simply chose to ignore the development.

Regulators permitted the use of hybrid instruments such as subordinated debt and trust preferred securities to serve as equity, thereby easing bank capital requirement. Under Basel Accord, "banks were permitted to hold as little as 2 percent common equity as a share of risk weighted assets."[300] "For European banks, the American model of minimizing capital and using high levels of leverage was something to be emulated, not scorned. Ultimately, common global tendencies produced a common global crisis."[301]

According to Fed Chairman Ben Bernanke, the world, primarily Asian countries, are awash in surplus savings that flow to the US where the US can spend it and thus maintain equilibrium. This is another version of the old story that the US capital account surplus creates the current account deficit. Capital is attracted to the US because it presents the most attractive investment destination, thus obliging the US to consume much and save little.

Unfortunately, US financial assets no longer offer superior returns. Most flows have gone into relatively low yield treasuries and mortgages. Anyway, according to Roche and Mckee, "surely the 20 percent fall in the dollar's trade-weighted index over the last three years (prior to 2008) is proof enough that the ex post widening of the current account deficit is not created by an ex ante inflow of foreign capital. If it had, the dollar would be appreciating not declining."[302]

In 2005 and 2006 cash surpluses that constitute the bulk of the liquidity pyramid have been chasing higher yields (often of securities with very low capital productivity, such as mortgage backed security) covering the US current account deficit. But this bloated the US financial system with liquidity that drove up asset prices, so keeping the US consumer borrowing and shopping:

> When a senator from the Republic of Kalmykia was caught shaking down a Russian airline, he was apprehended with a suitcase containing $300,000 in marked US bills. When Somali pirates ransom a ship, they demand that the ransom money be parachuted to them in dollars. Nearly three-quarters of all $100 bills circulate outside the United States attests to the dollar's dominance of this dubious realm.[303]

South Korea and Thailand set the prices of more than 80 percent of their trade in dollars even though only 20 percent of their exports go to American buyers. Fully 70 percent of Australia's exports are invoiced in Dollars even though fewer than 6 percent are destined for the United States. The principal commodity exchanges quote prices in dollars. Oil is priced in dollars. The dollar is used in 85 percent of all foreign exchange transactions worldwide. It accounts for nearly half of the global stock of international debt securities. It is the form in which central banks hold more than 60 percent of their foreign currency reserves. Today the US share of global exports is only 13 percent. The United States is the source of less than 20 percent of foreign direct investment, down from nearly 85 percent between 1945 and 1980. About $500 billion of US currency circulates outside the United States, for which foreigners have had to provide the United States with $500 billion of actual goods and services.[304] Even more important, foreign central banks now hold close to $18.5 trillion of the bonds of the US Treasury and quasi-governmental agencies like Fannie Mae and Freddie Mac.[305]

With cheap foreign finance keeping US interest rates low and enabling American households to live beyond their means, poor households in the developing world ended up subsidizing rich ones in the United States. The cheap finance that other countries provided the U.S. in order to obtain the dollars needed to back an expanding volume of international transactions underwrote the practices that culminated in the crisis. The United States lit the fire, but foreigners were forced by the perverse structure of the system to provide the fuel.

If this were not injustice enough, there is the fact that America's international financial position was strengthened by the crisis. In the course of 2007, the dollar weakened by about 8 percent on the foreign exchange market. But since our debts are denominated in our own currency, there was no impact on their dollar value. In contrast, our foreign investments, whether in bonds or factories, became more valuable as the dollar fell. The interest and dividends they threw off were worth more when they were converted back into dollars.

The dollars depreciation thereby improved the US external position by almost $450 billion. This largely offset the increase in US indebtedness to the rest of the world that would otherwise have resulted from our $660 billion current account deficit. It was almost enough to keep our debts to other countries stable, despite our consuming 6 percent more than we produced. Then, in 2008, in the throes of the most serious financial crises in 80 years, the federal government was able to borrow vast sums at low interest rates because foreigners figured that the dollar was the safest currency to be in at times of great turmoil. And again, in 2010, when financial volatility spiked, investors fled into the most liquid market, that for US treasury bonds, pushing down the cost of borrowing for the US government and, along with it the mortgage interest rates available to American households. This is what exorbitant privilege is all about.[306]

[2] Shadow Banking Money Acting as Liquid Sovereign Money at Par

The Uniform Agreement on the Classification and Appraisal of Securities Held by Depository Institutions,[307] directed the federal financial regulatory agencies to remove any reference to or requirement of reliance on credit ratings in the regulations and replace them with appropriate standards of creditworthiness, and to "use this statement for the classification and treatment of investment securities." The purpose of the new Agreement and revised regulations is to assure that asset backed securities held by banks are properly valued at fair value and properly classified when the underlying credits are impaired; the ratings agency classifications used by the banks having been demonstrably misleading and intentionally fraudulent in many cases.

The Agreement provides that: "Although Securities that do not meet the investment grade standard, as defined in applicable regulations, and for which the timely repayment of principal and interest is not certain, have investment characteristics that are distinctly or predominantly speculative and are generally subject to classification. For investment securities, the classification should be based on the instrument's worth as an earning asset assuming it is held to maturity. Therefore, the phrase "liquidation of the debt" in the classification definitions is synonymous with "payment of the obligation in full." Accordingly, if payment of the obligation in full is in question, it is no longer investment grade and management should classify the security:

> A Doubtful classification is appropriate when an asset has experienced significant credit deterioration and decline in fair value, but estimation of impairment involves significant uncertainty because of various pending factors. These factors could include uncertain financial data that may not permit the accurate forecasting of future cash flows or estimating recovery value. The use of the Doubtful classification is an interim measure until information becomes available to substantiate a more appropriate treatment.[308]
>
> Depository institutions should continually assess whether securities meet the investment grade standard. Throughout the term of an investment security, its credit risk profile can decline and improve as credit conditions change. Similarly,

> an institution's analysis should consider how potential adverse economic conditions can negatively affect an individual security. An institution's management expertise and the sophistication of its risk management and due diligence processes should be commensurate with the complexity of its investment portfolio holdings.[309]

The FDIC Uniform Agreement, prepared and implemented under *Dodd Frank*, is presented as an example of new effective bank regulation. This Agreement is apparently intended to assure the quality of mortgage-backed securities and their accurate presentation for asset classification and valuation purposes; these same securities being the largely defective overvalued credit derivatives lying at the heart of the financial crisis. The Agreement does not mention the fact that specific regulations establishing essentially the same substantive standards were in effect in 2001, and at the time of the financial crisis in 2008:

> 12 C.F.R. § 1.1 Authority, purpose, and scope; prescribes standards under which national banks may purchase, sell, deal in, underwrite, and hold securities, consistent with the authority contained in 12 U.S.C. 24 (Seventh) and safe and sound banking practices.
>
> 12 C.F.R. § 1.3 Limitations on dealing in, underwriting, and purchase and sale of securities.
>
> 12 C.F.R. § 1.5 Safe and sound banking practices; credit information required. A national bank shall adhere to safe and sound banking practices and the specific requirements of this part in conducting the activities described in § 1.3. The bank shall consider, as appropriate, the interest rate, credit, liquidity, price, foreign exchange, transaction, compliance, strategic, and reputation risks presented by a proposed activity, and the particular activities undertaken by the bank must be appropriate for that bank.

Notwithstanding the necessity for this sensible treatment of bank asset valuation and classification required in 2001 and now required under the Agreement, during the financial crisis the Wall Street banks consistently carried, and continue to carry illiquid, value impaired, toxic assets at par value without application of the disciplined valuation and classification required under the new agreement or under existing law and regulation. In fact, to avoid accountability for the capital losses due to value impairment on their balance sheets, the Wall Street banks have dumped the troubled assets onto the Fed's balance sheet at par, booking newly minted Federal Reserve notes in place of those toxic assets, the Federal Reserve Notes themselves backed by absolutely nothing. In this way the chain of bailouts, the "cover up" of losses and deliberate misrepresentation of the state of the American economy and financial system, the liquidity and value of the US dollar appears to have permanently deferred and delayed the accountability of the Washington Wall Street enterprise for the great financial crisis.

Importantly, neither the Agreement nor prior regulations provide for a discount of recorded value to reflect the risk and uncertainty of the immediate liquidity of those assets, yet they purport to serve the public purpose of maintaining the honesty, safety and soundness of American "sovereign money". This is the essence of the fundamental, tragic, conceptual and legal failure of America's banking and financial system leading up to and continuing in the wake of the financial crisis.

[3] *Repo Markets Create "Fake" Over-Valued Shadow Banking Money on a Massive Scale: Illiquid at Precisely the Time Liquidity Is Required*

The securities referred to in the regulations and the new Agreement serve as the foundation for the derivatives, which with the underlying securities provide the massive volume of high risk trading instruments that have infiltrated the nation's money market funds and serve as the fodder for high speed trading—money creation—through the even more massive phenomenon of perpetual overnight repo financing. Repos are in many ways the ultimate in the fraudulent misrepresentation of illiquid assets requiring effective discount for risk and uncertainty and resulting risks of illiquidity, as fully liquid assets at par value, the equivalent of sovereign money, the value and liquidity of which have been regulated by Congress, and by churning those assets over and over, through re-hypothecation, which means pledging the same assets over and over simultaneously to different parties in a pyramid of credit. Ordinary Americans would be jailed for such activity. "According to Yale Professor Gorton, in testimony to the Committee in February 2010, "This banking system—repo-based securitization—is a genuine banking system, as large as the traditional banking system. It is of critical importance to the economy." ... "Until recently, short-term repos have always been regarded as virtually risk-free instruments, Federal Reserve Chairman Ben Bernanke told a meeting of bankers in May 2008, after nine-months of turmoil in the repo market. Former Federal Reserve Chairman Alan Greenspan, writing in an April report on the panic, described repos as 'almost sacrosanct."[310] These statements were made despite the fact that the structure of repo financing is unsafe and unsound on its face. According to Gorton, the repo market is a critical cog in the wheel of finance. That may be. But the wheel of finance has become a giant Ponzi scheme financing Washington's and Wall Street's addiction to financial gambling. Gorton insists that without repo financing, traditional banks will not lend and credit, which is essential to job creation, will not be created. There is no evidence whatsoever that repo financing and the seemingly endless daisy-chain of repo re-hypothecation is essential for American job creation and such a statement is utterly irresponsible. There is no evidence that this credit creation machine is safe or sound or that it provides any economic or social benefits for the American public, while it subjects the public to enormous risk and loss.

The repo financing market largely consists primarily of 21 Wall Street Banks and other "big players" trading approximately 90 percent of $7 trillion in overnight borrowing every night (the actual numbers are uncertain because no one collects all the data).

Washington's and Wall Street's actions conducted under color of authority of unconstitutional relief from their duty to create and emit credit denominated in US dollars redeemable only by fiat Federal Reserve Notes as legal tender, have provided to Washington and Wall Street the opportunity that they have fully exploited to create money that has been debased, in many cases by as much as 60 percent, and in too many cases as much as 100 percent, enabling them to profit from such debasement while being protected against losses inherent in the debasement by holding the pubic hostage as institutions "too big to fail" lest the Washington Wall Street enterprise of banking and financial oligarchy collapse, and with it the real United States economy; forcing the losses to be borne by ordinary American citizens. Thus and thereby the Washington Wall Street enterprise abuses the vast power they wield over the American economy and perpetuate and protect their monopoly ability to concentrate wealth and power in the Wall Street Washington centered financial and economic system, that is in most respects disconnected from the real American markets and economy, creating an ever greater division and disparity of income and wealth to the detriment of and damage to the ordinary American public.

According to John Maudlin, "... the Fed now has three mandates instead of two, the third being that the central bank is now also supposed to be "responsible for the markets." This new duty, of course, is in addition to its intended role of ensuring price stability and full employment." Mauldin's observation assumes that all have forgotten, as seems obvious, Congress' purported delegation to the Fed of its mandate and duty to regulate the coining and value of sovereign money, and the Fed having purportedly delegated that mandate and duty to the Wall Street banks, the constitutional mandate—the highest law of the land, is now apparently out of sight and out of mind, with not even a footnote to show for it.[311]

"The Fed can be blamed or credited with controlling the prices of almost all assets over the last six years through Bailouts, Quantitative Easing, Operation Twist, and all other forms of economic stimulus. How the Fed goes about unwinding this unprecedented stimulus will do much to determine our economic destiny as a nation."[312] The phenomenon of the Fed, through the Wall Street banks as the Feds agents and partners, controlling the value of assets goes back to the disappearance of the last vestige of discipline provided by constitutional coined money, the value of which has been regulated by Congress—through repeated boom and bust cycles that have always left the American public poorer and the Wall Street Banks and those fortunate enough to tag along with the Washington Wall Street enterprise economy and financial system richer and more entrenched, and the most wealthy 1 percent of Americans even wealthier.

The specific failures of the Wall Street banks however, in their official role of following Federal Reserve created incentives designed to meet the Federal Reserve's stated political objectives, indeed, exceeding those incentives, unrestrained by impotent or compromised Federal and state examination, regulation and supervisory authorities which have ceded to the Wall Street banks "enlightened self-interest" through "self-regulation" in implementing Fed policies, have created a straight line of duty, wrongful conduct and breached duty leading from those failures directly to the financial crisis and to the losses suffered by the American public and identified by the Committee, the Fed, the GAO and by the Better Markets' analyses.

[4] *Intentional Misrepresentation of the Value and Liquidity of Shadow Money Through Shadow Banking*

Money at its most basic is a derivative that intermediates the respective value of goods and services in an exchange one step beyond immediate contemporaneous barter. All credit, representing a time deferral in the exchange transaction with risk and uncertainty attached to the element of time, is a derivative of the underlying value it represents, discounted to reflect the relevant risk and uncertainty of eventual liquidation and payment or loss in whole or in part. The risk and uncertainty borne by credit in exchange transactions is different and distinct with respect to each transaction supporting each credit. All credit instruments, or loans, are derivatives. So-called synthetic derivatives, or derivatives-cubed are derivatives. To the extent that derivative instruments, from gold or silver coins to CDO derivatives-cubed, across the spectrum of their complexity and opacity, can honestly and transparently connect their value over time as represented by, or correlated to a unit standard of value that can be reliably confirmed as liquid in the marketplace and may actually be generally relied on in the market with trust and confidence, constitutes money.

The distance between these derivatives is a matter only of the time, distance and degree of the connection of the derivative instrument to actual value, measured in reference to a regulated standard of value confirmed in the actual economic, as opposed to monetary, marketplace. Actual Federal Reserve notes, American legal tender; solely fiat money; is commonly considered to represent the American Dollar—America's "sovereign "money. Actual Federal Reserve notes constitute a largely insignificant proportion of US dollar denominated money globally, and do not actually constitute meaningful money in a legal, effective, equitable, fair, honest or functional sense.

The bulk of United States money consists almost exclusively of credit created through the banking system that derives its current face "represented dollar value" from the present day "represented dollar value" of anticipated future sources of the credits' repayment. This uncertain future anticipation of credit repayment as represented by the derivative credit instrument, may only consist of an electronic data entry denominated in US dollars. The peril of accepting a credit derivative at face value as liquid, negotiable money, without any legal, honest, trustworthy, creditworthy connection to the actual economic market place; without any legal, honest, clear understanding of the risk and uncertainty inherent in prospect of future repayment of the credit; and without any mechanism for immediate transfer and negotiation of the credit for a thing of value with immediate liquidity that is discounted to and represents a commonly accepted, trusted standard of value, is obvious.

The shadow banking system comprised largely of asset-backed securities and derivatives—structured finance—backed by dubious sources of repayment wholly inconsistent with the degree of liquidity and asset values represented, are at the heart of the crisis. Currently, according to *Derivatives: The Unregulated Global Casino for Banks*, citing *Zero Hedge* as its data source,[313] reports "the 9 largest banks shown [in the report] hold a total of $228.72 trillion in derivatives—Approximately 3 times the entire word economy" No government in the world has money for this bailout."

according to the most recent OCC quarterly report: Goldman Sachs has a current derivative exposure of more than $47 trillion dollars. JP Morgan Chase has a derivative exposure of $47 trillion dollars. Bank of America has a derivative exposure of more than $33 trillion dollars (Bank of America previously moved derivatives to accounts insured by the federal government in the amount of $53.7 trillion as of June 2011). Morgan Stanley has a derivative exposure of more than $28 trillion dollars. Citibank has a derivative exposure of more than $47 trillion dollars. Wells Fargo has a derivative exposure of more than $7 trillion dollars (this despite being subject to regulatory constraints on growth. Collectively, the top 25 banks own $222 trillion worth of derivatives.[314] That's just a little less than 15 times the national debt. The scope of the shadow banking system is detailed in, among a great number of other works, the Staff Paper No. 18, November 2008, *Understanding the Risks Inherent in Shadow Banking: A Primer and Practical Lessons Learned,* prepared by the Federal Reserve Bank of Dallas, and in the works of David Roche and Bob Mckee, *New Monetarism* (2007), *New Monetarism, New Edition* (2008) and *Sovereign Discredit: Why Sovereign Debt Risk is the Next Stage of New Monetarism* (2010).

Through Quantitative Easing the Fed purchased $85 billion of bonds each month: $45 billion in treasury bills and $40 billion of mortgage backed securities. The $40 billion each month in mortgage backed securities would amount to 9,600,000 jobs paying $50,000 per year. Unfortunately, more money does not equal more jobs. The newly printed money is not getting loaned out to consumers (as intended by the stimulus package) but stays with the banks and the banks invest the newly printed money in stocks for fast profits; pushing the stock market higher primarily to the benefit of the Wall Street banks and most wealthy 1 percent of Americans.

§3.06 THE FED AND SHADOW BANKING

As noted previously, and as quoted from Vieira, arguments have been made that the obligations created by *The Federal Reserve Act*, as amended, and the regulations that it and the other federal financial regulators have promulgated are reasonable in a regulatory context, but far too vague and nebulous to be used outside the regulatory context for which it was intended.

The vague and nebulous argument does apply to the Fed's general statutory objectives. "The Federal Reserve exercises unprecedented breadth and depth of power over money despite the fact that its official mission is quite limited: *The Federal Reserve Act* provides that the Board of Governors and the Federal Reserve Open Market Committee seek: 'to promote effectively the goals of maximum employment, stable prices, and moderate long-term interest rates.'" "Indeed, courts have held that the speculative nature of the issues involved precludes litigation over whether the FOMC's policies are actually responsible for the country's economic conditions—that is, the FRS's effects on the economy are not provable according to the laws of evidence."[315]

The Gramm-Leach-Bliley Act (GLBA),[316] unleashed the complex of institutions spanning completely unregulated institutions to those with multiple layers of regulatory, often with conflicting mandates. The locus of connection amongst all of these entities and regulatory authorities centers on the Fed, itself a nest of institutions and shareholders, representing in total every level and identity of financial enterprise that can be imagined. It is in this morass that US connection to the shadow banking system resides. Contrary to the holdings of the D.C. Court in Reuss v. Balles, the case for accountability for the financial crisis made in this work illustrates the present non-existent border between and amongst the formal largely federally regulated national banking and Federal Reserve systems and the amorphous inter-related shadow banking system. The Fed has been faced with criticism from all sides since its formation. Efforts to hold the Fed accountable for its actions were attacked in the Reuss case. The accountability sought from the Fed, among the other participants in the Washington Wall Street enterprise, differs entirely from the relief sought in Reuss.

The power and duty to regulate the value of money delegated by citizens to Congress, by Congress purportedly to the Fed and by the Fed, purportedly to the Wall Street banks is not subject to the same "too vague and nebulous" argument. Regulation of the value of money and credit is central to the concept of safety and soundness which concept lies at the heart of all state and national bank regulation and the duty of all parties in that chain of duty to honestly protect the public interest in integrity and stability of the American monetary, banking, financial, monetary and economic system. That set of obligations extends to the shadow banking system inasmuch as it has become integral to and enmeshed with the formal banking system.

As purportedly enlightened self-regulators, the Wall Street banks sold out the public interest for private profit at public expense. As to failure of the banks to adequately regulate the value of credit—money, there is ample specific evidence of specific failures in the official *The Financial Crisis Inquiry Report* (January 2011).

Testimony in debate over *The Federal Reserve Act* included statements such as the observation by Senator Reed that "the government can say whether it will issue money to the Federal Reserve Bank, but the money is never issued until [private] banker[s] ... believe [] the business of the country to be such as to warrant its issuance"—and a system in which, overall, it is [We the People's] money and ... credit which is to granted to secure ... accommodation[s] for private bankers to pursue private profits."[317]

Senator Work observed that "... Instead of taking away any part of the vast power for evil, now resting in the banks, [the bill] increases that power.... It affords no protection to the public interests but adds to the power of the banks. It assumes to control the banks it creates through the Federal Reserve Board. That board will have just about as much control over the practical daily business of the regional banks as the man in the moon. .... [The bill] provides for bankers banks, not peoples banks or government banks." "Senator Clapp concurred: 'I am very much inclined to believe that the men who have controlled the great credit system of this country have used their power in their own interest against the public ... ."[318]

Finally, Senator Borah addressed the important question: ".... [W]ho—the government or private banks—actually controls the emission of Federal Reserve Notes, and what significance the locus of control has.... The government itself has no power to put into circulation any currency unless the banks say that ... they need the currency....[I]n the power to issue those notes lies the power to inflate or contract the currency of the country to a very marked degree.....I think the power lies here for the banks of this country to contract or inflate the currency almost at will."[319]

The Board of Governors of the Federal Reserve system has represented to the American people and the world that Congress has delegated to it the power to create money through the Federal Reserve system and that it holds the responsibility to regulate the value of money so created through the ephemeral, and as it happens, the "association of loans with "value provided by individuals and business," based on valuations that deliberately misrepresent and overstate the liquid value supporting such credit—specifically, in the shadow banking system and therefor, because of their entwinement, the national banking and Federal Reserve systems.

[A] The Conceptual Abuse of Money Derivatives

So, sovereign money is a prime derivative of the standard by which it is regulated by the sovereign and by the integrity of the sovereign giving the sovereign money its imprimatur. So-called synthetic CDO derivatives, or derivatives-cubed are derivatives, ever more, progressively more thinly grounded in or correlated to the actual real commercial markets for goods and services. To the extent that money instruments derive their value by redeem-ability in gold or silver coins, to the extremes of derivatives-cubed redeemable only in debased Federal Reserve Notes or from insufficient collateral leaving a loss behind; across the spectrum of their complexity and opacity; only those money instruments that can, honestly and transparently connect their value as represented to a standard of value that can be reliably confirmed and freely liquidated and transferred in the market–place at the value represented by the instrument may actually be relied on with trust and confidence and constitute sound, safe, stable money. The distance between these derivatives is a matter only of time for liquidation, distance and degree of the connection of the derivative instrument to actual value, measured in reference to a regulated standard of liquid value confirmed in the actual economic, as opposed to monetary, marketplace. Actual Federal Reserve Notes, American legal tender; solely fiat money; is commonly considered to represent the American dollar. Actual Federal Reserve Notes constitute an insignificant proportion of US dollar denominated money.

The bulk of United States money consists almost exclusively of credit created through the banking system that derives its current face "represented dollar value" from the present day "represented dollar value" of anticipated future sources of the credits' repayment. This uncertain future anticipation of credit repayment as represented by the derivative credit instrument, may only consist of an electronic data entry denominated in United States dollars. The peril of accepting a credit derivative at face value as liquid negotiable money, without any trustworthy, creditworthy and confident connection to the actual economic market place; without a clear understanding of the risk inherent in prospect of future repayment of the credit; and without any mechanism for immediate transfer and negotiation of the credit for a thing of value that represents a commonly accepted, trusted standard of liquid value, is obvious.

According to John Mauldin's newsletter, July 30, 2014 *Big Banks Shift to Lower Gear:*[320]

> Derivative trading is largely being transferred to exchanges that guarantee fulfillment of the contracts as opposed to the highly-profitable over-the-counter derivatives that banks trade but with which investors or speculators have to look to counterparties to be good for losses. This is the "counterparty risk" problem. Still, the seven largest banks still accounted for 98% of the $215 trillion notional value of derivative contracts as of March 31, 85 percent of which were interest rate contracts.
>
> Still, regulators are concerned with derivatives. Those from 10 European and North American countries recently released a report that said many large banks and their regulators are still not ready to deal with difficulties in the huge derivatives market. They lack the information to consistently and accurately know who their counterparties are. Officials estimate that banks are up to three years away from having the necessary systems in place.

Through Quantitative Easing the Fed purchased $85 billion of bonds each month: $45 billion in treasury bills and $40 billion of mortgage backed securities. The $40 billion each month in mortgage backed securities would amount to 9,600,000 jobs paying $50,000 per year. Unfortunately, more money does not equal more jobs. The newly printed money is not getting loaned out to consumers (as intended by the stimulus package) but stays with the banks and the banks invest the newly printed money in stocks for fast profits; pushing the stock market higher primarily to the benefit of the Wall Street banks and most wealthy 1% of Americans.

[B] The Federal Reserve System Must Accommodate and Constrain the Shadow Banking System

The Federal Reserve System was not established to act in any congressionally mandated role to "coin money and regulate the value thereof" in accordance with any congressionally mandated standard of value. The stated purpose of the *Federal Reserve Act* was to furnish an elastic currency, to afford means of rediscounting commercial paper, to establish a more effective supervision of banking in the United States, and for other purposes.[321]

The Feds monetary policy objectives are to maintain long run growth of the monetary and credit aggregates commensurate with the economy's long run potential to increase production, so as to promote effectively the goals of maximum employment, stable prices, and moderate long-term interest rates.[322]

Although the Federal Reserve Board has represented from time to time, in writing, that it exercises its powers under a delegation to it by Congress of the congressional mandate to "coin money and regulate its value," there is no evidence of any such congressional legislative delegation of such power and duty. Because the Federal Reserve System does not have the express legal legislative imperative to "coin money and regulate the value thereof" and because its express legal, legislative mandate, duty and power is to act, primarily through money and market creation through credit expansion, interest rate manipulation and open market purchases of, now, assets of every stripe, for the limited purpose of effecting non-pecuniary social and political objectives, its entire existence and actions subvert and are directly opposed and antithetical to the constitutional congressional power and duty to coin and regulate the value of money in accordance with a defined, effective standard of value that ensures the equal protection for each individual's creation, preservation and protection of the value of the fruits of his or her labor, property and ability to participate in the American market economy on a fair, and equal basis under the American rule of law.

Although the legal exercise by Congress of its constitutional power and duty to regulate the value of money is a necessary condition for the Federal Reserve system and the national banking system to legitimately fulfill their respective statutory mandates; to the extent that they themselves impact the creation of money and regulation of its value without being subject to a legitimate constitutional standard of value, their policies and actions, most dramatically following the Nixon shock and continuing until today, morphed into a shadow banking system that is literally out of control, and are *directly antithetical and opposed to their respective official, legislative, social and political mandates.* As a matter of constitutional law, the existence, roles and actions of the Federal Reserve System and the national banking system are, and must be made specifically and unequivocally subject and subordinate to the constitutional mandate for Congress to exercise the power and duty delegated to it by the people to create and regulate the value of money in accordance with a legitimate, expressed defined and legitimate standard of value. All elements of shadow banking entwined with the formal US banking system must be subjected to the fundamental constitutional credit constraint of the primacy of a monetary unit, the value of which is regulated by Congress.

For that process to be effective, it must also include limitations on the creation of shadow money, the legal structures and incentives of which are aligned with the objectives of maintaining stable honest, safe and sound money; both sovereign constitutional money and shadow money substitutes. The model of 19th Century English central banking and system of shadow credit money substitutes provide a well-conceived stating point.

The pursuit by the Fed of its stated legislative mission at once has been shown to be largely ineffective and, in fact, has frustrated and rendered literally impossible the ability of the Fed or any federal financial regulatory authority to meet their "assumed mission" of the constitutional imperative for Congress to coin and regulate the value of money.

Admittedly, re-establishment of a proper constitutional mechanism for the creation and regulation of the value of money that provides the people with equal protection for each individual's creation, preservation and protection of the value of the fruits of his or her labor, property and ability to participate in the American market economy on a fair, and equal basis under the American rule of law would, and should dramatically limit the scope of the ability of the Federal Reserve System and the national banking system to continue business as usual facilitating the fleecing of American people by the Washington and Wall Street cabal while paying mere lip service to the their social and political objects that are the foundation for their respective legal existence.

The Monetary Commission of the Indianapolis Convention of 1900,[323] provides a useful compendium on the history of money in the United States and the various issues that faced Americans in 1900. The prime observation was that regardless of a tie of money to silver or gold, "most Americans wanted a more sound and stable money supply to use for the three basic roles that money plays in any economy. The report outlines the three "Functions of Money":

- A Standard or Common Denominator of Value
- A Medium of Exchange
- A Standard of Deferred Payments.

Regarding the first function, the Report stated that "a common denominator is as necessary in comparing the value of commodities as is a common language among many persons in a city to enable them to readily compare ideas." The needs and frustrations of Americans when it came to the nature of money were pretty basic and more related to economic and personal security than to an intellectual debate over the nature of money."[324]

The final version of the *National Currency Act*, enacted in 1864, created a Comptroller of the Currency responsible for the execution of all laws relating to the issue and regulation of a national currency secured by United States bonds. The Act authorized the formation of national banks. The Act did not require or pressure the national banks to redeem their paper money in specie. In practical effect, national bank notes were redeemable only in Greenbacks.[325]

The practical effect of the legislation, "...tied the government and the national banks together in a symbiotic political-economic relationship: In the banks, the government created a secure market for its bonds. The banks supported a government that would freely borrow, because the ready availability of government bonds allowed them to expand their issue of notes, and thereby their business of lending, and (at least initially) enabled them to redeem their notes in Greenbacks rather than specie. The government promoted, if not forced, the circulation of the bank's currency by making it legal tender for almost all payments to and from the government. And the bankers made a pretty profit: to be sure, they had to purchase the government bonds that secured the national currency. But they immediately received ninety percent of their investment back in the form of currency that they could lend at interest. So, the government monetized its debt, while the bankers collected interest on the bonds, and on their loans of the currency the bonds secured."[326] The final act also provided that these national banks, when so designated by the Secretary of the Treasury shall:

- Be depositaries of public money (except custom receipts)
- Be employed as financial agents of the government
- Perform all such reasonable duties as depositaries of public moneys and financial agents of the government as may be required of them.

Although the ratio of bonds to currency was nearly one-to-one, the banks' circulation and deposits were bottomed squarely on the principle of fractional reserves. Every national Bank was required to have at all times, ... on hand in lawful money of the United States, an amount equal to at least twenty-five [or fifteen, depending on the type of bank] per centum of the aggregate amount of its notes in circulation and its deposits—which, of course, implied that the bank could lend out the rest of its notes or create the remainder of its deposits with no reserves. ... Part of a bank's reserves, however, could consist of balances held in deposits in other national banks—thus allowing for an 'inverted pyramid' of credit expansion."[327] [See present day mechanisms used by banks to virtually eliminate reserve requirements]

The constitutionality of this new national banking system was never effectively challenged—it was assumed.[328]

The Civil War and the *Currency Acts* culminating in the *Currency Act of 1864* created the departure from constitutional discipline of money creation and valuation. The shadow banking system's eclipse of the protections of a stable, safe and sound banking system supported by the *Constitution* and protected by state and federal law has progressed to the point that the foundation and its protections have been simply ignored; swept away as archaic, historic relics, best forgotten. American and international dialogue regarding banking and financial crises and a new financial architecture in response to the still existing real threats of additional crises, even relatively immanent threatened new crises, has been largely limited to peripatetic and sporadic regulatory efforts at the jagged edge of bank regulation; niggling over largely ineffective limitations on financial institutions securities trading of shadow banking instruments and marginal adjustments of financial institution capital and liquidity requirements, all of which have been pared back and emasculated by the Washington and Wall Street enterprise, fueled by the well-oiled machinations of a well-oiled revolving door lobby of interchangeable bureaucrats with common self-serving objectives.[329]

§3.07 CONCLUDING OBSERVATIONS

Financial reform to date has been largely, practically, irrelevant to the resolution of the risk of another possibly even more destructive financial crises than the last one, from which we have yet to recover. This context of the irrelevant has been adopted as the only context for addressing national and global monetary and financial dysfunction. The only alternative to this misdirected effort is to shake-up and reframe the dialogue, to separate it from the available heuristic that has bound it to the pointless, and instead, to attack meaningful reform through the impetus of a return to fundamental first principles compelled by the American public's invocation of their rightful entitlement to protection of American law prosecuted through the judicial system and the judicial imposition of accountability on those who have caused this financial carnage: Washington and Wall Street.

Washington and Wall Street have worked together to inflict the financial crisis on ordinary Americans. It is not a matter of breach of contract. It is a matter of civil rights. And a matter of national security. It is of existential necessity. It is a course of abuse of their power through intentional representation of the value of money over a prolonged period, the effect of which has been to aggrandize wealth and power. In common vernacular, it is an intentional program of lying cheating and stealing. It is the ancient crime and tort of money debasement.

We turn next to the development and history of money debasement culminating in the financial crisis that has wrought monetary damages upon ordinary American households in excess of $20 trillion plus inestimable personal pain suffering and even loss of life. It has inflicted a burden on American that only Washington and Wall Street have largely avoided, and from which they have, in fact, ultimately prospered enormously. Money debasement. America led the process of institutional money debasement and has exported it throughout the global monetary and financial system. Enforcement of accountability for the damages inflicted by intentional money debasement will not be popular with Washington and Wall Street. If they cannot be compelled to follow the laws of the land and respect the long history of popular refusal, ultimately to suffer the degradations of money debasement and seek redress through violent means, it will be the greatest tragedy in world history; a tragedy that can be avoided only by our collective insistence on the adherence to the moral foundation for our social, economic and political system through enforcement of the laws of the land in which those principles are embedded.

CHAPTER 4

Money Debasement

§4.01 ANCIENT CRIME

Money debasement is an ancient crime. The ancient crime of money debasement constitutes an intentional, fraudulent misrepresentation of the liquid value of assets measured in units of sovereign money and an abuse of power by those that create it.

The United States of America was formed in a cauldron of war in the western world including exploitation of the 99 percent by the 1 percent; revolution by the 99 percent in a quest for accountability, redress and relief through America's mission to free itself and its society from the tyranny of the 1 percent. England won its war with France and debased its money to finance the victory. The debasement included restriction of private money in the American colonies, imposition of taxes in English currency and absence of money locally, requiring a resort to a local barter economy and the forced acceptance of trade credit from London, denominated in English money. The French lost the war with England, exhausted and ruined its money in the process and resorted to compulsory confiscation of gold and silver, forced loans from the nobility and ruinous taxation of the 99 percent. To add to the misery, in a fit of revenge, France further depleted its treasury to finance the American Revolution in the hope that the colonists would win and humiliate England.

Technically, 1788 was the year of France's last default, although, as we will see, post-revolutionary France experienced an epic hyperinflation that effectively led to the elimination of virtually all debts, public and private. Madison's and Martin's concerns were well-shared, were well founded and apply today just as they did at the inception of our government.[330]

The French experience came to a head virtually with the coincidence of the American Revolution with the French Revolution, the "Terror"; and mass execution of the 1% by the then new-fangled efficient execution machine called the "guillotine." That was an imposition of accountability: Old Testament punishment, retribution and deterrence in the manner feared by former Treasury Secretary Geithner.

The lessons of the time were taken by America's founding fathers, specifically Thomas Jefferson, author of the *Declaration of Independence* and James Madison, author of the *United States Constitution* and the *Bill of Rights*. The force of development of the English common law, beginning with the *Magna Charta*, and continuing to the time of the American Revolution, took a progressively stricter course of the prohibition of money debasement as a violation of the English publics' human civil right to honest money, ultimately making the debasement of money treason, a crime punishable by death. The American *Constitution* was the first organizational document for a modern nation-state that—so thought the authors and those adopting it—retained sovereignty in the people—not in government; prohibited money debasement and provided a specific congressional power and duty to provide honest money and regulate its value. This power and duty was intentionally and specifically, constitutionally, delegated by the American people to Congress—theoretically a democratically—a politically accountable body; thus and thereby avoiding the well-known scourge of money debasement historically perpetrated by the monarch as sovereign. Madison and Jefferson clearly understood that money debasement constituted a violation of the American citizens' natural, human civil right, in a democratic civil society, to a transparent government regulated medium of exchange, store of value, unit of account and standard for deferred payment. This human civil right formed an essential cornerstone in the foundation for the modern democratic civil society that is the United States of America.

Dylan Grice, formerly of Societe Generale has prepared a masterful short piece, *Short History of Currency Debasement*[331] widely circulated on the internet. Grice outlines the effects on a society and the consequences to the holders of economic power when the society is degraded and damaged by currency debasement, The only defect of this excellent short history is its failure to recognize that the power to create money and regulate its value, including also, the power to transparently devalue or revalue money, has been for practical, not legal purposes, ceded by the American Federal Reserve system to the Wall Street banks, through the Federal Reserve structure, and through the Fed policy of "self-regulation" for those powerful institutions.

Within the context of the short history of currency debasement beginning with the Great Roman Third Century Debasement, Wall Street and Washington's criminal and civil liability for the damages caused by the financial crisis is grounded in the *Magna Charta*, or great charter, that is the foundation for the common law of all of the English speaking peoples; specifically as developed in England and later in the American colonies and as embodied in the *United States Constitution*. Throughout history, societies have collapsed as a result of currency debasement. Examples cited by Grice and others include Rome, 3rd Century A.D; Britain, 1515—1659; France 1791-1795; Germany, 1914-1923 and today, globally.[332]

The English Kings engaged in the practice of debasing coinage under the authority of their "sovereign" power to do so. This debasement was accomplished by falsely certifying the intrinsic value of coinage, or by permuting the money standard, contrary to common law standards.[333] In 1215, by the *Magna Charta*, the English Barons at Runnymede in Sussex, England forced the English King John to acknowledge that the King of England, the sovereign, was bound by the common law of England. By the late 1700s, Parliament had defined the King's royal prerogative to regulate the value of money as "not including the authority to debase the coinage, either directly, or by transmogrifying the "sterling" standard."[334] The limitation on the royal prerogative imposed by *Magna Charta* was also held to prohibit the imposition of forced loans by its subjects (which is also the effect of currency debasement, a forced loan or tax exacted from the subjects without their consent), as an invasion of private property—theft, an affront to reason, infringement on men's liberties and a violation of due process of law, as secured by the *Magna Charta*.[335]

Notwithstanding the *Petition of Right* which confirmed this stricture of the common law, Charles I in 1640, through the exertions of the Earl of Strafford, seized currency from the mint as a forced loan, and then proceeded to "imbase," the coin with mixed brass, also referred to as a "debasement."[336] The Earl claimed in his defense, the urgent necessity—the political expedient—of payment of costs of shipbuilding. Or "Ship Money." Parliament was not impressed with by the citations of precedent offered by the Earl. He was convicted of his misdeeds, including currency debasement, and was executed, followed shortly by his master, Charles I.[337]

In the late 1700s, the constitutional struggle in America was between the people, as the sovereign, and the government, based upon the fundamental democratic principle of the public's denial of sovereign power to any legislature, executive official or judge. The result of this struggle enshrined in the *United States Constitution* certain principles, drawn from the common law, which only the people themselves could modify by formal constitutional amendment. The principle we are concerned with in this case is the constitutional prohibition of currency debasement through the adoption of fiat money or any other device that has the effect of debasement of the value of money.[338]

As both England and the United States directly addressed the evil effects of the debasement of money on the public welfare, in France, John Law, a Scottish economist who believed that money was only a means of exchange that did not constitute wealth in itself and that national wealth depended on trade, was appointed Controller General of Finances of France under King Louis XV. In 1716 Law established the Banque Générale in France, a private bank, but three-quarters of the capital consisted of government bills and government-accepted notes, effectively making it the first central bank of the nation. He was responsible for the Mississippi Bubble and a chaotic economic collapse in France. The wars waged by the King left the country completely wasted, both economically and financially. The resultant shortage of precious metals led to a shortage of coins in circulation, which in turn limited the production of new coins. It was in this context that the regent, Philippe d'Orléans, appointed John Law as Controller General of Finances. Since, following the devastating War of the Spanish Succession, France's economy was stagnant and her national debt was crippling, Law proposed to stimulate industry by replacing gold with paper credit and then increasing the supply of credit, and to reduce the national debt by replacing it with shares in economic ventures. Though they failed, his theories, ironically, live on 300 years later and "captured many key conceptual points which are very much a part of modern monetary theorizing." In May 1716, the Banque Générale Privée ("General Private Bank"), which developed the use of paper money, was set up by Law. Law would become the architect of what would later be known as "The Mississippi Bubble"; an event that would begin with the consolidation of the trading companies of Louisiana into a single monopoly (The Mississippi Company), and ended with the collapse of the Banque Générale and subsequent devaluing of the Mississippi Company's shares. The company's shares were ultimately rendered worthless, and the initially inflated speculation about their worth led to widespread financial stress, which saw Law dismissed from his post as Chief Director of the Banque Générale at the end of 1720. He contracted pneumonia and died a poor man in 1729. Some scholars believe Louis XV's decisions damaged the power of France, weakened the treasury, discredited the absolute monarchy, and combined with the financial distress inherited and resulting from Louis XV's wars and financial profligacy, contributed to the French Revolution, which broke out 15 years after his death. From 1776, Louis XVI actively supported the North American colonists, who were seeking their independence from Great Britain, which was realized in the 1783 Treaty of Paris. The ensuing debt and financial crisis contributed to the unpopularity of the ancien régime which culminated at the Estates-General of 1789. This crisis of money debasement, inflation and division of the rich and poor led to the Queen's famous response to the citizens' demand for bread—that if the people do not have bread "let them eat cake." The King and Queen both lost their heads by guillotine. As noted earlier, technically, 1788 was the year of France's last default. Post-revolutionary France experienced an epic hyperinflation that effectively led to the elimination of virtually all debts, public and private.[339]

Blackstone (1771-1773) in discussing the English common law forbidding the counterfeiting of coin, elaborates with respect to its corollary, the debasement of money: emitting and presenting as money that is not the full value it purports present: "clipping, washing, rounding or filing, for wicked gains sake, any of the money of this realm, or other money suffered to be current here, shall be adjudged high treason; and .... The same offence is described in more general words: *viz.* impairing, diminishing, falsifying, scaling and lightening; and made liable to the same penalties."[340] High treason, of course was punishable by death.

The *United States Constitution* established specific monetary powers and disabilities for each branch of government. The *Constitution* was adopted on September 17, 1787, by the *Constitutional* Convention in Philadelphia, Pennsylvania, and ratified by conventions in eleven States. It went into effect on March 4, 1789. Since the *Constitution* was adopted, it has been amended twenty-seven times. The first ten amendments (along with two others that were not ratified at the time) were proposed by Congress on September 25, 1789 and were ratified by the necessary three-fourths of the states on December 15, 1791. These first ten amendments are known as the *Bill of Rights*. The monetary powers and disabilities of the *United States Constitution* remain essentially as originally written.

The extension by the English Parliament in 1764 of the Act of 1751 permitted the "emission of Paper Bills or Bills of Credit" as "necessary or expedient ... in case of War or Invasion' and stipulated that any Colonial governor responsible for the "improper emission of legal tender bills of credit ... shall forfeit and pay the sum of one thousand Pounds, and shall be immediately dismissed from his Government, and for ever after rendered incapable of any public Office or Place of Trust."[341] Consistent with the English and American common law and the United States constitutional mandate, the *Coinage Act of 1792* accordingly "affixed the penalty of death for debasing the coinage."[342]

The history of constitutional law relating to the monetary powers and disabilities set out in the *Constitution*, however, is a history of almost continuous perversion of constitutional intent and language that has resulted in a national—and international system of money, credit and currency that rests in almost total conflict with the *Constitution*.

This subject has been detailed to the highest legal and academic standards by Edwin Vieria, Jr., in *Pieces of Eight*, 2nd Rev. Ed. (2002), (Vieira) a two-volume 1,722-page treatise on that subject. *Pieces of Eight* was largely out of print until highlighted by a column in the *Wall Street Journal* on May 29, 2010—as "... the most comprehensive account ever written of the legal history, from a strict constitutional perspective, of the money of the United States. An outstanding work of scholarship, unparalleled in its depth of research and rigor of analysis, *Pieces of Eight* undoubtedly must and will be recognized by all careful students of the subject as the definitive record—and the unanswerable indictment- of the United States' descent from the sound money of gold and silver established by the *Constitution* to the unsound and unconstitutional currency bottomed upon public and private debt that today masquerades as the 'dollar'." Dr. Vieira holds four degrees from Harvard: A.B. (Harvard College), A.M. and Ph.D. (Harvard Graduate School of Arts and Sciences), and J.D. (Harvard Law School). He has practiced law for more than thirty years, with an emphasis on constitutional issues.

The French Revolution, precipitated by money debasement, utilized largely to fund the American Revolution, among other highly visible acts of financial profligacy. The balance of the cost of the American Revolution was funded largely by "Continental" dollars—paper script, that were purchased by America's first coterie of wealthy bankers for pennies from destitute American soldiers and merchants in distress. The bankers promptly forced the Congress to redeem the largely worthless Continents with sound money, albeit partially, but sufficient to enable the bankers to reap enormous profits; beginning the practice of government and banking conjoint systematic depredation of the American public that continues today.

America's founding fathers were fully informed of the evils of currency debasement in England, France and in America. They intentionally provided legal protection for the American public against money debasement in the *Constitution*, primarily and specifically in Article 1, § 8, Clause 5, which provides that Congress shall have the power "To coin Money, regulate the Value thereof, and of foreign Coin, and fix the Standard of Weights and Measures." Facing the enormous cost of the Civil War, Congress began its slide down the slippery slope of political expedience, exploited the threat to American society posed by the war, for profit, by ignoring its constitutional duty to protect the public interest in sound money, first under the guise an existential emergency, and subsequently under successively less compelling guises, one after another. Congress has continued to ignore and subvert its constitutional imperative and duty to this day.

Money debasement under the guise of sovereignty is no longer accomplished in the main by the sovereign through clipping coinage, diluting coinage metal content or by diminishing coin size.[343] It is not even restricted to creating vast amounts of fiat currency by the sovereign. The overwhelming amount of unregulated money created with US government facilitation and incentives, is to be found in the explosion of debt in the "shadow banking system."[344] This includes dollar denominated trade and current account deficits, fiscal deficits and inflation in dollar denominated financial instruments well above the liquid value of the underlying collateral supporting the credit represented by those financial instruments. By increasing the amount of dollars in existence surreptitiously and letting the world discover the gap between face value and underlying liquid value of the credits' collateral support gradually, the government can create the illusion of greater prosperity measured in dollars than actually exists. Herbert Hoover concluded that "if the number of inches in the yardstick were lessened then there would be more cloth in the bolt."

§4.02 DEBASEMENT OF THE DOLLAR IS A MATTER OF FACT

Figure 4.1 US Dollar Purchasing Power / 1774-2012 (Log Scale)

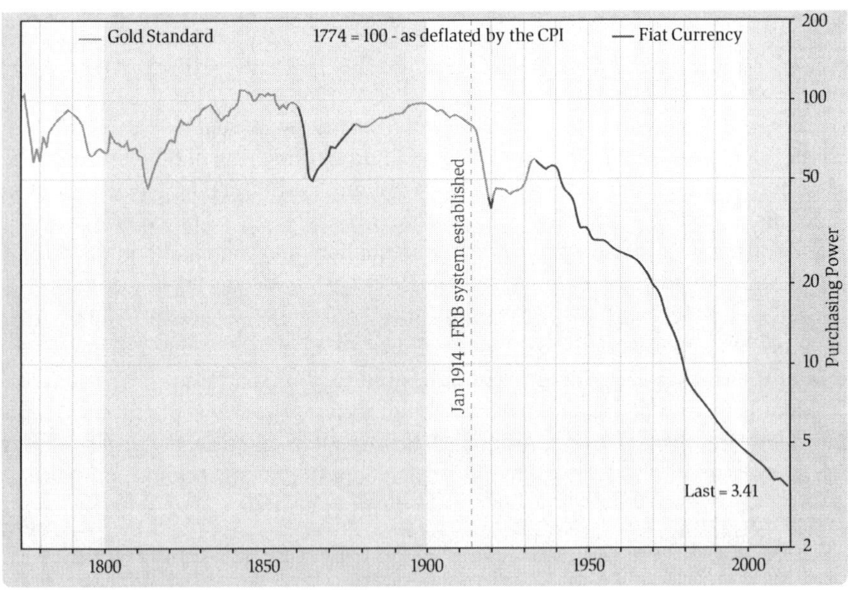

Current estimates in 2014 of the percentage debasement of the United States dollar run from 97 percent to 98 percent. Apart from the war periods prior to 1913, the entire debasement has occurred subsequent to the *Federal Reserve Act* and the establishment of the Federal Reserve System. Thus, money debasement—historically punishable as a capital crime—by the death penalty—in England and France, as well as under the first

American currency act, the *Coinage Act of 1792*[345]—shockingly, has now when taken in perspective, become the commonly accepted foundation of American fiscal and monetary policy. This perversion of principle, though now commonly accepted, is insane.

Government intervention in the economy through the Wall Street banks has resulted in a massive redistribution of wealth and income from the American public to Washington, Wall Street and the coterie of supporters and service providers that further their interests.

Figure 4.2 Average Income per Family

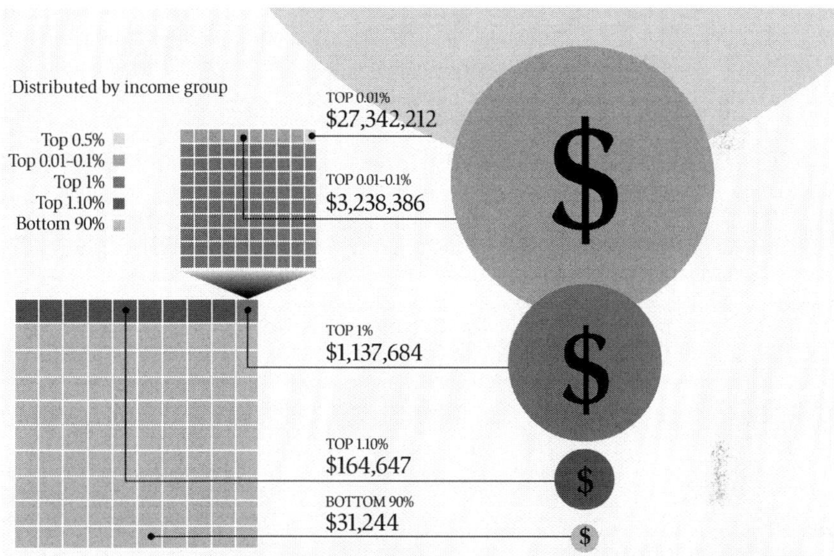

Figure 4.3 Household: Average and Change

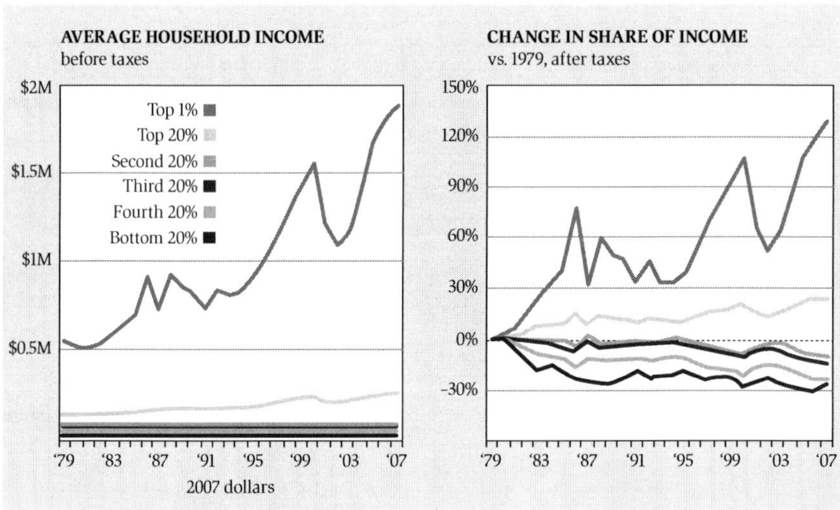

Source: Congressional Budget Office.

Figure 4.4 Wealth Distribution

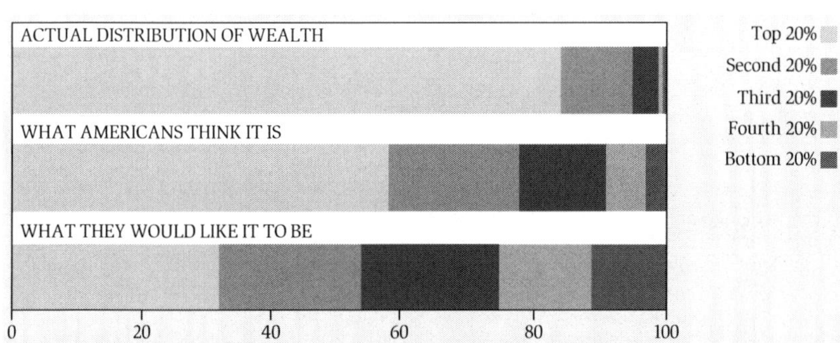

Source: Michael, Norton, Harvard Business School; Dan Ariely, Duke University.

As measured by FDIC data, the asset share of the largest banks has more than doubled from below 30 percent in 1984 to over 80 percent today, including a strong uptick since the 2008 financial collapse. During this same time frame, profits in the financial services sector increased significantly. Based on Bureau of Economic Analysis data, in the decades prior to deregulation, the financial sector share of total domestic corporate profits fluctuated from below 10 percent to as high as 16 percent. Beginning in the mid-1980s—as deregulatory efforts gained momentum—the financial sector share of domestic corporate profits increased steadily, finally reaching 30 to 40 percent of total

domestic corporate profits following the comprehensive deregulation of financial services under President Clinton in 1999 and 2000. This increase in the share of total private sector profits is significant, and it reflects the emergence of finance from an essential function in support of the broader economy—a notion central to the narrative described above—to an industry increasingly in service of itself.
According to John Mauldin in *Big Banks Shift to Lower Gear,*[346] "[a]t the end of 2013, the five largest institutions controlled 44.2 percent of total bank assets, up from 38.4 percent in 2007. As of March 31, 2014, those 107 institutions with over $10 billion in assets were only 1.7 percent of the total number but held 80.8 percent of all bank assets."

Dodd-Frank has bereaved banks of much of their origination in trading in futures, options and other derivatives. Derivative trading is largely being transferred to exchanges that guarantee fulfillment of the contracts as opposed to the highly profitable over-the-counter derivatives that banks trade but with which investors or speculators have to look to counterparties to be good for losses. This is the "counter-party risk" problem. Still, the seven largest banks still accounted for 98 percent of the $215 trillion notional value of derivative contracts as of March 31,[347] 85 percent of which were interest rate contracts.[348]

Still, regulators are concerned with derivatives. Those from 10 European and North American countries recently released a report that said many large banks and their regulators are still not ready to deal with difficulties in the huge derivatives market. They lack the information to consistently and accurately know who their counterparties are. Officials estimate that banks are up to three years away from having the necessary systems in place.

[A] Offshore Derivative Trading Has Escaped *Dodd Frank*

Michael Greenberger, Law School Professor, University of Maryland Carey School of Law, and Founder and Director, University of Maryland Center for Health and Homeland Security, former Director, Division of Trading and Markets, Commodity Futures Trading Commission, has described in great detail the extent to which Wall Street, its lawyers and lobbyists have effectively nullified the basic protections established by Dodd Frank to establish derivative trading transparency and constrain its excesses, in his paper published by the Institute for New Economic Thinking: *Too Big to Fail U.S. Banks' Regulatory Alchemy: Converting an Obscure Agency Footnote into an "At Will" Nullification of Dodd-Frank's Regulation of the Multi-Trillion Dollar Financial Swaps Market*, Working Paper No. (74 June 2018). Greenberger's abstract for the paper provides sufficient information for our present purposes. The entire paper is well worth the read. The abstract, in pertinent part, follows:

> The multi-trillion dollar market for, what was at that time wholly unregulated, over-the counter derivatives ("swaps") is widely viewed as a principal cause of the 2008 worldwide financial meltdown. *The Dodd-Frank Act* (Dodd Frank), signed into law on July 21, 2010, was expressly considered by Congress as a remedy for the deregulatory problems, in that market, that led to the crash. The legislation

required the swaps market, subject to US regulation, to comply with a host of business conduct and anti-competitive protections, including that the swaps market be fully transparent to U.S. financial regulators, collateralized, and capitalized. The statute also expressly provides that it would cover foreign subsidiaries of big US financial institutions if their swaps trading could adversely impact the US economy or represent an attempt to "evade" Dodd-Frank.

In July 2013, the CFTC promulgated an 80 page, triple columned, and single-spaced "guidance" implementing *Dodd-Frank's* extraterritorial reach, i.e., that manner in which Dodd Frank would apply to swaps transactions executed outside the United States. The key point of that guidance was that "guaranteed" foreign subsidiaries of US bank holding company swaps dealers were subject to all of Dodd-Frank's swaps regulations wherever in the world those subsidiaries' swaps were executed. At that time, the standardized industry swaps agreement contemplated that, inter alia, US swaps dealers foreign subsidiaries would be "guaranteed" by their corporate parent, as was true since 1992.

In August 2013, without notifying the CFTC, the principal swaps dealer trade association privately circulated to its member's standard contractual language that would, for the first time, "deguarantee" foreign subsidiaries. By relying only on the obscure footnote 563 of the CFTC guidance's 662 footnotes, the trade association assured its swaps dealer members that the newly deguaranteed foreign subsidiaries could (if they so choose) no longer be subject to Dodd-Frank.

As a result, it has been reported (and also has been understood by many experts within the swaps industry) that a substantial portion of the US swaps market has shifted from the large US bank holding companies swaps dealers and their U.S. affiliates to their newly deguaranteed "foreign" subsidiaries. The CFTC also soon discovered that these huge U.S. bank holding company swaps dealers, through their foreign subsidiaries, were "arranging, negotiating, and executing" these swaps in the United States with US bank personnel and, only after execution in the US, were these swaps formally "assigned" to the US banks' newly "deguaranteed" foreign subsidiaries with the accompanying claim that these swaps, even though executed in the US, were not covered by Dodd-Frank.

In October 2016, the CFTC proposed a rule that would have closed these loopholes completely. However, the proposed rule was not finalized prior to the inauguration of President Trump. All indications are that it will never be finalized during a Trump Administration.

[B] Dark Pools and High-Speed Trading[349]

Another area of concern to regulators is dark pools, private trading venues that do not disclose their activities publicly and account for 14 percent of all stock trading. Another 23 percent occurs in other off-exchange locales. The purpose of dark pools is to facilitate large institutional trading without exposure to high-frequency traders. Barclays bank runs Barclays LX, the country's second largest dark pool, which is marketed with the motto, "Protecting clients in the dark." But the New York Attorney General has charged that Barclays offered access to Barclays LX to high-speed traders. The bank is also accused of using other trading venues that benefit Barclays rather than its customers.

Under pressure from their institutional investor clients, many large brokers are routing trades away from Barclays LX and other dark pools. The SEC is investigating dark pools to determine whether they accurately disclose how they operate and whether they treat all investors fairly. Chairwoman White said in June that the size of off-exchange trading "risks seriously undermining" the quality of the US stock market. Goldman Sachs recently agreed to pay an $800,000 fine for mispricing 400,000 trades in dark pool Sigma X in 2011. The firm already reimbursed clients with $1.67 million."[350]

[C] Washington Wall Street Enterprise Profiteering from US Money Debasement

Following the crisis, Wall Street paid out $26.7 billion in bonuses, more than enough to double the salaries of Americans working full time at the minimum wage. According to *Bloomberg*, the "too big to fail" Wall Street banks enjoy an interest rate pricing advantage over other financial institutions; a subsidy, of approximately $83 billion per year. US banks now want to distribute more than $75 billion in "excess capital" to shareholders. There is no credible evidence that the Fed's massive Quantitative Easing program has benefited the public in any meaningful way, while inflating the Fed's assets to more than $4.2 trillion from $869 billion in August 2007.
There is clear evidence however, that the program has artificially kept interest rates down, creating and maintaining the interest rate spreads enjoyed by the Wall Street banks; taken toxic assets off their books without having to mark their values to liquid market value, thereby further enabling the banks to use the proceeds to continue to speculate in securities, driving the stock markets to inflated heights; and permitting the bankrupt FNMA and Freddie Mac to enjoy record profits and bonuses and "pretend" to repay governments bailout funds through funds created from nothing by the Fed and funneled to them as a part of the QE program.
The first among the beneficiaries of the intentionally fraudulent misrepresentation of the relative values of money, goods and services to the American public through the debasement of the US dollar are Washington and Wall Street. The American worker has seen the value of his or her honest labor, goods and services and savings shrivel. Deliberately manipulated interest rates have robbed the elderly and those with fixed income from a reasonable return on their savings—all to cover up Washington's and Wall Street's fraud. Younger generations of Americans have been left with a massive liability, created largely through wealth redistribution fostered by money debasement. The American public's demand for accountability means that Washington and Wall Street must be held liable in monetary damages under the American rule of law, punished for their wrongful conduct and deterred from future wrongful of that nature. That growing divide between the rich and you? It is not just in your mind, and it is certainly not just a couple years in the making:[351]

Figure 4.5 Average Incomes United States—1913-2012

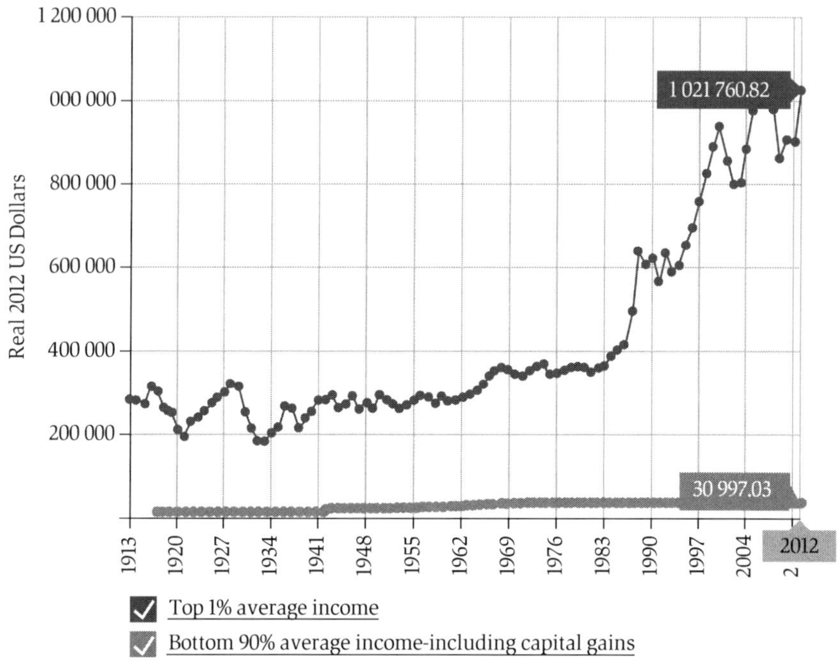

Sources: The World Top Incomes Database. http://topincomes.g-mond.parisschoolofeconomics.eu/; Piketty & Saez (2007).

This work does not present a case for income or wealth equality. It is simply a case for the proposition that Washington and Wall Street must be held accountable for their wrongdoing under the rule of law. It is that wrongdoing that has caused the dramatic increasing disparity in income and wealth and that same wrongdoing cased the financial crisis and the $20 trillion damages to ordinary Americans. The financial crisis does not call for the necessity of government political activism in income and wealth redistribution. That activism and redistribution have already occurred, accomplished and are ongoing through subversive, immoral and illegal activism and redistribution of income and wealth by Washington and Wall Street, conducted simply by stripping it away from the public through the raw exercise of concentrated power: through fraud and abuse of authority, trust and confidence. The American public can assert its legal rights to stop the iniquitous and increasing income and wealth disparity in America, based on fraud; recover damages for what they have had taken from them by way of damages and penalties for wrongdoing; rightful and acknowledged damages and legal penalties.

Bankers, politicians and bureaucrats might simply and sensibly find they are motivated to act with honesty and integrity if faced with the effect on this elite group of $20 trillion in damages, additional civil and criminal fines and time in prison, combined with a judicial mandate to meet their respective duties, standards of care and legal obligations. To date, Washington and Wall Street have dismissed any prospect of the force of public legal action and enforcement of the rule of law, and they continue to ignore and disparage the power of the American public under the rule of law. Washington's and Wall Street's liability under the current American rule of law is no longer the death penalty, but it is serious. It can and must be enforced. The mantra of Washington and Wall Street has been that, yes, the policies and actions that caused the financial crisis and more than $20 trillion in damages to the American public were wrong, possibly immoral but not criminal [or illegal]. That is incorrect.

The American rule of law exists. The people and the justice system need only actively implement and enforce it. Trillions of dollars of damages, penalties and prison time may have the wondrous effect of changing Washington and Wall Street's frame of reference, priorities and release a fresh attitude of remorse followed by a display of honesty and civic responsibility.

The failure of our judicial system to enforce the American rule of law has resulted in a fundamental failure of the American philosophical, social, political, and economic compact that is grounded in the American rule of law. President Obama has been quoted as advising the CEOs of the Wall Street Banks on March 27, 2009 that "[m]y administration is the only thing between you and the pitchforks ...."[352] As we will see., then US Attorney General Holder, without any evidence whatsoever, simply decided that protection of ordinary American households was too risky, but that saving the Washington's and Wall Street's presumed entitlement to protect their interests, included a free pass to continue to manipulate and debase the US dollar.

Congress has heretofore isolated itself from accountability through the nationwide scourge of rigid party politics, enforced through constituent electoral district gerrymandering, and irresponsible attempts to avoid accountability through "purported" delegation of duty to bureaucrats, while holding on to power as a political exercise with which to bargain for personal and institutional gain. The executive branch has isolated itself from accountability behind an impenetrable wall of entrenched bureaucracy and a quagmire of incomprehensible rule making and policies that serve only the bureaucrats and their special interests. As Winston Churchill famously observed: "If you have ten thousand regulations, you destroy all respect for the law."

As a result, Washington and Wall Street maintain a well lubricated revolving door between them that serves—not the public interest—but rather enables both Washington and Wall Street to maintain their unhindered exclusive trip down the yellow brick road to riches while the public interest languishes and withers.

§4.03 MONEY DEBASEMENT AND LAW

Why does the public need to advance its claims judicially under the American rule of law?

The public consensus is that, apart from a general dissatisfaction of the public with Congress (whose approval rating at this writing decline to around 9 percent in the wake of the financial crisis; just 13 percent currently[353]), the 7 percent honesty rating for members of Congress in 2012 was the lowest on record.[354] Although the public believes that Congress is dishonest, they do not realize that the *casus primus* of its dishonesty is its silent sanction of dishonest, debased money, yielding excess overvalued debt, the root of every financial crisis in our history.

Accountability for systemic financial crises has been a matter best kept quiet; left to expert's affected, staged concern and their questionable expertise in coping with the crisis. For Washington and Wall Street the most important objective for them, and they assure us, the best response to financial crises is to "move on," to "put the crises behind" using the threat of financial crises to further concentrate and expand their growth of power, wealth and income aggrandizement. For Washington and Wall Street, financial crises actually serve their constant desire for preservation and exploitation of the status quo on steroids. This perverse narrative of supposed support of public interest affords to Washington and Wall Street the time and distance enabling them to avoid the powerful forces of public retribution if the issues, roles, responsibilities and accountability were to be pointedly raised. The Washington and Wall Street rhetoric and narrative, then, is to simply put the crisis behind and get on with pursuit of the American dream, confident in our trust that they have served our interests, and without their efforts, each crisis would have been worse.

Congress has heretofore isolated itself from accountability through the nationwide scourge of rigid party politics, constituent electoral gerrymandering and irresponsible attempts to avoid accountability through delegation of duty to bureaucrats while holding on to power. The executive branch has isolated itself from accountability behind an impenetrable wall of entrenched bureaucracy and a quagmire of incomprehensible rule making and policies that serve the bureaucrats and their special interests. As Winston Churchill presciently observed: "If you have ten thousand regulations, you destroy all respect for the law."

As a result, Washington and Wall Street maintain a well lubricated revolving door between that serves—not the public interest—but rather enables both Washington and Wall Street to maintain their unhindered exclusive trip down the yellow brick road to riches while the public interest languishes and withers.

[A] Perverse Incentives

There are many perverse incentives to continued money debasement under the status quo of our economic, monetary, fiscal and financial systems:

- Traders in the market thrive on volatility, uncertainty and instability.
- Service providers in banking and financial services, including bankers, securities firms, insurance companies, ratings agencies, lawyers, accountants, appraisers and other valuation professionals, financial planners, contractors and the almost endless list of other commercial participants in the dispersion of the newly created money through credit creation down to the level of personal consumption, thrive on the increased volume of financial activity

that results directly from unrestrained creation of money and its flow through the American financial system.

- Bankers, including specifically and primarily, Wall Street bankers thrive on a protected and subsidized special relationship—a partnership with government.
- Bureaucrats, including specifically Federal financial regulators, thrive on an ever-increasing span of regulatory control, maximizing budget size and discretion, avoidance of responsibility for current developments and the possibility of being caught out on a mistake that would threaten the security of their sinecure.
- Members of Congress, its committees and politicians thrive on the attentions of special interests and unapologetically serve their interests in order to continue in office, cultivate post-service opportunities, garner campaign contributions and build a power base.
- The most prestigious lawyers and accountants in the country and their powerful clients have not done anything about accountability for the financial crisis because they all hope to benefit from the financial engineering activity—money creation—lying at the heart of the crisis, at someone else's—the America public's—expense. This band of prominent financial services clients and their advisors have resolved to deal with problems later—the indefinite date when some measure of accountability for their actions, might, cross their paths. The most prominent lawyers and accountants follow the money and the money creators; they go where financial services clients want to go. The largest and the most powerful and capable lawyers and accountants represent the Wall Street banks. They create and move money through financial engineering on a colossal scale—big deals, big prestige and the power that follows money. Von Mises was right. It's best for the bankers and their advisors to remain ignorant of the systemic tragedy that can be directly traced to their doors based on information that is, and has been, of public record. The theory is hardly what Americans would be entitled to expect from its most educated and powerful professionals and institutions—benefit if you can, as much as you can, and postpone the consequences. Someone else will have to deal with them later. That's just smart business.
- America, however, with the overwhelming hubris of the biggest bully on the block, continues to believe it can ignore the dramatic consequences of its abuse of its monetary institutions and policies and, what has been to date, the hegemonic power of the global dominance of the American dollar.

The prevailing hubris and arrogance of the Washington Wall Street enterprise's dominance in money matters has led to sloppy and myopic policies that have carried us too far from our Founding Fathers' admonition to base our government on sound, stable and honest money, the value of which is transparently regulated by Congress. A Congress that is democratically and legally responsible to the American public for the honest discharge of its constitutional duties and responsibilities. Without safe, sound, stable and honest money, every policy and act of our government is rendered unpredictable, because neither the American public nor the global financial community have an accurate, safe, sound, stable, honest unit of account to measure the economic impact of the American policies upon which those actions are taken. This failure opens wide the door to the vault holding the public's accumulation of the fruits of their labors and their honestly accumulated wealth and at each pass through the hands of those populating the Washington Wall Street enterprise, the value represented by ordinary American households is diluted and the literally stolen from each of them.

Throughout the history of financial crises in America the Wall Street banks have been bailed out, subsidized, preferred and protected by Washington. Washington and Wall Street have held the American public hostage through the ever-present specter and threat of an even greater, imminent and more damaging crisis, and the potential collapse of the nation's financial system, indeed the global financial system, if the Wall Street banks are not bailed out and treated preferentially as "too big to fail." The damages to ordinary Americans has simply been marginalized, intellectualized and ignored, as acceptable tail losses to be suffered by ordinary Americans. Ordinary Americans losses are thought by the Washington Wall Street enterprise as losses to be accepted as a normal consequence of business boom and bust cycles. So long as the Washington Wall Street enterprise is preserved and protected, all is well. The scattered complaints of individual American are derided and marginalized. Despite litigation and enforcement action arising from the financial crisis based on securities laws violations, the damages fines and penalties benefit the SEC and the holders to the securities in litigation, the collective results pale into insignificance in proportion to the losses suffered by ordinary Americans.

[B] Circumscribed, Managed and Minimized Financial Crisis Related Legal Accountability

Government imposed fines simply provide a small partial return of the benefits previously provided by the American government on behalf of the American public to the banks at taxpayer expense, and do little to nothing to punish the culpable parties past conduct or prevent the continuation of such conduct, and provides no justice to ordinary Americans at all..

Wall Street and Washington enjoy a symbiotic financial system all their own, providing for the creation and circulation of money, favors and opportunity in a revolving selfish circle that excludes and impoverishes the American public while enabling the closed Washington Wall Street enterprise and its circle of professional sycophants to prosper at public expense through an intentional policy of money debasement. There is no credible evidence that the preservation and preference of the Washington Wall Street enterprise based financial system and economy at the expense of and to the detriment of ordinary Americans is necessary to the protection and preservation of America's Main Street financial system and economy.

To the contrary, these wrongful actions are at the center of both the American Wall Street and American Main Street components of the financial crisis. Washington and Wall Street have protected themselves and the American public participants in the Main Street economy have been left, twisting in the wind, victims of the failure of legal accountability. The Washington Wall Street enterprise has violated the public's right to equal protection under the American rule of law and their right to due process before their wealth and property is appropriated—literally stolen from them through the mechanism of lying, cheating and stealing that is the nature of money debasement.

The causes of the financial crisis follow a pattern of money debasement repeated throughout history. The facts of this case have now been revealed in detail by the National Commission on the Causes of the Financial and Economic Crisis Inquiry in the United States in *The Financial Crisis Inquiry Report,* published in January 2011; the result of the Commission's review of millions of pages of documents, interviews with more than 700 witnesses and 19 days of public hearings conducted nationwide, as well as the existing work of a large body of congressional committees, government agencies, academics, journalists, legal investigators and many others.

In addition, SNL and other sources have publicly chronicled cases in which the top 6 Wall Street banks and been found liable for or settled allegations of fraud in the creation of money through the process of securitization which lies at the heart of the financial crisis that exploded from its epicenter in the shadow money and banking system. The legal record of these cases in litigation, in and of themselves, present incontrovertible evidence of the wrongdoing, not limited to the facts of each separate case, but more importantly, the course of conduct by these Wall Street banks, in concert with Washington government that, taken as a whole, constitutes a gross and intentional misrepresentation of the value American money, denominating the value of their assets, as debased through their financial engineering and structured financial products. The evidence of their wrongdoing is on file—in the public domain. SNL's charts follow:

Figure 4.6 Mortgage and Credit Crisis-Related Litigation and Settlement

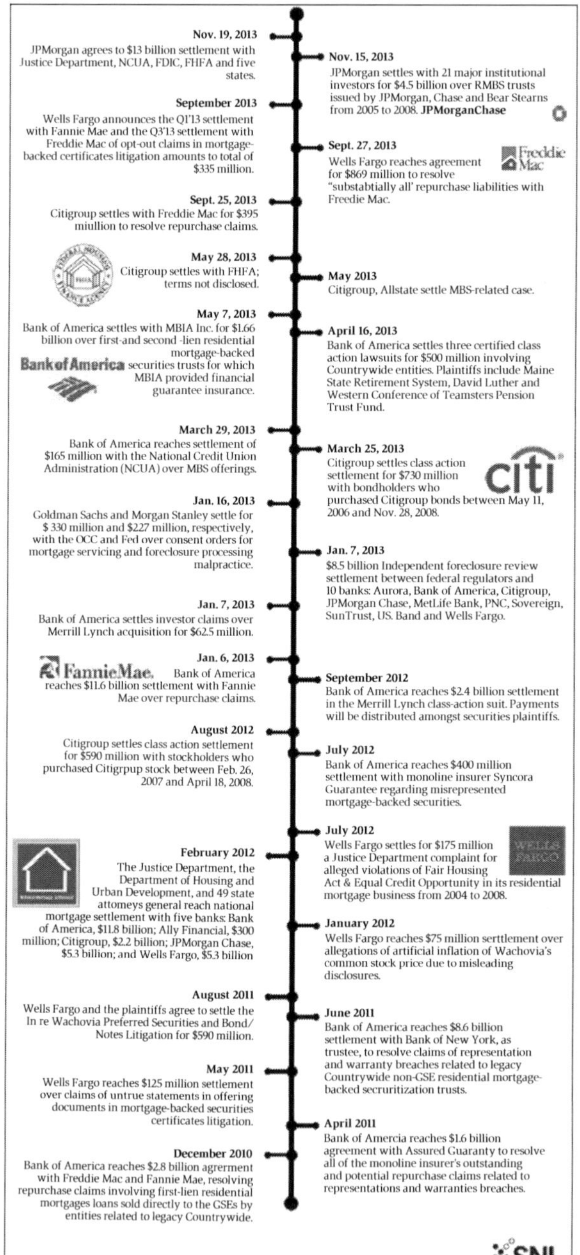

Source: SNL Financial
Credit: Cat VanVliet

Figure 4.7 Credit Crisis and Mortgage-Related Settlements for Selected Bank Holding Companies[1]

Amounts in millions of dollars unless otherwise noted

Company (ticker)	Total	2013 YTD Settlement	2013 YTD Details	2012Y Settlement	2012Y Details	2011Y Settlement	2011Y Details	2010Y Settlement	2010Y Details
Bank of America Corp. (BAC)	43,923.5	2,325.0	$1.66 billion, MBIA; $500 million, Maine State Retirement System, David H. Luther, and Western Conference of Teamsters Pension Trust Fund; $165 million, NCUA; TMST Inc.	16,174.5	$10.4 billion, Fannie Mae; $2.9 billion, OCC and FRB foreclosure review; $2.4 billion, Merrill Lynch class action; $400 million, Syncora; $62.5 million, pension funds over Merrill acquisition disclosures; $62 million, Maiden Lane II settlement	22,000.0	$8.6 billion, Bank of New York Mellon as trustee; $1.6 billion, Assured Guaranty; $11.8 billion, National Mortgage Settlement.	3,424.0	$624 million, New York state and municipal pension funds over Countrywide securities; $2.8 billion, GSEs.
Wells Fargo & Co. (WFC)	9,531.4	1,204.0	$869.0 million, Freddie Mac; $335 million, FHFA; Federal Home Loan Bank of Chicago; Federal Home Loan Bank of Indianapolis; Federal Home Loan Bank of Boston	2,125.0	$750 million in cash, $1.2 billion for foreclosure prevention, OCC and FRB foreclosure review settlement; $125 million, $50 million to community program, alleged violations of Fair Housing and Equal Credit Opportunity Acts.	6,090.0	$5.3 billion, National Mortgage Settlement; $125 million, mortgage-backed certificates litigation; $665 million, Wachovia Equity securities and bonds/notes litigation ($75 million equity, $590 million bonds/notes).	112.4	$100 million, Wachovia merger-related settlement with Citigroup; $12.4 million, Wachovia ERISA litigation with Wachovia employees.
JPMorgan Chase & Co. (JPM)	26,425.0	18,600.0	$4.5 billion, RMBS suit settlement with trusts issued by J.P. Morgan, Chase and Bear Stearns; $5.1 billion settlement with FHFA, Freddie Mac and Fannie Mae; $2 billion, DOJ; $1.4 billion NCUA; $515.4 million FDIC; $5.1 billion to states and consumers	2,525.0	$2.0 billion, OCC and FRB foreclosure review; $275 million, Bear Stearns shareholder litigation settlement; $297 million, SEC settlement of investigations into disclosures by JPMorgan subsidiaries and Bear Stearns entities.	5,300.0	National Mortgage Settlement. $3.7 billion for borrower relief, $500 million for refinancing assistance, $1.1 billion for cash payments.	NA	NA
Citigroup Inc. (C)	4,720.0	1,125.0	$730 million, Citigroup Inc. bond litigation; Allstate MBS-related settlement; $395 million, Freddie Mac; FHFA settlement over MBS sold to Freddie and Fannie	1,395.0	$305 million in cash, $500 million in foreclosure prevention, Independent Foreclosure Review; $590 million, Citigroup Inc. securities litigation.	2,200.0	$2.2 billion, National Mortgage Settlement.	NA	NA
Goldman Sachs Group Inc. (GS)	920.8	NA	NA	330.0	$330 million, FRB settlement over mortgage servicing and foreclosure processing.	13.0	$13 million in principal forgiveness, agreement in practice on mortgage servicing with New York State Department of Financial Services, Litton and Ocwen.	577.8	$550 million, SEC for ABACUS 2007-AC1 offering; $27.1 million, FSA for failing to notify of SEC ABACUS 2007-AC1 investigation; $650,000, FINRA for failure of timely U4 updates following SEC's Wells Notice.
Morgan Stanley (MS)	329.7	NA	Company et al settled class actions with King County, WA, Abu Dhabi Commercial Bank; participants announced settlement in Luther et al vs. Countrywide.; Central Mortgage Co. vs. Morgan Stanley Mortgage Capital Holdings litigation resolved	227.0	$227 million, FRB over mortgage servicing and foreclosure malpractice.	NA	Company reached agreement in principle to settle Lehman Brothers equity/debt securities litigation.	102.7	$102.7 million, assurance of discontinuance with attorney general of Massachusetts to resolve investigation into financing, purchase and securitization of certain subprime residential mortgages.
Total	85,850.4	23,254.0		22,776.5		35,603.0		4,216.9	

As of Dec. 5, 2013

[1] Includes the six largest bank holding companies by Q3'13 assets.

Data collected on a best-efforts basis from disclosures in public company documents and other releases. Totals or values represent approximations based on disclosures.

Values in chart are presented in financial periods in which companies report the values or conclusions of the litigation. Settlement amounts may not be accrued in the given period and in some cases may be subject to final court approval.

Comments are included to provide explanation and breakouts for a given company's value for a specific period.

Source: SNL Financial

Here is another SNL chart that illustrates the complexity and complicity of Washington and Wall Street in the web of shadow banking money debasement that fomented this crisis. Note that ordinary Americans appear nowhere in any of the foregoing or the following graphic analyses.

Figure 4.8 $Billions Paid in Settlements

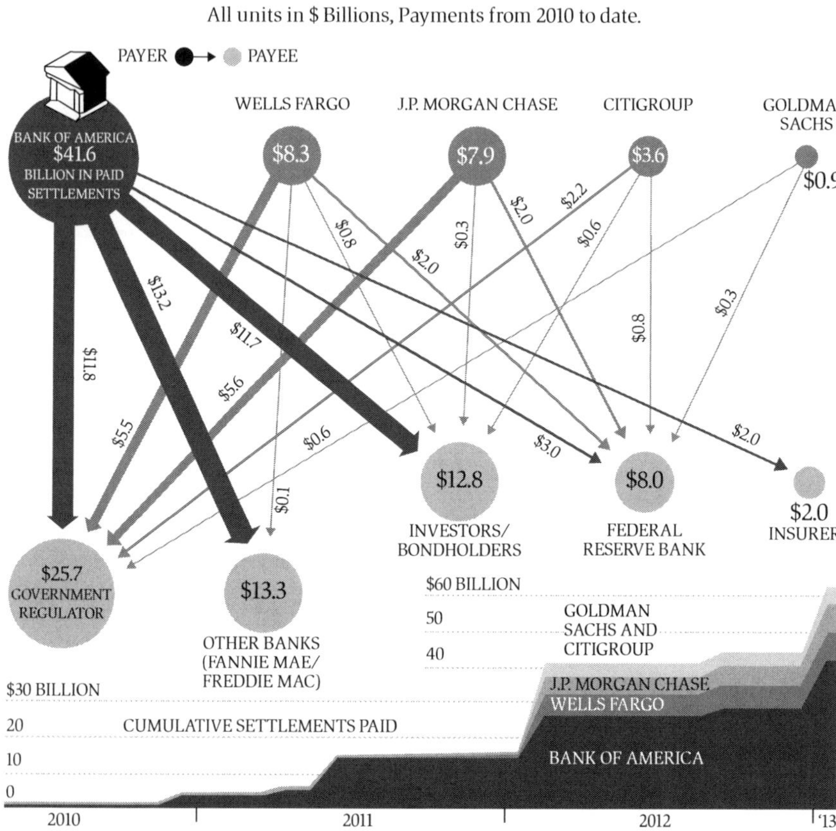

Source: SNL Financial.

[C] Money Debasement Causes Financial Crises Suffered Predominately by Ordinary American Households

Money is an abstract social construct and social compact useful to society when its value is regulated in relationship to an identifiable standard of value which can therefore be readily transferred and negotiated in the market economy. The standard of value used in recent centuries, the reference to which as a standard for regulation of the value of money has most often been, but need not necessarily be, precious metals such as gold or silver. The money need not itself be gold or silver. The concept that money itself must be comprised only of specie is a relatively recent concept propounded by John Locke as a ready remedy to then widespread money debasement and to ensure that the principles of democracy would not be eroded by government and captive monopoly banker money debasement, and resulting fraudulent concentrations of wealth and power. But in every event, the people must have trust and confidence that the money, whatever its form, can be safely transferred, negotiated and converted into a relative comparable value of goods and services in the marketplace.

When governments and banks abuse their power and the public trust; and as a result, confidence in money and its economic value in the marketplace is diminished and secretly, surreptitiously these powerful persons and institutions appropriate -incrementally steal—Americans money's value and take it for themselves by establishing overstated value in money, profiting from the process of launching it into the market where the public must accept it as legal tender that is not in fact supported by the value as represented; leaves the public with debased and devalued money while the Washington Wall Street enterprise keeps the profits; and ordinary Americans, while suffering the losses, bail out the perpetrators, insulating them from loss; concentrating the Wall Street banks power and wealth; and as a result, trust and confidence in government and the banking elite evaporate from the world of banking and commerce and, financial crises such as the ongoing 2008 global financial crisis are the result.

Since the beginning of civilization as we know it, and the development of numeracy and writing and then money in various forms in ancient Mesopotamia and in China thousands of years ago, money has served as the foundation for the development of civilization and the increased social and economic well-being it brings. The roles of the state and of banks created by the state, established to administer and finance state activities as well as the vital fundamental public and private interest in efficient, effective, honest, trusted and confident trade, savings and finance, have been crucial to the developments of civilization and complex economies accompanied by a seemingly ever increasing standard of living that in today's America has been called the "American Dream."

This same history also reflects a record of periodic abuse by the state and by banks of their artificially established legal monopoly on the creation of money and use of banks as a bifurcated tool of both government and civil society and their role in intermediating value through state and international economies. The abuse by the state and by banks of their official monopoly of money creation and thus concentration of wealth and power through the debasement of money; increases the amount of money without reflecting pecuniary value of any good or service—creating only a legal representation of something that purports to have a standard value, that, in fact represents in significant proportion, absolutely nothing; and then pocketing the money received in return that even as diminished and debased in value, represents more value received by the bank than value given by the holders of the fresh debased credit money. Sounds like a scam. In fact, it is a scam.

Secretly reducing the value represented by the monetary unit to enable the state and its banks to create more money for immediate use mainly to pay the (non-pecuniary, but allegedly socially useful or allegedly necessary) costs of war, social programs and financial profligacy (including bankers' profits, bonuses, lobbying costs as well as political contributions and subsidization of the costs of the revolving door of riches and opportunity between Washington and Wall Street); without facing the discipline of public debate and legislation that must precede legitimate taxation for the publicly identified purposes, and made subject to public scrutiny and informed consent, is not merely wrong, irresponsible and immoral; it is illegal. The public is susceptible to false assurances disseminated, in the present case, by Washington and Wall Street: that the monetary and economic policies forced on them are the work of trusted experts and in the public interest; that without their essentially unbridled control over these policies the public would certainly be worse off. When the citizens of the state become aware that the value of the fruits of their labor captured as money has been diluted and captured by the state and its state created and controlled partners and amanuenses, banks, outside of an honest and transparent system of taxation, their recourse is most often problematic, short of civil disobedience and then violence.

Wall Street's and Washington's dishonest behavior has been compounded by the recognition today that the hidden dispossession and transfer of the peoples' wealth has not been conducted simply to avoid accountability for immense, unmeasured and undisclosed non-pecuniary potentially beneficial social purposes without subjecting the amounts and purposes to public examination, debate and political action with corresponding political accountability.

No. No. In this financial crisis, Washington's and Wall Street's' mutual purpose has been to line their pockets and perpetuate their exclusive Washington Wall Street enterprise circle of prosperity through concentration of wealth and power, looting the public, and profiteering on a colossal scale.

This situation has been publicly reviled. Outrage has gripped the country; and yet the now obvious looting through lying, cheating and stealing by Washington and Wall Street, have, together, created a corrupt racket that dwarfs what we have come to know as the mafia—so-called organized crime. Today the corrupt racket is money debasement inflicted upon the American people, by the wealthiest, powerful and, at one time, trusted people and institutions of American society.

[D] *Ignorantia Affectata*

Not only are Washington and Wall Street, our experts in money matters, fully aware of the history and effects of money debasement, but further, both Washington and Wall Street have firmly adopted what Thomas Aquinas called the sinful practice of "cultivated ignorance," "*ignorantia affectata*": a pretended ignorance so useful that one protects it, keeps it from the light, in order to continue using it. Thus Washington and Wall Street pretend that they do not know about or understand the origins of and the lawful accountability for the financial crisis when they tell the American public so, even though the origins of the financial crisis and those accountable under American law for the damage caused by the crisis is, demonstrably, fully known to them. Washington and Wall Street caused the financial crisis and must be held accountable under the rule of law. Today's cultural and idiomatic equivalent to *ignorantia affectata,* comes to us in tired and ridiculous phrases such as *extend and pretend, kick the can down the road, deny and lie, delay and pray and so forth.* It is in this *ignorantia affectata* phraseology that Washington and Wall Street essentially admit to their conscious, intentional, ongoing deception of the American public so as to keep the clear foundation for their legal liability from the light of day; attempt to avoid their legal liability for conducting the largest, most profitable monopoly, cartel, literally and organized criminal racket, for as long as possible—forever if they continue to be as successful at *ignorantia affectata* as they have been to date.

There is then, consequently, an attitude in America that what has happened—the actions of Washington and Wall Street and the consequences of those actions, are somehow OK, legal; that the American people, are for some inexplicable reason, helpless in the face such wealth, power and claimed legitimacy. That is simply not so.

There has always existed some approximation of the 99 percent and the 1 percent consisting now of ordinary American households, on the one hand, and the power and wealthy elite in in and surrounding the Washington Wall Street enterprise on the other. People are not all equal. Some rise to the apex of society by the various combinations of genetics, physical stature, strength, intellect, cleverness; physical and geographic environment, deceit and luck. Those who have risen to the top echelon of a society have always used their resources and place in society to amass wealth and power to a greater extent than the rest of the American public. They have long preserved and protected their advantages through exercise of the power that their exalted positions command; and failing that, through the exercise of force; through violence. That the exercise of power and force has taken the form of violence external to the society, through the foment of war with other societies, such as the American Revolution, World Wars I and II and the regional wars in which America has been almost continually engaged during the past 60 years; or internal to the society, such as the American Civil War, each round of violence has been countenanced, if not authorized by Washington, financed by Wall Street and fought on the bloody ground by the American public, ostensibly to thereby counter real, or most recently, manufactured, existential threats to American society.

This war making enthusiasm has historically provided a rationalization for further concentrations of wealth, power and control by Washington and Wall Street, purportedly as an existential necessity and based on sacrifices purportedly made by them, as the elite; the wealthy and powerful, to protect the interests of the mass of the American public; a public too weak to protect themselves, too powerless individually, and on their own, to protect their American Dream, without the kind, self-less patronage of the wealthy and powerful. The narrative rings false and is un-American. Our democracy has been firmly established under the rule of law, precisely for the declared purpose of avoiding this hateful dynamic. As stated in the American *Declaration of Independence*:

> Prudence, indeed, will dictate that governments long established should not be changed for light and transient causes; and accordingly all experience hath shown that mankind are more disposed to suffer, while evils sufferable, than to right themselves by abolishing the forms to which they are accustomed. But when a long train of abuses and usurpations, pursuing invariably the same object evinces a design to reduce them under absolute despotism, it is their right, it is their duty, to throw off such government, and to provide new guards for their future security.

Americans are now reawakening to the abuses, usurpations and irreparable damages imposed by Washington and Wall Street on the American public through the great financial crisis and its predecessor crises occurring since the creation of America as the first social, political and legal experiment in modern democratic governance. The American public are reaching the outer limits of their range of tolerance of what they rightfully view as the abuse by the Washington and Wall Street partnership of their wealth and power, accomplished through abuse and repression of the American public, economically, through debasement of American money, through the euphemistic guise of "monetary policy."

Washington's and Wall Street's periodic abuse of the American public and usurpation of control over our economy are, and have always been, accompanied by displays of raw power and concentration of wealth; excesses of consumption; arrogance; hubris and the open disparagement, demeaning of the American public as "takers" not "makers"; and as somehow unworthy of a clear, fair, honest and open shot at achieving the American Dream. It is out of this foul miasma that American public have historically and repeatedly asserted their natural human right, as participants in civil society—their civil right—not to absolute equality—but to equality under the principles of civil society as expressed in the rule of law: the right not to be subjected to the effects of being lied to, cheated, and stolen from by the Washington Wall Street enterprise, with the fruits of ordinary Americans' labor and frugality taken from them without due process or equal protection of American law, through the demonstrably unequal and unlawful discrimination against them by a closed financial system represented by the Washington Wall Street enterprise, grounded in entrenched power.

This historical state of affairs is not news. The dynamics have been with us always; remain with us today; and will continue unabated without concerted public action under the American rule of law. The state of affairs has once again become intolerable to the American public and it is their constitutional right and duty to enforce our country's founding principles. Congress has failed us. The Executive branch, including all federal financial regulatory agencies and law enforcement agencies have failed ordinary Americans.

Maintaining a continuous state of war and physical repression of society is not cheap. Washington and Wall Street have historically used their wealth and power to operate a societal protection racket; whether the purported existential threats to society are real or posed, and whether they are internal or external. The Washington Wall Street enterprise finance their participants' aggrandizement of wealth and power through taxation, abuse of "tax breaks" and "loopholes," and on top of that, most perniciously, through debasement of money. Money debasement is not limited by its ancient origins. It has been defined in modern terms:[355]

> Currency debasement is the age-old process by which money is diluted such as mixing the gold in gold coins with a base metal to make more coins. Conceptually, it is creating money out of nothing. With paper money that is unredeemable for specie, i.e., fiat currency [the United States dollar], modern-day debasement takes the form of creating additional money, such as printing it. When private citizens create money out of nothing, it is called counterfeiting. Counterfeiting is always a crime, and government must act to stop it. When the government creates money

> out of nothing, thereby debasing the currency, it is described as Federal Open Market Operations, Monetizing the Debt, and Fractional Reserve Lending. Incredibly, society accepts such activity as a legitimate function of government.... One can make a prima facie case for the existence of current currency debasement from the reported increases in US currency in circulation over the past 45 years.

Modern day money debasement, in its essence, starts with an item of denominated currency; such as a dollar, in the form of printed paper, a journal or data account entry naming the denominated type of currency and the number of units represented, physically or electronically by the paper, digital or electronic record. Each unit of currency purportedly represents a certain amount of value that can be confirmed by reference to an outside thing, a standard. Historically, that thing has consisted of one or more precious metals of stable, enduring value and commonly recognized and accepted by society, thereby fixing a standard of value, regulating money values by reference to the standard, and limiting the creation of more money, including credit money, that can be supported in the economy by the limiting standard imposed through the ever-present discipline of conversion of money to the standard through redemption on demand.

[E] Money Debasement and The Supreme Court's Announced Monetary Law of the Land

The American *status quo* assessment of the US Supreme Court's position on the legitimate exercise by Congress of its power and to create and emit the nations' sovereign money, the value of which is regulated by Congress, is based in the Court's consideration of the enforceability of the certain contractual provisions which were at issue in the cases before it. These cases are referred to generally as the *Legal Tender Cases* and the *Gold Clause Cases*. These cases turned on the enforceability of contractual provisions. They did not turn on manner in which Congress might lawfully exercise its powers and duties under Article I, § 8, Clause 5 of the *Constitution*. The *Legal Tender Cases* and the *Gold Clause Cases*, in precatory language—dictum—, confirmed Congress' legitimate exercise of its powers and duties with respect to the creation, issuance and regulation of the value of money. The *Legal Tender Cases* adjudicated the enforceability of certain provisions of private contracts. The *Gold Clause Cases* adjudication the enforceability of certain provisions of contracts between the government as the issuer of bonds and private parties, the holders of such bonds.

[1] Legal Tender Cases

The United States Supreme Court in the *Legal Tender Cases*[356] stated expressly that we do not "assert that Congress may make anything which has no value money. ... It is, then, a mistake to regard the legal tender acts as either fixing a standard of value or regulating money values, or making that money which has no intrinsic value." The government had no power of making that money which has no intrinsic value. The Court further stated that "[t]his power of regulation is a power to determine the weight, purity, form, impression and denomination of the several coins, and their relation to each other, and the relations of foreign coins to the monetary unit of the United States."

[2] Gold Clause Cases

The United States Supreme Court in the *Gold Clause Cases,*[357] upheld the exercise by Congress of its Article I, § 8, Clause 5 powers as the basis for regulating the value of money. The exercise of those powers and duties was not at issue. The court stated the obvious point that Congress might alter the respective rights and obligation of private parties through the lawful exercise of such powers and duties. The Court held that the government, by eliminating the gold standard that defined the obligation of the government to repay the money it had borrowed, had essentially repudiated its obligations. The case turned, not on Congress foregoing powers and duties, but on its ability to borrow money. The Court confirmed that the government could not constitutionally abrogate its obligation as a debtor, and any such repudiation constituted a violation of the 14th Amendment provision that the validity of a public debt, lawfully undertaken, could not be questioned. Although the question whether the governments repudiation of its contract constituted a taking of the plaintiff's property without due process based upon *The Joint Resolution of the Congress of June 5, 1933*, 48 Stat. 113, that issue was not certified by the Court of Claims to the Supreme Court for consideration. But in the event, the plaintiff failed to prove damages.

These cases constitute the last word of the United States Supreme Court on the subject of the effect of the exercise by Congress of its power and duty to regulate the value of our money— dollar on terms of contracts between private parties and on obligations of the government for the payment of its lawfully incurred borrowings to private holder of that debt.

§4.04 A LEGAL CLAIM BASED ON THE INTENTIONAL TORT OF MONEY DEBASEMENT GOES TO THE HEART OF AMERICAS MORAL AND LEGAL FOUNDATIONS

When the United States government makes money that has no intrinsic value, and the holders or owners of the paper, or account entry representing their money cannot rely on the discipline imposed by the governments regulation of the standard of value based upon which the holder can redeem the legal tender representation of his or her unit values of money held in hand, commerce tumbles, often leading to financial crises. Upon the failure of the key constitutional requirement that the money be accounted for as a commonly accepted equivalent of publicly endorsed and legally prescribed, accepted, intrinsic value in accordance with the Article I, § 8, Clause 5 of the *United States Constitution* and the precedent established by the United States Supreme Court, in the *Legal Tender Cases* and the *Gold Clause Cases*, the value of the money is thereby debased. The representation of the value of the money or other assets or liabilities denominated and accounted for in that money constitutes false or fraudulent pretense, representation, dilation of the promise of value is money debasement. Today, in fact, the government has so far intentionally, unconstitutionally and tortiously failed and refused to regulate the value of the American dollar in relation to any outside standard of intrinsic value in furtherance of the Washington Wall Street enterprise. The amount of dollars in circulation has exploded and the scourge of money debasement is upon us. This debasement and the accompanying economic and financial dislocations constitute the financial crisis experienced by the American public, as opposed to the separate, discrete, financial crisis addressed by the Wall Street bailout and Washington's weak effort at financial reform under Dodd Frank.

Deliberate government (Washington) and banking (Wall Street) policies of money debasement lie at the heart of today's great financial crisis. Washington and Wall Street, together, have knowingly and intentionally executed, and continue to execute, the scheme or artifice of money debasement to obtain and concentrate under their ownership and control the moneys, funds, credits, assets, securities, or other property owned by American financial institutions or owned by American citizens and under the custody or control of American financial institutions, denominated in United States Federal Reserve Notes, by means of false or fraudulent pretenses, representations, or promises of the value of such moneys, funds, credits, securities and other property. Not only are Washington and Wall Street fully aware of the history and effects of money debasement and are America's self-appointed experts in money matters; but further, both Washington and Wall Street, have firmly adopted the sinful practice of "cultivated ignorance," *"ignorantia affectata."* Thus Washington and Wall Street pretend that they do not know about or understand the origins of and the moral and legal provision for their accountability for the great financial crisis under the rule of law, when they tell the American public so, even though the origins of the great financial crisis and those accountable under American law for the damage caused by the crisis, are fully known to them. Washington and Wall Street caused the great financial crisis through their greed for concentrated wealth and power. They must therefore be held accountable for their wrongdoing under the American rule of law.

§4.05 CIVIL AND CRIMINAL ACCOUNTABILITY FOR MONEY DEBASEMENT

The actions of individual Americans are subject to rigorous legal standards and sanctions imposed in cases of banking, securities and consumer fraud, and crime.

Politicians and the power elite throughout history have a well justified general reputation of duplicity and mendacity in money matters, accompanied by the continued ability to get away with it, time after time. Thus, the low regard in which they are held by the public. These "power elite" as well as the American public, seem to think that, no matter how outrageous the behavior of the power elite and no matter the level of outrage expressed by the American public, Washington and Wall Street are somehow exempt from the standards, laws and sanctions imposed on the rest of the American public in cases of banking, securities and consumer fraud and crime. And with the obvious political and financial success of the Washington Wall Street enterprise, the acceptance of practices of lying to, cheating and stealing from others as well- accepted, highly esteemed and emulated business and professional practices has spread throughout the banking, financial and political world. The closer one gets to the responsible individuals wielding power and garnering wealth in Washington and on Wall Street, the more difficult it is for ordinary Americans who have suffered deceit, misrepresentation or fraud through money debasement to successfully seek accountability and justice. They risk running afoul of the power held by the powerful public figures.

The customary and official method of dealing with the public figures and holding them accountable is generally thought to be for voters and shareholders to "throw the bums out." Unfortunately, congressional district gerrymandering and a rigid private dual-party political machine foundation has emasculated any semblance of the prospect of political accountability through the electoral process. That is dramatically confirmed in the current election cycle. The politicians who follow those thrown out, tend to be simply recycled from the base of lobbyists and special interests that control Washington and Wall Street, or otherwise fall into the age old patterns of active pursuit of self-interest held by their predecessors, in derogation of their formal and institutional responsibilities and their fiduciary duty to act in the public interest. This state of affairs is open, notorious and seemingly tolerated by the American public, for lack of leadership, organization and concentration of the power of the public based upon their shared collective interest and power, outside of the corrupt system dominated by the Washington Wall Street enterprise.

We are familiar with the generally held, some might say, cynical, view of Americans who find themselves at the end of acceptable levels of tail end losses consequent to the Washington Wall Street partnership's policies and actions; that there really "isn't anything we can do about it." It is just the nature of the system. The briefly popular, but largely ineffective, "Occupy Wall Street" movement and the more coherent and focused but intellectually questionable activity of the "tea party" movement; on essentially opposite ends of the political spectrum, both express public frustration with our collective inability to enforce responsibility and accountability for the harm caused by money debasement and systemic financial crises. Professor Paul Kennedy has thoroughly documented the historic consequences of successive societies' failure to enforce responsibility and accountability of the governing power elite through the mechanisms of civil society. When the gap between action and rhetoric becomes too great, mobs in fact do form, violence and war coalesce and heads actually do roll. Intellectual discipline and respect for the rule of law are abandoned. As President Obama once advised the nation's top financiers, Washington is the only thing standing between them and the pitchforks. That statement was apparently meant convey a sense that Washington in fact was protecting Wall Street from the consequences of its ongoing fraud. Actually, the Presidents statement simply served to clearly articulate Washington's active, intentional complicity in the Washington Wall Street enterprise. We certainly prefer that pitchforks will not be the answer. The modern equivalent is now more likely to be assault weapons, dirty bombs or other weapons of destruction. There is a middle ground that President Obama and the Department of Justice have simply ignored: the enforcement of existing laws against abuse of trust, power and money debasement by the Washington Wall Street enterprise. It is not too late.

When you get down to the essence of the issue, however, despite the widespread anger and frustration attendant to the loss allocation process in the ongoing American and global financial crises, we must be reminded that congressmen, federal financial regulators and their partners, the Wall Street banks and bankers, are not exempt from the legal standards and sanctions already provided for in our legal system. Their apparent insulation from the consequences of their actions is purely an illegitimate claim of perverse public policy, not supported by the American rule of law, and constitutes an act of raw unconstitutional usurpation of the sovereignty of the people of the United States and the irresponsible—and as we will indeed see—illegal—even criminal—exercise of unlawful political power by the American Congressional, bureaucratic and Wall Street power elite. How can this happen?

Today's cultural and idiomatic equivalent to Acquinas' *ignorantia affectata*, comes to us in phrases such as *extend and pretend, kick the can down the road, delay and pray, deny and lie,* and so forth. It is in this *ignorantia affectata* phraseology that Washington and Wall Street essentially admit to their conscious, intentional, ongoing deception of the American public, so as to keep the very clearly articulated legal foundation for their liability from the light of day; and to attempt to avoid their legal liability for as long as possible—forever if they continue to be as successful at it as they have been to date; and to continue to concentrate power, profit and wealth through their deception. The Obama administration admission that his administration was that has been standing between the public bearing pitchforks and Wall Street is a succinct admission of this very fact. If Washington does not assure the enforcement of the rule of law, by action of the DOJ or through judicial endorsement of private action under federal bank fraud, abuse of power and RICO statutes, history assures us that eventually the public will rise up, and this time they will be bearing far more destructive weapons than pitchforks,

[A] Surreptitious Insulation from Government Liability and Accountability

The Congress of the United States has determined, in its self-serving interest, under 28 US.C. § 2680, *Exceptions, of the United States Federal Tort Claims Act*, that as an exception to the ability of the public to hold government accountable for its wrongdoing—its torts—the government should be immune from claims for its deceit, its intentional misrepresentations in the communication of economic, monetary and financial information on which the recipient American households rely. For purposes of the exception insulating Washington from accountability, the definition of "misrepresentation" includes the failure to provide information as well as the providing of incorrect information. The deceit and misrepresentation exception has been applied to negligent as well as to intentional deceit and misrepresentations. Therefore, the person making the representation need not know that it is false, and the exception has been applied to complaints based on the government's failure to use due care in communicating information upon which the recipient relies. Similarly excluded from the coverage of the *Federal Tort Claims Act* are liability for damages caused by the fiscal operations of the Treasury or by the regulation of the monetary system.[358] Further, incredibly, Edwin Vieiera has pointed out that the Supreme Court, in United States v. Lee,[359] held that:

> "[n]o man in this country is so high that he is above the law. No officer of the law may set that law at defiance with impunity. All the officers of the government, from the highest to the lowest, are creatures of the law, and are bound to obey it.
>
> It is the only supreme power in our system of government, and every man who by accepting office participates in its functions is only the more bound to submit to that supremacy, and to observe the limitations which it imposes upon the exercise of the authority which it gives."

Nevertheless, as it apparently happens in today's real world, evidenced in the case of Mapco, Inc. v. Carter,[360] the court:

> F[und] no basis in constitutional history, judicial interpretation, political history, legal scholarship, or persuasive argument to conclude that ... a right ["to trust the federal government and to rely on the integrity of its pronouncements"] exists under the Ninth Amendment. Or any other provision of the *Constitution* of the United States.

As Dr. Vieiera noted further, "... through an exercise in relativistic or even solipsistic semantics, the court denied the existence under any possible circumstances of any possible constitutional right" to trust the ... government":

> Giving to the word "trust" the meanings, ... of assured reliance of confident expectation, it still describes a subjective condition of individual minds that simultaneously may be absent in some minds, and present in other minds in varying degrees, forms and substances. The concept of "trust" is not suitable for definition of a constitutional right enjoyed by all citizens or persons ...[361]

This is, of course, absurd.

[A]lthough Justices congratulate themselves on the "uniqueness of our *Constitution* and our system of judicial review: [that] courts at all levels are available and receptive to claims of injustice, large and small, by any and every citizen of this country," the reality remains that in Mapco (for one [exceptionally]egregious instance), the "courts at all levels," were anything but "receptive to claims of injustice"—even when those claims could be rejected only by repudiating the foundational doctrine that "a public office is a public trust." *In Pieces of Eight*, Dr. Vieira expands and explicates in excruciating detail his analysis of the web of legislative and judicial barriers to the application of traditional American justice to those who now hold the power in government over our money and its' debasement.[362]

The DOJ however has the authority and the obligation to enforce the criminal prosecution of the governmental defendants for their violations of criminal law based upon the facts and criminal laws referred to in this work. I advocate civil enforcement against the remaining defendants through American civil common law, constitutional and federal statutory law. So far, the DOJ has refused to enforce and prosecute applicable criminal law against either the government or the non-government defendants identified in this work for the civil and criminal intentional misrepresentation, fraud and abuse of trust and power described here. Former Attorney General Holder has taken the position that:

> ... [W]hen it comes to more complex transactions that involve more sophisticated traders—as opposed to run-of-the-mill "liar loan" cases or out-and-out Ponzi schemes—a criminal prosecution of an individual can be difficult, more complicated, to mount. This is true for any number of reasons—from possible advice-of-counsel defenses; to the adequacy or inadequacy of written disclosures; to the difficulty to establish materiality and intent. And in some instances, it is simply not possible to establish knowledge of a particular scheme on the part of a high-ranking executive who is far removed from a firm's day-to-day operations.[363]

When announcing his resignation as Attorney General at National Press Club event Tuesday, February 17, 2015, Attorney General Eric Holder gave the DOJ an opportunity to rewrite his legacy as the lead federal prosecutor who refused to take on some of the most notoriously larcenous bankers and politicians in history. Holder said he had given federal prosecutors a 90-day deadline to decide whether they can bring cases against individuals for their roles in the 2008 financial crisis. US attorneys who brought cases against institutions over misconduct in the pooling and sale of residential mortgage-backed securities have been asked "to try to develop cases against individuals and to report back in 90 days with regard to whether they think they can successfully bring criminal or civil cases against those individuals," Holder said:[364]

> I don't know if I'm making news now or not, but I asked the US Attorneys who made those cases and who are still involved in these RMBS cases over the next ninety days to look at their cases and to try and develop cases against individuals, and to report back in 90 days with regard to whether or not they think they will be able to successfully bring criminal or civil cases against those individuals.[365]

On December 15, 2011, at the referral of the Office of the United States Attorney for the Northern District of Texas, Dallas Division, I provided to the Dallas office of the FBI the essential facts and legal foundation for the claims covered in more detail in this work, as a "Potential Bank Fraud RICO case that is ripe for prosecution." To my knowledge, no action was taken by either the FBI or the DOJ, based on that information. The nature of these legal claims is not new knowledge.[366]

The elected and appointed members of our federal government—the holders of our public trust—individuals who are literally empowered and bound to protect our interests as American citizens above their own interests, as public fiduciaries—have so deteriorated in their sense of honor of the duties and responsibilities they have undertaken to the public; duties freely, clearly and unequivocally undertaken by them; and they have so deformed to the grotesque and perverted their sense of ordinary American's relationship with them as our government, through our consent to be constitutionally and lawfully governed, to the present demonstrably morally and legally bankrupt stage. They now hold themselves above the public without a twinge of conscience. Instead, they wield an unbridled arrogance, hubris and sense of entitlement combined with disregard—disdain—for the public interest, combined with unbridled expectation that they and their colleagues on Wall Street are literally entitled to lie to the public, cheat them, and steal from them with absolute impunity.

This present day is distanced only by the passage of time from the tyrants and despots of the past who, when they considered themselves impervious to public accountability under the rule of law, found themselves overtaken by angry mobs who wrought violent vengeance on them and literally paraded their heads on pikes as a graphic warning to others who might consider themselves as immune to public accountability through a perverse and ill-founded sense of natural and righteous nobility and entitlement.

This is the specter of "Old Testament retribution" that Tim Geithner, former United States Secretary of the Treasury, decried repeatedly in his recent book *Stress Test*. "[T]he Old Testament view" that "[t]he venal should be punished. The irresponsible should not be bailed out." He cites the appetite for "Old Testament vengeance," "Old Testament justice," "Old Testament impulses," "Old Testament populism," "Old Testament cravings," and so forth, no fewer than 18 times.[367]

Time magazine's Bill Saporito interviewed former Treasury Secretary Tim Geithner and, to this point, asked about beheading bankers (metaphorically): "You write about avoiding retribution against bankers, yet people are angry. Why didn't you go for a head on a stake just for show?" ([O]n the video, Saporito is more colorful: "You repeatedly talk about the need to avoid the sort of Old Testament retribution against bankers. People were angry at them. Why didn't you go for one head on a stake just for show?")[368]

Geithner's response: "Old Testament vengeance appeals to the populist fury of the moment, but the truly moral thing to do during a raging financial inferno is to put it out. The goal should be to protect the innocent, even if some of the arsonists escape their full measure of justice."[369] He might well have added, even if the Washington Wall Street enterprise is consolidated and strengthened; and oh, by the way, the *Constitution*, federal statutes and the common law are trampled to dust while ordinary Americans are left burdened with damages approaching $20 trillion.

[B] Creation and Direction of Money from Nothing to Disguise Money Debasement and Wealth Creation

In his Hayek Lecture for 2010, November 30, 2010, *Toward a common-sense currency*, Manuel Hinds, described what I have referred to as a "liquidity funnel" disguising money debasement as wealth creation, with another apt metaphor:

> The collapse of the Bretton Woods system in 1971 left in place the floating-currencies system, which grants central bankers' total freedom to print money at will. Floating currencies won the day because they conveyed a promise that, by allowing total freedom to create money in each country, they would promote global progress and employment, smooth out business cycles, and prevent bubbles and their associated crises. These expectations were based on what we can call the one-dimensionality of macroeconomic theory—the idea that demand is a homogeneous quantity which affects all sectors in the same proportion. Under

> this assumption, recessions come about because demand declines, negatively affecting the sales of all sectors in approximately the same proportion. This leaves all sectors with unsold inventories, impairing their ability to service their debts.
>
> If the world were actually like this, printing money would be like pressing the gas pedal of an automobile. It would increase demand equally for all sectors, which then would sell all their excess inventories, pay their debts, and start growing again. But in reality, the world is not like this. Printing money is like pressing a gas pedal that accelerates some wheels more than others. When the pedal is pressed to the floor, these disparate forces deform the vehicle. The problem of recessions is precisely this deformation. A deformed economy easily skids.
>
> These deformities initially take the form of bubbles, which increase demand for certain assets—say, dot.com shares, or houses, or commodities—leading to higher prices not in the entire economy but only in these particular assets. People overinvest in these sectors and feel increasingly richer while the boom is raging, generating a consumption binge that spreads the illusory gains of the boom to everybody else in the economy.
>
> Then, the bubble bursts and demand for the booming assets collapses along with prices. Demand does not contract uniformly, but in a distorted way. It contracts in a pattern dictated by the realities and feelings of people who have become poorer overnight. The last thing these people want is to continue buying the previously booming assets. So, the consumption binge comes to a stop. The economy seizes up because the troubled assets cannot be sold at their post-boom prices without defaulting on the loans that burden them. Banks stop lending because they do not know who is solvent and who is not. Thus, at the end of a boom and bust cycle, the economy gets deformed twice.

Ben Steil, in his Hayek lecture, *Hayek and the Dangers of Monetary Nationalism*, delivered at the same conference, followed the same line of thinking as Hinds but with yet a different metaphor:

> "To grasp what we are getting ourselves into, consider this analogy. Imagine you get into the shower, turn on the water, and nothing comes out. You call the plumber. He tells you there's a hole in the pipes, and that it will cost you a thousand dollars to repair it. You tell him just to turn up the water pressure instead.
>
> "Sound sensible? Well, this is the logic behind QE2, the Fed's strategy to keep flooding the money pipes until credit starts flowing freely again from banks to businesses.
>
> "You wouldn't expect this to work in your shower, and there's little reason to expect it to work in the commercial lending market. The credit transmission mechanism in the United States has been seriously damaged since 2007. There is a hole in the pipes. Small- and medium-sized businesses in this country are dependent on small- and medium-sized banks for access to vital credit, yet too many of these banks remain walking dead, unable to lend because their balance sheets are littered with bad commercial and real estate loans made during the boom years. The Troubled Asset Relief Program (TARP) was an opportunity to force banks to disgorge bad assets. This would have repaired the credit pipes. Instead, were obliged only to take equity injections from the government, equity they consider politically toxic, and they have therefore been focused on returning it at the earliest opportunity—not on using it to boost lending {Note that legal tender can be created only to serve as a medium for payment of debts, public and private; and that creating money for the purpose of serving as capital on the books

> of a bank is not authorized as a liability—debt}. The net result is that, even though the Fed has driven its short-term lending rate down to zero, most banks will only lend on vastly greater collateral and at much higher real interest rates than before the bust. So now we plow on with the cheap option: flood the pipes and see what comes out.
>
> "Make no mistake, something will come out. We've already seen the liquidity intended to boost domestic bank lending instead spill out through the cracks into markets as diverse as agricultural commodities, metals, and poor country debt."
>
> What is remarkable about this is that some of QE2's most prominent cheerleaders actually think it is all well and good wherever new demand shows up. After all, it is only "aggregate demand" that matters to the Keynesian faithful. To worry about the composition of demand, like a Hayekian, is silly. It only complicates the algebra. Nobel economist and *New York Times* columnist Paul Krugman, who today berates the Fed for not opening the sluice far wider, in August 2001, wrote that "The driving force behind the current slowdown is a plunge in business investment." Yet "to reflate the economy," he told us, "the Fed doesn't have to restore business investment; any kind of increase in demand will do." In particular, he continued, "Housing, which is highly sensitive to interest rates, could help lead a recovery." A year later, the Fed having not moved aggressively enough for him, Krugman divined that "[the Fed] needs soaring household spending to offset moribund business investment. And to do that [it] needs to create a housing bubble to replace the NASDAQ bubble." Wish granted.
>
> It is the great seduction of Keynesianism that its economics consists merely in the government's manipulation of national aggregates, and that the flagging animal spirits of the inscrutable entrepreneur need only be compensated for, quickly and painlessly, by government money-printing and spending. But we cannot afford a sequel to the crisis we are only just now unsteadily emerging from. The outside world, which relies on the US dollar as its primary trade vehicle and therefore reserve asset, cannot be expected to watch passively as dollars continue to spew forth into their currency, commodity, and asset markets, with no clear end in sight. The idea that freely floating exchange rates will take care of everything is contradicted by the post-1971 history of recurrent international financial crises, which compares abominably with the pre-1914 era of the classical gold standard. And it was Hayek who observed in the 1930s that floating exchange rates combined with monetary nationalism was a recipe for trade wars and political conflict.

The enormous increase in liquidity looking for a home in the US during this systemic financial crisis was funnelled into mortgage backed securities because they were:

- Directly promoted by the US government through legislation, regulation and the establishment of a massive transfer payment scheme through the Federal Housing Agencies and through the *Federal Income Tax Code*;
- Highly susceptible of being generated in large amounts;
- Purported able to be homogenized through standardized underwriting and documentation, bundled, sliced and diced into tranches and derivatives, that accurately and transparently disclosed their relative position in the process of risk identification, splitting and spreading the deconstructed investment for

investment by the parties best able to assess and price investment in each respective risk segment and component so created; and
- Supported by independent Rating Agency ratings and insurance that, on the face of each investment product, validated underlying asset values.

As the volume grew, the proportion of sub-prime volume grew disproportionately and quality diminished. The growth of the sub-prime component continued to be driven by purchased credit support or insurance, further slicing and dicing of varying constructed tranches of principle and interest and risk of default across a large number of credits, mixed and matched, all based upon financial models of questionable quality, always producing top quality tranches at each of the most senior levels. The lower tranches ended up being held in Special Purpose Investment Vehicles controlled by the prime brokers and Wall Street bank sponsors of the securities; theoretically off their balance sheets for financial reporting, compliance, and regulatory purposes; but most importantly to avoid liability attendant to the products they created.

[C] A New Risk-Free Economy

US deficits do not really matter, and in fact are a symbol of strength.[370] This is not a story about the economic surplus of emerging markets opting for investment in the superior returns of corporate America. It is a simple story of cash surpluses chasing higher yields (often of securities with very low capital productivity, such as mortgage-backed securities.

There are interesting parallels between the crises of the late 1980s and early 1990s and the current great American financial crisis. In the 70s and 80s the banking system served directly as the intermediary and let the Euro dollars and Petro-dollars escape the system. Now, the global open market intermediated the massive development and movement of monetized, securitized asset liquidity, "shadow banking money" wholly outside of the US financial, regulatory and supervisory system. Failure to underwrite and assess credit risk and impose liability for payment on transfer, even if credit is converted to and sheltered by structuring as a security, underlying the creation of an enormous amount of "credit money" outside of our monetary system is at the root of the current crisis. The primary failure is the abandonment of the principle of sound money upon which our country was founded. Both sound sovereign money and sound shadow negotiable credit money posing technically as securities without any discount mark to market to compensate for future risk and uncertainty.

To create and maintain sound sovereign money means that we must tie the US dollar as a sovereign money to a sound standard of value (it could well be that gold is the best option[371]), a specific standard measurable by quality and quantity, representative of and acceptable to ordinary Americans in exchanges of a market-based basket of products and services that is un-biased and reflects the most marketable commodities (non-financial assets) in the US market and international markets with our trading partners, as that may develop and change from time to time. The primary failure of the US to maintain sound sovereign money lies at the heart of this crisis, and of all financial crises since our nation's formation.

The failure to maintain honest, safe, sound sovereign money, the value of which is regulated by Congress in accordance with the *Constitution*, has been compounded by the distancing of credit money created liquidity from transparent underwriting of risk perception, including the time dimension of risk, from the actual assets that are the subject of the underlying market purchase and sale transaction supporting the creation of the credit money liquidity. The now defaulting borrowers buying houses with credit could not afford the houses or the terms of repayment of their debt. The assembly process of securitization stripped the essential characteristics of transferable credit money; that is, the endorsement liability of each successive transferring holder to the final holder, and the foundation of honesty, trust and confidence in payment that supported that liability.

No matter how far the financial assets that constitute the 90 percent of liquidity created outside the global banking system are distanced from the prime false assumption that each borrower or any assumed percentage of borrowers could pay their debt, in the end, the facts are now becoming clear. Regulatory and administrative "gaming" of accounting, legal, regulatory, fiscal and administrative policy funnel capitals into a specific asset class in the supposed interest of supporting economic growth, full employment and low interest rates. During the late 1980s, capital created through domestic fiscal deficits as well as global trade and current account deficits was funnelled through banks and thrifts back into US investments.

The massive movement of dollars was funnelled back into the US through bank loans secured by commercial real estate, oil & gas, highly leveraged transactions (junk bonds) and sovereign debt—through large transactions that could accept the velocity of money forced through the funnel.

Thus, money debasement has three fundamental components:

- Debasement of sovereign money unrestrained by regulation of its value.
- Debasement of credit money—shadow money, the vast bulk of money, by creating credit denominated in increasingly debased sovereign money; and
- Debasement of credit money by enabling its transferability through structured finance (primarily asset backed securities and derivatives) that strips the wrapping of endorser liability on transfer and that intentionally misrepresents the creditworthiness and collateral value underlying the credit enabled by securities laws unsuited to maintaining the safety and soundness of the credit money injected into the money supply denominated in units of sovereign money and rendered fungible in monetary terms, further debasing the value of all assets denominated in units unregulated sovereign money: Federal Reserve Notes.

[D] Risk and Uncertainty

A situation involving risk is one where probabilities can be assigned with confidence. A situation involving uncertainty is different—there are no precise probabilities to rely on.

In a situation characterized by uncertainty, our knowledge is based on a 'flimsy foundation' and is "subject to sudden and violent changes." This is especially true in the accumulation of wealth, which is the aim of all capitalist investment activity.

This ignorance of the public is the indispensable basis of the inflationary policy. It is a display of considerable naivety to recommend openly a monetary system that can work only if its essential features are ignored by the public.

The gold standard did not collapse. Governments abolished it and chose not to regulate the value of money by any other method in order to pave the way for inflation as acts of political expedience. Congress and the institutions it has created have the power, and with it constitutional responsibility, to maintain an honest, safe and sound, uniform and stable currency and to regulate its value (*Constitution* Article I, § 8, Clause 5).

The emergency that brings about inflation is that the people or the majority of the people, are not prepared to defray the costs incurred by their ruler's policies, first war—to project or protect political power; and second, social policies—to appease or promote special interests and gain political power. The people support these policies only to the extent that they believe that their conduct does not burden themselves. The mission of the government is then to convince the people that someone else—perhaps the "rich," will have to pay. Such practices take advantage of the masses' ignorance to cheat the ordinary people instead of trying to convince them. It is not just an accident that in our age, inflation has become the accepted method of money management. It is the expressed mission of the Federal Reserve System. Represented as the benign exercise of superior knowledge and skill in service of the public interest, the policies and actions of the Federal Reserve System are designed specifically to create inflation; it even has official targeted rated it seeks to create through the exercise of its "monetary powers"; it is the fiscal complement of statism and arbitrary government. It is the particular tool of a massive bureaucracy composed of competing regulatory agencies seeking to maximize budgets and minimize responsibilities by defining them away.

Anne O. Krueger, then Acting Managing Director International Monetary Fund, in an Address at the Money and Sovereignty Exhibit Opening, Washington, D.C., delivered April 15, 2004 said:

> Governments are often torn, because the ability to print money can offer important advantages, especially for those who want to avoid fiscal discipline.
>
> One of the Fund's most important tasks is to help countries achieve the macroeconomic stability that helps keep inflation in check and so maintains the domestic purchasing power of currencies. We are, in a sense, preaching the rewards of virtue: and in the context of this exhibition, it is interesting to see what Socrates had to say on this subject:
>
> > I tell you that virtue does not come from money: but from virtue comes money.

For the truth about money, to the extent accurately reported and not intentionally manipulated, and without including the effects outside the box circulating in the shadow banking system, see the following illustrations:

Figure 4.9 Cumulative Inflation by Decade Since 1913

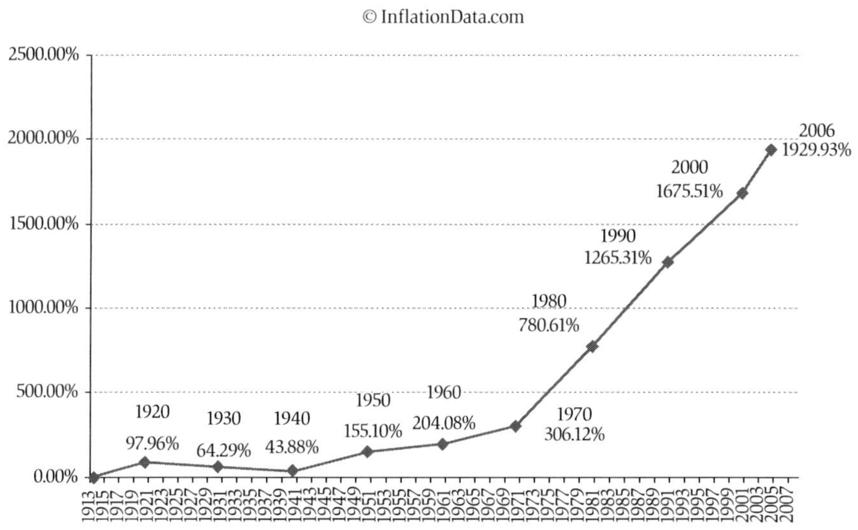

Figure 4.10 US Purchasing Power as Measured by Gold

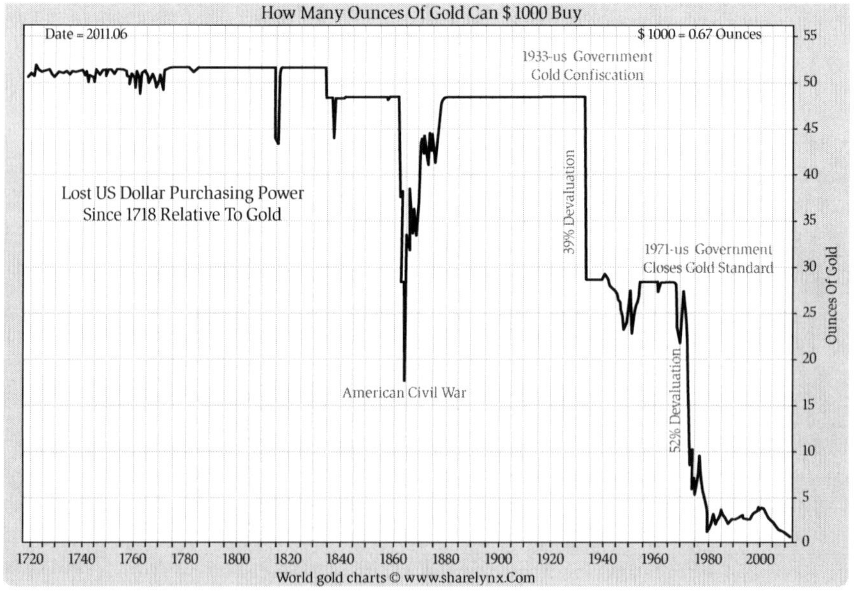

Figure 4.11 US Purchasing Power During the 20th Century

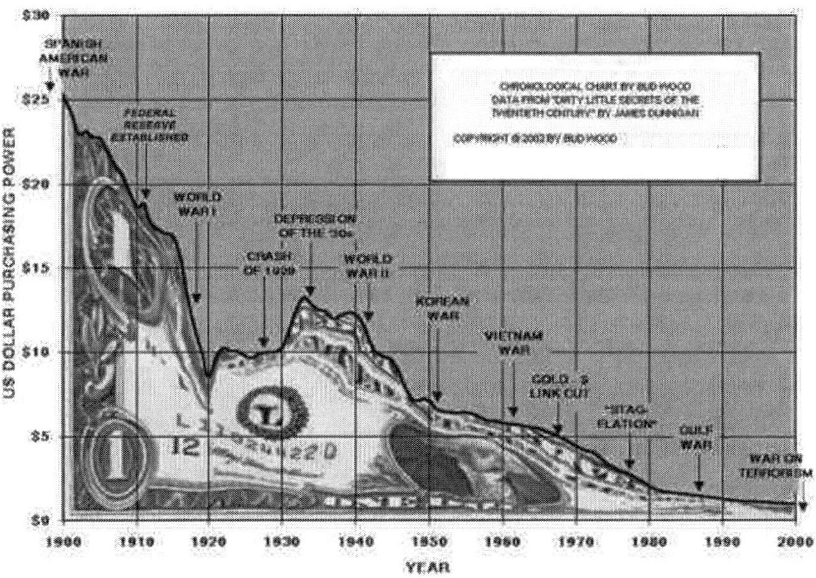

Government statistics are about the last place one should look to find inflation, as they are designed not to show much, investment manager David Einhorn argued in a May 26, 2010 *New York Times* commentary. "Over the last 35 years the government has changed the way it calculates inflation several times. According to the Web Site *Shadow Government Statistics,* using the pr-1980 method, the Consumer Price Index would be over 9 percent, compared with about 2 percent in the official statistics today."[372]

"When I boil what I've learned all down to one factor that drives the market and the economy, it is debt," Jerry Flum, CEO of Credit Risk Monitor observed. "Every dollar of debt moves a future purchase into the present. As credit grows, we spend more of it now. So, if you look at debt versus gross domestic product, we are already at record levels. We can also look at incremental debt versus incremental gross domestic product. In the 1950s, it took $1.50 in debt to produce an incremental $1 of GDP. Today it takes more than $6 in debt to produce $1 of GDP, so we are approaching the end of the game.[373]"

Following his history of the roles of debt and inflation in the economic history of the United States, Whalen reaches a sobering set of conclusions. "The real costs of two decades of Alan Greenspan at the Fed will be measured in the successive decades ahead. The failure of Chairmen Greenspan and other FOMC members to address the fiscal and monetary problems of the United States during his almost two decades at the Fed has left the United States on a trajectory for economic stagnation, hyperinflation and the attendant political and social costs of such policies.

The institutionalized crises affecting financial markets and the government's fiscal situation is inexorably moving the United States toward a more centralized and less democratic form of government. Without a change in the fiscal and monetary regimes of the United States, governments will continue to be the central player in the economy, surrounded by a heavily regulated 'private' market. Individual liberties and opportunities will become increasingly a function of administrative mechanisms, and decisions about major business transactions will be concentrated far beyond what was thought possible even two decades ago. This fundamental economic evolution, which has its roots in the Great Depression and the two World Wars, is occurring within the world's greatest democracy without an informed debate. The United States has lurched away from an ideal democratic republic to that of an authoritarian, bureaucratic, socialist state run by a junta of mercantilist oligarchs. If the United States cannot summon the will to grapple with the twin demons of public debt and inflation of asset values as a direct consequence of an official policy of money debasement conducted by and for the benefit of Washington and Wall Street, then it may be that America has lost the Cold War after all."[374]

The reliance on public debt and the unwillingness of Americans to live within their means since WWII are some of the primary threads in the narrative of the American Dream.[375]

As the ability of the private sector to generate jobs and real economic opportunities waned, the size of government and the public sector increased steadily. Indeed, today, the average wage of the public sector workers in America is twice that of workers in the private sector. The American addiction to inflation and debt is one obvious theme that emerges from our inquiry, an addiction that had contributed to financial market crises and overall volatility. One need only consider the erosion in the purchasing power of the dollar since the Great Depression to appreciate just how much of the economic activity in the United States reported during this period was an illusion Members of Congress and the public, for example, are horrified by the several trillion dollars' worth of assistance provided to banks by the Fed and Treasury since the start of the subprime crisis. If one inflates the several billion in Fed purchases of securities between 1933 and 1939 using the GDP deflator, plus Treasury purchases of Gold with newly minted greenbacks, the total in today's dollars goes into the double digit billions, illustrating the huge currency inflation since the 1930s. Put another way, every $1 spent in fiscal and monetary assistance in the 1930s is worth almost $14 in today's inflated money using the GDP deflator and over $16 using the consumer price index as an inflation measure. And remember that both widely accepted, officially defined measures of inflation understate the true erosion in the real value of the dollar.[376]

§4.06 MONEY DEBASEMENT REDISTRIBUTES WEALTH AND INCOME

Money debasement constitutes an intentional "imperceptible tax" to enable the unaccountable, unconstitutional, unlawful and secret income and wealth transfer and redistribution to benefit Washington politicians, bureaucrats, Wall Street bankers and the most wealthy 1 percent of the American public.

Dylan Grice, formerly of Societe Generale, in his Memo to Central Banks: *You're debasing more than our currency*, appearing online in John Mauldin, Newsletter October 26, 2012:

"At its most fundamental level, economic activity is no more than an exchange between strangers. It depends, therefore, on a degree of trust between strangers. Since money is the agent of exchange, it is the agent of trust. Debasing money therefore debases trust. History is replete with Great Disorders in which social cohesion has been undermined by currency debasements. The multi-decade credit inflation can now be seen to have had similarly corrosive effects. ... "Next to language, money is the most important medium through which modern societies communicate" writes Bernd Widdig in his masterful analysis of Germany's inflation crisis "Culture and Inflation in Weimar Germany." His may be an abstract observation, but it has the commendable merit of being true ... all economic activity requires the cooperation of strangers and therefore, a degree of trust between cooperating strangers. Since money is the agent of such mutual trust, debasing money implies debasing the trust upon which social cohesion rests.

The value strangers put on each other's contributions manifests itself in prices, and prices require money. So it is through money that we express the extent of our appreciation for the many different talents embedded in each thing we consume, and through money that our skills are in turn valued by others. Money, in other words, is the agent of this anonymous exchange, and therefore money is also the agent of the hidden trust on which it depends. Thus, as Bernd Widdig reflects in his book (which I urge you all to read), money ... "... is more than simply a tool for economic exchange; its different qualities shape the way modern people think, how they make sense of their reality, how they communicate, and ultimately how they find their place and identity in a modern environment."

Debasing money might be expected to have effects beyond the merely financial domain. Of course, there are many ways to debase money. Coin can be clipped, paper money can be printed; credit can be created on the basis of demand deposits which aren't there ... the effects are ultimately the same though: the implied trust that money communicates through society is eroded.

To see how, consider the example of money printing by authorities. We know that such an exercise raises revenues since the authorities now have a very real increase in purchasing power. But we also know that revenue cannot be raised by one party without another party paying. So who pays?

If the authorities raise taxes explicitly and openly, voters know exactly why they have less spending power. They also know how much less spending power they have. But if the authorities instead raise money by simply printing it, they raise the revenue by stealth. No one knows upon whom the burden falls. People notice only that they cannot afford the things they used to be able to afford, or they cannot afford the things which everyone else can afford. They know that something is wrong, but they just do not know what, why, or who is to blame. So inevitably they look for someone to blame.

So it is with monetary debasement, as Keynes understood deeply (so deeply, in fact, that it is ironic so many of today's crude Keynesians support QE so enthusiastically). In 1921 he said:

> By a continuing process of inflation, Governments can confiscate, secretly and unobserved, an important part of the wealth of their citizens. By this method they not only confiscate, but they confiscate arbitrarily; and, while the process impoverishes many, it actually enriches some .... Those to whom the system brings windfalls .... become "profiteers" who are the object of the hatred ... the process of wealth-getting degenerates into a gamble and a lottery. Lenin was certainly right. There is no subtler, no surer means of overturning the existing basis of society than to debauch the currency. The

> process engages all the hidden forces of economic law on the side of destruction and does it in a manner which not one man in a million is able to diagnose.

History is replete with Great Disorders in which currency debasement has coincided with social infighting and scapegoating. Despite the CPI inflation of the 1970s receding, our central banks have continued to play games with money. We have since lived through what might be the largest credit inflation in financial history, a credit hyperinflation. Where has it left us? Median US household incomes have been stagnant for the best part of twenty years (chart below)

Figure 4.12 US Household Income (2011 $s)

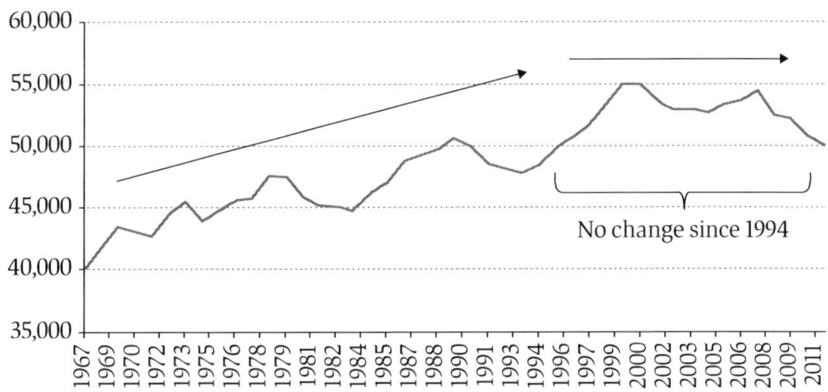

Source: Bloomberg.

Yet inequality has surged. While a record number of Americans are on food stamps, the top 1 percent of income earners are taking a larger share of total income than since the peak of the 1920s credit inflation. Moreover, the growth in that share has coincided almost exactly with the more recent credit inflation.

These phenomena are inflation's hallmarks. In the Keynes quote above, he alludes to the "artificial and iniquitous redistribution of wealth" inflation imposes on society without being specific. What actually happens is that artificially created money redistributes wealth towards those closest to it, to the detriment of those furthest away.

Figure 4.13 Income Distribution in the US

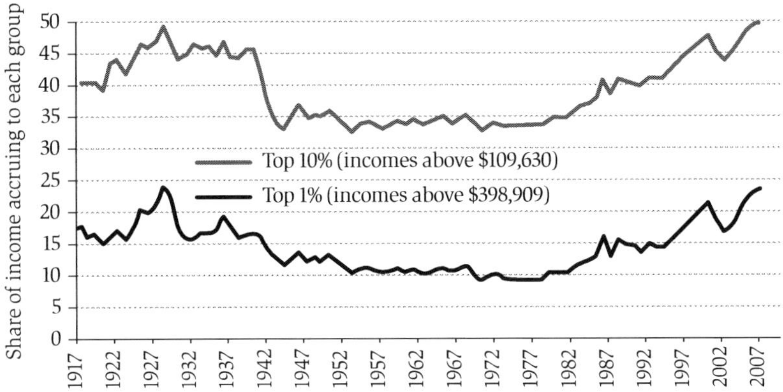

Source: Emmanuel Saez, University of California.

Richard Cantillon (writing decades before Adam Smith) was the first to observe this effect (hence "Cantillon effect"). He showed how those closest to the money source benefited unfairly at the expense of others, by thinking through the effects in Spain and Portugal of the influx of gold from the new world.

> "If the increase of actual money comes from mines of gold or silver ... the owner of these mines, the adventurers, the smelters, refiners, and all the other workers will increase their expenditures in proportion to their gains. ... All this increase of expenditures in meat, wine, wool, etc. diminishes of necessity the share of the other inhabitants of the state who do not participate at first in the wealth of the mines in question. The altercations of the market, or the demand for meat, wine, wool, etc. being more intense than usual, will not fail to raise their prices ... Those then who will suffer from this dearness ... will be first of all the landowners, during the term of their leases, then their domestic servants and all the workmen or fixed wage-earners ... All these must diminish their expenditure in proportion to the new consumption ..."
>
> (Quoted in Mark Thornton, *Quarterly Journal of Austrian Economics Vol 9, No 3* [Fall 2006], "Cantillon on the Cause of the Business Cycle")

In other words, the beneficiaries of newly created money spend that money and bid up the price of goods with their higher demand. Those who suffer are those who have to pay newly higher prices but did not benefit from the newly created money.

The credit inflation analog to the Cantillon effect has played out perfectly in recent decades. Central banks provided cheap money to banks, the cheap money artificially inflated asset prices, artificially inflated asset prices made anyone connected to those assets rich as we became a nation of speculators, those riches were achieved at everyone else's expense, and 'everyone else' has now realized what has happened and is understandable enraged ... as Keynes explained, "Those to whom the system brings windfalls .... are the object of the hatred."

And now the social debasement is clear for all to see. The 99% blame the 1%, the 1% blame the 47%, the private sector blames the public sector, the public sector returns the sentiment ... the young blame the old, everyone blame the rich ... yet few question the ideas behind government or central banks ...

I'd feel a whole lot better if central banks stopped playing games with money. But I can't see that happening anytime soon. The ECB has thrown the towel in, following the SNB last year in committing effectively to print unlimited amounts of money for the greater good. The BoE and the Fed have long since made a virtue of what was once considered a necessity, with what was once the unconventional conventional. As James Bullard told everyone a few weeks before the last Fed meeting, lest there be any doubt:

> "Markets have this idea that, there's QE1 and QE2, so QE3 must be the same as those previous ones. It is not that clear to me that this is the way this is going ... it would just be to do balance sheet policy as the exact analogue of interest rate policy."

In other words, the central banks' balance sheets are the new policy tool. As interest rates embarked on a multi-year decline from the 1980s on, central bank balance sheets are set to embark on a multi-year climb ...

Figure 4.14 Balance Sheet Policy as the Exact Analog of Interest Rate Policy

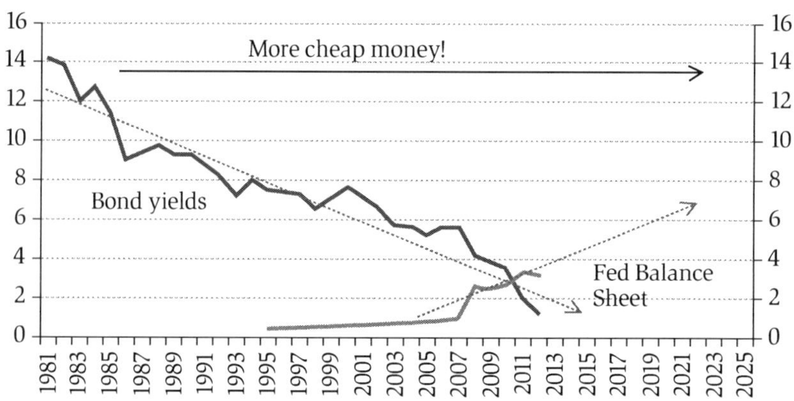

Source: Bloomberg, SC Cross Asset Research.

So as Nobel Prize winning experts in economics punch the air because inflation expectations have been rising since the policy was announced, "It's the whole point of the exercise" (Duh!) the BoE admits that QE has mainly benefited the rich, but vows to continue anyway.

§4.07 ORDINARY AMERICANS ARE THE AMERICAN SOVEREIGN

In *Beyond Sovereignty: Money and its Future*, March 5, 2010, Samuel Gregg quotes: "Adam Smith lamented in his *Wealth of Nations* (1776) that "in every country in the world . . . the avarice and injustice of princes and sovereign states abusing the confidence of their subjects, have by degrees diminished the real quality of the metal, which had been originally contained in their coins." In his famous critique of the *Treaty of Versailles, The Economic Consequences of the Peace* (1919), John Maynard Keynes observed: "Lenin is said to have declared that the best way to destroy the Capitalist System was to debauch the currency." History, however, illustrates that the greatest debauchers of money have not been Communist revolutionaries or even run-of-the-mill counterfeiters. The primary culprits have been entirely legitimate governments."[377]

> One reason traditionally given for the state's monopoly of the money supply is that it is an expression of national sovereignty. While sovereignty's meaning is endlessly debated, there is considerable agreement that sovereignty expresses a given government's supreme authority over a given territory. In the mid-fifth-century BC, for example, Athens compelled her allies to adopt Athenian coinage—a move that signaled Athens' expanding sense of the territorial boundaries of its sovereignty. The scholar who most developed the concept of sovereignty in the modern era, Jean Bodin (1530-1596), identified the right to issue coinage as a key element of sovereignty. In our time, some of the most contentious debates surrounding the euro have concerned its diminution of the national sovereignty of EU member-states adopting this transnational currency.[378]

According to Gregg:

> ... suggestions have been made to remove government from the business of money-supply altogether. In his well-known monograph, *The Denationalization of Money* (1976), the Nobel Prize economist Friedrich von Hayek sketched a powerful economic argument for ending the state's monopoly of the money supply. This has been developed by economists such as Jesús Huerta de Soto, whose *Money, Bank Credit, and Economic Cycles* (1998) contains a comprehensive plan for privatizing the money supply. One reason traditionally given for the state's monopoly of the money supply is that it is an expression of national sovereignty. But is a state monopoly of the money supply truly essential to sovereignty? It was not until 1914 that the United States legislated to mandate that only one bank would be privileged by the government to issue legal tender.
>
> Some clarification of the issues involved begins to emerge when we consider the purpose of money. Money's most basic function is to serve as a medium of exchange. From this is derived money's three other functions: a store of value, a unit of account, and a standard of deferred payment. It is not immediately clear why any of these functions necessitate a state monopoly of money. A different understanding of money, however, is often used to justify the state's monopoly of the money-supply. This is the idea that, besides the aforementioned functions, money is also a tool for the state's management of an economy.

The idea that manipulation of the amount and value of money can be used as management tool and process, the power to exercise which has been delegated to Congress and through it to the Board of Governors of the Federal Reserve System is wrong. The assertion and exercise of this power by Congress, the Fed, the federal financial regulators and all the other bad actors I have identified in this work created the foundation of the fundamental fraud that underlies every other fraudulent act described herein.

Gregg observes that the justification of wrong, irresponsible and likewise unlawful manipulation of the economy by manipulating the value of money "is further predicated upon the (much disputed) claim that the state can effectively steer an economy so that it serves the common good. The link to sovereignty is the state's need to invoke a unique authority that allows it to claim responsibility for managing economic activity within a defined set of territorial boundaries":[379]

> The problem is that there are many occasions when the state's regulation of the money supply involves the pursuit of goals that undermine money's ability to perform its other economic functions. The state's inflation, for example, of the money supply to reduce public deficits or finance a war economy can undermine money's ability to serve as a stable unit of value over long periods of time. Prominent modern examples include Germany after each world war or France during its Indo-China and Algerian wars.[380]
>
> The dollar, has long since escaped national boundaries. It is the world's reserve currency. When a senator from the Republic of Kalmykia is caught shaking down a Russian airline, he is apprehended with a suitcase containing $300,000 in marked US bills. When Somali pirates ransom a ship, they demand that the ransom money be parachuted to them in dollars. The fact that nearly three-quarters of all $100 bills circulate outside the United States attests to the dollar's dominance of this dubious realm.[381]
>
> South Korea and Thailand set the prices of more than 80 percent of their trade in dollars despite the fact that only 20 percent of their exports go to American buyers. Fully 70 percent of Australia's exports are invoiced in Dollars despite the fact that fewer than 6% are destined for the United States. The principal commodity exchanges quote prices in dollars. Oil is priced in dollars. The dollar is used in 85 percent of all foreign exchange transactions worldwide. It accounts for nearly half of the global stock of international debt securities. It is the form in which central banks hold more than 60 percent of their foreign currency reserves.
>
> Today the US share of global exports is only 13 percent. The United States is the source of less than 20 percent of foreign direct investment, down from nearly 85 percent between 1945 and 1980.
>
> About $500 billion of US currency circulates outside the United States, for which foreigners have had to provide the United States with $500 billion of actual goods and services. Even more important, foreign central banks hold close to $5 trillion of the bonds of the US Treasury and quasi-governmental agencies like Fannie Mae and Freddie Mac.[382]

With cheap foreign finance keeping US interest rates low and enabling American households to live beyond their means, poor households in the developing world ended up subsidizing rich ones in the United States. The cheap finance that other countries provided the US in order to obtain the dollars needed to back an expanding volume of international transactions underwrote the practices that culminated in the crisis. The United States lit the fire, but foreigners were forced by the perverse structure of the system to provide the fuel.

If this were not injustice enough, there is the fact that America's international financial position was actually strengthened by the crisis. In the course of 2007, the dollar weakened by about 8 percent on the foreign exchange market. But since our debts are denominated in our own currency, there was no impact on their dollar value.

In contrast, our foreign investments, whether in bonds or factories, became more valuable as the dollar fell. The interest and dividends they threw off were worth more when they were converted back into dollars.

The dollars depreciation thereby improved the US external position by almost $450 billion. This largely offset the increase in US indebtedness to the rest of the world that would otherwise have resulted from our $660 billion current account deficit... It was almost enough to keep our debts to other countries stable, despite our consuming 6 percent more than we produced. Then, in 2008, in the throes of the most serious financial crises in 80 years, the federal government was able to borrow vast sums at low interest rates because foreigners figured that the dollar was the safest currency to be in at times of great turmoil. And again, in 2010, when financial volatility spiked, investors fled into the most liquid market, that for U.S. treasury bonds, pushing down the cost of borrowing for the U.S. government and, along with it the mortgage interest rates available to American households. This is what exorbitant privilege is all about.[383]

Eichengreen call the American policy of exploiting its abuse and debasement of the American dollar as an "exorbitant privilege." This practice has gone far beyond the ancient and obsolete privilege of seigniorage. The fact that the American dollar may be the least of the worst money does not redeem its underlying corruption.

Money debasement under the guise of sovereignty is no longer accomplished in the main by the sovereign through clipping coinage, diluting coinage metal content or by diminishing coin size.[384] It is not even restricted to creating vast amounts of fiat currency by the sovereign. The overwhelming amount of unregulated money created with US government facilitation and incentives, is to be found in the explosion of debt in the "shadow banking system." (See Chapter 3) This includes dollar denominated trade and current account deficits, fiscal deficits and inflation in dollar denominated financial instruments. By increasing the amount of dollars in existence surreptitiously and letting the world discover this gradually, the government can create the illusion of greater prosperity measured in dollars than actually exists. Herbert Hoover concluded that "if the number of inches in the yardstick were lessened then there would be more cloth in the bolt."[385]

Another way to exercise political control without accountability is the use of public debt. "Over the past 150 years or so, over the history of international lending, payment of foreign loans almost never occurred." These "loans" were never really meant to be repaid. Even Great Britain, once considered the second-best sovereign credit risk after the United States, had defaulted on every foreign loan it had contracted since the end of the Boer War in 1902. Instead, every such loan has been subject to major currency devaluation, rolled over, suspended, rescheduled, or otherwise restructured, repudiated, reduced, cancelled, or forgiven. The more drastic steps, leading to eventual, partial or complete cancellation of debt have been surprisingly frequent.[386] As noted previously, technically, 1788 was the year of France's last default, although, as we will see post-revolutionary France experienced an epic hyperinflation that effectively led to the elimination of virtually all debts, public and private. No emerging market country in history, including the United States (whose inflation rate in 1779 approached 200 percent) has managed to escape bouts of high inflation.[387]

In America, we have lost sight of the nature and identity of our sovereign—from whence solely is derived the exercise of the key elements of sovereignty and any privilege of seigniorage. Devaluation of the currency has been and would be a political act in accordance with the power delegated by the sovereign public to Congress in the *Constitution*. Money debasement constitutes an intentional misrepresentation of the value of the dollar and assets the values of which are denominated in dollars, and this intentional money debasement effects Washington's and Wall Street's partnership in lying to, cheating and theft of value from the American public.

As opposed to kings, dictators and autocrats of every description who hold their power as sovereign through right of force, conquest and absolute rule, American sovereignty, and any privilege of seigniorage, lies in its citizens—not in the government; not in Congress; not in the Executive branch; not in the federal financial regulatory agencies; not in the Fed, our central bank; and certainly not in the Wall Street banks!

The sovereign powers exercised by these parties are derived solely from and limited by the *Constitution* of the United States. None of these parties has the slightest claim to exercise the rights of American sovereignty over the currency of the United States except as expressly delegated to them by the American public in the *Constitution*. The monetary powers and duties delegated by then American people to American government can and must be exercised, implemented and enforced by all branches of government purely in the interest of the people; not for privileged exploitation by Washington and Wall Street.

§4.08 CONCLUDING OBSERVATIONS

Debasement of American money by the Washington Wall Street enterprise and the financial crises caused by that debasement is wrong. And it is illegal. Money is the primary tool of society—of civilization, and certainly of government. It is inherently social. It defines almost all social relationships apart from the purely personal and emotional. The powers and duties attendant to the creation, emission and use of money are grounded in and are inseparable from the moral principles upon which societies and civilizations rest. Protestations that the intentional fraud of money debasement may be wrong—that is, it is immoral—but not illegal are hollow. It is clear from the first 4 chapters of this work that debasement is illegal—and it is immoral. We turn now to the connections between law and morality—and by virtue of its central importance to our society; a civilization based upon laws grounded in moral principles. The connections between and amongst American money, morality and law provide the essential framework for a prosperous developed civil society.

CHAPTER 5

Money and Morality

§5.01 THE PRIME WASHINGTON WALL STREET FALSE NARRATIVE

The primary false narrative proffered by the Washington Wall Street enterprise to deflect accountability for the financial crisis is that money debasement[388] is that the financial crisis (without mention of money basement as its underlying driver) immoral but not illegal. Money debasement is dishonest and therefore immoral. There appears to be no doubt about that. In America, sovereign money debasement is also illegal. This is so whether accomplished by coin adulteration or shaving; printing paper fiat money; or by electronically creating fiat money through accounting entries; wherever the value of sovereign money denominated under our present monetary system is not created and emitted by Congress; and where the value of the sovereign money is not regulated by reference to a proper, reliable, effective and external standard of value in which Americans may justifiably have trust and confidence.

The moral principles relating to money serve as the foundation for the law of honest, safe and sound money are brought to bear in two functions. The first function is the definition of a duties to create and maintain the three types of money that dominate our monetary and financial system: (i) sovereign money that dwells in our formal banking system; and (ii) credit money that dwells in our shadow banking system; and (iii) identification of the parties who are charged with the duties in each sphere.

§5.02 HONESTY VERSUS THE ENDS JUSTIFYING THE MEANS

The fundamental moral principle that lies at the heart of both types of money dominating our monetary system is honesty. The contention advanced by the Washington Wall Street enterprise is that financial crises, specifically the most recent great financial crisis, caused by money debasement is immoral but not illegal. It is indisputable that each and every American law is not directly tied to and based upon a correlative moral principle. Many laws amount to formalized conventions or norms that establish a framework for practical civil conduct. The fact that America is notorious for the promulgation of laws, rules and regulations supporting that framework must not obscure the direct connection between the moral principle of honesty and the constitutional mandate for honest, safe and sound money in Article I, §8, Clause 5 of the *Constitution*.

The tortured history of political expediency corrupting the morality of honest, safe and sound money is based on the classic rationalization that the ends justify the means.[389] Without a lengthy disquisition of the difficulties inherent in its extrapolation when applied to the most fundamental moral and legal social necessity of honest, safe and sound money, a brief clarifying comment is necessary. The primary end or consequence advanced by the Washington Wall Street enterprise as a justification for money debasement is that without resort to it in the case of an existential war, and if the war were lost, as a failed country, our money and country would also be lost. That existential justification has been given historically globally and in America from the American Revolution onward to today.

Historically, whenever the "existential war" exception has been exercised to justify money debasement and circumstances have departed from the initial threatening condition, those in political power, including the power over monetary matter, have simply extended, abused and distorted the underlying concept of necessity and flouted the law of money, continued the debasement and justified the advantages to be seized by the wealthy and powerful now identified as the Washington Wall Street enterprise as a practice of government, monetary and banking policies as business as usual.

[A] The Moral Foundation for Sovereign Money

Money debasement has historically been a capital crime punishable by death. Money debasement perpetrates a fraud on its holders. In American common law, money debasement is a tort and a crime. It is both immoral and illegal when conducted intentionally and knowingly by the Washington and Wall Street institutions that create American sovereign money under our present monetary system. The fact that that the intrinsic moral character of money is honesty appears now to be irrelevant. Washington and Wall Street institutions have assumed the power and have therefore assumed both moral and legal responsibility to maintain the integrity of American money in accordance with the *United States Constitution*, federal statutory law and American common law. They believe that they have met their monetary responsibilities.

Morality: "Honesty." "Honor." "Trust." "Confidence." The words expressing these moral virtues seem somewhat old fashioned—archaic. At first blush, many Americans take these moral virtues as anachronistic throwback concepts in an era of continuous, supposed positive and productive innovation in financial law and systems. Morality is now for suckers. In business, it is a sign of weakness.

Moral principles seem to have been relegated to history; obsolete. Gaming of the letter of the law for the most wealthy and powerful of clients occupies our greatest legal minds. Legal "reform," regulatory rulemaking as well as legal and regulatory enforcement discretion has produced a legal, regulatory and policy environment in which the law rests on blowing, shifting sands that occlude and confuse all efforts at imposition of accountability for financial crises.

Take time to look at the inscriptions displayed on public buildings across America, specifically, courthouses; and on college, university and law school campuses. The inscriptions generally communicate a series of moral principles that America's founders associated with law; the foundation for American society; a specialized field of study, and the grounding of an ancient, distinguished and honored profession. In the center of the gazebo in the center of the quadrangle of the Dedman School of Law at Southern Methodist University in Dallas, my *alma mater* and where I now teach, there is a cast bronze plaque that reads as follows:

> "History is a voice forever sounding across the centuries and the laws of right and wrong. Opinions alter. Manners change, creeds rise and fall, but the moral law is written on the tablets of eternity. For every false word or unrighteous deed, for cruelty and oppression, for lust or vanity, the price must be paid at last; not always by the chief offenders, but paid by someone. Justice and truth alone endure and live. Injustice and falsehood may be long-lived, but doomsday comes at last to them, in French revolutions and other terrible ways." James Anthony Froude.

Truth and justice. Falsehood and injustice. According to Froude and wise founders of the law school, the fulcrum of justice is honesty. When, as a society, our moral and legal grounding in truth and justice is systemically overcome by falsehood and injustice, doomsday comes at last.

Figure 5.1 Heads on Pikes[390]

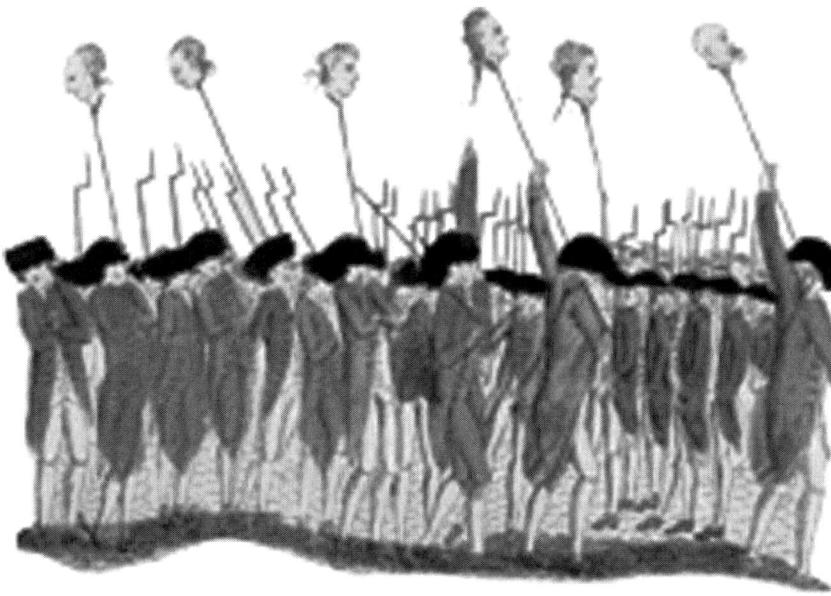

It is no surprise that Froude closes with a reference to the French Revolution. America may not have come into existence without enormous financial aid from the French, given in large part to spite the English, from whom we derive much of our moral and legal foundation. France's financial profligacy led to a disastrous debasement of French money that lay at the heart of the French revolution.[391] Royal dissembling to the French public in the face of desperate privation led to the bloody revolutionary response of French citizens to the French Queen's remonstrance to those outside the nobility who had no bread; that they should eat cake.[392] That exhortation is echoed today by the American elite's advice to the American public to simply quit being poor.[393] These exhortations, unless remediated in the enforcement of moral principles embodied in the law of money, abuse of trust and power, and fraud, leads to violence, bloodshed and ultimately, revolution overturning the exploitative government of the wealthy and powerful.

Apart from passing reference, today, the explicit connections between morality and the law may seem to have largely evaporated. The subject of ethics in law school has been relegated to short required courses on attorneys' codes of ethics. There are no classes in the subject of money, despite the fact that money provides the social, economic and legal foundation for all businesses as well as family units and American social and cultural survival at their most fundamental levels.

[B] Honor and Honesty Are Integral to American Sovereign and Shadow Money

The primary moral principles at stake in the context of this paper are honor and honesty. The etymology[394] of the word "honor" derives from twelfth century Anglo-French origins. The word indicates a position of dignity and distinction; having a good reputation; one of excellence, esteem, respect and nobleness of character or manners, attributable to the demonstrable performance of one's duty.

The word "honest" derives from the same etymological source. To be honest, is to be respectable, decent and specifically, to be "free from fraud." Beginning in the fourteenth century, the modern-day sense of being honest is to deal fairly, truthfully and free from deceit.

William Simpson in his book entitled *The Structure of Complex Words (1951)* takes us back further into history to the Latin noun "honos," likely derived from the adjective "honestus," possibly derived from the root word "onus," or burden, as if honor weighs us down morally. Such an interpretation is consistent with the apparent "throwing off the burden of honesty" in Washington and on Wall Street to free their energy for their unrestrained blind pursuit of power, income and wealth. The words honor and honesty lie entwined in the trail of definitions in various dictionaries, including the *New English Dictionary* and the *Oxford English Dictionary* that characterize the sense of Honesty as "not lying, not stealing, keeping promises and deserving and receiving social honour" therefrom.[395]

The first definition of the Latin word "honestas" given by the *Oxford Latin Dictionary* is: "Title to respect, honourableness, honour." Followed by: "Moral rectitude, integrity," in which sense it was frequently opposed to "utilitas," or expediency."[396] Utilitas or expediency follow the moral philosophy of consequentialism, as reference in the first Clause of this §5.01. This philosophy is contradistinguished from the principles of natural law that governed the founding of the United States and that is embodied in the American *Declaration of Independence* and in the *United States Constitution*. These founding documents, and American law of the land that is derived from the *Constitution* and the natural law principles embedded in our common law and formalized in federal statutory law establish the foundation for our moral and legal dedicated to and bound up in the Froude phrase "truth and justice."

Perforce, there is no longer any study or appreciation of the moral and ethical foundation, or even a legal and accounting comprehension of the nature of money in today's big data driven world of commerce, banking, and credit, and structured finance (securities, derivatives and repos) as tools of money creation.

We find ourselves in a new era of fintech, blockchain, cyber coin, and other technical innovations in money, banking and finance. These innovations are often presented as attempts to regain, and to meet the need for, transactional honesty and the trust and confidence in the financial world.[397] The first principles of honesty, trust and confidence in money matters are the moral principles governing the origins and present day state of the law of money, banking, credit and finance. Financial crises are direct results of American failures to enforce accountability of those who intentionally violate the law of money and openly disdain the identity, connection and importance of the moral virtues of honor, honesty, trust, integrity and confidence, as respected and incorporated in the American law of money and monetary systems.

[C] The Twisted Tension of Honor, Honesty, Truth and Justice Surrounding Money in America

As noted in the Introduction to this work, the age-old political, commercial methods of, and even legal assault on honor and honesty are dramatically manifested today by the conduct of individuals and institutions of trust and power in Washington and on Wall Street. Those at the center of power and wealth thrive on white lies, propaganda, spin, alternative facts, fake facts, fake news and pervasive "gas lighting."[398] Falsehood and injustice are the watchwords of the Washington Wall Street enterprise.

[1] Debasement of American Money

The debasement of American honest constitutionally protected sovereign money was driven in the first instance, as we have seen, by the then openly acknowledged assertion of existential necessity, expediency, as an exigency of war; specifically, the American Civil War. The deviation from the constitutional mandate for honest, safe and sound money was affected as a singular event, specifically and explicitly made purely temporary and to be redressed it its effects in a responsible manner consistent with preservation of American sovereignty at a known cost, in the shortest possible time. The justification of intentional debasement of the value of American sovereign money as a matter of existential expediency has now become intentionally embedded in our monetary system and structure as a political tool of manipulation that is expressed as American sovereign honest, safe and sound constitutionally compliant money has become an oxymoron. The practice of money debasement that originally constituted a capital crime in America is now the governing principle underlying our monetary, banking financial and economic system. Without honest, safe and sound sovereign money, we cannot hope to reach for the same characteristics of money in the shadow banking system.

Structurally securitizing, monetizing and presenting relative high yield illiquid assets at face value, notwithstanding the illiquid nature of assets incorporated in the structure in the shadow banking world of structured finance as liquid money-substitutes, crowds both regulated and shadow banking institutions balance sheets and directs the concentration of Washington and Wall Street's fountain of subsidized credit creation in those financial structures, the integrity of which at best have proven problematic. Neither the accounting nor the legal profession have questioned the progressive perversion of the American law of and accounting for money as honest representations of market values.

According to Seth Lobis, "[i]n the mid-sixteenth century, "honesty" was first used in what the *Oxford English Dictionary* refers to as the "prevailing modern sense"

— "Uprightness of disposition and conduct; integrity, truthfulness, straightforwardness: the quality opposed to lying, cheating, or stealing."[399]

The now prevailing dangerous resurgence of dishonesty has its grounding in both Washington's and Wall Street's historically oft expected but reluctantly and minimally tolerated, but clearly publicly disapproved propensity for disingenuous, deceptive and manipulative tactics in matters of money. Tactical monetary conduct that has been the purview of spin doctors acting as public relations and advertising experts, consultants and lobbyists based on practices of peripheral deceit and manipulation of public opinion, has now hardened into the official Washington and Wall Street code of dishonor and dishonesty, over-riding in practice America's moral and legal foundation. Dishonesty by money debasement is now the standard for American, and global, political and financial, and specifically monetary policy.

Common techniques for such dishonesty include: selective presentation of facts and quotes (cherry-picking); non-denial denials; non-apology apologies; the passive expression of "mistakes were made", distancing language acknowledging low quality or inappropriate handling of a matter or issue, but evading any direct admission or accusation of responsibility by not specifying the person or organization that made the mistakes (avoiding any implication of intent); using phrases that assume unproven claims or avoiding the question at issue; burying bad news in a bulk of verbiage or by manipulation of timing of disclosure; and by plain old misdirection and diversion.[400] Dishonesty can be accomplished by simple statements overwhelmed by disclaimers and qualifications—by the "small print." Dishonesty can be perpetrated by excessive simplicity of excessive complexity; by a "tweet" or by legislation consisting of hundreds of pages to be implemented by an unknowable number of regulations. "An article in the *New York Times* stated that the legislation is basically a 2,000-page missive to federal agencies, instructing regulators to address subjects ranging from derivatives trading to document retention. But it is notably short on specifics, giving regulators significant power to determine its impact—and giving partisans on both sides a second chance to influence the outcome."[401]

Honor and honesty are the moral principles that lie at the heart of every human social, political, economic, financial and legal relationship. Although honesty is the best policy is incorporated in the moral and legal framework of every society, we now live in a world of alternative facts and communication by twittered oxymoron. Black can be white. Bad can be good.

The word honesty derives from the word honor, meaning "respectable," "virtuous" and "decorous." The moral principles at issue in financial crises and accountability for their causes rest on the simple fact that the American people have given their trust and confidence in the integrity to Washington's and Wall Street's much-vaunted authority and expertise and their necessary acceptance of the honor extended to them by the public to conduct America's monetary affairs in an honest manner in positions of trust. In this sense, as detailed in the preceding chapters, Washington and Wall Street institutions, and those individuals who control them, occupy the positions of trusted fiduciaries to those who rely on them for honor, honesty and integrity in money matters.

One can conclude anecdotally that the prominence of moral principles throughout American culture has diminished throughout society, but most markedly in the banking, legal and accounting professions; both in observation and in practice:

> "The corruption of banking culture has been confirmed, not only by the mountains of evidence regarding bank fraud, but by independent research. The first confirmation came from a 2012 survey of British and American bankers. As we [*Huffpost*] reported at the time, one in six bankers said they were "fairly likely" to commit a banking crime if they could get away with it. Forty-five percent refused to rule it out if the payoff were big enough.
>
> "Researchers noted that 'nearly one-third of all financial services professionals reported feeling pressured by bonus or compensation plans to violate the law or engage in unethical conduct. Nearly one-quarter of the respondents felt similar pressure from other sources.'
>
> "Those findings appeared to find confirmation in a study published this month by the scientific journal *Nature*. The report, titled "Business culture and dishonesty in the banking industry," found that bankers were significantly more dishonest than employees of other industries — once they identified themselves as bankers.
>
> "In lay terms, bankers who were reminded of their own culture and business environment tended to cheat a lot. That was not true of any other profession or industry the researchers studied.[402]"

[2] Debasement of Honest Money Drives Debasement of Honesty Throughout American Society

A growing manifestation of intentional dishonesty in all walks of life has become a new normal. Advertising images, catch phrases, slogans, tweets and memes have become our language. Insistence on honesty in trade, commerce and finance has become just another impediment to profit maximization.

Today, the getting and having of money and the power it confers have a greater social value than honesty; and dishonest money is now the greatest tool for the amassing of power and wealth. It has become a new perverse social, political, economic, financial and legal foundation for our culture. Greed remains good. And the use of dishonesty to feed greed is even better.

Although every generation harkens back to the good old days when honesty was indeed the best policy, dishonesty in money matters has been a recurring component of social and economic crises since the invention of money. The current American experience of dishonesty as a virtue, used as a tool to concentrate power, income and wealth in the few while the condition of the many deteriorate or a best remain stagnant, is not an isolated, singular experience. America's financial crises suffered since its founding, and specifically during the past forty-five years, have been caused by dishonesty in money and finance, that has now spread, pervades our culture and has spoiled the American dream. The negative moral and ethical impact of rendering the language of money, by which every member of society seeks to provides for himself or herself, families, and our American society generally, through inherently dishonest actions, cannot be overstated. Social, civil, philosophical, religious, political, economic and financial aspects of life; all aspects of life in America, have become infused with dishonesty, to the point that dishonesty, whether subliminal or blatant, is held forth by many as a virtue. This is certainly true in Washington and on Wall Street. The stain of institutionally sponsorship of dishonesty is rotting America's collective moral fibre.

Jörg Guido Hülsmann, in his book entitled *The Ethics of Money Production* (2008), articulates the pervasive effects of monetary dishonesty:

> Money and financial questions come to play an exaggerated role in the life of man. Inflation makes society materialistic. More and more people strive for money income at the expense of other things important for personal happiness.
>
> Inflation-induced geographical mobility artificially weakens family bonds and patriotic loyalty. Many of those who tend to be greedy, envious, and niggardly anyway fall prey to sin. Even those who are not so inclined by their natures will be exposed to temptations they would not otherwise have felt. And because the vagaries of the financial markets also provide a ready excuse for an excessively parsimonious use of one's money, donations for charitable institutions decline.
>
> Then there is the fact that perennial inflation tends to deteriorate product quality. Every seller knows that it is difficult to sell the same physical product at higher prices than in previous years. But increasing money prices are unavoidable when the money supply is subject to relentless growth. So, what do sellers do? In many cases the rescue comes through technological innovation, which allows a cheaper production of the product, thus neutralizing or even overcompensating the countervailing influence of inflation. This is for example the case with personal computers and other products made with large inputs of information technology. But in other industries, technological progress plays a much smaller role. Here the sellers confront the above-mentioned problem. They then fabricate an inferior product and sell it under the same name, along with the euphemisms that have become customary in commercial marketing. For example, they might offer their customers "light" coffee and "non-spicy" vegetables—which translates into thin coffee and vegetables that have lost any trace of flavor. Similar product deterioration can be observed in the construction business. Countries plagued by perennial inflation seem to have a greater share of houses and streets that are in constant need of repair than other countries.
>
> In such an environment, people develop a more than sloppy attitude toward their language. If everything is whatever it is called, then it is difficult to explain the difference between truth and lie. Inflation tempts people to lie about their products, and perennial inflation encourages the habit of routine lying. We have already pointed out that routine lying plays a great role in fractional-reserve banking, the basic institution of the fiat money system [including money debasement institutionalized by Washington and Wall Street and presented as monetary policy that produces job and income growth, wealth accumulation and generally prosperity, which is demonstrably false.]. Fiat inflation seems to spread this habit like a cancer over the rest of the economy.[403]

Jessica Bennet, in a recent *Newsweek* article[404] observed that "[a]s Americans, we like to think we value the truth. Time and time again, public-opinion polls show that honesty is among the top five characteristics we want in a leader, friend, or lover; the world is full of woeful stories about the tragic consequences of betrayal. At the same time, deception is all around us. We are lied to by government officials and public figures to a disturbing degree; many of our social relationships are based on little white lies we tell each other. ..."

> We are a culture of liars, to put it bluntly, with deceit so deeply ingrained in our psyches that we hardly even notice we're engaging in it. ...

Another recent survey, by Junior Achievement, revealed that more than a third of teens believe lying, cheating, or plagiarizing can be necessary to succeed, while a brand-new study, commissioned by the publishers of Feldman's book,[405] shows that 18- to 34-year-olds—those Americans fully reared in this lying culture—deceive more frequently than the general population.

"Liars get what they want. They avoid punishment, and they win others' affection. Liars make themselves sound smart and savvy, they attain power over those of us who believe them, and they often use their lies to rise up in the professional world. Many liars have fun doing it. And many more take pride in getting away with it:

> [O]ne recent Duke University study found, as many as 90 percent of high-schoolers admit to cheating. Even lying adolescents are more popular among their peers.
>
> If everyone else is being rewarded for lying, don't we need to lie, too, just to keep up?[406]

There is and can be no honor derived from the vast scale of American money debasement.

§5.03 FAILURE OF HONEST MONEY AS A MORAL SOCIAL COVENANT

Financial crises and the legal context of those crises over the past forty-five years have persistently raised the question of the relevance of morality and ethics to the rule of law in money, banking and finance. But the connections of principles of morality and ethical practices to the phenomenon of the financialization of the American and global economies and the banking and financial systems that support them have been broken. They have been broken at the most fundamental conceptual level. The level of basic foundational moral and legal principles. Innovations in financial law and systems cannot be successful unless they are grounded in the moral and legal imperative of trusted, honest, safe and sound money. The algorithms, coding, computations and communication of financial data cannot be honest, accurate or true, if the underlying data is flawed. If the underlying data is flawed, the outcome the data's processing must necessarily be flawed. Financial data consists almost exclusively of numbers: numbers that represent units of account—monetary units. Money. If the data, in this case, monetary units of account are dishonest, or untrue, the information, knowledge and wisdom derived from the data will be dishonest or untrue and therefore misleading.[407] It cannot then be trusted.

The dishonesty of American money is baked into the monetary system prepared with the current recipe. Do not be misled by the international status of the dollar as the world's foremost reserve currency. It is simply the best of a very bad lot produced by an immoral system created by America in the modern era and exported throughout the global economy. Information has become misinformation, disinformation or error. Knowledge has become ignorance; and wisdom, folly. Without honest input and honest process, data output and decision-making based thereon must necessarily be false and the actions based thereon unjust.

Value is generally the degree of utility of a thing in satisfying, directly or indirectly, the needs or desires of human beings, called by economists "value in use;" or its worth consisting in the power of purchasing other things, called "value in exchange," calculated in money.

The concept of money is inseparable from the value it represents. For data representing monetary units to constitute an honest and true representation of the relative values of things, the value of the monetary unit must be regulated by reference to a common standard that is known to and accepted and trusted by the community it serves. Trust and confidence are the essential oils to a smooth running economic, monetary financial and thus commercial system.

Banking and commercial law and regulation have inexorably, progressively and intentionally weakened, ignored and finally broken the necessary socially and commercially known and accepted regulatory connection of monetary units to defined standards of value, and failed to honor and incorporate the moral principles and ethical practices of honesty, truthfulness and trust that are the intellectual and moral foundation of the law of money into our economic, banking and financial system. That failure goes to the heart of the otherwise inexplicable failure of accountability for the most recent great financial crises. Financial crises are inseparable from their origins in the falsehood and injustice of debased money.

Legal accountability for the series of financial crises since the Nixon shock in 1971, domestically and globally, have amply exposed the fact that Washington and Wall Street are riven by moral and ethical failures. These failures have been rationalized by self-serving pronouncements that the identified acts of moral and ethical failures are irresponsible, and wrong, but not illegal. As noted above, the financial crisis of 2008 has caused up to $20 trillion of damages to ordinary American households, while government and financial institutions have grown prospered. Damages globally have exceeded $40 trillion to $60 trillion.[408] *The Financial Inquiry Report*[409] chronicles the failures.

Washington and Wall Street have bombarded the American public with a series of false and misleading narratives to the effect that the great debasement of American money culminating in the great recession may have been wrong or immoral, but not illegal. These false and misleading narratives have undermined our economy and put our entire banking and financial system in peril. If we fail to address and rectify these false narratives in accordance with the American rule of law, innovations in financial law and systems cannot succeed in their expressed effects.

§5.04 FALSE NARRATIVE THAT MONETARY MORALITY IS SEPARATE FROM THE LAW OF MONEY

No banking law, regulation or exercise of or failure to exercise informed discretion by regulatory authorities; no financial crisis or existential emergency economic condition; and no failure by Congress to exercise its power and duty to provide honest and therefore safe and sound money, can take away Americans' moral and legal civil right to honest, safe and sound sovereign money, the value of which has been regulated by Congress.

The people's right to honest, safe and sound sovereign money is unequivocally grounded in the moral principles of natural law of honesty, truth and justice, as confirmed in the *Constitution* and as required by both common law and United States federal statutory law. Former Treasury Secretary Geithner has attacked and dismissed as what he describes as irrelevant, the:

> "[o]ld Testament view" that "[t]he venal should be punished. The irresponsible shouldn't be bailed out." In his recent book he cites the [ostensibly inapplicable public] appetite for "Old Testament vengeance," "Old Testament justice," "Old Testament impulses," "Old Testament populism," "Old Testament cravings," and so forth, no fewer than 18 times.
>
> "To Geithner, such impulses are the antithesis of his worldview—one that he believes relies on empiricism, pragmatism and reason. His 'Old Testament' crowd, by contrast, is driven by blind emotion, intuition and animalistic 'cravings' for heads on stakes. 'You could take [Goldman Sachs CEO] Lloyd Blankfein into a dark alley and slit his throat, and it would satisfy them for about two days,' former President Clinton told Geithner, as he recounts. 'Then the bloodlust would rise again.'[410]"

At a press conference in 2011, "President Barack Obama was forced to explain why there have been no prosecutions of Wall Street executives for their fraudulent actions during the run-up to the financial crisis. Asked by Jake Tapper to explain this behavior, Obama basically suggested that most of the actions on Wall Street weren't illegal but just immoral, and that his Administration worked to re-regulate the financial sector with the Dodd-Frank reform legislation.[411]"

President Obama first officially presented the proposition that the financial crisis, a crisis caused directly by dishonest communication of asset values denominated in debased money, was somehow wrong but not necessarily illegal. In his State of the Union Address in 2012, the President stated that:

> In 2008, the house of cards collapsed. We learned that mortgages had been sold to people who could not afford or understand them. Banks had made huge bets and bonuses with other people's money. Regulators had looked the other way or did not have the authority to stop the bad behavior.
>
> It was wrong. It was irresponsible. And it plunged our economy into a crisis that put millions out of work, saddled us with more debt, and left innocent, hardworking Americans holding the bag.[412]

Both President Obama and Secretary Geithner, giving voice to the shared views in Washington and on Wall Street, have asserted a distinction between the natural law moral principle of honest and true money, and the over-riding value and importance of apparent loopholes provided by banking law and regulations that could be "legally" exploited by both Washington and Wall Street to freely debase the money they create. The idea that immoral and illegal acts of money creation and emission through our banking system, as presently constituted could somehow be justified legally is a persistent thread in the literature relating to the law of money, banking and finance.[413] This unsupportable distinction goes directly to the failure of accountability of Washington and Wall Street for the financial crisis and for damages to American households of an estimated $20 trillion.[414]

[A] Coincidence of American Morality and the American Law of Money

Fortunately for the public, there is a direct identity of the moral principle of honest money with the constitutional, common law and federal statutory prohibition of fraud through money debasement. The money debasement that caused the financial crisis of 2008 was wrong, immoral and illegal. The intentionally false narratives spun by Washington and Wall Street, however, have been implemented through Washington and Wall Street failure to observe and enforce existing laws that are exact expressions of the moral principles of honesty and the legal duties of both Washington and Wall Street to refrain from abuse of the trust and powers extended to them by law, and through dishonest practices, to place their individual and institutional interests above the American public good. The moral principles expressed in the Old and New Testaments of the Christian Bible, the Ten Commandments, and I dare say, every compendium of moral principles, moral laws if you will, include honesty. Lying, cheating and stealing are prohibited. Money debasement is prohibited. These actions are both immoral and, demonstrably, illegal in the United States.[415]

The University of Oxford has recently published a paper in the *Journal of Anthropology* entitled "Is It Good to Cooperate? Testing the Theory of Morality-as-Cooperation in 60 Societies."[416] The upshot of the paper for present purposes, is that honest cooperation amongst a societies members "is always and everywhere considered moral … .[417]" This global conclusion is set within the more complete context of David Hume's classic statement of the universality of morality recognized in western societies:

> [M]oral judgments depend on an "internal sense or feeling, which nature has made universal in the whole species... and that as a result certain qualities—such as truth, justice, courage, temperance, constancy, dignity of mind...friendship sympathy, mutual attachment and fidelity... are the most universal, established principles of morals...esteemed universally, since the foundation of the world.[418]

Western societies are often characterized as equivalent to the Christian world. With that in mind, it is useful to note the position of the Catholic Holy See articulated in a well prepared Bulletin, N. 180517a, issued Thursday, 17.05.2018, entitled "'Oeconomicae et pecuniariae quaestiones' (Papal Bulletin, Considerations for an ethical discernment regarding some aspects of the present economic-financial system" of the Congregation for the Doctrine of the Faith and the Dicastery for Promoting Integral Human Development, dated Rome, January 6, 2018. The Papal Bulletin states:

> … the certainty that in every culture, there are multiple areas of ethical agreement that express a common moral wisdom and form the objective order upon which the dignity of the person is founded. From the solid and indispensable basis of such an order arise the clear and common principles that establish the fundamental

> rights and duties of the human person without which the control and abuse of the most powerful would come to dominate the entire human scene. This ethical order, rooted in the wisdom of God the Creator, is therefore the indispensable foundation for building a worthy community of persons, regulated by truly just laws. This is all the more evident where human beings, despite striving wholeheartedly for the good and the true, often succumb to vested interests, tyrannies, and iniquitous practices that cause grave suffering for all humanity, and especially for the weak and defenceless.[419]

In this extraordinary work the authors of the Papal Bulletin advocate the necessity that man return to fundament moral principles that constrain abuse of trust and power and dishonesty in realm of monetary affairs.

> ... it is clear that markets, as powerful propellers of the economy, are not capable of governing themselves. In fact, the markets know neither how to make the assumptions that allow their smooth running (social coexistence, honesty, trust, safety and security, laws, and so on) nor how to correct those effects and forces that are harmful to human society (inequality, asymmetries, environmental damage, social insecurity, and fraud).[420]
>
> ... it is impossible to ignore the fact that the financial industry, because of its pervasiveness and its inevitable capacity to condition and, in a certain sense, to dominate the real economy today, is a place where selfishness and the abuse of power have an enormous potential to harm the community.[421]
>
> What was sadly predicted a century ago has now come true today. Capital annuity can trap and supplant the income from work, which is often confined to the margins of the principal interests of the economic system. Consequently, work itself, together with its dignity, is increasingly at risk of losing its value as a 'good' for the human person and becoming merely a means of exchange within asymmetrical social relations. Precisely in this inversion of the order between means and ends, where work as a good becomes an 'instrument,' and money an 'end', the reckless and amoral 'culture of waste' finds a fertile ground."[422]

The Papal Bulletin goes on to state in extraordinarily clear language the existing disconnect between moral and legal principles wrought throughout the global economy, and specifically through the corruption of money and shadow money:

> "Thanks to globalization and digitalization, the markets can be compared to a giant organism through whose veins, like life giving sap, flow huge amounts of money. This analogy allows us to speak of the 'health' of such an organism when its means and structures are functioning well, and the growth and diffusion of wealth go hand in hand. The health of a system depends on the health of every single action performed. In a healthy market system, it is easier to respect and promote the dignity of the human person and the common good.
>
> "Correspondingly, every time unreliable economic-financial instruments are introduced and diffused, they put the growth and the diffusion of the wealth into serious danger creating systemic problems and risks that amount to the "intoxication" of the organism..."[423]
>
> "Experience and evidence over the last decades has demonstrated, on the one hand, how naive is the belief in a presumed self-sufficiency of the markets, independent of any ethics, and on the other hand, the compelling necessity of an appropriate regulation that at the same time unites the freedom and protection of every person and operates to create healthy and proper interactions, especially

with regards to the more vulnerable. In this sense, political and economic-financial powers must remain distant and autonomous and at the same time directed, beyond all proximate harms, towards the realization of a good that is basically common, and not reserved only for a few privileged persons.

"Such regulation is made even more necessary in view of the fact that among the major reasons for the most recent economic crisis was the immoral behavior of agents in the financial world, where the supranational dimension of the economic system makes it easy to bypass the regulations established by individual countries. Moreover, the extreme volatility and mobility of capital investments in the financial world permit those who control them to operate smoothly beyond every norm that does not aim at an immediate profit, often blackmailing by a position of strength even legitimate political authority."[424]

The perils of the disconnect between morality and law in money and banking are also described with are similarly articulated in the Papal Bulletin:

"[W]herever mere profit is placed at the summit of the culture of a financial enterprise, and the actual demands of the common good are ignored, every ethical claim is really perceived as irrelevant. This is reported today as a fact and is very much widespread even in the prestigious business schools. Every ethical claim is actually perceived as irrelevant and juxtaposed to the entrepreneurial action. This is very much highlighted from the fact that, in the organizational logic, those who do not adjust to business targets of this type are penalized both at the retributive level and at the level of professional recognition. In these cases, the objective of mere profit easily creates a perverse and selective logic that often favours the advancement of business leaders who are capable, but greedy and unscrupulous, and whose relationship with others is prevalently driven by a selfish and personal gain..."[425]

"All of these factors easily create and diffuse a profoundly amoral culture—in which one often does not hesitate to commit a crime when the foreseen benefits exceed the expected penalty. Such behaviour gravely pollutes the health of every economic-social system It endangers the functionality and seriously harms the effective realization of that common good, upon which is necessarily founded every form of social institution."[426]

Somehow, the practice of money debasement, which has historically been a capital crime, and which was punishable by death under the *American Currency Act of 1792*,[427] and in some countries by the penalty of the offender being half-hung, drawn and quartered, has now, presenting another glib oxymoron, and has found its central place as the basis for the monetary policy of the Federal Reserve System and of central banking systems, globally.

Immorality has infected our financial and economic system and that immorality is not separate from but is the essence of its illegality. We will turn to the relationship between morality and law. They may and have been addressed as sometimes separate by legal commentators. We will see how that separation is not applicable to the case of money debasement. Not only the moral accountability of the perpetrators of the debasement is necessary, but also civil and criminal legal accountability are necessary, before Washington or Wall Street will have any incentive to return to honest money under an honest monetary and economic system. Such a system is not only feasible but is legally required by the *United States Constitution* and the relevant decisions of the United States Supreme Court: the supreme law of the land.

It is our collective responsibility to revisit the moral and ethical foundations of commercial, banking and financial law and to provide legal and practical leadership to a renewal of recognition of and adherence to the moral principles and ethical practices upon which the American rule of law, the legal and accounting professions and judicial functions of our society are based.

Morality essentially means having and living according to a moral code; or principles of right and wrong. Basic morality condemns murder, adultery, lying, cheating and stealing. However, moral principles evolve with the evolution of society, sometimes differing noticeably in different cultures. Time also noticeably affects the idea of morality. Once prevalent moral principles are now considered outdated and irrelevant. Truth, honesty and respect of fiduciary obligations and limits on powers legally delegated to trusted and honored institutions and individual in Washington and on Wall Street are neither outdated nor irrelevant.

Financial crises are caused by money debasement, institutional lying about the value of money, perpetrated through the abuse of trust and monopoly power by Washington and Wall Street over money matters, the demonstrable effect of which is to steal the value of ordinary Americans' wealth and income to serve their own interests above and in derogation of Americans' right to honest, safe and sound money.

The philosophy of morality is ethics. Ethics explores the idea of morality and its place in society and addresses practical questions about morality. It is ironic that the volumes of banking law and regulation must, by their nature, be based on accurate information. Honest, truthful and reliable information. Information based on money. And prompt meaningful action based on that information. Yet, the basic language of money and banking has been corrupted; first, temporarily, in the name of existential necessity; then by benign neglect; and finally, by intentional abuse of trust, power and the establishment of a Washington and Wall Street enterprise centered on the unbridled aggrandizement of greed, power and wealth.

Money debasement is the most fundamental and far-reaching form of lying, cheating and stealing known to history. Money debasement makes each financial representation based on practices of money debasement a lie. When the misrepresentation of the value of money is knowingly institutionalized through practices that so blatantly constitute violations of natural law, moral principles, and ethical practices as well as constitutional and federal statutory law as well as common law, it is done intentionally. It is an abuse of trust and power by Washington and Wall Street. It is a breach by Washington and Wall Street bankers' fiduciary duty to place the public interest above their own selfish interests. It is intentional lying cheating and stealing. It is bank fraud.

[B] Connections, Identity and Inclusiveness of American Moral Law, Constitutional Law and Civil and Criminal Tort Law Relating to Honest Money

Connections amongst people, institutions, moral principles and laws have become a conundrum; in America, in particular. We have a tendency, reinforced by the increasing cultural dominance of big data as the primary force driving relationships and decision-making, to view individuals, facts and organizations in isolation, or in delimiting silos or isolated bundles of focus that increasingly ignore the fundamental and increasing interconnectedness of society. Commerce, economics, government and laws are inherently social and interconnected. The fundamental tool of interconnectedness of economics—commerce and government as social relationships—is money. For these social relationships to function successfully they must adhere to the fundamental principles that form the foundation for such relationships. Those principles establish the fundamental interconnectedness communicated through money. Those relationships must be based on the fundamental moral principle of honesty. Honesty observed leads to integrity, trust and confidence in one another. Without honesty as a fundamental moral, and legal foundation, civilizations cannot long endure. History is replete with examples of social collapse driven by the institutionalization of dishonesty manifest as an abuse of monopoly power over money by those entrusted with its safety, soundness and integrity, and the resulting infection of the entire culture with abuse of power and dishonesty.[428]

The pervasive discretion resting with bureaucrats is routinely interpreted to sell the outcome of the exercise of their discretion in exchange for admission to the revolving door to riches in the private sector, as opposed to satisfaction derived from devotion of their service to the public interest, as well as fair compensation. American public policy based upon tweeter feed, sound bites propounded by the powerful, greedy, selfish and lazy—communication at the highest reaches of government, banking and finance—is conducted on the level of sixth grade elementary school students. This development corrupts civilization rather than building and strengthening it. Technological developments based on communication through data selection, manipulation and simplicity in presentation, discourages complex thoughtful consideration, expression and connection to qualitative concepts, such as moral principles and ethical practices. Under these conditions, it is difficult to reconcile today's amoral, relativistic, data-based society with America's original, idealized moral foundation. These foundational principles and practices have been displaced by financial model outputs based on algorithms, incorporating and applied to selective data, as modern era substitutes for outdated moral principles, ethical practices and fundamental legal principles.

The increasing role of high-technology and data as instruments of social and economic connection can only be effective if based on the moral principle of honesty instead of what has evolved as a complex, institutionally embedded methodology of lying, cheating and stealing. There is no morality inherent in data. No trust; no confidence. Assumptions and effects are obscured by distance and structure offering limited opportunity for one to question or test data, develop knowledge or acquire wisdom that may support thoughtful decision making. Evaluation of data is progressively limited and manipulated. Therefore, diminishing useful information, knowledge and wisdom. Data itself provides no connection to real human efforts, goods or services. Data by itself, is sterile. Its origins, obscure. Its effects, profound. More data moving ever faster and through more relational complexity leaves the human mind, wisdom, discernment and judgment that define our social, economic, financial, legal, accounting and political compact behind. Its form in complex financial models, statistics, reports and public records supports and facilitates deep and widespread misrepresentation and misunderstanding. Crunching the numbers is a popular euphemism. It does not necessarily provide true information, much less knowledge or wisdom as a foundation for decision-make conforming to moral principles. Massive pro-forma disclosure of words and numbers does not provide a basis for moral and responsible decision-making. Honesty is the casualty. The triumph of big data is the death knell of moral integrity. The end game of data manipulation justifies all means. The disembodiment of morality. Social, political and economic principles are cast aside in the process. Lawyers and accountants are so tied to processes that they do not question underlying data, its source or meaning. America's legal and accounting professionals no longer provide an over-all moral framework for client decision-making or action. Big money equals big data for its own sake. Its manipulation to produce predictable effects quickly dispenses with the discernment of truth, accurate information, knowledge and wisdom in a moral context. Thoughtful consideration and assessment in social, political, economic and legal relationships have been stripped of the defining principles that support those relationships. Corruption and dishonesty are enshrined in big data.

The common, even defining trait of American society and culture originated as a loosely arrayed group of rugged individuals competing in a free market society where material success goes to the strong by virtue of the free exercise of their natural, God-given talents and hard work. The weaker and less materially successful members of American society therefore have only themselves to blame. It is only natural that in their individual drive for success, the strong and the successful exploit the weak and less successful. It is every man for himself. The ends justify the means.

Alexis de Tocqueville made the classic equation of the free condition sought by American immigrants with an aggregation of isolated autonomous individuals wresting their existence from the wilds of nature.[429] In fact, at the time Tocqueville made this definitional equation of American society he was largely correct. Based upon his observations, Tocqueville correctly anticipated developing social difficulties in America, including an increased tyranny of the ill-informed majority over thoughtful and informed minority, a preoccupation with material goods, and an unfounded appearance of the triumph of isolated individuals over the mass of society. He predicted the violence of party spirit now readily apparent in America political processes, and the judgment of the wise subordinated to the triumphant prejudices of the ignorant. These dangerous strains of thought are dominant in American society and politics today. They successfully serve the interests of America's corporate, banking and government power elite.

Much of today's thinking by American leaders is revealed in fragmented, segmented phrases—memes—expressed in clashing, jingoistic diatribes. Twitter feed. Not useful building blocks for informed policy or decision making. Not productive. Not instructive. Not wise. This abbreviated simplistic mode of communication will not stop until our social survival requires it. American leadership fears the use of too many words to express policy alternatives as well as the communication of conflicting thoughts and priorities. Apparently, this mode of discourse is perhaps considered to be "less politically correct." So here we are. Too many words. A *Constitution* that our leaders have never read. Laws and regulations that are disconnected, fragmented and impede rather than contribute to our national understanding of law and regulation in the context of our shared moral foundation. Numbers can be made to say anything, everything or nothing. Quants and computers rule.

It has been my experience that if one looks at the title and body of a federal government law, rule or regulation, one will inevitably discover that the body of the document serves the opposite ends from those expressed in the title. This manipulative practice intentionally serves to create and support, not clarity, but insider designed complexity and "loopholes" that support fertile ground for discretionary interpretation. Americas political, social and economic division is imbedded in practices of intentional deceit. These practices facilitate avoidance rather than compliance with or adherence to underlying foundational moral principles that serve the public interest. The best and brightest—and highest paid—attorneys, accountants, bankers and politicians are dedicated to the successful frustration of public policy, law and regulation based on fundamental moral principles. Winston Churchill famously observed that "[i]f you have ten thousand regulations you destroy all respect for the law." We certainly exceeded the ten thousand regulation quota. And we are none the wiser.

It is no mere coincidence that with the abandonment of the last vestiges of the regulation of American money that began with the existential necessity exception adopted to finance the Civil War and then the institution of fractional reserve banking, reached its denouement under the fractured protection of the *Bretton Woods Accords* and culminated with the Nixon shock in 1971. The development of banking law and regulation subsequently exploded in quantity and complexity as well as constriction in moral and legal effect. American banking and monetary laws, regulations and practices are riven with provision for unbridled regulatory discretion, often simply not exercised at all. That practice has been fully exploited—not in the public interest but in service of Washington's and Wall Street's interests. This explosion of banking law and regulation has oscillated between reactionary attempts at deregulation and reregulation that have unquestionably failed to supplant the simple, but now abandoned regulatory relationship between measured units of quality and quantity of goods or services on the one hand, and quantity and quantity of specie designated and enumerated, regulating the value of monetary equivalent units. The nature of the fundamental regulatory relationship is based on the moral imperative of honesty in the communication of value through money. The battle for honest money has concentrated on the periphery of the subject in recent times, leaving the moral principles and laws originally intended to affect those principles aside, as if somehow, they have been rendered obsolete and irrelevant.

The current apparent distinction made by American executive, legislative and central banking authorities between morality and the law relating to the honesty, safety and soundness of money, and therefore banking; since banks are now charged by the Federal Reserve System, under the auspices of the United States Congress, to "loan money into existence" that acquires value from individuals and business productivity, leaves an open door to discretionary interpretation and manipulation of money and banking.[430] The natural moral law principle of honesty that corresponds directly with banking and monetary matters is absent from Americas current monetary and banking system. That financial system fails to meet the constitutional mandate for congressional regulation of the value of money and the statutory and common law prohibition of abuse of trust and power by banks. The monopoly process of money creation by banks with the tolerance, indeed encouragement and facilitation by government, has been employed to perpetrate a scheme of lies and artifices intentionally designed to debase and misrepresent economic value; and through that scheme of lies and artifices, to cheat unsuspecting participants in the system and steal the value of their capital and labors through the crime and tort of money debasement. The monopoly has now also slipped out of control of government into the shadow banking system. Washington and Wall Street: intentionally, deliberately, have failed to establish any standard or mechanism for regulation of the value of American sovereign money—the United States dollar. Debasement is the inevitable consequence of failure to regulate the value of sovereign money and to subject credit money and money substitutes to the discipline of repayment in units of sovereign money, the value of which is properly regulated by reference to an external commonly accepted standard of value by which that money can be redeemed on demand, as well as by reference to and enforcement of historical principles of commercial law that attached accountability for repayment of credit money in an open, direct, honest and transparent manner.

This corruption is played out in Washington and on Wall Street. Their success, wealth and power have set modern standards. The Washington Wall Street enterprise model and standard of conduct given by example, not only permits but encourages and sanctions all Americans' exploitation of economic relationships through corruption. Lying, cheating and stealing have become a norm. Only those perceived as weak, losers and simple minded remain committed to the moral framework of honesty and integrity embodied in the American rule of law. They are not among the "players" in the big game of amassing wealth and power. Under the present iteration of America's legal and business upper crust, morality is treated as an outmoded relic, a hindrance to success, to growth, to the ability to meet the drumbeat of piling-up of data, numbers, and ultimately money and power. Morality does not reside in Washington or on Wall Street. Greed there remains good. Power for its own sake remains good. The limits of public delegation of trust and power to governments in the *Constitution*, and the handmaidens of government, Wall Street through the national bank and Federal Reserve System in their great work of money creation and debasement, have been worn away. Pursuit of wealth and power through lying, cheating and stealing is now a hallmark of success; publicly and unapologetically shouted from the rooftops; or at the very least on twitter and other social and public media.

Without the grounding of all social, political, economic and legal relationships in safe, sound and honest money, the tool that binds us together on the basis of the moral virtue of economic honesty, the moral and legal mandate for economic, monetary and financial honesty has now been abandoned to the realm of the archaic. Confidence in government and financial institutions; and their moral and legal accountability and integrity, will continue to erode, affecting every human relationship. Social, economic and political dysfunction and collapse will surely follow. History bears out the repetition of this sordid tale and the entirely predictable consequences. We are foolish and irresponsible to ignore, disparage and abandon the foundation of morality, ethics and laws upon which our great nation is grounded and upon which our individual and collective liberty, prosperity, health and happiness, and property rights are dependent.

All is not lost, however. As Tocqueville made his observations about the American democratic political framework and the society it defined, society continued to develop in America and in Europe to reflect increased population and increased urban concentrations of society and the harkening back to the social thinkers of ancient Greece and Rome by political and intellectual leaders on both continents.

Money debasement is an explicit betrayal and violation of deeply entrenched American principles of natural law and morality grounded in honesty in economic, monetary and financial relationships and transactions as the primary foundation for our democratic social compact. Washington's and Wall Street's collaborative efforts to simply roll over practical ethical rules that effect moral principles with a full sense of righteous entitlement have in fact, violated the American rule of law—formal rules enacted by Americas and subject to adjudication and enforcement, in the public interest and for the common good that relate to money—the primary social and economic connection establishing American society, its survival and civilization and the pre-conditional foundation of American government.

Ordinary Americans have expressed the fundamental natural law; the moral principles underlying American values, its social and economic compact and the principles governing American civilization and the role and integrity of money, in the *Constitution*: the law of the land. The American public exercises and enforces its social, economic and political compact of civil society based on the rule of law enforced through the mechanism and medium of money, through government, and its agents and partners, the Wall Street banks. American money and money globally, by extension and influence of American power and example, and has been near fatally corrupted by the American government and the Wall Street banks through persistent money debasement.

If we are to return to the American dream of economic opportunity for every American, the individuals and institutions in Washington and on Wall Street that have colluded to debase our money must be held accountable for their breach of the fundamental moral principal of honesty in the medium of exchange, under the rule of law in accordance with natural law and the moral principles and ethical practices that form the foundation for the American rule of the law of money.

American and global financial crises can be neither mitigated nor avoided without a return to and re-grounding according to the natural law, moral imperative, ethical practices, enforcement of the American rule of law including specifically the law of money, and thereby the re-establishment of the primacy of public sovereignty over government and its handmaidens in the corruption of American money—the Wall Street banks. Have we managed to evolve to the point where personal and institutional lying, cheating and stealing by Washington and Wall Street has become a moral, ethical and legally countenanced course of policy and action? Washington and Wall Street are apparently convinced that ordinary Americans have done so. Is honesty therefore obsolete—anachronistic? Has it become so only for Washington and Wall Street? Has the day arrived where the "goodness" in America—the "best" in America—is defined by the most powerful, the most ruthless, dishonest, lying, and cheating and stealing members of our society? Should ordinary Americans adopt the same set of moral, ethical and legal principles? Why not?

[C] Tort of Fraud Versus Fraud as Breach of Contract

The record of the United States Supreme Court pronouncements on the subject of the American law of money have been couched, not in terms of the legal attributes of money debasement, but on the effect of interpretation of the law of money as incorporated in specific contracts.[431]

Moral and legal accountability of Washington and Wall Street for their course of intentional misrepresentation of the liquidity and value of the money they create and emit, both in the supposedly regulated banking system or in the almost entirely unregulated shadow banking system, is not to be found in contract law.[432]

The American tale of money debasement differs from brutal physical repression through assault and battery only in that that the injuries to America's working households as a result of the great financial crisis of 2008 are primarily economic. "Physical assault, abuse and robbery" are the actions more commonly referred to and understood as torts. But make no mistake, the tort that has been inflicted by Washington and Wall Street on ordinary Americans public is as brutal as assault physical harm and physical robbery. The pervasive intentional bank fraud accomplished by lying to, cheating and stealing from ordinary Americans through the tort of intentional money debasement, is far more widespread and damaging than the more starkly visible harm caused by the torts of physical assault, battery and robbery could ever be. In fact, in the absence of legal enforcement of a case for financial crisis accountability, aggrieved ordinary Americans may turn to physical violence as their last option for justice in the face of the vast scale of American money debasement.

The torts of intentional fraud, abuse of trust and power and money debasement were conducted by Washington and Wall Street against the households of ordinary American people and has left in its wake unprecedented financial devastation as well as personal and physical trauma. The wounds of the people are no less visible or varied in the typicality of hurt and damage than the brutal torts of assault and battery. Victims of physical assault and battery might seek justice. So must the victims of the economic beating of the financial crisis. The conduct that led to the crisis continues unabated. The few defendants in a case for financial crisis accountability, numbering in mere hundreds, have inflicted their economic assault on a group of ordinary people numbering in the hundreds of thousands—millions—who so far have found no succor in those in the representative government they have entrusted with their protection.

Ordinary people in America and around the world, know that the damage by the economic assault led by Washington and Wall Street has been left un-redressed. Some have taken to Main Street and to the political arena, hoarding and wielding weapons, venting anger, fear and frustration in unfocused acts of violence. It is in this context that the case of the damaged ordinary American people against the economic brutality inflicted by the few upon the many must be heard and remediated under America's social and economic compact as enshrined in the American rule of law.

We must remember and reinvigorate the meaning of the words we use in the context of our discussion of moral principles and the law of money.

[1] Honesty

The depth and breadth of the strictures supporting the vital role of honesty as a foundation for civilized conduct and the rule of law is best described by the range of wrongs based in the tort of dishonesty.

[2] Lying

Money created through the American financial system, both the "official" banking system and the "unofficial" very real and enormous shadow banking system that dwarfs the official system in size and complexity, intentionally created by Washington and Wall Street, reflected as units of account of value, media of exchange, stores of value and methods of deferred payment of value over the past 45 years have consistently and misrepresented the information denominated in dollars contained in every account, financial statement and report conveying information denominated in US dollars, overstating the value of asset in each case in the face of ever declining correlation between the unit of measurement and any regulated standard of value—and resulting in the massive debasement of the value of American money.

[3] Cheating and Stealing

Washington and Wall Street have used the well-known and historically reviled process of money debasement to cheat the American public by the forced exchange of money having ever diminishing value for the fruits of their labor, sacrifice and savings. The stolen value, commandeered by Washington and Wall Street, has been squandered though years of political and financial payoffs for political and financial favors amongst politicians and bureaucrats; as well As Wall Street profits and bonuses; 'creating money debasement to fund their own prosperity as well as government profligacy. The American government has provided the illusion of a protection blanket for their partners in crime in the form of federal regulatory insulation from prosecution, losses and liabilities for their role in the Washington Wall Street greedy and illegal racketeering conspiracy enterprise to loot the American public.

[4] Common Law Torts of Deceit, Misrepresentation and Fraud

"Lies." According to *Black's Law Dictionary* (Black's): A "lie is an untruth deliberately told; the uttering or acting of that which is false for the purpose of deceiving; intentional mis[s]tatement (sic)." ... "Thou shalt not lie" (the Ninth Commandment of the *Bible*, 'Exodus" 20:16 common phrasing of "Thou shalt not bear false witness against thy neighbor").

Black's goes on to define the ancient common law wrong of "deceit" as: "a subtle trick or device, whereunto may be referred all manner of craft and collusion used to defraud another by any means whatsoever, which hath no other or more proper name than deceit to distinguish the offense. A 'deceit' is either (i) The suggestion, as a fact, of that which is not true, by one who does not believe it to be true; (ii) the assertion, as a fact, of that which is not true, by one who has no reasonable ground for believing it to be true; (iii) The suppression of a fact, by one who is bound to disclose it, or who gives information of other facts which are likely to mislead for want of communication of that fact; or (iv) a promise, made without any intention of performing it. To constitute a deceit, the statement must be untrue, made with knowledge of its falsity or with reckless and conscious ignorance thereof, especially if parties are not on equal terms, made with intent that the plaintiff act thereon or in a manner apparently fitted to induce him to act thereon, and the plaintiff must act on the statement in the manner contemplated, or manifestly probable, to his injury. The essential elements of 'deceit' are representation, falsity, scienter (intent), deception and injury."

Black's defines "misrepresentation" as: "Any manifestation by words or other conduct by one person to another that, under the circumstances, amounts to an assertion not in accordance with the facts." It is "An untrue statement of fact. An incorrect or false representation. That which, if accepted, leads the mind to an apprehension of a condition other and different from that which exists. Colloquially, it is understood to mean a statement made to mislead or deceive."

The same source defines "fraud" as: "An intentional perversion of truth for the purpose of inducing another in reliance upon it to part with some valuable thing belonging to him or to surrender a legal right; a false representation as a matter of fact, whether by words or conduct, by false or misleading allegations, or by concealment of that which should have been disclosed, which deceives and is intended to deceive another so that he shall act upon it to his legal injury." Also, it is a generic term, "embracing all multifarious means which human ingenuity can devise, and which are resorted to by one individual to get an advantage over another by false suggestions or by suppression of truth, and includes all surprise, trick, cunning or dissembling, and any unfair way by which another is cheated." Fraud is either actual or constructive. Actual fraud consists in deceit, artifice, trick, design, some direct and active operation of the mind; it includes cases of the intentional and successful employment of any cunning, deception or artifice used to circumvent or cheat another; it is something said, done or omitted by a person with the design of perpetrating what he knows to be a cheat or deception. Constructive fraud consists in any act of commission or omission contrary to legal or equitable duty, trust or confidence justly reposed, which is contrary to good conscience and operates to the injury of another. Or, as otherwise defined, it is an act, statement or omission which, if generally permitted, would be prejudicial to the public welfare, and yet may be unconnected with any selfish or evil design. Or according to Story, constructive frauds are such acts or contracts as, though not originating in any actual evil design or contrivance to perpetrate a positive fraud or injury upon other persons, are yet, by their tendency to deceive or mislead other persons, or to violate private or public confidence, or to impair or injure the public interests, deemed equally reprehensible with actual fraud."

Cheating is defined as: "[t]o [intentionally] deceive and defraud; ... contrary to the plain rules of common honesty."

Stealing is the: "[c]ommission of theft, that is the felonious taking and carrying away of the personal property of another... without right and without leave or consent of the owner."

Also, according to Black's, a "crime" is "A positive or negative act in violation of penal law; an offense against the State." Black's goes on to clarify that "The distinction between a crime and a tort or civil injury is that the former is a breach and violation of the public right and of duties due to the whole community considered as such, and in its social and aggregate capacity; whereas the latter is an infringement or privation of the civil rights of individuals merely." As opposed to ancient common law crimes, which no longer exist in the United States, crimes are created by statute. In the context of financial crises, the crimes have been primarily Federal crimes, although the same facts and circumstances may also constitute crimes or give rise to enforcement actions by state attorneys general under state law.

These definitions establish a framework to follow development of the moral and legal principles set forth in the *Constitution* and in state and federal statutory laws enacted to prevent and to punish bank fraud, securities fraud and consumer fraud and abuse of power through violations of trust [antitrust law, including bank anti-tying law], whether initiated through private rights of action or governmental civil or criminal enforcement actions. An examination of the overall context of the relatively recent great financial crisis in America and globally, one can discover a progression of laws and policies in derogation of the constitutional imperative that Congress create, emit and regulate the value of American sovereign money. Despite the clear language of the *United States Constitution* and the history of Congress' active management of the regulation of the value of the dollar, beginning with the *Constitution, The Coinage Act of 1792* and continuing with greater a lesser measure of success through the time of the Nixon shock in 1971, Congress did in fact consistently grapple with their constitutionally mandated power and duty. A combination of executive action and subsequent federal legislation essentially ended any semblance of Congress' recognition or fulfillment of its constitutional power and duty with respect to the "money question." Washington, Wall Street, the legal and accounting professions and those amongst the American public who are in the position to exploit congressional failure in their self-interest have done so; on the largest scale in history. False narratives promulgated in Washington and on Wall Street described in this and subsequent chapters provide cover for the big lie of asset liquidity and values supported by deliberate monetarization of illiquid asset without discounts to value reflecting risk and uncertainty of liquidation of underlying assets at par over time in the financial system.

Winston Churchill once observed that, "In wartime, truth is so precious that she should always be attended by a bodyguard of lies." Churchill's observation has been followed by Washington and Wall Street to entirely different and perverse ends. The existential threat of war is almost exclusively the predicate for the initial abandonment of moral law, offered up as a justification for the perversion of the law of money, through exploitation by government, bankers and corporate profiteers. Throughout American history proponents of the practice of lying, cheating and stealing from sovereign money debasement as a toll of war finance have found secure footing. The justification being that if we (read government and its financiers) is not permitted to lie, cheat and steal to finance war, we might lose and then have no country at all. By honoring the existential war exception to the natural law, and later constitutional, statutory and common law proscription of dishonest—lying cheating and stealing—through money debasement, Pandora's famous box is opened. The argument supporting the existential war exception ignores the alternative rights, powers and duties granted to government in the *Constitution* to conduct war if necessary and to finance it through open and transparent borrowing and taxation. Money debasement is not a necessity of war; it is an act of policy expediency, extended and exploited to enable the American elite of income, wealth and power to aggrandize their positions; concentrating income, wealth and power; and asserting their interests ahead of the interest of the ordinary public.

Through time, the so-called existential war exception to honest, safe and sound money has segued into an exception of political expedience and self-interested policies that serve only to protect the aggrandizement of wealth and power by Washington and their partners and financiers on Wall Street. The immoral, dishonest and illegal transformation, perversion and, finally, abandonment of the constitutional requirement of honest, safe and sound money has flourished under a progression of false narratives regarding money, morality and law; intentionally false narratives produced through political spin by the privileged sectors of our society, our experts on money and law, that are trusted and beholden to the American public to act in an open, honest, transparent and manner that respects our natural law foundation of moral principle and law as expressed in our founding documents, statutes, regulations and common law tradition. I have identified a number of false narratives, the adoption of which have been held out by Washington and Wall Street to justify a course of conduct that has damaged our country far beyond economics. These false narratives and the financial crises that occurred attendant to them have riven asunder our philosophical, social, political and legal compact.

Detailed exposition of all the false narratives employed by Washington and Wall Street as a part of their enterprise to loot the American public, is not possible here. In the Introduction I provided a listing of the most fundamental and damaging false narratives propounded by the Washington and Wall Street enterprise of economic tyranny, and provided comment with respect to the primary false narratives that drive to heart of the phantom narrative barrier that the Washington Wall Street enterprise has constructed to avoid legal accountability for the damages caused by the financial crises the enterprise has spawned and wrought upon the American public.

§5.05 UNIVERSAL OR NATURAL LAW, MORALITY, AND ETHICS AS A JURISPRUDENTIAL FOUNDATION FOR THE AMERICAN RULE OF THE LAW OF MONEY

The idea that morality is separate from the law has a history. The torts of intentional abuse of trust and power and fraud are at one with fundamental moral principles of honesty, equal protection and due process. Attempts to treat the legal and moral principles as separate; morality being applicable to the conduct causing the financial crisis; but neither criminal nor civil law being applicable, is simply wrong. It is another of the many false narratives spun by Washington and Wall Street to avoid legal accountability for the financial crisis.

[A] Legal Positivism Versus Natural Law: An Echo of Consequentialism Versus Universal Natural Law

The Papal Bulletin referred to earlier in this chapter unequivocally rejects the moral philosophy of "consequentialism", a big word that means the ends justify the means. That philosophy begs the question of whose ends and whose means. Legal positivism flags in support of universal natural law—the law of human civil rights.

Although legal positivism might be found to be appropriate with respect to particular laws or categories of law, the laws that define basic human civil rights are universal natural laws. One school of thought most often attributed to H.L.A. Hart, a British philosopher who was professor of jurisprudence at the University of Oxford, is the philosophy of legal positivism. His most important writings included *Causation in the Law* (1959, with A.M. Honoré), *The Concept of Law* (1961), *Law, Liberty and Morality* (1963), *Of Laws in General* (1970), and *Essays on Bentham* (1982):

> *The Concept of Law* (1961) is an analysis of the relation between law, coercion, and morality, and it is an attempt to clarify the question of whether all laws may be properly conceptualized as coercive orders or as moral commands. Hart says that there is no logically necessary connection between law and coercion or between law and morality. He explains that to classify all laws as coercive orders or as moral commands is to oversimplify the relation between law, coercion, and morality. He also explains that to conceptualize all laws as coercive orders or as moral commands is to impose a misleading appearance of uniformity on different kinds of laws and on different kinds of social functions which laws may perform. He argues that to describe all laws as coercive orders is to mischaracterize the purpose and function of some laws and is to misunderstand their content, mode of origin, and range of application.[433]

Hart's approach, generally referred to as legal positivism, is generally thought to be the source of a division; a separation of principles of morality from principles or provisions of law. According to Hart, there is no necessary logical connection between the content of law and morality, and that the existence of legal rights and duties may be devoid of any moral justification. Thus, his interpretation of the relation between law and morality appears to differ from that of Ronald Dworkin, who in *Law's*

Empire[434] suggests that every legal action has a moral dimension. Dworkin rejects the concept of law as acceptance of conventional patterns of recognition and describes law not merely as a descriptive concept but as an interpretive concept which combines jurisprudence and adjudication. He systematically demonstrates that his concept of political and legal moral integrity is the key to Anglo-American legal theory and practice:[435]

> Hart defines legal positivism as the theory that there is no logically necessary connection between law and morality. However, he describes his own viewpoint as a "soft positivism," because he admits that rules of recognition may consider the compatibility or incompatibility of a rule with moral values as a criterion of the rule's legal validity.
>
> Legal positivism may disagree with theories of natural law, which assert that civil laws must be based on moral laws in order for society to be properly governed. Theories of natural law may also assert that there are moral laws which are universal and which are discoverable by reason.[436]

Legal positivism generally holds that laws must derived from a sovereign authority and be enforceable by coercion. Although an extensive original analysis of the works of Hart and Dworkin is beyond the scope of this work, it is important to clarify here that their respective views do not present an irreconcilable conflict, as is often suggested in the voluminous body of scholarly work on the subject.

According to William C. Starr, a professor at Marquette University:

> It is a mistake to make generalizations about two opposing theories of law: natural law and legal positivism. Both theories level charges against the other. Some are perceptive; others are unfounded. What is less well known, but equally true, is that historically both the natural law defenders and the proponents of legal positivism have disagreed as much among themselves as with their opponents. If progress is to be made in legal philosophy by studying the works of important legal philosophers, it will be made by carefully examining the theories developed, rather than by attaching a label to the philosopher and then assuming certain things about that legal philosopher because the label has been attached.[437]

Speaking generally, "natural law finds that there is a necessary, not a contingent, relationship between law and morality. According to natural law theory, when there is a conflict between natural law and human law, natural law must take precedence. In this regard, natural law dictates that all human-made laws must be in accordance with fundamental natural law principles, such as Aquinas' notions of doing good, avoiding evil and promoting the common good. The natural law proponent believes that all law must be morally justified if it is to be legitimately called 'law' at all. Thus, any morally acceptable legal order must acknowledge natural law and incorporate its fundamental tenets."[438] The case made in this book incorporates both universal natural law principles and the principles of legal positivism. Systematic money debasement by the Washington Wall Street enterprise constitutes lying to, cheating and stealing from ordinary Americans and violates both universal natural law principles standing on their own as well as expressed in the *Constitution,* federal statutes and in American common law. There is nothing ephemeral or mystical in the global disapprobation of lying, cheating and stealing through money debasement. There is no exception to application of the American law of money forbidding intentional money debasement by the Washington Wall Street enterprise based on some nebulous and intentionally misleading rationalization that the end of protection of the status quo American and global financial system justifies the intentional exploitation and existential threat posed by the ongoing means of money debasement conducted by and in the sole interest of the Washington Wall Street enterprise itself.

The idea that honesty (one of the most fundamental of all moral principles applicable to social and economic conduct) in the expression of relative value of goods and services denominated in terms of sovereign money, as clearly provided for in Article I, § 8, Clauses 5 and 6 of the *Constitution* can be simply abandoned by subsidiary laws and regulations disconnected from the natural law moral requirement of honest money, is simply wrong and unsupportable.

While there may be laws that do not necessarily incorporate moral principles, the deliberate confusion of the bases for the distinction made under the applicable theories of jurisprudence articulated as natural law or legal positivism, must be addressed; not merely skipped over and ignored by Washington and Wall Street. An examination of the relevant distinctions between the legal positivism of Hart and the natural law theories of Dworkin as applied to the violation by the Washington Wall Street enterprise of the ordinary Americans' constitutional and common law right to the creation, emittance and maintenance of honest, safe and sound sovereign money through abuse of power does not lead to a conclusion that money debasement may be immoral but not illegal. According to Hart "[i]n any legal system, there may be cases in which existing laws are vague or indeterminate and that judicial discretion may be necessary in order to clarify existing laws in these cases. Hart also argues that by clarifying vague or indeterminate laws, judges may actually make new laws. He explains that this argument is rejected by Ronald Dworkin, who contends that judicial discretion is not an exercise in making new laws but is a means of determining which legal principles are most consistent with existing laws and which legal principles provide the best justification for existing laws."[439]

On the other hand, Alex Scott, in his article on H.L.A. Hart's *The Concept of Law*, provides a useful complementary statement of Hart's legal positivism and Dworkin's natural law theory. "A complete legal theory does not merely identify the rules of a legal system, but also interprets and evaluates them. A complete legal theory must consider not only the relation between law and coercion (i.e. the "force" of law), but the relation between law and rightfulness or justifiability (i.e. the "grounds" of law). Thus, Dworkin argues that a complete legal theory must address not only the question of whether the rules of a legal system are justified but the question of whether there are sufficient grounds for coercing individuals to comply with the rules of the system."[440]

The distinction that Scott draws in his brief paper highlights the source of the idea that although the grounds of the laws that prohibit the intentional abuse of trust and power, and fraud that govern the moral wrong and the legal civil tort and crime of money debasement through abuse of delegated powers may apply, but that for some reason, compliance with the laws may not be coerced. The reasons most often most often advanced for Washington and Wall Street's exemption form the coercive power of those laws is that the violations of law—of the moral "rightfulness or justifiability" of those laws, are superseded by the existential necessity of action by the Washington Wall Street enterprise to preserve our country and its economic and financial system. The determination of that existential necessity has been made, since the time of the American Civil War, by Washington and Wall Street, at the time of each succeeding financial crisis. The determination in each case has been justified by the opinions of financial, economic and monetary experts in Washington and on Wall Street. Americans have been exhorted to defer to the opinions and actions of those experts as being in the public interest—the experts know best. History informs us however that the economic, monetary and financial system preserved by these experts has been limited to a closed-system that benefits Washington and Wall Street primarily, which suffers the American public to bear the damages and losses inherent in that self-serving closed system. Protecting the Washington Wall Street enterprise closed system at the expense of the system in which ordinary Americans operate is not in the best interest of the American public.[441]

Money used in our modern society consists primarily of sovereign money; in the United States, the Dollar. By far the largest component of our monetary system consists of money created through our fractional reserve banking system. Recently, the money supply has been greatly expanded by an explosion of negotiable credit money. Historically, the supply of credit money negotiated in the market was limited to a relatively small circle of merchants, brokers and central banks; all familiar with and possessed of knowledge of and trust and confidence reposed amongst the parties involved, issuer and endorser personal liability for payment of the bills and notes negotiated, protections afforded by commercial law and the relative short term nature of the outstanding bills and notes cycle of maturity. The current explosion in the use of securitized debt; asset backed securities and derivative instruments all together providing a mass of liquid credit instruments posing as securities, without the historic protections of and limitations on the use of credit money poses a far more dire threat to America's existence than war.

The failure of Congress to exercise its power and duty to regulate the value of money as mandated by the *United States Constitution* has given rise to the ability of the Fed banking system to create credit denominated in sovereign money, leveraged through relaxation of banking laws and regulations relating to credit creation, leading to credit concentrations distorting asset values by virtue of the volume of credit directed to specific asset classes where credit concentrations have been incentivized. Formally, under our system of sovereign money, where the value of the dollar was regulated by Congress, the requirement of redemption of the sovereign money in terms of the values dictated by reference to the official external standard of value constrained debasement. Obviously, where paper dollars and assets whose values are denominated in dollars, and are unconstrained by regulated value, credit creation would, and has led to a steady progressive debasement of the value of the dollar. The process of securitization of credit and creation of derivative contracts based on the securities and traders of overnight repurchase financing arrangements, all denominated in dollars and created an ever increasing amount of assets denominated in dollars that has and continues to outstrip the values of the assets from which the credit instruments are derived. Thus, the abuse of trust and power by those who create this mass of credit money results in a systematic debasement of the value actually represented by both the credit money itself, as well as the sovereign money in terms of which the credit money is denominated.

Accordingly, the dollar value that the public attributes to goods and services in the real economy, and the asset values denominated in dollars as represented on the books and records of financial institutions and all other parties are consistently and progressively overstated.

This systematic overstatement of values directly caused by the intentional debasement of the value of the dollar by Washington and Wall Street, in their own self-interest, has led inevitably to recurring financial crises. Washington can lay claim to dollar denominated economic growth and Wall Street can profit through its creation and emission of enormous amounts of liquidity that overburden the associated asset base. When the value and liquidity supposedly represented by the financial assets collapses, Wall Street has consistently been protected from losses by Washington—with the American public bearing the cost of the realized threat of moral hazard incurred by the intentional conduct of the Washington Wall Street enterprise. The revolving door between Washington and Wall Street has created an identity of symbiotic interest amongst those institutions and the individuals who control them. This mechanism has enable Washington and Wall Street to lie about asset values, cheat the public by keeping the profits generated by their closed financial system and steal from the public by debasing the value of their income and assets through money debasement and enforcement of financial crisis losses on the participant's in the nations real economy.

Natural law, common law, constitutional law and statutory law as well as ancient standards of morality and ethics supply the legal framework to affect the social compact through the tool and medium of money. Washington and Wall Street have destroyed that compact. The dissociation of Washington's and Wall Street's conduct from the moral and legal requirements that bind them, under cover of a false flag of their superiority and the unrestricted discretion they claim under power of wealth and political position, has enabled Washington and Wall Street to over-run the established moral and legal restriction on their conduct in derogation of the rights and interest of the American people as sovereign.

H.L.A. Hart's conception of the law is a combination of primary rules and secondary rules overarched by what he calls the ultimate rule of recognition under English law, which is that "what the Queen in parliament enacts is law."[442] This conceptualization of legal positivism is alluded to by Washington and Wall Street as a basis for their exercise of unbridled discretion over the creation and emission of money. The value of American money is not regulated by Congress through banking laws and regulation or congressional, regulatory and institutional discretion, exercised in the public interest, politically and financially. Thee Washington Wall Street enterprise has given no consideration of the differing overarching and superseding supreme law of the United States. In American, the overarching supreme law of recognition is the *United States Constitution*, as implemented through law-making consistent with the limitations on the powers delegated by Americans in that document, all as interpreted by a majority of members of the United States Supreme Court.[443] A fundamental purpose of the *Constitution* is to protect and preserve the rights and interest of the sovereign people, through the exercise by Washington of limited powers that when undertaken, serve those public interests. The oft-repeated old saying [somewhat out of the context of the original quotation from Charles E. Wilson, then President of General Motors] that "what's good for General Motors is good for America" was a false narrative of coincident private and public interests, just as the present-day false narrative of saying that "what's good for Washington and Wall Street is good for America." In neither case the respective statement proved to be true.

Despite the seeming contrast between Hart's positivistic authoritarian supreme law of recognition residing in the English Parliament with the American natural supreme law of recognition residing in the people as sovereign as delegated to Washington's institutions on a limited basis in the *Constitution*, as interpreted by the United States Supreme Court, Hart does believe that law and morality have a very close relationship.[444]

§5.06 THE MORAL FOUNDATION OF ENFORCEMENT OF THE AMERICAN LAW OF MONEY

The focus on the natural law principle and moral virtue of honesty pervades the American legal system. It can be found as the driver in many areas of law that have developed in relatively recent history, including regulation of weights and measures, consumer protection law, including truth in lending, deceptive trade practices law, and specifically securities law. Honesty lies at the heart of property law, contract law, employment law, commercial law, tort law, antitrust law and criminal law. In the context of the law of money, two specific areas are relevant. Honest money is dependent on trust and confidence. The powers and duties of those empowered to create and emit money must do so honestly, submitting to the associated limitations on those who exercise such power and duty to do so in the public interest, and not to abuse those powers and duties for their own interests in derogation of the public interest.

[A] Washington's and Wall Street's Monetary Duties

Principles of common law, constitutional, civil and criminal statutory law that arise from the facts of the American public's case for accountability from Washington and Wall Street are basic legal principles.

Legal accountability, whether civil or criminal, implies the existence of defined moral and legal duties by specific individuals and institutions. Failure of the responsible parties to meet their respective defined duties, resulting in harm to others, when discovered, must be promptly followed by the imposition of stated consequences upon the respective parties for their illegal conduct in accordance with the American rule of law.

Most observers of America's financial crises and media pundits shy away from any discussion of specific individuals, with specific duties not met, or of legal accountability for the country's systemic great financial crisis. The individuals whose specific roles, duties, responsibilities and accountability might be discussed, examined and evaluated are among the most powerful in American government, business and banking. The idea of their potential civil and criminal accountability for systemic financial crises has been an idea best kept quiet, out of the media, and well away from the basic, fundamental processes of law in imposing civil and criminal accountability. For the past forty-five years, accountability has been left to special units or task forces such as those called for most recently by Presidents George H. W. Bush, Obama and the DOJ. Historically, these special units or task forces have been expensive, time consuming and largely impotent in identifying the true parties responsible for systemic financial crises and in holding them to account, under either civil or criminal law.

The public consensus is that, apart from a general dissatisfaction of the public with Congress (whose most recent reported approval rating for honesty and ethical standards at this writing hovers around 8 percent.[445] 2012's 7 percent honesty rating for members of Congress was the lowest on record.[446] Accountability for systemic financial crises is a matter best kept quiet; left to experts' concern and questionable expertise in coping with the crisis, but most importantly, to them at any rate, superseded by emphatic exhortations to just "move on." This consensus affords cover to the bad actors in Washington and on Wall Street to avoid accountability for the crisis, as well as the time and distance enabling them to avoid powerful forces of retribution if the issues, roles, responsibilities and accountability are pointedly raised. The rhetoric and the narrative are to put the crisis behind and get on with pursuit of the American dream. Washington and Wall Street, the "experts," the few who actually live the American dream will lead the way. The many will pay the price. Ordinary Americans will wish and hope to live the American Dream, but those wishes and hopes are in vain, without, unless and until they make a case for financial crisis accountability of the Washington Wall Street enterprise.

The authors and sources referred to in the Introduction to this work have documented clearly the origins and effects of systemic financial crises. They also describe the parties responsible for these crises. They do not describe or document the specific violations of the rule of law upon which these parties might be held accountable. Scholars uniformly conclude that somehow the American people will triumph over this latest, temporary challenge to the greatest nation and most successful economy on earth. In the final analysis, this may become so; but today it is wishful thinking. Ordinary Americans have uniformly shied away from description or documentation of the elements of the legal requirements applicable to the conduct of the parties, or suggest any action in response to that conduct, other than possible positive political policy reform by the powers of the few who are masters of the American financial systems that produced the political risk and the systemic financial risk that have led to systemic financial crises. Today, Washington and Wall Street have little incentive to serve the public interest, or any interest other than self-interest, in matters of economics, money and finance.

President Obama's criticism of federal financial regulators and Wall Street bankers was muted. Obama's Attorney General, Eric H. Holder, Jr., testified before the Senate Judiciary Committee in March, 2013, openly asserting the Obama Administration, DOJ and Federal Reserve policies of Wall Street Banks' special political—not moral or legal—classification as "too big to fail" and "too big to jail."[447]

"William Dudley, president of the Federal Reserve Bank of New York, and Sen. Sherrod Brown (D-Ohio), at a Senate Banking Committee hearing stated that: 'We were not willing to find those firms guilty before, because we were worried that if we found them guilty, that could somehow potentially destabilize the financial system,' Dudley said. 'We've gotten past that and I think it's really important that we got past that.[448]'" Dudley continued, while asserting that the culture of the New York Fed has changed, he insisted that Fed's bank regulators should not function as "the cop on the beat" looking out for misconduct.

> "There is an enforcement element to it, but I don't think our primary purpose as supervisors is really the cop on the beat," Dudley said. "Now that doesn't mean that if we see something, we should walk by and ignore it. I don't think that's the case at all."
>
> "You don't think you should be doing any investigations?" replied an incredulous Warren. "You should wait to see if it jumps in front of you?"
>
> "'Because I think our primary focus on supervision is ensuring that the bank is safe and sound, that it's run well,'" Dudley said."[449]

That the constitutional rights of ordinary Americans to honest money should be so trivialized by the President of the New York Fed; the federal regulatory responsible charged with the safety and soundness of the United States dollar and the financial system upon which it is based, is almost unimaginable. It has become the reality for ordinary Americans to the tune of approximately $20 trillion in damages. Note that the same William Dudley "spoke eloquently last year [2013] of Wall Street's 'apparent lack of respect for law, regulation and the public trust,' describing 'deep-seated cultural and ethical failures at many large financial institutions."[450]

Congress' role and responsibility have gone largely unmentioned apart from the findings of the National Commission on the Causes of the Financial and Economic Crisis in the United States, which have been uniformly ignored in Washington and on Wall Street. President Trump who promised to drain the "swamp" in Washington has in fact stocked it with no less than 6 Goldman Sachs' alum.[451] So far, political immunity has triumphed over moral and legal accountability for financial crises. Most Americans are not agitating for accountability or punishment in any organized way. They are angry; worried about their pocketbooks, educating their children, paying for mortgages, cars, healthcare and retirement. Americans just want the economic uncertainty to end. They want recovery of losses they have suffered as a result of the crisis if they can get it, and a return to normality. They want the American dream to continue, providing ever increasing prosperity. These are righteous demand that can be met openly and transparently under the American rule of law, but within the limits of reality and the rule of law.

This work gets to the bottom of ongoing systemic financial risk and financial crises and attach identified civil and criminal liability to those who are accountable under the American rule of law for the financial system and its workings and for the financial disasters they have visited upon the American public and the global economy. Has there been a failure of the rule of law? No. Has there been a failure of enforcement of the rule of law and imposition of civil and criminal accountability? Yes, without doubt.

Creation of systemic financial risk through unregulated creation of money, including specific credit, with no firm relation to a reliable outside standard of market value, to achieve short terms objectives of political expedience was, and remains, wrong. It was and remains irresponsible. But was it criminal? If so, how can the culpable parties be held to account under the American rule of civil and criminal law? Although systemic financial crises are grounded in wrongful and irresponsible conduct, neither the FDIC nor the DOJ, nor any other financial regulator or law enforcement agency have ever meaningfully investigated the possibility.

Systemic financial risk and systemic financial crises can be tied to one fundamental thing: the financial system. What is a financial system? It is a set of rules governing the facilitation of commerce through the use of money, including transferable credit, as an intermediator of the exchange of relative asset values.

When money does not function transparently, effectively and reliably as a unit of account of value; medium of exchange of value; a store of value; and a standard of deferred payment, systemic risk builds, value disparities are created and magnified through leverage and, if unchecked due to the abandonment of constitutionally mandated regulation of the value of money, the dysfunction of intermediation inexorably results in systemic financial crises.

When the value of money, including credit, is no longer regulated by ties to the reality of the relative value of goods and services in the real economy, money and credit become tools of deceit, misrepresentation and fraud in the communication of value through the financial system. Under those circumstances, it can no longer be trusted.

History confirms to us that eventually, commerce will grind to a halt, relatively speaking, unless the public can put confidence in the reasonable accuracy of the financial statements of those responsible for the integrity of our financial system.

[B] Weak, Ineffective and Unenforced Duties Comprising American Banking Law and Regulation

Bank lending and credit creation are limited by the legal and regulatory requirements that banks maintain the safety and soundness of their money on deposit through prudent standards of operating protection, careful risk assessment and maintenance of sufficient liquid capital to protect against the losses and costs presented by uncertainty, and the banks' ability to return money deposited with them through redemption of the receipt for their deposit in liquid sound money. Historically, banks duties to the public are the duties of a fiduciary. Banking laws and regulation have evolved to meet, and arguably to act as substitute specific laws and regulations in place of fiduciary duty.

Washington and Wall Street scoff at the idea that they are fiduciaries to ordinary Americans in monetary banking and financial matters. Washington and Wall Street continue to develop the complexity of banking in their financial self-interest as well as in obscuring the origin of monetary and banking law and regulation as bank fiduciary duties. Banking laws and regulations become ever more complex and more voluminous—yet they fail to address the fundament risk attendant to banking and known to bankers and governments for thousands of years: regulation of the value of money and protection of holders from debasement of the value of money. The disconnect of banking law and regulation from the fundamental historical protection provided by sovereign money, the value and liquidity of which is regulated by reference to a trusted independent standard simply separates the concerned public from concentration on the fundamental, intentional violations of law that lead to financial crises and have done for thousands of years. The strict standard of fiduciary duty of banks to customers and to the public has been largely supplanted and corrupted by banking laws and regulations riddled with weakness due to pervasive grants of regulatory discretion unbound by duty and by the complexity of banking law and regulations that have become unintelligible to the public, banker and regulator alike.

Financial innovation, driven by the rapid expansion of credit as money, unregulated in amount or value by reference to enforceable standards, fuelled by business innovation and powerful special interests dividing the banking function for competitive private institutional advantage, and not subjected to the discipline of redemption of such credit money instruments in constitutional sovereign coined money, the value of which has been regulated by Congress, has led to the wide and growing spectrum of banks and bank-like enterprises. These financial enterprises now play growing roles in the creation, emission and circulation of money through credit in our financial system. The politically protected immunity status of these financial institutions as too big to fail or jail has suffocated every attempt at enforcement of financial crisis accountability.

§5.07 CONCLUDING OBSERVATIONS

To get at first the principles, the violation of which led directly to the recent financial carnage and to establish fundamental civil and criminal accountability, we must look to the ancient and well-established legal doctrines of deceit, misrepresentation and fraud for which there are clearly defined principles of natural and common law that are the foundation for US statutory civil and criminal laws. Congress, federal financial regulatory agencies and the prime players in our financial systems, the Wall Street banks, to whom we look to maintain a safe and sound financial system, have explicit fiduciary responsibilities to the American public. They have collectively failed us. Washington's and Wall Street's lies, their false narratives and intentional financial misrepresentations are more than "little white lies", a "dodges" or "evasions."

As noted in President Obama's statement: "[r]egulators had looked the other way." But contrary to his statement, the regulators did have the authority to stop the bad behavior. They did not exercise their authority.

Arthur Schopenhauer (1788–1860) said that "all truth passes through three stages. First, it is ridiculed. Second, it is violently opposed. Third, it is accepted as being self-evident."

The financial ride constituting the "American Dream" held out to have no end, has collapsed. The continuation of the American Dream promised by both the Democrats and the Republicans at their 2012 and 2016 conventions, the 2018 mid-term elections and on offer in the present election cycle, is not likely. Ordinary Americans want what they have been promised despite the fact that the congress, federal financial regulators and the Wall Street banks have known all along that the public ride was unsustainable.

The American political and power elite should have said so; acted to regulate the value of money; limited the explosion of public and private debt unleashed by their legislation; and grounded their action in the *Constitution* and the readily accessible history of systemic financial crises. Variations of the reality of the American dream are achievable. A false vision of the American dream has been profiled, proliferated and misrepresented by Washington and Wall Street to pander to false and unsustainable public expectations. Thus, the division between the few and the many in America; a gulf of unsustainable income and wealth inequality is made ever wider and deeper.

Early in the most recent great financial crisis, Charles Prince, Citigroup's then CEO, famously said the bank was gladly lending even though there have been ample observations, from even the most modest of sources, that the credit market was overheated. "'When the music stops, in terms of liquidity, things will be complicated,' Prince told the *Financial Times*, 'but as long as the music is playing, you've got to get up and dance. We're still dancing.'"

Today, like ourselves, the French, British, Italians, Chinese, Greek, Argentines, Venezuelans and Spanish people protesting in the streets want to continue their ride of prosperity fed by low taxes, widespread tax avoidance, printing money without regulation off its value, and ever increasing public largess financed by unregulated credit creation, when faced with remedial policies of fiscal and monetary austerity brought down the Greek government. A return to a policy of austerity, notwithstanding the Euro zone's late efforts at their version of quantitative easing, may spare some governments.

The goal in each case is to point out the obvious facts that are already on the record, elicit their acceptance, create public pressure on makers and implementers of law and public policy to respect the obvious truths of the causes of systemic financial risk and crises, and to act responsibly, and legally, in accordance with their sworn duties.

To achieve that goal in the US it is necessary to concentrate public sentiment in support, in a demand, for the legal, judicial enforcement of the accountability of congress, federal financial regulators, federal housing agencies, rating agencies and the Wall Street banks for the crisis of 2008. It is necessary to implement serious fact-specific civil and criminal proceedings by federal and state attorneys general, with parallel civil class action proceedings as contemplated by this work, to enforce the accountability of Washington and Wall Street through judicial due process under the rule of law, and thereby extend equal protection of those laws to the members of the

American public. Without investigation and enforcement, followed by imposition of penalties for past bad behavior and as deterrence to future bad behavior by those parties, there will be no accountability for systemic financial crises. In the absence of accountability, the American public will therefore not likely see an effective return to first principles of sound money and a safe and sound financial system.

My objective here is to point out the obvious, elicit its acceptance, create public pressure on makers and implementers of public policy to respect the obvious truths of systemic financial risk and crises, and to act responsibly in accordance with their sworn duties.

To say that money debasement is "merely immoral" not "illegal" is not just disingenuous, it serves to compound and perpetuate the Washington and Wall Street intentional misrepresentation that is money debasement, through a false and misleading narrative. The self-evident nature of money debasement is not difficult, mysterious, or complex. It is quite simple by its nature and its predictable effects. It has, however, been surrounded and rendered opaque by political and legal mechanisms that impede its recognition and necessary accountability through Washington's and Wall Street's mysterious complex structured finance and ample confusing rhetoric.

Peeling the onion of political obfuscation leaves the fact and extent of money debasement crystal clear—and makes the necessary consequences that should follow, crystal clear and illuminated by both moral and legal principles.

Unfortunately, the individuals and institutions ordinary Americans have honored and entrusted with positions of leadership, and whose businesses are so empowered, enjoy protected monopolies over large scale money production. Washington and Wall Street have been charged with responsibility for maintaining a safe, sound and robust financial, monetary and economic system. But, the very same individuals and institutions have, over time, progressively and systematically, manipulated and abused their power over America's fiscal and monetary system, compromising the American legal and accounting systems and used their power to reconstruct in its stead a viciously corrupt system to suck the very life out of our economy; and create a wealth and income gap between Washington and Wall Street on the one hand and ordinary Americans on the other. Deconstruction and rebalancing of the American to provide honest, safe, and sound sovereign money is required by American law. Ordinary Americans must legally compel the constriction and subordination of the status quo system to the requirements of the American rule of law, as well as break up and disperse the present concentration of wealth and power now held in the Washington and Wall Street corrupt racketeering enterprise. These objectives can only be accomplished through the legal and judicial processes. Failing that; the objective will likely be accomplished in a ragged and destructive manner through bloody violence. The history of monetary affairs and financial crises over millennia confirms that one or the other of these consequences are inevitable. The choice is for ordinary American people to make; enforce the American rule of the law of honest money or face an effort to rebalance America through violence. The outcome rests first on the legal and judicial system; and failing that, the uncertain and threatening prospect of violence in an increasingly violent world riven with weapons far more destructive than ever previously known to man.

In 1913, the American banking system finally received a central bank on the European model. The US was the last great nation to introduce central banking. The original interpretation of the *Constitution* prevented it for more than a century, but the written word was unable to stem the tide of concentrated financial interests and their pro-inflation public relations campaigns. Central banks, by their nature serve their government and banks in a special relationship that amounts to a partnership, an enterprise that is highly vulnerable for exploitation of the many by the few. As such, the risk to the many must be contained by the self-protective action of ordinary Americans to limit that exploitation.

America must enforce its social compact today as required by natural law, moral principles, ethical practices and the American rule of law. The Federal Reserve System and its mandate must be aligned with the public interest and common good of American society in accordance with principles of natural law, morality, ethical practices and the American rule of law as the foundation for honest money.

CHAPTER 6

Degradation of the American Law of Money

§6.01 THE TORTURED PATH OF THE LAW OF MONETARY DUTIES AND ACCOUNTABILITY

Ordinary Americans are perplexed. The idea that money and banking are tools of fraud wielded by Washington and Wall Street remains unthinkable by ordinary Americans on many levels. They know something is wrong with the present monetary structure and policies; what is wrong specifically, they do not know. The literature addressing financial crises is notably lacking any penetrating analysis of the failure of law and accounting leading to the great financial crisis.

Our country was formed on a basis of safe, sound and honest money. The struggles of ordinary people who live and work for their family, community and their country are separate and distinct from the interests and priorities in Washington and on Wall Street; the denizens of which seek wealth and power at any cost. The struggle has been eternal. The positions of Washington and Wall Street are powerful. The institutions and individuals who occupy positions of power over the welfare of the public are entrusted with responsibility to put the public interest above their own. That is a fiduciary duty.

Black's confirms the fundamental moral and legal characteristics of a fiduciary, a fiduciary relationship and fiduciary duty. A fiduciary relationship is "one founded on trust or confidence reposed by one person in the good faith, integrity and fidelity of another." A fiduciary has a duty to act primarily for the benefit of those who have extended their trust and confidence to privileged individuals and institutions who create and control a society's money, who have accepted that trust and confidence, and especially those who have monopoly power in matters connected with the undertaking, and not for the fiduciary's own personal interest in derogation of the public interest. Scrupulous good faith and candor are always required. Fiduciaries must always act in complete fairness and may not ever exert any influence or pressure, take selfish advantage, or deal with those who have extended their trust in such a way that it benefits themselves or prejudices those who have relied on the honesty, good faith, trust, confidence and fidelity that forms the basis for the relationship. Business shrewdness, hard bargaining, and taking advantage of the forgetfulness or negligence of those who have are totally prohibited by a fiduciary. These concepts are ancient and straightforward. Governments and bankers are prime examples of fiduciaries. The power they have over the well-being of those who have entrusted with such trust and confidence, must be wielded with integrity and fidelity.

Washington and Wall Street viscerally recoil in outrage from any suggestion that they are fiduciaries in matters of the safety, soundness and honesty of money matters, including banking, shadow banking, without regard to whether the nature of the money is sovereign money or credit "shadow" money.

Washington and Wall Street have adopted a policy of lying cheating and stealing to meet their own interests. Ordinary Americans suffer under it and accept it because we cannot see any other viable, option. Sadly, many ordinary Americans have simply decided to join the zeitgeist in Washington and on Wall Street, and to glorify and aspire to benefits of lying cheating and stealing as a matter of policy. This is an exercise in the mistaken appraisal of dishonesty as virtue of competitive rugged individualism, self-reliance and self-interest. This exercise ignores the crucial role that honest, safe and sound money plays in binding our diverse culture together into the most prosperous and free country on earth. Because of Washington and Wall Street's open policy of money debasement and their adherence to a policy of monetary as well as fiscal manipulation to shelter the status quo, American society is deteriorating in front of our very eyes.

This work has examined the nature of money, shadow money and money debasement. We know that sovereign money debasement is both immoral and illegal. We know that the struggle between the "haves" and the "have nots" as context was clearly understood at the time our *Constitution* became our law of the land. Honest safe and sound money was constitutionally mandated and money debasement was a capital crime. How has the unthinkable come to pass?

Washington's and Wall Street's false narratives. We have examined and refuted the most dramatic false narrative that money debasement and resulting financial crises are immoral but not illegal. The work has examined and refuted the false narrative that the legal context at the time of the revolutionary war and the ratification or our *Constitution* somehow provided an open-ended endorsement of the unfettered ability of government and bankers to resort to money debasement as a legally and morally sanctioned public policy.

The following summary statements represent the most prominent of the ongoing series of Washington and Wall Street web of false narratives that, when aggregated, have formed and distorted the present American frame of reference for assessing the honesty and integrity of our banking and monetary system, as well clouding the firmly established moral and legal basis for Washington and Wall Street accountability for their wrongdoing. Each step in America's abandonment of honest, safe and sound money has been justified by successive determinations by Washington and Wall Street that each departure from honesty in money represents a case of the ends justifying the means and serving the public interest. But what ends? What means? The false narratives offered up by our experts in money and banking, Washington and Wall Street, suggest that the means and ends represented to the public by Washington and Wall Street are not honest. They are not in the public interest. The adherence to those false narrative does not protect the public from a fate imagined to be more damaging to ordinary American than the great financial crisis.

The means of money debasement is dishonest by its nature. The ends of aggrandizement of wealth and power by Washington and Wall Street has been accomplished by their intentional abuse of trust and power to misrepresent the systemic liquidity and asset values underlying and supporting our economy; by dishonesty. The exercise by Washington and Wall Street of monetary, as well as fiscal powers, are diametrically opposed to the public interest that they are intended to serve. Washington and Wall Street have not acted as fiduciaries. They have followed a well-documented path of lying to, cheating and stealing from those to whom they owe their fiduciary duties.

Let us consider the most egregious of the Washington and Wall Street false narratives as they developed from the seeds of our national formation.

§6.02 THE CONSTITUTIONAL FRAMEWORK FOR THE AMERICAN LAW OF MONEY

In any examination of the application law to a set of facts we must look first to the supreme law of the land, the American *Constitution*. Larry Becraft of Huntsville, Alabama has prepared an interesting *Memorandum of Law*, last updated August 29, 2009 regarding the issue commonly referred to as the "money" or "specie" issue, based in large part on Edwin Vieira, Jr.'s fine work, *Pieces of Eight, The Monetary Powers and Disabilities of the United States Constitution*, and "To Regulate The Value Of Money—An Analysis Of The Power Of Government To Create And Set A Value On Money," also By Edwin Vieira, Jr. The work of these gentlemen clearly establish that America's founding fathers had, quite literally, a fear of paper money, the value of which was not directly and legally connected with and regulated by an outside discipline of value. At the time of the Constitutional Convention of 1787, the outside standard of value was gold and silver specie, which came to be defined with great specificity. Excerpts from Becraft and Vieira follow.

Considering this vital bit of history, be mindful that the reason for America's founders' emphasis on correlation and discipline of the value of money by direct connection to gold and silver specie was to ensure against the debasement of the value of money. Gold and silver as an anchor of relative values of goods and services was the time tested and highest standard—the best practice—of the day. This subject, and the public concerns were the important driving issues of the day. They are likewise the important driving public issues facing the American public today and we struggle with global financial and therefore social, monetary and economic dysfunction.

Many of the court cases brought throughout the years to address the corruption of the dollar's function as American money have concentrated on the historical and legal foundation for use of gold and silver exclusively as standards to regulate the value of money. These foundations are convincing and compelling.

The United States has long since abandoned the use of gold and silver as standards of value for the American dollar. The historical trail of America's abandonment of an appropriate standard for regulation of the value of sovereign money is referred to in context throughout this work. It is apparent to many commentators that a return to a gold or silver standard of value is no longer considered practical or feasible in the context of modern economies and modern theories of monetary policy. A reversion to historical standards of value would not be considered to reflect what should be today's "best practice." Current critics of today's financial crisis who urge a return to the gold, silver or other metallic standard show themselves to be proponents of what is considered by Washington and Wall Street experts to be archaic, impractical and unfeasible; so, the arguments for reregulation of value through historical standards are ridiculed and marginalized; thus impeding the thoughtful consideration of practical and feasible alternatives—new "best practices"—for regulating the value of the American dollar in the many and diverse ways our money is created and used in today's global financial system.

The focus of this work is to establish a credible moral and legal case for the accountability of the Washington Wall Street enterprise for the tort of money debasement and the financial crisis it spawned in 2008 specifically. Without the establishment of meaningful legal accountability for the financial crisis on a scale commensurate with the damages caused by the crisis, it is clear that the public interest will continue to be subverted by perverse electoral process openly influenced and gridlocked by voting district gerrymandering. This process embeds a dual-party political system that is under the effective control of special interest lobbyists, whose power and influence is reinforced through a pervasive revolving door policy of aggrandizement and concentration of wealth and power that assures the continued dominance of our economic, banking, financial and monetary system by Washington and Wall Street.

Official policy in Washington and on Wall Street emphasizes to ordinary Americans that our pursuit of enforcement of their financial and legal accountability for the last financial crisis would lead to another economic and financial crisis of catastrophic consequence, and further, that as the recognized experts in all matters monetary, they know of no viable alternative substitute for the status quo. The enforcement of financial crisis accountability in Washington and on Wall Street would indeed have a catastrophic effect on their ability to maintain the existing status quo system of immoral and illegal Ponzi scheme finance from which they have prospered mightily. A new imminent, future financial and economic crisis however is virtually assured by the combination of continuation of the status quo, and the intentional cover up of the deferred and predictable effects of the continuation of political, fiscal and monetary policy through intentional money debasement.

History has clearly established that continuation of the status quo policy of Washington Wall Street enterprise's intentional money debasement will result, sooner or later in systemic change to affect a return to safe, sound and honest money. In today's world, this systemic change can be affected through public enforcement of systemic change through enforcement of moral and legal accountability under the existing American rule of law or through a breakdown in the American law and enforcement of Washington and Wall Street accountability through violence. In either event, a return to safe, sound and honest money through processes that are not Luddite in nature but rather control and effect the evolution of a modern day monetary, banking, financial and economic system that is not based on money debasement, is feasible. It may not be easy, and it certainly will not perpetuate the status quo. The necessary enforcement of accountability under and future application of the American rule of law would certainly result in a deafening hue and cry of anguished politicians, bureaucrats and Wall Street bankers who would suffer punishment for their wrongdoing and penalties to deter further wrongdoing; whose road to riches and power would be drastically circumscribed. In fact, much work has already been done in furtherance of viable alternatives to the status quo monetary system; almost any of which would be preferable to a system based on dishonesty and abuse of trust and power that are the dominant characteristics of the status quo. Washington and Wall Street cries that they know best is belied by the crystallization of immoral and illegal nature of the status quo, accompanied by the clear path to their legal accountability for damaging financial crisis driven by their immoral and illegal course of conduct as drawn in this work. The cry that there is no feasible alternative to the status quo is belied by the ongoing work of well-informed and concerned parties whose mission is to provide for the ongoing development and effect of a system driven by principles of monetary safety, soundness and honesty. This work is devoted to legal accountability which is the necessary consequence of the enforcement of existing law. The elaboration of existing law to effect its letter and spirit is a national mission that can lawfully be implemented with American ingenuity, moral foundation and legal and accounting acumen directed to clear objectives established by the *Constitution* and existing federal statutory and common law that respects our fundamental moral and legal traditions.

Since congress and the other branches of the federal government have apparently done such a bang-up job of completely vitiating their respective oaths of office and their "fiduciary responsibilities" as holders of the "public trust"—in a mockery of our system of justice under the American *Constitution* and the rule of law, ordinary Americans must then, explore the alternatives for the American public to hold Washington accountable for its failures:

> Indirectly, by breaking the corrupt compact of Washington and Wall Street to lie to, cheat and steal from the American public through unrestrained debasement of our money,
>
> - Directly, through dramatic legal action against Wall Street for up to treble the demonstrable $20 trillion in damages caused to the American directly attributable to the massive currency debasement knowingly effected by Wall Street, in combination with its government co-conspirators, that was the fundamental cause of the financial crisis,
> - Also, by wonderfully focusing the minds of the lions of Wall Street on the downside of the abuse of trust and power dropped into their laps by, or more realistically, ripped out of Washington's inept hands and unabashedly exploited by Wall Street for its benefit and the indirect benefit of the those at the center of

government in Washington, revolving in and out through the collegial gold lined revolving door on Wall Street, and
- Indirectly, by legally compelling Congress and the federal financial regulatory agencies to properly exercise their respective powers affecting Wall Street and our economy, and to meet their respective missions in fulfillment of their duties in accordance with and subject to the strictures of the *United States Constitution*, American common law and applicable federal statutes.

[A] Constitutional Principles and the American Rule of the Law of Money

Congress has the constitutional power, mandate, responsibility and duty to regulate the value of American money—the failure of which lies at the heart of the "illegal behavior" described in this work. The second instance appearing in the *United States Constitution* of a delegation of power, and with it the specific duty to regulate anything, after the commerce clause, appears in the *United States Constitution* in Article I, § 8, Clause 5, pertaining to regulation of the value and integrity of money.

Regulation of the value of money as a unit of account, store of value, medium of exchange and a standard of deferred payment, is a direct precondition to successful regulation of the amount and value of credit—which is also money. It is also a direct precondition to the successful and effective regulation of commerce by Congress provided for in Article I, § 8, Clause 2 of the *Constitution*, and to the ongoing ability of the United States to borrow money on its credit as provided for in Article I, § 8, Clause 2 of the *Constitution*. Similarly, Article I, § 8, Clause 6 of the *Constitution* (punishment of counterfeiting) is clearly intended to effect public delegation to Congress of the power and duty to preserve the integrity of America's honest, safe and sound money and government finance based thereon, that lies at the heart of the integrity of all American federal and state government fiscal activities. Article I, § 8, Clause 18 (the necessary and proper clause) of the *Constitution* is clearly intended to enable Congress to execute all the powers and duties delegated to it under Article I, § 8.

The extensive and deep intellectual foundation for this first principle of sound money, including credit, is amply documented in the literature. Congress and the federal financial regulators and the banks and other financial institutions who benefit from the special monetary charters and powers as a monopoly are the nation's experts with respect to our financial system. They have the power and duty and are accountable for maintaining sound money, sound credit and thereby an honest, safe and sound banking and financial system. A long history of congressional, regulatory and Wall Street banker intentional "wilful blindness," driven by short term high priority actions of political expedience, does not relieve their respective responsibility or accountability.

All the federal financial regulatory agencies have as their core responsibility the assurance and maintenance of an "honest, safe, and sound" banking and financial system. The long entrenched bureaucratic policies of intentional "willful blindness" designed to maximize discretionary power and avoid responsibility and accountability for polices when they lead predictably, repeatedly, and inexorably to systemic financial crises after crisis, must be exposed and subjected to the same moral and legal standards imposed on all other Americans. The depth of the systemic risk caused by Washington and Wall Street and the depth of our current financial crisis have been "covered up" by Fed policies of Quantitative Easing: QE 1, QE 2, "twisting" and now QE 3.[452] These policies are not based on any direct supporting constitutional authority, reliable predicating data, or analysis. They have not been subjected to full disclosure, transparency and debate. These policies exacerbate the recognized long-term problem of increasingly unsustainable levels of American public and private indebtedness. This current "cover-up" and the long course of conduct leading to the position in which we now find ourselves at present, is a direct and near mortal existential threat to the honesty, safety and soundness of America's economic, fiscal, monetary, banking and financial systems. Quantitative Easing, and the banking and monetary policies leading to the perceived necessity for its use, have been, and remain as a continuation of the Washington and Wall Street enterprise's intentional misrepresentations of systemic asset liquidity and value. That continuing conduct constitutes intentional lying, cheating and stealing. It is the end game of banking and monetary policy by intentional money debasement.

As the primary tools of congressional and regulatory implementation of fiscal, monetary economic and financial policy, the Wall Street banks have long enjoyed special monopoly status for such implementation, with profits and management compensation protected and losses deflected onto the American public by the Wall Street banks presumed status as "too big to fail." Their accountability has been deflected by their presumed status as "too big to jail." The management of the Wall Street banks have been willing participants and active protagonists in concert with congress and the federal financial regulators and the others included amongst those collaborating in Washington and on Wall Street in conduct that has been demonstrated over and over to be destructive to the American and global economic, banking and financial systems. The damage to the American public caused by the Washington Wall Street enterprise primarily falls upon those members of the public who are not members of the protected Washington Wall Street enterprise. The unprotected participants in the financial system: regional and community based financial institutions, commerce generally and every working citizen not included in the protected club; are left holding what the government, banking and financial power elite euphemistically call "acceptable levels of tail losses" suffered in pursuit of the greater good—that being in reality a perversion of the greater good. The Washington Wall Street enterprise notion of greater good is the concentration of wealth and power in Washington and on Wall Street.

As noted above, the second mention of the delegation of power by the American people to congress in the *Constitution* "to regulate" (there are only two specific references to regulation in the *Constitution*; the first being the regulation of commerce, the regulation of which can only be effective by regulation also of the value of money) is the power, accompanied by the duty, to regulate the value of our money. Without regulation of the value of our money, and its clarity as a unit of account, store of value, medium of exchange and a standard of deferred payment; accompanied by regulation of credit as measured by sound money as a stable and reliable unit of account, medium of exchange, store of value and a standard of deferred payment; the effect of all other powers delegated by the American people to and exerted by congress cannot be accurately measured, examined or rendered accountable by the American people.

The *Constitution,* Article I, § 8, Clause 5, provides that "The Congress shall have power to coin money, regulate the value thereof, and of foreign coin, and fix the standard of weights and measures."

The power "to coin money" and "regulate the value thereof" has been broadly construed to authorize regulation of every phase of the subject of currency and money. Each of the pertinent federal financial regulatory agencies and congressional committees acknowledge this construction of Article I, § 8, Clause 5 in the laws under which they were constituted and in the public representation of their respective roles, missions, and duties. Power delegated by the American people to congress under the *Constitution* implies the congressional duty to "well and faithfully discharge the duties of the office" and properly exercise that power. Congress and the federal financial and regulatory institutions it has created, and their instruments, the systemically vital Wall Street banks, have the power, and with it the constitutional duty, to maintain an honest, safe and sound, uniform and stable currency and to regulate its value as the foundation for an honest, safe, and sound banking and financial system.

The American public is entitled to rely, in good faith, and has relied in good faith on congress to fulfill its duties under the *Constitution* through its own actions as well as through its instruments, the federal financial regulatory agencies, and through management of the nation's banks and other systemically important financial institutions; to provide an honest, safe and sound banking and financial system through the safe, sound and prudent regulation of the value of US sovereign money and the accurate presentation of the regulated value of sovereign money in the statement in monetary terms of banks' and other financial institutions' assets and liabilities and in the statements in monetary terms of the budgets and accounts of America's municipal, state and federal governments and in the fulfillment of Congress' constitutional power and duty to "regulate" commerce.

[B] Money Debasement as a Capital Crime

Although *The Coinage Act of 1792* continued the common law treatment of currency debasement as a capital crime, punishable by death, that act has been largely repealed, and the last vestiges of prescribed accountability is now contained in 18 USC § 332:

> Debasement of coins; alteration of official scales, or embezzlement of metals. If any of the gold or silver coins struck or coined at any of the mints of the United States shall be debased, or made worse as to the proportion of fine gold or fine silver therein contained, or shall be of less weight or value than the same ought to be, pursuant to law, or if any of the scales or weights used at any of the mints or assay offices of the United States shall be defaced, altered, increased, or diminished through the fault or connivance of any officer or person employed at the said mints or assay offices, with a fraudulent intent; or if any such officer or person shall embezzle any of the metals at any time committed to his charge for the

purpose of being coined, or any of the coins struck or coined at the said mints, or any medals, coins, or other moneys of said mints or assay offices at any time committed to his charge, or of which he may have assumed the charge, every such officer or person who commits any of the said offenses shall be fined under this title or imprisoned not more than ten years, or both." See also, 18 USC § 331: Mutilation, diminution, and falsification of coins. "Whoever fraudulently alters, defaces, mutilates, impairs, diminishes, falsifies, scales, or lightens any of the coins coined at the mints of the United States, or any foreign coins which are by law made current or are in actual use or circulation as money within the United States; or Whoever fraudulently possesses, passes, utters, publishes, or sells, or attempts to pass, utter, publish, or sell, or brings into the United States, any such coin, knowing the same to be altered, defaced, mutilated, impaired, diminished, falsified, scaled, or lightened—Shall be fined under this title or imprisoned not more than five years, or both."

Although *The Coinage Act of 1792* has largely been repealed or replaced, Section 19 of the act arguably remains in effect and would, in theory, continue to apply in the case of "any of the gold or silver coins which shall be struck or coined at the mint." Since gold and silver coins are now minted only in commemorative form, the primary law of accountability contained in the act has been rendered toothless through the degradation of the American law of money. As ordinary Americans we are entitled to honest, safe, and sound sovereign money, the value of which is regulated by Congress, and the debasement of which should continue to be a serious, if not necessarily a capital crime.

Historically, money debasement is the emitting and presenting as money that is not the full value it purports to present, accomplished by impairing, diminishing, falsifying, scaling and lightening the value represented. While American money has devolved from constitutional coined money to paper legal tender made from nothing but paper and ink and coined Legal Tender money consisting of laminated embossed discs of sandwiched base metal, and most importantly, credit emitted by the Federal Reserve System and by their partners, the Wall Street banks, all within the Federal Reserve System, either physically or electronic denominated—and outside the official system in the shadow banking system, in paper credit documents hidden in securities posing as structured financial instruments—shadow money—represented by electronic impulses captured as digital electric accounting entries consisting of 1s and 0s that, once entered on public and private books of account, are redeemable thereafter only in corresponding points of electronic data or the pathetic composite base metal discs and paper items that constitute official American legal tender.

While Washington's and Wall Street's definition of money has been expanded far beyond that provided for in the *Constitution*, the definition of money debasement set forth in 18 USC § 331 and § 332 has remained fixed and has not been extended to correspond to the Fed's definition of "coined money' or to the actual money circulating through the Federal Reserve System or the shadow banking system and serving as liquidity, the regulation of all of which has been ostensibly delegated by Congress to the Fed, and by the Fed to its partners in the money creation business, the Wall Street banks. Instead of protecting the American public from the depredations of money debasement, the pertinent federal statutory law of debasement designed to protect the public interest has been rendered an anachronism; protecting the American public only from "depredations" and money debasement of "gold or silver coins struck or coined at any of the mints of the United States," and from defacement, alteration, increase or diminishment of the scales or weights used at any of the mints or assay offices of the United States through the fault or connivance of any officer or person employed at the said mints or assay offices, with a fraudulent intent. In today's world, 18 USC § 332 makes a mockery of congressional concern for the public interest.

Congress and the federal financial regulators have extended the meaning of money from gold or silver coins subject to and protected from debasement to sovereign fiat money redeemable only by itself. The standards for weights and measures designed to regulate the values of sovereign specie coined money or representative legal tender paper money and transferable credit money representing real bills of commercial exchange have been abandoned as irrelevant. The only meaning that can reasonably be taken from this statute [18 USC § 332] requires that it be construed to apply to money and its potential for debasement in accordance with its nature. Money, legal tender, as that term is presently construed by Congress and the federal financial regulators has been debased in value to a fraction of its stated purchasing value for goods and services in the marketplace. The graphic illustrations in this work demonstrate only the debased value expressed as purchasing power by Federal Reserve Notes and their predecessor official United Stated dollars, both on and off a metallic standard of specie by which the value of the currency was regulated, more or less, and does not reflect the debasement of dollar denominated money in the shadow banking system, as presently imbedded in the marketplace.

Liquidity has historically been set by the reserve ratios of the central banks and the size of their power money. Liquidity equalled power money multiplied by the inverse of the reserve ratio. Money is now shaped and sized by forces that were limited or non-existent in prior cycles. Neither Congress, its creature the Fed, nor its partners in crime, the Wall Street Banks, control the quantity, quality, value or price of money. The fog of liquidity created in the shadow banking system has reduced financial transparency to zero. Central bank-dictated reserves no longer set the credit multiplier, to the extent reserve requirements can any longer be considered useful. The definitions of reserves having been gamed so far as to reduce effective reserve requirements for most Wall Street Banks to zero. Raising (Fed policy) interest rates did not affect the cost of capital. The recent Fed reduction of the "policy" rates, on top of earlier reductions in response to the financial crisis has had no meaningful effect on the cost of capital. Once the cost of long-term capital rises above the natural interest rate, we should expect liquidity to contract sharply if the expansion and contraction phases are to remain symmetrical. When asset bubbles collapse, central banks, being unable to bear the economic costs then act asymmetrically.

Central banks have considered raising rates either to normalize them from easy monetary policy or to combat inflation, but at the first sign of asset price deflation, they have eased precipitously. The process, known as quantitative easing, has purported to control inflation, but for most American, whose needs are not included in the inflation index, prices of food, fuel and housing have risen dramatically. Housing prices have been re-inflated by artificially low interest rates and by output purchases by the Fed of government insured housing loans of $40 billion per month, purchased with money created from nothing, accompanied by Fed purchases of government bills at artificially low rates effectively manipulating and misrepresenting the values of assets purchased, and because money is fungible, the value of comparable assets outside the Feds portfolio. Thus, prices payable by ordinary Americans have risen, the shadow banking credit explosion continues with intentional support and action by Washington and Wall Street, and the winners in this fraudulent manipulation of asset values, prices and debasement of money are, yes, Washington and Wall Street. Thus, any pain of being invested in an asset bubble would be of short duration. This reinforces the markets' conviction that global monetary policy is asymmetric and biased in favor of investors and speculators. The massive resulting transfer of wealth to Washington and Wall Street and the wealthiest of Americans confirms the American public's worst fears.

The Fed's mandate to manipulate money and interest, and therefor asset values and liquidity, ostensibly to serve the public interest, has been corrupted through the influence of Wall Street banks and their captive congressional and bureaucratic servants and has eroded the fundamental American constitutional protection against fraud in money on the American public and our trading partners, through intentional debasement of American money.

The long list of additional federal criminal statutes enacted by congress that might reasonably be considered to support enforced by the DOJ to protect the American public from the fraud perpetrated by money debasement have only been ignored.

These criminal statutes include: 18 USC § 371 Conspiracy to commit offense or to defraud United States; 18 USC § 471 Obligations or Securities of United States; 18 USC § 472 Uttering Counterfeit Obligations or Securities; 18 USC § 491.Tokens or Paper used as Money; 18 USC § 1001 Statements or Entries Generally; 18 USC § 1005 Bank Entries, Reports and Transactions; 18 USC § 1016 Acknowledgment of Appearance or Oath;18 USC § 1018 Official Certificates or Writings; 18 USC § 1341 Frauds and Swindles; 18 USC § 1343; Fraud by Wire, Radio, or Television; 18 USC § 1344 Bank Fraud; 18 USC § 1346. Definition of "scheme or artifice to defraud"; 18 USC § 1349. Attempt and Conspiracy; 18 USC § 1505 Obstruction of Proceedings before Departments, Agencies, and Committees; 8 USC § 1621 Perjury Generally; 18 USC § 2073 False Entries and Reports of Moneys or Securities.

The Bank Fraud and Wire Fraud statues can be enforced under the Racketeer Influenced and Corrupt Organizations Act (RICO) 18 U.S.C. §§ 1961-1968. These statutes form the foundation for private enforcement by ordinary Americans of the financial crisis accountability of the Washington Wall Street enterprise.

The DOJ has only recently considered the application of bank fraud statutes and RICO to the fraud in the financial crisis—but have limited their interest to cases to be initiated by or on behalf of banks, ignoring the fundamental fraud of money debasement by the Washington Wall Street enterprise.[453]

§6.03 AMERICAN BORROWING VERSUS MONEY DEBASEMENT TO FINANCE EXISTENTIAL WAR

Congress and the institutions it has created have the power, and with it constitutional responsibility, to maintain a sound, uniform and stable currency and to regulate its value (*Constitution* Article I, § 8, Clause 5):

> The Congress shall have power to coin money, regulate the value thereof, and of foreign coin, and fix the standard of weights and measures.

James Madison, in *Federalist Paper No. 44* expressed his opinion that a further provision demanded to the effect that "the government should be affirmatively prohibited from issuing paper money was not necessary, as the prohibition was clear from the existing language as adopted."

Madison decried the Hamiltonian theory of the "special relationship" between wealth and centralized government that supported expansive executive powers over war and peace and therefore over the ability to unlock "the public treasures and to dispense them." This same interpretation was made by Maryland Delegate to the Constitutional Convention, Luther Martin.

In *Federalist Paper No. 48* James Madison warned that in a representative system, the people must be most wary of the legislature. Its actions are masked by complexity, and its access to the "pockets of the people" makes it especially dangerous. In "Vices of the Political System" he attributed to legislators three motives for seeking office: ambition, interest, and the public good, of which the latter is least and the second is most often in play. When self-interest is the motive, the legislator is especially energetic in gaining and keeping office. When a majority of legislators with like interests can form a majority, they can "join in a perfidious sacrifice" of the interest of their constituents so as better to serve their own. Elections might be thought to enable the public to rid themselves of this menace. But" base and selfish measures" are often "masked by pretexts of public good and apparent expediency." Other more "honest but unenlightened representatives" are then taken in by this masquerade and become its unwitting supporters."[454]

Madison's and Martin's concerns were well-shared, were well-founded and apply today just as they did at the inception of our government.

[A] Constitutional Powers and Duties

Edwin Vieira, Jr., makes his painstaking and powerful case through astute and clear linguistic analysis combined with explication of the constitutional context of the American government's powers and limitation in respect to regulation of the value of currency in *To Regulate The Value of Money—An Analysis Of The Power Of Government To Create And Set A Value On Money*:[455]

> In sum, the power "To * * * regulate the Value [of United States coin], and of foreign Coin" consists solely of a power of comparison and declaration: (i) comparing the amount of fine silver in particular silver coins to that contained in

the "Money-Unit or common measure of other coins in these states" (the "dollar"), and declaring this proportion in "dollar-values"; or (ii) ascertaining the amount of fine gold in particular gold coins, calculating the market-equivalent of fine silver, comparing the latter amount to the "Money-Unit," and declaring this proportion in "dollar"-values.

Thus, under the power "To coin Money," Congress has discretion to set the weight, purity, form, and impression of all silver, gold, and copper coins it mints (excepting, of course, the intrinsic value of the "dollar" itself). Whereas, under the power "To * * * regulate the Value," it has a duty accurately to determine the proportions of market value between the fixed "Money-Unit" and the coinage it, and foreign nations, mint. Insofar as the proportions of market value between various gold coins and the (silver) "dollar" are concerned, it may have been reasonable in the late 1700s and immediately thereafter to declare by statute the exchange-ratio customarily prevailing in the market between gold and silver—the transmission of financial information throughout the country, let alone the world, being both slow and uncertain. Even so, the Continental Congress recognized that, because "the proportional values of gold and silver at market are liable to vary," the government had a duty "whenever such variation shall have become sensible, * * * to make a corresponding change in the rates."

Today, with almost instantaneous transmission of sound market-data available, any rigid statutorily declared ratio of value between gold and silver is unreasonable, and therefore unconstitutional. Rather, in exercising the power "To * * * regulate * * * Value" under contemporary economic circumstances, the government should simply permit the value of domestic and foreign gold coinage to "float," as against the silver "Money-Unit" (the dollar), from one market level to another, as changing exchange-rates become "sensible" in commerce.

The Framers' consistent association of the power "To * regulate Value" with the power "To * * * fix the Standard of Weights and Measures," then, was no mere caprice. Although the purchasing-power of money varies with economic conditions, and ultimately is beyond the government's power to control, at any particular point in time the relationship of money to economic values parallels that of weights and measures to physical quantities. Just as the *Constitution* gave Congress the power "To * * * fix the Standard of Weights and Measures" in order to establish uniformity therein throughout the country, so, too, did it confer the power "To * * * regulate Value" in order (as much as possible in economic life) "to produce uniformity of value throughout the Union, and thus to preclude us from the embarrassments of a perpetually fluctuating and variable currency."... "[F]luctuating and variable," that is, in terms of political phenomena impinging on the market.

Now, a "Standard of Weigh[t]" must itself be a weight and a "Standard of * * * Measur[e]." So, too to regulate * * * "Value" implies the existence of a unit of "Value." Here, the two phrases "fix the Standard" and "regulate * * * Value" subtly diverge in shades of meaning, if not in ultimate intent: The phrase "fix the Standard" empowers Congress to define the basic units of Weights and Measures; whereas, the phrase "regulate the Value" empowers Congress only to apply the basic unit of "Value," which the *Constitution* elsewhere explicitly identifies as the "dollar," a known, historically fixed weight of silver.

Moreover, whereas the verb "fix" as applied to "Weights and Measures" implies "stability and confirmation," the verb "regulate" as applied to coinage implies adjustment. Here, then, is another striking example of the Framers' linguistic precision, in one phrase selecting the verb that connotes the establishment of permanent "Standard[s]," without which a system of "Weights and Measures" could not serve its purpose; and, in the other, choosing the synonym

> that connotes a process of inter-comparisons among changing forms of coinage, according to a set "Money-Unit," without which a monetary system involving both gold and silver could not achieve its end.
>
> In short, the Framers interpreted the constitutional "Value" of "Money" as something not subject to the vagaries of governmental edict—but rather, as Blackstone taught, as something identical with "the weight and standard (wherein consists the intrinsic value)." In short, the Framers interpreted the constitutional "Value" of "Money" as something not subject to the vagaries of governmental edict—but rather, as Blackstone taught, as something identical with "the weight and standard (wherein consists the intrinsic value)."

Once again, Mr. Vieira, like many experts in this subject, proves his case, essentially a case for a return to a metallic species standard of gold and silver. But that, in and of itself, is insufficient to aid our efforts today in establishing definitive recommendations or policy alternatives that will return America to the sound money foundation for our economy that America's founding fathers so clearly intended. Neither Vieira nor any other expert today has harnessed the case for constitutional regulation of the value of money with the law of accountability for having failed to provide safe, sound and honest money as so regulated.

The webs of false narratives addressed in this work have occluded any connection between the history and the legal and moral character of money with the crises we have faced in the last, now nearly 50 years. These false narratives have deprived ordinary Americans of the imperative of both moral and accountability Washington and Wall Street or failure to maintain the connection. Moral and legal accountability, together, are essential to establishing legal incentives for Washington and Wall Street re-establishment of the connection, compensating for damage wrought by Washington's and Wall Street's intentional promulgation, perpetuation as and exploitation of those false narratives to cover up abuse of trust and power in aid of the Washington and Wall Street criminal corrupt racketeering enterprise based on systemic intentional dishonesty. Enforcement of Washington and Wall Street legal and moral accountability is essential to deter future wrongdoing by Washington and Wall Street while opening the door and turning the lights of truth on our monetary system, illuminating a path to renewed public efforts to return to a moral and legal monetary system in America.

In his conclusion to "*To Regulate The Value Of Money*," Mr. Vieira states: "The foregoing analysis proves that there is no constitutional basis for using the power 'To * * * regulate the Value' of 'Money' for stimulation of the economy, redistribution of wealth, stabilization of the purchasing power of money, creation of 'legal-tender' substitutes for real 'dollars,' or for any of the other sundry monetary nostrums that politicians and their unelected 'expert' advisors have foisted, and continue to foist, on the American people. The sooner the people recognize this, the sooner something may be done to rectify the situation. If, however, the people remain ignorant, apathetic, and inactive, the politicians will 'regulate the Value' of American money to zero-just as one fiat currency after another, throughout the course of Western history, has collapsed into worthlessness-with all the serious economic, political, and social consequences such a collapse will entail."[456]

As you consider the foregoing and the following important bits of history and the balance of this work, please consider the importance of the establishment and maintenance of a methodology to regulate the value of money—the American dollar. The wrong, irresponsible and yes, criminal conduct that lies at the heart of the financial crisis is grounded on an unmistakable breach of the supreme law of the land—the *Constitution*. Failure to regulate the value of money has been known, ever since the invention of money—to result in the same kinds of lying, cheating and stealing that lie at the heart of the financial crisis—it runs through banking systems, shadow banking systems and the everyday economic wellbeing of every American citizens as well as our trading partners globally.

[B] The Constitutional Convention of 1787

Dr. Vieira and Larry Becraft documented and commented on America's efforts to address the issue of sound money in the formulation of the *United States Constitution*:[457]

> In May 1787, pursuant to a Congressional plan to revise and amend the Articles of Confederation, delegates from the various states met in Philadelphia. The union of the States created by the Articles had been imperfect and therefore a better organization of unity among them was needed. However, a substantial problem confronting all the States at that time was economic and was caused by the monetary system, therefore it was essential that the best monetary system possible also result from the work of the Convention.
>
> The best source of information available concerning the secret debates of the Convention is James Madison's notes. Insofar as the monetary provisions of the *Constitution* are concerned, Madison's notes reveal that on Thursday, August 16, 1787, the Convention was discussing the proposed *Constitution*'s provisions contained in Article 1, § 8, wherein Congress was to be given the power to "emit bills on the credit of the United States."
>
> Gouverneur Morris on this date moved to strike this proposed phrase from the *Constitution*. In response, Mr. Elseworth stated that he "thought this a favorable moment to shut and bar the door against paper money." He further stated that, "the mischiefs of the various experiments which had been made were now fresh in the public mind and had excited the disgust of all the respectable part of America. By withholding the power from the new government, more friends of influence would be gained to it than by almost anything else. Paper money can in no case be necessary. Give the government credit, and other resources will offer. The power may do harm, never good." Mr. Wilson commented that, "it will have a most salutary influence on the credit of the United States to remove the possibility of paper money." Mr. Read noted that he "thought the words, if not struck out, would be as alarming as the mark of the Beast in Revelations." Even more emphatically voiced was Mr. Langdon's remark that he "would rather reject the whole plan than retain the three words, 'and emit bills.'" The motion to strike these words from the *Constitution* carried by a vote of nine states in favor and two opposed. On Tuesday, August 28, 1787, the Convention was discussing the provisions contained in Article 1, § 10 of the *Constitution*. Mr. Roger Sherman and Mr. Wilson moved to amend the proposed Article 1, § 10 to include the words "nor emit bills of credit, nor make anything but gold and silver coin a tender in payment of debts." The discussion concerning this proposed amendment concerned only the portion regarding "emit bills of credit." In support of his motion, Mr. Sherman

stated that he "thought this a favorable crisis for crushing paper money," reasoning that "if the consent of the Legislature could authorize emissions of it, the friends of paper money would make every exertion to get into the Legislature in order to license it." The voting concerning the power to emit bills of credit was eight states in favor and two opposed. The remainder of the proposed amendment concerning gold and silver coin passed with no opposition.

The work of the Convention was completed on September 17, 1787, and the end result was the *Constitution of the United States of America*. In reference to the much needed revision of the monetary system, Congress had been granted the power to "coin money and regulate the value thereof," virtually the identical powers in reference to the currency which it possessed under the Articles, which did not include the power to declare a legal tender. Further, certain binding, absolute and uncircumventable prohibitions had been placed upon the states in Article 1, § 10, Clause 1, one of which limited the legal tender power of the States to gold and silver coin.

The chief architect of the monetary powers and disabilities contained in the US *Constitution* was none other than Roger Sherman, who had so ably expressed his opinion of paper money 35 years earlier and resoundingly condemned it. At the convention, virtually all the delegates held views identical with Sherman, and they were certain that paper money had been permanently prohibited by the "Supreme Law of the Land." The intent of the drafters of the *Constitution* was to grant to Congress the power to coin gold and silver which could be the only legal tender pursuant to Article 1, § 10.

Thus the *Constitution* was deliberately designed to insure gold and silver coin as the "money of the realm." The proposed *Constitution* was thereafter submitted to the states for ratification. In Maryland, a delegate to the Convention, a lawyer named Luther Martin who was probably one of the few men to oppose prohibitions upon paper currency, summarized the work of the Convention:

> By our original articles of confederation, the Congress have a power to borrow money and emit bills of credit, on the credit of the United States; agreeably to which, was the report on this system as made by the committee of detail. When we came to this part of the report, a motion was made to strike out the words 'to emit bills of credit.' Against the motion we urged, that it would be improper to deprive the Congress of that power. But, Sir, a majority of the convention, being wise beyond every event, and being willing to risk any political evil, rather than admit the idea of a paper emission, in any possible event, refused to trust this authority to a government, to which they were lavishing the most unlimited powers of taxation, and they erased that clause from the system.
>
> By the tenth section every State is prohibited from emitting bills of credit. As it was reported by the committee of detail, the States were only prohibited from emitting them without the consent of Congress; but the convention was so smitten with the paper money dread, that they insisted the prohibition should be absolute. It was my opinion, Sir, that the States ought not to be totally deprived of the right to emit bills of credit, and that, as we had not given an authority to the general government for that purpose, it was the more necessary to retain it in the States. I therefore thought it my duty to vote against this part of the system.

Thus, it is clear from both the proponents of the constitutional ban upon paper money and one of its most ardent foes that the clear design of the *Constitution* in reference to monetary powers was an absolute prohibition upon any paper money.

In New York, debate concerning ratification of the *Constitution* was heated. There, Alexander Hamilton, James Madison and John Jay came to the defense of the proposed *Constitution* by publication of a series of articles concerning the *Constitution* in New York newspapers. This series, now known as the *Federalist Papers*, contains virtually the best source of information concerning the interpretation of our *Constitution*. In Article number 44, written by Madison, the following comments were made regarding the intent of Article 1, § 10:

> The extension of the prohibition to bills of credit must give pleasure to every citizen in proportion to his love of justice and his knowledge of the true springs of public prosperity. The loss which America has sustained since the peace, from the pestilent effects of paper money on the necessary confidence between man and man, on the industry and morals of the people, and on the character of republican government, constitutes an enormous debt against the States chargeable with this unadvised measure which must long remain unsatisfied, or rather an accumulation of guilt which can be expiated no otherwise than by a voluntary sacrifice on the altar of justice of the power which has been the instrument of it. In addition to these persuasive considerations, it may be observed that the same reasons which show the necessity of denying to the States the power of regulating coin prove with equal force that they ought not to be at liberty to substitute a paper medium in the place of coin. Had every State a right to regulate the value of its coin, there must be as many different currencies as States, and thus the intercourse among them would be impeded; retrospective alterations in its value might be made, and thus citizens of other States be injured, and animosities be kindled among the States themselves. Thence the Union be discredited and embroiled by the indiscretion of a single member. No one of these mischiefs is less incident to a power in the States to emit paper money than to coin gold or silver. The power to make anything but gold and silver a tender in payment of debts is withdrawn from the States on the same principle with that of issuing a paper currency.

The success of the Federalist was evident in the fact that the proponents of the *Constitution* were successful in securing ratification in New York.

The adoption of the US *Constitution* in 1789 paved the way for the intended "more perfect union." An analysis of the method of construction of the constitutional provisions in reference to the currency powers thereof and of the contemporaneous expressions of these provisions leads to the unmistakable conclusion that the *Constitution* designed a monetary system based upon gold and silver coin, and the standard so built was enduring, perfect and immutable. The influence of Oresme, Cotton, Locke and Blackstone is easily perceived.[458]

§6.04 GREENBACKS, THE LEGAL TENDER ACTS AND NATIONAL BANKS AS PARTNERS WITH WASHINGTON IN THE CREATION OF MONEY

At the time of the Civil War, in response to the war emergency, Congress permitted the creation of "Greenbacks"; a fiat currency that was not backed by or redeemable at the time in constitutional coined money. The Greenbacks, however, were subsequently redeemed by constitutional coined money and by paper legal tender that was representative of and redeemable in constitutional coined money, pursuant to *The Legal Tender Acts.*[459] *The National Currency Acts of 1863 and 1864* (the Legal Tender Acts) had four primary purposes:

- To create a partnership between the national government and its creatures, the so-called 'National Banks', for the emission of paper currency and deposits payable on demand.
- To inflate the supply paper money and bank credit in a coordinated manner throughout the country.
- To float government bonds by making them the compulsory 'backing' for the National Bank's paper currency.
- And, ultimately, to coerce, curtail, and coopt the existing decentralized system of state banks, and perhaps even superseded it entirely with a nationwide cartel of congressionally chartered banks directed from a few major financial centers, and all closely tied to the Treasury in the most comprehensive structure of political banking ever seen in American history.[460]
- ... Congress was seeking an alliance, not just with any "capitalists"—who, after all, could simply invest in government bonds with no further ado—but with a certain privileged subset of "capitalists": to wit, bankers, who would employ the bonds in their peculiar business of expanding currency and credit ex nihilo. The specific legislative goal, then, was to create a new scheme of unabashedly political banking.[461]

That is, whereas the Independent Treasury had separated bank and state (or more descriptively) bankers and politicians, *The National Currency Act* [1863] integrated bankers and politicians, "identifying [bankers] with the government in the supply of currency to the nation." "So the Act marked the commencement of a full blown corporative state in the tortuous American Saga of political banking—by making it for the [bankers' and politicians'] mutual interest to sustain each other in generating public debt and issuing paper money in tandem.[462]"

Of course, in the event, the national banking system did not prevent future devastating nationwide financial panics. But rather than learning their lesson from these disasters, politicians and their special-interest clients used the panics to rationalize replacement of the national banking system with the even more corporative Federal Reserve System (as described below).[463]

In *The National Bank Act* debates, Senator Sherman observed that, "'although no nation can safely surrender to individuals or banks' the 'power to coin ... false money,' which 'ought to be exercised by the highest power in government' and 'only when the State is in danger,' nonetheless this special privilege can be exercised only pursuant to 'a combination between the interests of private individuals and the government'—thus admitting those select 'private individuals to share in the highest power in the Government.'"[464] Senator Sherman did not elaborate on how private banks, under State authority, could issue "false money" unchecked by the discipline of required redemption in specie. "So it always happens that whenever a wrong principle of conduct, political or personal, is adopted on a plea of necessity, it will be afterwards followed on a plea of convenience."[465]

Senator Henderson, "[d]rawing a cogent historical parallel, ... opposed *The National Currency Act* on the ground that Congress was attempting to square John Law's vicious circle: to create a viable system of money (the most liquid of all assets) on the basis of mere public debt (a liability that can become an asset only when its holder is actually paid) ... [T]he results of John Law's banking system will inevitably follow this. It cannot be otherwise. ... [Y]ou do not make money out of public credit; it is debt; it is not capital. It is a false idea that anything of that character is money ...."[466]

In 1863, there was as yet no settled policy by which the government assumed permanent control over national currency. The leading object of the national bank law, according to its sponsor, Congressman E. G. Spaulding, was to firmly establish a currency of uniform value and similitude—to facilitate the exchange of goods and services and collection of taxes—amply secured by gold bearing bonds deposited with the Treasury.

It was never intended by the originators of the Legal Tender Acts that the issue of an irredeemable paper currency become the permanent policy of the government. Congressman E. G. Spaulding, in introducing the bill in the House, said "...the bill before us is a war measure, a measure of necessity and not of choice." It was a temporary expedient to enable the country to "crush the rebellion" of the Civil War; to save the government and preserve our nationality—not a permanent policy of government. The expressed intention of the legislators was to redeem the paper currency for specie as soon as practicable after the cessation of the hostilities of the Civil War.

Just as the causes of the financial and economic crisis in the United States has been currently examined by The National Commission on the Causes of the Financial and Economic Crisis in the United States, *The Financial Crisis Inquiry Report*, published in 2011, the tortured history of congress' efforts to avoid its constitutional power and duty to "coin and regulate the value of money" is detailed in E.G. Spaulding's *History of Legal Tender* relating to the crisis of the Civil War; the *Pujo Report* relating to the crisis of 1907, the *Pecora Report* relating to the crisis of the Great Depression and the FDIC Report, History of the Eighties—Lessons for the Future, relating to the financial crisis of the late1980s and early 1990s. These reports are addressed, *infra*.

[A] E.G. Spaulding:[467] Civil War Existential Demand for War Exception to Permit Debasement

During the Civil War the money supply increased by 138 percent to pay for the war. The purchasing power of the Greenbacks fell by 65 percent. Wages were cut in half while prices doubled. For the south it was even worse. Almost all the Civil War was funded by printing fiat money. Confederate notes increased in volume by 214 percent per year. The volume of all the money including bank notes and checkbook money increased by over 300 percent per year. All the confederate states also printed their own fiat money as well. Within four years the prices hyper-inflated by 9,100 percent. Confederate bonds and notes were worthless. Once more the hidden tax of inflation was paid dearly by the public on both sides of the war.

The Civil War period of American history of money was a cauldron of turmoil. The country had run into financial difficulty as a result of the War of 1812 and had been forced to borrow to pay the war costs. The Civil War presented a far more challenging prospect. Not only was the US government forced to borrow to pay the costs of the Civil War but the cost exceeded the total amount of currency in circulation in the United States.

The issues became not only the issues of authorization of borrowing and terms of borrowing as contemplated by the *Constitution*, but also the issue of how the country could provide sufficient currency to fund the borrowing through coining money, the value of which was regulated by Congress, as required by the *Constitution*. Since borrowing money is the current monetization of commodities and profits measured in commodities and profits in the future, the government was forced, literally as a matter of maintaining its existence to substitute a paper promise of future commoditization of coined money to eventually redeem the current promises to the lenders—largely the American public. In this way the government created the money through instruments of credit, bearing interest, some of which was payable in specie, and which being ultimately redeemable at maturity in specie. The rights of holders of existing American paper money to redemption in specie on demand was suspended for the duration of the war, and until such time as the country could regenerate sufficient specie to commence the gradual process of redemption.

The fact that paper money was created to pay current expenses based on an uncertain future creation of value was not lost on the government or the public. Commodity money; specie, is a representation of current liquid value not future value. The purposes for which the new paper legal tender money was created did not represent concurrent exchanges of value or profit creating activities but rather represented, essentially a destruction of existing value and future profit, through immediate consumption in the destructive activity of war instead of the productive activity of commerce. The focus of the government and the public then was upon the necessary sacrifice of both current and future value and productive capacity, to pay the current costs of preserving the country of the United States. The government and all levels of American society were aware of the necessary sacrifices and the purpose of those sacrifices. The common desire was to spread the burden of sacrifice as evenly and equitably as possible without destruction of the economy and the public's future ability to repay the massive war debt, while maintaining the value and integrity of the legal tender paper currency through its ultimate redemption at full value in specie.

The establishment of legal tender and the temporary suspension of convertibility of that legal lender into and redeem-ability in gold under then then current *Currency Act*, in response to the existential emergency of the Civil War, inadvertently cracked the door open to exploitation and abuse by the new nations' banks to arbitrage their newly granted monopoly power over money creation to work subsequent concentrations of wealth and power in those bankers and their political partners and sponsors, in direct contradiction to the requirements of the *Constitution*.

Congressman E. G. Spaulding, who introduced *The National Banking Act* and *The Legal Tender Acts* in Congress, commented contemporaneously regarding the danger of shifting standards of value necessary to the regulation of value of the money, when created outside the needs of commerce. Spaulding clearly articulated the necessary considerations in regulation of the value of money that Washington and Wall Street have now so cavalierly cast aside, ignored and in so doing exploited the opportunity for debasement of state money; an evil that has occurred periodically throughout history with unavoidably disastrous results.

Spaulding clearly articulated the necessity for legal tender and its regulation of value through legal reference to legislatively established standards of value and clearly demonstrated that the adoption of the use of legal tender money during a time of emergency did not in any way do away with, dismiss, alter, affect, impair or impugn the constitutional requirement of government created money, the value of which is regulated by reference to a clearly articulated standard of value. At one time during the Civil War period Congress established a standard for regulation of the value of greenbacks provision for their redemption in government interest bearing bonds at market value:

> *This was not the issue of an irredeemable paper currency. There was a fixed standard and measure of value for the redemption of all these legal tender notes as they should be issued and re-issued from time to time. This was the standard of value fixed by the legal tender note bill. It was in effect a forced loan from the people to the government, but at a fair rate of interest for both the lender and the borrower* .... (Authors' emphasis added in italics)
>
> All the bonds and greenback promises to pay dollars, now outstanding, do not represent tangible property or means owned by the Government, but property in the possession of the people under its jurisdiction, and from which all this waste must be reproduced again, and the value restored, in order to bring us to the specie standard and enable us to pay the debt. In short, the debt must be paid from the earnings and income of the people, in some form of taxation to be enforced by the Government....
>
> *This was a radical change in the standard or measure of value within the United States, but it was a fixed standard established by law, and every business man could act upon it, and shape all his contracts and business transactions accordingly....* (Authors' emphasis added in italics)
>
> All became pecuniarily intrusted (sic) in its success, and they furnished the means to carry it on. The crushing of the rebellion was the people's triumph; and the people will in due time pay the debt, and thereby preserve the honor and good faith of the nation. ...
>
> To illustrate more fully. When individuals in commercial transactions give their notes, bonds or other promises to pay money, they usually receive in exchange either real or personal property, or labor, which is made valuable in some form to pay the obligation given for it. Not so with the war debt; the property received and services performed for the United States notes and obligations, outstanding, has not, in a financial sense, been employed in such a useful way as to furnish present value to pay them with, but on the contrary, it was consumed by the war. Hence the difference between a debt created for commercial purposes and a war debt. The one is generally for property or labor made useful, and productive,

> while the other is for unproductive labor or property consumed, wasted or destroyed not for any pecuniarily (sic) useful purpose ...[468]

Spaulding provided an excellent written record of the debates, correspondence and considerations surrounding the struggle to achieve fair and rational methods of financing the costs of the war through combinations of borrowing and money creation. The success of each aspect of the financing was to be determined by the support and willingness of both the government and the public to undertake payment of the current costs as well as the obligation for future deferred repayment of the debt through redemption of specie gained through future work and enterprise, without permanent debasement of the currency:

> "The value of the Union and the Government preserved in full vigor under the *Constitution*, cannot be estimated in dollars and cents. It is above all price. A vast continent, embracing territory and people, is now held under the control of a mighty central and consolidated Government, based upon the will of an enterprising, intelligent and powerful people. The mind of man is incapable of estimating the future progress and destiny of the American people under such a Government wisely administered. But in a financial and economical aspect, these vast sums expended present an entirely different view. Viewed simply as an economical question, the immense war debt represents only lives and property consumed. All the unproductive labor, vast material of war, provisions and supplies of all kinds are used up, wasted and blotted out of existence. This immense debt rolled up during four years of bloody war, stands out in bold demand upon the nation for liquidation from the future earnings and income of the people. Future labor and economy must furnish the means for its payment. This debt is the price of the Union and constitutional Government, but their value cannot be estimated in dollars...
>
> "This sum must be paid, principal and interest, not by the issue of new promises to pay it, but by the production of actual value, measured by gold and silver, the world's commercial standard, as well as the standard regulated by law.[469]

Very importantly, at this time the American government had no mechanism in place to affect the borrowing and redeemable currency issuance necessary to prosecute the Civil War. *The Legal Tender Acts* and *The National Banking Acts* were adopted to accomplish the vital, existential objectives of winning the war and reunification of the country. These were emergency acts, adopted based on expedience as a matter of survival. They did provide for the combination of government and banking then necessary for success in the war, and thus, inadvertently, set the stage for a dramatically expanding special relationship of the government with banks as a matter of necessity. What began as an arrangement of temporary convenience and expedience for national survival, a purely temporary arrangement, has subsequently been exploited by the banking industry and traded off by politicians and bureaucrats through the years in a manner that belies strictly temporary and expedient foundation of the relationship. The false narrative of the Civil War as precedent for the future necessity for money debasement, misrepresented both the nature of the relationship and the policy upon which it was based. It corrupted the values and public rights that had been protected so judiciously and transparently during the Civil War period.

The special relationship between Washington and Wall Street so necessary to the victory of the Union has now evolved into and resulted in policies and actions completely at odds with those embodied in common law, the *United States Constitution* and followed to the extent possible during the Civil War period. The clear and unequivocal understanding of and acknowledgment by Washington and the American public was that failure to return to the sound pre-war policies as soon as possible after the war would lead to the crime and corruption of money debasement and subsequent financial crises.

Each financial crisis subsequent to the Civil War has resulted in further deterioration of the rights of the American public to honest, safe and sound sovereign money, wrought by the government in Washington and by ever more powerful special partners on Wall Street.

Each financial crisis following the American Civil War has been followed by putative banking and financial reforms. But, contrary to the stated purposes of the reforms, they have instead resulted in further and ever more dramatic departures from the duties of Washington and Wall Streets as partners and public fiduciaries in the monetary foundation of our economy, and as fiduciaries and partners in the special relationship that now controls the creation, emission and value of the American dollar and that defines the monetary and property rights and interests of American public. The perversion and corruption wrought based upon the "false precedent" of the temporary, expedient policies following the Civil War, have been used intentionally, and fraudulently by the Washington and Wall Street partnership and monetary racketeering enterprise to justify each subsequent weakening of the publics' natural, civil, moral and legal right to honest, safe and sound money, in turn, leading to subsequent financial crises. As we follow the development of American fiscal, monetary and economic policy through its journey from the common law and constitutional mandate for honest, safe and sound money to the current policies firmly grounded in a policy of fraudulent misrepresentation of asset liquidity and values through abuse of power and money debasement, we will look back to the twisted departures from the foundation for the American Dream preserved during the Civil War through terrible struggle and sacrifice. It is now clear that subsequently, by stages, the public interest has been spurned and abandoned by Washington and Wall Street. Their enduring propensity to concentrate wealth and power in the hands of a narrowing group—the 1 percent—at the expense of the society at large, if not checked by the American public's enforcement of the accountability of Washington and Wall Street under the American rule law, will result in the widening of the gap in income and wealth between Washington and Wall Street on the one hand and ordinary Americans on the other. The seed of civil unrest are even now stirring, although few point the underlying cause of the unrest that is the lingering burden of loss and damage inflicted by the great financial crisis in the face of the growing concentration of wealth and power in Washington and on Wall Street.

[B] The *Legal Tender Cases* and Paper Money

The United States Supreme Court has held that *The Legal Tender Acts* do not attempt to make paper a standard of value. In fact, a close reading of the *Legal Tender Cases*[470] reveals that the legal issue of the ability of Washington and Wall Street to prosper through lying to, cheating and stealing from the American public through the age old device of money debasement was expressly reserved by the Court, not settled or decided in the *Legal Tender Cases*. The Court stated:

> *The legal tender acts do not attempt to make paper a standard of value. We do not rest their validity upon the assertion that their emission is coinage, or any regulation of the value of money; nor do we assert that Congress may make anything which has no value money.* What we do assert is, that Congress has power to enact that the government's promises to pay money shall be, for the time being, equivalent in value to the representative of value determined by the coinage acts, or to multiples thereof. (Authors' emphasis added in italics)
>
> The questions involved are constitutional questions of the most vital importance to the government and to the public at large. We have been in the habit of treating cases involving a consideration of constitutional power differently from those which concern merely private right. We are not accustomed to hear them in the absence of a full court, if it can be avoided. Even in cases involving only private rights, if convinced we had made a mistake, we would hear another argument and correct our error. And it is no unprecedented thing in courts of last resort, both in this country and in England, to overrule decisions previously made. We agree this should not be done inconsiderately, but in a case of such far-reaching consequences as the present, thoroughly convinced as we are that Congress has not transgressed its powers, we regard it as our duty so to decide and to affirm both these judgments.[471] ...
>
> *This power is entirely distinct from that of coining money and regulating the value thereof. It is not only embraced in the power to make all necessary auxiliary laws, but it is incidental to the power of borrowing money. It is often a necessary means of anticipating and realizing promptly the national resources, when, perhaps, promptness is necessary to the national existence. It is not an attempt to coin money out of a valueless material, like the coinage of leather or ivory or kowrie shells. It is a pledge of the national credit. It is a promise by the government to pay dollars; it is not an attempt to make dollars. The standard of value is not changed.*[472] (Authors' emphasis added in italics)

A case for Washington and Wall Street accountability for the financial crisis is not barred by the ultimate decision in the *Legal Tender Cases*. In fact, the *Legal Tender Cases* provide a substantial foundation for such a case. The Court's holding in the *Legal Tender Cases* has never been reversed. The government has the power and ability to borrow for its needs. The government does not have the constitutional power to debase American money for any reason, notwithstanding, the Court's claim that it may do so "when necessary to the national existence to promptly anticipate and realize the national resources." What was an unconstitutional but perceived necessary expedient existential act, transparently taken by Congress at that time, and later reversed has morphed into an unlawful implied power of Congress to debase American money at will. Although Congress may, however, devalue the value of money through appropriate, transparent legislation that changes or adjusts the constitutionally established standard of value as a part of its constitutional mandate to coin and regulate the value of money; and although it may use paper money as legal tender, redeemable in terms of money, the value of which is regulated by Congress, any devaluation, or revaluation as the case may be, must be accomplished transparently and lawfully, in respect to the fiduciary duty associated with the maintenance of honest, safe and sound American money. At least from the time of the Nixon shock in 1971 to today, the government has not declared that it must devalue or debase the dollar as necessary to the national existence. All branches of American government have simply acted as though any moral and legal requirement of protection of the honesty, safety and soundness of American money simply does not exist and its non-existence may not be questioned. This is not a case for technical posturing or hair-splitting in efforts at financial reform. It is a case of confirmation and enforcement of the fundamental first principles of our society. As it now stands:

> The Civil War, in short, ended the separation of the federal government from banking and brought the two institutions together in an increasingly close and permanent symbiosis. In that way, the Republican Party, which inherited the Whig admiration for paper money and government control and sponsorship of inflationary banking, was able to implant the soft-money tradition permanently in the American System.[473]

Action for accountability of Washington and Wall Street for the financial crisis is not barred by the ultimate decision in the *Legal Tender Cases*. In fact, the *Legal Tender Cases* provide a substantial foundation for such a case. As noted, the Court's holding has never been reversed.

The conclusive Supreme Court *Legal Tender Cases* confirmed the constitutionality of legal tender money, for the time being, only as an existential necessity, and only on the condition that it represents, and is redeemable in constitutional coined money, the value of which is regulated by Congress.

The *Legal Tender Cases*, however, have been wrongly construed to have established the constitutionality of the use of legal tender for the payment of all debts public and private, without the necessary attributes, which are:

- Redeemability in constitutional coined money, the value of which has been regulated by Congress.
- When created through bank credit, the credit must be adequately supported by sources of repayment, based upon a reasonable and prudent banker's determination that, considering the risk and uncertainty of the continued quality of credit, collateral and other sources of repayment over time until maturity, the credit, when repaid at maturity as originally stated, or earlier in the event maturity of the is lawfully accelerated, to provide liquidity to the holder who will then be repaid in money that is redeemable in sovereign American money, the value of which has been regulated in accordance with a congressional constitutional mandated honest, safe and sound standard of value.
- The money must provide the central features of uniformity and parity as an essential feature of congressional control of the currency; and providing an

> honest, safe, sound and uniform currency for the country; securing the benefit of it to the people.

These considerations properly observed are, and have always created the attributes of honest, safe and sound money that enables the money to serve its public purpose, thereby justifying the trust and confidence in the honesty, safety, and soundness of the money created and controlled by Congress; and by Congress' partners in the process, The Fed, the other federal financial regulatory authorities and the Wall Street bankers.

Following the Civil War, America experienced a series of financial panics—crises; in 1873, 1893 and then 1907. The crisis of 1873 followed a boom in railroad construction. Much of the craze in railroad investment was driven by government land grants and subsidies to the railroads. The railroad industry was the nation's largest employer outside of agriculture; involving large amounts of capital and risk. Cash from speculators caused abnormal growth in the industry as well as overbuilding of docks, factories and ancillary facilities. Too much capital was involved in projects offering no immediate or early returns.[474] The crisis of 1893 was a serious economic depression in the United States that began in 1893. Similar to the panic of 1873, it was marked by the overbuilding and shaky financing of railroads, resulting in a series of bank failures. Compounding market overbuilding and the railroad bubble was a run on the gold supply and a struggle over bimetallism, fractional reserve banking and global financial imbalances. The panic of '93 was the worst economic depression the United States had ever experienced at the time.[475] "Stock prices declined; 500 banks closed; 15,000 businesses failed; and farms ceased operation. Unemployment rate hit 25 percent in Pennsylvania, 35 percent in New York, and 43 percent in Michigan. Soup kitchens were needed to feed the destitute. People chopped wood, broke rocks, and sewed by hand with needle and thread in exchange for food. Women resorted to prostitution to feed their families."[476]

Murray Rothbard,[477] quoting John J. Klein in *Money and the Economy,* agrees that "The financial panics of 1873, 1884, 1893 and 1907 were in large part an outgrowth of ... reserve pyramiding and excess deposit creation by reserve city and central reserve city banks. These panics were triggered by the currency drains that took place in periods of relative prosperity when the banks were loaned up."[478]

[C] Financial Crisis of 1907: Establishment of the Federal Reserve System and Money Debasement—The *Pujo Report*

[1] Tension Between Sovereign Banking and Shadow Banking

The Federal Reserve has provided a somewhat self-serving account of the panic of 1907:

> The Panic of 1907 was the first worldwide financial crisis of the twentieth century. It transformed a recession into a contraction surpassed in severity only by the Great Depression. The panic's impact is still felt today because it spurred the

> monetary reform movement that led to the establishment of the Federal Reserve System. Moen and Tallman (1999) argued that the experience of the Panic of 1907 changed how New York Clearing House bankers perceived the value of a central bank because the panic took hold mainly among trust companies, institutions outside their membership.
>
> The central role of New York City trust companies distinguishes the Panic of 1907 from earlier panics. Trust companies were state-chartered intermediaries that competed with banks for deposits. Trusts were not, however, a central part of the payments system and had a low volume of check clearing compared with banks. As a result, they held a low percentage of cash reserves relative to deposits, around 5 percent, compared with 25 percent for national banks. Because trust-company deposit accounts were demandable in cash, trusts were just as susceptible to runs on deposits as were banks.
>
> Despite their minor role in the payments system, trusts were large and important to the financial system. Trust companies loaned large sums directly in New York equity markets, including New York Stock Exchange brokers. Trusts did not require collateral for these loans, which had to be repaid by the end of the business day. Brokers used these loans to purchase securities for themselves or their clients and then used these securities as collateral for a call loan—an overnight loan that facilitated stock purchases—from a nationally chartered bank. The proceeds of the call loan were used to pay back the initial loan from the trust company. Trusts were a necessary part of this process, because the law prohibited nationally chartered commercial banks from making uncollateralized loans or guaranteeing the payment of checks written by brokers on accounts without sufficient funds. The extra liquidity provided by trusts supported new daily transactions on the floor of the exchange. Runs on trust company deposits, however, short-circuited their role as the initial liquidity provider to the stock market.[479]

The Fed goes on to note the similarities of the financial crisis of 1907 and the great financial crisis of 2008:

> "The parallels between the crises in 1907 and 2008 are striking. During 2007-09, the financial crisis was centered on investment banks, institutions without direct access to the Federal Reserve System. In 1907, widespread depositor withdrawals occurred at New York City trust companies—intermediaries outside the New York Clearing House, the effective lender of last resort. In effect, both financial crises started outside the large banks serving as payments centers. Yet the crises created havoc within markets and among banks that were central to the payments system. Both crises challenged the existing mechanisms used to alleviate crises.
>
> "The trust companies in 1907 were like the shadow banks in the financial crisis of 2007-09. Short-term lending during the recent crisis came largely from some shadow banks (hedge funds and money market mutual funds) to fund other shadow banks (investment banks). As key liquidity providers for repurchase agreements, these shadow banks were the "depositors" providing funds for overnight lending to allow investment banks to finance the asset-backed security market, just as uncollateralized loans (overdrafts) by trust companies allowed brokers to purchase stock. Both the trusts and the shadow banks faced runs by their depositors and had to withdraw lending in short-term credit markets.[480]"

In the wake of the panic of 1907, the thrust of remedial action was directed intensely by Washington and Wall Street to the development of An American central bank, "an institution that could regulate the economy and serve as a lender of last resort to bail banks out of trouble."[481] The task for Washington and Wall Street then became to develop the details of the central bank and critically, to mobilize public opinion in support of the creation of the central bank. The duplicity employed by Washington and Wall Street gave rise to the modern string of false narratives that have supported and enabled the Washington and Wall Street objective of concentration of wealth and power by proclaiming that the mechanisms they employ are in service of the public interest. As is almost always the case, there then existed, and now exists, a kernel of truth in these false narratives. Just enough to enable Washington and Wall Street to give lip service to public interest whilst serving predominately their own interests at public expense.[482]

Murray Rothbard concludes his treatment of the panic of 1907 and mobilization for a central bank as follows:

> The financial elites of this country, notably the Rockefeller. And Kuhn, Loeb interests, were responsible for putting through the Federal Reserve System, as a government created and sanctioned cartel device to enable the nation's banks to inflate the money supply in a coordinated fashion, without suffering quick retribution from depositors or noteholders demanding cash. Recent researchers, however, have also highlighted the vital supporting role of the vital supporting role of the growing number of technocratic experts and academics, who were happy to lend the patina of their allegedly scientific expertise to the elites' drive for a central bank. To achieve a regime of big government and government control, power elites cannot achieve their goal of privilege through statism without the vital legitimizing, support of the supposedly disinterested experts and professoriat. To achieve the Leviathan state, interests seeking special privilege, and intellectuals offering scholarship and ideology, must work hand in hand.[483]

Thus, with the inception of the Federal Reserve System, begins the modern phenomenon of the Washington and Wall Street criminal corrupt racketeering enterprise. The Washington Wall Street response to the panic of 1907 presented the first iteration of the series of financial crisis reports conducted by Washington. The *Pujo Report* and each subsequent financial crisis report follow the same Washington narrative calling for protection of the public interest while, in tandem with Wall Street and in teamwork with the peripheral financial and political elites and the concentrated support of their acolytes in academia and the legal and accounting professions, Washington and Wall Street depart ever further from observance of and accountability for their march toward concentration of power and wealth.

[2] *The* Pujo Report

The facts, circumstances and legislative history leading to the *Federal Reserve Act* are detailed in the *Pujo Report—1913*.[484]

The primary issues addressed in the *Pujo Report* are:

- protection of the public interest;
- avoidance of undue concentrations of control in banking and finance;
- providing for and promote transparency, fairness and non-discrimination;

- prohibiting undue concentrations of control and officer and director self-dealing.

The *Pujo Report* recommended: transparency and non-discrimination in clearing associations' securities clearing; examination and supervision of clearing associations by public authorities; transparency and fairness in New York Stock Exchange transactions, prohibited wash sales and excessive margin investments and provide detail of customers and transactions to the Postmaster General; prohibited financial institution consolidation that would create undue concentrations of control; prohibited interlocking bank board directorates, interlocking stockholdings, voting trusts, securities holding companies, unsupervised and unregulated private bankers, officer and director self-dealing; acceptance of rewards for bank loans and public transparency of bank assets and stockholders; all to protect the public interest and to avoid undue concentrations of control in banking and finance; and to regulate the unwinding and reorganization of speculative railroad financing and investment the constituted the speculative bubble of the day—as asset backed securitization and derivatives are today's speculative bubble.

The litany of complaints and criticisms of Washington and Wall Street registered in the *Pujo Report* very closely correlates to the same complaints and criticisms registered today.

The litany of miscreants identified in the *Pujo Report* are eerily familiar, predecessors of today's Wall Street banks, including J P Morgan & Co., Bankers Trust, First National Bank of New York, National City Bank of New York, Kidder Peabody & Co., Kuhn Loeb & Co., Chase National Bank and National Bank of Commerce, among others.

[3] Jekyll Island, the Aldrich Plan and the Federal Reserve Act

As a response to the findings of the Pujo Committee, the Wall Street financiers of the day commenced an attack on the very foundation of United States money.[485] Murray Rothbard provided a concise description of this process:[486]

> In 1910 the Federal Reserve System was conceived during a highly secretive nine-day meeting in Jekyll Island, GA. Today in that same clubhouse in that private club on Jekyll Island there is a brass plaque that reads: *"In this room, the Federal Reserve System was created."* This meeting, held secret for many years, was publicized once the Federal Reserve was firmly established. All the men that were involved in the meeting have since written articles and books about those fateful days on Jekyll. But, at the time, it was a great secret and remained a secret for several years until the Federal Reserve was firmly rooted as the controlling force of our monetary system.
>
> The story starts when Senator Nelson Aldrich instructed six other well-known men to join him on his private train car in New Jersey in November of 1910. They were instructed to come separately. They were told to act like they did not know one another and to avoid all reporters. One man went so far as to carry a shot gun—not for defense, he planned to use the excuse he was going on a duck

hunting trip if questioned. It later came out in this man's biography that he never fired a gun in his life.

These men were told once on board the train to use only their first names because they didn't want the servants and wait staff to recognize them together. Two of the men even adopted code names.

Once on Jekyll Island, for nine days these men hammered out the details of the Federal Reserve System. For years after, these men firmly denied any such meeting had ever taken place. It wasn't until the Fed was established did they openly talk about it. They later wrote magazine articles, agreed to interviews, and even wrote books about the secret meeting.

The following men devised the Federal Reserve System:

- *Senator Nelson Aldrich*—Republican whip and Chairman of the National Monetary Commission. He was a business associate of JP Morgan. He was the father-in-law to John D. Rockefeller, Jr. and was grandfather of Nelson Aldrich Rockefeller who served as Vice President under former President Gerald Ford.
- *Abraham Piatt Andrew*—Assistant Secretary of the Treasury.
- *Frank Vanderlip*—President of the National City Bank of New York (largest bank in the country at the time). He represented the financial assets of Rockefeller.
- *Henry Davison*—Senior partner of the J.P. Morgan Company.
- *Charles D. Norton*—President of the First National Bank of New York.
- *Benjamin Strong*—Known as the "Lieutenant of JP Morgan," he was head of the J.P. Morgan Banker's Trust Company. Incidentally, Strong became the first head of the Federal Reserve.
- *Paul Warburg*—One of the wealthiest men in the world. He was a recent immigrant from Germany. He was a partner of the Kuhn, Loeb Company and represented the Rothschild banking dynasty in England and France. He had extensive knowledge of the banking system in Europe.

Together these men represented the interests of one-fourth of the wealth of the entire world.

"*The bill written to break the money trust was written by the money trust!* These are the men that created the creature we now know as the Federal Reserve System."

[a] The Plan Devised on Jekyll Island

"What's in a name?"

On Jekyll Island, the bankers discussed the type of system they wanted and how they would sell it to the public. They thought the name of the system was very important and decided to call it the *Federal Reserve System*. According to the later writings of the men who were in the meeting. This was their reasoning for the name:

Federal—Make it sound like a part of the government.

Reserve—Make it seem like there are reserves.

System—Make it sound like it was a diffusion of power. At the time the public was very concerned about a concentration of power in NY.

[b] *The Objectives Discussed in the 1910 Meeting*

"Why were these powerful bankers meeting in such secrecy? These men, representing the biggest banks in the world, wanted to reverse the trend of the erosion of power away from NY as the US economy was expanding to the South and to the West as our country grew. Established banks were experiencing heightened competition from new banks and wanted to control the competition before things progressed to a point where they could no longer maintain power.

"They wanted to reverse the trend of private capital formation. People and corporations were beginning to use their own savings instead of going to banks. These bankers had to decide how they could get people to come back and start relying on banks for loans again. Their answer was to create a means to artificially suppress interest rates below market levels:

> "Under a sound money system, interest rates are a product of supply and demand. But, the bankers wanted a way to artificially suppress interest rates so people depend on them for loans. The banks needed a flexible currency. One that was elastic. One where they could control interest rates and bring them down to levels below the market rate. Besides, if you are creating money out of nothing, you don't have to charge much interest to make a profit."

The bankers wanted a way to pass on losses in the banking system to the taxpayer without them knowing about it. These bankers were talking about "operation bailout" long before the current round of bailouts. During the meeting they discussed the prospects of not letting a bank or preferred firms fail.

[c] *Passing the Federal Reserve Act*

"Senator Aldrich came back to Washington and tried to pass the bill his banker buddies had drafted down on Jekyll Island. Against the urging of the bankers, Aldrich attached his name to the bill. He wanted to go down in history. However, since Senator Aldrich was a republican with ties to the big banks, the bill was the only thing that became history. It was easily shot down.

"However, Aldrich and the bankers did not give up. They were able to get two Democratic Senators Glass and Owen to sponsor a similar bill and added a few provisions (like one that said the Fed could not print money at will). The big bankers wanted the Federal Reserve bill passed, even with a few unfavorable provisions. They understood that once the system was established they would be able to change it over time and get it how they wanted.

"Here's where things get particularly interesting. Aldrich and Vanderlip both came out and gave speeches and wrote newspaper articles condemning the new Glass/Owen bill. They said this bill would ruin the big banks. This strategy worked to perfection.

Naturally, the average person fueled by populist rhetoric thought that if big banks did not like the new bill, then it had to be pretty good. BUT, at same time these bankers were publicly condemning the bill, they were privately financing the support of it. Talk about professional deception! Please see Eustace Mullins's *Secrets of the Federal Reserve* for more information.

"The Glass/Owen bill (the *Federal Reserve Act*) was passed December 22, 1913 and Woodrow Wilson signed the bill into law the next day.

"The bankers have been able to get the Federal Reserve System how they want it. Since the Federal Reserve Act has passed, it has been amended almost 200 times and hardly a person has given it any notice. They have greatly expanded the power of the Federal Reserve. They can now create money out of US Debt, Foreign Debt, Corporate Debt, and Mortgage Securities.

Since then [1913], the Act has been amended 195 times, expanding the power and scope of the System to the point where, today, it would be almost unrecognizable to the Congressmen and Senators who voted for it.—G. Edward Griffin; *The Creature From Jekyll Island.*"

(Authors' emphasis added in italics)

[d] So What Is the Fed?

The *Federal Reserve Act* formed a private banking cartel. This cartel is in partnership with the government. The Federal Reserve is:

- A corporation, chartered by Congress.
- A mechanism where Congress has been able to raise unlimited amounts of taxes through inflation without the people even knowing it.
- A method for the banks to earn perpetual interests on nothing.

The story of the Federal Reserve is the story of one of the biggest scams in the history of the world. This scam has been legitimized by law. The two partners of the Federal Reserve System are the big banks and the US Government—both are ripping off the citizens of America and the world.

The Federal Reserve is not Federal. It is not part of the government. It is a private banking cartel in partnership with the government to rip off the American people.

There are little to no required reserves backing the Federal Reserve Notes (our money). Our money is a fiat currency backed only by the confidence of the people. It is not a system. The creation of the Federal Reserve System concentrated power in New York more than ever and solidified the old order. The reforms of 1913 halted the diffusion of power and concentrated it in Wall Street.

[e] *The Creature from Jekyll Island*

The Creature from Jekyll Island: A Second Look at the Federal Reserve by G. Edward Griffin examines the creation of the Federal Reserve System that was devised during a secret nine-day meeting on Jekyll Island in Georgia in 1910.

In November of 1910, under the disguise of a duck-hunting trip, six men met at an exclusive private club on Jekyll Island here in Georgia, to write a Central Banking Act. The men who wrote the act were two Rockefeller men, two Morgan men, a Kuhn-Loeb partner; and Assistant Treasury Secretary. All Big Bankers![487]

Where do Americans stand today? If the origins and foundation principles of the Aldrich Plan and the Federal Reserve System have been made so public and they so obviously contradict the constitutional mandate for Congress to regulate the value of United States money, how has the Fed taken these facts and circumstances into account in response to the current financial crisis? Well. They have publicly celebrated their success—that is—their success in maintaining power and control in direct contradiction of the constitutional mandate for congressionally created money, the value of which is regulated by congress. The constitutional mandate has been cast aside once more, with emphasis and apparent relish.

In November of 2010, the Fed celebrated the 100 years of its existence: The Federal Reserve went back to Jekyll Island to celebrate the 100-year anniversary of the infamous 1910 Jekyll Island meeting that spawned the draft legislation that would ultimately create the US Federal Reserve. The title of the conference was "*A Return to Jekyll Island: The Origins, History, and Future of the Federal Reserve*," and it was held on November 5th and 6th in the exact same building where the original 1910 meeting occurred.

In November 1910, the original gathering at Jekyll Island included US Senator Nelson W. Aldrich, Assistant Secretary of the Treasury Department A.P. Andrews and many representatives from the upper crust of the US banking establishment. That meeting was held in an environment of absolute and total secrecy. 100 years later, Federal Reserve bureaucrats will return to Jekyll Island once again to "celebrate" the history and the future of the Federal Reserve:

> Sadly, most Americans have no idea how the Federal Reserve came into being. Forbes magazine founder Bertie Charles Forbes *was perhaps the first writer* to describe the secretive nature of the original gathering on Jekyll Island in a national publication....
>
> > *Picture a party of the nation's greatest bankers stealing out of New York on a private railroad car under cover of darkness, stealthily riding hundreds of miles South, embarking on a mysterious launch, sneaking onto an island deserted by all but a few servants, living there a full week under such rigid secrecy that the names of not one of them was once mentioned, lest the servants learn the identity and disclose to the world this strangest, most secret expedition in the history of American finance. I am not romancing; I am giving to the world, for the first time, the real story of how the famous Aldrich currency report, the foundation of our new currency system, was written... The utmost secrecy was enjoined upon all. The public must not glean a hint of what was to be done. Senator Aldrich notified each one to go quietly into a*

private car of which the railroad had received orders to draw up on an unfrequented platform. Off the party set. New York's ubiquitous reporters had been foiled... Nelson (Aldrich) had confided to Henry, Frank, Paul and Piatt that he was to keep them locked up at Jekyll Island, out of the rest of the world, until they had evolved and compiled a scientific currency system for the United States, the real birth of the present Federal Reserve System, the plan done on Jekyll Island in the conference with Paul, Frank and Henry... Warburg is the link that binds the Aldrich system and the present system together. He more than any one man has made the system possible as a working reality. (Authors' emphasis added in italics)

It was a system that was designed by the bankers and for the bankers. Now, the bureaucrats running the system are returning to Jekyll Island to congratulate themselves. Those attending the conference on November 5th and 6th include Federal Reserve Chairman Ben Bernanke, former Fed Chairman Alan Greenspan, Goldman Sachs managing director E. Gerald Corrigan and the heads of the various regional Federal Reserve banks. You can view the entire agenda of the conference right here. It looks like that there will be plenty of hors d'oeuvres to go around, but should the Federal Reserve really be celebrating their accomplishments at a time when the US economy is literally falling to pieces

Today, 63 percent of Americans do not think that they will be able to maintain their current standard of living. 1.47 million Americans have been unemployed for more than 99 weeks. We are facing a complete and total economic disaster.

Today, the Federal Reserve has more power over the economy than any other single institution in the United States. It is the Fed that primarily determines if we will see high inflation or low inflation, whether the money supply with expand or contract and whether we will have high interest rates or low interest rates. The President and the US Congress have far less power to influence the economy than the Federal Reserve does."[488]

[4] The Federal Reserve System

The Federal Reserve System and the national banking system are the nexus of the Washington and Wall Street partnership in exploitation of the American public and abuse of the power they wield.

The Federal Reserve System is the central bank of the United States. As noted, it was founded by Congress in 1913 to provide the nation with a safer, more flexible, and more stable monetary and financial system. Over the years, its role in banking and the economy has expanded. Today, the Federal Reserve's duties include conducting the nation's monetary policy by influencing the monetary and credit conditions in the economy in pursuit of maximum employment, stable prices, and moderate long-term interest rates; supervising and regulating banking institutions to ensure the safety and soundness of the nation's banking and financial system and to protect the credit rights of consumers and maintaining the stability of the financial system and containing systemic risk that may arise in financial markets.

Reasonable minds may differ on how we might identify, regulate and limit systemic financial risk to mitigate or avoid systemic financial crises. Many participants in the American financial system believe that the financial markets for financial products are essentially self-correcting and that the government should not interfere with the workings of the "invisible hand" of a free financial marketplace in an unregulated free market financial system. There are essentially two ways to regulate our financial system to mitigate or avoid systemic financial risk. Our American culture and those who oppose governmental intervention in "free markets" would have us enjoy a "self-regulated" financial system based on transparency of information and the discipline of the invisible free hand of the market based on complete information.

Although America does strive to achieve market transparency, and does the best job of providing such transparency of any of the developed economies in the free world; that does not suffice in the "financial" market place, or financial system, based on a monetary unit of value that is not regulated in reference to any standard.

We know that the neither the American nor the global financial system are really free markets. We know that we have a regulated banking system combined with a system of central banks, such as the Fed, supposedly charged with responsibility to the public to perform certain circumscribed, but non-transparent actions to control the amount and "quality" of money, including the amount of credit and the structure of credit as money in the economy. Although one might think the central bankers mandate would include some semblance of systematic regulation of the value of the money that is their *reason d'etre. The Federal Reserve Act*, as amended through the years, has never included the crucial constitutional requirement that the value of United States money be regulated; and it can be regulated only by the reference at some level to an independent—apolitical standard; and that functional regulation of value, fundamentally, can be enforced only through the required redemption of specified monetary units at the congressionally prescribed standard of value per unit, as established by Congress in an open, transparent and democratically accountable and responsible manner, after public date, accomplished in the interest of the sovereign citizens of the United States—not primarily Washington and Wall Street.

Again, just as the old phrase: "What is good for General Motors is good for America"[489] was offered up as a justification for corporate dominance, today, Washington and Wall Street contend that what is good for concentrating wealth and power through their corrupt racketeering enterprise is good for ordinary Americans. That, of course, is false equivalence in both cases.

The Fed's organizational mission (as opposed to the broader publicly stated mission as set forth in its organizational legislation, its written material, as well as other information on its public web site) is "to promote effectively the goals of maximum employment, stable prices and moderate long-term interest rates." They do this by a combination of the following, from time to time: increasing or lowering government spending; increasing or lowering government borrowing; changing the rate at which the government loans or borrows money; manipulation of exchange rates; taxation or tax breaks on imports or exports of capital into a country; raising or lowering bank reserve requirements; and regulation or prohibition of private currencies. As one can readily discern, none of these actions is consistent with a transparent, free market financial system. The tools of the Fed's trade then, are non-transparent actions of purely discretionary quasi-governmental intervention and manipulation, albeit ostensibly to serve legitimate social and political objectives; but in reality, without any public accountability, creating massive political risk threatening, by its very definition, to a strong foundation for systemic financial stability and safety and soundness of that system in a democratic civil society.

The Fed's organizational mission then, is not as expressed in its public statements. It is fundamentally circumscribed. As the Fed constantly reminds us and as we have seen in this current crisis, the Fed does not appear to have any specific organizationally founded tools to combat an excess of systemic financial risk. It does however claim the mandate, confirmed by legislation subsequent to its organization, that it can fulfill only by the introduction of broadly disseminated financial transparency, reporting the factual information necessary for market participants to understand the effects of its actions and actions of congress, the federal financial regulatory agencies and the Wall Street banks on the publics' reasonable expectation of a system of money that provides an honest, safe, sound and stable medium of exchange, unit of account, store of value and standard for deferred payment.

In fact, although control of systemic financial risk is not an organizational mission of the Fed, it does publicly represent that to be a material component of its mission on its official web site as:

> ... *supervising and regulating banking institutions to ensure the safety and soundness of the nation's banking and financial system and to protect the credit rights of consumers; maintaining the stability of the financial system and containing systemic risk that may arise in financial markets* (Authors' emphasis added in italics)

As the standard bearer for front line operational responsibility for our financial system—our central bank—the Fed is the first among all other parties culpable for our financial crises, apart from congress, creator of the Fed. Contrary to periodic calls to abolish the Fed—apparently congress has not seen fit to clarify the Fed's mission so that it cannot pretend it does not have the job of regulating the value of money, and, if it actually had that job, that it has the tools to do the job. Congress pretends it has dumped responsibility for systemic risk on the Fed. The Fed pretends that it does not have authority to meet that responsibility; but at the same time represents that it does.

The Fed does not call Congress out on the question because, theoretically, it is responsible to Congress. Both parties seem to find useful cover in the opacity and conflict. Neither institution has credibly proposed to clarify the line of authority, responsibility and accountability from congress and its committees to the Fed; from the Fed to the federal financial regulators; and from those financial regulators to the Wall Street banks.

Despite the Fed's statutorily limited role and correspondingly limited powers and tools to achieve specific but amorphous political and social objectives, the Fed purports to exercise an assumed power and claims to fulfill a largely undefined duty to assure bank safety and soundness, protect credit rights of consumers, maintain the stability of the financial system and contain systemic financial risk. All of the federal financial regulatory authorities, in one way or another, purport to have the same mission,[490] while lacking specific powers, authority and tools to meet that mission, and without any straightforward provision for accountability to or justice for the American people that suffer from their failure. The American people, apparently, are expected to unquestioningly believe that these banking experts can, have and continue to meet their mission. The facts betray the experts on all counts.

[5] Reserves Redeemable in Gold under the Federal Reserve Act

Section 16. of *The Federal Reserve Act* provided that "Federal Reserve Notes, to be issued at the discretion of the Federal Reserve Board for the purpose of making advances to Federal Reserve Banks through the Federal Reserve agents as hereinafter set forth and for no other purpose, are hereby authorized. The said notes shall be obligations of the United States and shall be receivable by all national and member banks and Federal Reserve banks and for all taxes, customs, and other public dues. They shall be redeemed in gold on demand at the Treasury Department of the United States, in the city of Washington . . . or in gold or lawful money at any Federal Reserve Bank."

[6] Reserves Redeemable in Gold Reduced to a "Fraction" of Deposits

Section 16. of *The Federal Reserve Act* was amended to provide that "Every Federal reserve bank shall maintain reserves in gold or lawful money of not less than thirty-five per centum against its deposits and reserves in gold of not less than forty per centum against its Federal reserve notes in actual circulation, and not offset by gold or lawful money deposited with the Federal reserve agent...."

[7] Reserves No Longer Redeemable in Gold

From 1913 until 1933 there remained a partial discipline of redeem-ability of the Federal Reserve Notes issued by the Board of Governors of the Federal Reserve to the Regional Federal Reserve Banks. Reserves are no longer required to be in gold, but only "lawful money," which has been determined by the United States Treasury to be simply Federal Reserve Notes, not redeemable in constitutional coined money, the value of which has been regulated by Congress.[491]

[8] Reserves No Longer Established by Law and Effectively Reduced to Zero

The determination of reserves is no longer specifically determined by law but by solely by the discretion of the Fed pursuant to 12 U.S.C. § 461. "Banks typically have 3% of their assets in cash in order to meet customer needs. Since 1960, banks have been allowed to use this "vault cash" to satisfy their reserve requirements. Today, bank reserve requirements have fallen to the point where they are now exceeded by vault cash, which means lowering reserve requirements to zero would have virtually no impact on the banking system. US banks are already operating free of any reserve constraints. The following graph shows reserve requirements falling to zero over the last fifty years. Federal Reserve Notes are no longer redeemable by specie; only by other Federal Reserve Notes:[492]

Figure 6.1 Required Reserves Minus Vault Cash (As Adjusted for Inflation)

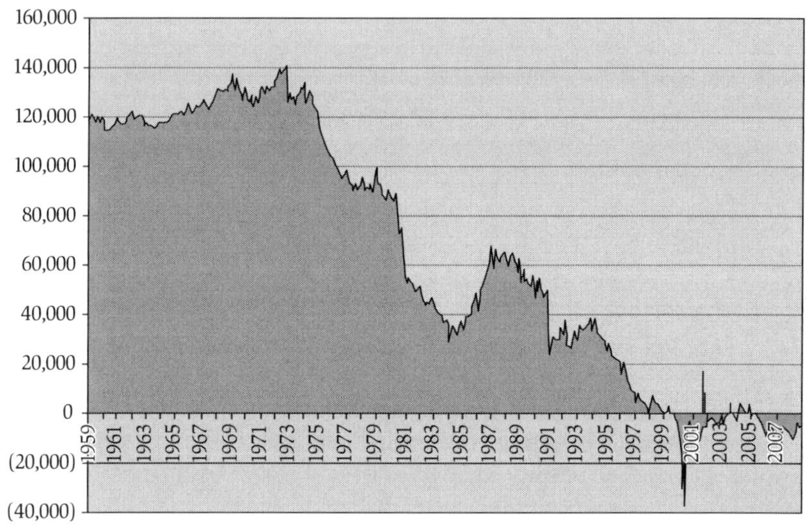

12 U.S.C.A. § 225a, effective December 27, 2000, amending *The Federal Reserve Act*, now requires the Fed to maintain long run growth of monetary and credit aggregates: "The Board of Governors of the Federal Reserve System and the Federal Open Market Committee shall maintain long run growth of the monetary and credit aggregates commensurate with the economy's long run potential to increase production, so as to promote effectively the goals of maximum employment, stable prices, and moderate long-term interest rates."

[9] The Federal Reserve Act: Too Vague and Nebulous to Enforce

Arguments have been made that the Fed's obligations under official regulations created by *The Federal Reserve Act*, as amended, are reasonable in a regulatory context, but far too vague and nebulous to be used outside the regulatory context for which it was intended.

The vague and nebulous argument does apply to the Fed's general statutory objectives. As noted earlier, and now worth repeating: "[t]he Federal Reserve exercises unprecedented breadth and depth of power over money despite the fact that its official mission is quite limited: "The Federal Reserve Act provides that the Board of Governors and the Federal Reserve Open Market Committee seek: 'to promote effectively the goals of maximum employment, stable prices, and moderate long-term interest rates.'" "Indeed courts have held that the speculative nature of the issues involved precludes litigation over whether the FOMC's policies are actually responsible for the country's economic conditions—that is, the FRS's effects on the economy are not provable according to the laws of evidence."[493]

"In our view, 'the links in the chain of causation between the [alleged constitutional violations] and the asserted injury [general inflation resulting from Fed exercise of monetary power] are far too weak for the chain as a whole to sustain [the appellants'] standing.' It is entirely speculative whether the influence of the Reserve Bank members is responsible for the FOMC's alleged pursuit of restrictive or erratic monetary policies. Moreover, in light of the complexity of the modern economy, it is also highly uncertain whether and to what extent such policies were responsible for the adverse economic conditions that allegedly resulted in harm to the appellants. Similarly, the appellants have given no indication as to how they can succeed in establishing that an overly broad delegation of power to the Federal Reserve System has had the consequence of undermining economic certainty and thereby increasing interest rates. Such general assertions are clearly inadequate to meet the constitutional requirement that parties allege specific facts sufficient to establish that their injuries are fairly traceable to the alleged violations. We think that courts lack both the competence and the authority to determine such abstract issues, which are better addressed through political and economic debate over the role of monetary policy in the national economy."[494]

Also, as I observed earlier, contrary to the holdings of the DC Court in Committee for Monetary Reform v. Board of Governors of the Federal Reserve System, the case made in this book is not to be prosecuted to remedy "restrictive or erratic" Fed monetary policies. It is important to recall this fact:

- This case is not asserted to essentially deal with a "broad, remedial social legislation" that is exercised and enforced by Congress or regulatory agencies. To the extent the case involves constitutional questions raised by existing legislation and regulatory structure, it nonetheless presents issues that must properly by addressed in the American judicial system.
- The case made in this book establishes in detail the duties and responsibilities of the culpable parties based upon specific official government reports over a period of specific action taken by the culpable parties.
- This book, the resources cited herein, including official government reports, together with expert testimony by nationally recognized experts, many of whom have been relied on by the Washington and Wall Street for their own purposes, provide specific facts sufficient to establish that the damages suffered by the American public are "fairly traceable to the alleged violations" by the culpable parties of the *United States Constitution*, federal statutory law and common law going back to the *Magna Charta*.
- The case made in this book does not constitute an assertion of an abstract principle of political or economic debate, but it is rather the assertion of specific, well-defined and well-supported claims made by Americans for enforcement by the judicial branch of the of United States government of the American rule of law. The fact that enforcement of the law by the judicial

system, dedicated to enforcement of the rule of the American rule of law, may subsequently lead to political controversy and debate over economic and monetary policies made by Congress, the Executive branch of government, including the federal financial regulators, and the Federal Reserve System, a quasi-governmental entity, as well as the Wall Street banks and other members of the Federal Reserve system, is entirely reasonable and to be expected and is one objective of such as case. Politics and the making and conduct of economic and monetary policies must, however, be made by the judicial system to be subject to the American rule of law. American political, economic and monetary policies activities are not exempt from the requirements of the *United States Constitution* or of applicable federal statutory law and common law.

- Edmund Vieira further pertinently observes that "if these matters are actually beyond rational investigation in a court of law, then the benchmarks the statutes set out cannot be classified as legal standards capable of controlling the actions of government agencies."[495]
- The false narrative that power and duty to regulate the value of money has been delegated by the American people to Congress, by Congress to the Fed and by the Fed to the Wall Street banks is not subject to the same "too vague and nebulous" argument. Regulation of the value of money and credit is central to the concepts of honesty, safety and soundness which lie at the heart of all national bank regulation and imposes the fiduciary duty on all parties in that chain of responsibility to protect the public interest in integrity of the American monetary, banking, financial and economic system.

As purportedly enlightened self-regulators, Washington and Wall Street sold out the public interest for private profit at public expense. The failure of the banks to adequately regulate the value of credit—money, and its liquidity is amply supported by specific evidence of specific failures in the official *The Financial Crisis Inquiry Report* (January 2011).

Testimony in debate over *The Federal Reserve Act* included statements such as the observation by Senator Reed that "the government can say whether it will issue money to the Federal Reserve Bank, but the money is never issued until [private] banker[s] … believe [] the business of the country to be such as to warrant its issuance"—and a system in which, overall, it is [We the People's] money and … credit which is to granted to secure … accommodation[s] for private bankers to pursue private profits."[496]

Senator Work observed that "… Instead of taking away any part of the vast power for evil, now resting in the banks, [the bill] increases that power.… It affords no protection to the public interests but adds to the power of the banks. It assumes to control the banks it creates through the Federal Reserve Board. That board will have just about as much control over the practical daily business of the regional banks as the man in the moon. …. [The bill] provides for bankers banks, not peoples banks or government banks." "Senator Clapp concurred: 'I am very much inclined to believe that the men who have controlled the great credit system of this country have used their power in their own interest against the public ...."[497]

Finally, Senator Borah addressed the important question: ".... [W]ho—the government or private banks—actually controls the emission of Federal Reserve Notes, and what significance the locus of control has.... The government itself has no power to put into circulation any currency unless the banks say that ... they need the currency... [I]n the power to issue those notes lies the power to inflate or contract the currency of the country to a very marked degree .... I think the power lies here for the banks of this country to contract or inflate the currency almost at will."[498]

The Board of Governors of the Federal Reserve System has represented to the American people and to the world that Congress has delegated to it the power to create money through the Federal Reserve System and that it holds the responsibility to regulate the value of money so created through the ephemeral, and as it happens, fraudulently accomplished, purported "association of loans with "value provided by individuals and business."

[10] What the Fed Does Not Do

The Federal Reserve System was not established to act in any congressionally mandated role to "coin money and regulate the value thereof in accordance with any congressionally mandated standard of value."

The stated purpose of *The Federal Reserve Act* was to "furnish an elastic currency, to afford means of rediscounting commercial paper, to establish a more effective supervision of banking in the United States, and for other purposes."

Although the Federal Reserve Board has represented from time to time, in writing, that it exercises its powers under a delegation to it by congress of the congressional mandate to "coin money and regulate its value," there is no evidence of any such congressional legislative delegation of such power and duty. Because the Federal Reserve System does not have the express legal legislative power to "coin money and regulate the value thereof" and because its express legal, legislative mandate, duty and power is to act, primarily through money and market creation through credit expansion, interest rate manipulation and open market purchases of, now, assets of every stripe, for the limited purpose of effecting non-pecuniary social and political objectives, its entire existence and actions subvert and are directly opposed and antithetical to the constitutional congressional power and duty to coin and regulate the value of money in accordance with a defined, effective standard of value that ensures the equal protection for each individual's creation, preservation and protection of the value of the fruits of his or her labor, property and ability to participate in the American market economy on a fair, and equal basis under the American rule of law. Although the legal exercise by Congress of its constitutional power and duty to regulate the value of money is a necessary condition for the Federal Reserve System and the national banking system to legitimately fulfill their respective statutory mandates; to the extent that they themselves impact the creation of money and regulation of its value without being subject to a legitimate constitutional standard of value, their policies and actions, most dramatically following the Great Depression, followed by the Nixon shock and continuing until today, are *directly antithetical and opposed to their respective official, legislative, social and political mandates.* As a matter of constitutional law, the existence, roles and actions of the Federal Reserve System and the national banking system are, and must be made specifically and unequivocally subject and subordinate to the constitutional mandate for Congress to exercise the power and duty delegated to it by the people to create and regulate the value of money in accordance with a legitimate, expressly defined and legitimate standard of value.

The pursuit by the Fed of its stated legislative mission at once has been shown to be largely ineffective and, in fact, has frustrated and rendered literally impossible the ability of the Fed or any federal financial regulatory authority to meet their "assumed mission" of meeting the constitutional imperative for Congress to coin and regulate the value of money.

Admittedly, re-establishment of a proper constitutional mechanism for the creation and regulation of the value of money that provides the people with equal protection for each individual's creation, preservation and protection of the value of the fruits of his or her labor, property and ability to participate in the American market economy on a fair, and equal basis under the American rule of law would, and should dramatically limit the scope of the ability of the Federal Reserve System and the national banking system to continue business as usual: fleecing of American people by the Washington and Wall Street criminal, corrupt, racketeering enterprise, while paying mere lip service to the legal, economic, social and political objects that are the foundation for their respective legal existence.

The Fed purports to provide financial services to depository institutions, the US government, and foreign official institutions, including playing a major role in operating the nation's payments system. The integrity of the nation's payments system is grounded in liquidity. By despoiling the payments system with shadow banking money equivalents created through structured finance, the Fed abrogated its responsibility and choked off payment system liquidity with unconstitutional money. The processes the Fed has adopted are in fact ephemeral.

Ephemeral or not—to the extent Congress' and the Fed's goals can be met in accordance with the requirements of the *Constitution* by meeting the duties prescribed under Article 1, § 8, Clause 5 "To coin Money, regulate the Value thereof, and of foreign Coin, and fix the Standard of Weights and Measures"—Congress and its creature, the Fed and its member Wall Street banks, have continuously conspicuously failed the American public ever since the inception of the Fed.

§6.05 FINANCIAL CRISIS IN 1929: END OF THE DOMESTIC GOLD STANDARD IN 1933—*THE PECORA REPORT – GLASS STEAGALL* – THE SEC, THE FDIC, AND MONEY

[A] Another Financial Crisis: Another Report

So much has been written on the subject of the Great Depression that one might confidently conclude that any reader of this work must have great familiarity with America's greatest, most infamous financial crisis. The facts, circumstances, legislation and conventional assessment of the judicial decisions leading to the Great Depression, as well as the legislation enacted in response to it are detailed in the *Pecora Report—Final June 6* (calendar day, June 16), 1934.[499] The *Pecora Report* details a recurrence of the same fundamental concerns expressed in the *Pujo Report, supra*:

> In the field of banking, three major principles have been dealt with in recent legislation, namely, the separation of monetary policy from banking, the creation of deposit insurance, and the separation of investment banking and the securities business from commercial banking. The *Pujo Report* distinguishes between investment companies and holding companies. Today the historic functions of investment companies and bank holding companies have again merged in the structure of the Wall Street banks. There remain for our immediate consideration, however, vital matters relating to the conduct and management of banking institutions, such as truthful and adequate financial statements, nature and diversification of loans and security, proper banking reserves, trust functions of banks, effective governmental examination of banks, employment of bank examiners, window dressing activities of banking officers, and other similar problems.
>
> Investment trusts conducted in accordance with the underlying principles responsible for their creation, diversification of investments with the view to investment return rather than capital appreciation may have a place in our investment system. The facility of perverted uses of these companies requires that these trusts be circumscribed with protective safeguards. The record indicates that it may be necessary to simplify the capital structure of investment trusts to prevent the organizers from usurping control and a disproportionate part of the equity and yield of these trusts; to limit and prescribe the concentration of securities in a particular industry; to prevent the diversion of these trusts from their normal channels of diversified investments to the abnormal avenues of control of industry; to prohibit pyramiding of investment trusts; to completely divorce investment trusts from investment banking; to eliminate the conflict of interest between investment managers and the public; to compel full and complete disclosure of the organization, capital structure, and management of the conduct of investment trusts.
>
> The magnitude of a corporation is no justification for its existence or propagation, nor reason for its abolition or curtailment. The determinative factor is social and economic utility. Holding companies serving no productive function but organized merely to pervert the use of controlled companies and to evade their legal limitations, are detrimental to the public welfare. Holding companies are a major problem meriting immediate consideration and action.
>
> Window dressing in financial reporting [by gaming accounting and banking rules and regulations] abuses of the interrelationships between and amongst commercial banking and investment banking, creation of unsafe and unsound

> banking and investment structures and practices, all fed by excessive compensation structures for bankers and excessive control by bankers over and concentrations of wealth have been a driver in every financial crisis experienced by this nation.[500]

[B] The *Pecora Report*

Primary issues addressed in the *Pecora Report*:

- Separation of monetary policy from banking;
- Separation of investment banking and the securities business;
- Truthful and adequate financial statements;
- Nature and diversification of loans and security;
- Proper banking reserves; abuses of group banking; abuses of bank investment affiliates;
- Violation of fiduciary trust functions of banks;
- Bank circumvention of the law;
- Ineffective governmental examination of banks;
- Income tax avoidance;
- Excessive profits to organizers;
- Excess concentration of control of wealth;
- Window dressing and false reports; and
- Other similar problems.

Once again, the litany of offending institutions perpetrating abuses of the American financial system includes predecessors of the Wall Street Banks, including J P Morgan & Co., Kuhn Loeb & Co., National City Co., National City Bank, Chase Securities Corporation and Dillon Read & Co., among others.

Notwithstanding the reports produced in the wake of our national series of great financial crises, Washington and Wall Street have assiduously ignored the historical findings and lessons studied and articulated as a result of repeated financial and economic crises and consequent investigations and reports, Washington and Wall Street have continued to perpetuate unconstitutional and tortious program of intentional money debasement in a quest for an ever more expansive vision of the American Dream, based on full employment and low interest rates. The great financial and economic crisis has not produced any semblance of the American Dream for the American people in this case. Washington and Wall Street have, however, successfully pursued their own Washington and Wall Street Dream of insatiable concentration of wealth and power Washington's and Wall Street's precipitation of this crisis has damaged the American public in the minimum amount of $20 trillion. Congress, the federal financial regulators and the "self-regulating" Wall Street banks have demonstrated repeatedly that they cannot be trusted to protect the American public's civil right to an honest, safe, sound, and transparent banking, financial and economic system.

[C] Congress' 1933 Repudiation of the Exercise of Its Constitutional Power and Duty to Coin Money and Regulate Its Value

Here's the Bill. Let's pass it. After a few minutes of debate and no amendments, it was passed.

The *Emergency Banking Act* was introduced on March 9, 1933, passed the same day and signed into law. Congressman Henry B. Steagall reportedly walked into the House chamber with the text of the legislation newly transmitted from the White House and waiving it in the air said "here's the bill. Let's pass it."[501]

After a few minutes of debate and no amendments it was passed, and the Senate soon followed suit. The first section of the law simply endorsed all the executive orders given by the President or Secretary of the Treasury since March 4. The law gave FDR the power to confiscate gold, seize banks, and impose currency controls. It also authorized the Treasury to issue $2 billion in new greenback paper dollars that were not convertible and instead were secured by the private assets of the US banking system.[502]

As in the case of the financial rescue of 2008, which was financed with trillions of dollars' worth of monetary expansion by the Fed, in the 1930s, elected officials were unwilling to raise taxes to pay the nation's bills. The economic emergency of the Great Depression gave our leaders sufficient political cover to disregard past precedents and established rules, and to print money with a level of recklessness that only a few years earlier would have ensured their political destruction.[503] Christopher Whalen observes, quoting Herbert Hoover, that "if the number of inches in the yardstick were lessened then there would be more cloth in the bolt."[504] FDR believed that by merely changing the dollar price of gold upward, the government would gain a "profit" of some $2 billion measured in greenback dollars. "Carter Glass immediately saw through the canard. 'That isn't a "profit" as you call it—it is nothing more than a bookkeeping markup.'"[505]

On June 5, 1933,[506] congress officially suspended the gold standard, abandoning any pretense to the regulation of the value of money; expressing its intent through an oxymoron: "To assure uniform value to the coins and currencies of the Unites States...." in other words, to regulate the value of US currency by ceasing to regulate the value of the US currency. The effect of this legislation was to strip the currency of any reference to external value and to thereby abandon the constitutional imperative to regulate the value of US money.

The Banking Act of 1935 completed the transition of the Fed from an institution that at least nominally paid homage to the gold standard and an asset-based currency, to one that was entirely devoted to a fiat currency that was not convertible into anything. Christopher Whalen, quoting Jane D'Arista in *The Evolution of U.S. Finance: Federal Reserve Monetary Policy, 1915-1935*:

> "Currently the American monetary system is composed of a series of procedures based on statutes and statutes based on procedures, which reflect no integral concept of money but, rather a series of residual concepts. Since at no point is any concept of money firmly repudiated, the system may be said to accommodate a process among alternatives. It preserves the procedural framework of an asset

currency system but in reality, is closer to fiat money." D'Arista writes that like *The Federal Reserve Act in 1913, The Banking Act of 1935* is silent on monetary policy and gives no guidance as to what metrics the Fed will use to judge the effect of its policy actions." This remains true today, when we cannot determine the amount of money in the financial system or regulate its value by reference to any stable external control, any representation by the Fed of the effects of its policies is inherently and intentionally a deceit, a lie, an intentional misrepresentation—a fraud on the American public—since there are no metrics for regulation of the value of the money used to measure the effects of its policies.[507]

In a 1937 book by Bernard J. Reis and John Flynn, *False Security: The Betrayal of the American Investor,* the authors chronicle "a financial zoological tour of structured financial instruments that could have come out of Wall Street in the late 2000s, but in fact were being sold in the period after WW I, a decade and more before the 1929 Wall Street Crash. Under the heading of investments, the public believed to be 'guilt edged'. Reis and Flynn take the reader through a dizzying collection of guaranteed mortgages, foreign bonds, investment trusts and real estate bonds. All manner of debt was in use during the 1920s and much of the apparent prosperity during the period resulted from the issuance of the debt. As had been the case during WW I, borrowing was employed by many Americans to enable all sorts of activity, from consumption to speculation, and the nations of Europe likewise continued to borrow in the United States to fund exports." The authors conveyed the bitterness and anger felt by many Americans in the 1930s in a comment at the end of their book:

> Simply stated, honesty plays little part in American business. Our morality, on the contrary, in a game of cards or in sports is irreproachable. And so it is that we are gentlemen of honor when engaged in life's pastimes, but devoid of it when engaged in serious pursuits. The public has a subconscious awareness of this state of immorality, but for some reason remains apathetic to it, and even condones it. True, a simple criminal act is condemned (and when simple it is invariably of small dimensions) but where large profits have accrued or an enormous institution erected on no matter how fraudulent a foundation we give it respect and applause.
>
> The authors found that of the $10 billion or so of mortgage-backed securities issued during the period, some $8 billion or original face amount were in default by the early 1930s when Congress launched various inquiries into the practices of Wall Street.[508]

The important point to take away from this period is that the very same type of mortgage-backed securities that caused the financial crisis of 2008 were actually first conceived and sold to the public a century earlier—and by many of the same banks and financial institutions—and to the same ultimate effect—financial crisis.

With the Civil War, WW I and WW II, and the Cold War, American used debt to finance military expenditures rather than carry the burden through increased taxation. This was not such a great evil after WW II since in absolute terms the level of military expenditure remained stable even as the overall economy expanded. The problem came several decades later, when non-military discretionary expenditures were likewise funded with federal debt, necessitating an expansion of the currency by the Fed. In that sense, not a great deal has changed since President Lincoln saved the Union and emancipated the slaves with a Grand Army financed with greenback dollars. The scale of the enterprise and the rate of erosion of the real value of the dollar have simply increased.[509]

More than pleasing the vanities of economists, an independent central bank that protects the value of money is the ultimate consumer protection agency.[510]

Once upon a time—specifically, between *The National Banking Act of 1863* and *The Banking Act of 1935*—the impairment or bankruptcy of a nationally chartered bank triggered a capital call. Not on the taxpayers, but on the stockholders. It was their bank, after all. Individual accountability in banking was the rule in the advanced economies. Hartley Withers, an editor of *The Economist* in the early 20th century, shook his head at the micromanagement of American banks by the Office of the Comptroller of the Currency—25 percent of their deposits had to be kept in cash, i.e., gold or money lawfully convertible into gold. The rules held. Yet New York had panics, London had none. Adjured Withers: "Good banking is produced not by good laws but by good bankers."[511]

The Federal Reserve System policy of self-regulation granted to its member banks: partners in the implementation of monetary policy and emission of money into the nation's banking and financial system, ceded and abandoned to those powerful banks enormous, unchecked and usurped unconstitutional power.

The systemically important, too big fail, too big to jail, too big to challenge Wall Street banks accepted and fully exploited and abused that usurped the trust and power over which they held sway, leading directly to the 2008 financial crisis and the trillions of dollars of damage to ordinary Americans.

[D] The Great Depression and World War II

The final unleashing of the process of money debasement leading inexorably to the subversion and ultimate destruction of honest money began during the Civil War as a matter of the financing of the winning of the war and to assure the continued existence of the country. Money debasement became progressively more damaging through each subsequent financial crisis brought on by continued chronic exploitation of the ordinary American people by Washington and the newly created national banking system; then overwhelmingly, with the establishment of the Federal Reserve System in 1913 that firmly entrenched fractional reserve banking and an ongoing iniquitous partnership—a criminally corrupt racketeering enterprise—between Washington and Wall Street. The enterprise that culminated when first, President Franklin Roosevelt, followed by a compliant Congress tagging along to do anything to avoid accountability for the Great Depression, that "just passed the bill" without reading, debating or deliberating over it or its likely effects. Washington and Wall Street thereby severed the existing connection between American money and a standard of value; and provided the rationale, however unconstitutional, for ignoring thereafter any attempt to congressionally, constitutionally, create money through the Federal Reserve and national banking systems, and for ignoring the constitutional imperative for Congress to regulate the value of money in accordance with an appropriate standard of value.

This remains true today, when ordinary Americans cannot determine the amount of money in the financial system or regulate its value by reference to any stable external control, any representation by the Fed of the effects of its policies is inherently and intentionally dishonest, an intentional misrepresentation—a fraud on the American public—since there are no metrics for regulation of the value of the money used to measure the effects of its policies.[512] Today's consensus, outside of Washington and Wall Street, is that the Fed has failed in its statutory mission, as is has failed in its corollary to maintain the honesty, safety and soundness of the banking and monetary system.[513] An honest, safe and sound monetary system and an honest, safe and sound banking system can only be successful based upon a foundation of honest money, the value of which has been constitutionally regulated by Congress by reference to a transparent, honest, effective, external standard of value.

Following a series of adjustments by Congress of the value of constitutional coined money following the Civil War, reflecting the continued explosion in creation of public and private credit and its increasing distance from: (1) trusted, known and creditable sources of repayment; and (2) mitigation of risk and uncertainty in prospects for liquidity through repayment when due, even under difficult and exigent economic times; thereby supporting trust and confidence in its transferability; Congress intentionally enabled this new money compounded credit excess, money debasement and concentration of wealth and power in Washington and Wall Street, to their benefit as well as the ultimate damage to and distress of the American public. In the face of the "emergency" presented by the Great Depression, and irrespective of the failures of the Federal Reserve, Wall Street and the national banking system to act in any meaningful way to regulate the value of money in accordance with an effective standard of value, Congress simply abandoned any semblance of the legal, constitutional exercise of its power and fulfilling its duty to coin money and regulate its value in *The Emergency Banking Act of 1933*, by completely and abruptly severing the ties and discipline of value of money through required redeemability of legal tender by constitutionally coined money, the value of which was regulated by Congress. There is no excuse for this abandonment. Its reasons are readily apparent: unconstrained greed, avarice and lust for power, topped off by political expedience, and protected by perverse and unjustified political doctrines of too big to fail and too big to jail.

[E] The *Gold Clause Cases*

The *Legal Tender Cases* and the *Gold Clause Cases*[514] briefly referred to earlier in this work, were all cases in contract, which only secondarily and sloppily touched on Congress' constitutional power and duty to regulate the value of money. The *Gold Clause Cases* are generally referred to together as standing for the proposition that Congress has unlimited power over matters of money. The holdings of the *Legal Tender Cases* and the *Gold Clause Cases* invalidated existing contract provisions that interfered with Congress' exercise of its power to regulate the value of money. Citing Veazi[515] the Court in the Norman Case confirmed that "[t]he authority to impose requirements of uniformity and parity is an essential feature of this control of the currency. The

Congress is authorized to provide 'a sound and uniform currency for the country,' and to 'secure the benefit of it to the people by appropriate legislation.'"[516] In other words, the *Legal Tender Cases* and the *Gold Clause Cases* confirm Congress' constitutional powers and duties with respect to maintaining honest, safe and sound money. The Court concluded that "[w]e think that it is clearly shown that these clauses interfere with the exertion of the power granted to the Congress, and certainly it is not established that the Congress arbitrarily or capriciously decided that such an interference existed."[517]

Professor Richard Timberlake, Professor (*Emeritus*) of economics and finance at the University of Georgia, quoting specifically from the Norman Case, expressed his take on the *Gold Clause Cases*, and commented as follows:

"The opinion of the Court's 5–4 majority stated that the primary and all-important issue 'is the power of Congress to establish a monetary system and the necessary implications of that power,' and 'to invalidate the provisions of existing contracts which interfere with the exercise of its constitutional authority' (294 U.S. 302). Chief Justice Charles Evans Hughes, who read the opinion, reviewed the *Legal Tender Cases* that had allowed Congress the power to make US notes (greenbacks) unqualified legal tender and granted it complete control over the monetary system.

"Hughes emphasized Congress's power 'To coin money and regulate the value thereof.' He held that 'the Court in the legal tender cases did not derive from that express grant [of power] alone the full authority of the Congress in relation to the currency. . . [but] in all the related powers conferred upon the Congress [that were] appropriate to achieve 'the great objects for which the government was framed—a national government with sovereign powers' (294 U.S. 303). Hughes here quoted and used without apology the argument of the infamous 1884 decision discussed above: 'The broad and comprehensive national authority over the subjects of revenue, finance and currency is derived from the aggregate of the powers granted to Congress.' The Congress is empowered, he quoted further from the *Juilliard* opinion, 'to issue the obligations of the United States in such form, and to impress upon them such qualities as currency for the payment of merchandise and the payment of debts, as accord with the usage of sovereign governments' (294 U.S. 304). Nothing in the *Constitution* implies any such power, nor does any statement suggest a possible inference leading to such a conclusion. Congress' monetary powers and duties and subject to the meaning of the words in Clause 5 of §8 Article II of the *Constitution* wherein it is granted and by the limitations of the Fifth and Fourteenth Amendments limiting Congress's ability to deprive Americans of their property rights without due process under and equal protection of the American rule of law.

"The majority opinion in 1935 simply treated these gross distortions of congressional power over money from the *Legal Tender Cases* as if they were quoted from the *Constitution* itself, and without re-examining the validity of the arguments. The majority opinion concluded: "We think that it is clearly shown that these [gold] clauses interfere with the exertion of the [monetary] power granted to the Congress"—that is, 'monetary powers' nowhere visible in the *Constitution* but conjured into existence by the Court decisions of 1871 and 1884 (294 U.S. 315–16).

"Therefore, Congress's Abrogation of the Gold Clauses stood. The creditors could be paid in any US currency that was legal tender, but they had no right to be paid in gold—gold clauses notwithstanding."[518]

Professor Timberlake, recently published *Constitutional Money—A Review of the Supreme Court's Monetary* Decisions.[519] Professor Timberlake's work follows on his earlier work and the work of others who have tread the same path.[520] Timberlake notes that the preceding works, by their nature, have limitations that inhibit their effectiveness. According to Timberlake, Bray Hammond's work showed "a misunderstanding of the Framers' monetary *Constitution* and its limits on the monetary powers of Congress," as well as "an uncritical acceptance of and apology for a central banking institution ... that is questionable." Gerald Dunne's work followed but did not question Hammond's analysis or assumptions." Although he "brought the monetary decisions of the Supreme Court into focus for the first time ... he was not an economist and he did not question the Court's authority or its clear violations of monetary precepts in the cases he reviewed." James Willard Hurst also was not an economist. His research was strictly limited to legal history. It lacks economic substance. Edwin Vieira's much acclaimed work also is largely limited to legal history and presented only "a limited account of the economic events and institutions of the times." Such has been the fate of most attempts to address the law of money in American. The analysis is limited. Connections to important related disciplines is weak to non-existent. Professor Timberlake's conclusions, like many other economists cited in this work, establish that there now exist many working alternatives to our present corrosive monetary system. Professor Timberlake's conclusion consists of "some suggestions for a constrained monetary system, including the possibility for the reinstitution of an authentic gold standard."

As is the case with Professor Timberlake's work, none of the other published works of lawyers, economists, philosophers or experts in other related disciplines that I have discovered have provided an analysis, historical context and examination of existence and foundation for specific legal actions that may be taken to force change and enforce the American law of money. Ordinary Americans are not impotent. America's current monetary system is grounded in abuse of trust and power, obscured by muddling dicta in the *Gold Clause Cases* ignoring the actual bases for the holdings in the *Legal Tender Cases*, to and thereby facilitate the ongoing and largely accepted American policy to facilitate of abuse of trust and power and lying, cheating and stealing. So far, we have simply suffered under this unconstitutional policy; accepting the status quo because we see no path to a viable alternative consistent with the American rule of law. The legal, accounting, economic and monetary experts in Washington and on Wall Street continue to maintain the status quo, even in the face of near continuous legal, banking and financial reform.

According to Professor Timberlake:

> [t]he Supreme Court's monetary decisions have become a casebook of primary material begging for examination and possible reinterpretation. While the decisions ... [reviewed by Professor Timberlake] are only a small fraction of the total judgments that the Court has rendered over this timespan, they have special

> importance in the economic world of markets because every transaction for goods, services, and capital also includes a sum of money.
>
> The Framers wrote the *Constitution* for the ages, and they provided for changes by means of a simple amendment procedure. Since the *Constitution* arranges for its own correction, it has no reason to be interpreted differently for different ages, social conditions, or other human circumstances. Judicial decisions that change the original meaning to fit some current social norm are illicit; they violate the substance of the document and destroy its reason for being.[521]

Professor Timberlake provides a very useful and detailed integration of the Supreme Court cases on the matter of money as well as an accompanying analysis of monetary policies and events. Timberlake concludes that the Federal Reserve System has interacted with the latter Supreme Court decisions to undermine the monetary protections provided by the *Constitution*; "and in so doing promoted continuous inflation and ongoing public uncertainty regarding the future (and one might say current) value of money (and one might include assets).[522]"

To say that the American law of money is well-settled and sound in the context presented by the current American monetary system is an oxymoron. The foundation of the American law of honest, safe and sound money is clear. Congress, the national banking system, the Federal Reserve System and the Supreme Court have managed to muddle the very clear law of money and manipulated the muddle to systematically debase American money for their self-interest through a classic Ponzi scheme implemented through a classic form of criminal corrupt racketeering enterprise.

Professor Timberlake provides a succinct statement of what should be obvious to any capable student of American monetary affairs. He suggests a possible structural remedy. What neither Professor Timberlake nor any other scholar of monetary law has done is prescribe a course of action; a legal case, by which the muddle may be cleared and Washington and Wall Street incentivized to restore an appreciation and the binding effect of the law of money on their policies and actions. The primary purpose of this work is to amplify the context of American monetary affairs and to prescribe the applicable legal remedies available to ordinary Americans as a class, as well as available to states attorney's general and the United States Department of Justice in the public interest.

Timberlake states that:

> "Settled and accepted US policy not only flouts the constitutional prohibition against fiat legal tender money—bills of credit—it also fails to provide any gold or silver money in any form. Courts of law will not even hear cases that would challenge the status quo. They throw out attempts to restore constitutional money as 'frivolous.' Somehow, between the time that the *Constitution* and the first ten Amendments were ratified, while the prohibited and the present, gold and silver money have disappeared, while the prohibited bills of credit—in this era, Federal Reserve Notes—have become conventional standard money. Congress and the Executive branch have often initiated the policies that that have reversed what once seemed to be eternal verities, while the Supreme Court decisions have sanctioned the changes and given them permanence.
>
> "This breach of explicit constitutional provisions, which appears illegal on its face, should have an excuse, or at least an explanation, intelligible to anyone and everyone. The present status of the monetary system seems, however, to have

been accepted at all levels—from the unschooled layman to the denizens of the Supreme Court—without serious argument, and without embarrassment at the obvious contradiction between what the *Constitution* specifies and what has come to exist today.[523]"

Professor Timberlake notes that the Supreme Court and the legal profession are understandably limited in their perspective to legal and political perspectives, while deferring to expert testimony from biased political and financial industry interests whose common objective is to maintain the status quo or to advance their self-interest. Timberlake does not condemn the judiciary for its failure to appreciate the historical, social, economic, and even the legal context for the nature and function of constitutional, safe, sound and honest sovereign money. He calls for inclusion of economic perspective in any subsequent money litigation, although he notes that such a project, might add credibility to future judgments and correct for posterity the mistaken judgments that are now part of accepted policy.

Professor Timberlake falls prey, however to the collective power of the web of accumulated false narratives spun by Washington and Wall Street, concluding that: "such a project may seem politically unrealistic," adding that "if no one suggests corrections to what has been handed down as the ultimate word from the court, manifestly incorrect or improper arguments become part of accepted law and endure forever."[524] He closes his work with the observation that his "review of the Supreme Court decisions on the monetary system does not suggest necessarily the re-establishment of a gold standard, but that some set of rules for monetary order be put in place—rules that remove hands-on 'guidance of human wisdom' from any control over the matter."[525]

Timberlake's excellent analysis, like that of most of the authors referred to in this work who have addressed the web of factors that lead to financial crises, accomplish several things:

- Chronicle the economic and monetary distortions that cause financial crises.
- Acknowledge that the American law of money as presently understood it literally unintelligible.
- Call for monetary reform to address the economic, monetary, legal and accounting that define and give substance to the American law of money.

Their work begs the question what action can and should be taken, under the American rule of law to make effective change? Leaving the most important question of all. What action can ordinary Americans take to provide meaningful incentives to the experts to return to ordinary Americans their just, constitutional civil right to honest, safe, and sound sovereign money and appropriate legal constraints on shadow money and shadow banking to protect the financial stability, safety and soundness of our economic and financial system?

The social, economic, financial and legal failures chronicled by academia can only be redressed and meaningful reforms made by compulsion conducted under the American rule of law. The web of false narratives clouding the issues has defeated any meaningful approach to voluntary action in the public interest. Compelling action based on the lessons of history in every sphere of thought governing the making and use of money can be enforced only by those to whom the power and duty act have been lawfully delegated, and in the face of their failure to act, by the people themselves, taken under the very laws designed for their protection. Successful and meaningful action can be taken only by explicating who amongst the American people have:

- the legal duty to act to create and maintain safe sound and honest American money;
- the power to act;
- the right and power to complain breach of the duty to so act; and who
- are entitled to redress from breach of that duty to act.

If those who have the legal and practical duty to act to assure the American people of a safe, sound and honest monetary financial and economic system, based on the foundation and framework of safe, sound, and honest sovereign money as required by law, will not act, the people must act under some iteration of the case made in this book, addressing and debunking the false narratives woven by Washington and Wall Street to obstruct their accountability and providing the entire foundation for the case with such thoroughness that the United States Supreme Court no longer has a place to hide from or escape their duty to enforce the plain language of American law, including the *Constitution* and cases they have decided that bear on their responsibility.

I must emphasize that a finding that congress had complete control over the monetary system and could make any paper money full legal tender, does not relieve congress of its constitutional duty to regulate the value of money so that, in the Courts own words, Congress thereby provides "a sound and uniform currency for the country," and ... "secure[s] the benefit of it to the people by appropriate legislation."[526] A currency so established by congress, the value of which is regulated by reference to an appropriate and effective external standard would in fact constitute honest money. That is Congress' constitutional duty. That duty is, in fact, confirmed by the *Legal Tender Cases* and the *Gold Clause Cases*. Since the Nixon shock in 1971, Congress has failed in its duty. That failure has been assiduously exploited by the Washington Wall Street criminal corrupt racketeering enterprise in their own interest, directly opposed to the public interest, by abusing the power and trust reposed in them by the American citizens lying to cheating and stealing from ordinary Americans through intentional money debasement.

§6.06 THE NIXON SHOCK AND THE OIL CRISIS

[A] Nixon and OPEC

The American oil crisis followed immediately from OPEC's actions in response to and as a direct result of President Richard M. Nixon's August 15, 1971 decision to close the gold window and abrogate the *Bretton Woods Accords*. Five weeks after the Nixon shock of August 15, 1971 OPEC met in extraordinary session in Beirut and passed its *OPEC Resolution XXV.140*, which reads:

> The Conference,
>
> Having considered the report of the Secretary General concerning the recent international monetary developments and their adverse effect on the purchasing power of the oil revenues of Member Countries;
>
> Noting that these developments have resulted in a de facto devaluation of the United States dollar, the currency in which posted prices are established, vis-a-vis the currencies of the major industrialized countries;
>
> Recalling Resolution XXI.122 which calls, inter alia, for adjustment in posted or tax-reference prices so as to offset any adverse effect resulting from de facto or de jure changes in the parity of monies of major industrialized countries:
>
> Resolves:
>
> 1. that Member Countries shall *take necessary action and/or shall establish negotiations, individually or in groups, with the oil companies with a view to adopting ways and means to offset any adverse effects on the per barrel real income of Member Countries resulting from the international monetary developments as of 15th August, 1971.* (Authors' emphasis added in italics)
> 2. that the results of negotiations shall be submitted to the next Conference. In case such negotiations fail to achieve their purpose, the Conference shall determine such action as necessary for the implementation of this Resolution.

"Such action as necessary," at least in my suspicion, included the 1973 Arab-Israeli War; the immediate impetus for the boost in oil prices. As their 1971 declaration shows, the sheiks of OPEC understood the implications of the closing of the gold window far better than the Western elites. The severing of the dollar's link to gold meant a great inflation was coming, despite of the US government's suppression of that inflation by wage and price controls to get past the 1972 election.[527]

A handful of economists understood what was taking place but could get no one to listen. Robert Triffin of Yale warned prior to 1971 that the huge accumulation of international reserves made a world-wide inflation inevitable. Under the Bretton Woods arrangements, the Federal Reserve in effect served as a world central bank, creating dollars that served as reserves for other banking systems. Its creation of reserves was in theory limited by a $35 gold price, and for a brief period the public could actually redeem gold at this price through the London Gold Pool. But the Gold Pool was dissolved in 1969, and the Fed would redeem gold only from other central banks, who were discouraged from presenting claims. So dollars created in financing the Vietnam War accumulated abroad. Finally, the Bank of England asked that its dollar holdings be protected against a devaluation of the dollar. This was taken as a demand for gold and led directly to the August 15, 1971 meeting, adoption of wage and price controls and the rest of the NEP. Again, the correct answer would be to keep the gold link but change the price, increasing it to provide the liquidity the world economy needed. This was in fact suggested by Jacques Rueff, but rejected by American elites because it would benefit France, which held large gold stocks, and South Africa, which produced gold.

Instead, US policymakers in the 1970s reversed the mistake of their counterparts of the 1920s. Where the latter had imposed a deflation, the former unleashed an inflation. Inflation of course always creates winners and losers. In this case, the Arab sheiks were clever enough to get to the head of the line, ensuring that they were the winners.

In the US, the results of this were wondrous to behold. The conventional wisdom declared an "energy crisis," deciding that its problem was that the earth's crust was running out of hydrocarbons. The US Department of Energy was created to provide better central planning than the oil companies could. The President of the United States blamed it all on "malaise" among the public. "The erosion of confidence in the future is threatening to destroy the social and political fabric of America," he told the public. His proposed answer was a six-point energy program, including quotas on imports, subsidies for oil shale and gasohol and standby gasoline rationing.

In December 1971 as part of a general revaluation of major currencies, devaluations were henceforth allowed 2.25 percent from the agreed exchange rate. But even the more flexible official rates could not be defended against the speculators. By March 1976, all the major currencies were floating—in other words, exchange rates were no longer the principal method used by governments to administer monetary policy. Gold became a floating asset. In 1971, it reached $44.20 per ounce; in 1972, $70.30 per ounce and still climbing. By 1972, currencies began abandoning even this devalued peg against the dollar, though it took a decade for all industrialized nations to do so.

In February 1973, the Bretton Woods currency exchange markets closed, after a last-gasp devaluation of the dollar to $44 per ounce, and reopened in March in a floating currency regime. Economic freedom seemed in tatters and political freedom seemed in danger. In 1980, the Western economic system seemed to have broken down. In that year, inflation ran at 13.5 percent measured by the consumer price index. A brief recession dawned, and unemployment averaged 7.1 percent. The prime rate reached a record 21.5 percent. Gold has recently traded at over $1,500 per ounce; oil has traded at over $140.00 per barrel. Prices continue to vacillate widely because the relative value of all trading currency denominations vary, with not one anchored to an external standard of value. The relative strength or weakness of different global currencies and the trading assets in which their value is denominated has been reduced to a guessing game, based on political propaganda and media spin.

Two key events in the re-emergence of these financial disturbances after almost three decades of stability were the 1971 decision by the United States to end the dollar peg to gold entirely and the re-emergence of sovereign borrowing to fund balance of payments deficits. In the case of the United States, funding external deficits did not require traditional borrowing because the government could simply finance these short falls via government debt and monetary expansion. The world did business in US dollars—a uniquely American convenience.[528] Other nations were not so fortunate. As two researchers at the Federal Reserve Bank of New York observed in 1998: "The current account deficit allows the United States to maintain a higher rate of investment spending than would be possible by relying on domestically generated savings alone. However, the corresponding foreign capital inflow is essentially a loan; therefore, it represents claims on future national income."[529]

Unusually, the decision to close the gold window was made without consulting members of congress, the international monetary system or even Nixon's own State Department, and was soon dubbed the "Nixon shock." As the crisis progressed,

President Nixon met with Treasury Secretary Connally and Office of Management and Budget Director George Shultz on August 2, 1971 to map out next steps. Tapes of their conversations on August 2 reveal Connally as the primary architect of the essential elements in the New Economic Policy (NEP) the President would announce on August 15. The State Department and the National Security Council were not represented at Camp David where, according to Kissinger, "a decision of major foreign policy importance had been taken about which neither the Secretary of State nor the national security adviser had been consulted." At no time was Congress or the Fed involved, nor did either respond to this policy statement that drove directly to the heart of Congress' constitutional responsibility to "to coin money" and "regulate the value thereof."

The Nixon shock represented a milestone in American economic development, where deficit spending was explicitly embraced to maximize employment even though the economy was not in recession or the nation at war. Nixon's final repudiation of gold and his explicit embrace of deficit spending to ensure full employment was a radical departure from the stated practice of either political party. Nixon delighted in a growing federal budget as he felt, just as (President) Johnson did, that more spending would insulate him politically.[530]

[B] Nixon's Opinion That His Critics Claim That the US Has a Problem of Too Much Liquidity, Is Just Bullshit!

President Nixon "*also opined that the problem of too much liquidity in the financial system was 'just bullshit.'*"[531] (Authors' emphasis added in italics)

The decision by President Nixon to devalue the dollar not only set the United States free of fiscal boundaries, but also set a very poor example for other nation states. As already noted, the flow of dollars into the global markets created a surfeit of greenbacks so large that they warranted a separate category—Eurodollars. And foreign nations began to borrow in dollars in the same way as had occurred between the two great wars.[532]

The Bretton Woods system provided for the IMF to make changes in the agreed exchange rates in the event of "fundamental disequilibrium." "This arrangement did not really address the underlying economic problems in the various nations, but merely obscured the reality with a veneer of government intervention."[533]

This arrangement worked—or appeared to function—for three decades after WW II, but only because it was underpinned and lubricated by the wonderful stuff of inflation and debt. The United States provided loans and grants to accommodate both domestic and international needs for liquidity.[534] "But rather than return to the gold standard or some other fixed discipline for maintaining the real value of global currencies, the *Bretton Woods Agreements* ... simply institutionalized global inflation under the aegis of the US dollar. And despite the mounting monetary chaos since then, the world's political officeholders have never seriously reexamined the inflationist assumptions that guided the authors of the *Bretton Woods Agreements*."[535]

One of the key measures of the global role of the dollar and inflation in helping to float the world economy after World War II was the growth of the offshore market in dollar deposits—the so-called Eurodollars. From $1 billion in 1950, the offshore market in US dollars grew to $10 billion at the end of 1965, $100 billion in 1990, over $5 trillion in 2000, and it reached more than $10 trillion by the end of 2009. More than the International Monetary Fund, the Federal Reserve System became the de facto liquidity provider to the world, a role now made explicit in the wake of the 2008 subprime crisis.

But when the Fed's domestic priorities as a liquidity provider are extended to the entire world, the result is the very global inflation and financial market instability that the classical economists warned against. When the military and strategic threat of the Cold War is layered atop the existing propensity to embrace statist solutions and mechanisms, the Bretton Woods framework has a certain logic—but only so long as the United States itself maintains fiscal discipline. Unfortunately, the United States never embraced fiscal discipline after WW I and instead created a culture of debt and deficits that has only grown with the succeeding decades. Under Bretton Woods, all the major currencies of the world were defined in dollars, thus when chronic external deficits brought the need to devalue the US dollar, the entire pegged arrangement disintegrated.

The Nixon shock represented a milestone in American economic development, where deficit spending was explicitly embraced to maximize employment even though the economy was not in recession or the nation at war.[536] Nixon's final repudiation of gold and his explicit embrace of deficit spending to ensure full employment was a radical departure from the stated practice of either political party. Nixon delighted in a growing federal budget as he felt, just as (President) Johnson did, that more spending would insulate him politically.

The decision by President Nixon to devalue the dollar not only set the United States free of fiscal boundaries, but also set a very poor example for other nation states. As already noted, the flow of dollars into the global markets created a surfeit of greenbacks so large that they warranted a separate category—Eurodollars. And foreign nations began to borrow in dollars in the same way as had occurred between the two great wars.[537]

[C] US Monetary Policy Became Officially "Money from Nothing"

By 1980 [legislation from 1916 through 1978[538]], Congress had licensed the Fed to issue Federal Reserve Notes based, in essence, on the credit of the United Stated, the credit of private parties engaged in actual commercial transactions and on the credit of state and local governments anticipating the collection of revenues.[539] In 1980, Congress enabled the Fed to monetize "obligations of, or fully guaranteed as to principal and interest by, a foreign government or agency thereof ..." thereby licensing the Fed to function as a global central bank capable of monetizing the public debt of the entire world.[540]

It is important to note, that as this daisy chain of monetization of debt winds endlessly, "... the Federal Reserve System imposes on the Treasury the last-ditch financial responsibility for the Wall Street banking cartel's excessive or imprudent emissions of Federal Reserve Notes. If the Federal Reserve regional banks fail, to the degree that the statutory "first and paramount lien on all [their] assets is insufficient to liquidate extant Federal Reserve Notes, the Treasury must make good on the losses, either by 'recei[ving the notes] ... for all taxes, customs and other public dues' or by 'redeem[ing the notes] in lawful money on demand."[541] This renders the Treasury and, ultimately the people "ersatz sureties,"... not only for all of the private parties and state and local governments, but also for all foreign governments and agencies the debts of which the bankers foolishly choose to monetize."[542]

Following the Nixon shock, amidst the scramble to adjust exchange rates to U.S. policy and action, according to Professor Barry Eichengreen "another committee was formed. The Committee of Twenty (with one finance minister or central banker for each of the twenty country groupings represented on the board of the International Monetary fund) sought to reconcile the desire for exchange rate stability with the need of currencies to move against the dollar. Its proposal for an "oxymoronic system of 'fixed but adjustable rates' went nowhere. This propensity of governments to pursue oxymoronic regulation by non-regulation to preserve political cover continues to this day."[543]

[D] Unconstrained American Money Debasement Created the American Banking and Financial System Crisis of the 1980s and 1990s

Starting in the mid-1980s, there was a gradual erosion of the limits of the regulatory segmentation imposed on the financial system under the 1933 *Glass-Steagall* legislation. This process has been called "deregulation." It was primarily the result of a decline in bank income that many thought would threaten the existence of commercial banks.

US commercial banks' share of the financial assets held by all financial institutions had fallen dramatically from around 50 percent in the 1950s to around 25 percent in the 1990s as banks suffered competition for both their deposit business (from thrifts and non-regulated money market accounts) and their commercial and industrial loan business (from commercial paper). Since existing regulations gave little possibility of entering new lines of business, flexibility had to be sought within existing regulations. Deterioration in segmentation has also worked in the opposite direction with securities firms and insurance companies linking up with certain types of depository institutions known as "nonbank banks," such as international Edge banks, industrial loan banks, credit card banks, and to link with deposit units through the acquisition of a single thrift, known as a "unitary thrift."

As banks sought new avenues of revenue aside from the disappearing business of borrowing retail deposits and lending to commercial firms, they thus moved more and more into securities. This led to an emphasis on proprietary trading (embarked upon by Bankers Trust) and into increasing their fee and commission incomes. In particular, as the savings and loan industry was imploding in the 1980s, banks increasingly expanded their construction lending, leading to the collapse in real estate of the end of the 1980s and to the Greenspan strategy of leaning against the wind, which basically means keeping short rates sufficiently low so that banks could rebuild their capital by riding the yield curve between short rates and medium-term rates on government securities.

Thus, the Wall Street driven banking system that emerged from the 1980s real-estate crisis was one that no longer serviced business lending and was no longer primarily dependent on net interest margins for its income, but on the ability of their proprietary trading desks to generate profits and affiliates to produce fee and commission income.

The late 1980s and early 90s real estate, S&L and banking crisis left collapsed property values. There were no buyers except vultures. There were no lenders. Re-regulation and capital impairment left banks and thrifts unable to lend. Other institutional lenders were also crippled by the fallout. Owners of large portfolios of commercial real estate looked to Wall Street to capture recovering values during mid-to-late 1990s. Partnership roll-ups into REITs took off. Wall Street liked the fees and quickly developed commercial property lending conduit programs that filled the gap left by traditional lenders. When traditional lenders—banks and thrifts—re-entered the market, they become conduit sponsors themselves. Increasing capital requirements imposed following the crisis encouraged banks to sell off their loans through conduit programs—supposedly getting the risk off their balance sheets while booking the fees (originate and distribute programs). These conduit programs remain a major factor in the property credit market. With REITs and conduit lenders' capital and loans chasing the same product—prices for their target property types have been driven up and yields have been driven down, despite lacklustre fundamentals. The buzz phrase for this phenomenon is "cap rate compression."

Wall Street liked the packaging process and the fees it generated, but commercial mortgages tend to be idiosyncratic, making it somewhat difficult to model and rate the derivative securities they were bundled into.

On November 12, 1999, President Bill Clinton signed into law the *Gramm-Leach-Bliley Act*, which repealed the *Glass-Steagall Act of 1933*. The repeal allowed commercial & investment banks to consolidate and paved the way for the explosion of the "off-balance sheet originate and distribute financing model." To amplify the effect of this legislation, the Securities and Exchange Commission in 2004 allowed investment banks to triple their leverage ratios.[544]

In the mid to late 1990s and ongoing to this year, Wall Street increasingly focused on residential mortgages as a product source. This was because the huge volume and homogeneity of the loans and documentation and the susceptibility of the assets to bundling, modelling, splitting into tranches and derivatives and re-bundling modelling and rating the derivatives into a multiplicity of individual investment vehicles and products that could be widely disseminated, produced huge fees as well as creating new markets and demand for those products; and in the process distributing interest rate and default risk more widely and efficiently. "At the beginning of 2008, the total value of mortgages in the United States was approximately 90 percent of GDP."[545]

Each level of bundling and splitting of the underlying assets into new assets with different attributes, created more fees and additional products. Each product was leveraged (often 40 or 50 to 1) in turn, by each subsequent level of investors. Each level of bundling, leverage and reselling ("layering") extended the asset further from the underlying source of fundamental value: income levels of homeowners available to make mortgage payments, which remained flat.

Mortgage companies proliferated and grew like Topsy. Other financial institutions joined the fray and all developed massive residential lending programs for home purchases and home equity loans, fuelling residential development and consumer spending. Demand for loan product induced by credit availability and artificially low interest rates drove the increasing volume of loan product, thus also driving loan originations up and loan pricing and underwriting of risk down. This process led to higher home costs and prices, begetting increased refinancing, pulling out additional cash for consumer spending and supporting the rapidly growing trend of trading up in housing. Loans went up. Household savings went down. Consumer spending went up—all sustaining our economy—holding at bay the threat of an unwinding of international financial imbalances represented by our enormous, growing and unsustainable fiscal, current account and trade deficits.

The bulge of liquidity driven by this ballooning class of securitized assets and their derivative assets converted into consumer spending and investment in financial assets is financed by an exploding fiscal deficit and by trade and current account deficits that have grown beyond any level considered sustainable by any country. This imbalance has continued and grown due to the desire, primarily of Asian and Middle Eastern economies and their central banks, to invest in US assets to keep the dollar strong and their currencies weak, thereby supporting their trade and export advantage and feeding the US consumer spending binge with cheap consumer products.

While this process continues, US fiscal policy has gone from Clinton-era fiscal surplus to a current, massive, fiscal deficit approaching $22 trillion. Residential loan-backed securities and derivatives have spread world-wide and now show up in what we all thought were safe, liquid "high-yield" money market funds. The booming demand for product has led to ever-reduced underwriting standards for loans and an ever-increasing proportion of subprime loan-backed securities and derivatives in the marketplace. The distance of the product from its fundamental underwriting source—not commercial tenant rental income but individual household income—has increased the predominance of mathematical quantitative models piled upon additional models and securities ratings piled on top of additional securities ratings.

Ultimately, common sense would tell you that with household incomes relatively flat, and real unemployment in excess of 9 percent and entrenched, the growing volume of the lower tranches of subprime asset based securities and their derivatives would begin to experience stress due to adjustment of artificially low introductory interest rates and periodic adjustment of adjustable rate loans, as interest rates increase. Although recent rate increases have been modest, and according to many authorities are still artificially low, and although spreads do not accurately account for underlying risks, the stress has been sufficient to generate stress in that market and, based on a contagion of fear and the investor "herd mentality," stop the subprime music. On August 9, 2007, the Fed had to flood the market with liquidity to offset bank's lack of confidence in the financial condition of their bank counterparties.

On March 12, 2008, Qatar and officials at the Gulf central bankers announced that they were discussing de-linking their currencies from the dollar to avoid the inflation use of the dollar is causing and portends to increase. This would lead to a currency devaluation or move to a currency basket to support their currencies. United States abuse of its power and hegemony and its oversupply of hubris will drive the market away from a dollar that is unsound and cannot be trusted. The only mitigating factor in this development is that the US has exported its monetary framework worldwide and all virtually all money systems amongst the developed economies suffer the same malady, to a greater or lesser degree.

[E] The Great Financial Crisis in 2008 and Ongoing Money Debasement

The National Commission on the Causes of the Financial and Economic Crisis Inquiry in the United States, presented their Official Account of the Causes of the Financial Crisis, in *The Financial Crisis Inquiry Report* (January, 2011) (the "Commission Report"). (The bulk of the Report's findings set out here are paraphrased from the original text.)

In the course of its investigation, the Committee reviewed millions of pages of documents, interviewed more than 700 witnesses and held 19 days of public hearings in New York, Washington, D.C., and communities across the country. The Commission also drew from a large body of existing work about the crisis developed by congressional committees, government agencies, academic, journalists, legal investigators, and many others. The Commission Report lays out the facts but does not identify defendants legal duties to the American public, the defendant's breach of those duties and the proximate cause of such breaches to the damage to the suffered by the American public and the Report does provide for or recommend any legal to recover the damages they have suffered, punish the defendants or deter them from now highly likely, future wrongful conduct.

In a 2010 interview with the Financial Crisis Inquiry Commission, Sandra Braunstein, the retiring Federal Reserve official who oversaw the regulator's lacklustre efforts to protect consumers in the years preceding the U.S. mortgage meltdown was asked whether the Fed should have done more in the early 2000s to rein in unfair or deceptive mortgage practices. Braunstein responded:

> *I really don't remember having thoughts along those lines.*[546] (Authors' emphasis added in italics)

It is abundantly clear that those amongst us in Washington and on Wall Street really do not remember having thoughts about accountability for their abuse of power and intentional bank fraud detailed in the public record. The Commission Report details in detail the indisputable facts of the crisis. The Commission's Report conclusions are clear and succinct. Amongst all of the sources supporting this work, the most dramatic example of experts' expression of opinions on the crisis while prescribing no legal mechanism to enforce accountably for the crisis, and with such accountability an alignment of interest with the law supporting meaningful reform to our monetary, banking and financial system.

The Commission concluded that "the financial crisis was avoidable. It was not unforeseeable or unavoidable as Washington and Wall Street would have us believe. Widespread failures in financial regulation and supervision proved devastating to the stability of the nation's financial markets. The sentries were not at their posts, in no small part due to the widely accepted faith in the self-correcting nature of the markets and the ability of financial institutions to effectively police themselves. More than 30 years of deregulation and reliance on self-regulation by financial institutions, championed by former Federal Reserve Chairman Alan Greenspan and others, supported by successive administrations and Congresses and actively pushed by the powerful financial industry at every turn, had stripped away key safeguards, which could have helped avoid catastrophe. ... In addition, the government permitted financial firms to pick their preferred regulators in what became a race to the weakest supervisor." .... Too often, they [financial regulators] lacked the political will—in a political and ideological environment that constrained it—as well as the fortitude to critically challenge the institutions and the entire system they were entrusted to oversee."[547]

The Committee went on to observe that "... the financial industry itself played a key role in weakening constraints on institutions, markets and products. It did not surprise the Commission that an industry of such wealth and power would exert pressure on policy makers and regulators. From 1999 to 2008, the financial sector expended $2.7 trillion in reported federal lobbying expenses; individuals and political action committees in the sector made more than $1 billion in campaign contributions. What troubled us was the extent to which the national was deprived of the necessary strength and independence of the oversight necessary to safeguard financial stability."[548]

The Committee additionally concluded that: "... there was a systemic breakdown in accountability and ethics. The integrity of our financial markets and the public's trust in those markets are essential to the economic well-being of our nation. The soundness and the sustained prosperity of our financial system and dour economy rely on the notions of fair-dealing, responsibility and transparency. In our economy, we expect businesses and individuals to pursue profits, at the same time that they produce products and services of quality and conduct themselves well. Unfortunately,—as has been the case in past speculative booms and busts—we witnessed an erosion of standards of responsibility and ethics that exacerbated the financial crisis. This was not universal, but these breached stretched from the ground level to the corporate suites. They resulted not only in significant financial consequences but also damage to the trust of investors, businesses and the public in the financial system."[549]

While the views of the Commission are directed system wide, the banking sector is replete with specific examples of bank and regulatory failures misconduct damaging trusting Americans.

The Committee concluded that "a combination of excessive borrowing, risky investments, and lack of transparency put the financial system on a collision course with crisis." ... "[T]he government was ill-prepared for the crisis, and its inconsistent response added to the uncertainty and panic in the financial markets. Collapsing mortgage-lending standards and the mortgage securitization pipeline lit and spread the flame of contagion and crisis." ... "The Federal Reserve neglected its mission 'to ensure the safety and soundness of the nation's banking and financial system and to protect the credit rights of consumers." ... "Over the counter derivatives contributed significantly to this crisis." ... "Credit rating agencies were essential cogs in the wheel of financial destruction."[550]

Nearly $11 trillion in household wealth has vanished. Ordinary Americans have suffered more than $20 trillion in damages.

§6.07 CONCLUDING OBSERVATIONS

A proliferation of inflation, stagflation, deflation and monetary uncertainty worldwide followed the Nixon shock and prompted an accompanying proliferation of banking law granting new bank powers and forbearance of the exercise of regulatory and legal constraints on the financial institutions, enabling them to take greater risks and, it was erroneous thought, to generate greater income to combat disintermediation fed by raging inflation driven by the Eurodollar Petro-dollar and regular American fiat dollars that washed through the global financial system following the Nixon shock. The deregulation that was hoped to cure the explosion of money debasement hiding in inflated asset values, resulted instead in a liquidity and financial crisis despite raging inflation, because the money debased value increases were not sustainable in the real economy. That recognition was accompanied by criminalizing the very bank activities, policies, practices and procedures advocate by Congress and the federal financial regulators, to little remedial affect, but thus and thereby exacerbating a devastating the financial crisis and betraying what ordinary Americans could expect from monetary and economic leadership in Washington and Wall Street.

America's early history of constant informed efforts to maintain honest, safe and sound money, monetary systems and stable economies in the public interest, were permanently abandoned and replaced with the Washington Wall Street enterprise and the present era of concentration of power and wealth in Washington and Wall Street through bailouts, subsidies, and other preferred financial assistance, quantitative easing and its variants, including the extension of the Fed's remit to including service as the last resort purchaser of toxic assets to clean up the Wall Street banks' income statements and balance sheets, driving their intentional misrepresentation of asset values that has protected their wealth and power while ordinary Americans are barely surviving financially. The Bretton Woods system consisting of global currencies' honesty, safety and soundness tied to the dollar accompanied by America's tie of the dollar to the gold standard as the then preferred standard for regulation of the value of the dollar was abandoned and we embarked on a process of money debasement as an unjust but explicit foundation for monetary policy. American led, and the global economies followed. Washington and Wall Street have crystalized into a corrupt criminal racketeering enterprise—the largest and most far-reaching criminal enterprise in history—disguised as the guardian of the ordinary Americans Dream. We turn now to the present era of monetary and economic dysfunction that has burdened ordinary Americans in this era, and thus portending the next crisis, which will likely be more severe than the great financial crisis of 2008.

CHAPTER 7

The Washington Wall Street Enterprise Web of False Narratives

The tension between the Washington Wall Street enterprise on the one hand, and ordinary Americans has been ongoing since the revolution era. The primary false narrative at issue today is the false narrative that has substituted shadow banking and shadow money for the disciplined constraints on sovereign and traditional credit money—shadow money and falsely presented them as equivalents. Washington and Wall Street have failed to examine the development of this process of dissociation of what we view as money from traditional constraints on money debasement of both sovereign money and credit money in their connection to underlying asset values dependent on the disparate assets' liquidity.

The fundamental false narrative spun by the Washington Wall Street enterprise is that shadow money can be treated as sovereign money; that sovereign money serves as a constraint on creation of excess credit shadow money, despite the fact that our sovereign money is in no wise regulated in value as required by the *Constitution*. This chapter examines a variety of important false narratives spun by the Washington Wall Street enterprise as a cover up for the primary false narrative that Washington and Wall Street have served the public interest in the lawful maintenance of honest, safe, and sound American money; both sovereign money and shadow credit money, under the American rule of law and cannot therefore be held accountable for the financial crisis.

§7.01 FALSE NARRATIVE: ORDINARY AMERICANS EXCESS BORROWING CAUSED THE FINANCIAL CRISIS

The US Congress' and the financial, regulatory, supervisory, and enforcement agencies' focus on banking and securities fraud and crime as the base cause of capital losses and bank insolvency is not without historical foundation. While speculative excess absorbs the money created by money debasement and the massive creation of unregulated indebtedness proves a fertile ground for financial and securities fraud and crime; the real crime underlying and creating conditions that support specific micro-economic and financial crime is the failure of our government to address the systemic issues that go to the heart of ordinary Americans' economic well-being: the actual debasement of our money through exploding levels of unregulated public and private debt. There is no longer any ground to be gained by governmental dissembling about liars, charlatans and cheats. Ordinary Americans' borrowing in the current era is driven by the US political objective of driving ever higher levels of acquisition of consumer goods financed by credit to fuel what we have been led to believe constitutes economic growth and prosperity. Ordinary Americans have responded to the political incentives to ever higher levels of borrowing, acquisition and consumption. The political concentration driving increased indebtedness has given rise to an explosive growth in the financial services industry including banking and shadow banking. Every form of debt that can be securitized is promoted by the financial services industry to reach out into the future and realize today the goods and services that current savings would normally pay for. Financiers monetize what would otherwise have been paid for in the future, by production of monetized debt financing the present-day expenditures while postponing the payment through undertaking the risk and uncertainty and associated cost in the future. The American and global economy have become dependent of this process of reaching out into the future with reckless disregard the risk and uncertainty inherent using monetized debt to grasp today that which is in the final analysis, dependent on structured finance driven in a regulated banking and shadow banking future that finances that are dependent on financial models based on past experiences that do not accurately reflect the discounted value on a current liquid basis of those obligations circulating in our monetary system due to the unknown vagaries of future risk and uncertainty. Once Washington and Wall Street had created a phantom of future value brought to the present through credit they are bound to continue and build and perpetuate the Ponzi scheme model in a vain effort to avoid a reckoning for having expended money today without recognizing that perils of future repayment of the debt. Thus, we continue to maintain unsustainable and ever-increasing amounts of public and private indebtedness. Ordinary Americans have been reduced to cogs in a wheel of burgeoning credit creation.

We must look instead to the disastrous abrogation of responsibility by Congress, the Executive administration, and our entire federal financial regulatory structure, including the Federal Reserve System and its dominant members, the systemically crucial Wall Street banks, for justice. They have failed in their respective moral and legal duties necessary to assure a prosperous American economy and society, by failing to: maintain honest, safe, and sound, liquid sovereign American money in accordance with Congress' constitutional requirements, as well as regulated and properly constrained public and private negotiable or transferable debt, and to thereby assure one of the highest American values—an honest, safe, and sound banking and financial system.

Ordinary Americans did not cause the financial crisis, except to the extent that their trust in the competence and the fiduciary roles played by Washington and Wall Street, to act in their interests, and to operate through an honest, safe and sound financial system in compliance with the American rule of law. The establishment and maintenance of a safe and sound banking and financial system is primarily and constitutionally dependent on the maintenance of a tie between money and liquid value, through reference of money to and regulation of its value by ties to the relative market value of goods and services as components of the real, as opposed the financial economy. The Washington Wall Street enterprise has done its utmost to obscure the duties that accompany the vast powers entrusted to them; and to preserve their elevated *status quo*. It is ordinary Americans' civil right to expect Washington and Wall Street to honor the powers and perform the duties entrusted to them under the American rule of law, and to honor their obligations in the best interests of those who entrusted them with such powers and duties. The Washington Wall Street enterprise having failed to meet their fiduciary duties and obligations, it only now behoves the body of ordinary American who have suffered by that breach of trust and power, to enforce their civil rights for redress under the American rule of law.

When I presented what became *Banks in Distress* as my doctoral thesis at the Centre for Commercial law Studies, Queen Mary College, University of London, one of my examiners noted that I listed professor Paul Kennedy's book *The Rise and Fall of the Great Powers*, in my bibliography. He asked why. I replied: "This has all happened before". Professor Kennedy chronicled the relationship between economic change, crises, and military conflict from 1500 to 1987— a continuing series of systemic financial crises arising out of money debasement, excessive public and private indebtedness and rampant inflation resulting, ultimately, in violence and warfare—time after time.

Systemic financial crises are not a new phenomenon and were not new at the time our nation's founders wrote the *United States Constitution*. Sovereign power after sovereign power has succumbed time and again to the handy tools of money debasement and creation of unsustainable public fiscal and current account and trade deficits as well as private indebtedness and ultimately, inflation of asset prices and then devaluation of unsustainable liquid asset values, as political expedients to satisfy short term political benefits for self-serving special political and economic interests. This series of policy and action failures by sovereign powers has been well chronicled in financial literature throughout the history of money. See, for example, Appendix B to Charles Kindleberger's book, *Manias, Panics and Crashes, A History of Financial Crises, Fourth Edition (Financial Crises from 1618 to 2000)*, the numerous charts created by Reinhart and Rogoff included in *This Time is Different*, the bibliography to each of my prior works as well as those in included in the more recent works addressing systemic financial risk and crises cited above and those referred to by David Kotok in his essay. Christopher Whalen, in *Inflated, How Money and Debt Built the American Dream*, provides an excellent current historical assessment of the evolution of United States financial system that is a worthy addition to Friedman and Schwartz' masterful *A Monetary History of the United States, 1867-1960*. Barry Eichengreen, in *Exorbitant Privilege, The Rise and Fall of the Dollar and the Future of the International Monetary System*, provides an excellent history and analysis of the facts of relatively recent history that have led to increasingly disproportionate influence of the American dollar as a global reserve currency and the accompanying disproportionate ability of the US to create vast unsustainable amounts of public and private debt without yet being called to account.[551] By one count, the United States experienced fourteen financial crises in the century preceding World War I, of which 1907 was the worst. Since 1907, Charles Kindleberger identifies an additional six financial crises occurring between 1907 and 2000. Add to that the dot.com crash in 2001 and the current financial crisis which has been ongoing since 2007. Felix Martin provides an excellent historical chronology of the social, economic and philosophical struggles by successive civilizations to maintain sound money since the first monetary systems were initiated four thousand years ago in ancient Persia. Systemic financial crises are not a new or recent phenomenon in America or around the world.

Current developments in the global economy reveal a growing conflict between those wish to balance the economy through forced fiscal austerity and balanced budgets and those who do not want to face the constrictions of a new fiscal policy of austerity. They have been used to the false promise of ever increasing economic growth and prosperity that has been based on massive debt creation, inflation and the prospect of lower taxation, or practices, as in Greece, of widespread and pervasive tax avoidance to which the Greek government has consistently turned a blind eye. No attention has been directed to the shocking US led but global abandonment of sovereign money the value of which has been regulated by reference to an appropriate outside standard of value. Similarly, although the practice of originate and distribute structured financial securities and derivatives slowed following the crisis, the volume of such transactions have reached new record highs.

Non-transparent levels of debt have been liberally used to avoid the limitations imposed on spending by the transparent connection of spending through transparent budgets to publicly disclosed, and legally approved levels of taxation, all of which can be measured and effected in terms of sound money. The American clear and constitutionally prescribed method of financing government, regulating commerce and regulating our financial system has been perverted by Congress' failure to agree upon budgets (For example, the Senate had not passed a budget resolution for 2011, 2012, or 2013, and passed the 2014 budget resolution on March 23, 2013—23 days before the deadline set by the *No Budget, No Pay Act of 2013*.[552] This was the first budget resolution passed by the Senate since a 2010 budget passed on April 29, 2009). America has created of a system of taxation that is incomprehensible and provides for an enormous perverse complex of tax loopholes, credits incentives, and off-budget guarantees and commitments commonly recognized to be riven with conflicts of interest and self-dealing. This legal, economic and political morass is exploited by Congress, federal financial regulators, Wall Street banks and a vast array of other wealthy elite special interests; that ordinary Americans cannot conceivably view as just or equitable. Congress, the federal financial regulators and the Wall Street banks have acted in concert to create the money necessary to finance their consolidation and growth of wealth and power through the perverted tax code; financing inside the banking and financial system by and for the benefit of the Washington and Wall Street cabal; as well as outside of the conventional banking and financial system through the burgeoning off-balance sheet and off-budget "shadow banking system."

This is not new information or brilliant analysis. It is a statement of the obvious. The American public knows this. They do not know what to do about it. Occupy Wall

Street—totally ineffective. Political campaigning and voting—rendered totally ineffective—coopted and compromised away by the ruling cabal and electoral gerrymandering. Concerns about "falling off the fiscal cliff", because Congress cannot or will not agree upon a budget and tax program to balance national income and expense has been routinely delayed and deferred by scaremongering claims that the government will be forced to shut down and the public will suffer. Even though Washington and Wall Street have failed to do their sworn duty as public servants, as the moment of new crisis becomes imminent, they may stay up all night for a couple of days and nights amid rancorous meetings the purposes of which are to protect their special interests and pretend to act in the public interest. After much argument, angst and amidst strongly worded public statements, Washington and Wall Street will likely defer any realistic solution by extending the status quo, protesting they thereby save the American public from certain doom, while garnering praise and congratulations from one another for a job well done and catastrophe avoided by their collective self-less sacrifice.

The American public knows that this process is wrong and irresponsible. They know that the constant systemic financial crises, fiscal crises and budget showdowns are a part and parcel of the same wrongful and irresponsible conduct by the bad actors in Washington and on Wall Street that they can call by name. They just do not know what to do about it.

When governments, financial regulators and financial institutions create expectations that deficits do not matter; that booming incomes, asset values, government benefits and entitlements, and individual prosperity, literally the American Dream, will follow a trajectory ever increasing may lead to temporary political support; the actual demonstrable historical results of these practices and expectations have been, time after time, over millennia, that where money, including money created through unsupportable levels of public and private debt, if not tied to actual relative market values of goods and services in the real economy; the ultimate result has consistently been widespread economic and financial depression, rising unemployment, increases in the gap between rich and poor, and all too often diminished respect for authority, civil disobedience, violence, revolution and war.

President Obama's proposed special unit of federal prosecutors and leading state attorneys general prosecuting cases of abusive lending and mortgage fraud has failed to touch on the subject of accountability for the damages to ordinary Americans caused by systemic financial crises. The little lies these special units are investigating so intently did not bring down our financial system down; it was the big lie: the lie that we can rely of the stable liquid value of our money as the cornerstone in the foundation of our economy: the lie that there is a free ride to the American Dream.

When ordinary Americans consider the words and application of the federal criminal fraud statutes, the current definitions and movements of what has now become money must be brought clearly to mind.

The Fed recognizes the bulk of private and public debt as money but does not measure the value or count the vast majority in amount of such money instruments or accounts, denominated in US dollars, for purposes of formulation of US monetary policy or for action in support of its stated mission. Despite the immense importance of regulating the value of US money, the Fed's official mission is "to promote effectively the goals of maximum employment, stable prices, and moderate long-term interest rates." This is not the same as a charge to maintain and regulate the value and liquidity of sound sovereign money. Subsequent chapters will examine more closely what the Fed, the other federal financial regulators, Congress, the congressional committees, housing agencies, rating agencies and other bad actors in this scenario represent as the respective public missions for which they are responsible.

Despite the Fed's attempts to exceed its mission through unprecedented open market purchases from the shadow banking system of assets outside the Fed's banking system, to support the values of those assets in a vain attempt to avoid the unavoidable but foreseeable consequences of its activities through the collective Washington and Wall Street criminal enterprise, the Fed has continued to systematically create money of every sort feeding the banking and shadow banking asset price bubble which is now on the verge of collapsing and will continue to do so until the markets clear of excess liquidity in relation to underlying asset values.

Money as a course subject is completely absent from law school curricula. The US *Constitution* and Supreme Court cases such as the *Legal Tender Cases* and the *Gold Clause Cases* have been simply ignored.

We are all familiar with the propensity of government to lose track of the meaning of the words they use. Communication in Washington and on Wall Street has been reduced to the constant exchange of insider gibberish and one indecipherable euphemism, meme or tweet for another to the point the public cannot really understand much of what they have to say. It is useful to turn to the common-sense meaning of the terms defining congressional power and responsible in the context of assessment of financial crisis accountability from the *Merriam-Webster Dictionary*:

- Coin: to create or invent money.
- Regulate: bring under the control of law or constituted authority; bring order, method, or uniformity.
- Value: fair return or equivalent in goods, services, or money for something exchanged; the monetary worth of something of relative worth, utility, or importance.
- Relative: referring grammatically to an antecedent; a thing having a *relation* to or connection with or necessary dependence on another thing qualifying an expressed or implied antecedent expressed as the ratio of the specified quantity (as an error in measuring) in comparison to the total magnitude (as the value of a measured quantity) or to the mean of all the quantities involved.
- Comparative: relating to, or constituting the degree of *comparison* in a language that denotes increase in the quality, quantity, or relation considered as if in comparison to something else as a standard not quite attained characterized by systematic comparison especially of likenesses and dissimilarities.

Power delegated to Congress under the *Constitution* implies the congressional duty to "well and faithfully discharge the duties of the office" and properly exercise that power.

The American public is entitled to rely, in good faith, and undoubtedly did rely in good faith on congress to fulfill its responsibilities under the *Constitution* through its own actions as well as through its instruments, the federal financial regulators, including the Board of Governors of the Federal Reserve System and the bank members of the Federal Reserve System, the Federal housing agencies, and participants in the Wall Street/Washington cabal to provide a safe and sound banking system through the safe, sound and prudent regulation of the liquid value of US money.

Congress and its members, individually, acting jointly and severally, have intentionally, knowingly and willfully and with reckless and conscious disregard of the consequences of their actions on the domestic and global banking and financial system as well as on the American citizens, failed in their duty to regulate the value of the dollar as a fiat currency as well as all other dollar denominated "money" instruments, specifically including mortgage and other asset backed securities and derivatives (including "repos"), that are treated by the financial and capital markets as currency or money in the broad and market-accepted meaning of the term, based in large part on the willingness of rating agencies to give assurance to the holders of such money of its correlation or connection to underlying confirmed asset value supporting the liquid value of such money. Thus these parties intentionally hid the dramatic debasement of the US dollar and the corresponding dramatic overstatement of the values of the assets into which the nation's banks, bank management, the Wall Street banks and the federal housing agencies funnelled such money, both through the formal US banking system regulated by the federal financial regulators and outside of it through the creation by these parties of an acknowledged but un-regulated "shadow banking system". This system consists of massive amounts of US dollar denominated financial assets that serve as uncounted money in the domestic and global economy, the value of which was unregulated and was, and remains uncertain, notwithstanding so-called assurances of value issued by the ratings agencies, in exchange for enormous compensation; by the federal housing agencies, Wall Street banks and bank management; to permit their lucrative origination and distribution of such money into the shadow banking system. Congress has acted in concert with the federal financial regulators, federal housing agencies and their respective policy making officers, jointly and severally, all intentionally, knowingly and willfully, and with reckless disregard of the consequences of their respective actions, to obtain political, institutional and individual personal benefits from not only permitting, but enabling and actively promoting the unregulated, unconstrained and immeasurable proliferation of money consisting of financial assets originated and distributed by the Wall Street banks. The values of these assets, denominated in US dollars, were dramatically overvalued and deemed more liquid than was the case, based in large part on the accompanying ratings opinions. These actions also include the failure to regulate the value of asset backed securities and derivatives and the deliberate concealment and misrepresentation of the predictable effects of such actions, which was indeed entirely predictable.

These actions have been the direct cause of the financial crisis that has caused massive losses to domestic and foreign financial institutions as well individuals, directly and directly; and which has been the direct cause of financial deterioration of the values of such money instruments, the assets supporting those instruments and of the jobs and economic well-being of the ultimate obligors of the mortgage and credit instruments underlying the corresponding securitization and derivative instruments.

Legal accountability, whether civil or criminal, implies the existence of defined moral and legal responsibilities by specific individuals and institutions. Failure of the responsible parties to meet their respective defined responsibilities, resulting in harm to others, must be promptly followed by the imposition of stated consequences upon the respective parties for their unlawful conduct in accordance with the rule of law.

Most observers of America's financial crises and media pundits shy away from any discussion of specific individuals, with specific responsibilities and accountability for the country's systemic financial crisis. The individuals whose specific roles, responsibilities and accountability might be discussed, examined and evaluated are among the most powerful in American government, business and banking. The idea of their potential civil and criminal accountability for systemic financial crises has been an idea best kept quiet, out of the media, and well away from the elemental processes of the law in imposing civil and criminal accountability. For the past forty-five years, accountability has been left to special units or task forces such as those called for currently by President Obama. Historically, these special units or task forces have been expensive and largely impotent to identify the true parties responsible for systemic financial crises and hold them to account, under either civil or criminal law.

§7.02 FALSE NARRATIVE: AMERICAN ECONOMIC AND MONETARY POLICY ARE NOT CONSTRAINED BY LAW

The Washington Wall Street enterprise has fed to ordinary Americans a false narrative that American economic theory and monetary policy are not bounded or constrained by morality or law. The Fed's mysterious goings on are best left to experts and their unbridled discretion, although they do not acknowledge any duty or accountability to ordinary Americans, rather, they are aristocrats of an amorphous "economy." Economic theory and monetary policy have made a mockery of banking and financial law, regulation, supervision and enforcement.

The continuing ebb and flow of the epic struggle in economic thought between the stylized theories of Keynes and Hayek has been corrupted and distorted by politicians, government and their collaborators, the financial powers of Wall Street, to serve their own as opposed to the public interest. Hayek and Keynes agreed that the government could provide a useful service by providing a civilized level of social services as well as economic stimulus to counter the tragedies attendant to normal business cycles driven by changes in technology, natural disasters, even war. These economists differed fundamentally in perspective in their focus on actions in the macroeconomic aggregates versus actions on a microeconomic individual basis. Each of these brilliant economists were driven and limited by their environment and their respective view of the effects of financial crises. The works of Keynes and Hayek are well known but not especially well understood. An excellent comparison and contrast of their respective views appears in Nicholas Wapshott's work, *Keynes Hayek, The Clash That Defined Modern Economics.*[553]

Hayek was driven by his witness to the devastation wrought in Austria by hyperinflation caused by government intervention in response to the financial consequences of WW I and the allies unrelenting demands for war reparations. Keynes was driven by his witness to the devastation wrought by chronic, entrenched mass unemployment resulting from the economic consequences of the Great War in Britain. Each of their respective views were of different sides of the same coin of monetary abuse that ultimately exacts its price for monetary distortions from the people—no matter who is the victor at war. Wars may benefit politicians or profiteers but drain productive society with predictable consequences. E.G. Spaulding articulated the issue brilliantly in his *History of the Legal Tender Paper Money,* an Appendix to his *Speech on the National Currency Bill,* February 19, 1863, noted above.

Thus, Hayek concerned himself with the consequences to the public economy of government intervention in the market—spending vast sums on activity that produce no value but rather enslave the public. Hayek's views were realistic to the point of cynicism and pessimism and measured the impact on an individual granular basis.

Keynes concerned himself with the flip side of the coin. He saw government intervention in the economy through spending as a driver to redirect and make productive the unproductive unemployed people and resources displaced and trodden down by the financial and economic consequences of war and financial crises. Each of these great economists harbored grudging appreciation of the others' views but feared the results of dogmatic doctrinal adherence to the other's policies through business and financial crisis cycles. Hayek feared the predictable consequences of government intervention and manipulation in the economy leading to the dominance of the state apparatus and tyranny over the public. He was vindicated in his concern. Keynes did not focus so much on how an economy entered into crisis or where to place blame and accountability, but rather on the possibilities for helpful action by government spending during and following a crisis to jump start demand and thus employment of the unemployed and underemployed workers and resources as a temporary and emergency policy. Both Keynes and Hayek conducted their analysis and policy formations based on a closed system where the numbers were known and transparent—or assumed to be so. They were concepts based on models.

Financial crises and our responses to them following the Nixon shock have been fraught with distortions of information, some unintentional, but most intentional, and intentionally manipulated by Washington and Wall Street to serve, not the public interest to prevent the devastation of the economy following government intervention in the prosecution of war or to serve the public interest to prevent the utter devastation of an economy and society through the financial consequences of the economic and societal distortions and damage resulting from war, or at this point in history, from raw unadulterated, unlawful, debasement of money for profit.

Washington and Wall Street have adopted the dark side of these well-meaning economists' prescriptions for financial response to economic crises; driven and dis torted them to serve their private profits, concentration and consolidation of power and wealth resulting in damages to the public inconceivable to either of these thought leaders; Keynes and Hayek.

There is no question about the utility of each strain of economic theory at particular points in time in the wake of financial crises. Neither theory has been effective when applied dogmatically through entire business cycles. The tensions between interest rates, credit money supply and inflation and government fiscal stimulus to counter unemployment, become academic when politicians face financial crises. The models have not panned out. The people are not looking for an economic, monetary and financial model that suits the Fed's quest to reconcile two conflicting theories, each having some validity at some point in time of crisis caused by the high cost of existential war, but neither is effective in the face of the pressure following crises brought about by Washington and Wall Street in their quest for increase in income and concentration of wealth and power in their own hands through abuse of trust and power accompanied by deception and dishonesty resulting in almost inconceivable damage to the public, domestically and globally. Washington, Wall Street, as well as their accountants and lawyers have simply turned a blind eye to the perilous foundation underlying the business of money, hoping as sitting US President Trump observed with respect to the current day exploding national debt: "[i]n an interview Thursday [May 6, 2016] on CNBC, Donald Trump broke with tired clichés about the evils of federal debt accumulation. 'I am the king of debt,' he said. 'I love debt. I love playing with it.' But he replaced fearmongering about debt with an even more alarming notion—a bankruptcy of the United States federal government that would incinerate the world economy. 'I would borrow, knowing that if the economy crashed, you could make a deal,' Trump said. 'And if the economy was good, it was good. So therefore, you can't lose.'"[554] More recently, when asked about the threat posed by the exploding level of public debt, President Trump "repeatedly shrugged it off, implying that he doesn't have to worry about the money owed to America's creditors—currently about $21 trillion—because he won't be around to shoulder the blame when it becomes even more untenable."[555]

§7.03 ALTHOUGH CONGRESS HAS THE POWER IT DOES NOT NECESSARILY HAVE THE DUTY TO REGULATE THE VALUE OF MONEY

Power delegated to Congress under the *Constitution* is inseparable from the congressional duty to "well and faithfully discharge the duties of the office" and properly exercise that power.

Ordinary Americans are entitled to rely, in good faith, and undoubtedly have relied in good faith on Congress' fulfilment of its responsibilities under the *Constitution* through its own actions as well as through its instruments, the Federal financial regulators and the Federal housing agencies, to provide an honest, safe and sound banking system through the honest, safe sound and prudent regulation of the value of US money.

Congress and its members, individually, acting jointly and severally, have intentionally, knowingly and willfully and with reckless and conscious disregard of the consequences of their actions on the domestic and global banking and financial system as well as on the American citizens, failed in their duty to regulate the value of the dollar as a fiat currency as well as dollar denominated "money" instruments, specifically including mortgage and other asset backed securities and derivatives that are treated by the financial and capital markets as currency or money in the broad and market-accepted meaning of the term, based in large part on the willingness of the rating agencies and purveyors of the structure of money substitutes to give assurance to the holders of such money of its correlation or connection to underlying confirmed asset value supporting the value of money. Thus these bad actors intentionally hid the dramatic debasement of the US dollar and the corresponding dramatic overstatement of the values of the assets.

These actions have been the direct cause of the financial crisis that has caused massive losses to domestic and foreign financial institutions as well individuals, directly and directly; and which has been the direct cause of financial deterioration of the values of structured money instruments, the assets supporting those instruments and of the jobs and economic well-being of the ultimate obligors of the underlying structured credit instruments.

§7.04 FALSE NARRATIVE: TRADITION REGULATION OF THE VALUE OF MONEY BY A STANDARD SUCH AS THE GOLD STANDARD IS AN ANACHRONISM

Washington and Wall Street have adopted the false narrative that sovereign money and the regulation of value by reference to an outside standard; such as the gold standard or bi-metalism is a barbaric outmoded anachronism. That idea has been obsolete really, from the 1930s. The mechanisms, policies practices and actions taken by the Fed are unquestionably embedded in its somewhat mythical stature. Honest, safe, and sound American money can be maintained by a combination of regulatory empowerment and enforcement of the redemption requirement established by Article 1 § 8 Clause 5 of the *United States Constitution* and the market discipline of application the legal doctrines historically circumscribing credit money as negotiable instruments in accordance with the principles underlying traditional commercial law, including the real bills doctrine.

The creation and regulation of the value of money has historically been grounded in the sovereign. In America, the sovereign American people have specifically delegated this power and duty to congress pursuant to Article 1, § 8, Clause 5. Clause 5 also includes the peoples' delegation to Congress of the power and duty to establish a system of weights and measures. Clause 6 grants to Congress the power and duty to provide for the punishment of counterfeiting the securities and current coin of the United States. The combined effect of these constitutional provisions is to set the framework for the establishment of United States sovereign money. Sovereign money was clearly contemplated by the *Constitution* to be coined precious metal, silver specifically, the value of which could, as was subsequently, regulated by congressionally prescribed specific characteristics of weights and measures of that coinage; the counterfeiting of which was to be punished in the manner prescribed by Congress. These ideas are very well articulated in Dr. Vieira's masterful and scholarly work, *Pieces of Eight*.

The founders of the United States and the framers of the *Constitution* were well aware, first, that that a sovereign coinage money, the value of which was regulated pursuant to the delegated democratic republic founded constitutional principles and processes was essential for the success of the new experiment in American government. This political, social, economic and legal philosophy and structure of individual sovereign power delegated by the people to Congress and the resulting control mechanism was directly attributable to the influential work of John Locke. Second, the founders of the American democratic republic and the framers of the American *Constitution* were also aware of the prevalence of the use of credit instruments as money, represented primarily by traded bills of account and notes, a practice that had been widely known and accepted as the "real bills doctrine." The duality of coined sovereign money based on specific standards of identities of the specified precious coined metals, disciplined by constitutionally mandated and specified weights and measures on the one hand, and the prevalent historical commercial use of credit money instruments and a well-defined process for clearing accounts based on the market-based negotiated values of so-called real bills that formed the two pillars of the American monetary system.

The *United States Constitution* established the foundation for American sovereign coined money to serve and universal common denominator of economic and financial transactions denominated in that official sovereign money.

While real bills, as negotiable instruments, were in common use as money on a practical basis, the negotiated value of such bills and notes were denominated and disciplined in terms of the regulated value of sovereign coined money. The regulation of the value of sovereign money provided the legal and economic discipline on the value of the bills and notes used as market-based credit money through the legal ability of holders of the bills and notes to redeem them at a bank at their respective discounted market values respecting risk and uncertainty associated with the specific bills and notes [not face value, since liquidity at par is viable only for sovereign coined money or legal tender redeemable at face value in sovereign coined money, which itself defines the highest degree of liquidity] in exchange for coined sovereign money, the value of which had been established and regulated by Congress on behalf of the sovereign American people.

The American failure—now also the global failure, of nations to regulate the value of their sovereign money has led to the predictable consequent inability of the market to reliably establish the value of credit money awash in the shadow banking system. Securitization and derivatives and other forms of structured finance that in recent times pose as credit money traded essentially at par, based not on direct value correlation but on credit and liquidity support devices which have been found to intentionally overstate, intentionally misrepresent both the value and liquidity of the instruments; the correlation with and accommodation of risk and uncertainty in future liquidation through payment in sovereign money, the value of which has been deliberately occluded and obscured by structure and complexity.

Much has been made by scholars of money and the *United States Constitution* about the implicit constitutional requirement that American constitutionally established sovereign money must be gold. Dr. Edwin Vieira is the first among many such scholars, as evidenced by his authoritative work, *Pieces of Eight*. One focus of Dr. Vieira's work is to condemn the use of Federal Reserve Notes that presently constitute "Legal Tender"—paper money. While it is true that our founding fathers and the framers of the *Constitution* emphatically rejected the use of commercial bills of credit and other forms of paper money, *i.e.*, real bills, as sovereign money; they were also fully aware of the prevalent use of real bills as a form of non-sovereign credit money, negotiable instruments traded in the commercial marketplace at market established discounts that varied by traders' underwriting of the risk and uncertainty attendant to the instrument at the time of the negotiated trade. The discipline intended by the authors of the *Constitution* was the discipline of sovereign coined money, the value of which had been regulated by a democratically elected Congress accountable to the American public. It is possible for the Fed to delegate its duty and responsibility to a quasi-governmental entity such as the Fed, provided that the delegation is accompanied by an appropriate stipulated standard and protects, not impairs, the civil right of ordinary Americans to the use of an honest, safe, and sound unit of sovereign money. The regulated value of sovereign coined money served, and must be restored to the legal position where it once again can serve as valuation discipline on the market-based value of the negotiated bills—real bills—*i.e.* "negotiable instruments" established through the bill holders' ability to redeem such bills for sovereign money at the time of trade. The prospect of redemption served as a discipline on and curb of overstated values of real bills denominated in units of sovereign money. The market-determined differential in the market value of real bills in comparison to the amount of sovereign money for which the bills could be redeemed in sovereign money, represented the market determined discount attributable to the perceived risk and uncertainty that such bills could be redeemed on demand for sovereign money at the bills' stated face value. That constraint and discipline cannot be stolen away by securitization of the credit accompanies by ratings agency opinions and structure as complex securities where they are widely transferred and negotiated as money substitutes; relying for liquidity on a matrix of contrived structure that emphatically does not serve as a viable substitute for the application of commercial law limiting of breadth and reach of circulation, personal knowledge accompanied by liability and accountability for repayment of the debt of each successor transferee, from the original maker and holder, together with each subsequent transferor through the final endorser to the holder who is entitled to redemption in liquid sovereign money. Each step in the use of bills and notes as money substitutes requires participation of parties who must each have made a knowledgeable, informed decision regarding the risk and uncertainty carried by the instrument, the maker and each endorser, thus establishing a discount in liquid value corresponding to the risk and uncertainty inherent in bringing illiquid future value to a current liquid state.

So, America has the constitutional imperative that Congress establish and regulate the value of American sovereign money on behalf of the American people. Congress has failed to fulfill its duty through the required exerciser of its constitutionally delegated power and duty, in any meaningful respect since the Nixon shock.

Next, America has the ancient historical practice of the use of real bills of credit, bills and notes; negotiable instruments, structured money substitute instruments, as the largest component of America's and global monetary and financial systems. As noted previously, Felix Martin provided an excellent chronicle of the development of societies' use of sovereign money as well as the simultaneous and complimentary use of credit-based money. Martin not only detailed the necessary attributes and role of effective honest, safe and sound sovereign money, but he also detailed the necessary attributes and role of effective honest, safe and sound credit money.

Just as America and today's circle of global financial and economic powers have failed, since the time of the Nixon shock, to honor the historic and American constitutional discipline of sovereign money the value of which has been lawfully and practically regulated by Congress in the best interest of all Americans. These same failed powers duties and practices have deliberately confused the respective roles of sovereign money and credit money. They have also failed to differentiate, distinguish and enforce the necessary attributes and characteristics of credit money to honestly serve the American and global monetary systems. The failure to anchor the value of credit money by structure and by a requirement for redemption in sovereign money, the value of which has been lawfully regulated by the sovereign led directly to the explosion in size and risk of the "shadow banking system."

The present policy of the Federal Reserve perpetuates the known limitations to the proper employment of the real bills doctrine as a defining concept for the widespread use of credit as money in today's monetary system. On top of the flagrant disregard of the constitutional imperative for Congress to create and regulate the value of sovereign coined money into which the ready liquidation of credit money instruments at an on-demand liquid discounted value, the Federal Reserve has so departed from the concept that the "real bills" acceptable for rediscount by the Federal Reserve now extend to the unconstrained central bank lending—and even purchase (as in quantitative easing) of the credit instruments employed by private parties engaged in actual commercial transactions, but today, most often hidden in securities bundling a hodgepodge of bundled non-homogeneous credit in stratified tranches embedded in structures that render valuation of liquid value of which is well-nigh impossible. The requirements for central bank re-discounting member bank credits and collateralizing open market based activity or lending as a last resort are now be construed by the Fed in its sole discretion (which it has stretched beyond all rational limits, considering the lessons of the history of money), and on the credit of foreign, state and local governments anticipating the collection of revenues, as well as "obligations of, or fully guaranteed as to principal and interest by, a foreign government or agency thereof ..." thereby licensing the Fed to function as a global central bank capable of monetizing the public debt and to serve as the lender and purchaser of last resort for the entire world. That is a long way from the real bills' doctrine. Shadow money substitutes have been stripped of any coherence presented by the concept itself or the constraints necessary to maintain monetary stability. These departures have been intentional, progressive and deliberate.

The Fed has abandoned its foundation discipline grounded in the real bills' doctrine and the gold standard. Congress has utterly failed to honor the American constitutional, statutory and common law constraints fiduciary power and duty to create and regulate the value of United States sovereign money as delegated to it by the American people under the United States *Constitution*. Washington and the Wall Street banks have structured credit extending to the sky until the data entries it represents have become realized to be illusory, largely a figment of truly uninformed "experts" imaginations.

§7.05 FALSE NARRATIVE: CONSTITUTIONAL MONEY, THE VALUE OF WHICH IS REGULATED BY CONGRESS IS OBSOLETE: IT HAS BEEN LAWFULLY—CONSTITUTIONALLY—SUPERSEDED BY FIAT MONEY

Since the Supreme Court's decisions in the *Legal Tender Cases*, 79 U.S. 457, 554 (1870) rendered by a politically manipulated court "packed" by President Grant, overruled the Court's 1869 decision in *Hepburn v. Griswold*, 75 U.S. 603, the judicial system has apparently abandoned its responsibility to protect the economic interests of the American public under the rule of law. It is fair to note that no American has pursued justice under the rule of law with sufficient clarity and purpose to rise to the level of Supreme Court consideration. The courts have subsequently characterized the public's claims of their right to honest, sound money and presented to them judicially, as a political question, not to be decided by the courts on the basis of separation of powers. The courts have made a mockery of justice by ignoring applicable law and avoiding their responsibilities, largely on purely technical grounds. The judicial system's unwillingness to afford redress for this legal issue appears to have permanently undermined and occluded the public's awareness of each citizens' natural human civil right as well as each citizen's constitutional, common law and federal statutory legal right to an honest, safe and sound banking and financial system. The courts have routinely engaged in misdirection and deliberate mischaracterization of facts and law, and profound dissembling in support of the apparent triumph of the political, and bureaucratic and financial mandarins in Washington and on Wall Street who feel free to create an endless supply of money out of nothing in order to serve their individual and private interests.

The government's power to tax and spend, however perverse and corrupt its exercise has become, is founded in the rule of law. The amount of taxes levied and the purposes for which the funds of the treasury are appropriated and spent, and the perverse tax incentives adopted by Congress as a crude method for conducting a systemic program of *quid pro quo* for financial support from special interests, are political determinations. Political accountability for fiscal irresponsibility and cronyism is not the subject of this work. Suffice it to say that accountability for financial crisis is not a political question but purely questions of fact and law.

The government's power to establish a fractional banking system is of questionable legality, but has become a not only simply an American, but a global phenomenon. In America the national banking system and fractional reserve banking were borne of the same necessity as the use of legal tender. The existential threat and emergency of the Civil War necessitated a mechanism to finance the government's prosecution of the war. The *Emergency Banking Act* and the *National Banking Acts* represented a legal resolution to a political problem.

The government's establishment of the Federal Reserve System, an action even more tangential to the imperatives of war than the *National Banking Acts*, was designed to increase the government's ability to finance its political activities. *The Federal Reserve Act* represented a purported legal resolution to a strictly political government desire to raise and spend more money than it could by the imposition of ever greater taxes. The Fed explicitly creates money not tied to any external, reliable, stable standard of value, in the form of credit. That credit money is leveraged through the Federal Reserve System and leveraged again through the fractional reserve banking system before being leveraged again by the ultimate borrowers of the money. So long as the credit consists of bilateral lending arrangement, the credit creation is purely a banking matter. When the credit created is purportedly and intentionally made transferable, liquid, as structured shadow money, it becomes a banking and monetary matter.

The credit machine initiated by the Fed has stoked Wall Street bankers' desire to create ever larger amounts of shadow money through transferable supposedly liquid credit, ostensibly for advancement of the Fed's public purpose of "maintaining long run growth of the monetary and credit aggregates commensurate with the economy's long run potential to increase production, so as to promote effectively the goals of maximum employment, stable prices and moderate long-term interest rates;" but in practical effect, to extract enormous profits through credit creation, money creation and money debasement. This intentional market intervention—euphemistically and now pervasively referred to and accepted as "monetary policy"—for the exclusive profit and benefit of Washington, Wall Street and their respective sycophants, has never fulfilled its promise. To the contrary, the Fed has demonstrably failed in its legislative purpose. Congress and the Wall Street banks have exploited this failure with reckless abandon. The federal financial regulators have been ineffective spectators; hoping eventually to get their own shot at the revolving door to Wall Street. All have contributed mightily to the financial crisis. The purported legal concept that the Fed's social and political objectives pursued through their partners, the banks, in the creation of money, the value of which is somehow "acquired from individual and business productivity" is wholly and fundamentally inconsistent with the constitutional requirement that Congress regulate the value of money; both sovereign money and shadow money to the extent it functions as dollar denominated credit money.

§7.06 FALSE NARRATIVE: THE CONSTRAINTS OF TRADITIONAL COMMERCIAL LAW CAN BE REPLACED THROUGH CONVERSION OF DEBT INSTRUMENTS INTO SECURITIES PROTECTED ONLY DISCLOSURE REQUIREMENT OF SECURITIES LAWS

Discussion of the real bills' doctrine has been relegated to bottom of government and Wall Street considerations regarding money, credit and financial crises. The nature and role of real bills as the dominant form of money throughout history from the time numeracy, accounting, confidence in counterparties and transferability of such bills became an accepted practice, continuing to the present day, begs a thorough examination of the impact of and deviance from the role of such transferable credit instruments have influenced the now widespread use of non-commodity money, structured shadow money, in its role as a contributor to financial crises.

The University of Minnesota and the Federal Reserve Bank of Minneapolis published a Staff Report in 1981 that describes an appreciation of the real bills doctrine as an academic footnote to the creation of the Federal Reserve System.[556]

> According to the real bills' doctrine, unrestricted intermediation either by private banks or by a central bank has beneficial economic effects and should be promoted by public policy. The doctrine proposes that there be unrestricted discounting of real bills—evidences of indebtedness which, in accordance with Adam Smith's definition in The *Wealth of Nations* (1937, p.288), are safe or free of default risk. As we interpret the doctrine, it asserts that one function of banks is to issue bank notes or similar liabilities that, because they are issued in small and standard denominations, are more easily held as assets by ultimate lenders than the bills being discounted. The keystone of the doctrine is that no government regulations ought to restrict the scope of such intermediation. In particular, the doctrine relies for its integrity on market forces constrained by the limitations of commercial law and the limitations of required redemption or payment at maturity in sovereign money, the value of which has been regulated by Congress. The enforcement of these constraints on abuse and fraud can be relied on to prevent excessive "credit creation" by private banks. Moreover, if there happen to exist regulations that inhibit private intermediation—for example, regulations that prohibit private banks from issuing bearer notes and that make the central bank a monopoly issuer of currency-like assets, then the central bank ought to conduct open-market operations or operate a discount window in a way that vitiates the restrictions against private intermediation. The central bank can accomplish this by freely rediscounting paper for private banks or by lending directly. By doing this, it brings together borrowers and lenders who otherwise might not be matched because of the restriction against private intermediation.[557]
>
> For a long time, the real bills' doctrine has been in disrepute, especially in the view of adherents to some form of the quantity theory of money. According to the quantity-theory view, certain liabilities are special: they are "money." The real bills' doctrine proposes to let fluctuations in the demand for private credit lead to fluctuations in the supply of "money." At best, according to the quantity theorists, under a real bills' regime fluctuations in the demand for credit will cause fluctuations in both the "money" supply and the price level. At worst, an economy

operating under a real bills' regime has no determinate price level or "money" supply.[558]

Quantity theorists take it for granted that it is desirable to avoid price level fluctuations and Wicksellian price level indeterminacy. They propose to accomplish this by legal restrictions on private intermediation. The legal restrictions are meant to separate "money creation" from "credit creation," that is, from the process of intermediation. Thus, for example, Friedman (1960, p. 21) hails the feature of the *National Banking Act* which taxed state bank notes out of existence and advocates 100 percent reserves against bank liabilities called demand deposits. Even Adam Smith, who, according to Mints (1945, p. 9), had provided the "most elegant statement" of the real bills' doctrine, advocated restrictions. Smith (p. 313) proposed leaving private banks unregulated except for two restrictions: they should not be allowed to issue notes in small denominations and all notes should be payable on demand.

One weakness in the quantity-theory view stems from the way that its adherents define "money." They define it by how it is used; all things which seem to be "means of payment" are defined as money. By defining money that way, quantity theorists ignore what may well be a more significant and operational categorization of liabilities by how they are backed, that is, by the characteristics of the balance sheets and prospective return streams of those who issue them. Further, as the proliferation of concepts like M1, M2, M3 ... shows, a definition of money as "means of payment" is difficult to render operational. The failure of "means of payment" to be an analytical category that sharply distinguishes one class of assets from everything else helps account for this proliferation and for quantity theorists' occasional search for empirically derived definitions of money. Such definitions have been based either on the degree of correlation that a particular collection of assets exhibits with the price level or nominal GNP, or on the degree of substitutability with currency that it exhibits.

That any such "means of payment" approach to defining money leads to difficulties can be illustrated by considering common-stock or money-market mutual funds. Everyone agrees that the function of such funds is to convert fund assets into other assets, shares in the funds, which are more easily held by lenders or savers. Under some circumstances, quantity theorists, who often favor laissez-faire in nonfinancial markets, endorse measures to restrict the scope of such intermediation. If fund liabilities become too convenient to hold, which is to say become too close to being "means of payment," then quantity theorists advocate intervention. At what point, though, do fund liabilities become too much like "means of payment?" In Friedman's view, state banks prior to the Civil War, which were in the business of intermediating state-issued bonds, had gone too far. Have money-market funds which allow check writing gone too far? Are repos a market segment that has gone too far? One weakness in the quantity-theory view is that it provides no principle for answering such questions.

Another weakness in the quantity-theory view is its willingness to base policy recommendations on claims about desirable time paths of the price level. Suppose fluctuations in something real give rise to fluctuations in the demand for credit. Presumably, it is desirable that this be reflected in movements of some prices, but which prices? The quantity-theory view advocates separating "money" from "credit." It asserts that a fluctuating credit demand ought to be reflected in a movement in interest rates and not in a movement of the price level. That, however, is not obvious.[559]

A discussion in terms of fiat currency seems relevant to contemporary monetary institutions. However, in much of the original debate between quantity

> theorists and real bills advocates, it was assumed that a commodity standard was in effect and in particular, a gold standard.[560]

The ongoing conflict between and amongst simultaneous circulation of commodity-backed sovereign money, circulation of sovereign fiat money, circulation of real bills and central bank market intervention in money and asset valuations through manipulation of interest rates and open market operations confirms the conundrum.

Thomas Humphry in an article published by the Federal Reserve Bank of Richmond, entitled "The Real Bills Doctrine, Economic Review,"[561] points up the long-existing conflict amongst experts in attempting to reconcile the concept of commodity based money, which has as its fundamental functions, service as sound sovereign money, in a classical sense, as well as the adoption by the founding fathers of their chosen mechanism to impose constitutional limitations on the ability of government to manipulate and debase money for the interests of politicians and bankers in derogation of the public interest. The Humphrey article is worthy of inclusion in some length because it demonstrates the recognition within the Federal Reserve Bank of Richmond, and thus the Federal Reserve Board and the Federal Reserve, of the difficulties and dangers inherent in the policies these experts have repeated over and over with the surreal expectations that somehow they might expect a different and better result. This false position lies at the heart of the consistent misrepresentation of the value of America's sovereign money that began in earnest at the time of *The Federal Reserve Act of 1913*, continuing until the present day.

Mr. Humphry states his case in summary as follows:

> With recession lingering and interest rates remaining high, one hears increasingly that the Fed should abandon its money growth targets and move to a policy of lowering interest rates to full employment levels [In the light of day in 2015, the conclusion that lower interest rates would necessarily correlate to growth in employment is highly questionable]. All would be well, we are told, if only the Fed would set a fixed low interest rate target consistent with full employment and then let the money stock adjust to money demand to achieve that desired target rate. In effect, this means that the Fed would relinquish control over the money stock, letting it expand as required in a vain effort to eliminate discrepancies between the market rate and the predetermined target rate.
>
> This low target interest rate proposal has much in common with the long-discredited real bills doctrine, according to which the money supply should expand passively to accommodate the legitimate needs of trade. Both views contend that the money supply is (or should be) essentially demand determined. Both see causality as running from economic activity to money rather than vice versa. And, in their simplest versions at least, both treat the price level and its rate of change as predetermined exogenous variables and deny that inflation originates in the central bank. In fact, both views prescribe positive monetary expansion even in the face of inflation, the one to allow real transactions to take place at ever-rising prices, the other in an attempt to lower interest rates to target levels. In essence, both tie the money supply directly to an uncontrolled nominal variable that reflects inflationary pressures-the volume of eligible bills offered for discount in the case of the real bills doctrine and the nominal market rate-target rate differential in the case of the interest-pegging scheme. Finally, because they link the money stock to variables that tend to rise in step with prices, both generate inflationary feedback mechanisms in which prices and money chase each other

> upward indefinitely. In these respects, at least, the interest-pegging proposal may be viewed as a recent variant of the old real bills doctrine.[562]

Mr. Humphry states his purpose in the article to: "trace the origin and historical evolution of the real bills doctrine and to show how that doctrine survives today in the interest-targeting scheme. Before doing so, however, it is necessary to spell out the essential features of the doctrine and to identify its underlying error."[563]
Mr. Humphrey predicates his analysis on a useful history of the real bills doctrine. Humphry's work enables an educated examination of that history and enables an evaluation whether either central bank interest manipulation or unrestrained negotiation of real bills, as defined historically, lead ultimately to, or contribute in a significant way to financial crisis, or are useful in resolving financial crises.
Humphrey describes the real bills' doctrine as follows:

> "Essentially, the real bills doctrine is a rule purporting to gear money to production via the short term commercial bill of exchange, thereby ensuring that output generates its own means of purchase and money adapts passively to the legitimate needs of trade. The doctrine states that money can never be excessive when issued against short-term commercial bills arising from real transactions in goods and services. More precisely, the doctrine contends that so long as banks lend only against sound, short-term commercial paper the money stock will be secured by and will automatically vary equiproportionally with real output such that the latter will be matched by just enough money to purchase it at existing prices.2 In other words, inflationary overissue is impossible provided money is issued on loans made to finance real transaction … .
>
> "The doctrine overlooks that the demand for loans depends not only upon the quantity of real transactions but also upon the level of prices at which those real transactions are effected. And rising prices would require an ever-growing volume of loans just to finance the same level of real transactions. Under the real bills criterion these loans would be granted and the stock of money would therefore expand. This monetary expansion would raise prices thereby requiring further monetary expansion leading to still higher prices and so on in a never-ending inflationary sequence. In this way, price inflation would induce the very monetary expansion necessary to perpetuate it and the real bills criterion would provide no effective limit to the quantity of money in existence. Here is the error of the real bills doctrine, namely the tendency to treat prices as given when in fact they vary directly with the money stock. Associated with this is the failure to perceive the two-way inflationary interaction between money and prices that results once money is allowed to be governed by the needs of trade.
>
> "The preceding has identified the flaw in the doctrine as its failure to take account of the price-money price feedback loop that renders the real bills mechanism dynamically unstable. As early as 1802 Henry Thornton had already recognized this inherent instability. Real bill's proponents, said he, 'forgot that there might be no bounds to the demand for paper; that the increasing quantity would contribute to the rise [in the prices] of commodities: and the rise of commodities require, and seem to justify, a still further increase.' More recently, Don Patinkin, referring to 'the vicious cycle of inflation (or deflation) generated by a policy based on the real bills doctrine,' identified the source of this instability:
>
>> "For the essence of this doctrine [Patinkin says] is that the banking system should expand credit in accordance with the "legitimate needs of business"- where these "needs" are measured in money terms, and thus increase

proportionately with the price level. [The result is] that any (say) upward price movement ... will—in accordance with the "real bills doctrine"—generate an increased supply of money which will enable the movement to continue indefinitely.

"In other words, the doctrine ignores the fact that the needs of trade are measured in nominal terms that rise in step with prices. Since monetary expansion raises prices and rising prices, by expanding the needs of trade, are allowed to generate further in creases in the money stock, the result is a vicious circle of inflation in which money and prices chase each other upward indefinitely. In short, because it ties the money supply to a nominal magnitude that moves in step with prices, the real bills doctrine provides no effective constraint on money or prices, both of which can rise without limit (see Box, pp. 6-7). Here is the fallacy of using one uncontrolled nominal variable (the money value of real transactions) to regulate another nominal variable (the money stock). This is the fundamental fallacy of the real bills' doctrine."[564]

A more recent commentary on the real bills doctrine, by Per Hortlund of the Stockholm School of Economics and the Ratio Institute, entitled "In Defense of the Real Bills Doctrine," published in the *Econ Journal Watch*, Volume 3, Number 1, January 2006,[565] pp. 73-87, was published on the cusp on the current great financial crisis. Hortlund surveys the historical foundation for the real bills doctrine as credit money laid out by the FRBR Staff Paper, as well as the commentary that followed, including the FRBR Humphrey article, and a series of related articles critical of the real bills' doctrine. Hortlund makes a number of not so subtle distinctions, that frankly, rather than represent the result of now customary economic sophistry, actually articulates important definitional distinctions and correlation of those distinctions to historical as well as present day distorted legal, economic and monetary policies. These policies have been intentionally engineered to operate for the benefit of Wall Street banking and Washington's pursuit of partisan political objectives, and have thereby intentionally clouded the clarity of well-known principles embodied in our *Constitution* that were constructed to provide for transparency in the creation and emission of money for the benefit of all American citizens.

According to Hortlund:

"The Real Bills Doctrine (RBD) roughly holds that a central bank should limit its operations to the discounting of short term commercial paper. To Timberlake, it was the Fed's faithful adherence to this doctrine that led to the contraction of the money stock in 1929–1932. The RBD has for a long time been criticized by economists in the quantity-theory tradition, who think that the central bank should focus on stabilizing the quantity of money rather than on acquiring only a certain type of assets. They, therefore, favor active open-market policies such as the monetization of government debt to ensure a stable quantity of money. It has also been criticized by economists favoring free banking, who think that competition in money issue will put better constraints on money creation. The scholarly activity of these economists has given rise to a 'tyranny of the status quo' regarding the unsoundness of the real bills doctrine. Some have even been so bold as to brand it a fallacy (Mints 1945, 30; Friedman 1960, 43; Humphrey 1982, 12; Selgin 1982; Bordo and Schwartz 1995, 469; White 1995, 122; Laidler 1995, 258; Timberlake 1993, 259; 2005, 219). The most recent example of this is to be found in Timberlake's piece. In this comment I want to defend the RBD against what I

> believe to be unjust charges brought against it in the literature. Although the RBD is not a monetary panacea, it may in practice be a useful rule of thumb that can improve the workings of a central banking system on the gold standard. Its particular merit is that it prohibits the monetization of government debt." (Hortlund, pp. 73, 74) ....
>
> > "Roughly, the RBD states that if the central bank issues money only against 'real bills', then the money stock will automatically conform to the demand for payment media (Mints 1945, 9). Much confusion in the discussion is due to vagueness of concepts. What constitutes a 'real' bill of exchange? According to Timberlake (2005, 205), the term "real bills doctrine" was coined by Mints, who derived the term from a passage of Adam Smith.
> >
> > "When a bank discounts to a merchant a real bill of exchange drawn by a real creditor upon a real debtor, and which, as soon as it becomes due, is really paid by that debtor, it only advances to him a part of the value which he would otherwise be obliged to keep by him unemployed and in ready money for answering occasional demands. The payment of the bill, when it becomes due, replaces to the bank the value of what it had advanced, together with the interest. The coffers of the bank, so far as its dealings are confined to such customers, resemble a water pond, from which, though a stream is continually running out, yet another is continually running in, fully equal to that which runs out; so that, without any further care or attention, the pond keeps always equally, or very near equally full. Little or no expence (sic) can ever be necessary for replenishing the coffers of such a bank. (Smith 1776, 304)

"This lengthy and somewhat obscure passage opens the way for two senses in which the term 'real bills' may be understood. In the first sense, a real bill is a bill that has arisen from an authentic transaction of goods. The primary function of an 'authentic' bill is to transfer ownership of goods. The credit function is secondary and attached to the transaction. When banks began to discount bills, so-called loan or accommodation bills emerged, which had the legal form of a bill, but without there being any goods transactions involved. For example, a merchant could write a bill on himself, promising to pay $100 three months hence, and then discount the bill with a bank, receiving, say, $98 from the bank in exchange for the bill. Real bills are opposed to this type of loan bills—the 'real' is synonymous with authentic and genuine, and opposed to "pseudo."

"In the second sense, 'real bills' are taken to be bills that represent 'real value.' Real is here opposed to nominal. The discussions by Timberlake (2005), and Humphrey (1982) is very much concerned with this sense of the term."[566] ....

The Real Bills Doctrine and the Productive Credit Doctrine

"The RBD should be distinguished from a number of related but distinct doctrines. One of them is what one might call the Productive Credit Doctrine (PCD). The RBD, at least in its original nineteenth century European form, is concerned with whether the bill arose out of authentic commercial transactions. It does not much concern itself with the *purpose* to which the debtor will put the money. Such purpose is more the concern of the PCD, which says that the central bank should extend credit only for "productive" commercial purposes (i.e., for buying capital goods or intermediate goods, but not for buying shares of company stock).

"Although related, the RBD and the PCD are conceptually distinct. Consider the following two events. First, a merchant that discounts a commodity bill, and uses the proceeds to buy stocks. Second, a merchant that discounts a 'loan bill,' and uses the proceeds to buy intermediate goods. The first event is in accordance with the RBD, but not with the PCD. The second is in accordance with the PCD but not with the RBD. This distinction is important and potentially substantive. Yet Meltzer (2003) consistently equates the two doctrines (for example, the index entry for the RBD on page 791 reads: 'real bills (productive credit) doctrine'). In Meltzer's account, and also in Timberlake's, the Fed's main concern in 1929–1932 seems to have been to avoid the granting of credit for the purpose of speculation, particularly in the stock market. In this regard its operators seem to have been guided by the PCD rather than by the RBD. That the PCD and not only the RBD played a role in the operations of the Fed is also seen from *The Federal Reserve Act* which defined "eligible paper" as 'notes and drafts, and bills of exchange arising out of actual commercial transactions . . . issued or drawn for agricultural, industrial, or commercial purposes' (Timberlake (2005, 207)).

"This definition of "eligible paper" encompasses not only the real bills criterion, but also the productive credit criterion. Because of this definition it is easy to conflate the two doctrines. However, in my view, they are conceptually distinct."[567]

Next Hortlund emphasizes the distinction between the RBD and PCD. The distinction is central to the deterioration of implementation constitutional constraints regulating the value of money, that commenced at soon as the Fed first abandoned the RBD in favor of the more expansive PCD and then implemented the ill-considered departure from any meaningful definition of money for constitutional purposes and any semblance of constitutional congressional regulation of the value of money by reference to a suitable external standard that must exist as a redemption on demand feature to discipline the creation of credit money under either doctrine.

> "Thus, in practice the substantive difference between real bills and productive credit may sometimes be only subtle. One may question whether it is not better to conflate the two, in the name of parsimony. However, I believe that under special circumstances the practical difference may be substantial. An analogy. In a frictionless world with no genuine uncertainty, one may create "synthetic" options out of dynamic portfolio strategies, thus substituting for "real" options. In the same way, productive credit may be considered a "synthetic" real bill that under normal circumstances work well. However, the productive credit rule is more forward looking than is the real bills rule. In times of genuine uncertainty, it may be more difficult to assess the purpose to which credit is to be used, and credit may be undersupplied. In uncertain times, therefore, bank policy according to the RB and to the PC criteria may yield different results.
>
> The Banking Principle
>
> "Also, the RBD should not be equated with the "Banking Principle." In writings on historical monetary doctrines, the RBD is thought to be but one of the "banking (school) principles" (Schwartz 1995, 149; White 1995, 121). The banking principle in the singular, however, is mostly associated with the view that banks, given only the constraint of gold redeemability, may safely be left to issue money according to their own criteria, and that external (quantitative) restrictions on banks—even

central banks—are unnecessary to stop them from overissuing (White 1995, 121). The underlying view is that redeemable bank-issued money is always and everywhere endogenous and demand-determined. There is a "law of reflux" at work, whereby unwanted money is always returned to the issuer—banks therefore do not have the power to over-issue money and can therefore never be the cause of inflation. The banking principle holds that money will always be demand-determined—even if it comes about through the central bank's monetization of government debt. The RBD, in contrast, holds that money will be demand-determined only if issued against real bills.

"Similarly, the RBD should not be equated with the "needs-of-trade doctrine." This doctrine holds it desirable for the central bank (or other banks) to have discretion to accommodate fluctuations in the demand for payment media (Schwartz 1995, 149). This is in contrast with what might be called the "quantity-doctrine," which holds that any quantity of money is always adequate to perform its task. The critique of the RBD by quantity- minded economists is often in reality a critique against the needs-of-trade doctrine. An important example is given next."[568]

Considering the United States in the period 1929-1932, Hortlund identifies the standard indictment of the role of the real bills doctrine in the Great Depression:

"[W]hether the Great Contraction was caused by the Fed's faithful adherence to the precepts of the RBD. Allegedly, the dynamic instability of the RBD now worked the other way. Insufficient quantities of real bills caused a decrease in the price level, which caused the volume of real bills to shrink even further, and so on in a downward spiral. To convict the RBD, it has to be shown: (a) that the Fed discounted all real bills (eligible paper) presented to it for discount; and (b) that these quantities were insufficient to sustain a stable quantity of money.[569]

The true real-bills central bank discounts *if and only if* real bills (eligible paper) is presented to it for discount. That is, the real-bills central bank acts according to these two rules:

Rule 1: Do not discount non-real bills (ineligible paper) presented for discount.
Rule 2: *Do* discount all real bills (eligible paper) presented for discount.

A central bank that does not follow *both* of these rules cannot be said to follow the RBD. For the RBD adherent, the real bills criterion provides a rule that renders monetary policy more or less automatic. The volume of real bills corresponds by itself in a desired manner with the "needs of trade," wherefore no discretionary evaluation or prudence on the part of the central bank is needed. The central banker's only task is to check whether the instruments presented for discount is on the list of eligible paper or not. Did the Fed follow the rules?

- *1914–1920*: Inflationary war-finance. The Fed was buying Treasury bonds. The Fed violated Rule 1.
- *1920–1929*: Price stabilization the goal of policy. The Fed engaged in open market purchases of Treasury bonds. Again it violated Rule 1.
- *1929–1932*: This is where the debate is. Was the Fed now taken over by RBD advocates such as Adolph Miller, who faithfully adhered to the RBD? To convict the RBD, it has to be shown that the Fed discounted all eligible paper presented to it, yet a deflationary spiral set in. Here Timberlake presents evidence indicating that the Fed actually acted contrariwise to the RBD. Quoting Clark Warburton, Timberlake provides a smoking gun that shows that the Fed violated Rule 2.

> [In the early 1930s the Fed Banks] ... virtually stopped discounting or otherwise acquiring "eligible" paper. ... Nor was this virtual stoppage ... due to any forces outside the Federal Reserve System. It was due to direct pressure [from the Federal Reserve Board] so strong as to amount to a virtual prohibition of rediscounting for banks which were making loans for security speculation, and a hard- boiled attitude towards banks in special need of rediscounts because of deposit withdrawals ... Federal Reserve authorities had discouraged discounting almost to the point of prohibition. (Warburton 1966, 339–340, quoted in Timberlake 2005, 216)

> "Assuming the accuracy of Warburton's account, we see clearly that the Fed did *not* operate according to the RBD. Nothing in the RBD says that the central bank should refuse to discount real bills in time of deposit withdrawals. On the contrary, this is the very time to do so, and for which the Federal Reserve System was set up. Anxious to make amends for past breaches of Rule 1, the Fed apparently erred in the other direction and grossly violated Rule 2. In so doing, its operators seem to have been inspired by the PCD rather than by the RBD.[570] ...
>
> "In sum, Timberlake successfully defends the gold standard against the view that it caused the Great Contraction. Timberlake is also successful when he puts the blame on errors in the monetary policies of the Fed. However, he is unsuccessful when he attributes the substance of those errors to the Fed's faithfully following the real bills doctrine. Timberlake's own account suggests the very opposite. From its inception, the Fed seems to have strayed from the real bills rules—at times by monetizing government debt, and at times by refusing to discount real bills. One may come away with the impression that if only the Fed's operators had followed the wise counsels provided by the system's founding fathers, everything would have been fine.
>
> "In my view, the current presentation therefore calls for a revision of scholarly understanding of the real bills doctrine. Admittedly, the RBD is waterproof neither in theory nor in practice, and is therefore probably not a sufficient guide for monetary policy. The RBD perhaps should come into use in systems with limitations on the quantity of base money—natural limitations in gold regimes and quantity rules in fiat money regimes. In such systems, however, one must seriously ask whether the RBD may not actually improve policy performance. Although not perfect, the RBD might be considered efficient, when compared with the performance of its rival doctrines."[571]

At the end of Hortland's paper, with appropriate academic modesty, Hortlund next poses a series of questions for the reader to ponder, as he concludes in his paper, that "show that the real bills doctrine is alive and kicking, and capable of generating important questions for future research." (Hortland, p. 84) This book however is a work of advocacy and I have taken the liberty of converting Hortlunds questions into statements that I believe are accurate reflections the points actually made by Hortlund and which support the positions taken subsequently in this book:

> "The classical gold standard period of 1870 to 1914 is acknowledged as one of the more stable periods of monetary history." ... The RBD was an integral policy of most central banks in this period. It be said that the RBD contributed to the stability of the classical gold standard era:
>
> 1. The history covered by Hortlund does not states an unambiguous case in which the RBD caused a major inflation. There ever been a major inflation that did not involve the monetization of government debt.

2. On the role of the RBD in the Great Depression, it cannot be shown quantitatively that the volume of eligible paper generated in the economy was insufficient to accommodate increased demands for currency in the early 1930s.
3. For free bankers, given that a free banking system is not politically feasible, there would be nothing wrong, with a rule that prohibits monetization of government debt for purposes of maintaining sound money and financial stability. In fact, a central banking system with such a rule be considered as a tool to serve sound money and financial stability, given a nominal anchor for sovereign money such as gold.
4. The monetarists' critique of the RBD significantly contributed to the adoption of government debt as the main instrument of monetary policy in the 1930s. This opened the way for unprecedented monetary expansion and inflation in period 1940 to 1990. Somewhat ironically, therefore, the monetarists, the champions of the fight against inflation, could rightly be considered some of the architects of the postwar inflations. In view of the historical record, would monetarists must be willing to revise their critique of the RBD. In practice, RBD-style "quality-rules" that emphasize restriction to certain types of assets would be more efficient than quantity rules, to limit inflation."[572]

The discussions included in this chapter point to a constant, though marginalized, professional and academic recognition that while the government has the constitutional power and authority to borrow money, it does not have the power and authority to monetize its debt without subjecting it to the discipline of redemption in accordance with the constitutional requirement of regulation of its value in accordance with an external standard of value, such as gold. Money then, might properly consist only of real bills discounted and rediscounted in accordance with the real bills rules identified by Hortland, following the 4,000 year history of the evolution of money set out in Chapters 2 and 3 of this work, and other paper money, made subject to the constitutional redemption discipline imposed by the constitutional requirements for creation and regulation of the value of money.

§7.07 FALSE NARRATIVE: CONGRESS HAS LAWFULLY DELEGATED TO THE FED AND THE FED HAS LAWFULLY DELEGATED TO WALL STREET THE POWER AND DUTY TO CREATE, EMIT AND REGULATE THE VALUE OF THE DOLLAR

Although the Federal Reserve Board has represented from time to time, in writing, that it exercises its powers under a delegation to it by Congress of the Congressional mandate to "coin money and regulate its value," there is no evidence of any such Congressional legislative delegation of such power and duty.

According to an official statement of the Fed Board of Governors, *"[t]he entire system is subject to oversight by the U.S. Congress because the Constitution gives to Congress the power to coin money and set its value—a power that, in the 1913 Act, Congress itself delegated to the Federal Reserve"*[573] … *"But one can search that act until his eyes fall out without finding a delegation of the 'power to coin money."* The delegation, if it can be said to have any legal basis or effect, is de facto: a ceding or relinquishment to or abandonment of the power, however undefined, by Congress to the Fed that the Fed has exploited to the fullest, for itself and through the entire national and global banking community. (Authors' emphasis added in italics)

Because the Federal Reserve System does not have the express legal legislative imperative to "coin money and regulate the value thereof" and because its express legal, legislative mandate, duty and power is to act, primarily through money and market creation through credit expansion, interest rate manipulation and open market purchases of, now, assets of every stripe, for the limited purpose of effecting non-pecuniary social and political objectives, its entire existence and actions subvert and are directly opposed and antithetical to the constitutional congressional power and duty to coin and regulate the value of money in accordance with a defined, effective standard of value that ensures the equal protection for each individual's creation, preservation and protection of the value of the fruits of his or her labor, property and ability to participate in the American market economy on a fair, and equal basis under the American rule of law. Although the legal exercise by Congress of its constitutional power and duty to regulate the value of money is a necessary condition for the Federal Reserve system and the national banking system to legitimately fulfill their respective statutory mandates; to the extent that they themselves impact the creation of money and regulation of its value without being subject to a legitimate constitutional standard of value, their policies and actions, most dramatically following the Nixon shock and continuing until today, they are *directly antithetical and opposed to their respective official, legislative, social and political.* As a matter of constitutional law, the existence, roles and actions of the Federal Reserve System and the national banking system are, and must be made specifically and unequivocally subject and subordinate to the constitutional mandate for Congress to exercise the power and duty delegated to it by the people to create and regulate the value of money in accordance with a legitimate, expressed defined and legitimate standard of value.

The pursuit by the Fed of its stated legislative mission at once has been shown to be largely ineffective and, in fact, has frustrated and rendered literally impossible the ability of the Fed or any federal financial regulatory authority to meet their sometime "assumed mission" of the constitutional imperative for Congress to coin and regulate the value of money.

Admittedly, re-establishment of a proper constitutional mechanism for the creation and regulation of the value of money that provides the people with equal protection for each individual's creation, preservation and protection of the value of the fruits of his or her labor, property and ability to participate in the American market economy on a fair, and equal basis under the American rule of law would, and should dramatically limit the scope of the ability of the Federal Reserve System and the national banking system to continue business as usual facilitating the fleecing of American people by the Washington and Wall Street enterprise while paying mere lip service to the their social and political objects that are the foundation for their respective legal existence.

The usual rhetoric employed by Washington and Wall Street intimates that the Fed is solely and supremely responsible for all matters involving American money; ostensibly based upon a congressional delegation of unbridled discretionary monetary powers. This false narrative is uniformly expressed in such a generality.[574] What does this narrative mean? It is, of course a story contrived and disseminated by Washington and Wall Street, from the creation of the Fed in *The Federal Reserve Act*, but largely over the past 45 years following the Nixon shock.[575] Edwin Vieira, the nation's foremost legal authority on the monetary powers and disabilities of the *United States Constitution* is of the opinion that "it is enough to grasp the fundamental principle that delegations of public powers to private parties are, in almost all conceivable cases, unlawful."[576]

Has Congress' establishment of the Federal Reserve System somehow attempted to effect a delegation of Congress' power and duty, as delegated to it in the first instance, specifically by the American people in the *United States Constitution*, to create and regulate the value of American sovereign money? Has the Federal Reserve System somehow attempted to affect a re-delegation, or sub-delegation of Congress' monetary power and duty to the Wall Street banks, permitting them to create and regulate the value of American sovereign money? However improbable on its face, and actually demonstrably false and legally ineffective, this daisy chain of abandonment of power and duty, and with it accountability, may have been, this fairy tale of a "Ponzi scheme" of supposed delegation of Congressional power and duty has become and remains the dominant narrative of how the value of the American dollar is regulated today—the false delegation narrative.

The Fed has intimated, from time to time that that constitutional congressional power and duty have been delegated to it by Congress. The Fed then turned to Wall Street under the Greenspan doctrine of Wall Street "self-regulation", protesting that it is not capable of regulating these enormous and powerful institutions. What has become of the fiduciary power, duty and accountability attributable to such power? Is any such delegation too vague to be enforced by the judicial system?

12 U.S.C.A. § 225a, effective December 27, 2000, amending the *Federal Reserve Act*, now requires the Fed to maintain long run growth of monetary and credit aggregates:

> The Board of Governors of the Federal Reserve System and the Federal Open Market Committee shall maintain long run growth of the monetary and credit aggregates commensurate with the economy's long run potential to increase production, so as to promote effectively the goals of maximum employment, stable prices, and moderate long-term interest rates.

Arguments have been made that the Fed's official regulations are the lawful product of its powers and duties created by *The Federal Reserve Act*, as amended, and are reasonable in a regulatory context, but far too vague and nebulous to be used outside the regulatory context for which it was intended. These arguments, covered by the false delegation narrative, now obscure the fundamental, clear and understandable constitutional imperative of honest, safe, sound, and transparent regulation of the value of money by Congress, with intentionally vague and nebulous rhetoric that, so far, has covered up the largest crime of bank fraud in the history of money and banking.

The vague and nebulous argument does apply to the Fed's general statutory objectives. "The Federal Reserve exercises unprecedented breadth and depth of power over money despite the fact that its official mission is actually quite limited: *The Federal Reserve Act* provides that the Board of Governors and the Federal Reserve Open Market Committee seek: "to promote effectively the goals of maximum employment, stable prices, and moderate long-term interest rates." ... "Indeed courts have held that the speculative nature of the issues involved precludes litigation over whether the FOMC's policies are actually responsible for the country's economic conditions—that is, the FRS's effects on the economy are not provable according to the laws of evidence."[577]

"In our view, "the links in the chain of causation between the [alleged constitutional violations] and the asserted injury [general inflation resulting from Fed exercise of monetary power] are far too weak for the chain as a whole to sustain [the appellants'] standing." It is entirely speculative whether the influence of the Reserve Bank members is responsible for the FOMC's alleged pursuit of restrictive or erratic monetary policies. Moreover, in light of the complexity of the modern economy, it is also highly uncertain whether and to what extent such policies were responsible for the adverse economic conditions that allegedly resulted in harm to the appellants. Similarly, the appellants have given no indication as to how they can succeed in establishing that an overly broad delegation of power to the Federal Reserve System has had the consequence of undermining economic certainty and thereby increasing interest rates. Such general assertions are clearly inadequate to meet the constitutional requirement that parties allege specific facts sufficient to establish that their injuries are fairly traceable to the alleged violations. We think that courts lack both the competence and the authority to determine such abstract issues, which are better addressed through political and economic debate over the role of monetary policy in the national economy."[578]

Contrary to the holdings of the D.C. Court in *Ruess v. Balles*:[579]

- Action to assure honest, safe and sound money in which the public may repose their trust and confidence may but does not necessarily have as its primary purpose to remedy "restrictive or erratic" Fed monetary policies.
- Insistence on the proper re-establishment of honest, safe and sound money, the value of which is regulated by Congress in the in the interest of the public welfare, is not asserted to essentially deal with a "broad, remedial social legislation" that is exercised and enforced by Congress over regulatory agencies. To the extent the this re-establishment involves constitutional questions raised by existing legislation and regulatory structure, however, it nonetheless presents not just legislative or regulatory issues, but rather, in the first instance a proper constitutional question that must be properly addressed in the American judicial system.
- Congress, the Fed and other federal financial regulatory authorities can and must establish in detail the duties and responsibilities of the parties whose mandate turns on honest, safe and sound money, based upon specific official papers, records and government reports over a protracted period of specific action. This does not equate to what has proved to be an ineffective *ex post facto* demand by financial regulators that banks increase income and capital, made at the time the banks suffer from asset devaluation and illiquidity

directly caused by persistent, continuous, unquestioned money debasement by the Washington Wall Street racketeering enterprise.

- Existing official government reports, together with expert testimony by nationally recognized experts, many of whom have been relied on by the Washington and Wall Street for their own purposes, provide specific facts sufficient to establish that the damages suffered by the American public caused by intentional representation of the liquidity and value of instruments actually constituting our money supply are "fairly traceable to the alleged violations" by Washington and Wall Street of the *United States Constitution*, federal and state statutory law and common law going back to the *Magna Charta.*
- The call for re-establishment of honest, safe and sound money does not constitute an assertion of an abstract principle of political or economic debate, but it is rather the assertion of the specific, well-defined and well-supported claims that can be made by the American public for enforcement of the *United States Constitution*, and the well-established American rule of law, by the Judicial Branch of the of United States government. The fact that enforcement of the American rule of law by the judicial system may subsequently lead to political controversy and debate over economic and monetary policies made by Congress, the Executive branch of government, including the federal financial regulators, and the Federal Reserve System, as well as other quasi-government entities and their fellows in the corrupt racketeering enterprise dedicated to money debasement, the Wall Street banks, is entirely reasonable, expected and is one objective of such action. Politics and the making and conduct of social, political, financial, economic and monetary policies are, as a matter of law, and must, as a practical matter, be made subject to constitutional challenge under our judicial system, upon petition, in accordance with and subject to the American rule of law. American social, political, financial, economic and monetary policy activities are not exempt from the requirements of the *United States Constitution* or of application of existing federal statutory law and common law.
- Edmund Vieria pertinently observes that "if these matters are actually beyond rational investigation in a court of law, then the benchmarks the statutes set out cannot be classified as legal standards capable of controlling the actions of government agencies."[580]

The "too vague and nebulous" characterization perfectly describes the existing presumption (the false delegation narrative) that the power and duty to regulate the value of money as delegated by citizens to Congress; has then somehow been purportedly delegated by Congress to the Fed at some indeterminate time and in some indeterminate manner; and that then such powers and duties have been, further, purportedly delegated by the Fed to the Wall Street banks at some purportedly indeterminate time and in some indeterminate manner. This vague and nebulous narrative cannot justify the takeover by the Fed and the Wall Street banks of total power over the nation's money. Congress does not have the right or power to affect such a narrative. Regulation of the value of money and credit is central to the concept of honesty, safety and soundness that lies at the heart of our banking, financial and monetary system. That concept lies at the heart of all federal bank regulation and the duties of all parties in that chain of duty, to honestly protect the public interest in the integrity of the American monetary, banking, financial and economic system that must, in turn, support our trust and confidence and the health of our civil society. The intentionally false Washington and Wall Street narrative of a daisy chain of uncontrolled delegation of congressional powers, duties or standards to the Washington and Wall Street corrupt enterprise of financial speculation does not, and cannot serve the public interest. It is an abomination.

§7.08 LEGAL REQUIREMENTS FOR CONGRESSIONAL DELEGATION OF POWERS AND DUTIES

[A] False Narrative of Congressional Delegation to the Fed

As noted repeated in this work, the American people delegated to Congress the power and duty to create sovereign money and regulate its value in the *United States Constitution* Article I, § 8, Clause 5 that provides that "The Congress shall have power to coin money, regulate the value thereof, and of foreign coin, and fix the standard of weights and measures."

Thomas Hart Benton,[581] in his *Abridgement of the Debates of Congress through 1850*, stated that:

> "Every legislative body, every person in vested with power of any kind, is morally bound to use only those means which are necessary and proper for the correct execution of the powers delegated to them.
>
> "In the selection of means to carry any of your constitutional powers into effect, you must exercise a sound discretion; acting under its influence, you will discover that what is proper at one time may be extremely unfit and improper at another. The original powers granted to the Government by the *Constitution* can never change with the varying circumstances of the country, but the means by which those powers are to be carried into effect must necessarily vary with the varying state and circumstances of the nation. We are, when acting to-day, not to inquire what means were necessary and proper twenty years ago, not what were necessary and proper at the organization of the Government, but our inquiry must be, what means are necessary and proper this day. The *Constitution*, in relation to the means by which its powers are to be executed, is one eternal now. The state of things now, the precise point of time when we are called upon to act, must determine our choice in the selection of means to execute the delegated powers."[582]

George Rothwell Brown, in his book *Leadership of Congress*, stated that:

> "... the delegated powers granted to Congress under Section VIII are not merely power conferred, but they are obligations laid upon Congress, the designation of acts which must be performed. Obviously, if Congress declined to exercise the power to "lay and collect taxes, duties, imposts, and excises, to pay the debts and provide for the common defense and general welfare of the United States," the government would cease to function; it could not exist. These delegated powers,

> therefore are not merely privileges, which Congress may exercise if it wishes, or decline to exercise if it so desires, but are sacred duties imposed upon Congress.
>
> "It is clear, first that the wording of the clause which states that each House "may" determine the rules of its procedure is such as to give to the word "may" the meaning of "shall"; and second that the powers and duties of Congress are inseparable; that the obligation to raise money and pay the debts of the nation could not be avoided, and that, therefore, no Congress could justify itself before the people for in ability to function which had rendered itself incapable of functioning through failure to avail itself of the constitutional authority to provide for its orderly management such rules as might be necessary to the full discharge of its duties."[583]

Subsequently, courts and commentators have addressed the issues implicit in the powerful language of Benton and Brown. David Schoenbrod, Professor, New York Law School, in his *"Delegation and Democracy: A Reply to My Critics,"* nicely summarizes the public policy debate, his views on and critique if the modern political trend and legal apathy supporting the delegation of constitutional powers and duties.

Schoenbrod begins with the observation that "[h]igh officials tell us that we can be proud to live in a democracy because we have elected them. That tale does not altogether convince voters today. Large majorities tell pollsters that government has somehow eluded their control. ... Although the *Constitution* established congressional responsibility as the main engine of our indirect democracy, members of Congress have evaded responsibility by delegating legislative powers to the executive branch. The result, as I [Schoenbrod] have argued, is that democracy suffers."[584]

Schoenbrod counters other commentators who have asserted "that delegation does no harm to democracy";[585] "democracy is a meaningless concept";[586] and that "delegation is a policy choice that Congress is entitled to make."[587] He responds to each of these contentions "after placing the question of delegation's impact on democracy in historical context."[588]

According to Schoenbrod, "[t]he effort to square delegation with democracy is pervasively futile because the drive for delegation, from the beginning of the twentieth century, stemmed from a desire to reduce government's accountability to ordinary voters."[589] He explains:

> "[t]hat democracy was undercut at the beginning of the twentieth century, according to Professor Wiebe [historian Robert H. Wiebe], by the rise of what he calls 'the national class.' The national class are the leaders and budding leaders of the institutions with clout on the national scene: the nationally oriented corporations and unions, the nationally oriented quarters of the professions and media, the nationally prestigious universities, and of course the federal government itself.
>
> "The national class thought that ordinary people should not have the power to hold government accountable. That power should come not from what ordinary people pride themselves on—self-support—but rather from what the national class had to offer -specialized knowledge. Members of the national class thought, and many still feel, that experts armed with science and insulated from politics were better equipped to govern than elected officials accountable to ordinary people."[590]

The shift of control has been affected first, by "discouraging voting by the lower classes,"[591] a familiar theme in political rhetoric, and second and most importantly for purposes of this work:

> [t]he national class sought to insulate the government from accountability at the polls. It campaigned to transfer governmental power from institutions that were most accountable to ordinary voters to institutions more in the control of the national class. It succeeded; power was transferred from the states to the national government and, within the national government, from Congress to the executive and the judiciary. From its inception, the core purpose of delegation was to undercut democratic accountability.[592]

"In spite of the generally populist rhetoric of the New Deal, according to "Thurman Arnold's *Folklore of American Capitalism* (1937), often cited as the New Deal's most significant commentary on government, derisively dismissed the very thought of popular rule. ... Policy itself fragmented into a multitude of exclusive dialogues among administrative officials, congressional committees, and powerful citizens. By the 1940s it was quite common for the same cluster of officials and citizens to write a law in private, then execute it in private, with just a quick public peek into the process as it was enacted. Few laws were designed for more than a tiny minority to comprehend."[593] Schenbrods and Arnold's observations resonate in the background in consideration of legal accountability for financial crises today.

According to Schoenbrod, through the pervasive delegation of power by Congress, America has devolved to the point that by reason of such widespread delegation, "[w]e now have war, regulation, and taxation without representation. ... For well over a century after the adoption of the *Constitution*, the Supreme Court held that the *Constitution* prohibits members of Congress from bestowing upon others their personal responsibility for enacting laws. When national class legislation began to delegate lawmaking authority to federal agencies at the turn of the century, there had to be a rationale to square the delegation with the *Constitution*."[594]

The first rationale was that Congress did not actually delegate power to make laws but only the power to enforce laws made by Congress. Schoenbrod notes, however that "[t]he supposed laws were, from [his] perspective, not laws at all because they provided no discernible rule of conduct. Nonetheless, this first rationale was more naive than disingenuous. The national class had the conceit that its expertise could pour meaning into these empty congressional formulations, and so doing was more akin to fact finding than lawmaking. Thus, the national class could think there was clear meaning in statutory standards that, to a modern mind, were hopelessly vague."[595] To the extent then that Congress and the Fed might like to think that the congressional fiduciary power and duty to create money and regulate its value could be discharged by Congress implicitly, and nowhere in law and by no means actually, delegation of that power and duty to the Fed or the Wall Street banks, the process in fact has perpetuated ongoing intentionally fraudulent money debasement, financial crises and damages almost inestimable, suffered by ordinary Americans while the powers that be escape not only unharmed but buoyed by ever increasing and concentrated power, income and wealth.

The second rationale, the "Intelligible Principle Test"[596] advanced in support of Congressional delegation of its Constitutional powers and duties to non-elected agency bureaucrats was addressed by the Supreme Court in 1928:

> In *J.W. Hampton & Co. v. United States*, decided in 1928, the Supreme Court held that Congress could delegate the power to make the law if it provided "an intelligible principle" to guide the agency lawmakers. The Court did not, however, explicitly admit that Congress could delegate the power to make law. That did not come until five years later, when it said that the statute in *Hampton* delegated legislative power in a "permissible" — that is, a minor — way. But the implication was clear in 1928. Even such a fervent believer in government by expert as President-elect Herbert Hoover reacted angrily at the departure from constitutional tradition: "There is only one commission to which delegation of that authority can be made. That is the great commission of [the voters'] own choosing, the Congress of [the voters'] own choosing, the Congress of the United States and the President. It is the only commission which can be held responsible to the electorate."[597]

The third rational was based upon the proposition that subsequent to delegation, Congress could always remediate agency law-making through remedial congressional legislation and thereby avoid any real harm to democracy, because, as the Supreme Court observed:

> "[B]ecause Congress retains the power to enact a statute, repealing whatever agency-made laws that it does not approve. This rationale reverses the burden that the Constitution places on those who want to expand the powers of government by imposing a new law. Under the Constitution, the proponents of the new law must bear the burden of getting it approved by the House, the Senate, and the President. Under the last rationale, inaction by either House is sufficient for the agency-made law to stay in effect. There are, of course, many ways to prevent a controversial bill from coming to the floor for a vote, and legislators are only too willing to avoid controversial votes. As a result, laws are sustained without any legislative accountability.
>
> "The Supreme Court understands perfectly well that legislators bear little responsibility for inaction, and so it refuses to rely upon legislative inaction in interpreting statutes. It is utterly unprincipled to claim that legislative inaction, somehow squares delegation with Article I of the *Constitution*. Indeed, the Supreme Court has come close to recognizing this much. In *INS v. Chadha*, it stated, '[t]o allow Congress to evade the strictures of the *Constitution* and in effect enact Executive proposals into law by mere silence cannot be squared with Art. I'.[598]

With the blessing of the Supreme Court then, Congress has purported to transform "its responsibility for the laws from a right of the voters to an option of the legislators."[599] The result of this apparent transformation is that:

> "[d]elegation has allowed legislators to rewrite the ground rules of democracy to help entrench themselves in office. They can pretend to deliver the best of everything to everyone by commanding agencies to promulgate laws to achieve popular statutorily prescribed goals. The statutes are framed so that legislators can skirt the hard choices. This permits legislators to claim much of the credit for the benefits of the laws but shift to the unelected agency officials much of the blame

for the inevitable costs and disappointments when the agency fails to deliver all the benefits promised.

"Delegation thus allows members of Congress to function as ministers, who express popular aspirations (through enacting lofty statutory goals) and tend to their flocks (by doing casework), rather than lawmakers who must make hard choices in passing laws. In a book that argues that delegation has enhanced legislators' chances of reelection, Morris Fiorina writes:

> "So long as ... congressmen ... function principally as national policy makers ... reasonably close congressional elections will naturally result. For every voter a congressman pleases by a policy stand he will displease someone else. The consequence is a marginal district. But if we have incumbents who deemphasize controversial policy positions and instead place heavy emphasis on nonpartisan, nonprogrammatic constituency service ... the resulting blurring of political friends and enemies is sufficient to shift the district out of the marginal camp.

"With delegation, legislators can escape being ejected from office except upon grounds that would oust a minister from the pulpit — scandal. In those exceptional cases when incumbents do lose an election, their defeat is far more likely to be caused by some escapade or chicanery than by how they shaped the law. Entrenched encumbency is a marker for what is a profound problem — that legislators have rewritten the ground rules of government to evade responsibility."[600]

The upshot of the growing tendency to, and in many cases a completely unfounded assumption of delegation of Congress's Article I powers and duties to government agencies and bureaucrats, according to Schoenbron, and with respect to which I agree, is that, even if it might somehow be correct to assert that delegation does not impair voters ability to vote for legislators with similar ideologies, it is wrong to conclude that there is no loss of democratic accountability caused by wholesale delegation by Congress of its constitutional powers and duties:

> "Even though legislators may personally share our ideological preferences, political incentives lead them to delegate in ways that do not produce laws that coincide with our views. For example, because they escape much of the blame for the inevitable costs of creating new federal lawmaking programs and also much of the blame for the inevitable failure of these programs to produce the benefits promised, legislators are skewed towards creating and enlarging an agency's lawmaking jurisdiction, making its goals more ambitious, its methods more intrusive, and its procedures more complicated. The upshot is that, in lawmaking, the national government, particularly the executive branch, increasingly takes jurisdiction over matters that might otherwise be left to the political branches of state or local government, the common law, or private ordering."[601]
>
> "While the problem is often too much regulation, sometimes it is too little regulation. Because legislators also escape blame for the resulting disappointments when agencies fail to deliver on statutory promises, Congress is insensitive to the delay and uncertainty that frequently results when the agency lacks the political muscle needed to make, expeditiously, the hard choices that Congress ducked."[602]
>
> ...
>
> "The early proponents of delegation were correct; it is a way to insulate the 'experts' from the pressures of elective politics. Once the 1970s arrived with their emphasis on participatory democracy and talk of 'power to the people,' the

rationale in favor of delegation has been repackaged to make it sound less elitist. While the talk is different, the walk still has all the swagger of 'power to the insiders.'"[603]

The transfer of power by the people, through Congress to "insiders" through unrestrained delegation of power, the purported transfers leave accountability for the exercise of that power in the dust. Delegation gives the electoral advantage to those who duck the difficult choices. It does not reflect much of a distinction between the political left or right so much as a distinction between insiders and outsiders in the power structure.

Schoenbrod addresses the assertion that delegation does not subvert democracy because the President and elected official responsible for the executive agencies are accountable for enforcement of the laws. The practical effect of broad Congressional delegation of its constitutional powers and duties is that "[s]o long as the agency does not profoundly anger large numbers of voters, and instead only slightly irritates large numbers of voters or badly harms only smaller numbers, it need not fear that Congress will take away its power."[604]

Is the delegation by Congress of its constitutional powers and duties a political question, unfit for judicial consideration of the enforcement of duties that follow the powers? Schoenbrod replies and I concur that "delegation is one of those policy choices that is controlled by the *Constitution*. Were all issues with policy implications off limits to the courts, they would largely be out of the business of constitutional review. The *Constitution* is a series of policy choices, often about how government should make policy. The *Constitution* is written precisely so that politicians cannot change these meta-policy choices." ... "Delegation is the reason, however, that it is only at the agency level that legislators or anyone else have any understanding of what is at stake. With delegation, legislation is mainly concerned with promising the best of everything to everyone, yet it is only when laws are passed that rights are actually linked to duties. Were Congress to make the law, the stakes would become apparent to legislators (and their constituents) at the legislative level, which is precisely why legislators avoid accountability and delegate." Schoenbrod goes on to clarify that:

> Delegation is the reason, however, that it is only at the agency level that legislators or anyone else have any understanding of what is at stake. With delegation, legislation is mainly concerned with promising the best of everything to everyone, yet it is only when laws are passed that rights are actually linked to duties. Were Congress to make the law, the stakes would become apparent to legislators (and their constituents) at the legislative level, which is precisely why legislators avoid accountability and delegate.[605]

The effects of the pernicious evolution of avoidance of Congressional accountability through the device of delegation is that "[t]he unorganized interests are the ones most prone to be harmed by delegation[;] and its corollary, [t]he broadest and most important public interests have little if any representation" Accordingly, [i]nherent in delegation is a bias towards more regulation, more centralized and complicated regulation, because lawmakers escape most of the blame for launching sweeping regulations that promise more than can be delivered and impose costs for which legislators would not take responsibility if they had to make the hard choice. In other words, society is deprived of the most direct means to decide how much it wants to be controlled by government. Rather, that decision is ceded, in substantial measure, to a government run by legislators who want to entrench themselves in office, agency officials who want to enlarge their budgets, and interest group leaders whose livelihoods and power grow in our thriving administrative state."[606]

Schoenbrod's analysis illustrates the evolution in American of the dangerous ever-growing phenomenon of government exercise of power for "insider" interests without accountability for the duties associated with and an un-severable part of the exercise of congressional constitutional powers that have been simply ignored. Certainly, accountability for congressional, federal agency and Wall Street "insider" accountability for the financial crisis has simply been left behind.

As we have learned so far, although Washington and Wall Street would have the American public believe the Congress has effectively and legally delegated the powers and implicit accompanying duties to create and regulate the value of American money to the Federal Reserve system and that the Federal Reserve system has effectively and legally delegated the powers and implicit accompanying duties to create and regulate the value of American money to Wall Street under the oxymoron of bank and bank regulatory agency "self-regulation"; there is, and there has been no legal delegations of such powers and duties. American money is neither created nor is its value regulated by Congress. Washington and Wall Street like it that way. The Washington Wall Street criminal racketeering enterprise blossoms and prospers.

If Congress had actually, legally made such a delegation to the Federal Reserve System in the first instance, and if the Fed actually somehow had the legal authority to abandon the powers and duties of creation and regulation of the value of American money to Wall Street through the unequivocally wrong and irresponsible mechanism of self-regulation, what legal requirements would apply to such a fantastic daisy chain, the sole purpose of which has not been to serve the public interest, but rather to benefit Washington and Wall Street insiders without public accountability?

Emblematic of the tension and polarization of interests encompassed by the concept of delegation of legislative power, the judicial treatment of the issue reflects the same unfortunate characteristics. The framers of our *Constitution* certainly did not contemplate further delegation of powers and duties specifically delegated to Congress in that founding document; and certainly not on the scale on which Congress has at least purported to delegate almost all of its powers and duties; leaving it to preside over a spoils system concentrated exclusively of the benefits to be secured under that system for both Washington and Wall Street.

Justia US Law has reproduced online a useful examination of the requirements for delegation of legislative power:[607]

> "The Supreme Court has sometimes declared categorically that 'the legislative power of Congress cannot be delegated,' and on other occasions has recognized more forthrightly, as Chief Justice Marshall did in 1825, that, although Congress may not delegate powers that 'are strictly and exclusively legislative,' it may delegate 'powers which [it] may rightfully exercise itself.' The categorical statement has never been literally true, the Court having upheld the delegation at issue

in the very case in which the statement was made. The Court has long recognized that administration of the law requires exercise of discretion, and that 'in our increasingly complex society, replete with ever changing and more technical problems, Congress simply cannot do its job absent an ability to delegate power under broad general directives.' The real issue is where to draw the line. Chief Justice Marshall recognized 'that there is some difficulty in discerning the exact limits,' and that 'the precise boundary of this power is a subject of delicate and difficult inquiry, into which a court will not enter unnecessarily.' Accordingly, the Court's solution has been to reject delegation challenges in all but the most extreme cases, and to accept delegations of vast powers to the President or to administrative agencies.'[608]

"The modern doctrine may be traced to the 1928 case *J. W. Hampton, Jr. & Co. v. United States*, 276 U.S. 394 (1928), where the Court emphasized 'that in seeking the cooperation of another branch Congress was restrained only according to 'common sense and the inherent necessities' of the situation.' This vague statement was elaborated somewhat in the statement that the Court would sustain delegations whenever Congress provided an 'intelligible principle' to which the President or an agency must conform.' (276 U.S. at 409) The 'intelligible principle' test of *Hampton* is the same as the 'legislative standards' test of A. L. A. Schechter Poultry Corp. v. United States, 295 U.S. 495, 530 (1935), and Panama Refining Co. v. Ryan, 293 U.S. 388, 421 (1935). 'As characterized by the Court, the delegations struck down in 1935 in the *Panama Refining* and *Schechter* cases were not only broad but unprecedented.'[609]

"The problem was that the Act [*National Industrial Recovery Act*] provided no guidance to the President in determining whether or when to exercise this authority and required no finding by the President as a condition of exercise of the authority. Congress 'declared no policy . . . established no standard, [and] laid down no rule,' but rather 'left the matter to the President without standard or rule, to be dealt with as he pleased.' At issue in *Schechter* was a delegation to the President of authority to promulgate codes of fair competition that could be drawn up by industry groups or prescribed by the President on his own initiative. The codes were required to implement the policies of the Act, but those policies were so general as to be nothing more than an endorsement of whatever might be thought to promote the recovery and expansion of the particular trade or industry. The President's authority to approve, condition, or adopt codes on his own initiative was similarly devoid of meaningful standards, and 'virtually unfettered.' This broad delegation was 'without precedent.' The Act supplied 'no standards' for any trade or industry group, and, unlike other broad delegations that had been upheld, did not set policies that could be implemented by an administrative agency required to follow 'appropriate administrative procedure.' 'Instead of prescribing rules of conduct, [the Act] authorize[d] the making of codes to prescribe them.'"[610]

"Since 1935, the Court has not struck down a delegation to an administrative agency. Rather, the Court has approved, 'without deviation, Congress' ability to delegate power under broad standards.'"[611]

With respect to any purported delegation by Congress to the Fed of its power and duty to create money and regulate its value, as we have seen earlier in this work, there exists an extensive, even exhaustive history and record of the nature of money and standards applicable to the regulation of its value, that takes into account the role of sovereign money such as that provided for in Article I, § 8 Clause 5 of the *Constitution* as well as the role of sovereign money in its role as a constraint on credit excess and a discipline through redemption requirements of the value of credit money denominated in units of sovereign money and created in the market in the form of negotiable bills and notes. To effect the public purpose of credit money, it must incorporate the common law requirements governing their use in an historically developed and commercially acceptable legal manner designed to protect the public interest in the economic and monetary system and thereby protecting the integrity of government and the constitutional civil, legal and moral compact amongst the governed.

For Congress to delegate its power and duty to create and regulate the value of sovereign money and through the exercise of that power and duty, in conjunction with common law and enabling legislation for such a purpose, regulation of the value of credit circulating as money in the economic and financial markets, would require sufficient specificity to enable the delegate to meet its duty—a constitutional fiduciary duty—to the public, through the exercise of the power so delegated and for which it must then be subjected to legal accountability.

Congress has not officially or implicitly delegated to the Fed the power and duty to regulate the value of America's sovereign money. Because the Fed does not have the constitutional power and duty to create and regulate the value of American sovereign money, it cannot further delegate such power and duty to its constituent banks and their partners and constituents in the credit markets.

Neither *The Federal Reserve Act* nor any other legislation officially and explicitly evidences any such delegation. Delegation cannot be somehow implicit in *The Federal Reserve Act* or any other legislation, because the requirement of sovereign money, created by Congress, the value of which has been regulated by Congress in accordance with a necessary standard, is *a priori*, a condition precedent to the Fed's lawful exercise of its expressed powers and duties in accordance with its creation and enabling legislation.

The Fed, however, by its organizing and enabling legislation, is empowered to create money in the form of credit and to establish, in conjunction with other federal financial regulators, standards for the extension, transferability and collection of credit. The Fed has the ability to create credit and denominate it in sovereign United States dollar units, whether as electronic data entry or other methods convertible to Federal Reserve Notes, i.e., Legal Tender. Legal Tender in the form of Federal Reserve Notes does not constitute constitutional sovereign money, the value of which is regulated by Congress. The Feds powers to create credit money and direct America's monetary system have been created by federal legislation, *The Federal Reserve Act*, as amended. The expressed primary purpose of *The Federal Reserve Act* is to "maintain long run growth of the monetary and credit aggregates commensurate with the economy's long run potential to increase production, so as to promote effectively the goals of maximum employment, stable prices, and moderate long-term interest rates."

That is, said another way, the Fed's purpose is to manipulate credit, credit money and money markets to achieve specific social and political public policy objectives, with an extraordinary degree of discretion and with little to no accountability. That purpose in no way incorporates a delegation of congressional constitutional power and duty to create the units of sovereign money, the value of which has been regulated by reference to an historical suitable standard of value, the historical purpose of which is to limit the ability of the state and the banking system to manipulate, first the value of sovereign money; and second, to enable the market, in accordance with the common law and statutory law of negotiable instruments and some semblance of the real bills doctrine, to regulate the use and value of credit money under the long established law of contracts, bills and notes and negotiable instruments, that meet the ancient disciplines on creation of credit money.[612]

Felix Martin correctly observed that today "currency is ephemeral and cosmetic: it is the underlying mechanism of credit accounts and clearing that is the essence of money."[613] This social technological concept is laid on the foundation of:

(1) An abstract unit of value in which money is denominated (in America, sovereign money, the US dollar, created, and the value of which is regulated by Congress).
(2) A system of accounts which keeps track of the individuals' or institutions' credit or debt balances as they engage in trade with one another.
(3) The possibility that the original creditor in a relationship can transfer their debtor's obligation to a third party in settlement of some unrelated debt.
(4) A bilateral credit relationship is simply a loan. "It is credit, but it is not money." It is when that credit—loan—can be passed on to a third party through "negotiation" and "endorsement" that the credit becomes money. Money is not just credit, but rather readily transferable credit. Quoting nineteenth-century economist and lawyer Henry Dunning Macleod, Martin observes that: "If we were asked—Who made the discovery which has most deeply affected the fortunes of the human race? We think, after full consideration, we might safely answer—the man who first discovered that a Debt is a Saleable Commodity."[614]
(5) For a seller to accept a buyer's credit instrument in payment, however, the seller must be convinced that:
    (a) The debtor whose payment obligation they are about to accept will, if it comes to it, be able to satisfy their claim—that the money's issuer is creditworthy.
    (b) The seller must also trust that third parties will be willing to accept the debtors credit obligation in payment as well—that it is and remain indefinitely, transferable—that the market for it is liquid (Herein lies the rub. The credit money must be not only transferability but must be transferable readily on a liquid basis, at a valuation denominated in terms of liquid sovereign monetary units).

According to Martin, then, "[d]epending on how powerful are the reasons to believe these two things, it will be easier or harder for an issuer's [debt] to circulate as money."[615] Martin refers to the process of negotiation and endorsement of a credit instrument through the system of processes of accounting and clearing a "financial jargon."

These two words represent more than jargon. The concept of "negotiation" describes the process of the seller and buyer reaching mutual agreement with respect to the value of the credit evidence to be transferred as money at the time of transfer.

The negotiation and mutual determination of the value of the credit item at the time of transfer, through "endorsement" requires that the buyer have both trust and confidence in the ability of the underlying issuer to repay his debt, and creditable independent evidence supporting that establishment of trust and confidence in the market value of the credit item.

In the absence of any other factors, that necessary evidence is found by the buyer in an examination and confirmation of the issuer's assets and liabilities and the issuer's ability to readily liquidate its assets in amounts and at values sufficient to repay his debt in accordance with its terms. Because that present determination must take into account the future risks and uncertainties that may adversely affect the issuer's future ability to so perform, the buyer must take into account the perceived risk and uncertainty of future performance by the issuer in determining the present value at which he will accept the transfer of the credit item through endorsement.

The negotiated value of the item presented is generally less that the face amount of the item, due to the corresponding assessment by the buyer of the present value of the item adjusted to reflect his assessment of the degree to which the items current liquidity is affected by future risk and uncertainty of payment off the item in full at maturity in accordance with its terms. The assessment and negotiation of the discounted present liquid value of the item is a precondition to its transfer to the buyer and his evaluation of his ability to transfer it on to unrelated third parties through the systems and process that constitute the socially acceptable monetary scheme at the time.

The challenge of conducting such transfers through negotiation and endorsement of credit items as money through the prevailing systems of valuation, accounting and decentralized transferability—that is repeated transferability of the item to successive, unknown third parties in an expeditious and efficient manner requires that the socially acceptable monetary system establish some governing concept or principle of confirmation of trust and confidence in a transferable credit item's present liquid value without the necessity of continued repetitive revaluation of the item at the time of each transfer of each item. The more confidence and trustworthy value and its homogeneity, the greater with be the efficiency, utility and reliability of the monetary system comprise of such credit items.

The Fed cannot legitimately or effectively exercise its powers and meet its duties centered on the manipulation of credit and credit money to achieve social and political objectives without the separate existence of sovereign, constitutional money, in terms of which the Fed's policies and actions can be understood and effected honestly and transparently and for which it can be held accountable.

The exercise by the Fed of its powers and duties, without: (i) the discipline imposed by the common denominator of redemption at a price/value level measured in terms of constitutional sovereign money; and without (ii) the enforcement of the ancient and well established laws regarding bills, notes and negotiability and thereby transferability at a liquid value confirmed and measured by reference to liquid transferable sovereign money, the value of which is regulated by Congress and which becomes the base tool for comparison and valuation of credit money, in terms of liquidity, and therefore also of liquid value and price that have evolved to discipline the creation of credit money.

It is indisputable that while Congress has failed to exercise its fiduciary powers and meet its fiduciary duties under Article I, § 8, Clause 5 of the *Constitution*, and not having lawfully delegated such power and duty to the Fed, the Fed then cannot simply somehow turn it over to Wall Street under the meaningless rubric of "self-regulation". The combination of Washington and Wall Street have conspired to misrepresent to marketplace, including the American public, that they have met the discipline imposed on honest, transparent, safe and sound credit money, and concomitantly, that the trading price of the instruments evidencing the credit money reflects the discount in value necessary to render the credit money liquid, even under conditions of strained liquidity when liquidity matters most. This false narrative and the money debasement it effected was manifest on enormous scale and lies at the heart of the great financial crisis. Washington and Wall Street have most egregiously lied to the public about the market value and liquidity of securitized credit, and derivatives, including repos traded in enormous sums on a short term basis without meeting the necessary disciplines on valuation and liquidity, thus cheating and stealing from the holders of sovereign money in addition to the holders of the undisciplined credit money, to the extent of the gap between face value of those instruments and the discount to valuation and liquidity disciplined by constitutional sovereign money values. When the gap is realized in terms of sovereign money, the illiquidity and overstatement of denominated value is recognized in the market and the bulk of sovereign money is thereby progressively further debased. Bubbles are made and bubbles are burst. In each case the result is driven by failure to regulate first, the value of sovereign money, and second the failure to regulate and discipline the liquidity and value of the assets and other sources of repayment underlying the credit offered up as shadow credit money.

Return now to the circumstances under which congressional powers and duties may lawfully be delegated:

> "Again and again, the Court has distinguished the two cases [mentioned above], sometimes by finding adequate standards in the challenged statute, sometimes by contrasting the vast scope of the power delegated by the National Industrial Recovery Act, and sometimes by pointing to required administrative findings and procedures that were absent in the NIRA. The Court has also relied on the constitutional doubt principle of statutory construction to narrow interpretations of statutes that, interpreted broadly, might have presented delegation issues. ... (*See, e.g.*, Fahey v. Mallonee, 332 U.S. 245, 250 (1947) (contrasting the delegation to deal with 'unprecedented economic problems of varied industries' with the delegation of authority to deal with problems of the banking industry, where there was 'accumulated experience' derived from long regulation and close supervision)."[616]

We must note, however, that despite this judicial finding, legal commentary and official papers and reports, from the *Federalist Papers*, E.G. Spauldings' treatise on *Legal Tender Laws and the Civil War*, the *Pujo Report* in 1913, the *Pecora Report* in 1934, the *FDIC Report* in 1997 to the *2011 Financial Crisis Inquiry Report*; from the American Revolution to the Civil War and on to the present day, have concluded and documented the fact that regulatory "accumulated experience" derived from "long regulation and close supervision" of money and banking have failed to protect the banking industry and the American public from financial crises driven by congressional failure to create and regulate the value of American sovereign constitutional money as well as shadow money substitutes. That is one of America's most important founding first principles and a fundamental prerequisite to the honesty, safety and soundness of the banking industry, the stability and integrity of our economic and monetary system and to the ability of the American public to hold their government accountable for policy and action under the American rule of law.

The broad delegation of "authority to deal with problems of the banking industry, where there was 'accumulated experience' derived from long regulation and close supervision" cannot overcome the massive fraud perpetrated upon the American public by the banking industry through congressional and regulatory abandonment—not the delegation—of congressional fiduciary power and duty delegated to Congress under Article I, § 8, Clause 5 of the *Constitution*.

Article I, § 8, Clause 5 is the law of the land, a first principle of democratic government and integral to an honest system of free enterprise. Enforcement of this important constitutional principle through the trail of its violation; holding all those in the chain of violation, exploitation and abuse accountable for the fraud they have effected in the absence of the proper recognition and performance of this vital constitutional fiduciary power and duty is one of the most import challenges to American society today. Our vast Washington governmental, political, bureaucratic regulatory and administrative complex and the Wall Street banking and financial system that now holds the American public hostage to its wealth, power and privilege can be rendered accountable only based upon enforcement of the American rule of law. Washington and Wall Street must be held legally accountable for their intentional breach of our American constitutional protection against the massive fraud on the American public perpetrated by Wall Street unleashed by the breach. As noted above, because of the nature of Washington's and Wall Street's wrongdoing, the experts that are in the best position of wealth, power and expertise to enforce financial crisis accountability are parties best able to defend themselves and thwart accountability, while ordinary Americans have been in no position to join the issue on a one by one, individual, well-informed basis, financed by a war chest sufficient to challenge the status quo. Only by joining together can ordinary Americans enforce the laws to which Washington and Wall Street, as fiduciaries to us in money matters, should rightly followed.

> Concerns in the scholarly literature with respect to the scope of the delegation doctrine have been reflected in the opinions of some of the Justices. Nonetheless, the Court's decisions continue to approve very broad delegations, and the practice will likely remain settled.
>
> The fact that the Court has gone so long without holding a statute to be an invalid delegation does not mean that the nondelegation doctrine is a dead letter.

> The long list of rejected challenges does suggest, however, that the doctrine applies only to standard less delegations of the most sweeping nature.[617]

[B] False Narrative: Fed Delegation to the Wall Street Banks

Congress has not officially or implicitly delegated to the Fed the power and duty to regulate the value of America's sovereign money. Because the Fed does not have the constitutional power and duty to create and regulate the value of American sovereign money, it cannot further delegate such power and duty to its constituent Wall Street banks and their partners and constituents in the credit markets. Finally then, we must recognize that not only has there been no legal sequence of delegation of the congressional power and duty to create and regulate the value of sovereign money, subsequent to the creation of the Fed, Congress did in fact continue to create and regulate the value of money until 1933. Thereafter, the *Bretton Woods Accords* provided a weak substitute for the proper and legitimate performance by Congress of its power and duty under Article I, § 8, Clause 5, the Nixon shock put an end to any semblance of regulation of the value of money in a constitutional manner.

The Federal Reserve System's action constitutes the final *de facto* and *de jure* ceding, abandonment of authority and responsibility, and effective abrogation of the federal government's ability, to control the nation's money supply and prevent its debasement, and, while Congress and the other federal financial regulators sat on their hands as, you might suppose, disinterested observers, left the entire mess in the hands of the Wall Street banks.

He [Fed Chairman Alan Greenspan] said in a May 2005 speech that:

> "[P]rivate regulation generally has proved far better at constraining excessive risk-taking than has government regulation." ... "Before the crisis intensified last month with the bankruptcy of Lehman Brothers Holdings Inc., Greenspan said markets should still be allowed to police themselves. I hope that one of the casualties will not be reliance on counterparty surveillance, and more generally financial self-regulation, as the fundamental balance mechanism for global finance," Greenspan wrote in the *Financial Times* in March." Today, the former chairman asked: "What went wrong with global economic policies that had worked so effectively for nearly four decades?" During his term at the Fed's helm, Greenspan repeatedly warned lawmakers against inhibiting markets, such as by tightening oversight of certain types of derivatives. Greenspan reiterated his "shocked disbelief" that financial companies failed to execute sufficient "surveillance" on their trading counterparties to prevent surging losses. The "breakdown" was clearest in the market where securities firms packaged home mortgages into debt sold on to other investors, he said.[618]

[C] False Narrative: The Greenspan Doctrine of Self-Regulating Wall Street Banks

The end of the Greenspan Doctrine was captured in Remarks by Chairman Alan Greenspan at a New York Economic Club dinner in 2009:

"The Greenspan Doctrine—a view that modern, technologically advanced financial markets are best left to police themselves—has an increasingly vocal detractor. His name is Alan Greenspan. As Fed chairman, Mr. Greenspan was a frequent opponent of market regulation. Sophisticated markets, he argued, had become increasingly adept at carving up risk themselves and dispersing it widely to investors and financial institutions best suited to manage it. The retired chairman has had to revise his views. In comments at a New York Economic Club dinner late Tuesday, the retired Fed chairman steered clear of much self-reflection on his role in the credit boom. But he did take a new swipe at the market's self-correcting tendencies and bowed his head to a new period of increased regulation. 'All of the sophisticated mathematics and computer wizardry essentially rested on one central premise: that enlightened self-interest of owners and managers of financial institutions would lead them to maintain a sufficient buffer against insolvency by actively monitoring and managing their firms' capital and risk positions,' the Fed chairman said. The premise failed in the summer of 2007, he said, leaving him 'deeply dismayed.' Self-regulation is still a first-line of defense, Mr. Greenspan said. But after the financial collapse of 2007 and 2008, 'I see no alternative to a set of heightened federal regulatory rules of behavior for banks and other financial institutions.' He said hoped it would come in the form of tougher capital requirements for banks. His comments echoed testimony of the former Fed chairman made last October, when he acknowledged his state of 'shocked disbelief' at the market turmoil. The former Fed chief also offered a sobering assessment of the losses now being nursed by investors around the world, which he tallied up to more than $40 trillion, when accounting for global stock declines, home prices declines and losses of unlisted businesses. 'The evaporation of the value of those 'paper claims' can have a profoundly deflationary impact on global economic activity,' he said. A rebound, he added, would likely be driven by a rebound in stock prices. Whenever that comes.'"[619]

In testimony before the Commission, former Fed Chairman Greenspan testified:

"The risk management paradigm nonetheless harbored a fatal flaw. In the growing state of euphoria, managers at financial institutions, along with regulators including but not limited to the Federal Reserve, failed to fully comprehend the underlying size, length, and potential impact of the so-called negative tail of the distribution of risk outcomes that was about to be revealed as the post-Lehman Brothers crisis played out," Greenspan said in his prepared remarks.

"For decades, with little to no data, almost all analysts, in my experience, had conjectured a far more limited tail risk. That led to more than a half century of significantly and chronically undercapitalized financial intermediaries, arguably the major failure of the private risk management system.

"The financial firms counted on being able to anticipate the onset of crisis in time to retrench. They were mistaken. They believed the then seemingly insatiable demand for their array of exotic financial products would enable them to sell large parts of their portfolios without loss.

"But that didn't happen—a lesson the U.S. learned several hundreds of billions of taxpayer dollars later."[620]

Greenspan finally concluded that the financial world has become too complex for federal financial regulators:

"Former Federal Reserve Chairman Alan Greenspan made the kind of admission this morning that may trouble those who assume that better regulators—rather

> than a wholesale rewriting of rules—will better protect Americans from a future financial crisis.
>
> "Regulators can't keep up with today's megabanks, he said. They're too complex. Regulators, in short, do not have a chance.
>
> "Greenspan, appearing before the panel convened to investigate the roots of the financial crisis, said that the 'ideal way' to supervise banks would be to go through its individual loan documents—the way supervisors used to police banks and financial firms before they grew so large.
>
> "But unfortunately, he lamented, that's no longer possible because firms are so complex."[621]

According to data from the Federal Reserve Bank of Dallas, the largest 0.2 percent of all banks—12 banks—now control nearly 70 percent of all banking assets:

> As of third quarter 2012, there were approximately 5,600 commercial banking organizations in the U.S. The bulk of these—roughly 5,500—were community banks with assets of less than $10 billion. These community-focused organizations accounted for 98.6 percent of all banks but only 12 percent of total industry assets. Another group numbering nearly 70 banking organizations—with assets of between $10 billion and $250 billion—accounted for 1.2 percent of banks, while controlling 19 percent of industry assets. The remaining group, the megabanks—with assets of between $250 billion and $2.3 trillion—was made up of a mere 12 institutions. These dozen behemoths accounted for roughly 0.2 percent of all banks, but they held 69 percent of industry assets.
>
> 105 banks (about 1 percent of the total banks in the US) now control close to 80 percent of all banking assets in the U.S. The top 105 banks control over $10.3 trillion in assets.
>
> Recently, two economists—Kenichi Ueda of the International Monetary Fund and Beatrice Weder di Mauro of the University of Mainz—estimated that prior to the 2008 collapse, the largest banks had a borrowing cost advantage, including the interest rate paid on their bonds and customer deposits, of 60 basis points relative to their competitors, and that cost advantage increased to 80 basis points after 2008. In a world of already low interest rates on bonds and bank certificates of deposits, 80 basis points, or almost 1 percent, is a substantial benefit.[622]
>
> Bloomberg used the Ueda/di Mauro data to calculate that the annual benefit to the largest banks totaled $83 billion, and reached the stunning conclusion that the annual benefit to the top five banks—JP Morgan, Citigroup, Bank of America, Wells Fargo and Goldman Sachs—totaled $64 billion, or an amount "roughly equal to their typical annual profits... In other words, the banks occupying the commanding heights of the US financial industry—with almost $9 trillion in assets, more than half the size of the US economy—would just about break even in the absence of corporate welfare. In large part, the profits they report are essentially transfers from taxpayers to their shareholders."[623]

The exercise by the Wall Street banks of the monopoly fiduciary powers entrusted to them carries the duty to the American public to exercise that power with reasonable care in a safe and sound manner to avoid foreseeable harm caused by their' failure to exercise such care; maintain the integrity of the banking system; maintain the relationship of value to money and so prevent the debasement of the American supply of money and the readily foreseeable damages to the American public caused by such debasement, which would, predictably result in systemic economic, financial and monetary instability and recession or depression.

While tougher capital requirements, leverage limitations and enforcement of existing statutory and regulatory requirements that federal financial regulators "go through its [banks] individual loan documents—the way supervisors used to police banks and financial firms before they grew so large" would go a long way toward effective regulation of financial markets to assure safety soundness and stability, the fundamental curb on excess risk taking in creation of credit that serves as money is the regulation of the value of money redeemable in relation to a clear, effective market based standard of value of the monetary unit.

Regulation and protection of the value of money to honestly serve the public need for honest, safe and sound money is the purpose of the *Constitution*'s congressional imperative to "coin money, regulate the value thereof, and of foreign coin, and fix the standard of weights and measures" and to thereby prevent the scourge of government and banker currency debasement that has plagued and reduced society after society since the invention of money itself, and is the primary and fundamental cause of the financial devastation of ordinary Americans in the great financial crisis, which has left Washington and Wall Street not only unscathed, but larger, more powerful and wealthier than ever. More than pleasing the vanities of economists, an independent central bank that protects the value of money is the ultimate consumer protection agency. Accountability to enforceable standards for regulation of asset values and liquidity is the ultimate regulatory agent.

Consider then relatively recent developments in Fed dialogue and pronouncements regarding financial stability:

> Monetary Policy faces "significant limitations" as a tool to counter financial stability risks, Federal Reserve Chair Janet Yellen said on Wednesday, adding that heading off the US housing bubble with higher interest rates would have caused major economic damage.
>
> "Weighing in on a global debate, Yellen reiterated her view that 'regulation—not rate policy—needs to play the lead role in combating excessive financial risk-taking. ... The potential cost ... is likely to be too great to give financial stability risks a central role in monetary policy discussions,' ... Analysts said Yellen was pushing back against some Fed officials who believe financial stability should be given a more prominent place in formulating monetary policy. ... 'is critical for regulators to complete their efforts at implementing a macroprudential approach to enhance resilience within the financial system,' she said. Yellen said building a stronger system was all the more important because economies around the globe could be in need of historically low rates for some time to come, whether due to scars from the financial crisis or deeper underlying economic shifts. Because of that, central banks could run out of room to cut rates more frequently when financial shocks hit, she warned.
>
> "Yellen cited a number of steps the United States had taken to strengthen its financial sector, including setting higher capital requirements for banks. In making her case that regulation should be in the forefront of fighting financial stability risks, she harkened back to the mid-2000s, when US housing prices were soaring. Yellen argued a 'very significant tightening' of monetary policy would have been

needed to stop the housing bubble from building, and that the cost would have been a very large increase in unemployment."[624]

The contrast Yellen was making was with the following recent remarks of Governor Jeremy C. Stein: International Research Forum on Monetary Policy, Washington, D.C. Governor Stein presented identical remarks at the International Monetary Fund 2014 Spring Meetings on April 13, 2014, and at the 2014 Financial Markets Conference on April 16, 2014.

"I would like to talk today about how one might explicitly incorporate financial stability considerations into a monetary policy framework. Doing so involves tackling two questions—one that is relatively easy and one that is much harder. The easier question is, should financial stability concerns, in principle, influence monetary Policy decisions? ... [T]he theoretical answer is a clear 'yes.' ... The second question is, how does one operationalize the theory? What sorts of data should one look to, and what sorts of empirical methods should one use, to calibrate by how much the stance of monetary policy should be altered relative to the case in which financial stability considerations are completely set aside? ...

"The generic argument rests on three assumptions. First, suppose that the Federal Reserve focuses only on its traditional dual mandate of maximum employment and price stability. To keep things simple, suppose further that these two goals are not in conflict with one another—say, because aggregate demand is weak, depressing both employment and inflation—so that we can boil things down to one objective: keeping unemployment close to target. ... Second, the argument assumes that there is some variable summarizing financial market vulnerability—I will be abstract for the moment and just call it FMV—which is influenced by monetary policy. That is, easier monetary policy leads to increased vulnerability as measured by FMV. Moreover, when FMV is elevated, there is a greater probability of an adverse event—some kind of financial market shock—that, if it were to occur, would push up the unemployment rate, all else being equal ....

"The third and final assumption is that the risks associated with an elevated value of FMV cannot be fully offset at zero cost with other nonmonetary tools, such as financial regulation. To be clear, this assumption does not imply that regulation is not helpful in reducing financial vulnerabilities—it only says that regulation is not a perfect instrument. These imperfections could stem from regulatory arbitrage; political-economy constraints; or the fact that too much regulation can also impede economic growth, just like overly restrictive monetary policy. Thus one way to think of my construct of FMV is that it is a stand-in for the level of financial vulnerabilities that remain after regulation has done the best that it can do, given the existing real-world limitations. ...

"First, when financial-sector leverage is high, the probability of a severe crisis in which multiple large intermediaries become insolvent is elevated—that is, we are more likely to have a replay of what happened in 2008 and 2009. Second, easy monetary policy is asserted to increase the incentives for the financial sector to lever up. And, third, focusing on leverage as opposed to asset prices avoids putting the central bank in the position of having to 'spot bubbles': Even if it is impossible for the central bank to know when an asset class is overvalued, the risks to the economy associated with overvaluation are presumably greater when intermediaries are highly levered. ...

"At the same time, this leverage-centric approach also has some drawbacks, which suggest that there is likely to be value in a parallel exploration of other tracks. For one thing, the effective degree of leverage in the financial system is not easy to measure in a comprehensive fashion. "One can certainly look at things like banks' capital ratios, but some of the important action, from a financial stability perspective, is likely to be in subtler forms of leverage that are either outside of the traditional banking sector or more prone to shape shifting. More to the point, recall that, for the purposes of informing monetary policy, one wants to focus on those sources of financial vulnerability that are least effectively dealt with via regulation. And the more reliably a form of leverage can be measured, the better a candidate it is for being handled with a regulatory or supervisory approach. In other words, if we were to see signs that banks' capital ratios were in danger of eroding, we would certainly want to do something, but it is hard for me to imagine that the something should involve monetary policy—the obvious first line of defense in this case would be to turn to our regulatory and supervisory tools. ...

"To restate my main point, I believe that measures of bond market risk premiums—for example, estimates of the expected excess returns on long-term Treasury securities relative to Treasury bills and on credit-risky bonds relative to Treasury securities—may turn out to be useful inputs into the monetary policy framework. These variables have the potential to serve as simple proxies for a particular sort of financial market vulnerability that may not be easily addressed by supervision and regulation. Again, however, let me emphasize the conjectural nature of these remarks. Even if this broad way of thinking about the problem turns out to be useful, there is a ways to go—in terms of modeling and calibration—before it can be used to make quantitative statements. Thus, at this early stage, I would not want to claim that one is likely to get policy prescriptions that differ significantly from those of our standard models. We will have to do the work and see what emerges.

"Finally, a more general theme that has been lurking in the background here is the sharp difference in perspective that subfields of economics sometimes bring to a given question. As I noted earlier, one of the central and most widely shared ideas in the academic finance literature is the importance of time variation in the risk premiums (or expected returns) on a wide range of assets. At the same time, canonical macro models in the New Keynesian genre of the sort that are often used to inform monetary policy tend to exhibit little or no meaningful risk premium variation. Even if most of the specifics of what I have had to say in this talk turn out to be off base, I have to believe that our macro models will ultimately be more useful as a guide to policy if they build on a more empirically realistic foundation with respect to the behavior of interest rates and credit spreads."[625]

The takeaway from this exchange of Fed positioning is that Yellen thinks financial stability is beyond the scope of the Feds primary focus on monetary policy and that financial stability and the goal of financial stability is more appropriately the focus of regulators macro-prudential focus on the stability of the macro-economy. Who might those regulators be? The Fed is responsible for the macro-prudential regulation of the systemically important financial institutions that create dominate and profit by the so-called macroeconomic system. The Fed has historically proclaimed that it is the macro-economic and macro-prudential global expert, and that domestic and global financial stability is its mission. While so doing and claiming the credit for its oracular financial acumen the Fed has been running its models supporting monetary policy based on what, as Chairman Greenspan admitted, "almost no data," certainly not the data necessary for its actions to have any relevance to its monetary policy, if it can be dignified as such, and no relevance whatsoever to domestic or global financial stability. To top it off, the Fed abandoned and turned over its regulatory, domestic prudential as well as global macro-prudential regulation, supervision and enforcement responsibility to the Wall Street banks that have laughed, laughed, pocked the profits and moved on. The Fed has monetized trillions of dollars of global toxic financial assets to protect the Wall Street banks and turned the United States financial regulatory structure into a global joke.

Governor Stein, on the other hand, recognized the importance of Fed focus of financial stability, which while laudable, he simply casts aside based upon the modelling difficulties, the difficulty of making Fed action "operational" and he simply side-lined asset value price differential based on the Feds, including the Wall Street banks' asset bubbles created by the unconstrained direction of the money they create into asset value bubbles that, by the time you get to CDOs cubed, have no ascertainable "FMV", Steins euphemistic acronym for asset value.

Compare the approach left to us by former Chairman Greenspan and later Fed Chair Yellen with the observations taken by researchers at the Federal Reserve Bank of Minneapolis and Johns Hopkins University, the only Fed paper I have discovered regarding currency debasement, *The Debasement Puzzle: An Essay on Medieval History*, Federal Reserve Bank of Minneapolis Quarterly Review vol. 21.no.4, 1997. The authors examine money debasement in time of Henry VIII. The paper makes three basic points: first, that following currency debasements, both old and new coins circulated side by side following currency debasements; second is that old and new coins were valued in circulation by their intrinsic content rather than their legal tender value; and third that minting volumes after reinforcement of the currency (the opposite of debasement) were also unusually large, about as large as after debasements.

The authors conclude that the fact of equal demand for re-coinage after both money reinforcements and debasements instead of simply taking the opportunity to reduce their debts through debasement exclusively was a puzzle that presented a "modeling" challenge to them—why did people hold money and re-coin even when it was debased, when it supposedly would have been in the holders best interest to trade debased money at face legal tender value to naïve or unsuspecting counterparties over whom they held a potential pricing advantage? In fact, the authors wondered why the holders of the debased money did not try harder to exploit the debasement. After an extensive scholarly analysis, the authors concern was that the anomalous behavior they viewed presented "modeling difficulties." The public sought re-coinage apparently against their own interest; ignoring the opportunity to trade existing debased or reinforced currency; and subjecting themselves to the large burden of cost associated with seignorage exacted by the sovereign for re-coinage.

Like federal financial regulatory authorities today, the authors did not imagine that the objective of the re-coinage under either circumstance was based on the peoples' desire to have and use with trust and confidence, honest, safe and sound money, to serve their honest and straight forward interests in trade and commerce. Their objective was not to game the system; but rather to use in in a safe and productive manner. An objective apparently not contemplated by the authors. The attraction of profits from gaming the system was in the hands of financiers, much like the Wall Street banks today. The authors failed to make any reference of their analysis to or connection of their analysis with the fact of current ongoing debasement of the American dollar today, which presents the same puzzle.

The public response is the same today as it was in the mid-1500s. The public wants honest, safe and sound money to enable them to conduct trade and commerce. The public is not knowingly in the business of dishonestly gaming money debasement, in effect lying to, cheating and stealing from the very customers or counterparties with which they most fervently desire to establish commercial or personal relationships of honesty, trust and confidence. That speculative gaming activity has been reserved to and relished by the Washington Wall Street enterprise.

Washington and Wall Street have adopted the policy of intentional misrepresentation of value through money debasement as a prime feature of banking, monetary and fiscal policy. The apparent over-arching importance to the Fed of manipulating their models to make them work and paper over their pervasive intentional misrepresentations provides nothing of value to the American public. In fact, that ongoing policy of deliberate dishonesty hidden by financial models, records and reports that are designed to be dishonest are the cause of the financial crisis. What is in the public's interest and is valuable to them today is a central bank that, through its primary instruments on Wall Street, fulfills its mission as represented to the public in its internet web site:

> [S]upervising and regulating banking institutions to ensure the safety and soundness of the nation's banking and financial system and to protect the credit rights of consumers; maintaining the stability of the financial system and containing systemic risk that may arise in financial markets.

Chairman Greenspan noted that "the "ideal way" to supervise banks would be to go through its individual loan documents—the way supervisors used to police banks and financial firms before they grew so large." Today, neither the Wall Street Banks nor their regulators, notably the Fed, go through the individual loan documents. They cannot be bothered to even make the most fundamental determination that the loan borrowers can repay their loans. New regulations proliferate repeating the regulatory standards for safety and soundness and the Wall Street banks and regulators alike simply ignore them, just as they have ignored the regulations already on the books. There now exists an impossible distance between the meaningless regulatory activities of the Fed and the federal financial regulators and the honest intermediation of value through the real economy based upon honest, safe and sound money, the value of which is regulated at all, much less regulated by Congress is accordance with the constitutional requirement for regulation in reference to an external standard that would thereby maintain the integrity, stability and reliability of the money and not be subject to continuous debasement. The Fed has been a failure; its policies inaccurate and unfounded; and its role meaningless to ordinary Americans. Based on this recognition, does the global financial system and its regulation require honest, safe and sound money to function? Can the systemically important global financial institutions deliver an honest, safe and sound money and financial system? How can central banks be restricted and controlled to give them the tools and incentives to achieve their missions? Exactly how can these missions relate to and support the responsibilities that global finance requires to operate in an honest, safe and sound regulatory context?

How can the people hold the central banks and the banks in the global financial system to account if they fail to perform as they have, almost universally?

As 2018 brought a new Federal Reserve Chairman, he sought to reassure markets of the priority of financial stability. New Federal Reserve Chairman Jerome Powell ... "said the central bank 'will remain alert' to any risks to financial stability, marking his maiden attempt to soothe financial markets. In brief prepared remarks at his swearing-in ceremony, Powell reminded the audience that Washington made enormous strides in its effort to strengthen the banking sector in the wake of the financial crisis. 'The financial system is incomparably stronger and safer, with much higher capital and liquidity, better risk management, and other improvements,' Powell said."[626]

Chairman Powell, in a speech at The Economic Club of New York, on November 28, 2018 entitled "The Federal Reserve's Framework for Monitoring Financial Stability", stated first that "[u]nder the dual mandate, jobs and inflation are the Fed's meat and potatoes. In the rest of my comments, I will focus on financial stability—a topic that has always been on the menu, but that, since the crisis, has become a more integral part of the meal." He went on to state that his "... main subject today will be the profound transformation since the Global Financial Crisis in the Federal Reserve's approach to monitoring and addressing financial stability. Today marks the publication of the Board of Governors' first Financial Stability Report. Earlier this month, we published our first Supervision and Regulation Report. Together, these reports contain a wealth of information on our approach to financial stability and to financial regulation more broadly." Powell also noted that "[t]he term "financial stability" has a particular meaning in this context. A stable financial system is one that continues to function effectively even in severely adverse conditions. A stable system meets the borrowing and investment needs of households and businesses despite economic turbulence. An unstable system, in contrast, may amplify turbulence and prolong economic hardship in the face of stress by failing to provide these essential services when they are needed most." Powell's recent emphasis on financial stability marks the same weakness in the Federal Reserve System's mandate that we experience in the Great Financial Crisis, and before that, the Great Depression:

> For Economic Club of New York trivia buffs, I will note that the second ever presentation to this club by a Federal Reserve official was about this very topic. The date was March 18, 1929. Weeks before, the Fed had issued a public statement of concern over stock market speculation and had provided guidance frowning on bank funding of such speculation. William Harding, a former Fed Chair and then president of the Federal Reserve Bank of Boston, defended the Fed's actions in his talk. He argued that, while the Fed should not act as the arbiter of correct asset prices, it did have a primary responsibility to protect the banking system's capacity to meet the credit needs of households and businesses. At the meeting, critics argued that public statements about inflated asset prices were "fraught with danger;" that the nation's banks were so well managed that they should not "face public admonition"; and, more generally, that the Fed was "out of its sphere." Of course, Harding spoke just a few months before the 1929 stock market crash, which signaled the onset of the Great Depression.

Greg Robb, in *Market Watch* reported in an article entitled "Powell says Fed 'will remain alert' to any financial stability risks" (February 13, 2018), that Powell indicated that the central bank "will remain alert" to any risks to financial stability, marking his maiden attempt to soothe financial markets. Powell observed that the banking system is "incomparably stronger" since the financial crisis. He implied that as to an anticipated Powell "put" for the stock market—do not even think about it.

> In his speech, Powell projected a steady-as-she-goes approach. While the challenges we face are always evolving, the Fed's approach will remain the same, he said. He noted that the global economy "is recovering strongly for the first time in a decade ....
>
> "We are in the process of gradually normalizing both interest rate policy and our balance sheet with a view to extending the recovery and sustaining the pursuit of our objectives," Powell said.
>
> "Powell said he would pursue interest rate policy "without concern for short-term political pressures." Analysts have speculated about the pressure President Donald Trump may put on the Fed, particularly if the economy softens. Powell said the Fed would not eliminate the regulations put in place since the crisis but may loosen them.

The plague of the status in the Feds eyes of financial stability as subordinated to its dual mandate of employment and interest rates insures that in the next crisis we will face the same conundrum posed by the Feds demonstrated policy of protecting the Washington Wall Street enterprise first in the name of financial stability which means protection of asset values, wielding the big stick of asset "puts" to the Fed accompanied by interest rate manipulation to support valuations, followed by tepid efforts to incentivize employment under the failed trickle-down theory following from the preservation of the all-important Washington Wall Street enterprise. Ordinary Americans will once again suffer the burden of money debasement driven financial crisis.

§7.09 FALSE NARRATIVE: THE FEDERAL SAFETY NET PROTECTS ORDINARY AMERICANS FROM THE RAVAGES OF MONEY DEBASEMENT BY PROTECTING BANK DEPOSITORS AND BANKS TOO BIG TO FAIL

When the efforts of the Federal Reserve failed to prevent the bank collapses of the 1930s, *The Banking Act of 1933* created federal deposit insurance. The subsequent evidence appears persuasive that the combination of a lender of last resort (the Federal Reserve) and the provision of federal deposit insurance has contributed significantly to financial stability and has accordingly achieved wide support within the Congress. Inevitably, however, such significant government intervention has not been an unmixed blessing.

The federal safety net for banks clearly has diminished the effectiveness of private market regulation and created perverse incentives in the banking system. To cite the most obvious and painful example, without federal deposit insurance, private markets presumably would never have permitted thrift institutions to purchase the portfolios that brought down the industry insurance fund and left future generations of taxpayers responsible for huge losses. To be sure, government regulators and politicians have learned from this experience and taken significant steps to diminish the likelihood of a recurrence. Nonetheless, the safety net undoubtedly still affects decisions by creditors of depository institutions in ways that weaken the effectiveness of private market regulation and leave ordinary Americans all too vulnerable to future failures of government regulation. As the history of American banking demonstrates, private market regulation can be quite effective, if government does not get in its way. Indeed, rapidly changing technology is rendering obsolescent much of the old bank examination supervision and regulation regime. Bank regulators are perforce being pressed to depend increasingly on ever more complex and sophisticated private market regulation. This is certainly the case for the rapidly expanding bank securitization and derivatives markets, and increasingly so for the more traditional loan products. The lessons of early American banking should encourage us in this endeavor.

> Powell, in closing, emphasized "that the rapidly changing technology that is rendering much government bank regulation irrelevant also bids fair to undercut regulatory efforts in a much wider segment of our economy. The reason is that such regulation is inherently conservative. It endeavors to maintain the status quo and the special interests who benefit therefrom. New ideas, new products, new ways of doing things, all of necessity, raise the riskiness of any organization, riskiness for which regulators have a profound aversion. Yet since the value of all wealth reflects its future productive capabilities, all wealth creation rests on uncertain forecasts, which means every investment is risky. Or put another way, you cannot have wealth creation without risk taking. With technological change clearly accelerating, existing regulatory structures are being bypassed, freeing market forces to enhance wealth creation and economic growth.
>
> "In finance, regulatory restraints against interstate banking and combinations of investment and commercial banking are being swept away under the pressures of technological change. Much the same is true in transportation and communications.
>
> "As we move into a new century, the market-stabilizing private regulatory forces should gradually displace many cumbersome, increasingly ineffective government structures. This is a likely outcome since governments, by their nature, cannot adjust sufficiently quickly to a changing environment, which too often veers in unforeseen directions. The current adult generations are having difficulty adjusting to the acceleration of the uncertainties of today's silicon driven environment. Fortunately, our children appear to thrive on it. The future accordingly looks bright."[627]

§7.10 FALSE NARRATIVE: SOVEREIGN MONEY AND SHADOW MONEY CAN SAFELY DWELL IN SEPARATE REGULATORY SPHERES

The American dollar has historically enjoyed global reserve currency status because its value has rested first of all, on its tie to gold, and importantly, on the strength of the government to accumulate credit from the American public through transparent taxation. The government has been recognized as legitimate and its money has enjoyed trust not only on commercial or legal, but on ideological and even spiritual grounds.[628] This is concept has been confused by the historical coincidence of the founding of our country with the aftermath of John Locke's recognition of and response to the "outbreak of mass criminal deviance unparalleled in English history" from the minted value of coins as measured against the standards of gold and silver. The debasement "amounted to nothing other than the robbing of unfortunate coin-users in broad daylight."[629] Locke's unorthodox conception of all money as a commodity, e.g. gold or silver, was propounded to limit the political authority of the sovereign, at that time, the authority of the monarchy, to alter the value of coined money without the holders consent, as a method to wield political power without the consent of the people. Locke contended that the only way to limit the "absolute, arbitrary unjust and unnatural" power of the sovereign and support a democratic form of government, was to strictly control the standard of the valuation of currency in relation to an external "immutable standard," e.g., the commodities of gold and silver; thereby forcing democratic-based consent to the extraction of value from the citizens through transparent taxation with the consent of the governed. The power of Lock's connection of political liberalism with his monetary doctrines not only survived but prospered. It did so notwithstanding the essentially concurrent Great Monetary Settlement represented by the formation of the Bank of England and the marriage of private banking and credit with sovereign money, the value of which was regulated by reference to specie, unleashing "the greatest force for economic and social progress in history."[630] This development recognized the proper role of sovereign money as a final settlement mechanism, while accommodating the increased and complementary role of negotiable credit as money. The distinct identity and characteristics of these two types of money has been lost. The value of sovereign money is no longer regulated as required by law. The legal protections necessary to the proper functioning of negotiable transferable credit have been abandoned. How will Americans react to the ongoing distortions of asset value and liquidity wrought by the legal decomposition of both sovereign money and credit money resulting in a total muddle of the principles of asset liquidity and value that are the foundational concepts underlying bankruptcy, the priority of claims and the equitable allocation of losses among those most culpable for the causes of the losses?

The connection of sovereign paper money backed by a gold and silver specie standard of value has become ineffective in the face of banks' and governments' ability to create debt far beyond their ability to reconcile its value with the immutable specie standard with its liquidity as a final immediate settlement medium. The fiduciary standard of duty and care of banks to perform their functions of credit creation and intermediation continues to be plagued by the essential conflict inherent in Locke's monetary doctrine. The government and the banks have simply overrun the Locke commodity standard for regulation of the value of sovereign money by reference to a specie/commodity standard. In so doing, they have abandoned their fiduciary responsibility for maintaining monetary and banking honesty, safety and soundness.

The duties of banks holding precious metals as money were essentially to assure that the money was safe—not lost or stolen; that the money was sound—that is, the depositor gets back what he put in—the same, if not identical—kind, amount and quality of specie deposited; and to maintain transparent and accurate accounts and receipts for deposit and withdrawal. They accepted deposits as fiduciaries.

For convenience, businessmen historically, from the time of the Mesopotamians, issued discounted bills of exchange and bills of credit redeemable at the discounted value of the bill, in specie by a depository bank, to avoid the burdensome requirement that businessmen transact business in heavy and unwieldy amounts of precious metals. This ancient practice was the beginning of money-based credit. These bills were traded at a discount reflecting the degree of trust, confidence and credit worthiness reposed by the negotiating bank in the issuer, the risk of safety and soundness of the depository bank and its holding bills convertible and redeemable on demand, "liquid" at the negotiated price of the bill in specie money.

Some readers of this work will recoil in horror at the suggestion that the accountability for the consequences of Washington and Wall Street enterprise's abuse of structured finance in the proliferation of credit backed securities, derivatives and repos, and the resulting "financialization" of the American and global economy, can be laid at their door. The conceptual and legal foundation for ultimate accountability is clear and its eventual recognition and imposition is inevitable. Washington and Wall Street violated their fiduciary duty to the American public through intentional separation of asset liquidity and value from any underlying standard of value for the money substitutes they created: (i) misrepresenting the monetary value they purport to evidence; and (ii) debasing the US dollar and corrupting the liquidity and value of all assets denominated in US dollars, including shadow money substitutes. This debasement caused the great financial crisis and to an ever-greater degree, each successive financial crisis following the American Civil War.

Shadow bankers, to the extent they do not find themselves a part of the Washington and Wall Street speculative monetary enterprise in shadow banking money and therefore subject to the now truncated bankers fiduciary standard in their financial, investment and trading activities, may also find that they have been victims of this dark enterprise in manipulation and misrepresentation of asset and money liquidity and value. They may also find that when the Washington and Wall Street enterprise's day of reckoning arrives, which it inevitably will, likely in the form of another financial crisis that Washington and Wall Street cannot simply paper over through manipulation of asset liquidity and values through quantitative easing, interest rate manipulations and collusion with governments, banks and central banks worldwide, there will be opportunities for well-informed hedge funds and private equity for speculative investment in and out of the bankruptcy processes, as party and counterparty liabilities for breaches of duties and standards of care are finally measured and allocated.

The essential function of sovereign money, the value of which is regulated as required by law, is to establish a *floor of trust and confidence* in the value and liquidity of money in its various capacities of use as: a medium of exchange; a unit of account; a store of value; and a standard for deferred payment. The function of sovereign money is assured by to regulation of its value in accordance with an outside verifiable standard, such as precious metal of a *stated quantity and quality as ensured by the sovereign.*

The essential function of credit money is to provide *elasticity* in the money supply. The credit money is denominated and payable in units of sovereign money, as and when due in accordance with the terms of the credit. *This elasticity comes with a cost: risk of default; and risk attendant to the passage of time. Both risks can result in a reduction in asset value or liquidity or both.* The function of credit money is assured by discounts in negotiated value to compensate for the risks as understood by and among a limited number of issuers, dealers, acceptors and bankers, all enjoying mutual shared information regarding all parties leading to mutual trust and confidence. The mutual trust and confidence is backed by the original liability of the issuer to pay when due and by the added "wrapped" liability of each party that endorses and transfers the credit as well as by the legal protections of banking and commerce that developed to regularize the documentation and process of prudently maximizing the liquidity and value of the credit transferred or employed as money in commerce.

When sovereign money and credit money fail to perform their function because their respective fundamental legal character is altered, who should bear responsibility for the booms and busts in asset liquidity and value caused by the economic distortions caused by the alterations worked upon the legal character essential to their respective proper legal functions?

To the extent that hedge funds and private equity investor have, wittingly or no, entered into the business of money creation, they should bear losses attributable to the consequent breakdown of asset liquidity and value affected by them and resulting in insolvency—their insolvency or that of a borrower from them or counterparty of theirs.

Banks, specifically the largest banks that dominate the Federal Reserve System and are directly responsible for and intimately involved in the business of money, banking, and the alignment of asset liquidity and value supporting money, banking and our economic and financial system clearly bear responsibility for the breakdown of the necessary alignment of liquidity and value. They are the privileged in that structure. They are the experts in the substance and process of money, banking, asset and therefore monetary liquidity and value and the honesty, safety and soundness of the money they originate and distribute and the integrity of all assets and liabilities denominated in units of that money.

Historically government intervention in monetary systems has been initiated based on right of conquest and sustained by threat of force. Sovereign money facilitated state assessment and collection of taxes. Control over money as an exercise of sovereignty provided an additional revenue source as well as an opportunity to increase revenue though debasement of quality and amount of specie—causing inflation, lack of confidence in the honesty, safety and soundness of money and constriction of trade due to uncertainty of values and liquidity of money, goods and services and their connection to one another. Sovereign money then can work for the people's free market economy, or it can subvert it. In America the people are the sovereign. Their will is that the government that they created regulate the value of their sovereign money. The peoples will has simply been perverted by their government servants for their own benefit, and the benefit of their partners and collaborators amongst the largest Wall Street banks in the Federal Reserve System.

§7.11 FALSE NARRATIVE: THE REGULATED MONETARY SYSTEM IS SEPARATE AND INSULATED FROM THE SHADOW BANKING SYSTEM

Hedge Funds and private equity investors, not satisfied with exploiting the disparities in asset liquidity and value presented by the explosion in money substitutes, largely originated by banks and affiliated investment banks, broker dealers and fed by primary dealers, have directly invaded the once exclusive lending territory of banks. The Wall Street banks have moved up to larger credits and sought to minimize the effects of the Dodd Frank inspired regulatory crackdown, leaving regional and community banks to compete with unregulated and aggressive competitors.

> Regulators' efforts to rein in Wall Street's biggest banks are in danger of backfiring. Guidelines aimed at strengthening lending standards are shifting the market for high-yield credit to less-supervised loan funds, raising alarm from the Financial Stability Oversight Council. Because the funds do not have depositors, some of their money comes from Wall Street banks, leaving systemically important institutions exposed to risks regulators hoped to avoid. Direct-lending funds, which raise money from institutional investors such as pension funds and insurance companies, surged to a global record last year of $29.9 billion, according to financial data firm Preqin. Loans by US business development companies, or BDCs, many of which have credit lines with banks, jumped to $55 billion in 2011 from $17 billion in 2010. Asset managers are reshaping the market for lending to midsize companies. Regulators continue to scrutinized large banks for risk, publishing strict guidance on leveraged lending in 2013 and subsequently. That's allowing non-bank funds, many with ties to private-equity firms, to fill the void by helping finance buyouts and indebted companies. The credit sustains jobs and businesses, but it is also operating beyond the oversight of bank supervisors.
>
> Firms like Fifth Street, KKR and Apollo are regulated by the US Securities and Exchange Commission. They aren't constrained by leveraged-lending guidelines that the Fed, Office of the Comptroller of the Currency and Federal Deposit Insurance Corp. issued in March 2013 to curb risky underwriting. "Erin Stattel, an SEC spokeswoman, declined to comment ... The guidance, which specifies that a deal pushing a company's debt level to more than six times a measure of earnings raises concern, has slowed issuance in the larger, broadly syndicated loan market where financing is arranged by banks and distributed to investors ... The FSOC, a panel created by the Dodd-Frank Act to coordinate supervision across regulators and headed by Treasury Secretary Jacob J. Lew, said in a report this week that firms 'not subject to the guidance' could originate more risky loans. 'The migration in credit origination outside of the banking system could result in a further decline in underwriting standards for those particular loans, which could result in larger losses in stressed conditions,' it said ... Karen Shaw Petrou, managing partner at Federal Financial Analytics Inc., a Washington consulting firm whose clients include the world's largest banks, said non-bank lenders haven't been tested by a recession or higher interest rates. Their loan growth is being driven by 'an absence of regulation' ... 'Nonbanks may fund a lot of corporate credit because they can—at least if market volatility allows,' Petrou said in a speech in October. The

absence of rules 'clears take-off. Safe landing?' she said. That's another question.'"[631]

The banks in the Federal Reserve System create money through lending by "associating it with value", ostensibly in compliance with bank regulatory standards, both specific requirements as well as the over-arching requirement that the banks maintain safety and soundness, disciplined by follow-on doctrines such as prompt corrective action and ultimately, resolution through FDIC receivership. Hedge funds and private equity, by borrowing from banks and lending outside the regulatory arena are reaching for yield and biting off risks that they have little experience in mitigating and creating money that is less associated with value than even the Fed has contemplated. The longer banks and hedge funds, private equity and other private unregulated lenders stretch the string tying credit to liquid value the greater is the risk to financial stability generally and to the solvency of borrowers and lenders at each level. The perils of shadow banking structured finance to asset liquidity and value are driven inevitably by the big Wall Street banks, however indirectly, and notwithstanding the potential greedy culpability of the creative hedge fund and private equity intermediaries for this speculative adventure in money creation. The markets controlling asset liquidity and values know no bounds.

Until relatively recently, credit was largely created directly incident to the purchase and sale of goods in trade between businesses and through small trade accounts. Credit creation was therefore directly tied to the creation of market-based transaction that continuously established and confirmed the liquid, safe, sound value of the credit created and the value at which it served as liquid form of money. The predominant use of larger credit arrangements was sovereign lending and borrowing to finance war—or simple financial profligacy. As balances on account at banks grew, money not required to be liquid for immediate use or redemption in specie also grew. Bankers increased the practice of lending money held on deposit for short periods of time and charging interest to compensate for the risk and uncertainty that the loans would not be repaid in time to meet requirements for redemption by depositors in an honest, safe and sound sovereign money in the ordinary course of business. The creation of credit through bank lending presented an expansion of the opportunity for bank profit through the assumption of greater risk and uncertainty.

Bank lending involves risk and uncertainty; risk—that the attributes and the valuation of collateral and other borrower resources for the repayment of the loan do not deteriorate. Since the abandonment of the last vestige of financial discipline over the creation of United States dollar denominate money, elements of financial risk and uncertainty domestically and globally has increased dramatically while at the same time asset and credit liquidity has been sustained by Washington's and Wall Street's proliferation of ever more complex financial structures that conceal and misrepresent the honest, safe sound and liquid value of the explosion of financial assets treated as money and falsely and fraudulently represented to be liquid at the values necessary to constitute safe, sound and liquid money at par, or face value.

Risk is generally recognized, allocated and protected against through establishment of loan to asset value ratios, debt service coverage ratios, operating ratios, asset operational requirements and accountability, net worth maintenance requirements, hedges against failure to pay when due through guarantees of payment and performance of action necessary to assure payment, insurance and calls for additional collateral or assurance of repayment under certain condition and constant reporting with respect to the status of conditions affecting repayment. This is a fertile field for regulators and lawyers. Uncertainty—in addition to risks to loan repayment that can reasonably be anticipated, evaluated and protected against, there is always uncertainty regarding the occurrence of events outside the strict lender/borrower/source of repayment relationship that can affect the timely and full repayment of a bank loan.

The uncertainty is most often political risk, changes in government incentives and inducements to the extension of credit, labor or other market disputes and conflicts, war, physical or weather calamities and other unforeseen events which present additional risk of loss. The protection banks maintain against uncertainty is bank capital, reserves and limits on leverage through minimum ratios. If losses in expected loan repayments are incurred, the banks' capital and reserves are supposed to serve as a buffer against which the loss can be charged, without impairing the banks' ability to redeem bank borrower deposits when due with honest, safe and sound money, the value of which has been established and regulated by Congress in accordance with its constitutional mandate. Leverage limitations should act as an overall bank cushioning against future losses due to risk or uncertainty, the most damaging of which during financial crisis is the evaporation of asset liquidity to meet unexpected broad based depository creditor demand for repayment in liquid constitutionally coined money, the value of which is regulated by Congress.

Bank leverage ratios are notoriously, ridiculously, inappropriately inadequate to serve their intended purpose. Bank reserve requirements have been whittled and gamed away by Washington and Wall Street to the point that functionally they are non-existent. Asset and credit liquidity have been deliberately and intentionally subverted as functions of honest, safe and sound credit banking and credit creation. The fundamental banking function is protecting those who use the banking and financial system from exposure to the risk and uncertainty inherent in creating liquid money in the form of credit backed by illiquid assets, at valuations that recognize and account for the necessary discount in valuation of illiquid assets when intermediated into the economy as liquid money. Washington's and Wall Street's position that the value of their assets have been truly and accurately presented in accordance with Generally Accepted Accounting Principles and banking law and regulation is false.

§7.12 FALSE NARRATIVE: SHADOW MONEY DOES NOT ACT AS SOVEREIGN MONEY

The Uniform Agreement on the Classification and Appraisal of Securities Held by Depository Institutions[632] directed the Federal financial regulatory agencies to remove any reference to or requirement of reliance on credit ratings in the regulations and replace them with appropriate standards of creditworthiness, and to "use this statement for the classification and treatment of investment securities."[633] The purpose of the new Agreement and revised regulations is to assure that asset backed securities held by banks are properly valued at fair value and properly classified when the underlying credits are impaired; the ratings agency classifications used by the banks having been demonstrably misleading and fraudulent in many cases.

The Agreement provides that "Although Securities that do not meet the investment grade standard, as defined in applicable regulations, and for which the timely repayment of principal and interest is not certain, have investment characteristics that are distinctly or predominantly speculative and are generally subject to classification. For investment securities, the classification should be based on the instrument's worth as an earning asset assuming it is held to maturity. Therefore, the phrase 'liquidation of the debt' in the classification definitions is synonymous with 'payment of the obligation in full.' Accordingly, if payment of the obligation in full is in question, it is no longer investment grade and management should classify the security.

> A Doubtful classification is appropriate when an asset has experienced significant credit deterioration and decline in fair value, but estimation of impairment involves significant uncertainty because of various pending factors. These factors could include uncertain financial data that may not permit the accurate forecasting of future cash flows or estimating recovery value. The use of the Doubtful classification is an interim measure until information becomes available to substantiate a more appropriate treatment.[634]
>
> Depository institutions should continually assess whether securities meet the investment grade standard. Throughout the term of an investment security, its credit risk profile can decline and improve as credit conditions change. Similarly, an institution's analysis should consider how potential adverse economic conditions can negatively affect an individual security. An institution's management expertise and the sophistication of its risk management and due diligence processes should be commensurate with the complexity of its investment portfolio holdings.[635]

The FDIC Uniform Agreement, prepared and implemented under *Dodd Frank,* is presented as an example of new effective bank regulation. This Agreement is apparently intended to assure the quality of mortgage-backed securities and their accurate presentation for asset classification and valuation purposes; these same securities being the largely defective credit derivatives lying at the heart of the financial crisis. The Agreement does not mention the fact that specific regulations establishing essentially the same substantive safety and soundness standards were in effect at the time of the financial crisis in 2008:

> 12 C.F.R. § 1.1 Authority, purpose, and scope; prescribes standards under which national banks may purchase, sell, deal in, underwrite, and hold securities, consistent with the authority contained in 12 U.S.C. 24 (Seventh) and safe and sound banking practices.
>
> 12 C.F.R. § 1.3 Limitations on dealing in, underwriting, and purchase and sale of securities.

12 C.F.R. § 1.5 Safe and sound banking practices; credit information required. A national bank shall adhere to safe and sound banking practices and the specific requirements of this part in conducting the activities described in § 1.3. The bank shall consider, as appropriate, the interest rate, credit, liquidity, price, foreign exchange, transaction, compliance, strategic, and reputation risks presented by a proposed activity, and the particular activities undertaken by the bank must be appropriate for that bank.

Notwithstanding the necessity for this sensible treatment of bank asset valuation and classification required in 2001 and now required under the Agreement, during the financial crisis and continuing to today, the Wall Street banks have consistently carried illiquid, value impaired, toxic assets at par value without application of the disciplined valuation and classification required under the new Agreement or under the prior existing safety and soundness statutes and corresponding regulations. In fact, to avoid accountability for the capital losses due to value impairment on their balance sheets, the Wall Street banks dumped the troubled assets onto the Fed's balance sheet at par, booking newly minted Federal Reserve Notes in place of those toxic assets, the Federal Reserve Notes themselves backed by absolutely nothing. In this way the chain of bailouts "covered up" losses and deliberately and intentionally misrepresents the state of the American economy and financial system. The accountability of the Wall Street banks and the federal financial regulators continues; another "can" "kicked down the road."

Importantly, neither the Agreement nor prior safety and soundness statutes and regulations provide for a discount of recorded value to reflect the risk and uncertainty of the immediate liquidity of those assets, yet they purport to serve the public purpose of "sovereign money. This is emblematic of the fundamental, tragic failure of America's banking and financial system.

These same securities referred to in the prior existing statutes, regulations and the new Agreement serve as the foundation for the derivatives that have infiltrated the nation's money market funds and serve as the fodder for trading—money creation—through the massive phenomenon of perpetual overnight repo financing. Repos are in many ways the ultimate in the fraudulent misrepresentation of illiquid asset as liquid assets at par value and by churning those assets over and over, through re-hypothecation, which means pledging the same assets over and over simultaneously to different parties in a pyramid of credit. Ordinary Americans would be jailed for such activity. "According to Yale Professor Gorton, in testimony to the Committee in February 2010, "This banking system—repo-based securitization—is a genuine banking system, as large as the traditional banking system. It is of critical importance to the economy." … "Until recently, short-term repos have always been regarded as virtually risk-free instruments, Federal Reserve Chairman Ben Bernanke told a meeting of bankers in May 2008, after nine-months of turmoil in the repo market. Former Federal Reserve Chairman Alan Greenspan, writing in an April report on the panic, described repos as 'almost sacrosanct."[636] These statements were made despite the fact that the structure of repo financing is unsafe and unsound on its face. According to Gorton, the repo market is a critical cog in the wheel of finance. That may be. But the wheel of finance has become a giant Ponzi scheme financing the Wall Street's addiction to financial gambling. Gorton insists that without repo financing, traditional banks will not lend and credit, which is essential to job creation, will not be created. There is no evidence whatsoever that repo financing and the seemingly endless daisy-chain of repo re-hypothecation is essential for American job creation. Such a statement is utterly irresponsible. There is no evidence that this credit creation machine is honest, safe or sound or that it provides any economic or social benefits for ordinary Americans, while it subjects them to enormous risk and loss.

The repo financing market largely consists primarily of 21 Wall Street Banks and other "big players" trading approximately 90% of $7 trillion in overnight borrowing every night (the actual numbers are uncertain because no one collects all the data).

The actions of the Washington Wall Street enterprise conducted under color of authority of unconstitutional relief from their duty to create and emit credit denominated in US dollars redeemable only by fiat Federal Reserve Notes as legal tender have provided to the Washington Wall Street enterprise the opportunity that they have fully exploited to create money that has been debased, in many cases by as much as 60%, and in too many cases as much as 100%, enabling them to profit from such debasement while being protected against losses inherent in such debasement by holding the pubic hostage as being institutions "too big to fail" lest the Wall Street Washington enterprise of banking and financial oligarchy collapse, and with it the real United States economy, and by forcing the losses to be borne by ordinary American citizens. Thus and thereby Wall Street and Washington perpetuate and protect their monopoly ability to concentrate income, wealth and power in the Washington Wall Street enterprise financial and economic system that is in most respects disconnected from the real American markets and economy, creating an ever greater division and disparity of power, income and wealth to the detriment of and damage to the American public.

According to John Maudlin, "... the Fed now has three mandates instead of two, the third being that the central bank is now also supposed to be "responsible for the markets." This new duty, of course, is in addition to its intended role of ensuring price stability and full employment." Mauldin's observation assumes that all have forgotten, [as seems obvious] the congressionally delegated mandate to regulate the creation and value of money. Having purportedly delegated that mandate to the Wall Street Banks, the constitutional mandate—the supreme law of the land—is now apparently out of sight and out of mind.[637]

"The Fed can be blamed or credited with controlling the prices of almost all assets over the last six years through Bailouts, Quantitative Easing, Operation Twist, and all other forms of economic stimulus. How the Fed goes about unwinding this unprecedented stimulus will do much to determine our economic destiny as a nation."[638] The phenomenon of the Fed, through the Wall Street banks as the Feds agents and partners, controlling the value of assets goes back to the disappearance of the last vestige of discipline provided by constitutional coined money, the value of which has been regulated by Congress—through repeated boom and bust cycles that have always left ordinary American poorer and the Washington Wall Street enterprise and those fortunate enough to tag along with them in the Washington Wall Street enterprise economy and financial system richer and more entrenched, and the most wealthy 1 percent of Americans ever more wealthy.

The specific failures of the Wall Street banks however, in their official role of following Federal Reserve created incentives designed to meet the Federal Reserve's stated political objectives, indeed, exceeding those incentives, unrestrained by federal and state examination, regulation and supervisory authorities—which have ceded to the Wall street banks "enlightened self-interest" through "self-regulation" in implementing Fed policies, have created a straight line of wrongful conduct and breached duty leading directly from those failures to the financial crisis and to the losses suffered by ordinary Americans and identified by the Committee, the Fed and the GAO.

§7.13 FALSE NARRATIVE: DODD FRANK HELD WASHINGTON AND WALL STREET ACCOUNTABLE FOR THE FINANCIAL CRISIS

[A] Dodd Frank Preceded and Did Not Respond to the Conclusions in the Report

The Report details the factual statements and conclusions with respect to the moral and legal failures that caused the financial crisis. Pursuant to the Report, the Commission apparently made what they considered to be appropriate referrals to law enforcement authorities. Nevertheless, no meaningful action was taken in response to those referrals and any meaningful Congressional response is non-existent. The combination of: (i) a Report that includes does not mandate a call for action; (ii) law enforcement agencies that continue to intentionally ignore their respective enforcement duties; (iii) Dodd Frank legislation passed before the indisputable facts were on the table; and (iv) failure of any Wall Street financial regulator to meaningfully and effectively mandate the enforcement of existing law, have left ordinary Americans with no alternative for enforcement of the moral and legal accountability of Washington and Wall Street, apart from organized, combined, individual, private legal action under existing law.

The actions of ordinary individual Americans are subject to the rigorous standards and sanctions imposed in cases of banking, securities and consumer fraud and crime. Washington and Wall Street have demonized ordinary Americans for causing the financial crisis. It is as though ordinary Americans caused the crisis. The focus of Washington and Wall Street programs established to vilify ordinary people for incurring excess indebtedness and failing to anticipate the collapse of asset liquidity and value that has been driven by Washington's and Wall Street's boom and bust monetary and economic policy is upside down and backwards. Before the dialogue can move from the moral failures that led to the financial crisis and continue to define public fiscal and monetary policy in America and lay out specific recommendations for a legal case for Washington and Wall Street legal accountability, we must take a look at the Commission Conclusions, as detailed in the Report.

[B] The Financial Crisis Inquiry Report

The Commission was created to "examine the causes of the current financial and economic crisis in the United States." In this report, the Commission presents to the

President, the Congress, and the American people the results of its examination and its conclusions as to the causes of the crisis. When the Report was issued, the Commission noted that "[m]ore than two years after the worst of the financial crisis, our economy, as well as communities and families across the country, continues to experience the aftershocks. Millions of Americans have lost their jobs and their homes, and the economy is still struggling to rebound. This report is intended to provide a historical accounting of what brought our financial system and economy to a precipice and to help policy makers and the public better understand how this calamity came to be."[639]

The Commission was thorough and its conclusions important. Unfortunately, The Report's conclusions have been largely ignored. The regulatory response to the financial crisis has been excruciatingly slow and timid. The aspects of Dodd Frank most restrictive on Wall Street have been gamed by Wall Street and the federal financial regulators so as to have been rendered largely ineffective.

> The Commission's statutory instructions set out 22 specific topics for inquiry and called for the examination of the collapse of major financial institutions that failed or would have failed if not for exceptional assistance from the government. This report fulfills these mandates. In addition, the Commission was instructed to refer to the attorney general of the United States and any appropriate state attorney general any person that the Commission found may have violated the laws of the United States in relation to the crisis. Where the Commission found such potential violations, it referred those matters to the appropriate authorities. The Commission used the authority it was given to issue subpoenas to compel testimony and the production of documents, but in the vast majority of instances, companies and individuals voluntarily cooperated with this inquiry. In the course of its research and investigation, the Commission reviewed millions of pages of documents, interviewed more than 700 witnesses, and held 19 days of public hearings in New York, Washington, D.C., and communities across the country that were hard hit by the crisis. The Commission also drew from a large body of existing work about the crisis developed by congressional committees, government agencies, academics, journalists, legal investigators, and many others.[640]

The Report is not the sole repository of what the Commission found. A website—www.fcic.gov—hosts a wealth of information beyond that presented in the Report. The web site contains a stockpile of materials, including documents and emails, video of the Commission's public hearings, testimony, and supporting research—that can be studied for years to come. Much of material footnoted in the Report can be found on the website. In addition, the Commission has stated that more materials that cannot be released yet for various reasons will eventually be made public through the National Archives and Records Administration. The Commission's work reflects the extraordinary commitment and knowledge of the members of the Commission who were accorded the honor of this public service. Note that the Commission treated its efforts to discover the truth of the financial crisis was a matter of honor, conducted in the public interest, to present a truthful and honest account of the crisis. These moral aspects of the service of the Commission and set out in the Report: honor, truth and honesty in the money matters that frame. These moral principles are largely absent from any other government action taken by Washington in response the crisis. The Commission benefited from the perspectives shared with commissioners by thousands of concerned Americans through letters and emails. The Commission also expressed its gratitude to the hundreds of individuals and organizations that offered expertise, information, and personal accounts in extensive interviews, testimony, and discussions with the Commission.[641]

The Commission concluded that there the crisis resulted from "a systemic breakdown in accountability and ethics." The Commission emphasized that the integrity of financial markets and the public's trust in those markets are essential to American economic well-being. The soundness and the sustained prosperity of the American financial system and our economy rely on the notions of "fair dealing, responsibility, and transparency." In our economy, Americans expect businesses and individuals to pursue profits, while they produce products and services of quality and conduct themselves well.[642]

Unfortunately, as has been the case in past speculative booms and busts, America has witnessed "an erosion of standards of responsibility and ethics that exacerbated the financial crisis. This was not universal, but these breaches stretched from the ground level to the corporate suites. They resulted not only in significant financial consequences but also in damage to the trust of investors, businesses, and the public in the financial system.[643]

The Commission placed special responsibility with "the public leaders charged with protecting our financial system, those entrusted to run our regulatory agencies, and the chief executives of companies whose failures drove us to crisis." These individuals sought and accepted positions of significant responsibility and obligation. Tone at the top does matter and, in this instance, we were let down. No one said "no."[644]

When the Commission began its work, some imagined that the events of 2008 and their consequences would be well behind us by the time it issued the Report. Yet, When the Report was published, more than two years after the federal government intervened in an unprecedented manner in our financial markets, and continuing until the present day, America finds itself still grappling with the aftereffects of the calamity. The American financial system is, in many respects, still unchanged from what existed on the eve of the crisis. Indeed, in the wake of the crisis, the American financial sector is now more concentrated than ever in the hands of a few large, systemically significant institutions.[645]

While the Commission was not been charged with making policy recommendations, the very purpose of the Report was to "take stock of what happened so we can plot a new course." In the Commission's inquiry, it found dramatic breakdowns of corporate governance, profound lapses in regulatory oversight, and near fatal flaws in our financial system. It also found that a series of choices and actions led America toward a catastrophe for which all were ill prepared. The Commission was of the opinion that these matters are serious matters; matters that must be addressed and resolved to restore faith in American financial markets; avoid the next crisis, and to rebuild a system of capital that provides the foundation for a new era of broadly shared prosperity. The Committee concluded that the greatest tragedy would be to accept the refrain that no one could have seen this coming and thus nothing could have been done. If we, ordinary Americans, accept this notion, Washington and Wall Street will continue and entrench the status quo that led the crisis; and yes, the factors that caused the financial crisis were not new, different or unforeseeable. If Washington and Wall Street are not held accountable for the financial crises they cause, the crisis will recur. The Commission stated that the Report should not be viewed as the end of the nation's examination of this crisis. There is still much to learn, much to investigate, and much to fix. This is our collective responsibility. It falls to us to make different choices if we want different results.[646]

Politicians and the power elite throughout history have a well justified general reputation of duplicity and mendacity accompanied by the continued ability to get away with it, time after time. Thus, the low regard in which they are held by the public. These "power elite" as well as the American public, seem to accept the explanation that, no matter how outrageous the behavior of the power elite and no matter the level of outrage expressed by the American public, the power elite are somehow exempt from the standards, laws and sanctions imposed on the rest of the American public in cases of banking, securities and consumer fraud and crime.

The closer one gets to the responsible individuals comprising the power elite, the more difficult it is for those who have suffered Washington's and Wall Street's deceit, misrepresentation and fraudulent debasement of American sovereign money to successfully find justice. Responsible Americans who seek to impose accountability on and to seek justice from Washington and Wall Street risk running afoul of the pervasive power held by these powerful public figures and the institutions they populate. The customary and official method of dealing with the public figures and holding them accountable is for voters and shareholders to "throw the bums out." Unfortunately, those who follow those thrown out, tend to fall into the age-old patterns of active pursuit of self-interest held by their predecessors, in derogation of their formal and institutional responsibilities.

We are familiar with the generally held, one might say, cynical, view of those ordinary Americans who find themselves suffering what we are assured are acceptable levels of tail end losses imposed by their policies and actions, that there really is not anything we can do about it. It is just the nature of the system. The briefly popular, but largely ineffective, "Occupy Wall Street" movement and the more coherent and focused activity of the "tea party" movement, express public frustration with our collective inability to enforce responsibility and accountability for the harm caused by American systemic financial crises. Professor Paul Kennedy has thoroughly documented the historic consequences of successive societies' failure to enforce responsibility and accountability of the governing power elite individuals and institutions through the mechanisms of civil society under the rule of law. When the gap between action and rhetoric becomes too great, the mobs in fact do form, violence and war coalesce, and heads eventually, and actually do roll.

When you get down to the essence of the issue, however, despite the widespread anger and frustration on the tail end of the loss allocation process in the ongoing American and global financial crises, we must be reminded that congressmen, federal financial regulators and their systemic tools, the Wall Street banks and bankers, are not exempt from the legal standards and sanctions already existing in our legal system. Washington's and Wall Street's apparent insulation from the consequences of their actions is an illegitimate claim of a perverse public policy not supported by the rule of law. This practical immunity is the product of an intentionally false narrative grounded in the notion that fraud is acceptable if it is perpetrated in existential circumstances to preserve our nation in time of war. We are now, and since 1971 has been in a perpetual state of war that has not threatened the existence of America. The Washington Wall Street enterprise course of intentional money debasement has not served to protect our existence under exceptional, existential circumstances, but rather the course of Washington and Wall Street intentional, fraudulent money debasement has become the primary tool exercised by Washington and Wall Street to concentrate economic power and amass wealth. The dominant false narrative presented in this chapter is that Washington and Wall Street fraud through money debasement is necessary for achievement of the American dream for ordinary Americans. The true narrative is that intentionally fraudulent money debasement constitutes an act of raw, immoral, illegal and unconstitutional usurpation of the civil legal right of the American people to honest, safe and sound American money and banking.

The idea that public policies of fraud conducted through fiscal, monetary and banking policy, law and regulation based on intentional money debasement is somehow good for ordinary Americans represents a level of blind acceptance of and refusal to confront the irresponsible, immoral and illegal exercise of political power by Washington and Wall Street.

§7.14 CONCLUDING OBSERVATIONS

Fear mongers who abound in the legal, accounting, political and economic communities react with disbelief and outrage to positions taken by some such as former United States Senator and Presidential candidate Ron Paul that America should return to an absolute gold standard. Glibly stated positions like this ignore: (i) the impossibility of 100 percent reserves of gold for paper money, which would not provide sufficient elasticity in the money market to serve the needs of the American economy; and (ii) the importance for a legally sound system of shadow credit money to provide the elasticity in the money supply sufficient to serve the American economy. That being said, the now totally dominant role played by credit as money in American and globally must be disciplined to reign in the Wall Street Washington enterprise that has high-jacked the American economy and the global economy through the unregulated and unaccountable exploitation of the trust and power reposed in them by the American public as "experts in matters of money" and the holders of American trust as well as a privileged monopoly power over American money and the American economy. The limited though crucial and indispensable role of monetary discipline through a constitutionally grounded redemption requirement that would apply to all credit money. Credit money substitutes should be limited essentially to credit money conforming to the real bills doctrine and expressly excluding monetized government debt and structured financial products, such as those lying at the heart of the financial crisis.

The state of sovereign money and credit money at the time of America's founding presented the very same archetype players in government and banking, and ordinary

Americans bore the brunt of damage, loss and suffering experienced then, and thereafter with each subsequent financial crisis. Each wave of American money debasement has been justified by the economic demands of existential war. The official reports following each crisis have recited essentially the same symptoms as causes and prescribed essentially the same government response that falls short of addressing the fundamental causation of money debasement produced by failure to regulate the value of sovereign money. That refusal to directly address the role of money debasement, demeaning of the legal attributes of transferable, or negotiable credit that are necessary for the money substitutes limited utility as credit money is contrary in its affects to the constitutional power duty to facilitate and regulate commerce and it inhibits congressional power and duty to provide the elasticity in the money supply that would serve to help moderate normal economic cycles. Each wave of American financial reform legislation has followed the same pattern of punitive remedial legislation, subsequently observed more in its breach than enforcement, and then followed by relaxation of the role of remediation of the crisis symptoms through administrative regulation and relaxation of financial regulatory and legal enforcement of the freshly enacted banking legislation and regulations.

We have progressed to our present state of money debasement and systemic financial crises by manipulation of America's ideal of honest, safe and sound money to a place where disparagement or diversion of enforcement of America's supreme law of the land through intentional manipulation of money and banking has become America's public policy. As America now stands, its entire monetary, banking, financial and economic systems are based on intention systemic fraudulent money debasement. The practice of money debasement prohibited by the American *Constitution* and established as a capital crime in 1792 has been transmogrified to a place where money debasement is our official monetary policy and abuse of trust and power is commonly expected. Dishonesty has become a popular, perverse virtue. Abuse of trust and power and dishonesty is now pervasive throughout modern culture. The quintessential American virtues of morality, law, and common sense have been stood on their heads.

This pattern of abuse of trust and power by government, bankers and speculators, has relentlessly worn away and subverted American morality, natural law, constitutional law, statutory and common law essential to the American foundation of protections mandated for its honest, safe and sound money, monetary, banking and economic systems. The destructive effects of continued money debasement now extend to the very heart of America's political democratic republic and a free enterprise economy. The American economy depends upon a system of safe, sound and honest money, which when effected, constrains the constant quest by Washington and Wall Street for income, wealth and power.

CHAPTER 8

False Narrative of Asset Liquidity and Value

The essence of insolvency for debtors and creditors, whatever their legal structure may be and whatever assets lie at the heart of their underlying business, turns on: liquidity; income or cash flow solvency; the ability of the entity in question to pay its debts as they become due; and balance sheet solvency; the value of the entity's assets in excess of its liabilities. These concepts are fundamental to insolvency law. They are also fundamental to roles and claim priorities of equity holders and credit holders in insolvency proceedings. Claim priorities reflect historical developments in law identifying the parties most responsible for and most capable of avoiding the necessity of seeking relief under insolvency laws and establishing claims priority that reflect the determination of such roles and claim priorities. The consideration of liquidity and value are expressed in monetary terms and units of money denomination is assumed. This is not new information.

The actual calculations supporting a determination of solvency or insolvency and the legal and accounting principles governing those calculations have historically been largely considered peripheral to the role of bankruptcy counsel in insolvency proceedings. These considerations have been primarily left to experts in valuation and accounting. Times have changed. Liquidity is not what it appears to be. Asset values are not what they appear to be.

We must broaden our understanding of all the factors that bear on liquidity, value and insolvency and loss. It is time to assess changes in perspective and treatment of the legal status, rights and remedies and priorities of claims amongst the various constituents in litigation over financial loss and damages as well as in insolvency proceedings brought upon us by developments in investment, finance and banking and monetary law and policy that are manifest in the series of disastrous financial crises over the more than 45 years following the Nixon shock.

Liquidity and value are driven now by the largest Wall Street banks and related or affiliated parties, including investment banks, primary dealers, hedge funds and private equity investors; all of whom operate to a greater or lesser degree in what is now referred to as the financial world of shadow banking. Most of you are aware that the banking industry is defined through state and federal law and regulation regarding charter, activities and conduct of banking. Shadow banking can be generally described as the conduct of banking activities largely outside of the state and federal legal and regulatory banking arena.

My colleague on a discussion panel concerning issues of asset liquidity and valuation, Stephen T. Crosson, MAI, SRA, FRICS, Principal an international valuation consulting firm, prepared and presented a short paper on the "Truths of Valuation"; valuation axioms that apply to any type of asset. The valuation methodologies detailed in the paper and discussion represented the starting point for prototypical determinations of asset liquidity and value before considering the matrix of new legal, accounting and monetary distortions that bear directly on changes, often abrupt changes, in asset liquidity, valuations and determinations of insolvency. These distortions have proven to be remarkably predictable in degree, if not in timing. The distortions may; or perhaps should, affect identity, classification and priority of claims in bankruptcy, the structure of plans of reorganization in bankruptcy court and a fresh focus of allocation of losses and damages suffered by the constituents in our economy resulting from financial crises under America's present corrupt monetary system.

The primary truths of asset valuation are grounded in asset holding period, time → liquidity; and in evidence of amount and timing of future income to be generated by the asset and multiples of current gross or net income (or rates of discount of future gross or net income) over the defined holding period before the expected liquidity event for the asset evaluated. Multiple rates and discount rates for present or future asset income are determined by valuation experts such as Mr. Crosson based on evidence and informed opinion.[647]

The common denominator for determination of holding periods (liquidity) and multiple of or discount rates applied to the present or future expected income of the asset, producing an asset value estimate, is the unit of measurement; money. The United States dollar. Lawyers generally, and commercial, banking and insolvency lawyers in particular, assume the stability, integrity and therefore utility of the dollar as a monetary tool upon which the validity of their role in insolvency resolution proceedings is grounded. Accountants do the same. All should know better. The banking, financial and monetary principles addressed in this work are not new, unknown or obscure, unless and except for those who simply choose not to concern themselves with the principles. Honesty is not obsolete. It has been hidden. Legally enforceable constraints on the exercise of trust and power of Washington government politicians and bureaucrats and Wall Street bankers who occupy positions of trust and confidence as ordinary Americans' fiduciaries, are vital to the welfare of all Americans and the continued existence of the United States as a developed economy and country.

Banks, and affiliated entities, such as money market funds, hedge funds, repo traders and private equity, in different ways and in different legal and accounting contexts, exploit dysfunction in monetary policy and action to distort asset liquidity and value in the market place and profoundly affect the timing and equity of constituents' interests in a bankrupt estate in bankruptcy court. They have done so since the time of the American Revolution. Thus, laws, rules and regulations have been set down for the protection of the public interest in and honest, safe and sound banking and monetary system. They must not be ignored.

Mr. Crosson's presentation focused on the fundamental valuation methodology consisting of the application of a rate or rates of multiple of an assets present gross income or net cash flow, based on established sources of evidence and expert opinion. This method concentrates on the risks and uncertainties attendant to the present liquid value of a stream of future income. While pricing information in active trading markets may seem compelling, very often dramatic changes in asset valuation occur primarily when assets become illiquid. It is precisely at the time that the liquidity of any asset is tested. It is also precisely the time that the value of the money unit in which the asset value denominated is also properly determined for purpose of its service as money or as a money substitute. In an insolvency proceeding that time is the filing date for initiation of insolvency proceedings. That day likely is a day when the assets of the bankrupt estate are likely to be least liquid; and when the value of money in which values are denominated, and the money's necessary attribute of liquidity are tested.

In new global financialized economy, markets are roiled during and following financial crises, and asset valuations shift dramatically. Many bankers and investors can find good hunting in exploiting liquidity and valuation distortions. When asset liquidity and values are manipulated, as they have been in the United States Federal Reserve System since the great recession, through contrived interest rate policy and quantitative easing, the hunting grounds have thinned out and potential yields shrunk. The liquidity and valuation manipulation is predominantly conducted by the United States Federal Reserve System, the national banking system, and throughout the world of shadow banking. The essence of money as an honest, safe, sound, stable tool managed through a comprehensive, but ever more complex bank legal and regulatory environment, has morphed into and become subsumed in a multi-trillion dollar pool of debt created, held and traded both within and without the Federal Reserve System, structured and disguised as securities and not subject to banking law and regulation that apply to credit. This is not news.

Dodd Frank[648] and the mountain of bank regulation it has spawned[649] has done little to change the dynamics that led to the great financial crisis.

Many opportunistic investors have expressed curiosity as to where all the bankruptcies have gone. Why are hedge funds suffering from collapsing returns and a dearth of deals; but not consequently presenting themselves as sources of bankruptcies? Why do some hedge funds, private equity firms and other investors act as banks, but are able to act outside the bank legal and regulatory matrix? Bankruptcy lawyers typically thrive during and following financial crises. Where are the bankruptcy opportunities? What are the constraints on the expected pool of opportunities? Where can investors find high yields? These questions are on the agenda of every participant in our banking, financial and economic systems.

Determination of asset liquidity and value are the starting point for any insolvency proceeding as well as for opportunistic investors that seek to capitalize on an asymmetrical understanding of money debasement on asset liquidity and value. Sorting out the roles and relative constituent culpability and consideration whether causes of value bubble bursting and liquidity evaporation as between banks, hedge funds, private equity and other constituents are legally actionable or should affect the amount and priority of any claims by banks, money market funds, hedge funds, repo traders, private equity investors or affiliated parties will present a new range of inquiry and strategy following the next financial crisis—which is surely inevitable. In fact, a sorting out those same roles and responsibilities in the wake of the great financial crisis continues to await informed immediate attention. A reading of the Commission Report prepared by the National Commission on the Causes of the Financial and Economic Crisis in the United States, published in January 2011, will confirm to any skeptic that neither debtors nor creditors, whether banks, money market funds, hedge funds, repo traders or private equity or any other significant constituent of our economy (all together, "shadow bankers"), in any case involving structured financial assets, will likely come to court with clean hands. All have sought profit in legal amnesia. Those determinations and allocations of losses and damages from financial crises should turn on the law of money, fiduciary duty and standard of care, whether on a case by case basis or in a general legal, policy, legislative, regulative context or, in bankruptcy litigation.[650] These subjects have been largely ignored in resolution of prior crises, including the great financial crisis.

In the wake of the most recent financial crisis, constituents in any sufferance of losses, damages or insolvency are buffeted by the pervasive exercise of legal, accounting and regulatory discretion in recognizing liquidity and valuation distortions as connected to amounts and timing of loss allocations and misdirection of identification and priority of debt holder and damage sufferer claims. The markets and therefore the incidence of insolvency proceedings have been directly impacted by the widespread adoption of policies known by such cliché's as "kick the can down the road, extend and pretend, deny and lie, delay and pray, too big to manage, too big to fail and too big to jail." These policies are grounded in the exercise of regulatory enforcement discretion, and in the effects of Fed monetary policy. Legal accountability for the damages caused by the financial crisis has not been addressed. Damages to ordinary Americans in the enormous sum of $20 trillion have been suffered, identified and simply swept aside.

The factual evidence and incidence of Wall Street banks income and balance sheet insolvencies has been ignored and papered over, disguising and deferring the clearing of losses imbedded in the market for financial assets specifically. These financial assets have acted and been treated as money and continued in that role. In an attempt to project an image of financial honesty, safety, soundness and stability, this fundamentally dishonest monetary policy process has served not to resolve market uncertainty, but rather to increase asset valuation concerns, distort underwriting and investment decisions and deprive the market of honest direction by its "free market" participants. It has left ordinary Americans holding the bag for $20 trillion in damages. They are mad as hell but see no recourse. There is recourse for the damages to ordinary Americans and it must be pursued by the American public to avoid a collapse of our way of life. Enforcement of accountability for American financial crises is the existential necessity to be faced; it is a war for the very security survival of the United States of America.

The interest, methods and practices of regulated banks on the one hand and unregulated affiliates and other large investors such as hedge funds and private equity funds on the other are no longer separate and distinct. The blurring of lines of differentiation of risk and reward amongst Washington, Wall Street and ordinary Americans is a perennial challenge.

Shadow bankers operate by different rules. Banks are heavily regulated by the OCC, the Fed, the FDIC, CFTC, SEC and state banking authorities. Determinations of bank solvency are driven by determination of bank safety and soundness and action taken under the bank regulatory requirement of prompt corrective action. These concepts, and the fiduciary duties of bankers and regulatory authorities pertaining to determinations of bank safety and soundness, and requirements of prompt corrective action by banks found to have violated standards for bank safety and soundness, are embodied in regulations relating to the various permitted banking activities, and are implemented through the timely enforcement of, or in too many cases, the failure to enforce legal and regulatory remedies available to address and resolve unsafe and unsound banking.

A reasonable man, much less an experienced banking attorney, would not consider the policy and action—or more precisely inaction—dictated by the prevailing bank regulatory policies of extending the day of reckoning and pretending that market-based asset valuations determined according the professionally accepted axioms, honestly or accurately support the valuations reported by the banks and their regulators, and bank borrowers. One might rightly suspect that asset valuations and income statements that are based on intentionally pretending, lying, denying asset value losses and characterization of materially overvalued and in many cases nonperforming assets as performing assets on bank books and regulatory reports constitute intentional misrepresentations, i.e., bank fraud. Does the exercise of unbridled bank and regulatory discretion extend to "supposedly" legally "sanctioned" bank fraud? What should a bankruptcy court make of the pervasive effect of institutional, intentional bank fraud, generally known to have been conducted over years prior to the ultimate necessity of facing proper asset valuation in bankruptcy, undistorted by a history of monetary debasement and financial manipulation?

Shadow bankers: the money market funds, hedge funds, repo traders, and private equity investors are generally corporate entities and have not been subject to the regulation of banks, but only to general corporate and securities law. Following the great financial crisis, the enactment of Dodd Frank and related laws and regulations, money market funds, hedge funds, repo traders and private equity investors are facing increased legal and regulatory limits and scrutiny imposed by the federal financial regulators. Shadow bankers, as a general rule, make no pretense of serving public interest and the law does not presume that they do. They each make speculative investment purely in the interest of profitmaking for the company's private interests. When these shadow banking enterprises, however, slip into the protected ambit of regulated banks, through affiliation, counterparty status or simply by force of sheer size and public reliance on those shadow bankers in their role in monetizing illiquid assets and expanding the money supply, they must then become subject to the discipline of regulation, including the ultimate regulation of the value of their money-like instruments by subjecting them to the discipline of repayment in dollars, the value, and therefore also the liquidity of which, are properly regulated by Congress in accordance with the law of the land.

Felix Martin presciently observed that "[b]y ignoring the essential link between the financial securities traded on the capital markets and the monetary system operated by the sovereign and the banks, academic finance built a theory of finance without the macroeconomy just as neoclassical macroeconomists had built had built a theory of the macro-economy without finance."

> What was critically missing was the insight of Bagehot, and Joplin and Thornton before him, of the importance of liquidity as a distinct property of credit—the property which makes it money when it exists, and inert bi-lateral credit when it does not. This was the crucial link between finance and the real economy that Bagehot and Keynes had sought so hard to emphasize, and the rationale for macroeconomic policy [and which should be also emphasized for macro-prudential regulation]—because the sovereign's liabilities enjoy a degree of liquidity to which no private issuer can aspire. Post war academic finance, however, gladly abandoned to the macroeconomists the morally and even theologically fraught topic of whether and how the sovereign might need to supply liquidity support in time of financial crisis. Scholars concerned themselves only with the unlocking of the secrets of how creditworthiness of financial claims traded on private markets affected their price. As such, it felt no need to complicate things with the additional element of liquidity, and before long, as one leading scholar has summed it up "[i]n the ... new formulation, it became impossible to conceptualize liquidity risk as a separate category of risk." Just as modern orthodox macroeconomics had ended up as a formal mathematical theory of how the moneyless doctrines of Say, Ricardo and their classical followers, so modern academic finance had ended up as a formal, mathematical theory of money in Utopia; a world with an infinite array of substitutable claims as shadow money substitutes, with no mention of sovereign money.[651]

At present neither scholars, bankers nor legal or accounting professionals refer to constitutional money created by Congress, the value of which is regulated by Congress. A deep analysis of how the "sovereign" money might be regulated and its liquidity assured, in a fair and equitable manner is beyond the scope of this work, although I have touched on the subject throughout. Martin's work and his sources are a good point of beginning of this understanding. Also, Professor Timberlake, as noted above, others, and specifically James Rickards in *The Death of Money—The Coming Collapse of the International Monetary System*[652] provide comprehensive analysis and recommendations detailing how the value of the dollar might feasibly be regulated. Dr Vieira also provides a specific legal mechanism for implementing constitutionally required regulation of the value of money.

The legal case presented in this work demands the funding, organization and leadership of America's, and the world's expertise to affect some such regulation in accordance with Congress' constitutional mandate, power and duty. The importance of getting to the point where the American and the global financial systems and their regulators can define and effectuate a new monetary system incorporating liquid "sovereign" money, the value of which is regulated by reference to a flexible, or elastic but reliable and constant outside standard in domestic and global finance can only be included on the agenda when Washington and Wall Street have an incentive to put it on the agenda and are forced to come to the table. Unfortunately, enforcement of the rule of law by ordinary Americans; the award and recovery of massive damages caused by the Washington and Wall Street enterprise's respective failure to follow the American rule of law; adding treble damages penalizing them for their intentional illegal acts; and finally, providing a material deterrence to future illegal conduct, is now the only way to ordinary Americans can hope to initiate the process of prosecuting a legal case for financial crisis accountability that will lead to realignment of the priorities of vested interests and the status quo.

The academic foundation for economic analysis and action is over-run during times of economic crisis by political interests focused almost exclusively on creating economic growth and combating unemployment through use of the least intellect, little understanding or appreciation of the historical record of the causes of financial crisis, and the most blunt exercise of political power taken in the political and financial self-interest of the concentrated political power, wealth and control in Washington and on Wall Street enterprise. Following each successive financial crisis in American history, Washington and Wall Street have been "blamed" but not held accountable. Instead their interests have been progressively promoted, expanded and concentrated. The public has borne the burden. Despite successive assurances that in the end the taxpaying public has been protected, that protection has been shown to be essentially an economic shell game of financial reporting manipulation. Ordinary American public's damages have been suffered, not as taxpayers, but as ordinary Americans living everyday lives, who are not on the payroll or a direct constituent of Washington or Wall Street. Main Street ordinary Americans are damaged directly and personally by the financial crises driven by the Washington and Wall Street enterprises actions. The abuse of trust and power and dishonest policies and actions have perversely become estimable characteristics of the American success story. The values held in Washington and on Wall Street conflict directly with the most fundamental traditional American principles of mutual trust, honesty, equality, respect for individual rights, and integrity and adherence to the rule of law.

The use of fiscal and monetary policy in pursuit of political and social objectives on an aggregate basis has proved to be impotent and wasted on the level of real results in the real economy on an individual basis, for ordinary Americans. This would be bad enough if the policies were simply well-intentioned but largely ineffective—other than to support a rationalization that without the action taken, the results would have been worse.

This work does not concern itself with the philosophical rut of exploitation of the differences between the different, but frankly complementary lines of economic thought represented by Keynes and Hayek. Both have been maligned and betrayed by the failure of the rule of law that sets the boundaries for the exercise of both fiscal and money policy in America, without regard to any doctrinal views of economic thought. Both Keynes and Hayek would likely be appalled at the low point our government has now reached in its perversion and abuse of economic theory. When Keynes and Hayek disagreed over the role, degree and desirability or necessity of the regulation of business, both of these leading lights of economic theory would have agreed, and in fact did agree that any role of government in economics must be subject to measurement and evaluation in terms of money, the value of which is transparently regulated by reference to an effective external standard of value in accordance with the rule of law. The standard need not be forever fixed and "immutable" as some pedants have demanded. The standard must, however, be established, and changed when necessary to accommodate economic and financial change, in a transparent, politically and legally accountable manner, in the interest of all Americans, not just the Washington and Wall Street enterprise.

This book has demonstrated the perils of abdication of congressionally mandated power and duty to create and regulate the value of money in the interest of ordinary Americans, and the damage wrought by the Washington Wall Street enterprise's in its essentially unconstrained abuse of trust and of political and financial power leading to debasement of the United States dollar, the world's reserve currency. Money debasement led to the collapse of any semblance of financial discipline of the value of money upon the elimination by Nixon's executive action rendering impotent and moot the Bretton Woods international financial institutions mission to regulate the value of money globally based on a reliable standard of value. The essential mission of these institutions evaporated in the face of the Nixon shock. These international financial institutions, whose missions were to foster global financial stability, have devolved into just another set of global financial intermediaries, banks, funded by taxpayers for purely political purposes, dispensing financial favors globally and playing their part in the furtherance of the global money debasement manufactured in and exported by America to the rest of the world.[653]

The BRIC[654] countries are now attempting to resuscitate the influence of global financial institutions that would serve their interests, and not the interests of Washington and Wall Street. Their desire appears to be misplaced in that they may simply be attempting to replicate their own version of these anachronistic institutions, cobbled up in the current function of, in many cases, ineffectively consolidating financial resources from its members to feed the financing of projects of questionable public value and bailing each other out from the effects of their public financial profligacy without the disciple of the *Bretton Woods Accords'* original mission of maintaining global financial stability by the disciple of a requirement of currency convertibility and redemption under a clear standard of value that would both supply the level the economic and financial field, and promote the honesty, trust and confidence that are conditions to global financial stability.[655]

The balance of the respective roles and responsibilities of individuals, financial institutions and governments in stabilizing and promoting economic growth and employment has been rendered largely irrelevant by the handing over of power and control over the creation and value of money to the entrenched financial powers in Washington and on Wall Street, to be exploited and abused for their self-interest, shorn of any semblance of fiduciary duty or responsibility to the public to provide "sovereign" money in accordance of the rule of law by which the economic policy debate can be explored and refined in service of the American public. Neither Keynes' nor Hayek's economic theories can remedy the financial and economic damage wrought by the exploitation and unlawful abuse of trust and power by Washington and Wall Street through the debasement of American money.

Over the past forty-five years, following the Nixon shock, banks including investment banks, have taken over and corrupted the fundamental mechanisms for discussing, debating, creating, implementing and evaluating fiscal and monetary policy. By coopting Congress and the Executive branch of American government through political contributions, lobbying and the blandishments of the revolving door between Washington and Wall Street, they hold the American public hostage to the undisguised threat of departure from the abusive politically invocation of immunity of Washington and Wall Street as "too big to fail and too big to jail"—in effect too big and powerful to be held legally accountable. The record of history tells us that at some point in time, the ordinary American people will take the law into their own hands and take to the streets. The street crowds' condemnation of governments and bankers in Greece, Italy, Spain, Portugal, Venezuela and other countries is the cry of "financial genocide." It follows from the enormous and growing gap that has developed between the very small number of "haves" and the ever expanding group of "have nots" worldwide. Violent reprisal and revolution do not yet appear to present a real threat to entrenched financial and economic power; but history has shown repeatedly and inevitably that complacency reins until the mobs actually come knocking on the doors of the elite to fetch them for the quick trip to street justice and accountability, following the failure of the rule of law. Ultimately, accountability for money debasement will be meted out in either a civil manner under the rule of law, or by a raging bloody mob.

The financial high jacking of the American economy by Washington and Wall Street through the great financial crisis has robbed the American public of more than $20 trillion, the global economy of $40 up to estimates as high as $60 trillion, accompanied by untold human suffering and injustice. Most importantly, Washington and Wall Street have intentionally taken every opportunity to subvert the American public's ability to hold government accountable for their actions under the rule of law.

The American judicial system is the last line of defense against the predations of Washington and Wall Street. If the courts fail to provide the most fundamental protection of the American public under the *Constitution*, the common law and federal statutory law, the integrity of American civil society will be permanently threatened. The violence of civil strife and war that has followed as the effects of money debasement historically, and now bubbling up currently in the fringe EU countries and South America, is inevitable. Perhaps not necessarily next month or next year—but inexorably. It is the fundamental duty of the American public, through the American judicial system, to act to compel Washington and Wall Street to recognize and respect their privileged status as monopolisers of power over American money, and as such, fiduciaries to ordinary Americans. The enforced subservience of the Washington Wall Street enterprise's self-interest to the interests of the ordinary American public in honest, safe and sound money under America's founding principles and the American rule of law. The strident cries of financial genocide can resonate in America just as they do in Spain, Greece, Italy, Portugal, France, Venezuela, Argentina and yes, even now, beginning in the United States.

§8.01 AMERICAN ECONOMIC, FISCAL, MONETARY THEORY POLICY AND ACTION ARE SUBJECT AND SUBORDINATE TO THE AMERICAN RULE OF LAW

When the Fed was formed and continuing until today, the Fed's powers and duties under the *Federal Reserve Act* have been and are in all respects, subject and subordinate to the congressional constitutional imperative to create as well as regulate the value of money in accordance with a democratically mandated, transparent, effective, legitimate external and constant standard of value. The Fed does not possess the power and duty to regulate the value of money, despite the fact that it has often represented to the American public that the Fed has that power and exercises it in the public interest. In 2005 the Fed, through its Chairman Alan Greenspan, simply acknowledged that, not only did the Fed not have the capability to regulate the value of money and credit, but yet purported to delegate the congressional constitutional power and duty to create and regulate the value of money, in the form of credit created within and without the regulated banking system (the very same power and duty that the Fed did not legally possess and therefore did not have the legal authority and capability to exercise, fulfil, abuse or to delegate to any other party), to the very Wall Street banks that have raided the American public, fattened themselves on the fruits of the American economy fed by intentional money debasement.

Enforcement by the American people of their legal rights under the common law, the *United States Constitution* and federal statutes that have been enacted to give the American public the power and legal right to enforce the financial crisis accountability of Washington and Wall Street and obtain justice for abuse of trust and their monopoly power to force us to choke down a form of money that embodies the pervasive intentional lies and misrepresentations of the value that the money purports to present, and which effects the organized institutional theft of the property right of honest asset value from the people.

If the power and duty have been delegated by Congress to the Federal Reserve, under the structure of the Federal Reserve System, the only connection of Federal Reserve Notes to value of any kind is established through the process of credit creation by the member banks, primarily and specifically through the Wall Street banks; powerful institutions that, in fact, control the banking and financial system in the United States. This is true regardless, and in spite of, the concerns expressed in the E.G. Spaulding's *History of Legal Tender Paper Money*, the *Pujo Report*, the *Pecora Report, the FDIC Report* and the *Commission's Report*. Each of these government reports decries the evil effects of concentration of banking, financial and economic power in the hands of a few Wall Street banks without effective regulation. None of these reports have led to any meaningful accountability or change. Each report has, in fact, been followed by a "doubling down" of the combined and concentrated income, wealth and power of the Washington Wall Street enterprise as a civil and criminally corrupt racketeering enterprise. The Fed has purportedly delegated to the Wall Street banks the power and duty to create and regulate the value of money through the Federal Reserve's official policy of "self-regulation" of the systemically important, "too big to fail and too big to jail" Wall Street banks.

As primary structural components in the Federal Reserve system, the Wall Street banks have created trillions of dollars of credit represented by Federal Reserve Notes (primarily electronic data entries of assets and liabilities denominated in units of measurement as United States dollars) not redeemable in constitutional coined money, the value of which has been regulated by Congress; and which Federal Reserve Note "dollar" data entries were created irrespective of the American legal requirement of honest, safe and sound provision for such credit to be redeemable through the collateral and other sources of repayment, supposedly protecting the holders by "associating" "value" with such credit. This vague and ineffective policy and practice has evolved without any regard to the constitutionally required discipline on the amount and value of credit created by the Wall Street banks. This arrangement has wholly abandoned the legal requirement that credit be redeemed in Federal Reserve Note dollars, which, as such, must also then be redeemable in constitutional coined money, the liquid value of which has been regulated by Congress.

The Wall Street banks have unlawfully exploited their ability to created vast amounts of credit through mortgage or other asset backed securities, derivatives, including credit default swaps, repos and other structured finance vehicles that the Wall Street banks have represented to represent the full face value of the instrument, when in fact the losses behind the "empty portions such credit," not supported by or associated with value, have in many cases exceeded 60 percent of the face amount of the credit, resulting in a permanent debasement of the dollar denominated credit, to the extent of the imbedded losses.

Wall Street banks, in complicity with their partners in the Federal Reserve system, including the Board of Governors of the Federal Reserve System and the Federal Reserve Bank of New York under the direction of the Federal Reserve Open Market Committee, have attempted hide—and continue to attempt to "cover up" these imbedded losses through the exercise of the "Greenspan put," either through "bailout structures" or subsequent programs of "quantitative easing", by selling the toxic credits, including their embedded losses, to the Federal Reserve at par, without recognition of the losses embedded in pricing, in exchange for new Federal Reserve Notes or their electronic data entry functional equivalents; once again, stripped of any transparent connection of the par value of such credits to liquid market value of the credits to the sources of repayment or ultimately, through required redemption by constitutional money, the liquid value of which has been regulated by Congress. The Fed policy of maintaining artificially low interest rates has not led to economic recovery. The recovery, still nascent to most Americans, has been entirely of their own making. The maintenance by the Fed of artificially low interest rates, however, has been another of their many tools used to manipulate and misrepresent the value of the toxic assets taken by the Fed off the balance sheets of the Wall Street banks. The cost of the artificially manipulated low interest rates comes out of the pockets of the retired Americans and other citizens dependent on fixed incomes that are based on conservative investments that are highly interest rate sensitive. The new money so created has fed even more speculative investments, such as the stock markets, housing, automobiles and other consumer goods. Ordinary Americans flat levels of wages and income cannot be hoped to discharge the skyrocketing volume of new credit. The conse quences of inability to pay will fall first on ordinary Americans solvency, then ripple back up the chain of money debasement leading to the predictable collapse of asset liquidity, then value, and ordinary Americans will then experience and suffer the next financial crisis.

Washington's and Wall Street's usurpation and abuse of the trusted power to create money through an exclusive monopoly power, wholly discretionary, unaccountable, and completely unrestricted by meaningful monetary and banking law and regulatory policy will reach a breaking point and the results will be catastrophic.

§8.02 DEREGULATION, LIQUIDITY AND ASSET VALUES

The bulk of global liquidity consists of money now generated entirely outside the purview of our government's authority and responsibility to maintain a safe and sound currency and regulate its value. Our government has continued to pontificate, wrap its actions in mystery and concentrate its narrowed focus on what has become nearly a financial and economic irrelevancy—the actual "official" US dollar—what David Roche refers to as "Power Money." The Treasury, the Comptroller of the Currency and the Federal Reserve System have all ignored the bulk of money—the mass of global liquidity driving our global financial imbalances, and, with the collapse of underlying value, creating liquidity crisis. That money—liquidity—is simply out of the bureaucrats' sight and out of their mind—literally. Our elected representatives, the President, and Congress have busied themselves with a strictly politically motivated massive government bailout or bribe of the public of approximately $168 billion in cash and tax credits, while the Chairman of the Fed, Ben Bernanke spoke of dropping money from helicopters to resolve our liquidity crisis. Our government has been and remains ignorant, myopic, politically greedy, needy for support by special interests, and is doomed, along with ordinary Americans, to continue to fall victim to the law of consequences of deliberate short-term acts of political expediency—in deliberate abrogation of congressional trust, power and duty to regulate the value of our money.

As to Europe, in the time leading up to the great financial crisis, the statute for the European Central Bank, predictably "emphasized independence, insulation from political interference, and a mandate for price stability." ... "Its ability to finance deficits was limited, like the Bundesbank. Countries should first bring down their inflation, budget deficits, and debts in order to participate. Budget deficits would have to be limited to 3 percent of national income, government debts to 60 percent. Exchange rates would have to be held stable."[656]

So stated the *Treaty of Maastricht*[657] agreed to in 1991, but not effective until 1999, neatly coinciding with passage of the *Graham-Leach-Bliley Act*, and the resulting explosion of public and private indebtedness that led to and constitutes the crisis. The *Maastricht Treaty* is admirable for going to the heart of centuries of financial crises fed by unwarranted explosions of public and private indebtedness. Its legacy, however, has been a short history replete with exceptions to the rules, disregard of the rules, and a constant scramble to hold the EU together. The rules did not stop the rash of global tendencies leading to a global crises. Europe is much in the news as of this writing, with bailout negotiations dominating the European political and financial landscape. The focus of the political and financial world on the crisis in Europe, as it is being dealt with publicly, has begun to ignore the continuation of the crisis in America, hidden from view by "kicking the can down the road", "extend and pretend" supported by the slender thread of the dollar's unwarranted status as the world's reserve currency—the currency that continues to be viewed as a safe haven in the whorl of global financial meltdown.

Barry Eichengreen has observed that "[a]t the root of the crisis lay financial irregularities unchecked by adequate regulations."[658] Professor Eichengreen goes on to note that "the originate-and-distribute model, and the perverse incentives it created, was an important factor in what started out as the now quaintly sounding 'subprime crisis' and developed into the most serious global credit crisis in 80 years. And as for what enabled all involved to act on these incentives, the answer is simple: inadequate regulation."[659]

As we will see, despite Professor Eichengreen's conclusion, the enabler of this crisis has not solely been inadequate regulation—in fact it has been the deliberate, intentional disregard by Washington and Wall Street of the well documented history since the Nixon Shock of near continuous financial crises driven by unsustainable levels of public and private debt. The failure of regulation is not simply a failure of bank regulations, but the fundamental failure of congressional regulation of the value of money pursuant to its powers and duties under the *United States Constitution*. This is true, notwithstanding Reinhart and Rogoff's lament about the comic—but now tragic—and ultimate criminal, concealment and cooking of the books by both Washington and Wall Street, thereby misrepresenting levels of private and public indebtedness, the perverse effects of asset value and money inflation and deflation, and the damaging effect of government fiscal and monetary incentives directing the creation and application of that debt, fuelling asset bubbles, and asset values that were demonstrably unsustainable at the time they were created to support the debt creation.

Washington and Wall Street are the experts that have proclaimed, and ordinary Americans have trusted, that they are, in fact, fully capable, qualified and willing to fulfill their collective responsibilities for avoiding systemic financial crises. They have necessary information—it has existed for hundreds—thousands—of years. They have the legal, regulatory and operational mandate to act on that information. They have simply ignored the mandate, role, duty, responsibility and the information sitting in clear sight in order to maximize their respective personal and their institutional interests, and they have intentionally disregarded the entirely predictable effects of their actions on the American and global public, who must rely on the integrity and stability of the financial system to support themselves, their families, communities, and yes—the welfare of those in Washington and on Wall street who have betrayed us all. "If flawed regulation was the spark, then central bank policy was the accelerant."[660]

Professor Eichengreen quotes Donald Kohn, vice chairman of the Federal Reserve Board, in 2008 "not long after things went south. In a broader sense, perhaps the underlying cause of the current crisis was complacency. With the onset of the 'Great Moderation' back in the mid-1980s, households and firms in the United States and elsewhere have enjoyed a long period of reduced output volatility and low and stable inflation."[661] Even with reduced volatility and through this channel, complacency, Eichengreen notes that "there was always the belief that the Fed under Greenspan would intervene to put a floor under asset prices in order to prevent a destabilizing crash." By 1998, "the 'Greenspan put'—the idea that the Greenspan Fed was ready to effectively guarantee a minimum level of asset prices—had become a part of the financial lexicon."[662] Artificial support of asset prices has never been an accepted function of a central bank.

> But the idea crystallized when the Fed cut rates to 1 percent following the collapse of the tech bubble. Fed Chairman Greenspan spoke in 2002 on the subject of asset prices and monetary policy. The Chairman argued that asset bubbles are hard to identify while they are developing, making it impractical to direct monetary policy against them. He went on to suggest that there is no such difficulty of detecting bubbles after the fact and that the role of monetary policy is to limit the destabilizing consequences. Investors came to believe, rightly or wrongly that because the Fed would intervene in time of financial crisis, it was no longer necessary to worry about the slim possibility, the so-called tail risk, of asset liquidity and prices collapsing. The danger of large losses being less, the temptation to take on risk was more. And there was nothing to restrain the risk takers, what with the Federal Open Market Committee and the regulators, including the Fed, itself, in denial of their ability to detect bubbles, much less to limit their growth.[663]

Of course, the Greenspan put was has been exercised by Fed Chairman Bernanke on a scale never before envisioned. There has not appeared to be any regulatory inadequacy preventing the Fed from this unprecedented intervention, ostensibly to avoid a financial meltdown, but more importantly for Washington's politicians, regulators and Wall Street banks, it is and continues to be a convenient cover up of the depth and true causes of the crisis. In fact, the Fed is ill suited to provide any meaningful assistance to ordinary Americans in the effort to mitigate the crisis or protect the interests of the American people from losses counted in the trillions of dollars.

> When after World War II the United States stationed large numbers of troops in Europe and Asia, our allies there saw supporting the greenback as an appropriate quid pro quo. Today, in contrast, China, our largest foreign creditor, is not a close ally. In many parts of the world, the American security umbrella is neither as essential as it once was nor, it would seem, as welcome. It is not so obvious that the best way for foreign countries to ensure their security is to prop up the dollar. All this makes America's creditors increasingly critical of America's exorbitant privilege.[664]

This phenomenon emerged with the development of Petro-dollars, Eurodollars and super-dollars during the 1970s and 1980s. Our government's disastrous efforts—acts of government intervention in market forces—to exert some control over the effects of the burgeoning liquidity and asset value inflation unleashed after the abandonment of the *Bretton Woods Accord*, are detailed in *Banks in Distress*, G N Olson (2000).

[A] Deregulation: Again

The *Riegle Neal Interstate Banking and Branching Efficiency Act—1994;*[665] *Home Ownership and Equity Protection Act 1994;*[666] *Economic Growth and Regulatory Paperwork Reduction Act 1996;*[667] and the *Graham Leach Bliley Act of 1999* all contributed to relaxed supervision, facilitated conflicts of interest—affected how regulators are paid and how bankers are paid—aligning their interests against the public interest. The legislation resulted in Fed Lite—a euphemism for non-existent regulation by the Fed and non-existent self-regulation by the Wall Street banks, creating enormous tail risk in the financial economy, the collapse of which damaged the American real economy.

The damage suffered by the American public represents the real financial crisis. The much-publicized financial manipulations of the Wall Street banks may have been addressed by Washington through their crisis cover-up for the benefit of the Washington Wall Street enterprise. Much less attention has been focused on the real financial crisis suffered by the American public. Virtually no attention has been focused on the necessity and foundation for legal accountability of Washington and Wall Street to the American public.

[B] Regulation of Money and Banks

The essence of regulation of money and banks is the public's need for the honesty, safety and soundness of Americans money in the hands of banks—not strictly safety and soundness of banks themselves. Regulation of bank safety and soundness is a corollary only of the honesty, safety and soundness of money. Banks were charged with the fiduciary duty to protect depositors against loss or theft of their money or its debasement as to kind, quality and quantity. For the money to be safe and sound it must also be liquid: readily transferable at the stated value. Liquidity and trustworthiness of value are the essence of money.

Herein lays the rub. In order for banks to facilitate the use by of bills of credit and bills of exchange redeemable in specie, it was essential to establish uniformity of units of specie as to kind, quality and amount; liquid money- available in the here and now—as a clear representation of value readily transferable in the marketplace in units or money measurement denominated in an honest, safe and sound final settlement medium, even in times of uncertainty or distress, where the market value of goods and services might fluctuate in relationship to the relative consistency of the liquidity and value of the money. Historically, this arrangement worked well enough, subject to occasional theft, dishonesty of bankers and bankers' debasement of specie or issuance of fraudulent bills of credit or exchange, resulting in bank failure. The growth of the importance and amount of money in circulation created an immediate and growing tension between depositors of money with banks and the states' perceived need for ever increasing revenue to finances wars, excesses of consumption and the power that wielding large amounts of wealth represented by money can bring. As a matter of political expediency and in the shadow of the threat of exercise of power backed by force, the interest of the state in money and banking was first and foremost to exploit the nature and limitations of specie as money in support of the representation and projection of the power won by conquest and maintained under threat of force. State interest in banks, banking and money, previously purely a market-based convenience, then necessarily grew apace. Currency counterfeiting and debasement became a political way of life in authoritarian state societies.

Development of widespread use of specie as money and credit based on and redeemable in specie as sovereign money historically has been limited by the owners' requirement that their money be kept safe and sound and honestly accounted for by the depository bank. And to meet those requirements, it became the role of the sovereign to create liquid money, available on demand, in specie to preserve the integrity, safety and soundness of its value. The greatest ongoing threat to the safety and soundness of money, liquid, readily transferable money, has become acts of government intervention to serve the Washington Wall Street enterprise as opposed to the public interest, first in money—then in banking.

Washington and Wall Street's misrepresentation of financial asset values and liquidity, specifically since the abandonment of the *Bretton Woods Accords* and the explosion of banking law and regulation as a miserable failed substitute for the discipline of the redeemability of legal tender in the form of Federal Reserve Notes posing as sovereign money, or at a minimum, regulation of its value in accordance with constitutional requirements, has resulted directly in the conduct by Washington and Wall Street of progressive systemic fraud in each successive financial crisis during the period.

[C] Safety and Soundness Means Asset Values and Liquidity Are Measured Against Independent Standards and Recorded Honestly

Although the safety and soundness of money and banking are ostensibly assured through banking law and regulation, they are only selectively enforced and thus provide a very poor substitute for the publics necessary ability to privately enforce: (i) the fiduciary liability of banks and bankers to their depositors and the public; (ii) the conservative valuation of sources of repayment of debt in amounts discounted considering risk and uncertainty of repayment during times of financial difficulty and illiquidity; and (iii) the constitutionally mandated issuance of American sovereign money, the value of which, including the essential attribute of liquidity, is regulated by Congress.[668] That is, regulated by reference to an external, standard; by something rather than nothing; something other than the unfettered discretion of the Fed, exercised, if at all, by select reference to specific segmented banking activities, practices and attendant risk of actual experience of loss. The concept of monetary and therefore, bank safety and soundness and financial stability, has been reduced to a web of intentional representations by Washington of the "safety and soundness of money, banks and the entire financial system," all lumped together, without any demonstrable basis in fact and without clear differentiation between sovereign money, credit money created in a regulated system and unregulated shadow banking credit money posing as securities. This complex and undifferentiated process has been found by Washington and Wall Street to be in their best interests; as opposed to the public interest. The overriding self-interest of Washington and Wall Street, acting symbiotically of course, goes straight to the heart of the breach of their fiduciary duty to the American public with respect to the integrity, liquidity and value of money and the honesty, safety, soundness and stability of our economy, monetary and financial system.

Banking law and regulation are designed to assure that banks are responsible and accountable for maintaining honest, safe and sound monetary conditions through the conduct of their banking activities and practices, including the creation of what passes for sovereign money—credit money created through the Federal Reserve System. Elements of risk to bank safety and soundness attendant to any banking activity or practice must be identified and mitigated by the bank. Bank regulators are not strictly responsible for a particular bank's safety and soundness. Bank regulators are, however, responsible and accountable for the overall honesty, safety and soundness of the banking system; including all of the constituents of the banking system, taken as a whole, and including specifically, the ability of the financial system to provide money that serves its well established purposes in the real economy: intermediating value amongst participants in the real economy, personally unknown to one another, through the medium of liquid, readily transferable money, in increments of stated standard common value, regulated in relation to a common standard of value and readily accepted as such in the real economy. This responsibility cannot be met by aspirations and words alone. Credit money, whether created or retained in the Federal Reserve System or in the shadow banking world of money substitutes, must be anchored to liquid, honest, safe and sound sovereign money, the value of which in regulated by reference to a suitable outside standard publicly accepted with trust and confidence.

The expressed purpose of banking law and regulation, supervision, examination and financial institution compliance is to establish the foundation for intermediation of the money value of assets that are liquid when deposited and assets that are generally illiquid, providing an opportunity to put the deposited money to work through investment while maintaining the discipline and liquidity of the assets to provide liquid redemption of deposits in accordance with their terms, even in, and especially in, times of market illiquidity and uncertainty. The banking laws and regulations that provide the foundation and establish the standards for the honesty, safety and soundness of banks and provide for the liquidity of money, are matters of law. They are expressly intended to protect the public interest under circumstances where they cannot protect their own interests due to enormous and complex structure of the financial markets; the importance of these financial markets to government finance; and the governments requirement that the public use the form of sovereign money legally mandated by the government for payment of all debts, public and private. In exchange for the purported benefits of a government controlled financial system, as distinguished from what has now became a somewhat quaint historical and now fundamentally impractical private financial system, and based upon their open exploitation of what should be a fully informed consensual foundation of mutual trust and confidence supporting money, banking and finance, Washington and Wall Street have hijacked the system to serve their own interests as opposed to the public interest. What was intended to create a fiduciary relationship between Americans with banks has been flipped to a relationship of predator and prey. Washington and Wall Street, the predators, have openly betrayed the trust and confidence reposed in them by the public prey and they have flouted the requirements of the *Constitution*, common law, federal statutory law as well as the vast body of banking rules and regulations established to protect "bank safety and soundness" in the public interest and. The predators have made a laughingstock of the federal financial regulators, which have uniformly been coopted to serve primarily the interests of Washington and Wall Street in denigration of the public interest. This condition evolved gradually over time and now actually appears to be unquestioningly accepted by the ordinary American prey as representing the best "state-of-the-art" banking legal, accounting, regulatory and commercial practices.

Each bank regulatory agency has its own perspective on and guidance with respect to different risks to bank safety and soundness attendant to specific banking activities and practices. Federal and state bank regulators are working to promote regulatory consistency through the Federal Financial Institutions Examination Council "[t]o encourage the application of uniform examination principles and standards by state and federal supervisory agencies"; ... and to "prescribe uniform principles and standards for the Federal examination of financial institutions."[669] Despite this mandate, the regulators have been distinguished by their inconsistency, lax enforcement and by the failure of their efforts to produce an honest, safe and sound banking system in America. The Commission Report documents the American regulatory failure in excruciating detail.

Each bank may engage in a broad range of banking activities and practices that receive more or less regulatory interest, attention and action than another due to the circumscribed original role of the respective regulatory agency and a specific bank's market activities and practices. Bank regulatory agencies should be interested in mitigation of risk of, and threats to systemic monetary, bank and financial safety and soundness. Regulators should provide guidance with respect to honest, safe and sound activities and practices, depending on the banking activities in which a bank is or may become engaged across the narrow lines of demarcation of the missions of the separate, often competing and conflicting bank regulatory agencies. The guidance must include and accommodate the effect on all money liquidity and value of the volume, velocity and concentrations of regulated credit money as well as the connections between that credit money and the proliferation of unregulated money substitutes in the shadow banking system, all as anchored in properly created and regulated sovereign money. They have notoriously failed to do so. The regulatory arbitrage engaged in by all participants in the financial marketplace, whether regulated or not, contributes directly to that failure.

A bank's overarching concern about liability due to unmitigated risk is that when loss is realized, the loss may impair earning and capital resulting in an unsafe and unsound bank condition; and most importantly for the law of bank safety and soundness, a trigger—based on very broad regulatory discretion that has now unfortunately lost the trust and confidence of the American public and the global financial community, leading to prompt corrective enforcement action by the bank's regulators, ranging from simple memoranda of understanding with respect to prompt corrective action up to bank receivership and criminal prosecutions. Each bank has a duty to its depositors and customers engaged with it in banking activity to conduct its banking business in an honest safe and sound manner that will protect it and them from loss in connection with the bank's specific activities.

The banks accomplish, or should accomplish, if they were to meet their responsibilities, their official objective of safety and soundness, by making an assessment of risk factors inherent in each specific banking activity and practice in which it engages or to which it is exposed and then by following "proven practices and established procedures" to mitigate those risks, regardless of the differences between and among individual regulatory fiefdoms.

The regulated banking and financial system serves as one of its functions, the creation of credit that is treated as liquid money, the liquid value of which is accepted in the market place as money, but which is backed by assets and future sources of repayment that do not possess the attributes of liquidity and value that corresponds to the liquidity and value of the credit that serves as liquid money. Banking law and regulation serve to establish the conditions under which financial institutions can invest money deposited with them in illiquid assets while remaining fully able to meet the liquidity and money value the holders of the banks liabilities who are entitled to redeem the money in accordance with the terms of the deposit, even in, and especially in times of general market uncertainty and restricted liquidity of generally illiquid assets backing the credit at par value. The reliability of this expectation of money holder's liquidity at par value is essential to bank and financial system honesty, safety and soundness. Washington and Wall Street are charged with the duty to assure that each citizen's money deposited in the financial system controlled and dominated by Washington and Wall Street is available to them on demand, or at the stated time for its redemption at a stable, safe and sound regulated monetary value. In our global economy, specifically in the American economy, the public's, Wall Streets' and Washington's performance of their respective duties is paramount to their ability to serve their public functions and to enable them to enjoy the specific benefits their honest performance confers upon them as legally privileged participants. These banking entities have basic fiduciary responsibilities to the public that supersede their respective private interests. In exchange for their faithful and honest performance of this fiduciary duty, Washington and Wall Street, by virtue of their privileged monopoly status in the process of money creation, are each able to obtain the profits and funding to meet their respective expectations for the financial system. The faithful and honest performance of this fiduciary duty cannot be met in the absence of the discipline of a sovereign money, the value of which has been regulated by Congress, by law, to serve as a common denominator of asset liquidity and value.

If credit based monetary liquidity was limited in circulation to close, intimate circles of counterparties that shared mutual trust and confidence in the liquid value of the transferable asset, or negotiability of the credit, including the liquidator of the credit obligors, the national and global economies would grind to a halt. Failure of Washington and Wall Street to meet their fiduciary obligations to assure the limitations on negotiability of credit and other money derivatives and to establish discipline on the liquid value of such credit instruments, has been followed by widespread intentional concealment and misrepresentation of losses in the recorded values of assets in the regulated banking system, including Federal Reserve Notes themselves.

[D] Limitations of Banking Law and Regulation

Bank lending and credit creation are limited by the requirements of depositors of the banks maintenance of the safety of their money on deposit through prudent standards of operating protection, careful risk assessment and maintenance of sufficient liquid capital to protect against the losses and costs presented by uncertainty, and the banks' ability to return through redemption of their deposit in liquid sound money. Banking laws and regulation have evolved in a vain attempt to meet these requirements. In the crucible of financial crises over the past forty years, banking laws and regulations have failed the people. Banking laws and regulations have proved to be no substitute for accountability for meeting Washington's and Wall Street's prime fiduciary duty. Financial innovation, driven by the rapid expansion of shadow credit money, unregulated in amount, value or liquidity, fueled by business innovation and powerful special interests. The Washington Wall Street enterprise has divided the banking function amongst themselves for competitive advantage, leading to the wide spectrum of banks and bank-like enterprises, all of whom now play growing roles in the creation of money through credit. Credit, the liquidity of which is necessary to meet depositor creditor demand in a crisis, has been disguised by complexity and opacity of structured financial products and by the extension of the distance to value realizable in the actual real world market place. The values and liquidity of those credit instruments, all derivatives of real-world value to greater or lesser degree, have been intentionally misrepresented to the public.

Each bank supposedly protects against threats to money and bank honesty, safety and soundness through conducting only those banking activities and practices within the bank's approved banking powers and authorizations, in accordance with proven practices and established procedures that are the subject of bank regulation. A reasonable prudent banker will exercise common sense as a matter of risk assessment to consider resources of all of these regulators as well as other financial regulators to seek over-arching best guidance, prudential considerations and practices to protect against risk to honesty, safety and soundness of money or bank. The banking laws, regulations, rulings, interpretations, opinions guidance policies and that could and should be considered and followed with respect to avoid loss—they collectively define the standards and duties of care applicable to the bank, which must be observed and enforced to provide ordinary Americans the functional equivalence of compliance with the fiduciary standard.

Each type of regulator has developed historically and may tend to narrow focus often leading to banks' attempts to game regulators.

Each bank is subject to multiple regulators for various purposes and must take the initiative to look across regulatory silos to seek best guidance, prudential considerations, proven practices and established procedures under bank regulatory standards, including in this case fiduciary standards, considering the specific banking activity involved and the nature of its specific role and practices as an intermediator in that activity.

§8.03 AN INDEPENDENT REGULATED CONSTITUTIONAL STANDARD OF VALUE IS ESSENTIAL FOR THE CREATION AND CIRCULATION OF CONSTITUTIONAL, TRUSTED, HONEST, SAFE AND SOUND SOVEREIGN MONEY IN AMERICA

I have used the term liquid as an adjective to the term money. I have qualified the term money with the attributes of safety, soundness and liquidity for emphasis. Money, by its definition, must be safe, sound and liquid. Money substitutes created through "structured finance" by Washington and Wall Street and passed off as constitutional sovereign money has rather debased the value of money to the tiniest proportion of its historic value imaginable. This debasement is not a devaluation, which could be accomplished by Congress constitutionally. Instead, the debasement is hidden by Washington and Wall Street. It has been covered up. The damage done by this debasement constitutes ordinary Americans great financial crisis. The damage done to ordinary Americans persists. Washington and Wall Street, the perpetrators of the debasement are now bigger and wealthier than ever. Ordinary Americans have suffered up to $20 trillion in damages, by Washington's own calculation.[670] By way of contrast, at the time of this writing, the nation's top 10 banks hold assets of $11.9 trillion. The bank capital supporting the top 10 bank's assets at Basle III tier I capital in general at 10%, approximately $1.2 trillion, is a miniscule as compared to the $20 trillion damages they have caused to ordinary Americans.[671]

[A] Creation and Regulation of the Value of Money

What is the constitutional source and character of money? What is the constitutional rule for valuation of one form of money in terms of another? And, what authority—if any—does the government possess to manipulate the purchasing-power of sovereign money and shadow money substitutes, which are ever so tightly entwined in America's economy?

As noted throughout this work, and worth repeating, is the fact that these questions are answered in Article 1, § 8, Clause 5 of the *Constitution*, which provides that Congress shall have the power "To coin Money, regulate the Value thereof, and of foreign Coin, and fix the Standard of Weights and Measures"; and in Article 1, § 10, Clause 1 of the *Constitution*, which provides (in relevant part) that "no State shall ... coin Money; emit Bills of Credit"; [or] "make any Thing but gold and silver Coin a Tender in Payment of Debts."

But, then, asks Edwin Vieira, the world's foremost authority on monetary powers and disabilities under the *Constitution*, where in the *Constitution* resides the "legal tender" power that Article 1, § 10, Clause 1 prohibits to the States and Congress? The Tenth Amendment answers this question, by identifying the locus of the latter authority as "reserved * * * to the people. The States cannot make anything but gold and silver coin a 'Tender' because of Article 1, § 10, Clause 1. Congress cannot make anything but gold and silver coin a 'tender' because of Article VI, Clause 2 (in addition to the common-law interpretation of Article 1, § 8, Clause 5)."

Political concentration and abuse of Americans trust and sovereign power to create and regulate the value of money, as constitutionally delegated to Congress, and policies of economic expediency entailing basic and pervasive manipulation and misrepresentation of asset values and liquidity benefiting Washington and Wall Street have driven the corruption, debasement and demise of American honest, safe and sound money; then and therefore, threatening honest, safe and sound credit, banks, and monetary systems, an honest, safe and sound economy and honest, safe and sound jobs, incomes, family security and a clear shot at the hard-won American dream. The ephemeral American Dream historically has been thought to be earned through energy, strength, persistence and hard work on a level and honest playing field, based on fair rules of the game—the American rule of law. Those in Washington and Wall Street have grasped their version of the American Dream on a foundation of abuse of trust and power and of lying to, cheating and stealing from ordinary Americans.

The demands of various existential wars, or wars promoted as existential by Washington and Wall Street as such, as well as public and business demands for government support for government expenditures and monetary incentives to political and social action, have exceeded the government's ability and the ability of the banking system to continue to provide for honest, safe and sound American money backed by gold and silver specie. The failure culminated in the Nixon shock. America has since been left, without what can be considered in its historical meaning, honest, safe and sound money.

Credit expansion is no longer limited by any requirement that credit be repayable in sound money or that deposits with banks and other financial intermediaries be redeemed in sound money. Credit expansion is no longer limited by any requirement that it be regulated by or through the banking system, historically the holder and lender of sound money deposits and loans repayable in sound money. Banks, historically the holders, protectors and intermediators of honest, safe and sound money for the use and benefit of the business and mercantile community, have lost their primary mission. The money held and created by banks is no longer limited to money that is the same kind, amount and quality, including liquidity, as that deposited, loaned or repaid. The basic concepts of honesty, safety and soundness have been perverted to relate strictly to banks only, not money, and not to relate at all to non-bank unregulated credit creators and financial intermediaries in the shadow banking world. Banks now hawk services and processes for money and credit exchanges for businesses and consumers, for fees.[672] These activities and services are a fertile source for providers of bank regulation, legal and accounting services, but they are not really germane to the present necessity of making a case for financial crises accountability.

[B] The Meaning of Safety and Soundness

After years of clear understanding of the importance of safe and sound money, which was maintained and facilitated by banks, Americans now face continuous departures from the constitutional imperative of sound money to order to expand credit to finance so-called existential wars and support for the American economy. Since the Nixon shock of 1971, the words honesty, safety and soundness have become a sort of floating talisman with no object. Money is now purely fiat money and the obligation to maintain the honesty, safety and soundness of anything at all has been tagged and transitioned to the banks under 12 U.S.C. 1818 and 1831; and 12 C.F.R. Part 30, Effective July 1, 2001; Appendix A: G. Asset quality; and H. Earnings; and 12 C.F.R. Part 1, Investment Securities, specifically § 1.5, regarding safe and sound banking practices. Bankers are now charged to maintain acceptable levels of asset quality [asset quality includes liquidity in relation to market value, discounted value of future cash flows and the ready transferability of the asset at the stated value in a liquid manner] and earnings, determined by bank examiners in retrospect purely from a micro-prudential and supervisory assessment of specific bank books and records. These requirements for safety and soundness, and the correlated standards and duties of care applicable to Washington and Wall Street have been intentionally ignored and subverted by their collusion in the intentional and ongoing racketeering and corrupt enterprise based on abuse of Americans trust reposed on them and the power delegated to them to exploit a program of intentional misrepresentation of asset values and liquidity, colloquially referred to as extend and pretend, delay and pray, kick the can down the road, too big to fail too big jail too big to manage, as though these silly idiomatic phrases somehow validate, legalize and sanction, the Washington Wall Street enterprise actions that actually constitute a massive fraud on ordinary Americans.

[C] The Degradation of Bank Safety and Soundness to a Euphemism

Banking law and regulation is driven by considerations of bank safety and soundness. The original standard of safety and soundness in traditional banking was a fiduciary standard; the bank held the depositors' specie money as a fiduciary, and the banks' duty was to keep:

- Money safe—not lost, stolen or misappropriated (standard violated in this case—money misappropriated)
- Money sound—depositor gets back what he put in—same, if not identical—kind, amount and quality

The essential characteristic of the money itself was, and remains—it is liquid, readily transferable at par, in a safe and sound condition.

The value of the money was but is no longer protected by the doctrine of safety and soundness as functional equivalents of a bank and government fiduciary standard. Much of the money created as credit over the past years has been unsafe and unsound in that it was not essentially liquid at the values recorded by the Wall Street banks that created it at par. From time to time—times of financial crisis, the markets suspect or recognize that money backed by the supposed asset values that support the valuation of the credit as recorded on the books of the Wall Street banks, are not liquid at par value and the result is a liquidity crisis. The crises continue until the markets become convinced that the losses in credit money's recorded par value have been recognized on the holders' books and that the losses in value are recorded in the reduced—discounted par value amounts that render the money liquid at a new reduced par value.

Unsafe and unsound, and therefore illiquid, conditions are now considered to be evidenced by actual or threatened bank capital and earnings impairment caused by unsafe and unsound banking activities and practices as determined pursuant to banking law and regulation. Support for the value and liquidity of banks assets, including bank capital, and bank earnings, lies in compliance with the common law, the *Constitution* and banking law and regulation to ensure liquid values supporting the value of the dollar and dollar denominated asset; and specially in time of asset illiquidity and financial crises. As demonstrated in this work, the Washington Wall Street enterprise has simply abandoned the ancient standards for the safety and soundness of sovereign money as well as what were old fashioned bills and notes but now are structured shadow money substitutes. Even the noted banking experts, Carnell, Macey and Miller in their banking law text, comment in a somewhat naïve manner reflecting the deliberate institutional obfuscation of the doctrine of safety and soundness of liquid money as follows:

> Despite its plural phrasing, "safety and soundness" represents a single concept-centered on financial health but often with overtones of the sort of prudent management practices needed to keep a healthy bank healthy. The pairing of "safety" with "soundness" follows the old English practice of linking synonyms to form such stock expressions as "fit and proper," "free and clear," and peace and quiet.[673]

This comment illustrates the widespread fundamental ignorance of the nature of money and therefore banking and the legal principles that have governed money and banking for millennia, even amongst recognized experts in banking law and regulation.

During and as a result of the great financial crisis, losses in bank asset values have not been recorded. They continue to be carried on holders' books, in large part on the books of the banks, and other market participants, based upon a false representation of liquidity at par provided by the Feds purchase of the banks toxic sub-par value instruments at par, with money created out of nothing, thereby continuing to monetize credit that is artificially inflated in value. The only liquidity provided has been the artificial liquidity provided by the Fed based upon money created out of nothing and by the common practice of other federal financial regulators to allow financial institutions as well as the Fed to continue to hold assets, the value of which is below par, to avoid recognizing the embedded losses and to continue to carry those assets on their books at the inflated value of those assets in excess of the liquid value. This regulatory practice is commonly referred to as extend and pretend, kick the can down the road, deny and lie, delay and pray, etc. These practices mirror on a regional and community level the so-called bail out and cover up of losses in the recorded par value of credit money at the Wall Street bank level, all orchestrated and implemented by the Fed.

This practice is not innocuous, useful or honest. It constitutes intentional misrepresentation of the value of the assets of every financial institution in the United States and therefore a misrepresentation of the value of every asset, the value of which is recorded in dollar denominated terms. The Fed support of artificially low interest rates and artificially high liquid asset values comes at a steep cost. American savers have been punished by low rates of interest on deposits. They have effectively subsidized the policy of extend and pretend. Washington and Wall Street have been protected from the necessity of recognition of imbedded losses on their balance sheets and have instead, by effectuating and abusing their monopoly enterprise trust and power over the creation of and regulation of the value of money in violation of their fiduciary duty and the limitations attendant to that power, have continued to build and consolidate power and further distance themselves from ordinary Americans in wealth and income, who have been forced the pay the price, and bear the losses.

If a bank's capital or earnings are impaired or threatened with impairment, as in financial crisis, the bankers in question will be expected to have clearly identified the specific nature of the banking activity or practice in question and identified the risk factors inherent in such specific banking activities or practices, and then by taking recommended action in accordance with the duty and standard of care it owes to the bank's counterparties and the public to mitigate that risk of loss.

The bank is required to look to all laws, regulations, rulings, interpretations, opinions guidance policies and procedures that could have been followed, irrespective whether mandatory in application, to avoid capital and earnings impairment as well as to unsafe and unsound activity of condition in connection with each banking activity in which it is engaged and the potential of an unsafe and unsound bank condition. These resources identify the range of risk and they collectively define the actions the bank should take to meet the banks' applicable standards of conduct, and duty of care.

Unsafe and unsound bank conduct of specific banking activity or practice is, or more appropriately should be a trigger for bank regulatory enforcement action—based on actual or potential effect of such conduct on the bank.

Bank activities and practices are unsafe if they expose bank to danger; unsound if they are not based on proven practices or established procedures; unsafe and unsound if they are imprudent and carry an abnormal risk of harm.[674] The bank activities, practices policies and procedures are dishonest if they further the ongoing debasement of the US dollar.

Now that all money is debt, money deposited in a bank constitutes transfer of ownership of money from depositor to bank subject to bank liability to depositor for withdrawal or transfer. Since deposited money is now normally owned by bank subject to the depositors contractual right of withdrawal. Depositor accounts are insured by FDIC. Safety and soundness as a general matter relate to the depositors interest in the safety and soundness of the bank having the liability instead of the safety and soundness of the money itself. The bankers' regulatory safety and soundness mandate is to "identify problem assets and prevent deterioration in those assets" and to "maintain systems that are commensurate with the institution's size and the nature and scope of its operations to evaluate and monitor earnings and ensure that earnings are sufficient to maintain adequate capital and reserves."

Bank asset quality and earnings, however, are measured in terms of money that has no disciplined or regulated relationship to any standard of value consisting of external goods or services or any asset with stable and market accepted value, or any combination thereof that has ongoing stable and reliable intrinsic worth. Asset valuations are based on GAAP standards (as they may be modified by regulation) of asset fair market value rather than on the constitutional mandated valuation regulated in accordance with a transparently calculated value derived by reference to a standard of value for sovereign money established by Congress in accordance with the *Constitution*. Credit money created and held on the books of banks as assets constitutes the creation of currency—that means money for current use—use in the here and now—in other words liquid money—liquid and currently transferable in the market at its par value as represented on the books and records of the banks, and the public representation of the honesty, safety and soundness of the state of our banking, financial, and monetary system taken as a whole.

Recognizing the disconnect of the safety and soundness of money from the safety and soundness of banks as our primary money intermediators; Americans will be further distressed by the disconnect of the regulated banking business from the exploding proliferation of shadow credit money creators and intermediators, and therefore creation of non-transparent web of finance through an almost unlimited series of evolving enterprises, within and without what we have traditionally viewed as banks.

The primary objective of these enterprises is to create as much money as possible—pass it on into the financial system, collecting enormous profits, fees and compensation without having any meaningful responsibility for the safety and soundness of the credit money so created. There is no defined and disciplined tie between the money created and liquid value in the real economic marketplace. That is how trillions of dollars in credit have been created backed only by asset values inflated by the force of credit creation itself and tied to computer models based on scant underlying credit and market information and without proper consideration of the actual market requirements for asset liquidity or the requirement for asset liquidity as a prime factor in valuation of banks assets. As Felix Martin noted, the value assets sold and purchased in the market on a bilateral basis is determined by the seller and purchaser on the same basis as asset fair market value of determined in accordance with GAAP valuation standards. Bank assets however are different. They represent the creation of money freely transferred and negotiable amongst a vast number of unrelated parties unknown to one another and who are in position to repose trust and confidence in the creator of the money. The public relies on the law and the keepers and enforcers of the law of money and banking to assure and endorse the honesty, safety and soundness of liquid dollar denominated money. As such, dollar denominated money created by banks should be valued on a liquidation basis—meaning that it can be reliable used as money measurement of liquid value in the market place with public trust and confidence. As previously noted, GAAP provides a mechanism for such determinations of appropriate value under appropriate circumstances, such as the valuation of bank created assets that purport to serve as money.

Collateral for credit repayment is no longer trustworthy because there no longer exists any enforceable obligation of the credit creator to return or redeem the credit in sound sovereign money.

The predominant role of the bank in its holding and intermediation of customer money is purely depository, including payments and clearing functions and lending. A reasonable and prudent banker's duty is to keep money deposited with and owned by bank safe and sound for benefit of the depositors, subject to and with assurance that Bank can meet liability to depositors for withdrawal. Conduct leading to loss that could have been avoided by bankers as prudent and diligent business persons, making reasonable inquiries and reasonable business judgments on a fully informed basis and after proper deliberation—is unsafe and unsound conduct in violation of 12 U.S.C. 1818 (a) and 1831 (p) 1; and 12 C.F.R. Part 30, effective July 1, 2001.

[D] The Bank Regulatory Policy of Extend and Pretend

The policy of "extend and pretend" was adopted by the FDIC and the interagency group of "financial regulators" on or about October 30, 2009, to delay the day of reckoning for bank loss recognition and the resulting deterioration of bank capital and earnings and thus safety and soundness, attributable to bank non-performing assets (NPA). The financial regulators simply harkened back to their successful use of the same policy in the 1990s to avoid a flood of scheduled bank failures, by simply by not marking the value of the NPAs to market value, and by financing and covering up the losses. At the end of 1991, more than 1,000 banks were slated for closure, in addition to the 1,617 bank and 1,300 thrifts that had already failed. That systemic threat to the economy simply evaporated. To avoid the messy prospect of additional bank failures and pressure on the FDIC insurance fund, during 1991 and 1992, the financial regulatory authorities imply ignored the problem publicly, and privately, Washington and Wall Street simply kept the prime rate at about 6% while bringing the discount rate to 3%. A full 300 basis points. Huge profits were pumped into the banking industry by holding short term rates down and encouraging banks to borrow and invest the proceeds in Treasury securities yielding 5% to 6%, thus monetizing the losses through Fed leverage. The economy picked up from a negative growth rate in 1991 to expansion of more than 4% in 1994. The inception of extend and pretend established in the 90s returned with a vengeance following the great financial crisis of 2008. The lucky bankers on the troubled bank list in 1991 simply escaped accountability.[675] The banks that made the hit list early on did not. Those banks on the hit list included every major banking institution in Texas. The policies of existential self-preservation and monetary expedience established during the Civil War have progressed to the point that our monetary policy is now firmly grounded in institutional fraud and an almost complete absence of Washington and Wall Street accountability for asset liquidity and value manipulation and misrepresentation.

The policy of extend and pretend has once again given banks time to build capital from investors and retained earnings from investing cash balances and the interest spread between Fed Funds borrowing and Treasury Bill and Fed Term Deposit Certificate[676] investment yields, facilitated by the Fed's purchase of toxic assets from the Wall Street banks at book value pursuant to the policy of quantitative easing. This "cover-up" of and preferential protection against loss recognition have driven continued and mounting domination by Wall Street of the financial markets in terms of market share and profitability while the balance of the economy and the American people suffer. After raising this new capital to meet new and higher capital standards, Wall Street banks have not traded the capital for losses hidden by the policy of extend. They have simply increased and transferred the money equivalent of the "bid-ask" gap to the Fed. As Wall Street accomplished its cover up of losses incurred during the 2008 financial crisis and began to prop up their income statement and balance sheets, and with the blessing of Washington, began to feel free to use newfound magic liquidity, the banks were able to monetize for themselves the largely Fed generated economic support of Wall Street by embarking on a widespread practice of stock buy-backs, enriching the remaining investors and widening the gaps in power, income and wealth between the haves and have-nots.

Active adherents of the bank regulatory sponsored process of extend and pretend may find that regulatory support deteriorates as the extent of the causes and effects of money debasement are asserted by the American people. Auditors, attorneys, shareholders and creditors of financial institutions have been lulled into complacency by the reported effects of the regulatory policy of extend and pretend have not yet been willing to look to Congress, The Fed, or bank regulatory authorities for any redress. The losses have become out of sight and out of mind. Moral Hazard reigns. As the true state of money debasement emerges in the next crisis, Wall Street financial institutions and their officers and directors will find themselves subject to real blame, responsibility and liability, both civil and criminal, for understated losses and overstated earnings, asset values and liquidity in a new environment where the comfort of government policy does not protect them against the external liabilities created to third parties by adherence to that program: an ongoing program of intentional, deliberate understatement of reported imbedded capital losses and overstated artificial asset values, capital and earnings.[677]

The adoption of the practice of extend and pretend—the phrase itself suggesting knowing and intentional misrepresentation of the capital and earnings, asset value and liquidity positions of any bank following the practice—should be found to be a direct systemic threat to bank safety and soundness. The OCC's stated mission is to preserve safety and soundness. The fact that the FDIC and other bank regulatory authorities, including the Fed and the OCC, proposed and endorsed the practice of extend and pretend will ultimately provide no solace. The liabilities inherent in the policy of extend and pretend must be borne by the Wall Street banks and their executives that have adopted that policy with Washington's blessing, as members of the Washington Wall Street enterprise, and when, in retrospect, they are found to have deliberately failed to properly disclose timely charges to capital and earnings, and instead exploited ordinary Americans through the policy and practice of money debasement. The foundational concept of the fiduciary duty of money creators to the public historically developed in accordance with well-established mechanisms to assure the alignment of asset liquidity and value in money. When the losses inherent in the dysfunctional capital markets must be faced all at one time, as extend and pretend comes to a disquieting end, there will be no shortage of injury, blame and claims of loss and liability.

Investors who have responded to bank calls for additional capital will not be pleased to discover that the capital raised to support bank stability, growth and ongoing safety and soundness have been applied to cover losses hidden from view by the policy of extend and pretend. Bank adherence to an unsafe and unsound bank regulatory policy of money debasement and intentional understatement of potential losses in an attempt to delay the recognition of the effects of those losses, leaves looming problems for the industry and the American economy, but perhaps opportunities for hedge funds and private equity speculative investment strategies.

The losses inherent in misalignment of asset liquidity and value in commercial real estate immediately after the great financial crisis was graphically evident:

Figure 8.1 NCREIF Property Index

The NCREIF Property Index chart appeared on the NCREIF Website until March of 2009, when the Total Return Line literally fell off the chart and the display of the chart was discontinued. With a return of stability, the chart has returned. The now current NCREIF Property Index chart follows:[678]

Figure 8.2 NCREIF Annual NPI Return History

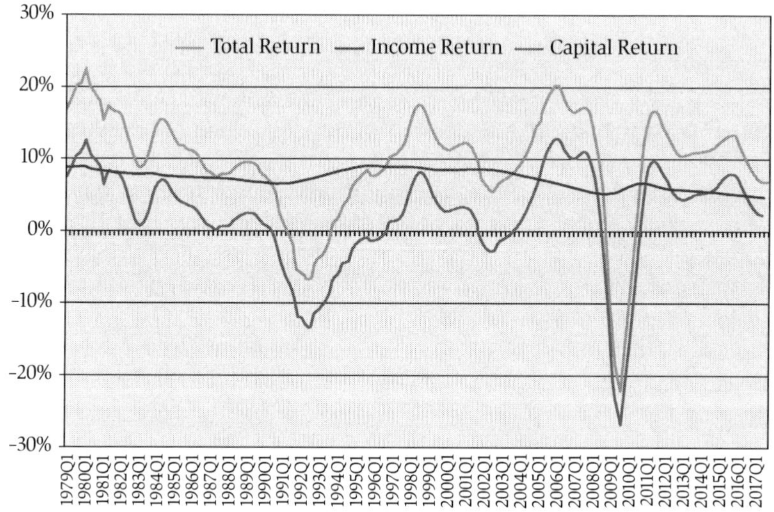

The NCREIF Property Index chart dramatically illustrates the gap between income return and capital return during times of systemic liquidity and capital adequacy crises. The properties in the NCREIF Index are fully completed income properties, including apartments, office buildings, retail shopping centers, and R&D/office and warehouse/industrial buildings. All are valued un-leveraged to avoid valuation discrepancies due to the effects of leverage on valuation. Capital Returns and Total Returns shown in the preceding chart fluctuate independently of Income Returns during crisis periods. That is because collapsing values are not related to property income profiles, but rather correlate to the availability of capital, or liquidity, in amounts and with velocity during times when asset valuation is uncertain because the unit of account for capital—money—is uncertain, due, in each crisis period shown on the chart, to the unwinding of asset bubbles caused by domestic and international financial imbalances that represent money debasement, intermediated through constantly evolving financial innovations outside of traditional bank regulatory mandates.

The gap between Total Return and Income Return, if calculated and charted with respect to properties consisting of NPA would be even more dramatic, due to increasing vacancies, deteriorating rents and income, and the distressed condition of NPA properties generally as distinguished from the NCREF Indexed Properties.

The "liquidity crunch" in the dysfunctional capital market in 2008 was not caused by a lack of cash. Indeed, the investment community was and remains awash in cash—excess liquidity. The dysfunction in capital markets, especially with respect to generally illiquid assets such as commercial real estate and also mortgage backed securities and derivatives based on underlying illiquid assets not marked to liquid market value, is attributable to the fact that the cash sloshing about at the time was the result of creation, outside the regulated banking system, of vast amount of shadow credit money, the proceeds of which have been introduced into the market as cash equivalence, the value of which (both the credits and the cash) became distorted through a boom in structured financial products that so distanced the liquidity created from any connection to asset values in the real economy that the connection to the market was literally broken. The result has been massive money debasement and financial crisis. The cash was there but the connection to market values was not. Prospects for re-establishing the connection continue to be uncertain in the long term; especially in an environment where Wall Street is insulated by Washington from the effects of their enterprise. Predictably, many asset classes, including commercial real estate have returned again to boom levels, sustained in part by the wash of liquidity and the Washington sleight of hand policy designed to inspire economic growth, but which has simply increased higher levels of speculation and creation of asset value bubbles that are destined, ultimately, to burst.

Until the connection between cash and market value of assets in the real economy is re-established through the reduction of excess liquidity and regulation of the value of money by Congress as mandated by the *Constitution*, and debts are collected or written down, assets are disposed of through new connections to the market value in the real economy and losses are recognized; the markets, will remain uncertain and will not clear—will not be liquid. Bank assets will continue to deteriorate in value and levels of NPA, valued properly under bank regulations and GAAP to reflect the uncertainty (dysfunction) in the capital markets resulting from money debasement, through delayed through the policy of extend and pretend, will ultimately increase, increasing the threat to bank safety and soundness and destabilizing capital markets, again.

Washington's protection of Wall Street preserving their mutually beneficial enterprise and financial system is of little comfort to the American people, who continue to struggle to emerge from the dark shadow of the $10 to $20 trillion loss imposed on them by the Washington Wall Street enterprise.

§8.04 BANK ASSET VALUATION, LIQUIDITY, SAFETY AND SOUNDNESS AND THE FLAWED CERTAINTY OF GENERALLY ACCEPTED ACCOUNTING PRINCIPLES

Walter Bagehot, a 19th century English banker and commentator who understood our current and longtime conundrum in the world of banking and finance, opined that: "*men of business in England do not like the currency question. They are perplexed to define accurately what money is: how to count they know, but what to count they do not know.*" (Authors' emphasis added in italics) This was true in Bagehot's day and it is true today—and this truth is even more convoluted in its manifestations today. It is especially true—starkly evident—in the application of Generally Accepted Accounting Principles (GAAP) to banks, financial institutions and to government agencies. An extended treatment of GAAP and their effect on asset value and liquidity are represented on the books and records of GAAP compliant entities is beyond the scope of this work. The conventional view is that compliance with GAAP and any other applicable regulatory additions to GAAP for regulated entities, or for the government, assures the accurate representation of the financial status of those entities. Accounts must acknowledge, however, that manipulation of the liquidity and value of the unit of account on which all their accounting treatments are based, cannot but materially affect the validity of their accounts.

Washington and Wall Street will undoubtedly seek refuge from the duties and responsibilities outlined in this work in the safe haven of compliance in reporting with GAAP requirements. GAAP provides the banks' mechanisms to count and account for asset and liability values denominated in units of American sovereign money. That is the "how to count." The accountants share the fundamental failure of understanding "what to count" with the bankers' failure. The "what to count" of course is the value of things calculated and communicated through the honest safe and sound tool of money. When the tool of money is corrupted, manipulated and debased it invalidate the tool of money as the basis for their exertions in "how to count" asset, liabilities, income, expenses and losses by accountants and bankers. This failure and the intentional misrepresentations it enables serves the bankers interests as well as the interests of their captive and coopted professional service providers, including accountants, lawyers, rating agencies and valuation professionals in the Washington Wall Street enterprise program of intentional misrepresentation of liquid asset values and corresponding liability values and earnings on banks' balance sheets and income statements.

The benefits to the participants in this ongoing practice of intentional misrepresentation of asset liquidity and value denominated in American money through its debasement is demonstrated throughout this work.

Impairment of bank safety and soundness is measured by the deterioration of bank capital and bank earnings.[679] Increasing impairment of bank safety and soundness requires bank management to make and implement a plan of prompt corrective action with respect to non-performing assets (NPA) to mitigate deterioration and to provide an accurate foundation upon which to rebuild both bank capital and earnings.

The fair market value of bank assets is determined primarily pursuant to GAAP ASC 820 level 1 and level 2 inputs. As an example, consider that losses in asset values confirmed by level 1 and level 2 inputs are generally recognized by the banks and valuation experts. These Level 1 and Level 2 losses can be separated and distinguished between losses attributable to experience in the real economy and losses attributable to causes of bid ask gap during a liquidity crisis leading to high discount rates or low multiples applicable to asset market valuation.

Financial institution valuation policies and regulatory policies are generally based on: (i) micro-economic valuation process; (ii) micro-prudential regulation; and (iii) closed "silos" of analysis limited to a regulatory "silo," individual institution "silo-based" ignorance of the overwhelming impact on assets, institutions and financial system of level 3 "unobservable" inputs, such as money debasement, which can be made observable.

Current legal and financial policies, processes, procedures and documentation masterfully identify and allocate level 1 and level 2 and legal risk of loss and financial restructure efforts enforce these allocations. Current legal and financial policies, processes, procedures and documentation utterly fail to acknowledge, identify and allocate the level 3 risks of loss through money debasement identified in this work.

Financial institution safety and soundness is grounded in the establishment of processes that protect bank capital and earnings and therefore must deal with the level 3 valuation inputs that have created the bid-ask gap and support current market "liquidation" values of assets that are created as credit money.

Bid-ask gap in bank asset valuation is attributable to GAAP ASC Level 3 unobservable inputs, including the effects of macro-economic failure, macro-prudential failure and systemic failure, all supposedly grounded in so-called exogenous events, in the view of the federal financial regulators. In fact, the mysterious complex exogenous events are simply market recognition of the state of currency debasement reflect in intentionally exaggerated value of assets and their liquidity. The systematic intentional creation by Washington and Wall Street of artificially exaggerated and overstated—intentionally misrepresented—asset values and liquidity through systematic currency debasement is the fundamental cause of capital market dysfunction and liquidity crises. It is illegal.

Asset value and liquidity losses are imbedded and must either be recognized on liquidation into dysfunctional capital market or with respect to assets held until capital markets clear the foregoing, but held at a restated valuation recognition to the extent of overstated asset value and liquidity caused by money debasement. Washington and Wall Street can eliminate uncertainty in level 3 inputs leading to capital market dysfunction discount by creating distinctions, documented causes and effects and thus a much higher level of certainty. Washington and Wall Street could document the differential between fair value and market value, by isolating and deducting in its calculations the extent of discount rates attributable to level 3 inputs; i.e., leaving current liquidation value.

Fair value under *GAAP ASC Topics 820 and 825* "is the price that would be received to sell an asset or paid to transfer a liability in an orderly transaction (that is, not a forced liquidation or distressed sale) between market participants at the measurement date under *current* market conditions" (Authors' emphasis added in italics). This emphasis reinforces that fair value is a current market-based measurement, not a hypothetical future market-based measurement Although the presumption under *ASC 820 and 825* is that fair value is a not *forced liquidation or distressed value*, that presumption is qualified, in the case of NPA that are required to be the subject of a plan of prompt corrective action to meet safety and soundness requirements, by the necessity of inclusion in level 3 non-observable inputs of shorter market exposure periods dictated by the safety and soundness requirement of prompt corrective action through NPA disposition, as well as by the inclusion of higher discount rates and lower comparable auction cash prices and vulture cash prices as both level 2 and level 3 inputs to the determination of the NPA fair value. *The NPA fair value must recognize the heavy punitive discount directly attributable to the liquidity crunch in the capital markets currently accessible by purchasers of NPA.*

Although the application of other GAAP or international accounting standards is also beyond the scope or this work, see, for example, the work of Ray Ball, The University of Chicago Booth School of Business, Sudarshan Jayaraman, Olin Business

School, Washington University in St. Louis and Lakshmanan Shivakumar, London Business School, *Mark-to-Market Accounting and Information Asymmetry in Banks*,[680] August 12, 2012, exploring the relation between mark-to-market (MTM) accounting under SFAS No. 115 and SFAS No. 159 for securities and information asymmetry among bank investors. The point of reference, however, is not for their detailed analysis exploring the appropriate accounting methodology to accurately reflect liquid value of debt securities on historical cost or a mark to market basis, but to note their complete absence of consideration of the effects of Washington and Wall Street manipulation of the integrity of liquidity and values of assets denominated in Federal Reserve Notes through money debasement that corrupts its function as a unit and measurement of value in an account. The accounting profession has apparently decided to ignore this fundamental flaw, just as the legal profession has decided, for the time at any rate, to ignore the constitutional mandate for the regulation of the liquidity and value of United States sovereign money and its crucial role in disciplining the creation of credit money within and without the regulated Federal Reserve System.

So far, Washington and Wall Street have simply ignored the regulatory and accounting requirements for recognition of potential impairment of earnings and capital due to loss recognition for NPA, simply by covering up the specter of loss through Fed interest rate and value manipulations though discount rate policy, abuse of regulatory discretion and through massive bank asset purchases at par value as quantitative easing.

Bank assets should be valued at a pricing discount based on ASC 820 level 3 unobservable inputs, including anecdotal "unobservable"—inputs meaning inputs not articulated by typical documentary sources—based on previous liquidation cycles and current forced liquidations. Put simply, the proper valuation must recognize the effects of money debasement on the values of bank assets attributable to excess credit creation. For bank assets to constitute liquid assets and therefor suitable for use as credit money, the valuations must take into consideration previous liquidation cycles driven by the factors that create a bid-ask gap during periods of constrained market liquidity and demonstrable calculation of the degree of money debasement.

During financial crises, asset purchasers wait for regulatory pressure to force widespread asset liquidation and increasingly discounted pricing to meet competitive liquidation demand. Capital markets normally force allocation and realization of loss to financial institutions forced to clear balance sheets of NPA at liquidation value. This asset liquidation value is a more accurate representation of the money value of the asset on a liquid basis. To the extent the liquidation value is less than the book value of the asset the liquidation will result in a loss to be charged against the bankers required shock absorbers established to bridge the gap in valuation caused by term and therefore liquidity value mismatches. That is the essential function of the banking industry.

Shadow banking entities may also be subject to GAAP liquidity and valuation distortions in their financial data, but they are free to explicate the sources of those distortions and trade off them. What is suitable as a trading strategy based upon—even dependent upon information asymmetry attributable to money debasement, should not be a suitable strategy for regulated banks that control our money supply as the foundation for the safety soundness and stability of our regulated banks and the American economy.

Asset purchasers price the uncertainty in and confusion between level 1, 2 and unobservable level 3 valuation inputs determined under *GAAP ASC Topics 820 and 825* through blind discount rates. It is the bankers' responsibility to always maintain the shock absorber cushions and protections against illiquidity and accompanying capital inadequacy crises through prudent establishment and maintenance of capital and reserves, leverage limitations and regulatory compliance designed to enforce bank safety and soundness. Although Mr. Crosson's paper and commentary referred to earlier in this work speak for themselves, I believe that his concentration on gross income or net cash flow multiples method of asset valuation, when applied comprehensively through the levels and complexities of structured finance, are designed to achieve these same valuation objectives based on market-based evidence.

Washington and Wall Street are collectively responsible as fiduciaries to the American public for maintaining the integrity of American sovereign money as a functioning tool. This is not an outrageous expectation. Washington and Wall Street simply do not like it. The mass of literature regarding causes of financial crisis concur that they are caused by credit excess. Credit creators want to create more credit rather than less. They want to make more money and grasp more power than less. Their interests are directly opposed to the prescription for honest, safe and sound money, the value of which has properly regulated by Congress. History informs the scholar that credit creators ultimately will have to face the constraints on credit creation implicit in the regulation of the value of both sovereign money, and then necessarily shadow money, as a matter of law, or they will be forced to face it extra-legally, possibly violently.

§8.05 BANKS AND BANKERS DUTY AND STANDARD OF CARE

[A] The Reasonable and Prudent Banker

The reasonable and prudent banker, among other duties, must[681] "exercise sound and prudent judgment." The banker has a duty of loyalty and care. Bankers must be:

(i) prudent and diligent business persons; ...
(ii) make reasonable inquiries [and] ...
(iii) make reasonable business judgments on:
- a fully informed basis;
- after proper deliberation.

One would think that a reasonable and prudent banker then would be knowledgeable of the common law and common sense status of banks, bankers as well as bank regulatory, supervisory and enforcement agencies whose existence purports to stand in for protection of the public interest as fiduciaries to the public, and that as such, would be aware of the threats to their professions of the liquidity and valuation distortions created within the Federal Reserve System and also within and without the shadow banking system. One would think that banks and bankers would know that the public interest in the honesty, safety and soundness in the banking industry is dependent on the legal definitions and complementary but inter-related functioning of: (i) sovereign money, the value of which is regulated by Congress, providing the fundamental anchor for monetary liquidity and value; (ii) credit money created through and accounted for in the Federal Reserve System; and (iii) shadow banking money substitutes.

Regulators apply the regulatory standards of safety and soundness subjectively, based on a retrospective factual analysis and assessment of the bank's activities and practices. In addition, although both Washington and Wall Street will take issue with the additional specific duties and high fiduciary standards of care upon which the powers they wield are grounded, they are subject to the requirement of the *United States Constitution* and to the formal re-establishment of their historical grounded ultimate fiduciary duty to the American public.

Consequently, and in the affirmative, Congress, the federal banking authorities and bank management must be proactive and anticipatory in demonstrating to regulators its awareness of and serious concern for all laws, regulations, rulings, interpretations, opinions, guidance, policies and procedures that could have been followed by the bank, including their source in the *Constitution* and in the principle of fiduciary duty to their sovereign, the American people, irrespective of whether mandatory in application, to avoid dishonest, unsafe and unsound banking activities and practices leading to losses. Washington and Wall Street management awareness and concern of and legal commitment to the honesty, safety and soundness of money and banking must be carefully documented.

Both Washington and the Wall Street banks have failed to meet their legal duties and standards of care, and they have avoided accountability for that failure with the knowing complicity of their colleagues in Washington and on Wall Street.

The Federal Reserve System and the other federal financial regulators are responsible to the public as fiduciaries for the safety and soundness of our monetary and financial system and for the active consideration off and protection of the public interest from threats to safety and soundness of the system flowing from congressional and regulatory failure and Wall Street's intentional exploitation of the totality of Washington and Wall Street's failure to constantly monitor, assess and control the debasement of American money created through the monetary, legal and regulatory system that they control and which they are mandated to enforce.[682]

The Wall Street banks and bankers are the nation's experts in money and banking. Congress and the Federal Reserve System have abandoned to Wall Street all power over the creation of American money and regulation of its value. Congress, the Fed and the federal financial regulators and enforcement agencies, including the DOJ, SEC and CFTC have failed in their mandate, duty and standard of care required to be exercised in the public interest, and have for themselves absolved Wall Street banks and bankers of accountability for their actions in the exercise of this power through a deliberate intentional policy of "too big to fail and too big to jail." The intentional fraudulent debasement and misrepresentation of the value of American money by Washington and Wall Street and their mutual absolution of accountability for profi teering from their enterprise of lying to, cheating and stealing from the American public through the ancient but reviled practice of money debasement has been followed and exacerbated by their mutual continuing perpetuation of their enterprise in denying and covering up the connection between their gross concentration of wealth, income and power and the losses of wealth, income, trust and power suffered by the American public and the additional tort damages they have suffered and continue to suffer at the hands of Washington and Wall Street. Washington's and Wall Street's moral and legal failures and self-conferred absolution from their wrongdoing does not, however, limit, alter, affect or impair the American public's ongoing legal right to the enforcement of the rule of law, recovery of damages, imposition of punishment and deterrence to future wrongdoing by Washington and Wall Street.

[B] Bank Duties and Standards of Care

This may come as a surprise to most lawyers, banking and bankruptcy lawyers in particular, that banks by their nature are fiduciaries.

F.A. Mann, in his seminal international foundational work entitled *The Legal Aspects of Money, Fourth Edition* (1982), while finding the Bretton Woods System[683] to have been "necessarily and universally disregarded"[684] and therefore only of "historical interest,"[685] Mann then goes to the conceptual heart of the role of the gold standard, or any other specie based standard established for the purpose of regulating the value of money. The central importance of the necessity of the legal regulation of the value of money by reference to a metallic standard such as the gold standard is the forced alignment of the liquidity and value of the paper money substitutes with the metallic standard which is the final settlement measurement standard. When the regulation of the value of money by reference to and independent standard of value, e.g., the gold standard, is cast aside, in Mann's words, "[t]his is the birth of the 'fiduciary issue,' which is independent of gold."[686] To the extent any monetary issue was not backed gold, the standard substituting for the English "self-regulating" gold standard became a fiduciary standard applicable to the issuer, imposing on the issuer the obligation to make the backing of the fiduciary note issue as good as gold.

According to Mann, "[a]lthough or perhaps because the fiduciary issue is no longer backed by gold, the government retains complete control over it. Yet, 'the government's function in issuing notes is simply the passive one of ensuring sufficient notes are available for the practical convenience of the public.'"[687] On the one hand, while these fiduciary issues are no longer specifically backed by specie, it remains the fiduciary obligation of the issuer of the paper currency legal tender money substitute (whether issued by the government, banks or private individuals) to assure the public that the value of the fiduciary notes issued do not "materially deviate from their nominal value expressed in terms of metallic currency."[688]

In America, the consideration expressed by Mann, finds expression as the necessity to treat the issuers of money substitutes as trustees of the fiscal affairs of the people and the state. As such, they are the proper subject of regulation as fiduciaries. In the *Law of Financial Institutions, Fifth Edition,* Professors Richard Scott Carnell of

Fordham University, Jonathan R. Macey of Yale, and Geoffrey P. Miller of New York University (Carnell Macey Miller),[689] looked to a particularly eloquent case for government regulation of banks and other financial institutions, as trustees of the fiscal affairs of the people and of the state. Schaake v. Dolley, 119 P. 80 (Kan. 1911) was decided by the Supreme Court of Kansas, with the Opinion written by Justice Burch, in the wake of the financial crisis of 1907 which ultimate brought the Federal Reserve System to ordinary Americans in 1913:

> Banks are indispensable agencies through which the industry, trade and commerce of all civilized countries and communities are now carried on. The banker is the universal broker over whose counter the exchanges of supply and demand are, in the final analysis, effected. *The capital which he has invested and the returns which he receives upon it are insignificant in importance relative to the advantages which society at large derives from the conduct of the banking business, and the evil consequences of unsound banking are distributed between the banker and the general public in like proportion. Banking ... has ceased to be, if it ever was, a matter of private concern only, like the business of the merchant, and for all purposes of legislative regulation and control it may be said to be, if "affected with a public interest." The public patronage which the banker invites and receives is of such a character that he becomes in a just sense a trustee of the fiscal affairs of the people and of the state.* If a merchant can not meet his bills promptly the general public is not disturbed. He is not ruined at once, and if he should fail the effects are limited to comparatively few persons. If a bank is unable to meet a check drawn upon it the refusal to pay is an act of insolvency. Its doors are closed, its business is arrested, its affairs go into liquidation and the mischief takes a wide range. [Borrowers must pay off their loans], whatever their readiness or ability to do so. Further advances cannot be obtained. Other banks must call in their loans and refuse to extend credit in order to fortify themselves against the uneasiness and even terror of their own depositors. Confidence is destroyed. Enterprises are stopped. Business is brought to a standstill. [Foreclosures occur.] Property is sacrificed and disaster spreads from locality to locality. All these incidents of the banking business are matters of common knowledge and experience. They clearly distinguish banking from the ordinary private business, illustrate its public nature and show that it is properly subject to the police power of the state, vested in its legislature .... (Authors' emphasis added in italics)

Similarly, Walter Bagehot observed in *Lombard Street*, the threat to banking posed by the then new and revolutionary technological development of the shadow money instrument of the check, or "cheque":

> As long as the Bank of England note was currency required for business circulation, this restriction was open to criticism as the infliction of a cast-iron fetter where elasticity was most or all desirable; *and the advantages of the German system, which provided for an expansion in the issue of notes against securities-the fiduciary issue as it is generally called-when money is in great demand, was frequently held up as an example for England.* But now that it is more clearly perceived that the money of England is the cheque, which can be multiplied to an extent which is only limited by the prudence of bankers and the security that their customers may be able to provide, and that the Bank of England note itchiefly used as part of the banking cash reserve, the opinion commonly held in the City that the restrictions on its issue imposed by Peel's Act should be carried still further, and *that that part of the issue which is fiduciary, or based on securities, should gradually*

> *be abolished, the securities behind it being replaced by gold.* Since most of the profit on the fiduciary issue goes to the Government the difficulty of introducing any change tending towards its abolition is redoubled; but as a matter of theory it is safe to say that a majority of well-informed City opinion is now in favour of making the Bank of England note a pure and simple bullion certificate. And this change of opinion concerning the only law which seriously restricts the banker in the conduct of his business is striking evidence of the extent to which English banking has been modified by the development of the use of the cheque. It has been revolutionized rather than modified, for the cheque has freed banking from the fetters of the Bank Act.[690] (Authors' emphasis added in italics)

The policies and actions of Washington and Wall Street leading to and following the great financial crisis of 2008 were, and remain knowingly and intentionally conducted in deliberate disregard of the clearly established and applicable historical legal duties, responsibilities and standards of care for ensuring the integrity of money and its necessary alignment of asset liquidity and value as a final settlement mechanism; placing the interests of the holders of notes ahead of the issuers.

The monetary distortions wrought by widespread booms in the creation of shadow banking credit money substitutes led inevitably to bust and financial crisis when the dramatic misalignment of liquidity and value became obvious notwithstanding the layers of structure designed to cover up the gap.

[C] External and Internal Costs of Breach of Duty to Honestly Regulate the Value of Money

The distinction Schaake v. Dolley, *supra,* draws between banks and other firms parallels the distinction economists draw between external and internal costs. "The *internal costs* of an activity are those borne by the person conducting the activity. The *external costs* are those borne by others. Bank failures can have significant external costs (e.g., on depositors, borrowers and local communities), which furnish some of the most important rationales for regulating banks." In America, and now globally, the regulation of banks safety and soundness through comprehensive banking law and regulation, while well-intended, although often disjointed and largely ineffective, has functionally replaced the discipline of required redemption of the dollar in coined money, the value of which is regulated by Congress. The historical, traditional standard for the regulation of the value of the dollar consisted of its relation to the value and specified quantity and quality of primarily gold or silver; but now, in relation to nothing, literally. Even if the feature of redemption is removed from the equation, the fiduciary obligation of the issue remains to assure the value of the money substitutes' correlation to the nominal value of the monetary standard, thus maintaining the necessary alignment of asset liquidity and value in the money substitutes service as safe and sound money, as bankers historically understand it and as required by the *United States Constitution.*

Banks are inseparable from money—their existence is based on the need for money. The privileged success and extraordinary profitability of Wall Street banks and other federally insured or "systemically protected" financial institutions are driven by

Washington's greed for money not available through the open and transparent legislative process and open, transparent and honest taxation. That greed is met by Washington and Wall Street enterprise's complex "structured" separation of the money substitutes they originate and distribute, injecting them into the monetary system as shadow banking assets, from the liquidity necessary to support their value as money substitutes in accordance with their constitutionally regulated value by redemption in, or by reference to a credible independent specie standard, e.g., the gold or other metallic standard.

Money market funds, hedge funds, repo traders, private equity investors and other speculators that simple trade on the volatility introduced by the corruption of the asset liquidity and value of shadow banking assets introduced by Washington and Wall Street into the monetary system, are just that, traders, not fiduciaries responsible for the safety and soundness of the American monetary and banking system.

Concerns about hedge funds include: "large size, elite investors, lack of transparency, perceptions of predatory behavior, high risk and periodic spectacular failure, complexity, perceived false promises of easy money, volatility, and attacks on established interests—can foment popular fear of a new breed of shadowy financial players. The populist anti-hedge fund spin almost writes itself: a wealthy, backroom, elite group of investors, driven by selfish greed, takes excessive risks with cheater-style trading strategies that imperil the health of our banks and our corporations—our entire economy. And popular fear created pressure for government regulation of the industry."[691]

[D] Shadow Banks Duties and Standards of Care[692]

Wulf A. Kaal and Dale Oesterle, in their "The History of Hedge Fund Regulation in the United States," *Handbook on Hedge Funds*, Oxford University Press (2016), provide an excellent summary regulatory background for assessing the relative freedom of hedge funds and private equity funds from a history and complex matrix of duties and standards of care, as distinguished from those of banks.

> At the beginning of the industry in the early 1950s, organizers of hedge funds designed the funds to be exempt from the public offering registration requirements of the *Securities Act of 1933*, the periodic reporting requirements of the *Securities Exchange Act of 1934*, the registration requirements of the *Investment Company Act of 1940*, and the registration requirements of the *Investment Advisers Act of 1940*. The exemptions gave United States hedge funds substantial freedom in their investment activities.
>
> The typical hedge fund manager raises money from wealthy individuals and institutional investors using an exemption for "private offerings" under the *Securities Act of 1933* in Rule 506 of Regulation D. Most early hedge funds satisfied the exemption by marketing themselves only to "accredited investors," institutional investors, insiders, or natural persons with a net worth of over $1 million or income over $200,000 for each of the last two years. Funds that used Rule 506 were prohibited from using any form of "general solicitation or general advertising."

The SEC applied a "pre-existing, substantive relationship" test when deciding that the general solicitation rule has not been violated.[693]

Hedge funds were careful to avoid classification as a financial market player that is specifically regulated by the federal legislation. A hedge fund is not an underwriter, a market maker, or a broker-dealer (market intermediary). A bank or investment subsidiary of an operating company is not a hedge fund. Hedge funds were also careful to limit investors to fewer than 500 to avoid the periodic reporting obligations of Section 12 of the *Securities Exchange Act of 1934* and SEC Rule 12g-1.[694]

The most important regulatory exemption for hedge funds is *the Investment Company Act of 1940,* applicable to mutual funds. Hedge funds either have fewer than 100 investors or have only investors that are "qualified purchasers," i.e., individuals who own over $5 million in investments or companies with over $25 million in investments. Exempt hedge funds may use investment techniques that are forbidden to registered investment companies; the most notable being "shorting," or betting on decreases in value in asset classes.[695]

Hedge fund investment strategies are generally complex, involving a combination of several coordinated trading positions to make the desired market play. In a "convertible arbitrage," for example, a hedge fund goes long in convertible securities (bonds or shares that are exchangeable for another form of securities, usually common shares, at a pre-set price) and simultaneously shorts the shares. In a "merger arbitrage," a hedge fund buys target company stock and shorts the stock of the purchaser. In a "global macro" play, a fund takes a long position in one country's currency and shorts the currency of another (this is also done with government debt). In a "market neutral" play, a fund takes offsetting long positions in undervalued companies and short positions in overvalued companies.[696]

Hedge funds can also structure their operations to avoid the regulation as a "commodity pool" by the Commodity Futures Trading Commission (CFTC). New CFTC rules exempt pools that sell only to sophisticated participants, "accredited investors" under Regulation D or "qualified purchasers" under the Investment Company Act. Hedge funds avoid regulation under the Employee Retirement Income Security Act (ERISA) by limiting the ownership interest of any employee benefit plan to less than 25 percent of the fund.[697]

Since the growth of the hedge fund industry increased dramatically in the 1980s, the SEC repeatedly attempted to require registration of hedge fund advisers. Dodd-Frank mooted prior efforts to regulate hedge funds by explicitly authorizing the SEC to register hedge fund advisers.

Title IV of the *Dodd–Frank Act* is entitled the *Private Fund Investment Advisers Registration Act of 2010* (PFIARA). PFIARA authorizes the SEC to bring hedge funds under regulatory supervision. Dodd-Frank authorized the SEC to promulgate rules requiring registration and enhanced disclosure for private equity and hedge funds managers. As part of the new rules, the SEC introduced controversial reporting obligations that would require the disclosure of strategies and products used by the investment adviser and its funds, performance and changes in

> performance, financing information, risks metrics, counterparties and credit exposure, positions held by the investment adviser, percent of assets traded using algorithms, and the percent of equity and debt, among other matters.
>
> The Act mandates hedge fund adviser registration to increase record keeping and disclosure. Under PFIARA, hedge funds with more than $150 million Assets Under Management (AUM) are required to register as investment advisers and to disclose information about their trades and portfolios to the SEC. Dodd-Frank also directs the SEC to set up rules for the registration and reporting of hedge fund managers who were previously exempt from registration. By registering hedge fund advisers, the SEC may collect necessary information to curtail those who operate in the "shadows of our markets," prevent fraud, limit systemic risk, and provide information to investors.
>
> Title IV of *Dodd-Frank* also requires registered investment advisers to maintain records and any other information that may be necessary and appropriate to avoid systemic risk. Advisers are required to provide confidential reports with respect to certain information related to systemic risk, such as trading practices; trading and investment positions; the amount of AUM; valuation policies; side letters; the use of leverage, including off-balance sheet leverage; counterparty credit risk exposures; and other information deemed necessary. PFIARA also makes it mandatory for registered advisers to maintain records and any other information the SEC and the systemic risk regulators may deem necessary.[698]

The newest regulatory threat to hedge funds is a change in the tax code which would, if enacted, dramatically increase the taxes paid by successful hedge funds on their returns. The increased taxes, unless mitigated though clever planning, could reduce hedge fund returns and make them less competitive with other forms of intermediated investments.[699]

Recently, concerns about slowing global growth, supply gluts in commodities markets, and shifts in exchange rate and monetary policies abroad have led to significant price swings across a range of financial assets as US interest rates have remained low.[700] It is worth noting that US financial regulators and market participants made progress in addressing a number of structural vulnerabilities highlighted in the Financial Services Oversight Council's previous annual reports:

> "The Federal Reserve finalized a rule requiring that global systemically important banks (G-SIBs) increase their holdings of common equity relative to risk-weighted assets (RWAs) and proposed standards for mandatory long-term debt and total loss-absorbing capacity for G-SIBs. The Federal Reserve and the FDIC completed their review of the 2015 resolution plans of eight of the largest, most complex US bank holding companies (BHCs). The agencies jointly determined that five of the firms had submitted plans that were not credible or would not facilitate an orderly resolution under bankruptcy and have notified these firms of the deficiencies in their plans. The Federal Reserve and the FDIC informed all eight firms of the steps they must take in response to the agencies' findings. The International Swaps and Derivatives Association (ISDA) expanded the scope of its Universal Resolution Stay Protocol to cover securities financing transactions. In February 2016, the CFTC and the European Commission announced a common approach to the supervision of central counterparties (CCPs) operating in the United States and the European Union (EU). U.S. prudential regulators and the CFTC issued rules establishing minimum margin requirements for swaps that are not cleared through

> CCPs. The SEC finalized rules setting forth reporting requirements for securities-based swaps and establishing a process for the registration of securities-based swap dealers and major securities-based swap participants. The OFR, Federal Reserve System, and SEC collaborated on pilot projects to improve the collection and analysis of data on securities financing transactions. These and other actions undertaken over the last year can be expected to make the largest, most interconnected financial institutions more resilient, improve regulators' and firm managers' ability to manage potential distress at such institutions, and reduce the impact of contagion that may arise from interconnections among firms and markets. Despite these important, positive steps, this report identifies a number of structural vulnerabilities and emerging threats in the US financial system that require action from market participants, regulators, and policymakers.
>
> "In addition, the Council continued its analysis of potential financial stability risks that may arise from certain asset management products and activities. Based on this work, the Council identified areas of potential financial stability risks and, in April 2016, publicly issued a written update regarding its evaluation. Since May 2015, the SEC has issued several proposed rules affecting the asset management industry. The SEC has proposed rules to enhance data reporting for registered investment companies and registered investment advisers of separately managed accounts, strengthen liquidity risk management programs and disclosure for registered funds, and limit the amount of leverage that registered investment companies may obtain through derivatives transactions.
>
> "Lastly, the Council remains focused on taking steps to appropriately address threats to financial stability. Recently, a federal court rescinded the Council's designation of a nonbank financial company for Federal Reserve supervision and enhanced prudential standards. The government is appealing the court's decision. The Council's authority to designate nonbank financial companies remains a critical tool to address potential threats to financial stability, and the Council will continue to defend vigorously the nonbank designations process."[701]

The FSOC's Report highlights the efforts in Washington and on Wall Street continue to nibble at the edges of the systemic risk that leads to financial crisis. When the next crisis arrives, these intense, detailed, specialized, technical reforms will hold little weight to sorting out losses and accountability in the web of shadow banking.

In the wake of the great financial crisis, money market funds, which were then near fatally threatened by runs on redemption, leading to liquidity and therefore asset valuation crises. Their status as "cash equivalents" was imperiled. The SEC enacted rules[702] effective October 14, 2014 that, at 893 pages, are briefly summarized by the SEC as follows:

> "The Securities and Exchange Commission ("Commission" or "SEC") is adopting amendments to the rules that govern money market mutual funds (or "money market funds") under the Investment Company Act of 1940 ("Investment Company Act" or "Act"). The amendments are designed to address money market funds' susceptibility to heavy redemptions in times of stress, improve their ability to manage and mitigate potential contagion from such redemptions, and increase the transparency of their risks, while preserving, as much as possible, their benefits. The SEC is removing the valuation exemption that permitted institutional non- government money market funds (whose investors historically have made the heaviest redemptions in times of stress) to maintain a stable net asset value per share ("NAV"), and is requiring those funds to sell and redeem shares based on the current market-based value of the securities in their underlying portfolios rounded

to the fourth decimal place (e.g., $1.0000), i.e., transact at a "floating" NAV. The SEC also is adopting amendments that will give the boards of directors of money market funds new tools to stem heavy redemptions by giving them discretion to impose a liquidity fee if a fund's weekly liquidity level falls below the required regulatory threshold, and giving them discretion to suspend redemptions temporarily, i.e., to "gate" funds, under the same circumstances. These amendments will require all non-government money market funds to impose a liquidity fee if the fund's weekly liquidity level falls below a designated threshold, unless the fund's board determines that imposing such a fee is not in the best interests of the fund. In addition, the SEC is adopting amendments designed to make money market funds more resilient by increasing the diversification of their portfolios, enhancing their stress testing, and improving transparency by requiring money market funds to report additional information to the SEC and to investors. Finally, the amendments require investment advisers to certain large unregistered liquidity funds, which can have many of the same economic features as money market funds, to provide additional information about those funds to the SEC."

At this writing money market funds total $3 trillion. At the time of the financial crisis in 2008, "[t]he total held in money funds, which had hit a record high of $3.535 trillion on Sept. 9, plummeted to $3.288 trillion 10 days later, when the government [rescue] plan was unveiled."[703]

In the light of the history of regulatory supervision and enforcement experienced during the crisis which, despite a flurry of rulemaking, the integrity of cash money equivalents in the next crisis remains very much in question.

With respect to repo trading, the Paul Volker and *The Volker Alliance Report* that "the uninsured short-term debt markets grew dramatically in the years leading up to the 2008 financial crisis, reaching a pre-crisis peak of roughly $18 trillion, or about 120 percent of US gross domestic product and more than four times the amount of insured deposits."[704]

Volker continues, "[p]ut simply, uninsured short-term funding remains a threat to financial stability. As interest rates normalize, incentives to engage in even more short-term borrowing and lending will return. Despite recent reforms, the financial system will remain prone to funding runs and make failure resolution all the more difficult. Reforms that directly target run-prone funding structures are required to ensure the health and well-being of the financial system and the broader economy. In a speech earlier this year, Mr. Tarullo [a Fed Governor at the time] said, 'I continue to believe that the post-crisis work to create a solid regime to protect financial stability cannot be deemed complete without a well-considered approach to regulating runnable funding outside, as well as inside, the regulatory perimeter.'"[705]

Shadow bankers do not serve the public interest in a comprehensive manner comparable to that articulated in Schaake v. Dolley. Hedge funds and private equity investors do not, their primary function, create money and provide depository and transactional clearing services to the public. They are not a part of the Federal Reserve System. What happens then, or perhaps what should happen when the activities of shadow bankers invade the territory of heavily regulated banks? These private parties are already heavily involved in investment in and trading of shadow banking assets through networks or affiliated parties and counterparties. As I note below, they are also beginning to encroach on the lending functions typically the province of regulated bank lenders. As the asset side of all of these regulated and largely unregulated entities began to overlap and resemble one another, since all, or substantially all of their assets are denominated in US dollars or are at risk of currency of exchange into dollars, the safety and soundness of the dollar and thus the safety and soundness of the American banking system and economy are impacted by the risks of asset liquidity and value infused collectively into the system. Who then, should bear the increased risk attendant to the increased gap in alignment of asset liquidity and value with the profile of aligned liquidity and value necessary to a well-functioning money system?

§8.06 SYSTEMIC RISK, BANKING AND FINANCIAL CRISES

The customary view of systemic financial risk concentrates first, on a financial shock that has a simultaneous impact on a number of financial institutions and financial markets. The second customary view refers to the chain reaction problem, the possibility that the failure of one bank will affect other banks.

This limited view of systemic financial risk focuses on a limited number of transmission vehicles, i.e., banks, without focus on the nature of the initiating shocks that trigger financial crises or taking into account the magnifying effect of those "external" shocks through the non-regulated shadow banking system. The shadow banking system incorporates no meaningful constraints on money creation, credit creation or ongoing enforceable ties to asset quality and earning to support—or even connect on the most remote basis—the safety and soundness of the credit created based on the asset quality and earnings necessary to be converted to sound liquid money to redeem the credit on demand at maturity.

Bank capital standards, lending underwriting requirements and constant regulatory examination for bank safety and soundness are all subverted by the consequences of failure to regulate the value of money, Systemic crises result from:

- Unregulated creation of money without regulation of money as a unit of measure leads to asset valuation, including liquidity, distortions which, in turn, leads to credit bubbles, liquidity crises and inflated valuation of assets that are the focus of the credit creation.
- Asset value distortions become unsustainable without a continued flood of credit to support inflated values based on their artificially supplied characteristic of liquidity.
- When the connection between the volume of credit and the underlying use value of the affected assets supporting the credit becomes apparent, the uncertainty of valuation and liquidity of both credit and assets blocks market movement.
- A market freeze in response to valuation uncertainty renders the credit and related assets illiquid—resulting in a liquidity crisis.
- Credit money loses the essential and central characteristic of liquidity at par value upon which the use of money is lost. It is lost at precisely the time that liquidity of credit money at par value is essential.

- When the affected credit and assets become illiquid in the market place their values collapse resulting in a solvency crisis for those holding the credit and/or underlying assets.
- Profits from the creation of credit money are harvested by the defendants Washington and Wall Street.
- Losses attributable to the intentional misrepresentation of the value and liquidity of credit money are forced upon the hapless holders of dollars and dollar denominated assets and on American taxpayers, as money debasement and fiscal folly.

Systemic financial crises based on credit and liquidity distortions due to failure to regulate the value of money persist so long as the valuations of the credit and related assets are not reconciled to relative use value in the market and true market value. Euphemistic expressions for the intentional misrepresentation of the value and liquidity of credit money include phrases such as "collateral transformation" and "structured finance." In fact, the processes represented by these phrases are actually the mechanisms of intentional fraud through which asset values and liquidity are simply manufactured through regulatory, legal and accounting manipulation, resulting in overstated asset values and liquidity and money debasement.

Considering the establishment of bank fiduciary duties, the importance of the specter of heavy external costs or losses suffered by the American public to whom such fiduciary duties were owed, and consequently by the banks other external constituents such as the depositors, the FDIC, bank shareholders, and the public, who are the proper beneficiaries of the state and federal legal requirement of prior regulatory approval for the Wall Street banks to conduct their banking and money creation and intermediation activities, and to the other banking law duties, standards, conditions, restrictions and sanctions would have prevented the losses suffered by the American public but also the other external losses yet to be suffered due to the banks actions as contemplated by the Schaake case and contemplated to be protected by the *United States Constitution* and the state and federal bank legal and regulatory regime.

In the systemic financial crises occurring since the Nixon shock in 1971, loss experience in the credit and underlying assets fed by the credit creation bubble have averaged 40 percent to 60 percent. Losses of this magnitude are not sustainable by banks or by shadow banking enterprises. Bank credit and asset underwriting, supervision and examination and assessment of capital adequacy performed on a micro-basis, pales into insignificance under the weight of losses from unrestrained creation of credit money whose value is not regulated, safe and sound and liquid. The losses presented in systemic financial crises of the magnitude experienced in the banking crises of the 1980s and 90s and the current crisis are not sustainable by banks or other financial and business institutions.

Washington and Wall Street have not met the applicable legal, regulatory and banking standards and duties of care. So, the losses have not been recognized and sustained. What does this mean for the concept and enforcement of bank safety and soundness and a bank regulatory scheme base on the standard or safety and soundness?

The concept of safety and soundness has moved from safety and soundness of money, to safety and soundness of banks to safety and soundness of a system that maintains safety and soundness by removing threats to bank safety and soundness presented as threats to income and capital adequacy by redefining the standards—using new words—or by bailouts, subsidies and other structural support of the largest and most powerful of banks,—now including any business with sufficient size and financial impact on the economy that politicians, bankers and regulators sacrifice institution level regulation and enforcement of safety and soundness to financial systemic stability; and those standards have been sacrificed to current political stability of the status quo—though Washington's publicly acknowledged policy of protection of Wall Street banks as too big to fail and too big to jail.

Compounding the valuation and economic distortions and damage inflicted on the American and global economies by systemic financial crises, the policy, legislative and regulatory response to the crisis has not been to force accountability in accordance with the rule of law.

The response has been to compound the ongoing misrepresentation of credit and asset liquid values through intentional proliferation of money and credit whose value is not regulated, by continuation of the policy of too big to fail, simple misrepresentation of values on institutional balance sheets with the complicity of the institutions, the financial regulators and congress, transparent and non-transparent bailouts of the largest most powerful institutions, repayment of bailout funds through additional non-transparent bailouts and, finally the ongoing Fed programs of quantitative easing.

These programs are purported designed to hold interest rates down to promote employment. Their effect is to continue a program of interest rate subsidies to financial institutions to enable them to rebuild capital and gradually absorb losses and to systematically purchase overvalued assets from those institutions at par to avoid loss recognition at the financial institution level and transfer the losses ultimately to the national debt and the American public.

The protected parties may not fare so well in the next financial crisis. And there will be a next financial crisis. There will be opportunities for hedge funds and private equity investors in exploiting the financial distortions now embed in our financial system Those opportunities do not lie ultimately in the participation in the ongoing extension of these financial distortions buy picking up in lending where the banks left off. Hedge funds and private equity may not have the benefit of a federal safety net through the Fed discount window or from the FDIC during the next crisis.

§8.07 CHAIRMAN ALAN GREENSPAN AND THE FAILURE OF BANK REGULATION

The following are excerpts from a live blog of the testimony at The Financial Crisis Inquiry Commission's hearings in Washington, DC:[706]

The US banking system has been "undercapitalized" for the past "40 to 50 years," former Federal Reserve Chairman Alan Greenspan told a panel today in Washington convened to investigate the roots of the financial crisis.[707]

In response to a question about the Fed's failure to guard against megabanks becoming so large and interconnected that they posed a systemic risk—risks that pose threats to the entire financial system—Greenspan said the Fed was not alone in that regard. Rather, he said, *everyone—the financial industry and their regulators at the Fed—failed to appropriately appreciate how badly banks were guarding themselves against risk.*

"Once the Fed realized how poorly the banks' risk management systems were, Greenspan realized how poorly they were capitalized—money, in short, that banks keep on hand to protect themselves from going under in the case of huge losses. In fact, the banking system has been "undercapitalized" for the past 40 to 50 years," he said.

Put another way: for the past few generations, *the US banking system has not been holding enough money to guard itself from insolvency, putting taxpayers at great risk in case a panic were to materialize*—a lesson painfully learned in 2008. When regulators judge banks to be undercapitalized, the banks are told to shore up their capital or shed potential sources of future losses, like sour loans or underperforming businesses. If they can't, they're shut down. Most of the time, it's an open-and-shut case.

The risk management paradigm nonetheless harbored a fatal flaw. In the growing state of euphoria, managers at financial institutions, along with regulators including but not limited to the Federal Reserve, *failed to fully comprehend the underlying size, length, and potential impact of the so-called negative tail of the distribution of risk outcomes* that was about to be revealed as the post-Lehman Brothers crisis played out, Greenspan said in his prepared remarks. '*For decades, with little to no data, almost all analysts, in my experience, had conjectured a far more limited tail risk. That led to more than a half century of significantly and chronically undercapitalized financial intermediaries, arguably the major failure of the private risk management system.*'"

"The financial firms counted on being able to anticipate the onset of crisis in time to retrench. They were mistaken. They believed the then seemingly insatiable demand for their array of exotic financial products would enable them to sell large parts of their portfolios without loss." But that did not happen—a lesson the US learned several hundreds of billions of taxpayer dollars later.

"Former Federal Reserve Chairman Alan Greenspan made the kind of *admission this morning that may trouble those who assume that better regulators—rather than a wholesale rewriting of rules—will better protect Americans from a future financial crisis. Regulators can't keep up with today's megabanks, he said. They're too complex. Regulators, in short, don't have a chance.*"[708]

Greenspan, appearing before the panel convened to investigate the roots of the financial crisis, said that the *"ideal way" to supervise banks would be to go through its individual loan documents—the way supervisors used to police banks and financial firms before they grew so large. But unfortunately, he lamented, that's no longer possible because firms are so complex. "We are reaching far beyond our capacities,"* Greenspan told the Financial Crisis Inquiry Commission. "It's not a simple issue of 'Let's regulate better,'" he said. "It's a different world." "The complexity is awesome," he noted. Instead, regulators need to rely on banks' counterparties—those they do business with—as a first line of defense.

"But that failed in 2008, Greenspan admitted. Counterparties were left holding the bag when the firms they did business with—like Lehman Brothers and AIG, for starters—nearly went belly up (Lehman ended up declaring bankruptcy).

> Taxpayers were forced to bail the firms out—money that in AIG's case went straight to its trading partners, like the billions that went to Goldman Sachs—in what some members of Congress have called a "backdoor bailout." *"If you cannot depend on counterparty surveillance," Greenspan warned, regulators are much less effective. So, in effect, it really doesn't matter who's regulating—the industry has to step up its self-regulation by keeping counterparties in check."*
>
> *"You found that your view of the world, your ideology was not right, it was not working?"* said Rep. Henry A. Waxman (D-Calif.), the committee chairman.
>
> *"Absolutely, precisely," Greenspan said. "You know, that's precisely the reason I was shocked, because I have been going for 40 years or more with very considerable evidence that it was working exceptionally well."*
>
> Greenspan alternately defended his legacy and acknowledged mistakes. Waxman asked whether the former chairman was wrong to consistently oppose regulating the multitrillion dollar derivative market that has contributed to the financial crisis. "Well, partially," said Greenspan, before stressing the difference between credit-default swaps and other types of derivatives. *With the global financial system unraveling, economists and political leaders are coming to doubt some of Greenspan's most closely held views: that markets can exact self-discipline, that central bankers should generally not try to prick bubbles in the price of houses or tech stocks, that a policymaker's most powerful tool to encourage growth is to stay out of the way. Even Greenspan seemed genuinely perplexed yesterday by all that had happened, hard-pressed to explain how formerly fundamental truths about how markets work could have proved so wrong.*[709]
>
> (Authors' emphasis added in italics).

In the final analysis, lack Greenspan has acknowledged the failure of discretionary regulation by both Washington and Wall Street. America's failure to support financial stability by regulating the value of sovereign and conforming structured financial instruments to the disciplines attached to traditional commercial law imposed financial liability on issuers and transferors or endorsers of debt, whether transferred as debt or in the financial structure of marketable securities. Wall Street would prefer to avoid such financial accountability. Their lobbyists stand ready to persuade Washington that it is in Washington's, Wall Street's and the lobbyists best interest to enable Wall Street to avoid liability and accountability for losses caused by their creation and emission of virtually unlimited amounts of bank credit and shadow bank credit money. The public interest being entirely outside the consideration of the meaning of financial stability.

§8.08 CONCLUDING OBSERVATIONS

Washington's and Wall Street's conduct portends the next crisis. The Dodd Frank legislation was designed in part, to deal specifically the corrosive effect of financial derivatives on the American public—the primarily driver during this crisis of currency debasement and economic collapse on Main Street American. Notwithstanding the specific intent of Dodd Frank, the old Washington Wall Street cabal remains alive and well and is concentrating efforts to roll back the protections through amendments and through corruption of the rule making process, making a mockery of any consideration of the public interest:

"In March, as US bank regulators were framing a new rule that would affect the $630 trillion derivatives market, JPMorgan Chase & Co sent five bankers from New York and London to Washington to raise some fine points about the impact of the financial reform. In a jargon-laden, 23-slide presentation, the JPMorgan bankers walked regulators through the complexities of how their decisions would affect the arcane market, according to documents and a person familiar with the meeting. On July 2, the US Federal Reserve released the final rule. Of three requests made by JPMorgan—which were backed widely by other banks and lobby groups—regulators rejected the first, adopted the second and split the difference on the third. The episode highlights the less antagonistic approach Wall Street is taking as it tries to blunt the force of the *Dodd-Frank Wall Street Reform and Consumer Protection Act*, the 848-page legislative response to the financial crisis. Sunday marks the three-year anniversary of its passage. Bank executives, lawyers and lobbyists now portray themselves as concerned parties trying to help stretched technocrats, who face the task of writing hundreds of complex rules to regulate high finance. The current strategy contrasts with the knock-down, drag-out fights that occurred during the legislative process—and even afterward, as bank lawyers battled agencies in court, and lobbyists fought to repeal Dodd-Frank in Congress. ...

"Rules being fashioned now can make a difference of billions of dollars in profits for banks. How they are written will also determine the stability of the financial system and the ability of the world to avoid another crippling crisis in the future. "The lobbyists might be less vocal, but they are constantly deploying their forces by visiting regulators," said Mayra Rodriguez Valladares, managing principal of MRV Associates, a firm that advises banks and regulators on implementing the new rules. In the derivatives market, for example, reform broadly calls for banks to hold more capital against risky positions. The rules, such as the ones JPMorgan met with regulators about in March, will determine how much money banks have to set aside to protect against trading losses and how risk is calculated. That means every little detail counts, especially for banks like JPMorgan, Citigroup Inc, Bank of America Corp and Goldman Sachs Group Inc, which together control more than 90 percent of the U.S. derivatives markets. "The American banks are going to fight this tooth and nail because their derivative positions are huge beyond belief," said Rodriguez Valladares. ...

"Shedding more light on the opaque derivatives market was a central tenet of the Dodd-Frank law, but it has been difficult for an agency that saw its tasks vastly expanded while its budget stayed the same. Scott O'Malia, one of the CFTC's four commissioners, said the agency is still unable to analyze the data. With just a handful of people working on the problem, he expects it to take "a lot of time and a lot of staff effort" to fix it. There is a less sunny view of the industry's rulemaking dialogue with regulators as well. Several sources referred to "regulatory capture" and "revolving doors," in which bankers become too friendly with regulators, who water down rules and later get cushy jobs on Wall Street. Resigned to reform, Wall Street tries a different tack in DC."[710]

On Wednesday, October 30th, 2013, a crucial vote was taken in the US House of Representatives, on whether there should be meaningful regulation of the types of till-now unregulated financial derivatives that brought down the world's economies in 2008. In order to be able to get this legislative measure, which is a bill to repeal Section 716 of the *Dodd-Frank Act*, to pass in the Republican House with some Democratic votes, and not only with Republican votes, Wall Street's operatives literally lied through their teeth.[711] In other words, Wall Street and its agents blatantly lied here. In fact: Barney Frank, Sheila Bair, and Maxine Waters vigorously condemned this Republican bill.

> Barney Frank said: "Citigroup wrote a bill that's about gutting a provision of Dodd-Frank called 'swaps pushout' that says you can't have derivatives in the place where you have your grandma's savings account ... insured. ... I wanted to be able to kill it." He regretted that he was not able to get it killed.
>
> Bair said: "I opposed the original [Blanche] Lincoln Amendment" in the Senate, "as it would have pushed all derivatives activity completely outside of regulated bank holding companies. ... I do not support efforts to repeal section 716. ... This [misrepresentation] is really annoying."
>
> Waters herself had been one of the only 6 members of the House Committee on Financial Services who voted against this measure even being put to a House vote (53 members on that Committee voted for it to go to a vote of the full House). On October 30th, she yet again voted against it, when the full House finally did take it up.
>
> There is thus no real question that Wall Street and its agents were lying to say that those three—each one of whom had helped actually to lead in support of enforcing Section 716 of the Dodd-Frank Act—endorsed repealing that key provision.
>
> ... [O]nly 122 members of the U.S. House of Representatives voted against repealing this crucial protection of U.S. Taxpayers—this crucial provision to not extend to Wall Street's gambling casinos the federal insurance that was originally intended only for ultra-safe savings accounts and checking accounts. (That roll-call is where you will see Maxine Waters' floor-vote against the repeal-measure.) There were 292 "Aye" votes, including 222 Republicans, and 70 Democrats. There were only 122 "No" votes, including 3 Republicans, and 119 Democrats. (One of the 70 Democrats who voted to gut Section 716, and so, in effect, to hold the U.S. public again vulnerable to bailing out the Wall Street mega-banks if their gambles go bad, was congressperson Debbie Wasserman Schultz, the friend of Hillary Clinton that Barack Obama chose to head the Democratic National Committee; so, the corrupt Democratic Establishment were in league with virtually all Republicans on this. The only 3 clean Republicans here were: John Duncan of Tennessee, Walter Jones of N.C., and Thomas Massie of Kentucky.)
>
> 119 Democrats and 3 Republicans voted against extending federal insurance to Wall Street's casinos. 222 Republicans and 70 Democrats voted in favor of extending federal insurance to Wall Street's casinos.
>
> No House vote in recent memory could be a clearer indication of the identities of the members of the House of Representatives who actually represent Wall Street, and of the members who represent the public that elected them.
>
> Wall Street evidently owns 292 members of the U.S. House. Only 122 members are not owned by Wall Street.
>
> Its something worth making note of. Apparently, at least 292 members of the U.S. House are corrupt—they are the ones whose owners are, clearly, the mega-financial institutions, who benefit from this taxpayer-funded gravy-train for the most elite category of gamblers.[712]

The Washington Wall Street enterprise revolving door feeds and nurtures their mutually beneficial partnership in currency debasement.

Why has so little been done about banks' market manipulation? The LIBOR scandal is a major example. Nothing has been done to replace this manipulate-able (and manipulated) figure, a fictional number that remains the basis of a more than $300 trillion market. And every day we are exposed to new stories of banks manipulating one market or another—most recently, energy and ethanol credits. The list of issues goes on.

The causes of much of this neglect are all too obvious: congressional lobbying combined with a revolving door, with too many people in the administration too closely tied to the financial sector. The banking industry has a well-oiled propaganda machine, trying to convince everyone that all is well, if only we could dial the clock back. The administration too has a well-oiled propaganda machine, trying to convince everyone that, having pulled the economy back from the brink, they are well on the road to creating a financial sector that will support sustainable and shared prosperity. But Americans know otherwise.[713]

CHAPTER 9

Enforcement of Financial Crisis Accountability

§9.01 NATURE OF CLAIMS FOR FINANCIAL CRISIS ACCOUNTABILITY

Why do ordinary Americans need to band together to advance the claims for damage directly caused by financial crises judicially under the American rule of law? Congress, the Fed, the DOJ and the array of federal financial regulars have quite simply refused to follow and enforce existing law. The FDIC has established standards for reasonable prudent banker. These same standards should also apply to financial regulators and Congress. Duty is inherent in delegation of power to the empowered and in the exercise of that power in the interest of those who delegated the power under the rule of law.

Each individual officer, director and manager on Wall Street or in the corridors of power in Washington has at some point determined that he or she has met their applicable duty and standard of care and that their individual and institutional deliberations decisions and action have complied with those standards, in the performance of their honored and trusted roles as experts in American monetary matters. They have publicly and continuously assured their constituents they deserve and have honored the trust Americans' trust; that the people may rest assured with confidence that the experts to whom Americans have honored and entrusted with exclusive power over the integrity, honesty safety and soundness of their sovereign money, have met their moral and legal duties; and that they have placed the interests of their constituents above their own narrow self-interest in aggrandizement and amassing of wealth and power. They have done so knowing full well, without doubt, that failure to meet their moral and legal duties in the exercise of their power inevitable results in financial crises and massive financial and economic damage to and accompanying widespread suffering of their constituents.

The facts clearly confirm that the privileged and trusted individuals and institutions have demonstrably, intentionally, and repeatedly failed to meet their clear moral and legal duties and standards of care. Washington's and Wall Street's progressive hegemony over and corruption of American money has been accompanied by increasing abuse of their power and resort to policies and actions that are based on lying, cheating and stealing. Washington's and Wall Street's failures to act morally and legally have caused every financial crisis in American history. These parties have effectively insulated themselves from array of damages they have inflicted on those outside of Washington and Wall Street. Ordinary Americans now face the continuing debasement and confiscation of their wealth and income, economic stagnation, untold personal suffering, exacerbated by the ever-widening wealth and income gap between American society and the privileged few on Wall Street and in Washington.

The policy and decision patterns predicating American financial crises have occurred and recurred over millennia, ever since governments and bankers discovered that money debasement conducted progressively and insidiously was the ticket to more and more wealth and power for them all. It is Washington's and Wall Street's now entrenched sense of entitlement to abuse their delegated and entrusted powers over money matters to lie, cheat and steal themselves into positions of wealth and power historically claimed by tyrants and despots, rather that trusted and privileged public servants.

These patterns are well known in the literature of the history of money, banking and government finance, most often conducted by tyrants and despots. This abuse of power is worked by the banks and government exploiting the trust and confidence reposed in them. They have been able to do so without moral or legal accountability based upon their monopoly roles as experts in all aspects of money, credit, law, accounting, and the lawful discipline and representation of the value of money and accordingly the liquid value of the assets denominated in the official units of American sovereign money that supports the entire American and global monetary systems. Neither Washington nor Wall Street have been willing to acknowledge their duties, standards of care or their abuse of power willingly.

Ordinary Americans exercise of their legal rights under the American rule of law through the judicial process is the last best hope for escaping the historically inevitable violent and bloody consequences of the tyrannical and despotic triumph of Washington government's and Wall Street bankers' abuse of power through money debasement of money.

Washington and Wall Street continue to maintain that their compliance with laws that would serve to curb financial crises would, in fact, cause future financial crises. They discount their wrongful conduct as merely immoral but justified by exigence circumstances; the exigent circumstances being not the service of the public interest consistent with their power, but rather their continued march to financial and economic domination of the American and global economies without accountability. Washington and Wall Street continue to assure the public that they have, in fact, met the duties that are inherent in their powers as our trusted experts in matters of money and the economy. Washington and Wall Street continue to adjure the public that they are doing the best they can and that we just trust them. Despite the hope of financial reform under *Dodd Frank*, Washington and Wall Street have refused to tolerate any meaningful legislative action imposing on them liability for their intentional misrepresentation of the values of assets constituting our monetary and financial system that caused the recent financial crisis. They have continued to exploit their self-promoted and self-interested insulation from accountability by continuing and compounding their false narrative of the moral, legal and honorable exercise of their powers.

The record chronicled in this work confirms that Washington's and Wall Street's actions causing financial crises have been taken through abuse and exploitation of the powers they have seized, through an ongoing program of dishonesty and misrepresentation of facts and law; entirely predictable, self-righteous and self-serving actions intended specifically to further their enterprise of self-interested amassment and concentration of wealth and power.

Washington and Wall Street's brazen disregard of the moral and legal significance and historically justified priority of honest, safe and sound money as the most fundamental and vital foundation for our virtuous compact as Americans under the rule of law is outrageous. When the seizure of power develops incrementally, and the conditions to and limits on the wrongful and illegal exercise of such power are progressively and openly ignored and subverted, it hardly seems possible for Americans to examine, explicate and connect the factors attendant to how money matters have gone so wrong, with such devastating consequences.

The moral and legal framework for American money and the perversion and manipulation thereof, though an enterprise wide abuse of power seems overwhelmingly complex. The complexity is real. The fundamental moral and legal principles against which the complexity must be measured and constrained under the American rule of law are simple.

This work details the historical moral and legal principles and the corrosive effects of Washington's Wall Street's formation of a corrupt racketeering enterprise developed through the abuse and exploitation of power in violation of these primer moral and legal principles. The Washington/Wall Street enterprise has been perpetrated to further, control and conceal the great wrongs that they have done under a scam of immunity through manufactured policies of "too big to fail or to jail," and abuse of power and trust through privileges of immunity through sovereignty. The sovereignty at issue here lies not in Washington or on Wall Street. It remains with the citizens of American who must now fight to defend it. The fight will be carries under the rule of law failing that, through violence.

Although it is Washington's responsibility to enforce the law of American money and it is Wall Streets' responsibility to comply with the letter, as well as the moral and substance, the spirit, of that law, Washington and Wall Street's intentional disregard of the longstanding and undisputed benefit to all Americans of the necessary compliance with the rule of law, the non-compliance has been downplayed and subverted. Wall Street's program of money debasement supported by Washington failure to act lawfully under cover of fraud and deceit, leaves private judicial action by Americans outside of Washington and Wall Street as the only remaining civilized option to impose the accountability of Washington and Wall Street for the financial crises and the $20 trillion of damages.

Judicially imposed legal accountability, privately enforced, is the last best hope for Americans to incentivize compliance with the existing American law of money. If Americans fail to grasp this hope through private judicial action, history has confirmed that eventually, probably sooner than later, the moral imperative will out and change will be wrought, accountability imposed and the America economic field will be leveled, outside of the rule of law, through violence and bloodshed that recaptures the people's powers over American sovereign money and allows no alternative but the dismantling and destruction of the corrupt monopoly, racketeering enterprise that is choking-off American economic dynamism. The recapture by Americans over the integrity, honesty, safety and soundness of their sovereign money, whether accomplished through action under the American rule of law or through violence, must result in a renewed, transparent and simple compact of honor, honest money under the rule of law resting on the moral foundation that first made the American dream possible.

The causes of the financial crisis follow a pattern repeated throughout history. As previously noted, the facts of this case were revealed in detail by the National Commission on the Causes of the Financial and Economic Crisis Inquiry in the United States (the "Commission") in *The Financial Crisis Inquiry Report*, published in January 2011 (the "Report"). It is interesting to note that the Dodd Frank financial reform legislation was passed January 5, 2010, approximately one year before Congress had in hand the facts and conclusions necessary to guide its law-making activity. As noted previously, between the vague nature of the legislation and its inclusion of provision for a wide range and number of interpretive regulations as well other detailed and discretion based operational details, there is very little in the legislation that could conceivably address the causes of financial crises as detailed in this work or in the Report

§9.02 THE TORTURED PATH OF THE LAW OF MONETARY DUTY AND ACCOUNTABILITY

Ordinary Americans are perplexed. The idea that money and banking are tools of fraud wielded by Washington and Wall Street remains unthinkable by ordinary Americans on many levels. They know something is wrong with the present monetary structure and policies; what is wrong specifically, they do not know. The literature addressing financial crises is notably lacking any penetrating analysis of the failure of law and accounting leading to the great financial crisis.

Our country was formed on a basis of safe, sound and honest money. The struggles of ordinary people who live and work for their family, community and their country are separate and distinct from the interests and priorities in Washington and on Wall Street; the denizens of which seek wealth and power at any cost. The struggle has been eternal. The positions of Washington and Wall Street are powerful. The institutions and individuals who occupy positions of power over the welfare of the public are entrusted with responsibility to put the public interest above their own. That is a fiduciary duty.

Black's confirms the basic fundamental moral and legal characteristics of a fiduciary, a fiduciary relationship and fiduciary duty. A fiduciary relationship is "one founded on trust or confidence reposed by one person in the good faith, integrity and fidelity of another." A fiduciary has a duty to act primarily for the benefit of those who have extended their trust and confidence to privileged individuals and institutions who create and control a society's money, who have accepted that trust and confidence, and especially those who have monopoly power in matters connected with the undertaking, and not for the fiduciary's own personal interest in derogation of the public interest. Scrupulous good faith and candor are always required. Fiduciaries must always act in complete fairness and may not ever exert any influence or pressure, take selfish advantage, or deal with those who have extended their trust in such a way that it benefits themselves or prejudices those who have relied on the honesty, good faith, trust, confidence and fidelity that forms the basis for the relationship. Business shrewdness, hard bargaining, and taking advantage of the forgetfulness or negligence of those who have are totally prohibited by a fiduciary. These concepts are ancient and straightforward. Governments and bankers are prime examples of fiduciaries. The power they have over the well-being of those who have entrusted with such trust and confidence, must be wielded with integrity and fidelity.

Washington and Wall Street viscerally recoil in outrage from any suggestion that they are fiduciaries in matters of the safety, soundness and honesty of money matters, including banking, shadow banking, and whether the nature of the money is sovereign money or credit "shadow" money.

Washington and Wall Street have adopted a pervasive policy of lying cheating and stealing to meet their own interests. Ordinary Americans suffer under it. We accept it because we cannot see any other viable, option. Sadly, many ordinary Americans have simply decided to join the zeitgeist in Washington and on Wall Street, and to glorify and aspire to benefits of lying cheating and stealing as a matter of policy. An exercise in the mistaken appraisal of dishonesty as virtue of competitive rugged individualism, self-reliance and self-interest. This exercise ignores the crucial role that honest, safe and sound money plays in binding our diverse culture together into the most prosperous and free country on earth. Because of Washington and Wall Street's open policy of money debasement and their adherence to a policy of monetary as well as fiscal manipulation to shelter the status quo, American society is deteriorating in front of our very eyes.

We have examined the nature of money, shadow money and money debasement. We know that sovereign money debasement is both immoral and illegal. We know that the struggle between the "haves" and the "have nots" as context was clearly understood at the time our *Constitution* became our law of the land. Honest safe and sound money was constitutionally mandated and money debasement was a capital crime. How has the unthinkable come to pass?

Washington's and Wall Street's false narratives. We have examined and refuted the most dramatic false narrative that money debasement and resulting financial crises are immoral but not illegal. We have examined and refuted the false narrative that the legal context at the time of the revolutionary war and the ratification or our *Constitution* somehow provided an open-ended endorsement of the unfettered ability of government and bankers to resort to money debasement as a legally and morally sanctioned public policy.

The following summary statements represent the most prominent of the ongoing series of Washington and Wall Street web of false narratives that, when aggregated, have formed and distorted the present American frame of reference for assessing the honesty and integrity of our banking and monetary system, as well clouding the firmly established moral and legal basis for Washington and Wall Street accountability for their wrongdoing. Each step in America's abandonment of honest, safe and sound money has been justified by successive determinations by Washington and Wall Street that each departure from honesty in money represents a case of the ends justifying the means and serving the public interest. But what ends? What means? The false narratives offered up by our experts in money and banking, Washington and Wall Street, suggest that the means and ends represented to the public by Washington and Wall Street are not honest. They are not in the public interest. The adherence to those false narrative does not protect the public from a fate imagined to be more damaging to ordinary American than the great financial crisis.

The means of money debasement is dishonest by its nature. The ends of aggrandizement of wealth and power by Washington and Wall Street has been accomplished by intentional misrepresentation of the systemic liquidity and asset values underlying and supporting our economy; by dishonesty. The exercise by Washington and Wall Street of monetary, as well as fiscal powers, are diametrically opposed to the public interest that they are intended to serve. Washington and Wall Street have not acted as fiduciaries. They have followed a well-documented path of lying to, cheating and stealing from those to whom they owe their fiduciary duties.

Let us consider the most egregious of the Washington and Wall Street false narratives as they developed from the seeds of our national formation.

§9.03 DENIAL OF DUE PROCESS UNDER AND EQUAL PROTECTION OF THE LAW

Washington and its agents and partners on Wall Street have denied to the people due process and equal protection of the law:

> "It is now the settled doctrine of this Court that the Due Process Clause embodies a system of rights based on moral principles so deeply imbedded in the traditions and feelings of our people as to be deemed fundamental to a civilized society as conceived by our whole history. Due Process is that which comports with the deepest notions of what is fair and right and just.[714]" Due process is violated if a practice or rule "offends some principle of justice so rooted in the traditions and conscience of our people as to be ranked as fundamental."[715]
>
> The content of due process is "a historical product" that traces all the way back to chapter 39 of *Magna Carta*, in which King John promised that "[n]o free man shall be taken or imprisoned or disseized or exiled or in any way destroyed, nor will we go upon him nor send upon him, except by the lawful judgment of his peers or by the law of the land." The phrase "due process of law" first appeared in a statutory rendition of this chapter in 1354. "No man of what state or condition he be, shall be put out of his lands or tenements nor taken, nor disinherited, nor put to death, without he be brought to answer by due process of law."[716] As expanded, it read: "No free man shall be taken or imprisoned or deprived of his freehold or his liberties or free customs, or outlawed or exiled, or in any manner destroyed, nor shall we come upon him or send against him, except by a legal judgment of his

peers or by the law of the land."[717] The 1225 reissue of the same text also added to chapter 29 the language of chapter 40 of the original text: "To no one will we sell, to no one will we deny or delay right or justice." This 1225 reissue became the standard text thereafter. England's brilliant and profound constitutional historian, [Henry] Hallam, has well said *Magna Charta* is the keystone of English liberty. "After all the past, is it needful to say what it means to deny right or justice to any man?"[718]

"The insertion of these words into the *Magna Charta* was intended to fix England's custom under King John of bringing gifts or payment to the King in order to obtain justice before his courts, or extorting fines from suitors or causing delay or denial to right of justice. In other words, under the 40th chapter the right to justice was no longer dependent upon the prerogative of anyone but the law of the land itself. This makes it easy to understand what protection of the laws the phrase speaks of: Equality of all people before the law where people receive the same protections of law against arbitrary injustice regardless of how rich, poor or color of skin."[719] The words of the 40th Chapter of the *Magna Charta*: "*We will sell to no man, we will not deny or delay to any man right or Justice*" provide the foundation for the American Legal Doctrine of the peoples' right to equal protection and due process under the law, including specifically, the *Constitution*, the "law of the land." Due process and equal protection under the American rule of law are grounded in the 5th and 14th Amendments to the *Constitution*. A complete treatment of these doctrines is beyond the scope of this this work.

Ordinary Americans are entitled to the equal protection of the United States *Constitution* against the debasement of their money by the corrupt monopoly racketeering enterprise of Washington and Wall Street in violation of Article I, § 8, Clause 5 of the *Constitution*. Washington and Wall Street may not collude and act to deprive ordinary Americans of the value their money purports to represent, and they may not conduct an open program to siphon off, literally steal, that value for their purposes and profits, without affording to the them due process of the American rule of law and without an explicit grant of equal protection to them. The web of protections afforded to Washington and Wall Street to insulate them from the consequences of their actions as a corrupt racketeering enterprise have been woven by abuse of power and by intentional bank fraud. Due process and equal protection are not to be found in a program of systemic fraud and abuse of power. Washington and Wall Street may not be permitted to engage in an ongoing and massive program of intentional misrepresentation of the value of assets in the banking system and the true state of that systems safety and soundness, which is the foundation for each and every economic transaction denominated in United States money.

The Wall Street banks are required to play their part in the coining of money and regulation of its value through the Federal Reserve and national banking systems in a constitutional manner that necessitates its regulation in accordance with a legitimate standard of value. Instead, Washington and the Wall Street Banks have intentionally ignored their constitutional imperative and abridged Americans civil right to enjoy the constitutional protection of the value of their money by reference to an external standard of value.

Washington and Wall Street have substituted an ever deteriorating and debased unit of money on their balance sheets, their books and records and in every transactional intermediation they conduct, the money unit they use is intentionally and inherently continuously made defective and corrupted; and more so, daily, by ever the increasing pace and amount of money ever more debased in value and character that serves to dispossess ordinary Americans of the value of the fruits of their labor. The intentional misrepresentation of value through the debasement of money enables Washington and Wall Street to unlawfully grasp it for their own profit without any semblance of due process and by the subversive and concealed manner of their deprivation of the American public of their property without due process of and equal protection under the American rule of law. The corrupt monopoly, cartel and racketeering scheme perpetuated by Washington and Wall Street deprives ordinary Americans of their right to equal protection of the constitutional right to coined money, the value of which has been regulated by Congress in accordance with a legitimate standard of value that will not admit its secret and intentional debasement. Any refusal by the courts to hear and resolve this case will constitute a denial of the peoples' right to justice through the enjoyment of their right due process and equal protection under the American rule of law; the law of the land.

The case made in this work made on behalf of the American public and the remedies to be sought in the case do not involve political questions. According to Manheim, "under the political question doctrine an issue, even a constitutional one, which the Court feels is best resolved by one of the other branches of government may denied judicial review under the political question doctrine. These issues are generally political in nature, and the court feels that the political system of accountability is the best mechanism to resolve the issues, as opposed to a mandate from the courts. Often, these issues are either given wholly to another branch of government in the *Constitution*, or there is a lack of judicially manageable standards for resolving it, or for a number of other reasons." As noted earlier, the enforcement by the public of the law of the land does not raise a political question. The intentional systemic abuse of power and bank fraud by the Washington and Wall Street corrupt racketeering enterprise is political only because it is illegal. Enforcement of the existing law of the land, including the *United States Constitution* simply confirms the moral and political standards already embodied in that law.

§9.04 ABUSE OF POWER: ANTI-TRUST, ANTI-MONOPOLY AND ANTI-TYING LAW

Federal anti-trust, anti-monopoly law addresses Washington's and Wall Street's abuse of power.

The Great Depression and the Washington and Wall Street abuses of power chronicled in the *Pecora Report* of 1934 led to the *Glass–Steagall Banking Act of 1933*, the *Securities Act of 1933*, and the *Securities Exchange Act of 1934*, also led to the *Robinson Patman Act of 1936*, building on the *Clayton Antitrust Act and the Federal Trade Commission Acts, both of 1914*, and the *Sherman Antitrust Act of 1890*. These laws form the bulk of federal laws and are, generally speaking, designed to protect the numerous and weak of economic society from domination by the concentrated monopoly power of the few. Banks, specifically the Wall Street banks, have been largely ignored in the application of anti-trust, anti-monopoly laws. To the extent applied their focus has been on mergers and acquisition of bank holding companies and have been viewed through the perspective of Federal bank regulatory authorities. According to a paper by the Federal Reserve Bank of Kansas City, "[t]he *Federal Deposit Insurance Act* ('FDIA'), the *Bank Holding Company Act* ('BHCA'), and the *Change in Bank Control Act* ('CIBCA') provide for the antitrust review of bank and bank holding company transactions and change in control notifications. The wording of the antitrust sections in these acts is similar and incorporates the standards set out in the *Sherman Antitrust Act* and the *Clayton Act*."[720]

Despite the overarching objective of the antitrust-antimonopoly laws to protect our marketplace from abuse of power derived from enterprise size and market dominance, the too big to jail and too big to fail rhetoric emanating from Washington currently has managed by bypass any semblance of accountability of Washington or Wall street for the collective abuse by these elites of the power, trust and confidence reposed in them by ordinary Americans. Notwithstanding the web of legislation potentially, or theoretically applicable to the imposition of accountability for these governmental and, primarily financial institutions, for the financial crisis, abuse of power has simply been accepted as business as usual. Once again a false narrative of the immunity of Washington and Wall Street for the predations they inflict on ordinary Americans is assumed to be a fact. Rising political figure and law professor at Duke University has speculated publicly, but not definitively on the potential application of the "antitrust framework" to the too big to fail banks.[721] The application of legal restrictions on institutional abuse of power however, could find no more fertile ground than application to Washington and Wall Street to curb the abuse of their power as a monopoly cartel for the exploitation of honest American money through institutional, systemic money debasement:

> The anti-tying provision was specially designed to address Congress' concerns with the banking industry, but there are other antitrust statutes that can be used against banks and other commercial enterprises. The *Sherman Act* was enacted in 1890 to prevent all types of antitrust violations, from monopolies to price-fixing to tying. Section 1, which prohibits all contracts, combinations and conspiracies in restraint of trade or commerce, is codified at 15 U.S.C. § 1.185 Section 3 of the Clayton Act (15 U.S.C. § 14), enacted in 1914, also prohibits tying arrangements; however, it applies only to the sale or lease of goods, not services. The Federal Trade Commission Act, section 5 (15 U.S.C. § 45), also enacted in 1914, has been used against antitrust violators, but it is much broader, encompassing all forms of unfair competition.
>
> These antitrust statutes are related to the BHCA, although they are different in many ways. Nonetheless, they can be used in conjunction with the anti-tying provision to address antitrust violations by banks and other financial institutions.
>
> To establish a *per se* illegal tying arrangement under the Sherman Act, a plaintiff must demonstrate: (1) two separate products or services, with the sale of one (the tying product) conditioned on the purchase of the other (the tied product); (2) a seller having sufficient economic power with respect to the tying product to appreciably restrain competition in the market for the tied product; and (3) a tie-in affecting a "not insubstantial" amount of interstate commerce. There are circumstances, however, when two products may be sold together; for example, when there is a business justification for doing so, such as quality control.

> While the other antitrust statutes can be used against banks, it is easier to prevail on an anti-tying provision claim because there are fewer elements to prove. A plaintiff could lose under one or more statutes though, for different reasons. In both *Clark v. United Bank of Denver Nat'l Ass'n*193 and *Pappas v. NCNB Nat'l Bank of N. Carolina*,194 the plaintiffs lost on Sherman Act claims for failing to prove sufficient market power of the defendants, and lost on BHCA claims because the conduct fell within the scope of "appropriate traditional banking practices."[722]

Fortunately, the issue of Washington and Wall Street abuse of monopoly power is not totally subsumed in institutional dissembling. BHCA, 12 U.S.C. § 1972 prohibits a bank from extending credit, leasing or selling property, or furnishing any service on the condition or requirement that the customer provide or obtain something else in the process, or refrain from obtaining something else from a competitor of a bank. In short, 12 U.S.C § 1972 prohibits three types of conditional transactions:

(i) traditional tie-in arrangements;
(ii) reciprocal arrangements whereby the customer agrees to provide the bank with something of value in exchange for the bank's product or service; and
(iii) exclusive dealing arrangements.

Not all bank tie in arrangements are *per se* illegal under this section. Congress provided a limited exemption in 12 U.S.C. § 1972 for transactions exclusively involving four so-called traditional banking services—specifically, loans, discounts, deposits, or trust services. This exemption only applies, however, where all of the components of a particular transaction fall into one or more of the four enumerated categories. If any of these so-called traditional banking services are tied to another service offered by the bank, the exemption does not apply. Finally, even within the four exempted bank service categories, the bank is still subject to treble damage actions under the antitrust laws. 12 U.S.C. § 1972 provides for substantial civil penalties to be enforced and collected in the case of a national bank, by the Comptroller of the Currency; in the case of a State member bank, by the Federal Reserve Board; and in the case of an insured non-member State bank, by the Federal Deposit Insurance Corporation.

Private right of civil action against any "Institution Affiliated Parties" is available to enforce criminal laws under 12 U.S.C. § 1972 and recover treble damages. 12 U.S.C. § 1975 provides for a private right of action by a bank customer that may recover treble damages and costs including reasonable attorneys' fees. The law applies to Institution Affiliated Parties, including officers and directors of institutional corporate defendants, making them personally, and individually responsible for the damage they have caused. To establish a tying arrangement generally, a bank must require a customer of the bank to accept from or provide to the bank, the holding company of such bank, or a subsidiary of the bank's holding company, additional credit, property or service. In this case:

(1) Condition 1: The Wall Street banks
(2) Condition 2: Agreed to handle their customers' banking relationship—if and only if

(3) Condition 3: The customers and their counterparties throughout the economy agreed to:
   - accept and rely on a unit of money which the Wall Street banks knew represented;
   - a debasement of the value of the money units in which the transactions were denominated; and– ("accept property from the BHC").

The Wall Street banks customers and their counterparties throughout the American public have agreed to accept debased units of money notwithstanding and without knowledge of the money's defect in presentation of an actual debasement, an intentional reduction of its value, thereby "accepting credit or property from and providing credit or property to the bank."

Washington and the Wall Street banks have all benefited from the proliferation of progressively more debased and defective money to serve their own individual objectives of concentration of wealth, power and control over the economy through their monopoly racketeering cartel while incrementally and continuously redistributing the incomes, savings and wealth of the American public to the combined sphere of power and control of the ever expanding criminal enterprise combination.

§9.05 BANK FRAUD AND RICO

Under RICO, 901(a) of the *Organized Crime Control Act of 1970,* Chapter 96 of 18 U.S.C. §§ 1961-1968, a person who is a member of an enterprise that has committed any two of the foregoing crimes (bank fraud included) within a 10-year period can be charged with racketeering.

Bank fraud through intentional criminal and civil misrepresentation under (among other defined predicate acts under RICO) 18 U.S.C. § 1341 (relating to criminal mail fraud), 18 U.S.C. § 1343 (relating to criminal fraud by wire, radio, or television); and 18 U.S.C. § 1344 (relating to criminal financial institution fraud):

> 18 U.S.C. § 1341. Frauds and swindles. Whoever, having devised or intending to devise any scheme or artifice to defraud, or for obtaining money or property by means of false or fraudulent pretenses, representations, or promises, or to sell, dispose of, loan, exchange, alter, give away, distribute, supply, or furnish or procure for unlawful use any counterfeit or spurious coin, obligation, security, or other article, or anything represented to be or intimated or held out to be such counterfeit or spurious article, for the purpose of executing such scheme or artifice or attempting so to do, places in any post office or authorized depository for mail matter, any matter or thing whatever to be sent or delivered by the Postal Service, or deposits or causes to be deposited any matter or thing whatever to be sent or delivered by any private or commercial interstate carrier, or take or receives therefrom, any such matter or thing, or knowingly causes to be delivered by mail or such carrier according to the direction thereon, or at the place at which it is directed to be delivered by the person to whom it is addressed, any such matter or thing, shall be fined under this title or imprisoned not more than 20 years, or both. If the violation affects a financial institution, such person shall be fined not more than $1,000,000 or imprisoned not more than 30 years, or both.

18 U.S.C. § 1343. Fraud by wire, radio, or television Whoever, having devised or intending to devise any scheme or artifice to defraud, or for obtaining money or property by means of false or fraudulent pretenses, representations, or promises, transmits or causes to be transmitted by means of wire, radio, or television communication in interstate or foreign commerce, any writings, signs, signals, pictures, or sounds for the purpose of executing such scheme or artifice, shall be fined under this title or imprisoned not more than 20 years, or both. If the violation affects a financial institution, such person shall be fined not more than $1,000,000 or imprisoned not more than 30 years, or both.

18 U.S.C. § 1344. Bank fraud Whoever knowingly executes, or attempts to execute, a scheme or artifice—(1) to defraud a financial institution; or (2) to obtain any of the moneys, funds, credits, assets, securities, or other property owned by, or under the custody or control of, a financial institution, by means of false or fraudulent pretenses, representations, or promises; shall be fined not more than $1,000,000 or imprisoned not more than 30 years, or both.

A RICO criminal claim requires proof of four elements, all of which are proved without doubt by the facts appearing as a matter of public record:

- the existence of an enterprise affecting interstate commerce;
- that defendants were employed by or associated with the enterprise;
- that the defendants participated, directly or indirectly, in the conduct or affairs of the enterprise; and
- that the defendants participated through a pattern of racketeering activity that must include the allegation of at least two racketeering acts.

Private right of civil action is available against any "enterprise associated person" to enforce criminal laws under RICO and recover treble damages. Persons injured by reasons of a RICO violation have a civil cause of action under the terms of the act. 18 U.S.C. §§ 1962(c), 1964(c) provides for liability in civil suits brought by any person injured "in his business or property" by a RICO violation, with a compulsory award of treble damages, costs, and attorneys' fees and makes it unlawful for *"any person" who is employed by or associated with 'any enterprise' affecting interstate commerce to 'participate, directly or indirectly, in the conduct of such enterprise's affairs through a pattern of racketeering activity, Making these parties personally, individually, responsible for the damages they have caused."*[723] (Authors' emphasis added in italics)

Also, under RICO, 18 U.S.C. § 1961 B, "racketeering activity" includes any act which is indictable under 18 U.S.C. § 1511 (relating to the obstruction of state or local law enforcement), 18 U.S.C. § 1512 (relating to *tampering with a witness, victim, or an informant*), 18 U.S.C. § 1513 (relating *to retaliating against a witness, victim, or an informant*; relating to possible *acts of interference or retaliation by targets of assertion by Washington or Wall Street of the complaints contemplated by this strategy under RICO*. See also, 18 U.S.C. § 1505 (relating to obstruction of proceedings before departments, agencies, and committees); 18 U.S.C. § 1510 (relating to *obstruction of criminal investigations*); and 18 U.S.C. § 2073 (relating to *false entries and reports of moneys or securities*). The Feds mandate to manipulate money and interest, ostensibly to serve the public interest, has been dramatically corrupted through the influence of Wall Street banks and their captive Congressional and federal financial regulator servants. The intentional manipulation of asset values and liquidity has eroded the fundamental American constitutional protection against fraud on the American public and our trading partners, accomplished through debasement of American money. The long list of additional federal criminal statutes enacted by Congress that might reasonably be considered to support enforced by the Justice Department to protect the American public from the fraud perpetrated by money debasement have only been ignored. These criminal statutes include: 18 U.S.C. § 371 Conspiracy to commit offense or to defraud United States; 18 U.S.C. § 471 Obligations or Securities of United States; 18 U.S.C. § 472 Uttering Counterfeit Obligations or Securities; 18 U.S.C. § 491.Tokens or Paper used as Money; 18 U.S.C. § 1001 Statements or Entries Generally; 18 U.S.C. § 1005 Bank Entries, Reports and Transactions; 18 U.S.C. § 1016 Acknowledgment of Appearance or Oath;18 U.S.C. § 1018 Official Certificates or Writings; 18 U.S.C. § 1341 Frauds and Swindles; 18 U.S.C. § 1343; Fraud by Wire, Radio, or Television; 18 U.S.C. § 1344 Bank Fraud; 18 U.S.C. § 1346. Definition of "scheme or artifice to defraud"; 18 U.S.C. § 1349. Attempt and Conspiracy; 18 U.S.C. § 1505 Obstruction of Proceedings before Departments, Agencies, and Committees; 8 U.S.C. § 1621 Perjury Generally; 18 U.S.C. § 2073 False Entries and Reports of Moneys or Securities. As noted above and presented in more detail in the Appendix, the Bank Fraud and Wire Fraud statues can be enforced under the *Racketeer Influenced and Corrupt Organizations Act* "RICO" 18 U.S.C. §§ 1961-1968. The Department of Justice has only recently considered the application of bank fraud statutes and RICO to the fraud in the financial crisis—but have limited their interest to damage to banks rather that damage caused by banks, ignoring the fundamental fraud of money debasement.[724] (Authors' emphasis added in italics)

I have identified the legal elements of ordinary Americans' moral and legal case against Washington and Wall Street for damages caused by the financial crisis. The foregoing federal statutes pertaining to bank fraud conducted by unconstitutional abuse of powers are cited and described briefly.

The simple statement of the ordinary Americans' legal case is that Washington and Wall Street acting in concert, as a corrupt racketeering enterprise, have systematically and intentionally abused the powers entrusted to them to fraudulently debase American money, and to thereby lie to, cheat and steal from ordinary Americans the value of the fruits of their honest labor and capital as wages, income from accumulated assets, that are necessary to the existence and wellbeing of their families. There is but little of legal importance more vital to ordinary Americans than honesty in their monetary affairs. The status quo in American money matters is the financial and economic equivalent to sufferance of physical assault, battery and yes, even murder.

Washington and Wall Street must account for their abuse of power through fraudulent money debasement by payment of damages and punishment to deter future wrongdoing, motivate and set the ground rules to restore honest, safe and sound money to the American people as is their basic human, civil right.

[A] Origin of the Washington Wall Street RICO Enterprise

The racketeering enterprise in this case is an association in fact between and among all of the named defendants. The racketeering activity of the enterprise adversely affects interstate enterprises and this adverse impact proximately caused injury to the plaintiffs' through the financial and economic crisis. Such racketeering activity includes at least two acts of racketeering within ten years of each other, and that the predicate acts had a common relationship and continuity. When the United States *Constitution* was ratified, the country had no currency, no central bank and no banking system. The *Constitution* clearly provided that Congress had the power and duty to coin money, regulate the value thereof, and of foreign coin, and fix the standard of weights and measures. The clear intention of the authors of the *Constitution*, in particular James Madison, was that the coin be metallic specie and that use of paper currency be prohibited. Congress followed this intent, sometimes effectively and sometimes less so, until 1971 and the abandonment of the *Bretton Woods Accords*.

The country developed the use of paper currency backed by specie to facilitate commerce as well as to enable the government to more efficiently finance and implement the system of transfer payments inherent in the function of a central government. The requirement of currency in specie and paper currency backed by specie has been suspended periodically, substituting the use of purely fiat currency, under extraordinary circumstances of war requiring the creation of money to finance war, without the use of which to enable the successful waging of war the country and *Constitution* would cease to exist. These suspensions were extraordinary and expressly designed to be temporary acts of expediency. In each case, the value of the fiat currency was discounted in the marketplace to reflect holder and counterparty doubts of value and liquidity of the fiat money through redemption, both essential elements of sovereign money.

As the magnitude and diversification of the country's economy grew, Congress created a national banking system and later, a so-called central bank, the Fed, to facilitate the distribution and effective utilization of sovereign money. The United States banking system has developed in accordance with the Hamiltonian view that there exists and should exist and "special relationship" between the government whereby banking institutions, in exchange for privileges granted to the banks to create sovereign through leveraging bank deposits and credit money denominated as sovereign money, through loans, and to intermediate that money throughout the country to finance economic growth, control inflation and maximize employment.

[B] Application of Common Law and the *Restatement (Second) of Torts* § 874A[725]

In addition to the statutory causes of action described above, when a legislative provision protects a class of persons by proscribing or requiring certain conduct but does not provide a civil remedy for the violation, the court may, if it determines that the remedy is appropriate in furtherance of the purpose of the legislation and needed to assure the effectiveness of the provision, accord to an injured member of the class a right of action, using a suitable existing tort action or a new cause of action analogous to an existing tort action. The *Restatement (Second) of Torts* § 874A (1979), updated October 2013, Division 11. Miscellaneous Rules, Chapter 43; Rules Applicable to Certain Types of Conduct § 874A Tort Liability for Violation of Legislative (Constitutional) Provision, and the comments to § 874A detail the connection between the foundation of honesty as principle of natural law and moral law in the *Constitution*, as well as federal statutory and common law.

Restatement (Second) of Torts § 874A (1979), updated October 2013, Division 11. *Miscellaneous Rules*, Chapter 43. *Rules Applicable to Certain Types of Conduct* § 874A *Tort Liability for Violation of Legislative (Constitutional) Provision* applies to the tort of money debasement in violation of Article I, § 8 Clause 5 of the *Constitution*; the 5th and 14th Amendments to the *Constitution* protecting plaintiffs right to due process under and equal protection of the law and under the *Constitution*, federal bank and wire fraud statutes, asserted under the federal RICO statutes federal bank anti-tying (anti-monopoly—anti-trust) statutes.

In addition to the statutory causes of action described above, when a legislative provision protects a class of persons by proscribing or requiring certain conduct but does not provide a civil remedy for the violation, the court may, if it determines that the remedy is appropriate in furtherance of the purpose of the legislation and needed to assure the effectiveness of the provision, accord to an injured member of the class a right of action, using a suitable existing tort action or a new cause of action analogous to an existing tort action.

As used in § 874 A, according to Comment "a. Legislative provision," the term "legislative provision" includes constitutional provisions, such as Article 1 § 8 Clause 5 of the *United States Constitution*. The term "legislative body" is correspondingly used to designate Congress, administrative agencies, and the people or particular agency or organization promulgating a *Constitution* or establishing rules binding on members of the organization, including the appropriate Committees of Congress, the Board of governors of the Federal Reserve Board and the Federal Reserve District Banks.

As used in § 874 A, according to Comment "b. Express provision for remedy," The typical case falling within this Section is one involving a criminal statute that proscribes certain conduct and imposes a criminal penalty but says nothing about civil responsibility. In a case of this nature, it is obvious that the legislative body must have: (1) intended that civil liability be imposed; (2) intended that there be no civil liability; or (3) not contemplated the issue at all and therefore have had no specific intent regarding it. The civil and criminal statutes referred to in this work and cited as applicable to this case contemplate that civil liability for damages can be established by private action. A common law tort claim under § 874 A reinforces the statutory emphasis of the availability of this right and supports the plaintiffs statutory case against the defendants.

As used in § 874 A, according to Comment "c. No express provision for remedy", the typical case falling within this Section (874 A) is one involving a criminal statute that proscribes certain conduct and imposes a criminal penalty but says nothing about civil responsibility. In a case of this nature, it is obvious that the legislative body must have: (1) intended that civil liability be imposed; (2) intended that there be no civil liability; or (3) not contemplated the issue at all and therefore have had no specific intent regarding it. If the court determines that the legislative body did actually intend for civil liability to be imposed or not imposed, whether the intent is explicit or implicit, then the court should treat the situation as if it had expressly so provided. If this was the intent of the legislative body, a study of the text of the provision, including the title and preamble, if any, will often disclose the fact. Tracing the legislative history may sometimes prove helpful. It is the right of every American citizen to litigate in the Federal courts to enforce their rights and protections under the *Constitution* of the United States. Under the English common law, currency debasement was considered high treason, punishable by death. The *Coinage Act of 1792* "affixed the penalty of death for debasing the coinage." Considering the history of currency debasement and its application to the modern economy, the constitutional requirement for Congress to coin money and regulate the value thereof as well as the original congressional intent of 18 U.S.C. § 331: Coins and currency, and U.S.C. § 332: "Debasement of coins; alteration of official scales, or embezzlement of metals",—which follows on from the historical proscription of money debasement, a civil action for enforcement of the *Constitution* as well as these criminal statutes falls within the contemplation of § 874 A.

As used in § 874 A, according to "Comment d. Action by the court," if the court has reached the conclusion that the people of the United States, in establishing and adopting the *Constitution* of the United States, and granting specific enumerated powers and duties to Congress as in the power and duty to coin money and regulate the value thereof, the grant of the power and duty establishes actual intent either to establish a civil remedy to protect and enforce duty attached to the Congressional power as this Honorable Court must find in this case, the issue is settled, and this Honorable Court is warranted in declaring that it is complying with the legislative—or more specifically, constitutional, intent. Enforcement of 18 U.S.C. § 331 and 18 U.S.C. § 332 have languished and atrophied in the face of the abandonment by Congress of its constitutional responsibilities and the general uncertainty regarding Congress' purported delegation of its constitutional responsibilities to the Fed and the less than transparent role of the Wall Street Banks in implementing the purported Federal Reserve system responsibility to "coin and regulate the value of money."

James Madison's notes on the constitutional debates, in the Federalist papers and other contemporaneous commentary, clearly show how the framers of the *Constitution* "would have dealt with the concrete situation" if it had had the situation before it in the way in which it is now before the court. Perhaps more frequently, the figurative search for legislative intent involves looking for the policy behind the legislative provision, attempting to perceive the purpose for which it was enacted, and then, having ascertained that policy or purpose, determining the most appropriate way to carry it out and identifying the remedy needed to accomplish that result. In this case, the intent of the framers of the *Constitution* was to forbid the use of paper money and to protect the American public from the corrosive effects of money debasement and to avoid the social, political, economic and financial tragedies that have historically resulted from government programs of money debasement.

As used in § 874 A, according to "Comment f. Relationship to other torts." If, in a particular case, the court determines that it is appropriate to provide a civil action in order to effectuate the policy behind a legislative provision that civil action will normally sound in tort. A tort action is the form of civil relief that grants damages or injunctive relief for harm wrongfully inflicted upon or threatened to an interest of the injured party. (Cf. § 870). The cause of action will ordinarily be assimilated to the most similar common law tort. Common law torts were created by the courts, and they are still subject to being modified by the courts. If a legislative provision indicates the existence of a significant public policy within the jurisdiction, the courts, in furtherance of that policy, may judicially make modifications in the elements of a common law tort.

As used in § 874 A Comment "g. Special problems regarding federal legislation." There is a doctrine of "federal common law" in areas of distinctively federal concern. This doctrine has application in matters such as one in which the United States Government is involved because of its facilities or personnel, but in cases of this nature the federal courts have noted that their role is of narrower scope and more modest than that of state courts engaged in reshaping common law rules governing relations between private individuals ... Predominantly, however, the federal courts address areas of federal private remedy in terms of carrying forward a federal statute or a provision of the *United States Constitution*. All of this means that the federal courts have been much more inclined to treat the problem covered by this Section by discussion of the court's implying the right from the legislative intent. Justices of the Supreme Court have indicated their realization that there may not be any specific legislative intent controlling the court and that principles of statutory construction will not alone solve the problem. But a civil action for damages or for injunction is a particular remedial mechanism normally available in the federal courts; and the power to authorize damages or injunctive relief as a remedy for the vindication of a federal constitutional or statutory right is not exclusively in the hands of Congress but exists inherently in the courts. As said by Justice Harlan, concurring, in *Bivens v. Six Unknown Named Agents of Federal Bureau of Narcotics*, (1971) 403 U.S. 388, 403, n. 4, "The notion of 'implying' a remedy therefore, ... can only refer to a process whereby the federal judiciary exercises a choice among traditionally available judicial remedies according to reasons related to the substantive sound policy embodied in an act of positive law." Chief Justice Burger has spoken of "judicially creating a damages action ... to ensure the fulfillment of" the legislative purposes. *Piper v. Chris-Craft Industries, Inc.*, (1977) 430 U.S. 1, 41. The approach to the problem may perhaps be posed by suggesting that the legislative body, by creating the substantive right has authorized the court to provide, if necessary, a suitable remedy to make it effective. In essence, therefore, the principle set forth in this Section applies in the federal courts as well as the state courts. ... In the absence of a general federal common law tort of negligence in which to substitute the statutory rule of conduct for the general standard of reasonable care (see Comment e), the courts may find it necessary to supply a new cause of action in negligence instead of modifying an existing cause

As used in § 874 A Comment "h. Factors affecting the determination of whether the court should provide a tort remedy." The primary test for determining whether the courts should provide a tort remedy for violation of the legislative provision is whether this remedy is consistent with the legislative provision, appropriate for promoting its policy and needed to assure its effectiveness. Among the factors to which a court may be expected to give consideration in determining whether a tort remedy is appropriate and needed are the following:

(1) The nature of the legislative provision. How specific is the legislative provision in its regulation of conduct? In this case, both the court and the defendants were fully aware in advance that their conduct was prohibited? The legal, historical and constitutional foundation for this case involve a fundamental right to honest money and an honest, safe, sound and stable banking and financial systems based on constitutionally mandated "sovereign" money, the value, including liquidity of which, is regulated by Congress by reference to an external of standard of value, including liquidity.
(2) The adequacy of existing remedies. Consideration is given first to the remedies provided for in the legislative provision itself. The remedies provided for in the statutory claims in this case are sufficient to effectuate the policy of the legislation, but in the face of concentrated defense of these claims anticipated by the most powerful, wealthy, vested interests in this country, the courts' notice of the common law foundation for the constitutional and statutory claims is vital to the protection of the plaintiffs rights and interests. In this case multiple causes of action and multiple remedies are appropriate and are sought by the plaintiffs.
(3) The extent to which the tort action will aid or supplement or interfere with, existing remedies and other means of enforcement. In this case, the tort action is entirely consistent with the statutory claims made by the plaintiffs.
(4) The significance of the purpose that the legislative body is seeking to effectuate. How important is the policy behind the legislative provision? The plaintiffs' interest is a fundamental interest intended to be protected by the constitutional law of the land and the defendants' representatives charged with the protection of their fundamental and statutory rights are complicit in the wrongful action complained of in the case.
(5) The extent of the change in tort law. The plaintiffs' claims do not change tort law. The tort claims are made to substantiate and clarify the foundations of the plaintiffs' constitutional and statutory claims and appropriate to ensure that the plaintiffs' fundamental rights under the common law of tort, as well as constitutional and statutory law, implementing the common law principles of tort law as embodied in the *Constitution* and in federal statutory law are preserved and enforced in protection of the plaintiffs rights under the entire American rule of law.
(6) The burden that the new cause of action will place on the judicial machinery. This case presents a singular challenge to an ongoing course of wrongful conduct pursued by the most wealthy and powerful interests in the country in violation of the ancient common law, constitutional and statutory laws established to protect the public interest such the plaintiffs interests from such conduct, and the enforcements of those laws. The courts imposition of accountability for the violations of law and the granting of redress to the American people is of paramount importance. The facts are largely uncontested. Their application of the law of the land by the American Judiciary, as distinguished from, contrasted with and as opposed to the congressional and executive deference shown to these powerful defendants is a test of our American form of government and the primacy and effectiveness of the rule of law in America.

As used in § 874 A Comment "i. Scope of the legislative purpose." In this case the principles underlying the constitutional and federal statutory claims advanced by the plaintiffs are embedded in the common law, the *Constitution* and the legislative history of the statutes upon which plaintiffs' claims are based. The plaintiffs' claims and the facts upon which they are based defeat and repudiate any contention by the defendants that their privileged positions somehow afford to them some unwarranted immunity for their massive, ongoing, wrongful and corrupt conduct that has caused the greatest public damage of any criminal enterprise in history, including wars. The American judiciary must confirm that the principle set out in the 40th Chapter of the *Magna Charta* "we will sell to no man, we will not deny or delay to any man right or justice."

[C] Moral and Legal Character of Honest, Safe, and Sound United States Money

Money is a unit of account, standard and store of value and as a standard for value in deferred payments of credit. Value is not a property or characteristic of any one thing, in and of itself. The establishment of value is determined by an evaluation of one thing in terms of another thing. The establishment of value is a foundational concept permitting voluntary exchanges of things of value between two or more people. The relationship between people who exchange one thing for another thing is inherently social, on one hand, and economic on the other. The trust, confidence, honesty and integrity of these two kinds of relationships is essential to the establishment and maintenance of a harmonious and prosperous civil society. The fundamental objective and effectiveness of these social and economic relationships is the honest presentation of each thing to be exchanged with honesty so that an agreement with respect to value for exchange can be fairly determined. Honesty is the base for trust, confidence and integrity in economic relationships. Honesty as a moral virtue is the cornerstone of a just society. This is not surprise. Honesty is a virtue commonly understood in terms of commerce, justice and religion. A social and economic exchange is affected with honesty by full disclosure and assessment of the kind, quality and quantity of things in relationship to one another. With it, commerce and productivity thrive. Without honesty, uncertainty reluctance and hesitation in commerce often leads to isolation and distrust, and all too often, conflict violence and war. The development and use of money for its defined purposed in a civil society requires honesty in the translation of the value one thing in relationship to units of money, which must in turn be transferable to the value of the thing to be exchanged in terms of money. The moral values of society and its laws relating to commerce require honesty as the essential attribute of a successful medium of exchange, whether the exchange of value is made currently or deferred in whole or part over time. Honesty is central to the well-functional practice of exchanges of things where the relative value of things must be measured based on units grounded upon a common, mutually accepted standard. That is the essence of regulation of the value of money by reference to the best, most trusted of a standard. When commercial exchanges are made, the parties to the exchange must be honest, not only in tendering the kind, quality, and quantity of the item or items to be exchanged, but the medium through which they are exchanged must be honest. The honesty of the medium is determined in relationship to the most commonly trusted and accepted common standard of value in which all of the members of the society have confidence.

It is no accident that the use of standards based on gold and silver has an ancient and historical basis. The justification for the historical preference for gold and silver as the reference point for a monetary standard of value is well documented. Only within the past fifty years has governments in the US and globally dismissed gold and, and by implication, silver as "barbarous relics," unsuitable to serve as standards of value for the regulation of money. The critics of specie as standards for regulation of the value of money assert that, "there is not enough gold to support finance and commerce"; ... "the gold supply does not grow fast enough to support world growth," "gold caused the Great Depression," "gold has no yield, and gold has no intrinsic value."[726]

James Rickards, among other writers and commentators, has addressed and established the un-supportability of these the identified purported deficiencies of specie as suitable for standards for regulating the value of money and assuring the honesty of money for its social and economic purposes.[727] The use of specie, paper and digital data entries as money developed. The book details how the universe of shadow banking has overwhelmed and literally destroyed the use of any suitable and honest standard for the regulation of the value of money in the US, and globally. It describes the effects of stripping any trusted and honest standard of value for the regulation of the value of money from US dollar. The result has been a massive fraud on those who must use sovereign legal tender paper money and credit money denominated in those dollars; even those who voluntarily choose to use one sovereign legal tender paper money as opposed to any other; having made the determination that the money of choice may be the best of the bad available choices. This book establishes the basis for a determination that the intentional and fraudulent debasement of the United States dollar is a matter of fact. Because of the current process of money creation in the United States is conducted primarily by a combination of private market credit money production, i.e., banking system finance and shadow banking finance, by Wall Street in partnership between with the Fed; and public money production, i.e., public finance, by the Treasury Department in Washington in partnership with the Fed, Washington, including the Treasury and the Fed, and Wall Street bankers reap the profits inherent in the US money distribution system.

Jörg Guido Hülsman has produced an excellent work entitled "*The Ethics of Money Production*."[728] Hülsman's work, among things, describes the price and value distortions of fiat money through its production and distribution and absorption by the market:

> [T]he process through which money production tends to increase the price level is spread out in time. It therefore affects the different prices at different points of time—there is no simultaneous increase of all prices. Furthermore, there is no reason why prices should change uniformly or in some fixed proportion to the change of the money supply. Hence, money production entails a tendency for

> prices to increase, but this increase occurs step by step in a process spread out through time and affects each price to a different extent.[729]

In fact, the dominant characteristic in the distribution effect leading up to the great financial crisis was to concentrate money production and price increases in residential and commercial real estate and the chain of service providers participating in that "asset boom," described as it occurred as a "wealth" effect; confusing price increases with value increases, so that when the asset bubble burst, asset values and prices that were unsustainable by underlying market fundamentals suffered enormous losses for ordinary Americans, while the interests of Washington and Wall Street were and continue to be bailed out by a succession of emergency lending, bailouts, quantitative easing to artificially support values artificially low interest rates and time. Washington and Wall Street were too big to fail or jail. Not so for ordinary Americans:

> In addition to the unequal treatment of the money creators as opposed to ordinary people who must by law utilize this inherently defective monetary tool, [t]here is however another distribution effect of the production of money.
>
> This effect is far more important than the one we have just described because it does not depend on the market participant's expectations. It is an effect that the market participants cannot avoid by greater smartness or circumspection. To understand this distribution effect we must consider that exchange and distribution are not disconnected activities. In the market process, they are but one and the same event.
>
> Brown sells his apple for Green's pear. After the exchange, the distribution of apples and pears is different from what it otherwise would have been. Every exchange thus entails a modification of the "distribution" of resources that would otherwise have come into being. It follows that any production of additional goods and services is bound to have such an impact on distribution. The new supply of product redirects the distribution of wealth in favor of the producer.
>
> Consider the case of money production. Here too the additional quantities that leave the production process, when sold, first benefit the first owner: the producer. He can buy more goods and services than he otherwise could have bought, and his spending on these things in turn increases the incomes of his suppliers beyond the level they would otherwise have reached. But the additional money production reduces the purchasing power of money. It follows that it *also* creates losers, namely, those market participants whose monetary income does not rise at first, but who have to pay right away the higher prices that result when the new money supply spreads step by step into the economy.
>
> Money production therefore *redistributes real income from later to earlier owners of the new money*. As we have pointed out, this redistribution cannot be neutralized through expectations. Even the market participants who are aware of it cannot prevent it from happening. They can merely try to improve their own *relative* position in it, supplying early owners of the new money, preferably the money producer himself.
>
> This distribution effect is a key to understanding monetary economies. It is the primary cause of almost all conflicts revolving around the production of money... [I]t is therefore also of central importance for the adequate moral assessment of monetary institutions.[730]

Ordinary Americans do not understand that the production and distribution of money, the value of which is not regulated by reference to an external standards, will find their savings and income distorted, reduced in relative terms as compared to the growing wealth and income of Washington and Wall Street, who, acting together as a well-oiled enterprise, have monopoly power over money and wealth creation as well as protection from loss or accountability. This distribution effect, is the method by which Washington and Wall Street are able to intentionally misrepresent the effects of their actions, cheat and steal from ordinary American, producing a wealth and income gap of inequality on an unprecedented scale. The tool is dishonest money.

When evaluating the importance of honesty—a moral virtue—in the creation and use of money, the American public has been intentionally misled as to: (i) the importance of honest money, the immorality of Washington's and Wall Street's failure to use honest money, whether sovereign money such as the US dollar, credit money, or securities based on structured credit money; and (ii) the undisputable fact the creation and emission of that dishonest money constitutes tortious and criminal actionable as a matter of United States law.

[D] The Washington Wall Street Enterprise Has Denied to the American People Due Process and Equal Protection of the Law

The doctrines of due process and equal protection of the law are addressed in some detail in Suffice it for here to make a few observations. "It is now the settled doctrine of this Court that the Due Process Clause embodies a system of rights based on moral principles so deeply imbedded in the traditions and feelings of our people as to be deemed fundamental to a civilized society as conceived by our whole history. Due Process is that which comports with the deepest notions of what is fair and right and just."[731] Due process is violated if a practice or rule "offends some principle of justice so rooted in the traditions and conscience of our people as to be ranked as fundamental."[732]

The content of due process is "a historical product" that traces all the way back to chapter 39 of *Magna Carta*, in which King John promised that "[n]o free man shall be taken or imprisoned or disseized or exiled or in any way destroyed, nor will we go upon him nor send upon him, except by the lawful judgment of his peers or by the law of the land." The phrase "due process of law" first appeared in a statutory rendition of this chapter in 1354. "No man of what state or condition he be, shall be put out of his lands or tenements nor taken, nor disinherited, nor put to death, without he be brought to answer by due process of law." [See, W. McKechnie, *Magna Carta—A Commentary on the Great Charter of King John* 375-395 (Glasgow, 2d rev. ed. 1914)]. The chapter became chapter 29 in the Third Reissue of Henry III in 1225. *Id.* at 504, and see 139-159. As expanded, it read: "No free man shall be taken or imprisoned or deprived of his freehold or his liberties or free customs, or outlawed or exiled, or in any manner destroyed, nor shall we come upon him or send against him, except by a legal judgment of his peers or by the law of the land."[733] The 1225 reissue also added to chapter 29 the language of chapter 40 of the original text: "To no one will we sell, to no one will we deny or delay right or justice." This 1225 reissue became the standard text thereafter. England's brilliant and profound constitutional historian, [Henry] Hallam, has well said *Magna Charta* is the keystone of English liberty. "After all the past, is it needful to say what it means to deny right or justice to any man?"[734]

"The insertion of these words into the *Magna Charta* was intended to fix England's custom under King John of bringing gifts or payment to the King in order to obtain justice before his courts, or extorting fines from suitors or causing delay or denial to right of justice. In other words, under the 40th chapter the right to justice was no longer dependent upon the prerogative of anyone but the law of the land itself. This makes it easy to understand what protection of the laws the phrase speaks of: Equality of all people before the law where people receive the same protections of law against arbitrary injustice regardless of how rich, poor or color of skin."[735] The words of the 40th chapter of the *Magna Charta*: "*We will sell to no man, we will not deny or delay to any man right or Justice*" provide the foundation for the American legal doctrine of the peoples' right to equal protection and due process under the law, including specifically, the *Constitution*, the "law of the land." Due process and equal protection under the American rule of law are grounded in the 5th and 14th Amendments to the *Constitution*. A complete treatment of these doctrines is beyond the scope of this this work.

Ordinary Americans are entitled to the equal protection of the *United States Constitution* against the debasement of their money by the monopoly racketeering cartel of Washington and Wall Street in violation of Article I, § 8, Clause 5 of the *Constitution*. Washington and Wall Street may not collude and act to deprive the people of the value their money purports to represent, and conduct an open program to siphon off, literally steal, that value for their purposes and profits without affording to the public due process of the American rule of law and without an explicit grant of equal protection to ordinary Americans. Washington and Wall Street may not engage in an ongoing and massive program of intentional misrepresentation of the value of assets in the banking system and the true state of that systems safety and soundness, which is the foundation for each and every economic transaction denominated in United States money by the people.

The Wall Street banks are required to play their part in the coining of money and regulation of its value through the Federal Reserve and national banking systems in a constitutional manner that necessitates its regulation in accordance with a legitimate standard of value. Instead, Washington and the Wall Street Banks have intentionally ignored their constitutional imperative and abridged the peoples' privilege to enjoy the constitutional protection of the value of their money by reference to an external standard of value. Washington and Wall Street have substituted an ever deteriorating and debased unit of money on their balance sheets, their books and records and in every transactional intermediation they conduct, the money unit they use is intentionally and inherently continuously made defective and corrupted; and more so, daily, by ever the increasing pace and amount of money ever more debased in value and character that serves to dispossess the people of the value of the fruits of their labor. The intentional misrepresentation of value through the debasement of money enables Washington and Wall Street to unlawfully grasp it for their own profit without any semblance of due process and by the subversive and concealed manner of their deprivation of the people of their property without due process of and equal protection under the American rule of law. The corrupt monopoly, cartel and racketeering scheme perpetuated by Washington and Wall Street deprives the people of their right to equal protection of the constitutional right to coined money, the value of which has been regulated by Congress in accordance with a legitimate standard of value that will not admit its secret and intentional debasement. Any refusal by the courts to hear and resolve this case will constitute a denial of the peoples' right to justice through the enjoyment of their right due process and equal protection under the American rule of law; the law of the land.

The claims made by ordinary Americans and remedies sought in this case for financial crisis accountability do not involve political questions. According to Manheim, "under the political question doctrine an issue, even a constitutional one, which the Court feels is best resolved by one of the other branches of government may denied judicial review under the political question doctrine."

Not only has Congress failed to resolve the issue in accordance with the *Constitution*, it has conspired with the other defendants in the racketeering enterprise complained of here by the plaintiffs. Although issues of fiscal and monetary policy may be generally political in nature, and the court may feel that the political system of accountability is the best mechanism to resolve the issues, as opposed to a mandate from the courts, the crime and economic assault of money debasement conducted by Congress in a racketeering enterprise is a matter of legal accountability of the defendants as participants in a racketing enterprise, for intention injury in fact caused by the enterprise against the plaintiffs in this case.

The American establishment of congressional monopoly power and duty to create a national currency and to regulate its value in reference to an appropriate standard of value was settled by ratification of the *United States Constitution*. The first currency act enacted by Congress in 1792 created the American unit of money and established legitimate standards for its value. The act also provided that the debasement of the value of money was a capital crime punishable by death. The successive currency acts adopted by Congress prior to the Legal Tender Cases were acknowledged by the United States Supreme Court as proper regulation by Congress of the value of money in accordance with Congress' constitutional imperative.

§9.06 PUBLIC POLICY AND COMMON LAW PRECEDENT FOR THE CASE FOR FINANCIAL CRISIS ACCOUNTABILITY

[A] Common Law Evolution into Statutory Laws Regarding Securities Fraud and Crime as a Public Policy Precedent

The law applicable to securities fraud and crime do not strictly apply to the fraud and crime in the emission of money and regulation of its value, but the same first principles do apply. The SEC and the federal courts have emphasized that manipulation, in essence, interferes with the free forces of supply and demand, and, thus, the integrity of the market. The SEC consistently has stated that investors are:

> [e]ntitled to assume the prices they pay and receive are determined by the unimpeded interaction of real supply and real demand so that those prices are the

> collective marketplace judgments that they purport to be. Manipulations frustrate those expectations. They substitute fiction for fact . . . The vice is that the market has been distorted and made into a "stage-managed performance."[736]

The prohibitions against manipulative and deceptive acts under Section 10(b) and Rule 10b-5 apply to all securities, not just those registered on a national stock exchange. The SEC and the federal courts have established that pure manipulation—that is, merely undertaking acts to raise or lower the price of a security—constitutes a "manipulative or deceptive device" and a "scheme to defraud."

Section 17(a) of the *Securities Act of 1933*,[737] as amended, is also a general antifraud provision and applies to manipulation in the over-the-counter market. Section 17(a) proscribes material misrepresentations or omissions, any scheme, device or artifice to defraud, or any fraudulent or deceitful transaction, practice or course of business, in the offer or sale of securities.

Section 9(a) of the *Exchange Act*[738]specifically prohibits various manipulative practices. For example, Section 9(a)(1) prohibits the use of "wash sales" and "matched orders" for the purpose of creating a false or misleading appearance of active trading in any security registered on a national exchange. Section 9(a)(2) prohibits manipulation of prices by any person, acting alone or with others, who for the purpose of inducing others to buy or sell a particular security, effects a series of transactions in the security which creates actual or apparent active trading in the security or causes a rise or decline in the price of the security.

[B] Common Law Evolution into Statutory Consumer Protection Law as a Public Policy Precedent

The basis for the application of consumer fraud and consumer protection laws as an extension of the common law of deceit is well accepted.[739] Jean Braucher details the basis for application in Arizona Legal Studies, in a 2006 *Discussion Paper No. 06-43 Deception, Economic Loss and Mass-Market Customers: Consumer Protection Statutes as Persuasive Authority in the Common Law of Fraud.* Although money is excluded from the definition of a consumer product under consumer protection laws, the objectives of consumer protection law apply in this case.

According to Bruacher, "before the modern campaign for state consumer protection began, President Kennedy urged in a speech in 1962 that consumer rights to choice, information, and freedom from deception are matters of national interest.[740] Encouraged by the Federal Trade Commission,[741] state legislatures took up these principles and wrote them into law, typically providing both for state level public enforcement and private rights of action."[742]

"The popularity of consumer protection reflects a transformation of norms; deception in the marketplace may be common, but it is no longer considered acceptable behavior. As a result, the idea of a civil obligation not to use deceptive practices is hardly novel."[743] "Consumer protection statutes are sometimes restricted to household consumers, but mass-market customers buying for other uses are often subject to the same disadvantages when entering into transactions or seeking contractual relief for being cheated. Even a large business cannot afford to investigate for possible deception in every small purchase nor can it afford to pursue contract remedies when a small problem comes to light; it is more efficient for the law to recognize an obligation in sellers not to deceive their customers and to provide remedies that effectively deter that behavior. Tort law has a role to play that is different from contract. This is why the common law of fraud should be open to development by following the trail blazed by consumer protection statutes. It should not ossify or lie dormant because some of the most compelling fraud cases are now better pursued using a statutory theory":[744]

> Consumer protection is smart, popular policy, empirically well-grounded and part of minimum decency. Consumer protection in its myriad forms makes sense in an economy that measures its health by consumer confidence to go forth and spend exuberantly.[745] There has long been good evidence that, no matter what law professors and judges think consumers ought to do, most are not wary. For example, most consumers accept what the law considers obvious puffing as "completely true" or "partly true."[746] Furthermore, most consumers who feel cheated lump it without even complaining to the seller, let alone going to a lawyer.... [I]f there is a problem with consumer protection law, in this view, it is that it is seldom enforced, with the poor bearing the brunt of the ease with which con artists and slick operators can get away with their scams. The result is not only inefficiency but redistribution from the relatively worse off to the relatively better off.[747]
>
> The type of interest protected by the law of deceit is the interest in formulating business judgments without being misled by others—in short, in not being cheated. Generally, the law of deceit is limited to misrepresentations that mislead another into an unwise judgment in some business enterprise resulting in financial loss.[748]
>
> When the facts are peculiarly within the knowledge of the defendant and inaccessible to the plaintiff, commercial dealings between the parties must come to a halt unless the plaintiff can put confidence in reasonable accuracy of the defendant's statements. So, courts sometimes impose a duty of care when the defendant had peculiar knowledge or expertise.[749]

Congressional and regulatory failure leave judicial action as the last bastion to protect the public interest from financial crises; financial crises caused by broad-based abuse of trust and power, and failure of Washington and Wall Street to meet their duties and standards of care.

§9.07 CLASS ACTION IN *PARES PATRIAE* BY ONE OR MORE STATES ATTORNEYS GENERAL

The prosecution of a case for financial crisis accountability might be made by ordinary Americans as a class through private action directly, or through a representative, such as an action in *parens patriae* by one or more states attorneys general, on behalf of ordinary Americans resident in various states brought for Wall Street and Washington enterprise accountability.[750] State Attorneys General may prosecute a civil case based on the facts and law addressed in this book, in state or federal court.[751]

Throughout the history of money and banking, and particularly throughout America's history of money and banking, both Washington and Wall Street have, step by step, eroded the constitutional, statutory and common law protections for ordinary Americans against financial crises driven by intentional fraudulent money debasement through proliferation of outright misrepresentation of the rule of law. The Washington Wall Street enterprise has enacted laws and regulations that conflict with and purport to render obsolete ordinary Americans' moral and legal civil rights. The Washington Wall Street has proceeded openly, unapologetically, and unjustifiably ignoring and refusing to enforce existing laws applicable to abuse of trust and power, to commit fraudulent money debasement. Since the Nixon shock in 1971, Washington and Wall Street have promulgated a blizzard of banking laws, rules and regulations, that have been public represented to protect the honesty, safety and soundness of American money; but which, perversely have accomplished the opposite. Untangling the complex web of false narratives woven by Washington and Wall Street is complex on its face. But as Winston Churchill is to have said: "If you have ten thousand regulations you destroy all respect for the law." So, it has been in the area of banking and monetary law and regulation. The complexity in destruction of the law of safe and sound money and its moral foundation in honesty have been chronicled in the Commission's Report and in this work.

§9.08 DEFINITION OF A CLASS OF PLAINTIFFS IN A CASE FOR FINANCIAL CRISIS ACCOUNTABILITY

The plaintiff class consists of the either the American individuals or households of all American individual depositors, customers and counterparties of federally insured or regulated financial institutions and all American individuals or households whose credit or loan accounts at federally regulated depository financial institutions whose accounts and banking activities are denominated in United States official sovereign money, United Stated Federal Reserve Notes, within the ten year period preceding the publication of the Commission Report and who have suffered one or more of the actual or threatened injuries in fact objectively itemized by the government and expert reports as having been suffered by plaintiffs in common with one another, to a greater of lesser degree, and which are redressable by the remedies sought in this case, excluding however, any household including any executive employee, officer or director or controlling shareholder of any entity constituting a defendant in this case.

Estimates of the number of members of public who may qualify as members of the plaintiff class range from 155,559,000 to 159,068,557 ordinary people.

"According to the U.S. Bureau of Labor Statistics, there are 11,742,000 working age Americans that are officially unemployed. In addition, the US Bureau of Labor Statistics says that there are 89,967,000 working age Americans that are 'not in the labor force.' That is a new all-time record, and that number increased by a whopping 663,000 during the month of March alone. When you add 11,742,000 working age

Americans that are officially unemployed to the 89,967,000 working age Americans that are 'not in the labor force,' you come up with a grand total of 101,709,000 working age Americans that do not have a job." *More Than 101 Million Working Age Americans Do Not Have A Job* By Michael Snyder, on April 7th, 2013.

The Federal Reserve Bank of Dallas in 2013 estimated damages ranging from $50,000 to $120,000 per household, for a range of total damages of $6 trillion to $14 trillion based on their assumption of 120 million households. The United States Census, 2010—2014, prepared by the United States Department of Commerce estimates American households of 116,211,092 (http://www.census.gov/quickfacts/table/HSD 410214/00 estimates total U.S.).

The Dallas Federal Reserve Bank (Staff Paper NO. 20. July 2013 and *Economic Letter* Vol 8, NO. 7. September 2013), The U.S. Department of the Treasury (*The Financial Crisis Response in Charts*, April 2012—estimates $19.2 trillion in lost household wealth, or $160,000 per household based upon 120 million households), and the United States Government Accounting Office (*Report to Congressional Requesters, Financial Regulatory Reform—Financial Crisis Losses and Potential Impacts of the Dodd Frank Act*, January 2013, citing at page 20, The Federal Reserve's Survey of Consumer Finances' estimate of damage in the form of lost median household net worth of $49,000 per household, between 2007 and 2010) have all calculated loss, cost or damage by reference to American households. In addition, Better Markets in its reports on the cost of the crisis, dated, September 15, 2012 and July 2014, estimate, loss, cost or damage by house hold and on a gross basis, more than $12.8 trillion ($106,667 per household) in 2012, and more than $20 trillion ($166,667, per household) in 2015, respectively. Accordingly, the government would find it convenient to face a plaintiff's class composed of approximately 120 million American households, suffering damages of $83,334 per household, identified and calculated by the criteria set forth above.

The defendants effectively selected and defined the plaintiff class by: (1) the selection of the power they chose to usurp and abuse, the power to create sovereign money, the value of which is not regulated in accordance with the requirements of the *United States Constitution*, emitted through the Federal Reserve and national banking systems based upon the United States dollar as the medium for the discharge of all debts, public and private, and which is the exclusive American unit in use to denominate accounts, serve as a medium of exchange, a store of value and as a standard for deferred payments; and (2) the selection of the weapon they chose to wield in their economic and financial assault on their targeted victims, the tort of debasement of the dollar as used in all of its capacities, and specifically by the ordinary people and households of America who have looked to the powerful, privileged governmental, economic and financial institutions of America, Washington and Wall Street, to protect their interests in accordance with the law of the land. Instead, Washington and Wall Street combined as a criminal, corrupt racketeering enterprise to loot the value represented by the dollar through the weapon of fraudulent debasement, to profit and benefit the enterprise from that fraud and to shift the accompanying losses and damages onto unsuspecting ordinary working American households. A beating with the economic and financial cudgel of money debasement leaving economic losses and damages as the largest measurable component of the wounds, broken bones, cuts, bruises and ruined lives of ordinary working American households.

§9.09 ORDINARY AMERICANS HAVE SUFFERED DISCRETE, PALPABLE INJURIES IN FACT CAUSED BY THE WASHINGTON WALL STREET ENTERPRISE

[A] The Wall Street Defendants

- Goldman Sachs & Co, and Lloyd C. Blankfein, Chief Executive Officer and Chairman;
- JP Morgan Chase & Co., and James Dimon, Chief Executive Office
- Bank of America, and Ken Lewis, former Chairman and Chief Executive Officer;
- Morgan Stanley, and John J. Mack, Chairman and Chief Executive Officer;
- Citigroup, and Vikram Pandit, former Chief Executive Officer;
- Wells Fargo & Company, and John Stumpf, President and Chief Executive Officer; and
- Federal National Mortgage Association, or Fannie Mae; and
- The Federal Home Loan Mortgage Corporation, or Freddie Mac.
- All other executive officers and directors of the Wall Street Defendants in office during the applicable period of limitations in this case.

[B] The Rating Agency Defendants

- Moody's Corporation and Moody's Investors Service
- Standard & Poor's and Standard & Poor's Financial Services LLC,
- A.M. Best Company
- Fitch and Fitch Group
- And all other executive officers and directors of the defendant ratings agencies in office during the applicable period of limitations in this case.

Plaintiffs can seek damages, penalties and costs from the Wall Street defendants and the Rating Agency defendants.

[C] The Washington Defendants

- United States Congress;
- The Federal Reserve System;
- The Board of Governors of the Federal Reserve System;
- The Federal Reserve District Banks;
- The Office of the Comptroller of the Currency;
- The Securities and Exchange Commission;
- The United States Department of Justice;

- Commodity Futures Trading Commission

Plaintiffs can seek equitable relief against the Washington defendants. The defendants as a group, the Washington Wall Street enterprise, have acted in concert as a corrupt "racketeering enterprise" under the *Racketeer Influenced and Corrupt Organizations Act* "RICO" 18 U.S.C. §§ 1961-1968. A case for financial crisis accountability filed in federal court will have to comply with the *Manual for Complex Manual for Complex Litigation, Fourth*, Federal Judicial Center 2004, as it may be amended or replaced.

§9.10 PRACTICAL, TECHNICAL AND PROCEDURAL ISSUES

There are number of substantive, technical and procedural issues that will likely be posed in any case for financial crisis accountability. As a practical matter these issues must be dealt with and pled in depth and detail, and as such are beyond the scope of this work. The following general descriptions of some of the most pertinent issues and accompanying brief analysis may be useful to any ordinary American who may wish to pursue a specific action to enforce financial crises accountability. The case made in this work can be made if ordinary Americans are willing. If the following assessment of these issues is outside your interest, please skip the following and go directly to the Concluding Observations in Chapter 10, *infra*.

[A] Immunity Issues

Pursuit of the legal accountability of congress, federal financial regulatory agencies including the Fed, and the individuals that make their policies, is complex and involves issues of immunity and special procedures such as the *Federal Tort Claims Act*, 28 U.S.C. 1346(b); 2671-2680, as amended, and the *Federal Administrative Procedures Act*, 5 U.S.C. Subchapter II, as amended, among other laws that limit redress against public officials and governmental entities and agents. For purposes of the case for accountability made in this work,I do not address these complexities conclusively, but instead the reader should consider the practical effects of the case made on politicians and bureaucrats alike, as well as the impact the case on their Wall Street partners of the massive liabilities to which they are subject, and to the granting of the possible equitable remedies outlined in this work. The result would not likely be business as usual. At the very least a case for financial crisis accountability would reframe the status quo and open Washington and Wall Street to the necessity of compliance with the American rule of law as the preferable alternative to economic leveling, economic balancing and moral accountability wrenched from them through violence.

[B] Statutes of Limitation

[1] Limitations: Abuse of Power—Anti-tying

With respect to a bank abuse of power anti-tying cause of action based on 12 U.S. Code § 1972, 12 U.S. Code § 1977—Limitation of actions; suspension of limitations: (1) Subject to Clause; (2) [tolling provision], provides any action to enforce any cause of action under this chapter shall be forever barred unless commenced within four years after the cause of action accrued. One can take the position that the prohibited action is ongoing and that causes of action accrue on an ongoing basis. Some causes of action under other applicable anti-trust laws may be subject to different limitations periods. Any case filed based on the theories presented in the foregoing book must consider the applicable limitations periods.

[2] Limitations: RICO Bank Fraud

The statute of limitations for mail fraud and wire fraud prosecutions is five years (18 U.S.C. § 3282), except for mail and wire fraud schemes that affect a financial institution, in which case the statute is ten years (18 U.S.C. § 3293).
Consider that a scheme may extend back beyond the limitations period; the gist of the offense is the use of the mails, and if the prohibited use of the mails was within the period, the prosecution is timely. *See* O. Obermaier and R. Morvillo, *White Collar Crime: Business and Regulatory Offenses*, § 9.04[5], at 9-67 (Rel. 2, 1991) (citing cases); *cf. United States v. Garfinkel*, 29 F.3d 1253, 1259 (8th Cir. 1994) (mail fraud scheme may continue after mailing). That a scheme may extend back beyond the limitation period does not preclude prosecution of an offense committed in furtherance of the scheme within the period.[752]

[3] Tolling

"Courts in several Circuits have held a continuing tort or conspiracy may serve as grounds for equitable tolling in civil RICO cases." A First Circuit decision holds that a continuing tort sufficient to toll the statute of limitations is characterized by continual unlawful acts, not continuing ill effects from the original act. A Second Circuit court specifies plaintiffs must allege at least two acts of racketeering activity occurring within 10 years of each other, and that such acts must be related and pose a threat of continued criminal activity. Advancing what sounds like a modified version of the "Last Predicate Act" rule, the same court recognized a "separate accrual" rule whereby a new claim accrues, and the limitations period begins anew each time plaintiff discovers, or should have discovered, a new injury. Similarly, in considering the "continuing conspiracy" exception, a Fifth Circuit court held that each time a plaintiff is injured by an act of the defendant, a cause of action accrues to recover damages and, as to those damages, the statute of limitations runs from the commission of the act. (See further discussion of this issue at Jeffrey Harrington, *HG.org Legal Resources*, "Limitations Period in Civil RICO Litigation, Discuss of statute of limitations in civil RICO litigation" (undated).

[C] Standing and Class Certification

To meet the requirements for federal legal standing and to meet the requirements of Rule 23 of the Federal Rules of Civil Procedure (2019) for certification of the plaintiff class for certification of the plaintiffs' class action in this case, each named plaintiff and the plaintiff class representative and must provide credible evidence, proof, of their injury in fact that is the defendant corrupt racketeering enterprise' intentional fraudulent debasement of American money as exhibited in one or more if not all of the foregoing symptoms of the great financial crisis. Reports of government agencies and other expert sources have identified and concluded, based on well informed and diligent consideration of the extensive factual foundation now appearing in the public record, and with respect to which the plaintiffs can move that the court in the case take Judicial Notice under Rule 201 of the Federal Rules of Evidence, that the great financial crisis that constitutes the defendants injury in fact to the plaintiffs is the intentional fraudulent money debasement suffered by the plaintiff class of ordinary American households. Those injuries have been, and continues to be inflicted upon the plaintiffs by the defendant Washington Wall Street corrupt racketeering enterprise. The threshold issue of standing in this case prosecuted as a class action requires consideration of the requirements of Rule 23 for class certification, including the named lead plaintiff(s) standing. Considerations of standing and class certification require a statement of the substantive legal basis for the case as well as sufficient factual information to satisfy the threshold requirements.

In the following discussion, I have drawn on the work of Professor Karl Manheim, Loyola Law School, James Keenley, Esq., David Marcus, 1885 Society Distinguished Scholar; Professor of Law, The University of Arizona, James E. Rogers College of Law, the authors of the *Justia* article referenced above, as well as other experts in the doctrine of justiciability, standing and Rule 23 Requirements, to provide an overview of the application of the apposite legal principles applicable the case as outlined here.

The legal requirements to establish plaintiff and class standing and Rule 23 compliance for class certification are uncertain at best. Current case law suggests that a comprehensive statement of the case and its factual foundation in the initial complaint provides the strongest foundation for class certification. The technical requirements of Rule 23 are beyond the scope of this work. The following iteration of the principles affecting standing in a class action case for financial crisis accountability are included for context and completeness of the framework for the initiation of such a case.

[1] Threshold Issues Regarding Standing

I do not profess expertise in the complex subject matter. But I have learned that currently, particularly in the light of generalized reaction to distinctions now being drawn between the import of *Brown v. Board of Education of Topeka (No. 1.)* 347 U.S. 483 (1954), as affected by the relatively recent case of *Wal-Mart Stores, Inc. v. Dukes*, 131 S. Ct. 2541 (2011) (Wal-Mart), the initial knee jerk reaction to the this case is to recoil, intimidated by the complexity and confusion of the necessity of satisfaction of the threshold requirements of standing. Wal-Mart seeks to present a specter of massive "anti-business" class actions "economically damaging to business interests" heard by "populist judges" who may allow "gargantuan verdicts" against American corporations, leading to stock devaluation, and perhaps even bankruptcy, followed by and leading to economic "blackmail" and "substantial costs" forcing defendants to settle the claims "irrespective of the merits" that "would undermine a company's ability to make company-wide decisions necessary to forge a strong internal culture, and that this disruption could 'mean the difference between a thriving business ... and a corporate train wreck.'" This self-serving hyperbole must be dissolved in the face of the facts and law of the case for financial crisis accountability. The compensatory damages and punitive damages to be prayed for in the case are provided for by federal statute and directly follow the statutory foundation. The equitable relief of declarative judgment and injunction to be prayed for in this case are entirely appropriate to the case and consistent with the long history of class action relief sought in cases at this level of existential national significance.

"[T]he concept of 'Art. III standing' has not been defined with complete consistency in all of the various cases decided by this Court . . . [and] this very fact is probably proof that the concept cannot be reduced to a one-sentence or one-Clause definition." *Valley Forge Christian College v. Americans United*, 454 U.S. 464, 475 (1982). "Generalizations about standing to sue are largely worthless as such." *Association of Data Processing Service Orgs. v. Camp*, 397 U.S. 150, 151 (1970).

Success in meeting the threshold requirement in this case requires a reframing and marshalling of the varied procedural requirements, the confused state of applicable law, and most importantly the impact of the fundamental facts of the case and specific legal issues invoked to seek redress. It appears that the threatening implication of the Wal-Mart case is that it has somehow turned the law of standing and class action certifications upside down. The case filed and the judicial consideration of the plaintiffs' case requires a verified statement of the material connection of the facts of the case to the plaintiffs and the defendants in the supporting the plaintiffs motion for class certification, accompanied by fear and intimidation that might well follow the hint of institutional embarrassment by the well documented, publicly chronicled reprehensible conduct shared by Legislative and Executive branches of government as they have directly participated in and supported the clearly criminal, and also civil, tortious activities of the defendant Washington Wall Street corrupt racketeering enterprise.

The attitudes displayed and the actions taken by the Legislative and Executive branches of United States government that give rise to this case are characterized, at best and in the most charitable light, by studied, calculated indifference to and entrenched bureaucratic disdain for the suffering, the injuries in fact, of the plaintiffs as supported by the voluminous publicly documented evidence. The facts of the case, however confirm that the participation by the Congress and the Federal Reserve System, and federal financial regulators imbedded in the Executive branch of government have been active and intentional participants in the Washington Wall Street brazen corrupt racketeering enterprise complained of by the plaintiffs.

[2] Standing Generally

Perhaps the most important element of the requirement of adverse parties may be found in the "complexities and vagaries" of the standing doctrine. "The fundamental aspect of standing is that it focuses on the party seeking to get his complaint before a federal court and not on the issues he wishes to have adjudicated":[753]

> The "gist of the question of standing" is whether the party seeking relief has "alleged such a personal stake in the outcome of the controversy as to assure that concrete adverseness which sharpens the presentation of issues upon which the court so largely depends for illumination of difficult constitutional questions."[339] This practical conception of standing has now given way to a primary emphasis upon separation of powers as the guide. "[T]he 'case or controversy' requirement defines with respect to the Judicial Branch the idea of separation of powers on which the Federal Government is founded. The several doctrines that have grown up to elaborate that requirement are 'founded in concern about the proper—and properly limited—role of the courts in a democratic society.'"[754]
>
> Standing as a doctrine is composed of both constitutional and prudential restraints on the power of the federal courts to render decisions, and is almost exclusively concerned with public law questions as determinations of constitutionality and review of administrative or other governmental action. As such, it is often interpreted according to the prevailing philosophies of judicial activism and restraint, and narrowly or broadly, in terms of the viewed desirability of access to the courts by persons seeking to challenge legislation or other governmental action. The trend in the 1960s was to broaden access; in the 1970s, 1980s, and 1990s, the trend shifted to narrow access by stiffening the requirements of standing, although Court majorities were not entirely consistent. The major difficulty in setting forth the standards is that the Court's generalizations and the results it achieves are often at variance."[755]

Putting it more frankly, "Standing doctrine generally and the injury-in-fact test in particular have not received a warm welcome from the academic community. Commentators widely assert that the doctrine is applied in an inconsistent, if not incoherent, manner. Many claim that federal courts use standing doctrine to dodge difficult questions, or as an unprincipled device to dispose of cases for unstated substantive reasons without actually analysing the questions under review. Even one of the Court's own referred to standing as naught more than 'a word game played by secret rules.' Determinations that plaintiffs lack injury-in-fact appear to have effectively cut off certain constitutional provisions from judicial interpretation or enforcement. This has led some scholars to argue that the injury-in-fact test is inconsistent with the constitutional design. Nearly all the seminal injury-in-fact cases occur in the context of lawsuits commenced by private parties to challenge public/government action or inaction. Scholars, in turn, have focused their analysis of the injury-in-fact requirement on how it impacts the ability of private plaintiffs to assert public rights. What is lost in this discussion is the impact injury-in-fact doctrine has on jurisdictional issues in private disputes. Perhaps this is because the big question in the Article III inquiry-whether an alleged injury is sufficiently particularized or concrete to invoke the federal judicial power-is not particularly meaningful in lawsuits between private parties because such disputes do not present the constitutional separation of powers concerns that arise when the federal judicial power is invoked against other public bodies. In a typical two-party private dispute, the only meaningful standing inquiry ought to be whether the plaintiffs claim rests on a legal right created in positive law. If not, the plaintiff's case is dead on arrival, regardless of the Article III issues. We should not be surprised that injury-in-fact jurisprudence has had little, if any, discernible effect on the conduct of bilateral private lawsuits in federal court."[756]

[3] Not a Citizen Suit

Citizen suits will not be granted standing. A first impression upon consideration of the case for financial crisis accountability is that as the case "looks like a citizen suit", the plaintiffs would not have standing. "Persons do not have standing to sue to enforce a constitutional provision when all they can show or claim is that they have an interest or have suffered an injury that is shared by all members of the public. ... [where] '[t]he only interest all citizens share in the claim advanced ... is one which presents injury in the abstract.... [The] claimed nonobservance [of the [constitutional] clause], standing alone, would adversely affect only the generalized interest of all citizens in constitutional governance.'"[757]

The initial characterization of the plaintiffs in this case as an aggregation of American citizens in pursuit of a claim of redress for a common shared injury in the abstract is not correct. Much of this work serves to counter that false initial impression from a variety of perspectives of moral principles, legal principles, substantive law and facts that are well documented in the public domain.

The plaintiffs in a case for financial crisis accountability do not advance their claims as an abstract matter and as generalized citizens of the United States. Each household is likely, but not necessarily, composed of resident citizens. Their citizenship of these ordinary people is not the determining characteristic of their inclusion in the class of plaintiffs. The respective plaintiff parties are the American households of ordinary people injured in fact as a direct result of specifically identifiable wrongful, tortious actions taken by the defendants, not acting in common—as common defendants, but rather acting in concert as a criminal, corrupt racketeering enterprise under RICO. Recognition that the group of ordinary American people who have been financially and economically brutalized, as a class, avoids many of the Rule 23 and standing issues and complications raised by characterization of the composition of the class of plaintiffs merely citizens in the abstract, makes an undifferentiated legal claim in the abstract against simply common defendants, involving mere generalized factual patterns.

The conduct by the defendants as a criminal corrupt racketeering enterprise as contemplated by RICO is substantively and legally distinct from a "multi-defendant common practice lawsuit," and as such it avoids many of the Rule 23 and standing issues and the complications raised by such a distinct characterization of the defendants.

In this case, the plaintiffs are not required to establish that each plaintiff member of the class has suffered an injury in fact fairly traceable to each named defendant. The plaintiffs in this case are prosecuting their claims of damages and equitable remedies for a shared fundamental injury in fact, a crime of financial and economic assault by abuse of trust and power and fraud, fairly traceable to the conduct by all of the defendants, as a group, a racketeering enterprise under RICO (jointly and severally between and amongst the Wall Street and Rating Agency defendants only as to damages, penalties and costs) through the infliction by the Washington Wall Street racketeering enterprise of defendants on each member of the class of ordinary American household plaintiffs, of one or more of a specific set of damages from the injury in fact fairly traceable to the defendants Washington Wall Street criminal corrupt racketeering enterprise. The defendants actions establish a common nexus of the intentional continued practice of progressive abuse of trust and power in misrepresentation of the value of all of their property as denominated in United States dollars or dollar denominated instruments or accounts, which, when discovered, created the great financial crisis—an unprecedented brutal financial and economic assault on American households. Even though the typical nature and factual patterns of specific damages resulting from the common shared injury in fact of the great financial crisis is applicable to and suffered in person by each individual comprising each American household plaintiff, is varied amongst a series of readily identifiable and identified typical factual patterns of actual losses and damages described in the existing body of documentation of the factual evidence. The plaintiffs can move the court to judicially notice that individual losses and damages suffered by each respective household are virtually impossible to quantify of an individual case by case basis for all plaintiffs.

In the present case of financial and economic assault through intentional fraud of abuse of trust and power to intentionally cause money debasement, there can be no doubt that the injuries are injuries in fact. The strongest and most able among the plaintiffs fought back to protect themselves and their own. Others sought help and support from the leaders of the land, whose half-hearted efforts were compromised by their complicity in and tolerance of the economic and financial brutality. The economically and financially weak and infirm were doomed. All suffered the litany of damage and loss detailed by category in the existing factual evidence; each to a greater or lesser degree; but nonetheless, real loss and damage that may never heal. The people were left weakened, reeling, submissive and fearful. They were all hurt. Some more than others. But all of them have been and continue to be hurt.[758]

Individually, one by one, the plaintiffs, as a practical matter, could not dare hope for justice where the Government defendants are, for the most part, legally or practically immune to individual plaintiff claims, or because the Government defen dants have protected their Wall Street and Rating Agency defendants as partners in the racketeering enterprise, rendering them essentially immune to such claims, so far, as too big to fail or to jail.

As note earlier in this work, the DOJ has only recently considered the application of bank fraud statutes and RICO to the fraud in the financial crisis—but have limited their interest to damage to banks rather than damage caused by The Washington Wall Street enterprise, composed of all of the defendants in this case, ignoring the fundamental shared injuries in fact of from abuse of trust and power to conduct intentional money debasement, the financial crisis consequent which have been suffered by the plaintiffs in common. (See, *Feds Weighing New Strategy To Criminally Charge Wall St. Bankers Tied To Housing Bust,* Reuters By Emily Flitter, Posted: 07/17/2013 2:42 pm EDT) (Note: the author provided an initial outline of the case presented in this work to the Dallas office of the FBI at the direction of the United States Attorney's office for the Northern District of Texas on December 15, 2011) The DOJ among all of the other Government defendants are riven with conflicts of interests fed by the fruits of their participation in or complicity with the Washington Wall Street racketeering enterprise at the heart of this case. It is important to note that the defendants damaging conduct as a racketeering enterprise has been, not unexpectedly, covered up and their accountability for it has been insistently frustrated.[759]

Confirmation of plaintiffs basis for certification by the court of the plaintiffs as a class under Rule 23 of the Federal Rules of Civil Procedure, including standing in this case, as noted above, is largely a judicial exercise that is not conducted under any real degree of clarity under the specific language of Rule 23 or under the current state of applicable case law. Since I am not a specialist in the law of standing or Rule 23 requirements, for purposes of this work I have relied on secondary sources published by experts. The predominant recommendation all the experts is that the cautious plaintiffs' counsel in preparation of the initial complaint will:

- Track the specific Rule 23 requirements for class certification, including the establishment of plaintiffs' standing as a class in the complaint.
- Track the requirements not just by their recitation but also by inclusion in the complaint of proof of each element.
- The initial filing be accompanied by plaintiffs' motion for court certification of the existence of the class and the class representatives.
- The initial filing be accompanied, in this case at any rate, by plaintiffs' motion that the court take judicial notice under Rule 201 of the Federal Rules of Evidence of the factual foundation for the case documented and appearing in the official and public documents referred to in this memorandum and recited in support of the conclusion that the plaintiffs are entitled to certification of the class and confirming that plaintiffs have standing to prosecute their claims as outline here. See Rule 201 and the accompanying notes as well as Paul J. Kiernan, *Better Living Through Judicial Notice*, published in the American Bar Association publication *Litigation*, Volume 1, Fall, 2009.

[4] Justiciability

The plaintiffs' damages, collectively the single largest component of damage comprising the financial crisis, are fairly traceable to their cause: intentional money debasement conducted by the defendants as a racketeering enterprise through the creation of sovereign money, the value of which has not been regulated by Congress, and the shadow banking system composed largely of unsupportable credit, packaged and securitized, then monetized through the use of securities ratings and derives based on those securities and even on derivatives, which predictably resulted in the body of damages that constitute the financial crisis suffered by the plaintiffs as a class, as opposed to and distinct from the other forms of fraud such as securities fraud that have been the subject of specific litigation between and amongst the government, Wall Street and investors in specific securities or other structured financial instruments. The Washington Wall Street enterprise's unrestrained creation of credit money in the form of securities and derivatives as structured financial products, primarily, enabled these institutions to systematically overstate and inflate the value of assets and earnings on their balance sheets and operating statements as well as required financial reporting, while simultaneously debasing and diminishing the value of their respective liabilities, held by bank depositors and other creditors. Because money is fungible and the value of which is not property regulated by Congress, both the inflated assets treated, traded and exchanged, and as recorded as money simultaneously inflated asset values denominated in the credit created and debased the overall money supply. The asset bubble and debased state of money were connected by the market, the credit money value liquidity and value plummeted. The Washington Wall Street enterprise has largely been protected as too big to fail or to jail, and depositors and holders of dollars and dollar denominated assets were left with debased money and collapsed asset values that would no longer offset the amount of the credit money upon which it was based. The collapsed asset bubble and the manifest money debasement resulted directly in actual losses to the owners of the underlying assets, as well losses in all assets denominated or priced in debased dollars but also consequential, related and intertwined losses that rippled through the American economy and America's households. The uncertainty of assets and money substitute credit money value and liquidity as absorbed by the market constitutes the financial crisis. The Washington Wall Street enterprise has largely avoided loss recognition and absorption and legal accountability. That is not so for ordinary American American households.

The relief sought by the plaintiffs as a class detailed later in this work would, if granted, provide accountability for the financial crisis. The plaintiff class' "zone of interest" encompasses the plaintiffs' common, shared legal civil right to relief from the defendants' past and ongoing abuse of trust and power to conduct intentional tortious, fraudulent, debasement of American money. Article III of the *United States Constitution* states that the judicial power of the federal courts extends only to cases and controversies which arise under the *Constitution*, federal laws of the United States and its treaties.

The suggested legal actions for financial crisis accountability described in this work present an actual ongoing dispute, not hypothetical legal questions. They are based upon concrete demonstrable facts, application of the common law, The *United States Constitution*, federal and possibly state statutory violations and constitutional violations—violations of the law of the land—and not "upon some fanciful situation which may not have presented a complete picture of the controversy." These legal actions present a controversy that requires resolution; the opponents are true adversaries, and any opinion in the case would not simply be advisory. The facts are clear and comprehensive. The substantive law is clear and unambiguous. The injuries in fact are visible and palpable. The damages have been publicly acknowledged and calculated. Only judicial action and enforcement is required. There is a substantial likelihood that the legal actions described in this work would have a material effect on the defendants' wrongful conduct; and the defendants could not simply ignore the court's ruling. In any situation where the opposing party could ignore the ruling, then the opinion lacks finality and is in effect advisory. The damages, penalties and costs recoverable by the plaintiffs in this case are so large that defendants ignoring the ruling of the court could only result in the insolvency and collapse of the Washington and Rating Agency defendants, and civil tumult impairing the legitimacy and effectiveness of the Government defendants followed by the prospect of a social revolution. The judgments of the courts in this case will determine the primacy of the American system of government as one founded on the Constitution, the rule of law—the law of the land. Declaratory judgments are justiciable as long as they present a real controversy. Declaratory judgments that meet these criteria are themselves justiciable. This case contemplated by this work would include a prayer for declaratory judgment in aid of the other equitable relief sought by the plaintiffs.

The legal actions described in this work are not moot. They are ripe and appropriate for consideration by the courts. The United States Supreme Court, in the *Legal Tender Cases* noticed briefly in the final words of its opinions in those cases, the relevant issue of congressional creation and regulation of the value of sovereign money in relationship to standards having intrinsic value under, and as contemplated by Article I, Section 8, Clause 5 of the *United States Constitution*, despite the lack of necessity of that notice to the decision by the Court in those cases. The Court stated that "[t]he questions involved are constitutional questions of the most vital importance to the government and to the public at large." The potential of far reaching consequences was noted to be crucial not only to the Court's considerations of law specifically at issue in the *Legal Tender Cases*, but also to the related issue of the constitutional nature of sovereign money, the necessity for congressional regulation of its value by reference to a standard that possess intrinsic value, and the constitutional protections against its debasement. The defendant Washington Wall Street enterprise has successfully been, able to ignore the law, it has broken the law and profited mightily from illegal conduct for many years; all while while hiding and covering up their illegal actions by abuse of their members' respective positions of trust, power and purported special expertise. The Washington Wall Street enterprise intentionally misled and deluded the ordinary people of American until the first blows in the economic and financial assault of the great financial crisis rained down upon them.

The damages claimed by the plaintiffs have been determined and calculated by the written public reports of the federal government and the Federal Reserve System.

The equitable relief sought by the plaintiffs is specifically contemplated by the *United States Constitution* and the *Legal Tender Cases*. The relief to be sought by the plaintiff ordinary Americans in the case described in this work does not include any determination of the validity or constitutionality of the *Federal Reserve Act* or the Federal Reserve System. The case would seek only a ruling and judgment that the provisions of the *Federal Reserve Act* and the activities of the system are subject to and are not exempt from the laws upon which the plaintiffs' case is founded.

The legal actions suggested in this work reflect a profound disagreement between the American public and the Washington Wall Street enterprise combination of defendants, operating as a criminal corrupt racketeering enterprise. These legal actions are not premature nor are they based on an abstract disagreement. The facts are concrete, demonstrable and appear in the public records of the various defendants and in the works of the many expert scholars and commentators cited in this work. The public records also include the significant body of government studies and reports pertaining to the financial crisis as well the court records of the great number of fraud litigation cases documented by SNL relating to Wall Street banks' fraud in connection with the financial crisis. The defendants' fraudulent conduct of a broad course of intentional misrepresentation of asset values is a matter of fact. The fraud works not only on the holders of the securities that have been the subject of litigation, but also on the entire body of plaintiffs whose income and wealth have been debased as a direct result of the money debasement made by the defendants in the creation of an enormous body of unsupportable credit, including the credit underlying the securities that were the subject of the reported litigation documented by SNL as well as official government sources, as they were monetized and injected as sovereign money into the heart of the American economic and financial system.

The standing doctrine provides for a determination by the court that a person lacks standing, meaning that person is not the proper party to bring the issue before the court for adjudication. The standing doctrine is viewed as a tool that promotes both the separation of powers amongst the three branches of government and judicial efficiency. Separation of powers is achieved through limiting the issues the judiciary hears, thus limiting review of the other branches of government. The limiting of cases before the courts promotes judicial efficiency, and this limiting also improves the decision-making ability of the judiciary through ensuring that a specific controversy exists and that an advocate with a stake in the outcome is present to pursue the matter.

The studies and reports prepared by the government and the Commission as well as volumes of works of recognized experts published since the financial crisis began and the record of court cases arising from the financial crisis have identified the defendants named in this case as the parties primarily, fundamentally, and collectively accountable for the financial crisis. The acknowledged experts and the existing public judicial record have provided fundamental analyses and comprehensive support for the legal claims and causes of action to be asserted in this case contemplated by this work. The published studies and reports specifically identify and quantify the number of plaintiffs in the plaintiff class, define the common injury in fact suffered in fact by the plaintiff claimants, the injuries in fact of the intentional, tortious, fraudulent debasement of their money comprising their experience in the great financial crisis, and the published reports and studies further detail the typical shared factual patterns of loss and damage directly suffered by them as the direct consequence; as part and parcel of their shared injuries in fact in.

Money's most basic function is to serve as a medium of exchange. From this is derived money's three other functions: a store of value, a unit of account, and a standard of deferred payment. Money is certainly a commodity unlike any other economic good. But there is no obvious reason why attempts to undermine money's ability to perform these functions could not be addressed through the ways that we address most other economic crimes. As noted by the distinguished nineteenth-century English jurist and civil servant Lord Farrer, "contract law, tort law, and criminal law are more than sufficient to adjudicate such matters without invoking any special law of legal tender." In this case, the plaintiffs, as a class, have turned to the *United States Constitution*, and to tort law as expressed in federal statutes as supported by *the Restatement (Second) Torts* § 874 A, and common law to address what Lord Farrer recognized as a tort, as well as the corresponding economic crimes provided for in the same statutes.

[5] Case or Controversy

Article III of the *Constitution* states that the judicial power of the federal courts extends only to cases and controversies which arise under the *Constitution*, federal laws of the United States and its treaties. This remains the overlying principle by which the courts determine whether or not an issue is justiciable as a case of controversy and the requirement a case or controversy has led to the judicial establishment of the justiciability doctrines. These doctrines are used to determine whether a case or controversy actually exists, and if one does then the issues are considered justiciable:

> Constitutional Standards: Injury in Fact, Causation, and Redressability. While the Court has been inconsistent, it has now settled upon the rule that, "at an irreducible minimum, the constitutional requisites under Article III for the existence of standing are that the plaintiff must personally have suffered some actual or threatened injury that can fairly be traced to the challenged action of the defendant, and that the injury is likely to be redressed by a favorable decision." For some time, injury alone was not sufficient; rather, the injury had to be "a wrong which directly results in the violation of a legal right," that is, "one of property, one arising out of contract, one protected against tortious invasion, or one founded in a statute which confers a privilege." The problem was that the "legal right" language was "demonstrably circular: if the plaintiff is given standing to assert his claims, his interest is legally protected; if he is denied standing, his interest is not legally protected." The observable tendency of the Court, however, was to find standing frequently in cases distinctly not grounded in property rights. (In the case presented in this work, however, note that the violation of the plaintiffs' legal rights to protection from abuse of trust and power and intentional money debasement are clearly demonstrable and the requirement is thus has nonetheless been met).
>
> In any event, the "legal rights" language has now been dispensed with. Rejection occurred in two administrative law cases in which the Court announced that parties had standing when they suffered "injury in fact" to some interest,

> "economic or otherwise," that is arguably within the zone of interest to be protected or regulated by the statute or constitutional provision in question.[361] "Now political, environmental, aesthetic, and social interests, when impaired, afford a basis for making constitutional attacks upon governmental action. ... Nonetheless, the Court has also in constitutional cases been wary of granting standing to persons who alleged threats or harm to interests which they shared with the larger community of people at large, a rule against airing 'generalized grievances' through the courts, although it is unclear whether this rule (or subrule) has a constitutional or a prudential basis. And in a number of cases, the Court has refused standing apparently in the belief that the assertion of harm is too speculative or too remote to credit."[760]
>
> Of increasing importance are the second and third elements of standing, causation and redressability, recently developed and held to be of constitutional requisite. There must be a causal connection between the injury and the conduct complained of; that is, the Court insists that the plaintiff show that "but for" the action, she would not have been injured. And the Court has insisted that there must be a "substantial likelihood" that the relief sought from the court if granted would remedy the harm.[761]
>
> "Although the two tests were initially articulated as two facets of a single requirement, the Court now insists they are separate inquiries. ... To the extent there is a difference, it is that the former examines a causal connection between the asserted unlawful conduct and the alleged injury, whereas the latter examines the causal connection between the alleged injury and the judicial relief requested."[762]

The plaintiffs' claims arise under Article I, § 8, Clause 5, of the *Constitution*, the due process and equal protection and taking clauses of the 5th and 14th Amendments to the *Constitution*, 18 U.S.C. § 1341 (relating to criminal mail fraud), 18 U.S.C. § 1343 (relating to criminal fraud by wire, radio, or television); and 18 U.S.C. § 1344 (relating to criminal financial institution fraud); the *Racketeer Influenced and Corrupt Organizations Act* "RICO" 18 U.S.C. §§ 1961-1968, and the bank anti-tying provisions of *The Bank Holding Company Act*, 12 U.S.C. §§ 1972—1975, all supported in the courts consideration by the *Restatement (Second) Torts*, § 874 A.

> Prudential Standing Rules. "Even when Article III constitutional standing rules have been satisfied, the Court has held that principles of prudence may counsel the judiciary to refuse to adjudicate some claims. It is clear that the Court feels free to disregard any of these prudential rules in cases in which it thinks exceptionable circumstances exist... The Court has identified three rules as prudential ones, only one of which has been a significant factor in the jurisprudence of standing. The first two rules are that the plaintiff's interest, to which she asserts an injury, must come within the 'zone of interest' arguably protected by the constitutional provision or statute in question and that plaintiffs may not air 'generalized grievances' shared by all or a large class of citizens. The important rule concerns the ability of a plaintiff to represent the constitutional rights of third parties not before the court."[763]
>
> ...
>
> "[A] plaintiff may still lack standing under the prudential principles by which the judiciary seeks to avoid deciding questions of broad social import where no individual rights would be vindicated and to limit access to the federal courts to those litigants best suited to assert a particular claim."[764]
>
> "Congress may grant an express right of action to persons who otherwise would be barred by prudential standing rules. Of course, Art. III's requirement

> remains: the plaintiff still must allege a distinct and palpable injury to himself, even if it is an injury shared by a large class of other possible litigants. ... That is, the actual or threatened injury required may exist solely by virtue of 'statutes creating legal rights, the invasion of which creates standing, even though no injury would exist without the statute.'"[765]

In this case, the claims of the plaintiffs and the plaintiff class of injury by the defendants' abuse of trust and power to effect intentional fraudulent debasement of money are supported by the complete range of each and all of their legal rights spanning the common law, the *Constitution* and federal statutes. The injury in fact to each plaintiff and to the plaintiff class as a group are all distinct and palpable by any construction of that phrase, as detailed by the facts of the case as evidence and proof.

> Standing to Assert the Constitutional Rights of Others. "Usually, one may assert only one's interest in the litigation and not challenge the constitutionality of a statute or a governmental action because it infringes the protectable rights of someone else. ... But there are several exceptions to this part of the standing doctrine that make generalization misleading. Many cases allow standing to third parties if they demonstrate a requisite degree of injury to themselves and if under the circumstances the injured parties whom they seek to represent would likely not be able to assert their rights."[766]

In this case, the interests asserted by the named plaintiffs are the same interests in the litigation as the interest of each class member. As a part of the class certification, the court should find that each of the plaintiffs is likely not be able to assert its rights on a case by case basis. That is, of course a requirement for certification of the class and thereby directly meets and satisfies this standing concern.

Standing to sue on statutory or other non-constitutional grounds challenging the lawfulness of governmental action has a constitutional content to the degree that Article III requires a "case" or "controversy," necessitating a litigant who has sustained or will sustain an injury so that he will be moved to present the issue "in an adversary context and in a form historically viewed as capable of judicial resolution." Liberalization of the law of standing in this field has been notable. The "old law" required that in order to sue to contest the lawfulness of agency administrative action, one must have suffered a "legal wrong," that is, "the right invaded must be a legal right," requiring some resolution of the merits preliminarily. An injury-in-fact was insufficient.[767] In this case, the plaintiffs' case is based upon a legal right grounded in the common law, the *Constitution*, and federal statures as well as injuries in fact consequent to ongoing violation of those legal rights by the defendant Washington Wall Street criminal, corrupt racketeering enterprise. The plaintiff ordinary American households can present the case in an adversary context and is in a form historically viewed as capable of judicial resolution as contemplated by the *Legal Tender Cases*, by the remedies provided for by federal statute, as additionally supported, although not required to be so supported, by the *Restatement (Second) Torts*, § 874 A. The preliminary resolution of the merits in the case for financial crisis accountability firmly grounds the case as based on the defendant Washington Wall Street corrupt racketeering enterprise' legal wrong to the named plaintiffs and to each member of the plaintiff class, directly resulting in distinct and palpable injury in fact to each such plaintiff and to each member of the plaintiff class.

"A 'legal right' could be established in one of two ways. It could be a common-law right, such that if the injury were administered by a private party, one could sue on it; or it could be a right created by the *Constitution* or a statute. The statutory right most relied on was the judicial review section of the *Administrative Procedure Act,* which provided that '[a] person suffering legal wrong because of agency action, or adversely affected or aggrieved by agency action within the meaning of a relevant statute, is entitled to judicial review thereof.' Early decisions under this statute interpreted the language as adopting the 'legal interest' and 'legal wrong' standard then prevailing as constitutional requirements of standing, which generally had the effect of limiting the type of injury cognizable in federal court to economic ones.

"In 1970, however, the Court promulgated a two-pronged standing test: if the litigant (1) has suffered injury-in-fact and if he (2) shows that the interest he seeks to protect is arguably within the zone of interests to be protected or regulated by the statutory guarantee in question, he has standing. Of even greater importance was the expansion of the nature of the cognizable injury beyond economic injury, to encompass 'aesthetic, conservational, and recreational' interests as well. 'Aesthetic and environmental well-being, like economic well-being, are important ingredients of the quality of life in our society, and the fact that particular environmental interests are shared by the many rather than the few does not make them less deserving of legal protection through the judicial process.'"[768]

In *Sierra Club v. Morton*, 405 U.S. 727, 734 (1972), "[m]oreover, said the Court, once a person establishes that he has standing to seek judicial review of an action because of particularized injury to him, he may argue the public interest as a 'representative of the public interest,' as a 'private attorney general,' so that he may contest not only the action which injures him but the entire complex of actions of which his injury-inducing action is a part." *Id.* at 737-738, noting *Scripps-Howard Radio v. FCC,* 316 U.S. 4 (1942); *FCC v. Sanders Brothers Radio Station*, 309 U.S. (1940). *See also Gladstone Realtors v. Village of Bellwood,* 441 U.S. 91, 103 n. (1979); *Havens Realty Corp. v. Coleman*, 455 U.S. 363, 376 n.16 (1982) (noting ability of such party to represent interests of third parties).

> "Much debate has occurred in recent years with respect to the validity of 'citizen suit' provisions in the environmental laws, especially in light of the Court's retrenchment in constitutional standing cases. The Court in insisting on injury in fact as well as causation and redressability has curbed access to citizen suits, but that Congress may expansively confer substantial degrees of standing through statutory creations of interests remains true."[769]

The defendant Washington Wall Street criminal corrupt racketeering enterprise injuries in fact inflicted on each member of the plaintiff class in this case includes economic injury as well as the entire complex of actions of which the injury-inducing action is a part, as contemplated in application by the Court.

[6] Advisory Opinions

Since Article III mandates that the judiciary only has power over cases and controversies, the Supreme Court has held that where a case or controversy does not exist, the judiciary is not to issue any advisory opinion regarding the matter. This prohibition against advisory opinions helps to serve separation of powers: by not issuing advisory opinions, the federal judiciary is keeping the courts out of the political process and leaving that process solely to the discretion of the legislative and executive branches. Additionally, by not issuing advisory opinions, the judiciary is conserving its resources for cases that need adjudication.

"Three basic requirements must be met so that the judiciary may hear a case and issue an opinion that would not be advisory.

"First, the case needs to present an actual dispute, not a hypothetical legal question. By requiring an actual dispute, the judiciary is ensuring that any decision issued in the case is the final one because it was based upon concrete facts and not upon some fanciful situation which may not have presented a complete picture of the controversy. The specific facts supporting the plaintiffs' claims are outlined in this memorandum and supported in detail by the factual material of which the court may take, must take, judicial notice, upon the plaintiffs' motion and clearly present an actual dispute.

"The second requirement is that the dispute is between adverse litigants. Adversity, or "Adversariness" is required to ensure that the case brought before the courts truly involves a controversy that is in need of a resolution; if the opponents are not true adversaries, then any issued opinion would be advisory. All the standards relating to whether a plaintiff is entitled to adjudication of his claims must be evaluated "by reference to the Art. III notion that federal courts may exercise power only 'in the last resort, and as a necessity,' . . . and only when adjudication is 'consistent with a system of separated powers and [the dispute is one] traditionally thought to be capable of resolution through the judicial process.'" (Justia, p. 2, citing *Allen v. Wright*, 468 U.S. 737, 750, 752 (1984) (quoting *Warth v. Seldin*, 422 U.S. 490, 498 (1975)) (quoting, respectively, *Chicago & G.T. Ry. v. Wellman*, 143 U.S. 339, 345 (1892), and *Flast v. Cohen*, 392 U.S. 83, 97 (1968)). For the strengthening of the separation-of-powers barrier to standing, *see Lujan v. Defenders of Wildlife*, 504 U.S. 555, 559-560, 571-578 (1992)). "[T]he 'case or controversy' requirement defines with respect to the Judicial Branch the idea of separation of powers on which the Federal Government is founded. The several doctrines that have grown up to elaborate that requirement are 'founded in concern about the proper—and properly limited—role of the courts in a democratic society"[770]:

> Standing as a doctrine is composed of both constitutional and prudential restraints on the power of the federal courts to render decisions, and is almost exclusively concerned with such public law questions as determinations of constitutionality and review of administrative or other governmental action. (Citing C. Wright, *Handbook of the Law of Federal Courts*, 60 (4th ed. 1983). As such, it is often interpreted according to the prevailing philosophies of judicial activism and restraint and narrowly or broadly in terms of the viewed desirability of access to

> the courts by persons seeking to challenge legislation or other governmental action. The trend in the 1960s was to broaden access; in the 1970s, 1980s, and 1990s, it was to narrow access by stiffening the requirements of standing, although Court majorities were not entirely consistent. The major difficulty in setting forth the standards is that the Court's generalizations and the results it achieves are often at variance.[771]

The plaintiffs, as a class, have suffered approximately $20 trillion in damages for which they seek, compensation, penalties as a deterrent to future wrongful conduct, and equitable remedies to protect the honesty, safety and soundness, as well as the integrity and value of their money from the ongoing, continuous, notorious predations of the defendants as a criminal, corrupt, racketeering enterprise. The plaintiffs and the defendants could hardly adopt a more adversary posture to the courts than is presented in ordinary Americans case for financial crisis accountability. Further, the United States Supreme Court in the *Legal Tender Cases* (See, *infra.*) specifically contemplate hearing the Article I. § 8, Clause 5 constitutional issue presented in this case regarding plaintiffs' constitutional, statutory and common law civil right to protection from and against the scourge of money debasement that ordinary Americans have experienced as the great financial crisis.

The last requirement is that if a decision is issued in favor of the claimant, there is a substantial likelihood that it would have some effect. In any situation where the opposing party could ignore the ruling, then the opinion lacks finality and is in effect advisory. Declaratory judgments are justiciable as long as they present a real controversy. Declaratory judgments that meet these criteria are themselves justiciable. *Aetna Life Insurance Co. v. Haworth*, 300 U.S. 227 (1937). Because of the large amount in controversy, damages, penalties and costs awarded to the plaintiffs would be a very large amount, even when limited to a proportion that would not spark a financial Armageddon, a prospect to be considered for judicial approval as being in the best interest of the class, and which, imposed in conjunction with the equitable remedies sought by the plaintiffs, including declaratory judgments as well as a judicially mandated, supervised and managed plan to assure the implantation by the defendants of corrective action to mitigate past wrongdoing and minimize future money debasement as required by applicable law is clearly justiciable.

[7] Mootness and Ripeness

Mootness and ripeness both deal with the existence of an actual controversy; mootness with whether the controversy has terminated, and ripeness with whether it is ready for adjudication. A case will be declared moot if the defendant dies during a criminal trial, if the plaintiff dies during a civil action and the action does not survive the death (usually by statute), and if the parties settle between themselves before a final judgement is entered. In these situations, the issues are no longer redressable. Exceptions do exist to the mootness doctrine which allow a case to be heard: (i) where secondary injuries exist that may be addressed by the court; (ii) cases which involve a wrong that is capable of repetition and likely to evade review; (iii) where an illegal practice has been terminated but it could be resumed at any time; and (iv) in a properly certified class action suit. The facts of this case clearly and indisputably confirm the ongoing and continuing nature of the defendants' racketeering enterprise and the court may take judicial notice of the ongoing public distress with the failure of any responsible authority to halt or temper the ongoing effect of the economic and financial assault by the defendants upon the plaintiffs complained of in the case presented in this work.

Cases are declared not ripe because the injuries are either too speculative or they may never occur. The rationale behind the ripeness doctrine is that a court should not issue premature judgements based on abstract disagreements. *Abbott Laboratories v. Gardner*, 387 U.S. 136 (1967). The injuries suffered by the plaintiffs at the hands of the defendants have been chronicled, calculated, counted and apportioned in the exhaustive public sources cited herein. The plaintiffs' injuries are real and actual, and they are continuing. They are not speculative. The damages caused by those injuries have already occurred and are continuing. Ripeness typically arises when pre-enforcement review of a statute is sought, at which point the considerations are examined, and both must be present in order for an issue to be ripe. First, the plaintiff must show that a hardship is likely to be suffered in the absence of a judgement. This hardship could be caused by the law as it will eventually be applied, by collateral injuries, or because compliance with the law causes the hardship, and the only other choice is to break the law with the resulting consequences of being prosecuted. This case does not present a claim for pre-enforcement review of any statute. The second consideration is whether the issues are fit for a judicial decision. An issue that specific facts would assist in the judicial consideration will be found not ripe, while an issue is ripe when it is mostly a question of law, one which does not depend on context. This case is ripe and involves the application of existing United States law and such a case is specifically contemplated and found appropriate for judicial consideration by the United States Supreme Court in the *Legal Tender Cases*. The Court specifically noted that the issues to be raised in a case such this case were important, worthy and suitable for judicial consideration and were not contemplated to be considered and resolved in those cases only because those specific issues had not been properly brought before the Court for its consideration.

[8] Judicial Restraint

Judicial restraint has two aspects to its nature. The first is the use of discretion in granting certiorari, and the second is a set of prudential rules used to deny a party standing in a particular case. Currently, the Supreme Court has the power to deny certiorari in any case. Congress, however, has the power under Article III to require Supreme Court review for any issue.

The prudential restraint rules focus on whether the plaintiffs' own rights are being asserted, or whether someone else's rights are being asserted. There is no general third party standing, except in cases of the 1st Amendment and where a special relationship exists between the injured party and the party asserting the right. The special relationships which are permitted to exert third party standing are very limited.

A close relationship is required between the third party and the right being asserted, such as an association which is closely tied to the claimed right or a party which has a zone of interest encompassing the right. Congress may also change any of these rules since they are not based within the *Constitution*.

[9] Political Question Doctrine

The political question doctrine is also addressed in the body of the book's foregoing text. An issue, even a constitutional issue, which the Court feels is best resolved by one of the other branches of government may denied judicial review under the Political Question Doctrine. These issues are generally political in nature, and the court feels that the political system of accountability is the best mechanism to resolve the issues, as opposed to a mandate from the courts. Often, these issues are either given wholly to another branch of government in the *Constitution*, or there is a lack of judicially manageable standards for resolving it, or for a number of other reasons. See *Baker v. Carr*, 396 U.S. 186, 217 (1962) (Baker). These principals have been applied in such areas as the republican form of government clause in Article IV, § 4, foreign relations, and Congress' control of its own internal processes.

In *Baker v. Carr*, Presidential argues that the case must be dismissed because its resolution will require the court to decide a political question. A federal court has no authority to review a political question. See *Marbury v. Madison*, 5 U.S. 137, 170, 2 L. Ed. 60 (1803). ("Questions, in their nature political, or which are, by the *Constitution* and laws, submitted to the executive, can never be made in this court.") The political question doctrine protects the separation of powers and prevents federal courts from overstepping their constitutionally defined role[772] ("The nonjusticiability of a political question is primarily a function of the separation of powers."); *Aktepe v. United States*, 105 F.3d 1400, 1402 (11th Cir. 1997) (Aktepe) (noting that the political question doctrine is "derived from the separation of powers").

In Baker, the Supreme Court set out the six indicia of a political question:[773]

- a textually demonstrable constitutional commitment of the issue to a coordinate political department; or
- a lack of judicially discoverable and manageable standards for resolving it; or
- the impossibility of deciding without an initial policy determination of a kind clearly for non-judicial discretion; or
- the impossibility of a court's undertaking independent resolution without expressing lack of the respect due coordinate branches of government; or
- an unusual need for unquestioning adherence to a political decision already made; or
- the potentiality of embarrassment from multifarious pronouncements by various departments on one question.

A case may be dismissed on political question grounds if—and only if—the case will require the court to decide a question possessing one of these six characteristics. See *Id.* ("Unless one of these formulations is inextricable from the case at bar, there should be no dismissal for non-justiciability on the ground of a political question's presence."); see also Aktepe, 105 F.3d at 1403. ("For invocation of the political question doctrine to be appropriate, at least one of these characteristics must be evident.") If the case would require the court to decide a political question, it must be dismissed for lack of jurisdiction. See *Made in the USA Found. v. United States*, 242 F.3d 1300, 1319 (11th Cir. 2001) (dismissing suit barred by political question doctrine for lack of jurisdiction); *Occidental of Umm al Qaywayn, Inc. v. A Certain Cargo of Petroleum*, 577 F.2d 1196, 1201 (5th Cir. 1978).

"Presidential argues that adjudication of the instant case, involving an accident that occurred in Afghanistan during wartime, will require the district court to decide a political question. It is undoubtedly true that military activities often give rise to political questions. In one case involving the military, we observed that '[t]he interjection of tort law into the realms of foreign policy and military affairs would effectively permit judicial reappraisal of judgments the *Constitution* has committed to the other branches.' Aktepe, 105 F.3d at 1404. Nevertheless, it is clear that not even military judgments are completely immune from judicial review. See *Gilligan v. Morgan*, 413 U.S. 1, 11-12, 93 S. Ct. 2440, 2446-2447, 37 L. Ed. 2d 407 (1973) ('[I]t should be clear that we neither hold nor imply that the conduct of the National Guard is always beyond judicial review or that there may not be accountability in a judicial forum for violations of law or for specific unlawful conduct by military personnel, whether by way of damages or injunctive relief.'[774]) ('[I]t is error to suppose that every case or controversy which touches foreign relations lies beyond judicial cognizance.'). Accordingly, we must apply the Baker factors to determine whether the suit against Presidential will require the district court to reexamine a military judgment; and if so, whether the military judgment is the kind that warrants application of the political question doctrine."

[D] Will the Case Involve a Decision That Has Been Constitutionally Committed to Another Branch?

The first Baker factor asks whether there is "a textually demonstrable constitutional commitment of the issue to a coordinate political department."[775] This factor recognizes that, under the separation of powers, certain decisions have been exclusively committed to the legislative and executive branches of the federal government, and are therefore not subject to judicial review.

The United States Supreme Court statement in the *Legal Tender Cases* that the "argument presented in support of the position that the unit of money [sovereign constitutional money] value must possess intrinsic value," derived from Article I, § 8, Clause 5 of the *Constitution*, has deserved and received the Court's most careful consideration. In the *Legal Tender Cases*, a case of far-reaching consequences, the Court heard the case and "thoroughly convinced as we are that Congress has not transgressed its powers," issued its ruling. The Court recognized the over-riding importance of the issue of creation and regulation of the value of money as a Congressional power and duty, despite the fact that the arguments on this issue were heard by the court but not ruled on solely because the issue was not presented for a ruling. One must conclude that the Court, having heard the argument and recognized the vital importance of the issue and the argument to the government and to the public at large, would not decline to hear the same argument and would decide the same issue were it to be properly framed and presented to the Court for disposition, precisely because, in the case presented in this work, Congress has "transgressed its powers" and duties through its participation in the defendants' criminal, corrupt racketeering enterprise.

[E] Does the Suit Involve a Lack of Judicially Discoverable and Manageable Standards?

The second Baker factor applies when there is "a lack of judicially discoverable and manageable standards for resolving" the case.[776] In Aktepe, "we found that the political question doctrine applied, in part because there are no judicially manageable standards to apply to the training activities of the United States military.... [C]ourts lack standards with which to assess whether reasonable care was taken to achieve military objectives while minimizing injury and loss of life."[777]

In the case contemplated by this work, as its contribution to the success of the defendants' racketeering enterprise, Congress "transgressed its powers" by providing no intrinsic standard for the value of the dollar, failing to delegate such duty and power to any other party with suitable standards to govern its conduct in accordance with applicable law, leaving the Washington Wall Street racketeering enterprise free to exploit the failure of regulation of value of the dollar by its intentional debasement of the dollar in fact, injuring every member of the plaintiff class. Congress having eliminating any discoverable and manageable standard for regulation of the value of American sovereign money in accordance with a standard of intrinsic value, the Court could fill that void on its own motion, or on plaintiff's motion, establish an equitable, transparent, judicially mandated plan whereby Congress could meet its constitutional mandate voluntarily in conjunction with all of the named defendants, without usurping Congressional power and duty and without any embarrassment or lack of respect to Congress or any of the other government defendants. The Court has already recognized and confirmed the vital importance of the legal issue of assurance of the constitutional necessity that Congress avoid "transgressing its powers," by meeting its power and duty to regulate the value of the unit of American money in accordance with a standard possessing intrinsic value as required of it under the *Constitution*, as well as the vital importance of the issue and the argument to the government and to the public at large.

[F] Other Baker Factors

"Finally, Presidential has not yet demonstrated that the other Baker factors apply to this case, for essentially the same reasons discussed above. As the case appears to be an ordinary tort suit, there is no 'impossibility of deciding without an initial policy determination of a kind clearly for nonjudicial discretion.'"[778] There is also no evident "impossibility of a court's undertaking independent resolution without expressing lack of the respect due coordinate branches of government."[779] "Presidential has not shown that the suit will implicate a decision made by a coordinate branch of government. For the same reason, there is no 'unusual need for unquestioning adherence to a political decision already made' or "the potentiality of embarrassment from multifarious pronouncements by various departments on one question.' Presidential simply has not shown that the case implicates any "political decision" or decision made by any other 'department ... of government.'"[780]

In the plaintiff's case, although Congress has the constitutional power and duty to create and regulate the value of American money, Congress does not now meet its constitutional mandate, "transgressing its powers," but instead Congress permits the Wall Street banks primarily, amongst other credit creators, through the conduct of the Washington Wall Street defendants criminal corrupt racketeering enterprise, to create money without reference to any standard of intrinsic value and to emit and conflate that valueless money throughout the Federal Reserve and national banking systems and throughout other domestic and global financial systems, and most germane to this case, in their hands of ordinary American households that rely of the United States dollar to fulfill its promise of protection of money value to them. Congress has, in fact, permitted and participated with the Wall Street defendants and other defendants in this case to actively debase the dollar, such as it is—now paper money not regulated in value by any sense of meaning. In fact the American dollar is completely disconnected from any standard of intrinsic value. Congress, in addition to the other members of the Washington Wall Street enterprise has exploited its refusal to regulate the value of American money pursuant to a suitable standard of intrinsic value, to the extent the causation of the great financial crisis driven debasement of the dollar culminated in plaintiff's injuries in fact complained of in the case to be made as contemplated by this work. It is inconceivable that the Court would decline to hear the argument and the issue of the constitutional congressional imperative to regulate the value of the unit of money in accordance with a standard possessing intrinsic value, and to thereby compel Congress and the Executive, including the Fed and other financial regulators, supervisors and enforcers, to protect and defend the civil and constitutional rights of Americans to an honest, safe and sound dollar, against the scourge of debasement. Congressional failure lies at the heart of the financial crises that inevitably follow money debasement and the injuries in fact suffered by the plaintiffs.

The DOJ Fraud Section has emphasized time after time that its mission is to bring those who lie cheat and steal to justice. Money debasement is the embodiment of lying, cheating and stealing by the defendant Washington Wall Street criminal corrupt racketeering enterprise on an unprecedented and intolerable scale The DOJ has failed the people, the ordinary people, the American households, plaintiffs in case for financial crisis accountability. The DOJ has ignored its stated formal mission to protect the American people under the rule of law. The government defendants in this case, the purported protectors of the public interest, have found, without any discernible foundation in fact or law and without a real shred of realistic justification acceptable to the people, that the Wall Street defendants are too big, too powerful, too important to fail or to be jailed. They are also admittedly too big to manage. As too big to manage they are also too big to play any meaningful role in the restraint on intentional money debasement that may be profitable for them but is toxic to ordinary Americans. The protection of the plaintiffs in this case under the common law—the will of the people issuing from their lives; protection from the vast harm caused by pervasive institutional lying, cheating and stealing through abuse of power and trust and intentional money debasement has been abjectly abandoned by Congress, the Wall Street banks and the other members of the Washington Wall Street enterprise. This conduct of legally and morally indefensible. The Wall Street defendants have simply purchased from paid ransom to the government defendants for political and legal immunity, making a mockery of the American public's rights to equal protection under the law, due process of law in remediating their grievances and finding justice in the form of a case for financial crisis accountability under the American rule of law. Enforcement of the plaintiffs' rights under the American rule of law *is not a political act.* The practical immunity from legal accountability for the financial crisis extended by the DOJ and the Federal financial regulators to Washington and Wall Street protecting them from the consequences of their actions *is a political act.*

In summary then, the textually demonstrable United States constitutional commitment of the governments' powers and duties to protect of the interests of plaintiffs in this case from the scourge of intentional fraudulent money debasement through intentional abuse of the trust extended to them and the powers delegated to them falls on all branches of government political departments. The Washington defendants include primarily Congress; the special non-governmental creature of the United States Congress comprising the Federal Reserve System, including specifically, the defendant Wall Street banks; and the federal financial regulatory agencies forming a part of the United States Executive Branch of government. The Judicial System, represented by the United States Supreme Court, has specifically stated and acknowledged in the *Legal Tender Cases* the importance of the integrity of constitutional created sovereign money, the value of which has been regulated by Congress in accordance with a standard of intrinsic value, "involve constitutional questions of the most vital importance to the government and to the public at large," which includes, of course the ordinary Americans as members of the plaintiff class in this case.

There are clearly mandated judicially discoverable and manageable standards for resolving the constitutional issues through the equitable relief to be sought by the plaintiff class in this case; by the defendants' compliance with such standards, that can be incentivized by the courts assessment of monetary damages from the nongovernmental members of the Washington Wall Street enterprise in the form of compensation, penalties and costs. The nongovernmental members of the Washington Wall Street enterprise responses to the judicially imposed remedies will directly affect and impair the ongoing continuation of the Washington Wall Street enterprise and will be integral the willing compliance by the Government defendants with the requirements of such equitable relief.

The United States Supreme Court has made the initial policy determination that the issues raised in this case are specifically and clearly suitable for resolution through the judicial process and exercise of judicial discretion, all as contemplated by the United States Supreme Court in the *Legal Tender Cases*.

The court's undertaking independent resolution of these issues in the manner in which the plaintiff class has prayed for relief does not expressly constitute a lack of the respect due coordinate branches of government. Whatever lack of respect may be attributed and directed to coordinate branches of government in this case are directed not by the court or the judicial system, but rather by the public record of conduct by those branches of government that are replete in the existing documentation, proof and evidence that forms the factual foundation for this case, with respect to which the court may simply take judicial notice, without further comment or characterization.

There exists no unusual need for the courts unquestioning adherence to a political decision already made. To the extent political decisions may be relevant to this case they have been made by the framers of the law and now reside not as political decisions, but rather as the *Constitution* and the law of the land, or in the status of decisions taken by the other branches of government in violation of the *Constitution* and the law of the land. Political decisions made by the defendants to violate existing American laws to the damage of the plaintiffs in this case require does not unquestioning adherence to and acceptance of such illegal acts by the court but, to the contrary, those decisions and actions form the gravamen of the plaintiffs' case and the result should be well considered justice under the American rule of law the results must be unquestionably followed, accepted and adhered to by the other branches government.

Any potentiality of embarrassment from multifarious pronouncements on the money question by various departments on that one question would derive only through the active historically recorded transgression by those departments of their respective constitutional powers and duties pertaining to that question. If the possibility of any such embarrassment to those departments is ever to be realized, the grounds for such possibility have already been realized in the public record and through public discourse and such potentiality, if it did exist, would rest solely upon the existing record and admissions of those departments and not upon the dispassionate and due deliberations upon the issue by the judicial system's enforcement of financial crisis accountability under the existing American rule of law.

There is, however, a clear legal basis and a legal case for plaintiffs holding the defendants accountable for their lying cheating and stealing that caused the great financial crisis and the damages it has wrought on the plaintiffs; under the common law, under the *United States Constitution* and under the federal statutes, itemized earlier in this work. These laws exist to protect the people from organized combinations of the rich and powerful that have seized the power lie, cheat and steal and abuse the trust and confidence reposed in them and intentionally inflict the injurious consequences of their wrongdoing on ordinary Americans, the plaintiffs in this case.

§9.11 CONCLUDING OBSERVATIONS

Have we become so cynical that we accept the fraudulent policy of extend and pretend rather than insist that Washington and Wall Street, and yes, the legal and accounting professions, return, not to some previous golden age of perfect monetary systems? Does the body of ordinary Americans insist on conduct of America's existing monetary, economic and banking system in accordance with existing law and the moral and legal principles that underlie and support the law? Financial crisis accountability is about Washington' and Wall Street's simple honor of the limited delegated powers of government and the fiduciary duty of both Washington and Wall Street to maintain an American system of honest, safe and sound money and banking as required by existing American law. Any legal reform considered in pursuant to the granting of the equitable remedies to be sought in the case for financial crisis accountability must be based on proven disciplines of asset valuation. We can no longer trust, or credibly, consciously and intentionally turn away from the effects of the Washington Wall Street enterprise's abuse of trust and power, violation of existing law that is based on the proposition that ordinary Americans can achieve national economic prosperity based upon policies of money debasement and intentional asset liquidity and value manipulation that serve, not the national interest, but rather the selfish interests of Washington and Wall Street. Washington's and Wall Street's policies are designed to manipulate and misrepresent asset liquidity and value, not to protect them. Monetary policy may be necessary, but it must be made subject and subordinate to the discipline and fundamental principles that govern the historical, proven functions of clearly delineated tools of sovereign money, regulated credit money and the prudent use of securitization and derivatives to facilitate credit supporting economic growth and efficiency—not boom and bust speculation.[781]

Readers may also conclude that the fundamental issues of enforcement of existing American law accompanied by focused attention to the remediation of the well-documented failures of our banking and monetary system, may ultimately be addressed, and even resolved, on a sensible, honest and legal basis in the context of bankruptcy proceedings. The ultimate issues of asset liquidity and valuation are central to bankruptcy. In theory, claims to assets or their proceeds in bankruptcy are arranged in priority, placing those least culpable for the debtors' losses at the highest level of priority, and those most culpable at the lowest level. The competing interest of claimants may be most well suited to fight through the priorities and loss allocation considering the changed dynamics of debtor creditor relationships that have been revealed during financial crises over the past 45 years since the Nixon shock. Consideration of the nature of money, its role in measuring and intermediating asset liquidity and value, the perversion of that role through the abandonment of traditional sovereign money, the progressive loosening of credit created in the Federal Reserve System and the explosion of shadow banking money substitutes provide a new battleground for financial equity and justice. Bankruptcy attorneys, debtors and creditors in bankruptcy courts are perhaps best suited to take on the implications of distorted asset liquidity and value and loss sharing and allocation where the rubber meets the road, so to speak. Washington and Wall Street are not likely to voluntarily address their role in and assume accountability for the mess they have created.

Shadow bankers are not agents of the Federal Reserve System. Their business models, though varied and often complex, are driven by informed speculative investment. Greater risk for a higher yield. That risk and yield are generally found in market dysfunction and asymmetry. The ultimate unwinding of the great financial crisis, likely in the context of the next crisis,[782] or as a result of the prosecution of the case for financial crisis accountability made in this work, will provide great opportunity to those who can participate in and capitalize on the current asset liquidity and value mal-alignment and represent the market's contribution to such a realignment, in accordance with the legal principles that are fundamental to that alignment. The realignment may open the door to new successive opportunities for speculative investment, not in the world of a financialized economy, but in a productive real economy.

America has an enduring history of alignment of natural law and moral law with its constitutional, statutory and common law traditions. There can be no doubt that honesty is a principle of natural law and one of the greatest of moral laws. and Honesty in economic and financial matters is central to the integrity, trust and confidence that must lie at the heart of each and every successful socio-economic system. America has taken great pride it its tradition of openness, honesty and transparency. Our money historically has inspired trust and confidence world-wide.

Honest money is a founding principle for the American political, economic, financial and legal system. America as a nation depends for its continued socio-economic balance based on the rule of law in the breaking down concentrations of wealth and power in politics, business and in banking. The progressive tendency of government and banking to attack and erode the natural, moral and legal principles that protects ordinary Americans and their institutions as embodied in the American rule of law is profoundly un-American. The American public will have its heritage one way or the other. It will be respected in accordance with the application of the American rule of law through our judicial system, affording every American due process and equal protection of the law, or the public will have its heritage through the wrenching process of revolution. Such an unfortunate outcome is not laughable. The money question lay at the heart of the strife leading to the *Magna Charta*, the American Revolution and the French Revolution. The quotation from James Anthony Froude, *infra,* could not be more apt.

Consistent with the concerns and objectives expressed in the *Report of the Monetary Commission of the Indianapolis Convention*, Congress passed the *Gold Standard Act of 1900*. In the preamble to this legislation, the document provided that the Act was "to define and fix the standard of value, to maintain parity of all forms of money issued or coined by the United States, to refund the public debt and for other purposes." The Act again imposed a gold standard as "the standard unit of value, and all forms of money issued or coined by the United States shall be maintained at a parity of value with this standard, and it shall be the duty of the Treasury to maintain such parity."

The *Gold Standard Act of 1900* clearly provided a "common denominator as necessary for the comparison of the value of commodities." "Fiat money provides not such common denominator."

The absence of such a common denominator also makes possible the creation of money substitutes such as have flooded the market in geyser of liquidity in the shadow banking system in the form of: (i) securitized assets with the most tenuous of ties to asset values, accompanied by (ii) a pyramid of derivative money substitutes piled on those securitized instruments, once again, having no meaningful tie to underlying real assets in the real economy; and (iii) being in themselves purely financial assets, functioning as money substitutes on the balance sheets banks and other financial institutions, including money market funds.[783]

The intentional misrepresentation of the value of a societies' money by the state and its bankers works a fraud on the holders of the money who find that the money cannot be exchanged for the value promised. Societies have long attempted to protect themselves from the fraud of money debasement. By the time a society discovers the extent of the intentional misrepresentations in money and accounts expressed in books and records, made by governments and banks to further their private interest in successful money debasement, rather than honor the trust and powers reposed in them by the public; and by the time that the public apprehends the extent of fraudulent debasement of its money, compounded by the secret theft and transfer of its value to the state and its bankers; and the extent of the fraud and theft becomes intolerable; the only remedy available to the citizens has most often civil disobedience, mob violence and war.

Money now consists overwhelmingly of credit, as has largely been the case throughout history. Early in American history, demand for credit to pay the costs of Civil War prompted Congress to establish the national banking system, greenbacks and fractional reserve banking to facilitate the creation of state credit. The value of that credit was assured by the requirement of the credit by interest bearing bonds and their ultimate redemption in gold, both principal and interest, under specific standards of congressionally constitutionally established standards of value. Since that point in time in American history, Congress' commitment to meet its constitutional mandate to regulate the value of American credit money has literally, progressively, evaporated. The combination of Washington and Wall Street and the concentration of wealth and power in that combination has subverted the public interest in the trust and confidence they rightfully expect from Washington and Wall Street, and they have subverted ordinary Americans reliance on the integrity of government and bank fiduciary grounded monopoly over money and all its characteristics. As the value of American money has literally plummeted. Washington and Wall Street continue to misrepresent their interest in the benefits money debasement secretly confers on them and the great injury it does to the people, American households and the American economy.

According to Washington and Wall Street, they are the experts in charge; we must trust them; they have Americans' best interests at heart; and without their self-serving ministrations the American public would surely be even worse off than ordinary Americans are now.

The important point to take away from this period is that the very same type of mortgage-backed securities that caused the great financial crisis of 2008 were actually first conceived and sold to the public a century earlier—and by many of the same banks and financial institutions—and to the same ultimate effect—financial crises.

Liquid money must be backed by liquid value. Methods of accomplishing this in absence of constitutional standards have been intentionally gamed on so many levels that must be return to the fundamental monetary equation and its American constitu tional foundation. No matter what standard or standards are selected and no matter how the standard or standards are established they must be free of manipulation by banks or government on nontransparent basis. The only way to move to such a positive development is to predicate it by imposition of accountability for failure to have done so for past 45 years. This case, whether made by the DOJ or, the DOJ having failed and expected to continue to refuse to make the case, then by ordinary Americans who have been so grievously damaged by such failure, must be advanced.

It is self-evident that abuse of trust and power through the lying, cheating, and stealing, in the mechanism of money debasement, are manifestly: (i) intentional; and (ii) misrepresentations. They are so by definition and as matters of fact.

An action by ordinary Americans to enforce legal accountability upon the Washington Wall Street enterprise for the financial crisis cannot simply be advance as punishment and retribution. It must provide for a feasible alternative to the status quo, incentive to address the alternative and a methodology to return to us honest, safe, and sound American money and a stable economic, monetary, and financial system that conforms to existing American moral and legal principles, the American rule of law, and gives rise to well-justified public trust and confidence in that system. The next and final chapter of this book embodies my modest recommended course of action necessary to provide the inspiration to justly achieve that trust and confidence.

CHAPTER 10

Concluding Observations

§10.01 WASHINGTON AND WALL STREET ARE ACCOUNTABLE FOR THE FINANCIAL CRISIS

Washington and Wall Street have lied tous ordinary Americans; they cheated and stolen the value of the fruits of our labor and our modest stores of value, through a systemic web of false narratives and intentional misrepresentations, enabled by an abuse of trust and power of almost inconceivable depth and breadth. The characterization of Washington and Wall Street conduct as lying, cheating, and stealing is not in the manner of exaggeration or a polemic. The protection of ordinary Americans civil rights is essential to realization of the self-evident truth that all men are created equal; that we are endowed with certain unalienable rights, among these are life, liberty and the pursuit of happiness; and that to secure these rights, we have established a government based on the *United States Constitution*; including the right to transparent, honest, safe and sound money, the value of which is regulated by Congress; and that we may not be deprived of life, liberty, or property, including specifically, but without limitation, the value of our sovereign constitutional money without due process of law; nor shall our private property be taken for public use by the government or any agency thereof, without just compensation; and that, without due process of law we shall not be denied the equal protection of the laws, including the protections afforded by the *Constitution* and the American rule of law.

The stated mission of the DOJ has been created to protect, preserve and enforce American legal rights. Specifically, the Fraud Division of the DOJ has stated specifically on its official web site that its mission is to protect us from those who lie to, cheat and steal from us. The DOJ Fraud Section boasts that it plays a "unique and essential role in the DOJ's fight against sophisticated economic crime." The American money debasement revealed in this work is the very essence of such sophisticated economic crime. Just as the mission statement has now disappeared from the Fraud Division's web site, the actual performance of its fight against the sophisticated economic crime of money debasement has disappeared from its policies and conduct in response to the great financial crisis.[784]

Washington and Wall Street have promulgated a body of misrepresentations to the American public, false narratives that go to the heart of our monetary and financial system, economy and the, possibility, perhaps the reality of the American Dream. The misrepresentations are perpetrated in every Federal Reserve Note and every report filed by every federally regulated financial institution and published throughout our financial system by writing, electronic data entry and communicated by mail, wire or electronic communication mechanisms. The misrepresentations are now idiomatically characterized, through what Washington and Wall Street hope appear to be, innocuous, euphemistic phrases such as extend and pretend, kick the can down the road, too big to fail, too big to jail, too big to regulate—as though somehow Washington and Wall Street have the right to engage in a long term intentional policy and course of action constituting abuse of trust and power as well as lying to, cheating, and stealing from the American public. Washington and Wall Street do not have that right. They have not been held accountable to the American public for that conduct. As President Franklin Roosevelt once said, "Repetition does not transform a lie into the truth." At the same time, Roosevelt took American off the gold standard with the complicity of Congress, the Federal Reserve System and the National Banking system. America then embraced a monetary policy based on non-transparent fiat money manipulation to achieve institutional, and individual self-interest.[785] That monetary policy was abandoned briefly when the Bretton Woods institutions were established and acted as a tertiary, but reasonably satisfactory American amanuenses in service of financial stability for a period of twenty-seven years, in an attempt to corral the value of American money in its capacity as the world's reserve currency. America unilaterally abandoned the constraints of *the Bretton Woods Agreements* in 1971 in what became known as the Nixon shock. That was the end of any American congressional attempt to regulate the value of the dollar as required by the *Constitution*.

Asset values are now openly manipulated by Washington and Wall Street. The policy of Quantitative Easing did not help the American economy. It helped the institutions from which the Fed purchased overpriced assets. The public record is replete with government reports containing official acknowledgments that asset values and liquidity have been and continue to be intentionally manipulated. Intentional manipulation and misrepresentation of asset values and liquidity by Washington and Wall Street has become accepted government policy.[786] It is as though Washington truly believes that a massive program of intentional misrepresentation of asset values and liquidity, fraudulent debasement of money, protection of their own interests as a group through manipulation and abuse of regulatory discretion and legal forbearance, bailouts, subsidies and Quantitative Easing meets the moral, legal constitutional requirement of a transparent, honest, safe, and sound monetary, banking and financial system. This program is commonly accepted by the American public. Washington and Wall Street continue to steal value from the Americans, concentrating wealth, power and control in the Washington Wall Street closed economic circle, as though that conduct represents a legitimate exercise of public policy. It is no wonder that Washington and Wall Street have been able to perpetuate their policies and practices of intentional abuse of the trust, power and confidence Americans have delegated to them and to continue the policies and practices unchecked.

Quite simply, the people, have not called the question of financial accountability and justice under the American rule of law for the tragic consequences of financial crises.

The Federal Reserve System, a creature of Congress, the active members of which are the national banks as well as state charted banks that are members, and among them are the Wall Street banks, actually controlling the economy. The Federal Reserve System is represented by Washington and Wall Street to the American public to be the embodiment of monetary, banking and financial expertise, responsibly wielding their power, authority and duty to transparently protect the value of American money and the financial system it represents through the exercise of its monetary powers. That is simply untrue.

§10.02 WASHINGTON AND WALL STREET HAVE ACCOMPLISHED THEIR CONCENTRATION OF INCOME, WEALTH, AND POWER THROUGH ANCIENT CRIME OF MONEY DEBASEMENT

"Wall Street sheriff Preet Bharara directed both barrels at JPMorgan Chase ..., and he aimed his sights high." ... "The difficulty inherent in precisely valuing certain kinds of financial positions does not give people a license to mislead or cover up losses," he said. "That goes double for handsomely paid executives at public companies whose actions can roil markets and upend an economy." ... "Capitalism works best when its participants do not lie and cheat. Capitalism works best when its biggest beneficiaries play by the same rules as everyone else," Bharara said.[787]

Historically, money debasement is the emission, presentation and circulation of any form of money that does not possess the full value it purports to represent. Money debasement is accomplished by impairing, diminishing, falsifying, scaling and lightening the value represented. While American money has devolved from constitutional coined form of "sovereign" money to paper legal tender sovereign money made from nothing but paper and ink, and coined legal tender money consisting of laminated embossed discs of sandwiched base metal.

While the working definition of money has been expanded far beyond the sovereign money provided for in the *Constitution*, the definition of money debasement set forth in 18 U.S.C. § 331 and § 332 has remained anachronistically fixed, and has not been extended to correspond to the Fed's definition of "coined money" or to the actual money circulating through the formal banking and the shadow banking systems and serving as "liquidity"; liquid value on which society can rely with trust and confidence. Money is now data, electronic date with no real discernable connection to Americans real lives.

The regulation of money of is said to have been delegated by Congress to the Fed and by the Fed to its partners in the money creation business, the Wall Street banks.

Instead of protecting the American public from the depredations of money debasement, these institutions have simply ignored the *Constitution*, common law and statutory law forbidding the tort of money debasement. The American rule of statutory law established to protect the public interest has been rendered a glaring anachronism. The current statutes pertaining by their definition to the tort and crime of money debasement, have seemingly become irrelevant. They are thought to protect the American public only from "depredations" and money debasement of "gold or silver coins struck or coined at any of the mints of the United States," and from defacement, alteration, increase or diminishment of the scales or weights used at any of the mints or assay offices of the United States through the fault or connivance of any officer or person employed at the said mints or assay offices, with a fraudulent intent. In today's world, 18 U.S.C. § 332 makes a mockery of any pretense of Washington or Wall Street concern for protection of the public interest in honest, safe and sound money and banking. It makes a mockery of our legal, economic, financial, monetary, social and political systems. It makes a mockery of most Americans' hopes of achievement of the American Dream.

Congress and the federal financial regulators have extended the meaning of money far from gold or silver coins subject to statutory debasement. The standards for weights and measures designed to regulate the values of specie coined money have been abandoned as anachronistic. The only true meaning that can be taken from American law prohibiting money debasement requires that it be construed to apply to present day American money and its potential for debasement in accordance with its nature. Money, as that term is presently construed by Congress and the federal financial regulators, has been debased in value to a fraction of its historical stated purchasing value for goods and services in the marketplace. The following graph demonstrates only the debased value expressed (in this chart, by comparison the Swiss Franc, a relatively stable currency and measure of asset value and liquidity) as purchasing power by Federal Reserve Notes and their predecessor official United States dollars, both on and off a metallic standard of specie by which the value of the currency was historically regulated, more or less, and does not reflect the debasement of dollar denominated money in the shadow banking system, as presently recognized in the real marketplace:

Figure 10.1 US BLS Consumer Price Index NSA (CPUSAM) Versus Switzerland Franks per Dollar (USDCHF)

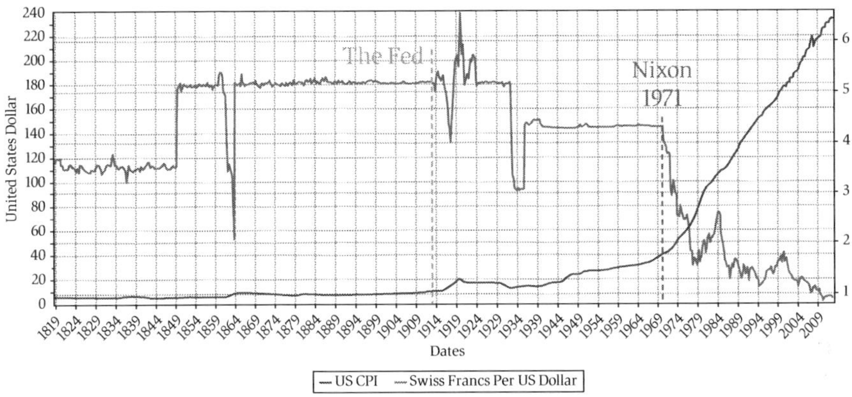

In the present era of central banking, liquidity has historically been set by the reserve ratios of the central banks and the size of their power money. Liquidity equaled power money multiplied by the inverse of the reserve ratio.[788]

Money is now shaped by forces that were limited or non-existent in prior cycles. Neither our Congress, its creature the Fed, nor its partners in the tort and crime of money debasement, the Wall Street banks, actually control the quantity, quality, liquidity and value of money. The fog of monetized structured financial products, securities, derivatives and liquidity created in the shadow banking system has reduced financial transparency to zero. Central bank-dictated reserves no longer set the credit multiplier, to the extent reserve requirements can any longer be considered useful. The definitions of reserves have been gamed so far as to reduce effective reserve requirements for most Wall Street banks to zero. Raising (Fed policy) interest rates did not affect the cost of capital in the capital markets. The recent Fed reduction of the "policy" rates, on top of earlier reductions in response to our liquidity crisis, had little effect on the cost of capital. Once the cost of long-term capital rises above the natural interest rate, we should expect that liquidity, and therefore values, to contract sharply if the expansion and contraction phases are to remain symmetrical. When asset bubbles collapse, central banks, being unable to bear the economic costs act asymmetrically.[789]

Central banks have considered raising rates either to normalize them from easy monetary policy or to combat inflation, but at the first sign of asset price deflation, they have eased precipitously. The dialogue of policy vacillation continues as this book is written. Quantitative Easing has purported to control inflation, but for most Americans, whose fundamental needs are not included in the core inflation index, including prices of food and energy and housing (under-reported) have risen dramatically. Housing prices have been re-inflated by artificially low interest rates and by continuing output purchases by the Fed of government of insured housing loans of $40 billion per month, purchased with money created from nothing. Even though the current Fed policy rhetoric is the unwinding of Quantitative Easing and the unwinding of its balance sheet, the unwinding has been minimal and asset purchases continue. Thus, prices paid by ordinary Americans have risen, creating a false impression of increasing wealth. The Fed embarked on a program of balance sheet reduction (unwinding) while housing prices are simultaneously exhibiting weakness. Unwinding appears to be on hold.

The shadow banking credit explosion continues with intentional support and action by both Washington and Wall Street. The winners in this fraudulent manipulation of asset values, liquidity, prices and debasement of money are Washington and Wall Street. Thus, any pain of being invested in an asset bubble would appear to be of short duration. This view reinforces the markets' conviction that global monetary policy is asymmetric and biased in favor of investors and speculators. The massive resulting transfer of income, wealth and power to Washington, Wall Street and the wealthiest one percent of Americans confirms the American public's worst fears.

This work has revisited the foundational concepts of bank fraud and crime specifically applicable to the use of credit as money and presents a re-evaluation of the role of accountability for bank fraud and crime as an aspect of new thinking in global finance and its regulation. Ordinary Americans must challenge and condemn the current institutionally accepted narrative and assumption that financial reform should focus on the systemic institutional harm government and financial institutions may face and have suffered; and the corollary narrative and assumption that their suffering has been due to fraud inflicted upon them by, yes, ordinary Americans.

The publicly recorded facts of damages caused by Washington and Wall Street to ordinary American citizens invoke the application of specific principles of common law, constitutional, civil and criminal statutory law. These basic legal principles exist outside of and rise above the bureaucratically controlled banking and financial regulatory context.

Legal financial crisis accountability, whether civil or criminal, implies the existence of defined moral and legal duties binding specific individuals and institutions. Failure of the responsible parties to meet their respective defined duties, resulting in harm to others, when discovered, must be promptly followed by petition for relief, remedies, damages, penalties and meaningful institutional and policy reform. Americans are entitled to the prompt imposition of well-established and long-standing appropriate consequences upon the respective culpable parties for their wrongful, immoral, and illegal conduct in accordance with the American rule of law. While Washington's federal financial regulatory authorities have broad discretion to enforce laws, rules and regulations, they have declined to do so for political reasons and for self-preservation. The fiduciary standard historically applied to bankers and government under the rule of law has been replaced by vacillating regulatory discretion that has proved to be a failure in fact, in application and enforcement of existing American law that rises higher than the false dignity of regulatory discretion that is shot through Americas monetary, economic, banking and financial systems.

Washington and Wall Street have proudly proclaimed that taxpayers have been repaid and suffered no loss from massive government bailouts. The fact is that Wall Street has simply appeared to repay the publicly identified bailouts through some obvious, but primarily through non-transparent government subsidies circling through the monetary system referred to as Fed "monetary policy," "discount window lending" and "open market operations," conducted outside of the limited scope contemplated for their use, based upon the usual cry of necessity in response to an unprecedented existential crisis.

The official sounding narrative of existential necessity offered to the public in the interest of "financial stability," has passed by uncritically, without scrutiny or accountability. Washington and Wall Street created the great financial crisis and have been the primary beneficiaries of these extraordinary illegal policy departures. Once the departure is made by Washington and Wall Street in one financial crisis, it becomes the norm from which the departure is necessitated in response to each next succeeding financial crisis. Washington and Wall Street have always emerged from American financial crises bigger, more powerful and wealthier. Washington and Wall Street have simply cooked the books. Any suggestion that taxpayers have been repaid for the cost and protected from the damage caused by the financial crisis is farcical when examined in the light of a Federal Reserve balance sheet that ballooned to nearly $4.5 trillion at week end July 2, 2014, that funded what amounts to a cover-up of Washington and Wall Street legal culpability, and left domestic damages to the American people estimated by the government of up to $20 trillion; and damages to people outside of America estimated by the Fed as in excess of $60 trillion. As of this writing, the balance sheet remains at just under $4.5 trillion, with an actual accomplished unwinding of the impact of Quantitative Easing on the balance sheet at this writing of only approximately $100 billion. As investments mature and are retired, the proceeds have been used to continue to purchase additional securities to support prices and therefore underlying asset values, notwithstanding rhetoric of unwinding and news of Fed interest rate hikes, rates remain artificially suppressed. Suppressed interest rates constitute an additional form of price support price for the value and liquidity of the securities which the Fed continues to purchase. This price support and value and liquidity manipulation constitutes intentional value misrepresentation and serves to contribute to increasing asset valuation bubbles reflected on the balance sheets of not only the Fed, but also banks and shadow banks and ordinary Americans. That is bank fraud.

Recognition of systemic risk as the cause of systemic financial crises is one thing. Defining it, doing something about it by rooting out who has done what that was wrong and irresponsible in creating systemic financial risk and systemic financial crises; and most importantly, holding them to account under the rule of law is another thing entirely. We cannot move to long term solutions to its structural financial instability without a change in perspective brought about by public display of enforced legal responsibility, accountability, and disincentives to further bad acts such as those at the root of the financial crisis. The case made in this book for financial crisis accountability is the last option available to restore monetary balance without resort to active civil disobedience, violence and war.

The sustainability of global finance as a useful and honest tool will ultimately be determined by whether governments and financial institutions can be held accountable under the rule of law for their course of bank fraud and crime that has directly caused financial crisis after crisis. There is no issue more important to Americans current and future well-being than the recognition of and legal redress for the great financial crisis through the imposition Washington and Wall Street accountability to the American public achieved through the judicial system.

§10.03 ENFORCEMENT OF FINANCIAL CRISIS ACCOUNTABILITY DOES NOT POSE AN EXISTENTIAL THREAT TO AMERICA

The Washington Wall Street mantra of too big to fail and too big to jail springs from the idea that systemic bank failures attributable to intentional systemic money debasement and criminal prosecution of the government and financial elite in our country would be so destructive that the effects of enforced legal accountability would pose an existential threat to America as a nation.

Most observers of America's financial crises and media pundits shy away from any discussion of specific individuals in Washington and on Wall Street, whose specific legal duties, fiduciary duties, to their respective institutions and to the American public to maintain a transparent, honest, safe and sound banking, financial and monetary system were not met, and caused the great financial crisis. Washington and Wall Street must, therefore, be held legally accountable individually, personally, for the damages they have done to ordinary Americans. The individuals whose specific roles, duties, responsibilities and accountability might be discussed, examined and evaluated are among the most powerful in American government, business and banking. The idea of their potential civil and criminal accountability for systemic financial crises including the great financial crisis has been an idea best kept quiet, out of the media, and well away from the reach of basic, fundamental processes of law in imposing civil and criminal accountability.

For the past forty-five years, accountability has been left to special units or task forces such as those called for by Presidents George H. W. Bush, George W. Bush and Barak Obama, and by the DOJ in the years immediately following each financial crisis during their respective terms in office. Historically, these special units or task forces have been expensive, time consuming and largely impotent in identifying the true parties responsible for systemic financial crises and in holding them to account, under either civil or criminal law. Their history of illusory effect provides credence for the perpetuation of the web of false narratives exposed in this work that have so far protected Washington and Wall Street as: immune; too big to fail, and too big to jail.

The naming of names of the individuals that caused the financial crisis and the specification of violations of American law that have worked bank fraud and crime upon the American public has been scrupulously avoided, except for named Wall Street executive officers during the at the time of the financial crisis. This book presents a current recognition of the existence and validity of legal standards for accountability and justice that apply to Washington and Wall Street; and provide for and sustain the American and global standards of integrity, trust and confidence necessary to money and banking as fundamental components of domestic and global commerce. These legal standards are as old as money and banking. One simply cannot deny that transparency, integrity, honesty, trust and confidence in money and banking are the very essence of public interest. These factors apply to every member of every civilized society every day.

Efforts in the public interest in the years following the financial crises of the past 45 years to impose legal accountability on those responsible for the financial and human devastation wrought by the crises have largely been expressions of public frustration and anger that do not intelligently or strategically advance the process. Washington and Wall Street have the power and resources to divide, minimize, marginalize and coopt private, public as well as legislative and regulatory action to impose legal accountability on those responsible for the crises. So far, Washington and Wall Street have successfully wielded their power and resources. There has been a lot of talk by frustrated Americans demanding accountability without really understanding what it means or how to get it. Simply complaining goes nowhere. Politics as usual and talk about moral hazard and moral suasion have proved to be empty options.

A look at the effective options available to impose accountability on Washington and Wall Street under the rule of law clearly reveals that the American public must directly confront the most powerful individuals and institutions in the country. That means economic claims against and recovery of damages, in compensation and as punishment, from Wall Street, and indirectly, Washington, for their specific legal wrongdoing, and for deterrence of their ongoing and likely future wrongdoing. Legal action designed to hold Washington and Wall Street accountable under the rule of law can only succeed within a context of public support. That means public education through a sophisticated, experienced public relations, public media, social media and grass roots organization backed by resources commensurate with the resources wielded by Washington and Wall Street.

According to SNL's December 9, 2013 report, the top 6 Wall Street banks were spending on average $1 billion per quarter on attorneys' fees and expenses in defense of fraud claims. According to Reuters, "The financial sector spent $2 billion on political activity from the beginning of 2015 to the end of 2016, including $1.2 billion in campaign contributions—more than twice the amount given by any other business sector, according to the study from Americans for Financial Reform. That works out to $3.7 million per member of Congress and is the most ever tracked by the group, which analyzed spending data going back to 1990. Furthermore, the actual amount is probably higher, because it did not include so-called 'dark money': funds donated to political advocacy by nonprofit groups."[790]

Ordinary Americans must place their legal action in the context of a widespread apolitical public demand for Americans' civil right to transparent, honest, safe, and sound money, banking and finance as the foundation for the American economy. So far, threats of criminal prosecutions and civil actions have been scarce and muted. The invention, development and implementation of the use of words, numbers, writing and accounting are the hallmarks of civilization. For millennia, civil societies have risen and prospered based upon the emblematic honesty and integrity of these immensely important tools. These tools must capture and preserve, in a tangible way, the abstract concepts they represent and support public trust and confidence in the systems upon which ordinary Americans livelihoods depend. Just as the honest use of these tools is vital to a healthy and growing society, correspondingly, the concentration of power and control over, and the abuse, corruption and dishonest use of these tools by the wealthy and powerful has periodically and predictably brought down one great civilization after another.

The fruits of the division of labor and specialized abilities amongst a society's members enables them to maximize their individual and societal well-being through trade and commerce, finance, and savings and accumulation of the value of work from the most productive time of life, to protect against risk, uncertainty and the inevitable effects of age and debility. The sanctity of these property rights is grounded on the careful, honest and professional use of the ancient tools of words, writing and laws, together with numbers and accounting systems, necessary to create money and credit and to memorialize the relationships they represent and preserve, and to protect and enforce the personal rights and duties that instruments of money and credit represent. These property rights are protected by the *United States Constitution*. The public's trust and confidence in the honesty and integrity of money and credit and the parties to the counter-party relationships that these concepts establish is a fundamental condition to societies' acceptance of the characteristics of transferability of instruments of credit amongst an extended array of counterparties in trade and commerce. Societies' trust and confidence is the prime condition to the transparent, honest and effective service of money as a unit of measurement, store of value, medium of exchange, and standard of deferred payment, in a reliable series of exchanges of value over time. Thus, social stability and prosperity depend directly on maximization of public trust and confidence in the transparency, honesty, safety, soundness and integrity of money, credit and justice under the rule of law, are the foundation of their broad-based use through the ability of institutional and individual parties, counterparties and by society in general.

Money and credit, the lubricants of commerce that have firmly established their place in modern society, continue to rely on the public trust and confidence in their issuers. Banks were conceived essentially, to endorse the public confidence in the money and credit they create and emit as well as to support and validate the transferability of those instruments beyond the relatively small circle of trust and confidence that, in early developing societies, could only be maintained as personal relationships amongst a relatively small group of individuals. The growth of America as civilized and powerful nation state and Americas requirement for the finance of the exercise of powers in the public interest have, historically and predictably, led to abuse of the fiduciary powers and duties entrusted to the experts in Washington and on Wall Street at the center of our society. Intentional perversion and corruption of the basic tools of words, writing, laws, numbers and accounting systems, including the technology, that support the money and credit of accepted reliable and stable liquid value is intolerable. If that perversion and corruption continues unchecked by ordinary Americans, our commerce and civil society will deteriorate into a state of growing fear and distrust of the institutions on which our society depend. The people and the prosperity of America's economy and civil society will correspondingly suffer, not just in Washington and on Wall Street where the focus of crisis resolution and remediation has been centered, but on Main Street, amongst ordinary Americans who have been left holding the very large bag of losses.

A dangerous combination of the ability of the nation state to magnify its spending power through use of banks as a vehicle for money debasement, combined with the greed of banks, eager to cast aside their character as men, women and institutions acting as fiduciaries to ordinary Americans at the heart of our bedrock of honest trade, commerce and finance, has hurled the public interest under the bus of money debasement for short term individual greed and profit. This travesty of justice has evolved through a simple set of trade-offs. Government abuse of public trust and power granted to it solely in service of the public interest, accomplished through a massive misrepresentation of all aspect of banking, money and credit to gain addition wealth at the expense of the public; plus government tolerance, nay encouragement and active facilitation of the processes of powerful Wall Street banks embedded in financial support of government, for aggrandizement of the personal power of government officials and a turn through the revolving door at the Wall Street banks, to pick up their share of wealth held there, systematically loots the public through money creation and debasement. This travesty of justice has been accomplished through both fiscal excess exempting the rich and powerful through perversion of the federal tax structure, manipulative trade barriers and tariffs, as well as through the unfounded and unjustified protection of the Wall Street banks against the horrors otherwise created in the lives of ordinary Americans public by the ongoing cycle of financial crises.

The great financial crisis has admittedly been caused by massive, unrestrained creation of excess credit unsupported by collateral dishonestly valued as liquid and thus freely transferable without diminution in value, represented by the respective issuers as appropriate instruments suitable to serve as money. Shadow banks, supported by Wall Street are in the market to monetize every conceivable asset, without regard to traditional notions of value or liquidity. The instruments themselves, divorced from real economic activity, such as cyber or crypto currency anticipated to reach $84 billion by the year 2024, are backed by absolutely nothing. At least tulips in the tulip mania bubble were actual tulips. Government fiat money, although its value remains unregulated, is theoretically (and demonstrably ineffectively) backed by the perceived but unqualified and unquantified creditworthiness of the state. So far, The American dollar remains the best among the global cast of ever-weakening fiat moneys. That status is changing as other countries reduce dollar reserve holding and diversify risk away from the American dollar.

The banking euphemism for the process of monetization of illiquid (or even nonexistent things on the fringes of unregulated monetization) is called "collateral transformation." Collateral transformation is simply an exercise in word play that enables bankers to represent illiquid collateral as liquid collateral without having actually performed the central, primary bankers' mission of providing collateral valuation discounts, adequate capital, leverage limitations and other appropriate, transparent, safe and sound underwriting conditions and limitations sufficient to protect against the risks and uncertainties of collateral asset illiquidity at the recorded face value of a credit instrument.

Collateral asset value bubbles build predicated on ever loosening credit liquidity and valuation standards and the bubbles expand exponentially when the weakened standards permit the continued creation of excess credit backed by collateral of ever diminishing value and liquidity until the represented truth and honesty of the collateral value and liquidity and thus the credit instruments value and liquidity for use in trade and commerce as money, are no longer sustainable at reported value without resort by Wall Street to Washington's intervention and support of continued excess credit creation, or alternatively the recognition, allocation and absorption of the losses embedded in the credit instruments the value and liquidity of which has been thus misrepresented. Traditionally, when the represented value of money has been debased, as is the direct intentional effect of excess credit supported by asset value bubbles and liquidity misrepresentation, the losses should be expected to be recognized, allocated, absorbed in accordance with the rule of law. That has not occurred.

Washington, including the Fed, has provided trillion of dollars in secret loans to support the illiquidity of overvalued assets allowing the banks to sell them to the Fed at par, avoiding losses. Subsidizing loss recognition, in timing and amounts, creates a deliberate illusion of financial stability. When the legal effect of the collective action and acceptance of these vast expenditures of new credit excesses is recognized as fraud in the representation of the value and liquidity of money held by the public, as opposed to Wall Street banks, ordinary Americans are cheated out of the true value of what they have created and earned, in order to non-transparently subsidize Wall Street, including government sponsored enterprises such and FNMA and Freddie Mac. Through this cooking of the books, Washington and Wall Street have created a pretense, an intentional misrepresentation that the crisis is over—that all is well, when that is false. The crisis may be temporarily over in Washington and on Wall Street, but the American public has faced and borne up to $20 trillion in losses, as opposed to Washington and Wall Street who have hidden behind their web of false narratives, shrouded with the benefits of cooked books, secret loans and subsidies. The financial benefits from this process have simply been redirected into asset bubbles that continue to allow Washington and Wall Street to prosper while the income and wealth of ordinary Americans continue to languish.

The profits have been privatized by Washington and Wall Street. The losses have been socialized amongst the American people. This is not simply an inescapable, and unfortunate, inevitable, consequence of good government—it is intentional fraud and misrepresentation by Washington and Wall Street of the value of money on its books and in every account of money and credit in America. The Board of Governors of the Federal Reserve characterizes the process of money creation in its public description of banks creating "money that acquires value from individuals + business productivity," under the authority of the Federal Reserve System, without any connection to any actual external standard of value. The banks, with and through the misrepresentation of the value of the credit money they have created, and through collusive action, Washington and Wall Street have conducted a massive program of abuse of trust and power to lie, cheat and steal from the American people.

Washington and Wall Street have captured massive support from and participation by lawyers, accountants, economists, bureaucrats, lobbying groups, academics and all manner of suppliers of other services to Washington and Wall Street, or those who aspire to do so. The largest financial institutions in the world and their supporters have joined forces and resources to avoid accountability and justice for financial crises.

Without American enforcement of legal accountability for the underlying fraud worked though our financial system through an imposition of justice under the rule of law as a foundation for integrity, transparency, honesty and confidence in the global financial system, any attempt at meaningful monetary, banking or financial reform is a chimera.

Through this vast institutional complex of self-serving manipulation and misrepresentation, the members of the American public have been deprived of the true value of their honest labor, goods, services, and their saving held to protect them against the uncertainty of the future, as well as the certainty of old age and debility. The American public have been sentenced to a future of stagnant wages and limited future prospects with high embedded levels of under and un-employment. America's younger generation faces a bleak future burdened by unsustainable levels of public and private debt and a bleak, smudged palimpsest of the American dream. The record of government and bank losses of value have been misrepresented, papered over, and subsidized with the complicity of the legal and accounting professions. Washington, Wall Street and their servants now have more power, control and wealth than ever before.

The credit excesses driving money manipulation has been primarily centered in the proliferation of the financialization of our economy created to facilitate speculation by Wall Street and the shadow banking system, with direct participation and support by Washington. That being said, there is little evidence that curtailment of money debasement in search of speculative profits benefiting Washington, Wall Street and the wealthiest Americans would lead to economic catastrophe that would directly threaten America's existence. Money debasement is the very real existential threat to America. There is ample evidence that ongoing money debasement directed by Washington and Wall Street through the status quo is a direct threat to American civil society and to American national security.

America is experiencing an unprecedented and growing gap in wealth and income between our financial and government elite who continue to prosper and the balance of ordinary Americans who continue to suffer from the financial crisis:

Wealth:

Figure 10.2 Concentration of Wealth United States and Political Division and Dysfunction in the United States

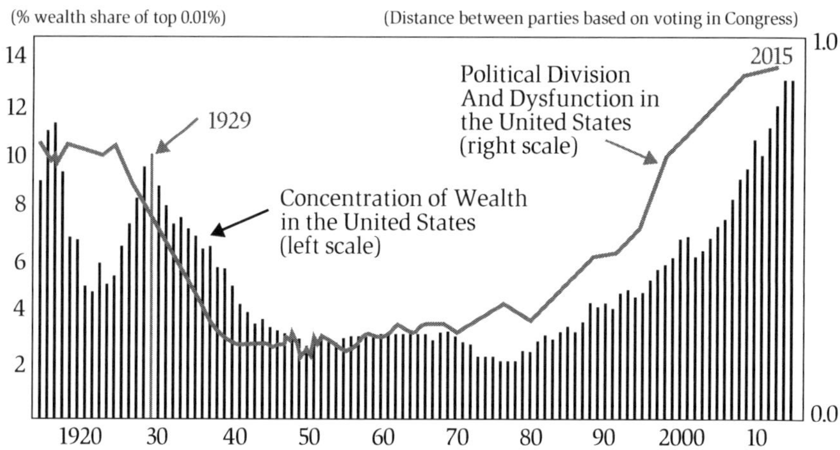

Income:

Figure 10.3 Average Household Income—Change of Share in Income

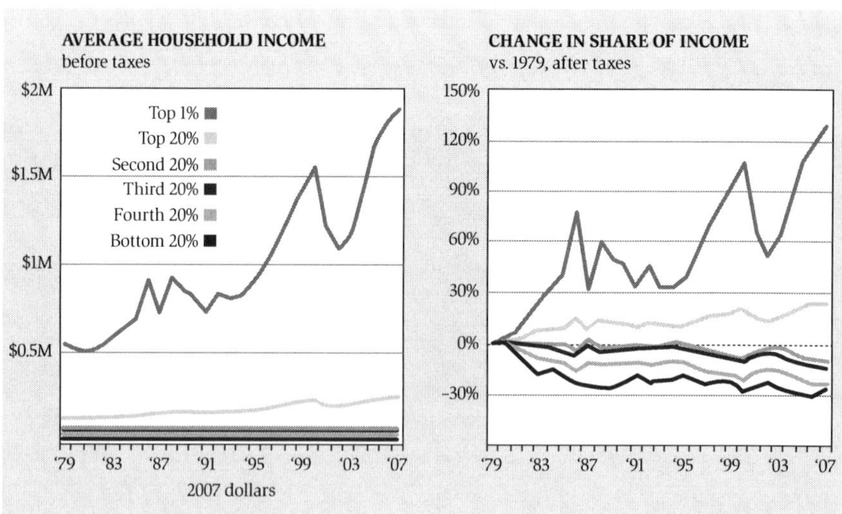

Source: Congressional Budget Office.

Most legal commentators and courts considering the role of the Federal Reserve System and the exercise of its monetary powers, have characterized the public's claims of their right to transparent, honest, safe and sound money as a political question, not to be decided by the courts, based on the doctrine of separation of powers. The courts have made a history of the mockery of justice; avoiding judicial responsibilities, largely on purely technical grounds. The judicial system's unwillingness to afford redress for this legal issue appears to have permanently undermined and occluded the public's awareness of each citizens' natural human civil right as well as each Americans constitutional, common law and federal statutory legal right to a transparent honest, safe and sound banking and financial system. The courts have routinely engaged in misdirection and deliberate mischaracterization of facts and law, and profound dissembling in support of the apparent triumph of the political, and bureaucratic and financial mandarins in Washington and on Wall Street who feel free to create an endless supply of money out of nothing in order to serve their individual and private interests. That legal miasma has been based largely on intentional misreading of the *Legal Tender Cases* and the *Gold Clause Cases*. As we have seen, these Supreme Court cases not only confirm Congress' constitutional power and duty to regulate the value of American money, they also confirm that issues relating to that power and duty are expressly suitable to resolution by the courts and the judicial system.

The government's power to tax and spend, however perverse and corrupt its exercise has become, is founded in the rule of law. The amount of taxes levied and the purposes for which the funds of the treasury are appropriated and spent, and the perverse tax incentives adopted by Congress as a crude method for conducting a systemic program of *quid pro quo* for financial support from special interests, are political determinations. Political accountability for fiscal irresponsibility and cronyism accomplished in an arena that has evolved away from and pretense of transparency is not the subject of this work.

The government's power to establish a fractional banking system is of questionable legality, but has become not only an American, but a global phenomenon. In America the national banking system and fractional reserve banking were borne of the same necessity as the first use of fiat legal tender. The existential threat and emergency of the Civil War necessitated a mechanism to finance the government's prosecution of the war. The *Emergency Banking Act* and the *National Banking Acts* combined with a return to constitutional regulation of the value of money represented a legal resolution to a political problem.

The government's establishment of the Federal Reserve System, an action even more tangential to the imperatives of war than the *National Banking Acts*, was designed to increase the government's ability to finance its political activities. The *Federal Reserve Act* represented a purported legal resolution to a strictly political government desire to raise and spend more money than it could by the imposition of ever greater taxes. The Fed explicitly creates money that is not tied to any external, reliable, stable standard of value, in the form of credit. That credit money is leveraged through the Federal Reserve System and leveraged again through the fractional reserve banking system before being leveraged again by the ultimate borrowers of the money. So long as that credit consists of bilateral lending arrangement, the credit creation is purely a banking matter. When the credit created is purportedly made transferable, liquid, it becomes a monetary matter and a matter of constitutional law.

The credit machine initiated by the Fed has stoked Wall Street bankers' desire to create ever larger amounts of money through transferable supposedly liquid credit, ostensibly for advancement of the Fed's public purpose of "maintaining long run growth of the monetary and credit aggregates commensurate with the economy's long run potential to increase production, so as to promote effectively the goals of maximum employment, stable prices and moderate long-term interest rates"; but its practical effect has been to extract enormous profits through credit creation, money creation and money debasement. This intentional market intervention—euphemistically and now pervasively referred to and accepted as "monetary policy"—has proved to be for the primary profit and benefit of Washington, Wall Street and their respective sycophants, and it has never fulfilled its expressed public promise. To the contrary, the Fed has failed in its stated public purpose. There exists little to no evidence that the Fed ever has met its official mission.

A set of distinguished scholars, George Selgin, Department of Economics Terry College of Business, University of Georgia William D. Lastrapes, Department of Economics Terry College of Business, University of Georgia, and Lawrence H. White, Department of Economics George Mason University, in a CATO Working Paper entitled *Has the Fed Been a Failure?*, revised, December 2010, concluded, in part, that: "Some proposed alternative arrangements might plausibly do better than the Fed as presently constituted. We conclude that the need for a systematic exploration of alternatives to the established monetary system is as pressing today as it was a century ago." At the head of the body of the paper, referring to the Fed, the authors quote Milton Friedman (1988): "No major institution in the US has so poor a record of performance over so long a period, yet so high a public reputation."

Congress and the Wall Street banks have exploited the Fed's failure with abandon. The federal financial regulators have been ineffective spectators; hoping eventually to get their own shot at the revolving door to Wall Street. All have contributed mightily to financial crises. The concept that the Fed's pursuit of social and political objectives through their partners in the creation of money, the Wall Street banks, the value of which is somehow "acquired from individual and business productivity" can form the foundation for an honest, safe, and sound monetary system is diametrically opposed to the constitutional requirement that Congress create, emit and regulate the value of American money in accordance with suitable standards of value.

The Nixon shock of 1971 that permanently disconnected the US dollar from any outside standard of and discipline on value was purely political and was a violation of law. Not a peep of protest was heard from Washington or Wall Street. All American historical developments in matters of central banking, bank regulation, monetary policy, banking and shadow banking, and achievement of systemic financial stability involve political questions to a greater or lesser degree. All these political issues and questions can be honestly identified, described, debated, decided and resolutions implemented with public accountability only if based on sound sovereign money that is an honest legal tool of measurement of liquid transferable value. The *Constitution* empowers and requires Congress to establish uniform standards ascribed to the quantity, quality or purity, capacity, volume, or dimensions of anything. The establishment of uniform weights and measures is a mechanical process, validated by convention and by Congress as a matter of law. These standards must be constant and enduring. One the most important and profound powers delegated to Congress by the public, with respect to which it owes the public its highest duty, the classic definition of a fiduciary duty, is to regulate the value of American sovereign money by reference to such a standard.

Similarly, the *Constitution* empowers and requires Congress to coin money and regulate its value. The establishment of standards of value, as differentiated from standards of weights and measures, is not simply mechanical. The market values of things measured in standard weights and measures change constantly, in relation to other things and in relation to the thing or things measured in standard weights and measures that may be determined from time to time by Congress, to be the standard against which the value of money is regulated. Gold, silver, nickel and copper, as such materials were subjected to and disciplined by uniform standards of weights and measures, long served as standards for the regulation of the value of money.

Despite Edwin Vieira's masterful work in *Pieces of Eight*, the value of his work is constrained by his insistence that the standard of value for American money must be based on a specific commodity: the gold standard. The importance of his work is to have demonstrated that the *United States Constitution* requires Congress to regulate the value of money, and to have meticulously documented the course of their failure to do so. The offer or recordation of units of money that in a transactional exchange of value have, or purport to represent a certain standard value or the use of things measured in units of weights and measures of a certain standard that are less than the standard represented are therefore, by definition, misrepresented. The debasement of money is by definition an act of misrepresentation. Congress, and those instrumentalities it employs to meet its constitutional responsibilities to maintain standards to regulate and ensure accurate representation of units of the weight or measure of things or the values of units of money, and that lie with respect to accuracy of the representation, cheat the recipient through deception and steal from the recipients through deception.

There have always been difficulties associated with regulation of the value of money. Times have changed. Markets and technology have changed and evolved. The principle of transparent, honest, safe, and sound, money and the law with respect to money, the value of which is regulated in the public interest, however, have not changed. The regulation of the value of money is not mechanical. It is difficult. It requires the application of intellect and reason. It is not a political exercise, but it must be a transparent publicly conducted exercise. It requires flexibility and judgment rendered publicly. It is not impossible. It requires Congress to meet its constitutional duty. Failing that, Congress must now be judicially mandated to do its job as a matter of law. To the extent federal banking regulators have aided and abetted Congress' failure to regulate the value of money, they must be judicially mandated to act in accordance with the law. To the extent the Wall Street banks have conspired with members of Congress, federal financial regulators and others to exploit their privileged status; to lie to, cheat and steal from the American public through the creation, issuance and representation of debased money, they must be judicially compelled to pay just compensation for damages, as well as exemplary damages as punishment and to deter their continuation of such illegal conduct.

Protection of the public interest and right to a transparent, honest, safe and sound banking, financial and economic system by enforcement of Washington's and Wall Street's common law, constitutional and statutory legal duties is not a political issue. To the contrary, the issue is the most fundamental and important legal issue, case and controversy affecting every United States citizen as well as our global trading partners and their constituents today. Although political issues have been raised and will continue to be raised and resolved by law, this is a case where the political issues have been previously raised and resolved by law. America's citizens have a natural human civil right as well as a constitutional, common law and federal statutory legal right to a transparent, honest, safe and sound banking and financial system that is focused primarily on financial and monetary stability, supported by public trust and confidence, the prevention or minimization of financial crises and the avoidance of the harm inflicted on Americans by financial crises. Americans have, apparently unjustifiably, entrusted great power and great responsibility to Washington and Wall Street to maintain a level playing field upon which to pursue ordinary Americans financial well-being.

The tensions inherent in regulation of the value of sovereign money and its effect on the interests of different portions of the community were addressed by William Gouge in 1883, and resonate today:

> Our American Bankers have found that for which the ancient alchymists [*sic*] sought in vain; they have found that which turns every thing into gold—in their own pockets; and it is difficult to persuade them that a system which is so very beneficial to themselves, can be very injurious to the rest of the community. They exclaim, as perhaps some of the rest of us would exclaim, if we were in their situation, "every thing goes on very well": thus verifying the remark of Say, that some persons who, under a vicious order of things, have obtained a competent share of social enjoyments, are never in want of arguments to justify to the eye of reason such a state of society. If the same individuals were to-morrow required to cast anew the lots assigning them a place in society, they would find many things to object to.
>
> Not a few who have no interest in Banks, are equally devoted to their support. They appear to think that if Bank notes were withdrawn, there would be no money in the country—no credit—no trade. They have a vague notion that the wealth of the country is chiefly, if not entirely, owing to the Banks.
>
> This is not surprising. The institutions to which men have long been accustomed, they believe to be necessary to social order. Church establishments were once regarded in this light, and hereditary nobility also. The distinguished writer whom we have just quoted, says:
>
>> Certain individuals who have never caught a glimpse of a more improved state of society, boldly affirm that it cannot exist: they acquiesce in established evils, and console themselves for their existence by remarking that they could not possibly be otherwise—in this respect reminding us of the Emperor of Japan, who thought he should have been suffocated with laughter on hearing that the Dutch had no king. The Iroquois were at a loss

to conceive how wars could be carried on with success, if prisoners were not to be burnt.

Some of our countrymen who are aware of the evils of the Banking system, seem to think all discussion of it superfluous, apparently regarding it as a system so deeply rooted that it must exist in perpetuity. What always has been, always will be: but we know of no reason why Banking should be exempt from the vicissitudes which usually attend human institutions. Banking with convertible paper has been known in England for about one hundred and forty years, and in the United States for about fifty. England, in prohibiting the issue of all notes of a less denomination than twenty-four dollars, has begun to retrace her steps. In the United States we are far behind England in this respect, yet Bank notes may, fifty years hence, be found only in the cabinets of the curious. The penny notes which were issued by the Bank of North America about the year 1790, are already regarded as rarities by the virtuosi.

Banking, it must be admitted, is deeply interwoven with all the business, the interests, operations, and even the rights of society, public and private. But so was the feudal system, which had an effect, in the middle ages, similar to that which the paper system has in modern times. Like the feudal system, the paper system divides the community into distinct classes, and impresses its stamp on morals and manners. In the progress of society it may be as necessary to pass through the one as it was to pass through the other; but the feudal system is giving way in Europe to enlightened reason, and it may, at least, be hoped, that the paper system will not last forever in America. ...

We may say, it is true that paper money has always produced evil, but it is because it has not been properly managed. But, if there is not something essentially bad in factitious money, there seems to be something in human nature which prevents its being properly managed. No new experiments are wanted to convince mankind of this truth.

Any new paper money that we may devise must be issued either by individuals, by corporations, or by the Government. If it should be issued by individuals, it would not be a new experiment, for that has been tried in Scotland. Of the result, an eye witness shall speak for us. Mr. McCulloh, in his *Historical Sketch of the Bank of England,* recently published, says, "the example of the Scotch Banks may here be referred to. They are most liberal of their advances so long as they conceive they run no risk in making them; but the moment alarm and discredit begin to make their appearance, they demand payment of every advance that is not made on the very best security; they cease, in a great measure, to discount; and provide for their own safety by ruining thousands of their customers."

Such must ever be the effect of 'convertible' paper. Commercial credit is an excellent thing, but it requires metallic money as an accompaniment, to prevent its being carried to excess.

If we give to corporations the power to issue paper money, we produce other evils. The very act of establishing a money corporation destroys the natural equilibrium of society. As is remarked by Raymond, "sound policy requires that the natural equality of men should be preserved as far as practicable: and it is the duty of Government to preserve this natural equality, so far as equal laws and equal rights and privileges will preserve it; to keep all the members of the community as distinct and independent as possible; to preserve the individuality of the citizens, and to discourage, as far as

> practicable, all associations for the purpose of giving to those combined an artificial power."[791]

The United States Supreme Court, in the *Legal Tender Cases* and the *Gold Clause Cases,* confirmed that the value of money created by Congress was then and continues to be regulated by the applicable currency acts. The Court invalidated existing contract provisions that interfered with Congress exercise of its power and duty to regulate the value of money. The case for financial accountability made here is not a case in contract. It is a case in tortious abuse of trust and power through intentional bank fraud. The case does not seek to constrain Congress' power to regulate the value of money. It is, in fact, a case that requires Congress to regulate the value of money; to openly, transparently exercise its constitutional power and meet its constitutional fiduciary duty to protect the American public interest in transparent, honest, safe and sound sovereign money. Today, there exist no applicable, relevant or effective currency acts providing for the creation of constitutional money, the liquid value of which is regulated by reference to any appropriate external standard. Ordinary Americans must mandate it through legal action and the American judicial system.

At least from the time of the Nixon shock in 1971 to today, the government has not even troubled itself to declare that it must debase the dollar as necessary to the national existence. This is not a case for technical posturing or hairsplitting between lawful transparent money devaluation by congressional action and non-transparent and damaging money debasement that enriches Washington and Wall Street while inflicting enormous damages on ordinary Americans, taking their property value without equal protection under the law or the exercise of due process under law. It is a case of fundamental first principles and the legal right of America's citizens not to be lied to, cheated or stolen from by their government or its enterprise with the Wall Street banks. The case of money debasement and its role as both the cause and effect of financial crises is ripe for consideration as contemplated by the Supreme Court in the *Legal Tender Cases* and in the *Gold Clause Cases,* and for confirmation of Congress' mandate to regulate the value of our national money in the public interest.

A failure by the judicial system to properly fulfill its constitutional duty to preserve, protect and defend the American rule of law in the public interest—not the singular interests of Washington and Wall Street—will eventually, but certainly, shred the remaining threads holding American society together. The next sounds heard in Washington and on Wall Street would then not be mere words, but may then be the sounds of crowds and tumbrels rattling onto the National Mall, into the streets of mid-town and the lower reaches of Manhattan; bundling politicians, bankers and bureaucrats along to a modern day appointment with the "national razor," in a modern day American version of Place de la Concorde; followed by a lively parade of American citizens, figuratively not literally, bearing miscreants heads prominently displayed on pikes.

The authors and sources referred to in the Introduction have documented the origins and effects of systemic financial crises clearly and thoroughly. They also describe the parties responsible for these crises. They do not, however, describe or document the specific violations of the rule of law upon which these parties might be held accountable. Scholars, academics and bureaucrats uniformly conclude that somehow the American people will triumph over the latest, temporary challenge to the greatest nation and most successful economy on earth. We may hope that this may occur purely because of the virtue, resilience, diligence, drive and productivity of ordinary Americans. Today that is wishful thinking. Historians of and commentators on financial crises uniformly shy away from description or documentation of the connection of the facts of financial crises to the elements of the law applicable to and supporting Washington and Wall Street accountability, the imposition of damages for the injustice suffered, retribution and incentives for deterrence of future tortious, criminal conduct by Washington and Wall Street.

Without legal accountability, the anonymous destruction and reconstruction of American property rights rewarding Washington and Wall Street and punishing ordinary Americans cannot be reversed. Through the effects of the Washington and Wall Street web of false narratives woven in self-service, ordinary Americans are fed the rhetoric of hope in the possibility that Congress and the Fed, and the Executive, including the federal financial regulatory, supervisory and enforcement agencies will somehow remediate the damage done and reduce the risk of future financial crises. So far, the individual and institutional powers that are masters of the American economic, fiscal, monetary and financial systems that produced the political risk and the systemic financial risk that caused the systemic financial crises are way ahead in what must seem to them to be a jolly good game. We are given to hope that Washington will take more than the usual weak initiative and make more than the usual mythical political monetary and financial policy reform. Those same hopes haven been proven false and unfounded, time after time.

President Obama's criticism of federal financial regulators and Wall Street bankers for their role in the financial crisis was muted; and Congress' role and responsibility have gone largely unmentioned. The DOJ has public abandoned its duty to enforce the law forbidding abuse of power and bank fraud. Most Americans are not agitating in any organized way for justice and accountability. They remain angry; worried about their pocketbooks, educating their children, paying for mortgages, cars, education, healthcare and retirement. Americans just want the economic uncertainty to end. They want recovery of losses they have suffered as a result of the crisis, if they can get it, and a return to normality. They want the American dream to continue, providing ever increasing productivity and prosperity. These are righteous demands that can be met openly and transparently under the American rule of law, but within the limitations of an honest, safe and sound monetary and banking system.

Although it is clear that systemic financial crises are grounded in wrongful and irresponsible conduct, neither the FDIC nor the DOJ, nor any other financial regulator or law enforcement agency have ever meaningfully investigated the possibility of enforcement of legal accountability for that conduct and the harm it has done to ordinary Americans. They have not done so in connection with the current crisis or any prior crisis during the last 45 years.

This is no incidental issue. It is the primary issue. The $20 trillion in damages suffered by ordinary American families is approximately equal to the American national debt. It is larger than the total assets of the Wall Street banks. Trebled under

RICO, the damages are $60 trillion. Americans can never be recompensed in full for their damages. They can, however, shift the damages to the Washington Wall Street enterprise to the maximum amount that serves the public interest, and leaves us with a banking system that serves ordinary American banking needs that does not remain a corrupt, organized criminal, racketeering enterprise that has, of itself, become a vast systemic speculative game.

Systemic financial risk and systemic financial crises can be tied to one fundamental thing: the financial system. What is a financial system? It is a set of rules governing the facilitation of commerce through the use of money, including credit, as an intermediator of the exchange of disparate assets of varying and relative asset values.

When the value of money, including credit, is no longer regulated by ties to the reality of the relative value of goods and services in the real economy, money and credit become tools of speculation, deceit, misrepresentation and fraud in the communication of value through the financial system. Under those circumstances, it can no longer be trusted. Those who control the system can no longer be trusted.

Commerce will eventually grind to a halt, relatively speaking, unless the public can safely place their confidence in the reasonable, honest, accuracy and soundness of the financial statements of those responsible for the integrity of our financial system.

§10.04 WEAK, INEFFECTIVE AND UNENFORCED BANKING LAW AND REGULATION PROVES NO SUBSTITUTE TO THE RECOGNITION AND ENFORCEMENT OF WASHINGTON AND WALL STREET FIDUCIARY MONETARY POWERS AND DUTIES

Weak, ineffective and unenforced banking law and regulation are no substitute for Washington's and Wall Street's fiduciary duty to the American public to maintain a transparent, honest, safe and sound sovereign money and monetary system.

Bank lending and credit creation are limited by the legal and regulatory requirement that banks maintain the banks safety and soundness as well as the safety and soundness of their money on deposit through prudent standards of operating protection, careful risk assessment and maintenance of sufficient liquid capital to protect against the losses and costs presented by uncertainty, and the banks' ability to return money deposited with them through redemption of the receipt for their deposit in liquid, honest, safe and sound money, without diminution of value. Historically, banks duties to the public are the duties of a fiduciary. Banking laws and regulation have evolved to meet, and arguably (primarily by Washington and Wall Street) to act as substitutes, in place of the general nature of fiduciary duty to the public, and developing along with the complexity of banking to clarify what have historically been bank fiduciary duties. Banking laws and regulations become ever more complex and more voluminous—yet they fail to address the fundament risk attendant to banking and known to bankers and governments for thousands of years: regulation of the value of money and protection of holders from debasement of the value of money. The disconnect of banking law and regulation from the fundamental historical protection provided by sovereign money to the public, the value and liquidity of which is regulated in accordance with fiduciary duty to the public, and by reference to a trusted, independent standard, simply separates the focus of a concerned public from their concentration on the fundamental, intentional violations of law that lead to financial crises, and have done for thousands of years. The strict standard of fiduciary duty of banks to customers and to the public has been largely supplanted and most certainly corrupted by banking laws and regulations riddled with weakness due to pervasive grants of regulatory discretion unbound by duty and by the complexity of banking law and regulations that have become unintelligible to the public, bankers and regulators alike.

Financial innovation has driven the rapid expansion of credit as money, unregulated in amount or value by reference to enforceable standards, fueled by business innovation and powerful special interests conflating and incorporating acknowledged speculative investment with traditional transparent, honest, safe and sound banking functions. This phenomenon has led to the wide and growing spectrum of banks and bank-like enterprises that morph from banking to shadow banking. These financial enterprises now play dominant roles in the creation, emission and circulation of money through credit in our financial system.

§10.05 FIRST PRINCIPLES OF MORAL AND LEGAL ACCOUNTABILITY FOR ABUSE OF POWER AND INTENTIONAL FALSE MISREPRESENTATION OF ASSET VALUE THROUGH MONEY DEBASEMENT

To get at first the principles, the violation of which led directly to the great financial crisis and to establish fundamental civil and criminal accountability, we must look to the ancient and well-established legal doctrines of abuse of trust, and power, and intentional deceit, misrepresentation and fraud. These legal doctrines are clearly defined principles of natural and common law that are the foundation for the *United States Constitution* Article I, § 8 Clause 5, as well as federal statutory civil and criminal laws. Congress, federal financial regulatory agencies and the prime players in our financial systems, the so-called Wall Street banks, to whom we look to maintain a transparent, honest, safe and sound financial system, have explicit responsibilities to the American public. The Washington Wall Street enterprise has failed ordinary Americans. Washington and Wall Street have intentionally lied to the American public. The lies are more than "little white lies," "dodges" or "evasions."

As noted in President Obama's statement: "[r]egulators had looked the other way," But contrary to his statement, the regulators did have the authority to stop the bad behavior. The regulators did not exercise their authority.

Arthur Schopenhauer (1788–1860) said that "all truth passes through three stages. First, it is ridiculed. Second, it is violently opposed. Third, it is accepted as being self-evident."

The financial ride constituting the American Dream held-out to have no end, has collapsed. The rejuvenation of the American Dream promised by both the Democrats and the Republicans at their 2012 and 2016 conventions, and on offer in the current election cycle, is not likely. The people want what they have been promised, despite the fact that the Congress, federal financial regulators and the Wall Street banks have known all along that the promised public ride was unsustainable for ordinary Americans, as long as these powerful individuals and institutions constituting the Washington Wall Street enterprise hold the reins of power.

The American political and power elite should have acknowledged that fact; acted to regulate the value of money; limited the explosion of public and private debt they unleashed; and grounded their future action in the American rule of law and the readily accessible history of systemic financial crises. The reality of the American dream is achievable. A false vision of the American dream has been profiled, proliferated and misrepresented by Washington and Wall Street to pander to false and unsustainable public expectations.

Early in the most recent crisis, Charles Prince, Citigroup's then CEO, famously said the bank was gladly lending even though there had been ample observations, from even the most modest of sources, that the credit market was overheated. "'When the music stops, in terms of liquidity, things will be complicated,' Prince told the *Financial Times*, 'but as long as the music is playing, you've got to get up and dance. We're still dancing.'"

Today, as in America, the Greeks, Spanish, Italians, Argentinians, Venezuelans, Turks, French, British, German and throughout Eastern Europe, Latin America and the Balkan States, ordinary people are protesting in the streets. They all want to continue a ride of prosperity fed by low taxes, widespread tax avoidance, printing money without regulation of its value, and ever increasing public largess, financed by unregulated credit creation and manifest by concentration of wealth and power in government bankers and other financial elite. Aspirations of ordinary people to the same advantages has faded. A return to a policy of austerity required through membership in the European Union has brought down the Greek government. Spain, Italy and Portugal may follow. These protests often combine with protests against immigrants seeking an economic haven in a world of civil strife, political and gangland violence.

This work references the obvious facts that are already on the record, elicits their acceptance, and with good fortune, may serve to create public pressure on makers and implementers of law and public policy to respect the obvious truths of the causes of systemic financial risk and crises, and to act responsibly, and legally, in accordance with their sworn duty. Freed from manipulation, deception and misrepresentation of money value, under the honest and transparent system provided by the American rule of law, ordinary Americans can adjust their economic expectations to the honest results of competition in a free market, based their labor, ingenuity and dedication. Social safety nets for health, education and general welfare can be honestly debated, appraised and applied without the distortions imposed by money debasement. The measure of our personal and public welfare is now based on the fraud and deception of money. Accordingly, fraud and deception are shot though American culture and those who do not employ fraud and deception are derided. That is un-American, a betrayal of our values and a corruption of the American rule of law.

To achieve the goal of a transparent, honest, safe and sound economic system it is necessary to concentrate public sentiment in support, and in a demand, for legal, judicial enforcement of the accountability of Congress, federal financial regulators, federal housing agencies, rating agencies and the Wall Street banks for the great financial crises. It is necessary to implement serious fact-specific civil and criminal proceedings by federal and state attorneys general, with possible parallel civil class action proceedings, to enforce the accountability of Washington and Wall Street through judicial, due process under the American rule of law, and thereby extend equal protection of those laws to the ordinary American public. Without investigation and enforcement, followed by imposition of penalties for past bad behavior and as deterrence to future bad behavior by those parties, there will be no accountability for systemic financial crises. In the absence of accountability, the American public will therefore not likely see an effective return to first principles of honest, sound money and a safe and sound financial system. Without American legal action, prospects for meaningful action in service of such a system on a global basis are slim to none.

My objective here is to point out the obvious, elicit its acceptance, create public pressure on makers and implementers of public policy to respect the obvious truths of systemic financial risk and crises, and to act responsibly in accordance with their sworn duty and the rule of law.

Congress has acted in concert with the federal financial regulatory agencies and the management of systemically important financial institutions, the "Wall Street banks," and their respective policy making officers, in concert:

- Intentionally, knowingly and willfully, and with "willful blindness" to and reckless disregard of the consequences of their respective actions on the financial wellbeing of the American public, financial institution shareholders, depositors and customers, workers and consumers.
- To obtain political, institutional and individual personal benefits from not only permitting, but enabling and actively promoting the unregulated, unconstrained and immeasurable proliferation of instruments of money denominated in US dollars.
- Resulting in systemic debasement of the currency, overstatement of asset values and relative associated liability values; which, when becoming unsustainable.
- Resulted in uncertain and deteriorating value of all assets and liabilities in our economy.
- While exporting the financial uncertainty and resulting financial crises around the world through dollar denominated financial relationships with our trading partners.

As noted by Gregg in his assessment of the relevance of the concept of sovereignty to today's financial crises, "[m]oney's most basic function is to serve as a medium of exchange. From this is derived money's three other functions: a store of value, a unit of account, and a standard of deferred payment. Money is certainly a commodity unlike any other economic good. But there is no obvious reason why attempts to undermine money's ability to perform these functions could not be addressed through the ways we address most other economic crimes. As noted by the distinguished nineteenth-century English jurist and civil servant Lord Farrer, contract law, tort law, and criminal law are more than sufficient to adjudicate such matters without invoking any special law of legal tender." As it happens, we Americans can look to the constitutional imperative for Congress to regulate the value of our money as well as to a wealth of civil and criminal law that proscribe abuse of trust and power, breach of fiduciary duty, manipulation and debasement of the dollar as medium of exchange, a store of value, a unit of account, and a standard of deferred payment through deceit, misrepresentation and fraud. Development of the common law of deceit, misrepresentation and fraud grounds and sets the context for the analysis of the factors involved in systemic financial crises leading to civil and criminal liability and to the basis for actions to impose liability and accountability for these torts and crimes.

This is not new information or brilliant analysis. It is a statement of the obvious. The American public knows this. They do not know what to do about it. Occupy Wall Street—has been ineffective. Political campaigning and voting—has been rendered ineffective; coopted and compromised away by the politicians of all persuasions and by pervasive electoral gerrymandering and the over-riding quest for fund raising from special interests. A classic example of banana republic governance. Prospects of "falling off the fiscal cliff," because Congress cannot or will not agree upon a budget and tax program to balance national income and expense has been routinely delayed and deferred by scaremongering claims that the government will be forced to shut down and the public will suffer if pork barrel backroom compromises are not accepted as the normal course. Even though Washington and Wall Street have failed to do their sworn duty as public servants, as the moment of crisis becomes imminent, they stay up all night for a while, conduct rancorous meetings the purposes of which are to protect their special interests and pretend to act in the public interest. After much argument, angst and amidst strongly worded public statements, Washington and Wall Street usually defer any solution by extending the status quo, protesting that they have thereby saved the American public from certain doom, and garnering praise and congratulations from one another for a job well done and catastrophe avoided by their self-less sacrifice.

The American public knows that this process is wrong and irresponsible. They know that systemic financial crises, fiscal crises and budget showdowns are a part and parcel of the same conduct by the bad actors in Washington and on Wall Street that they can call by name. They just do not know what to do about it.

§10.06 THE ESSENCE OF CIVIL AND CRIMINAL ACCOUNTABILITY FOR FINANCIAL CRISES

The actions of ordinary Americans are subject to rigorous legal standards and sanctions imposed in cases of abuse of trust and power in cases of banking, securities and consumer fraud and crime.

Politicians and the power elite throughout history have a well justified general reputation of duplicity and mendacity accompanied by the continued ability to get away with it, time after time. Thus, the low regard in which they are held by the public. These "power elite" as well as the American public seem to think that, no matter how outrageous the behavior of the power elite and no matter the level of outrage expressed by the American public, the power elite are somehow exempt from the standards, laws and sanctions imposed on the rest of the American public in cases of banking, securities and consumer fraud and crime.

The closer one gets to the responsible individuals comprising the power elite, the more difficult it is for those who have suffered to successfully seek justice. They risk speaking the truth to and running afoul of power. The customary and official method of dealing with the public figures and holding them accountable is for voters and shareholders to "throw the bums out." Unfortunately, those who follow those thrown out, tend to fall into the age-old patterns of active pursuit of self-interest held by their predecessors, through the portals of the Washington Wall Street revolving door of prosperity. We are familiar with the generally held, some might say, cynical, view of those American citizens and company shareholders who find themselves suffering what the power elite view as acceptable levels of tail end losses imposed by their policies and actions; that there really is not anything we can do about it. It is just the nature of the system. The briefly popular, but largely ineffective, "Occupy Wall Street" movement and the more coherent and focused activity of the "tea party" movement, expressed public frustration with our collective inability to enforce responsibility and accountability for the harm caused by Washington and Wall Street driven systemic financial crises. Professor Paul Kennedy has thoroughly documented the historic consequences of successive societies' failure to enforce responsibility and accountability of the governing power elite through the mechanisms of civil society. When the gap between action and rhetoric becomes too great, the mobs in fact do form, violence and war coalesce and heads do actually roll.

America's status as a developed economy is now openly challenged. In a new *book, The Vanishing Middle Class: Prejudice and Power in a Dual Economy,* Peter Temin, Professor Emeritus of economics at MIT, finds that "the U.S. is no longer one country, but divided into two separate economic and political words." Lynn Parramore, Senior Research Analyst at the Institute for New Economic Thinking, begins her review of Professor Temin's book with the assertion that "*America is Regressing into a Developing Nation for Most People.*" Temin's trenchant observations and conclusions however do not extend to advocacy of any plan of action to ameliorate the situation. He foresees America not only reverting to developing country status; but he also contends that America is "increasingly ripe for serious social turmoil that has not been seen in generations." Emmanuel Saez Professor of Economics at UC Berkeley, who has researched the phenomenon of cyclical growth of income and wealth inequality in depth, from the beginning of the use of money as a social and cultural tool form ancient Mesopotamia to the present, has shown pertinently that income and wealth inequality in America have reached the highest level since 1928.

The progression in this pernicious cycle of growing disparity of income and wealth in America has increased dramatically since the 1970s. Stanford Professor

Walter Scheidel, in his recent book *The Great Leveler*, argues that income and wealth inequality are essentially an inevitable byproduct of civilization, the only remedy to which appears to be societal upheaval, produced by war, disease, state collapse or revolution. "Inasmuch as policy measures have worked, they were usually rooted meaningfully in one or more of these violent shocks." On a more optimistic note, Scheidel notes that although policy alone is unlikely to curb the widening gap, in the US there are still plenty of policies that can be implemented successfully. Scheidel argues that the reduction of inequality achieved by welfare states, communist revolutions and confiscatory taxes required by world wars were one-offs. Paul Mason, in a review of Scheidel's book, commented that:

> Social democracy wishes to suppress inequality in a controlled, consensual way, using the very state the elite has fashioned to entrench it; heading off pestilence, state failure and violent revolution. The vast wealth being generated in the highly technologically efficient society of the 21st century must, contrary to Scheidel, offer the possibility of an even greater redistributional space in which social democracy can operate.
>
> The only problem is, for 30 years, social democracy lost the will to redistribute (other than upwards to its allies in the yachting and mafia fraternities). Since around 2011, with the mass revolts of technologically empowered and educated people, the world has been offered the possibility of a break from the cycle of relentless inequality. In effect it turned the offer down—and in saying no to a future of social justice it has, for now, opened the door to the past: to kleptocrats, mafiosi, politicians whose imaginations are trapped in that tight space between the golden tower and the golden shower.[792]

America is on the verge of a new financial crisis. The bases for the next crisis are already in place. The divisions in and polarization of American society are readily apparent, as well as being nascent, if not obvious, in every other developed nation. America's example has been exported throughout the global financial and monetary system with disastrous effects. All of the destructive developments described by Professor Temin, Thomas Picketty, Saez, Scheidel and other authorities on finance and economic matters, have ignored the fact that the modern era of social dysfunction and polarization can be traced in their origin to the collapse of any modern political interest in honest, safe and sound money that followed the Nixon shock in 1971. Money in America is created and controlled by the "haves": Washington, Wall Street, and the largest finance, technology and electronics industries. The "have nots" are all of the rest of us; you, your family, friends, and neighbors; the 99 percent of Americans not among or beholden in some way to the "haves."

The response of ordinary Americans to the current state of affairs, particularly in the years immediately following the great financial crisis of 2008, has been righteous anger based on the betrayal of their interests by those to whom they entrusted political and economic power. A "change in policy" is neither required nor sufficient to redress the Washington Wall Street enterprise's intentional violation of ordinary American's civil right to honest, safe and sound money. Legal action, based on existing law, to enforce that civil right is the only available and viable alternative to the specter presented by Professor Scheidel:

> "Only specific types of violence have consistently forced down inequality," Scheidel writes. War has to be total; revolution has to be ultraviolent and socially pervasive; state failure has to lead to violence so intense that "it wipes the slate clean." Ditto the social effects of pandemics.
>
> "This account of the emergence of systemic inequality follows the classic materialist schema: only with the emergence of a durable economic surplus in early societies do you get archaeological evidence of inequality—that is where social status begins to map on to economic status. States, defensible and transferable forms of wealth, hereditary elites and the rituals to endow them with status emerge together, Scheidel's review of the evidence shows, to create the 'original 1%'—from ...' ancient Mesopotamia to the present day."[793]

There is no readily apparent forum through which ordinary Americans can seek fairness, redress, recompense and justice. Congress has been gerrymandered into paralysis. The federal financial regulators have been corrupted and serve almost exclusively the interests of the regulated, and the preservation of the revolving door admitting so-called public servants to the comfort of waiting positions in the industries they have so assiduously served and protected. The public; ordinary Americans, have been left out. The FBI and the DOJ have simply left the building. The crises have been legal crises. Their resolution lies in the enforcement of the rule of law and the judicial process. Ordinary Americans, for the sake of themselves, their families and futures must act to enforce the rule of law.

Despite the failure of America's governmental and financial elites to protect ordinary Americans' civil right to honest, safe and sound money as required by law, the last and most often ignored focus for Americans' imposition on Washington and Wall Street of moral, legal, financial and equitable accountability for financial crises damage to ordinary Americans, remains our civil right and duty, as American's, to initiate direct action based on the rule of law and our system of justice. The DOJ has refused to act based on purely political considerations; this despite their self-proclaimed responsibility for the redress of government, finance and business "lying, cheating and stealing." Recent financial crises are the greatest and most profound incidence of institutional and individual conduct of intentional lying, cheating and stealing in history.

The people, however, have direct private rights of legal action available to them. Moral and legal accountability is the necessary predicate for any shift in the *status quo* that can make practical reform feasible and establish proper incentives to meaningful monetary, and therefore social, economic, and political reform a reality. Failing that, ordinary Americans will be facing the serious social turmoil anticipated by Professor Temin. History informs us that that such turmoil most often means violence and war.

Without a tether of credit to the discipline of honest, safe and sound sovereign money restraining excess and unsupported credit creation, ordinary Americans have no shelter from the Washington Wall Street enterprise's, as well as other institutional and corporate "haves' economic, social, cultural and political predations.

When you get down to the essence of the issue, however, despite the widespread anger and frustration on the tail end of the loss allocation process in the ongoing American and global financial crises, we must be reminded that congressmen, federal financial regulators and their systemic tools, the Wall Street banks and bankers, are not exempt from the legal standards and sanctions already provided for in our legal system and the legal history upon which it stands. Their apparent insulation from the consequences of their actions is purely an illegitimate but actively assumed claim of perverse public policy, not supported by the rule of law. How can this happen?

America, led by financial, economic and monetary experts in Washington and on Wall Street, have driven headlong into dominant use of the tools of big data accumulation feeding back through high tech systems and mathematical algorithms as unworthy substitutes for wisdom and value judgments. The old canard that the numbers do not lie is a profound falsehood. The numbers are highly manipulated, and that manipulation goes to the heart of the intentional financial misrepresentations that reverberate through our society resulting directly in financial fraud and financial crises. No less a luminary than Henry Kissinger recently commented on the implications of that fact on matters of fundamental, thoughtful, wise, moral, legal and thoughtful decision making. *The Atlantic*, "How the Enlightenment Ends, Philosophically, Intellectually—In Every Way—Human Society Is Unprepared for the Rise of Artificial Intelligence," Henry A. Kissinger (June 2018 Issue)

As Kissinger notes: "Truth becomes relative. Information threatens to overwhelm wisdom." As a matter of fact, it has repeatedly overwhelmed wisdom. The supporting facts are replete throughout the literature and, specifically, in the *Financial Crisis Inquiry Report*. Kissinger notes that the purpose of financial data systems:

> ... is to ratify knowledge through the accumulation and manipulation of ever-expanding data. Human cognition loses its personal character. Individuals turn into data and data becomes regnant.
>
> Users of the internet emphasize retrieving and manipulating information over contextualizing or conceptualizing its meaning. They rarely interrogate history or philosophy; as a rule, they demand information relevant to their immediate practical needs.

Political leaders, and their partners on Wall Street, are ostensibly serving their own interests as well as the public interest, in a manifestly dangerous and damaging manner, through *The National Bank Acts*, the *National Currency Act* and the *Federal Reserve Act*, all as amended, that are charged with the primary constitutional duty to regulate the value of the dollar so it may serve as an honest, safe and sound currency binding our society and culture, have all abjectly failed in their overriding constitutional duty to Americans. Kissinger further notes:

> The ability [of Washington and Wall Street] to target micro-groups has broken up the previous consensus on priorities by permitting a focus on specialized purposes or grievances. Political leaders, overwhelmed by niche pressures, are deprived of time to think or reflect on context, contracting the space available for them to develop vision.
>
> The digital world's emphasis on speed inhibits reflection; its incentive empowers the radical over the thoughtful; its values are shaped by subgroup consensus, not by introspection. For all its achievements, it runs the risk of turning on itself as its impositions overwhelm its conveniences.

We must all come to understand that our economic and monetary systems have mutated from their intended purposes to a game of numbers manipulation that is rigged favor of Washington and Wall Street. The game embraces a subversive, damaging illegal policy and practice of deliberate, intentional abuse of trust and power, and fraud that has led to financial crises and a crisis of income and wealth diversion and concentration that threatens our national existence.

Commentators on the financial crisis have uniformly reached common agreement on the facts of the case for financial crisis accountability. None have heretofore made the case under the rule of law set out here in this work. Failure of the American justice system to deliver justice in this case based upon the legal and moral imperatives expressed in and consistent with the *Constitution* and in the vast array and variety of American laws designed to protect the public from and provide a constitutional check upon the massive fraud committed by the wealthy and powerful Wall Street "money interests" in combination with the informed, intentional participation and complicity of government, will result in loss of legitimacy of the courts and our system of justice. The Washington Wall Street enterprise's corrupt criminal racketeering enterprise is not the product of rugged individualism, hard work and simply being smarter than ordinary Americans.

The Washington Wall Street enterprise's cohesion is a conveniently and opportunistically shared set of mutual objectives and including accumulation of wealth and power. Objectives shared by many in America. Washington and Wall street are supported in their enterprise by their collective ability to share and abuse the power entrusted to openly and unapologetically defraud the public through intentional misrepresentation of asset value and liquidity through money debasement supported by a web of shared and complementary false narratives and selective law enforcement and have enrolled a pyramid of self-interested financial institutions, companies, and the nation's most prestigious attorneys and accountants who share, or desire to share in the benefits of the enterprise. How long can you get away with? How far out can you go? Go as far as you can get as much as you can. That's it. Be a winner. Not a loser.

§10.07 THE FALSE PROMISE OF COMMITTEE AND REGULATORY INVESTIGATIONS AND REPORTS

Another of the many false narrative spread by Washington and Wall Street and bought into by many ordinary Americans is that government is primarily responsible for perpetual economic growth in America. To the contrary, Washington's and Wall Street's shared fiduciary duty to the sovereign American people who have enabled their existence and granted to them the powers they wield, is to provide and protect a legal environment of economic and financial transparency, honesty and stability, integrity, safety and soundness. Individuals and businesses provide growth. The connection of government policy to economic growth of the American society and economy as a whole is tenuous at best. As conducted today, it has devolved to a corrupt criminal racketeering enterprise that is exploitative, divisive and destructive of the public interest. That is not a rant. It is simply the truth. The trend of Washington and Wall Street to perpetuate this immoral and illegal conduct can be reduced and conformed to our moral foundation, the American *Constitution* and rule of law, only with the enforcement of historically necessity of accountability of power and financial elites for the damages they cause through their conduct.

When commentators are faced with demands by ordinary Americans for financial crisis accountability; Washington and Wall Street respond that they are doing the best that can be done, that recrimination is counterproductive and the continuation of the cycle of regulation and deregulation of banking through more laws, rules and regulations that protect and advance the status quo is the only viable response to financial crisis. Common sense tells us that continuation and doubling down on the existing monetary legal, economic, financial and banking regime is doomed to result in the continuation of financial crises that the system has already produced.

Advances in technology and cries by Washington and Wall Street of continuing existential justification for their existing enterprise of exploitation in the face of a clear record of damage to the public interest only serves to reinforce Washington's and Wall Street's ongoing practices to create their perpetual economic growth, becoming ever more disconnected from individual and business productivity.

§10.08 FINANCIAL CRISIS ACCOUNTABILITY CAN BE FOUND IN OUR EXISTING AMERICAN LAW, ACCOUNTING AND OUR JUDICIAL SYSTEM

The vital role of the American courts and justice system is to protect, perpetuate, convey and enforce the American rule of law. That law provides the remedies.

[A] Equitable Justice and Equitable Relief

Proactive preservation, protection and enforcement of ordinary Americans' common law, statutory and Constitutional civil right to transparent, honest, safe and sound money by:

- Declaratory judgment

  By Declaratory Judgment order that certain Acts of Congress unconstitutional. The Federal banking laws, rules and regulations contained in Title 12 of the United States Code based on *The National Banking Act of 1913*, *The Federal Reserve Act of 1913*, *The Emergency Banking Act of 1933*, *The Banking Act of 1935*, as amended, as well as other banking laws and regulations, are unconstitutional to the extent they permit the creation and emission of legal tender in the form of Federal Reserve Notes or debt denominated in Federal Reserve Notes that are not fully redeemable in constitutional coined money, the value of which has been regulated by Congress.
- Order to cease and desist

  Order Washington and Wall Street to cease and desist from wrongful and unconstitutional debasement of the money of the United States.

- Writ of mandamus

  Command affirmative action by Washington and Wall Street to meet the requirements of the *United States Constitution* relating to the power and duty to create, emit and regulate the value of money and prevent its ongoing debasement under a judicial plan for affirmative action under the supervision and subject to the jurisdiction of the court.

[B] Award of Compensatory Monetary Damages as Retributive Justice

Determine and award damages sustained by the ordinary Americans as a result of the violations of law set forth above, from Wall Street; holding Wall Street accountable to ordinary Americans for their damages. Washington will have to cope with the prospect of Wall Street's financial condition and subject themselves to a withering public examination of their conduct as well as well-focused public consideration of their failures in public service.

[C] Calculation of Money Damages and Penalties as Retributive Justice

The Federal Reserve Bank of Dallas in 2013 estimated damages ranging from $50,000 to $120,000 per household, for a range of total damages of $6 trillion to $14 trillion based on their assumption of 120 million households. The United States Census, 2010–2014, prepared by the United States Department of Commerce estimates American households of 116,211,092 (http://www.census.gov/quickfacts/table/HSD410214/00 estimates total U.S.).

The Dallas Federal Reserve Bank (Staff Paper No. 20. July 2013 and *Economic Letter* Vol. 8, No. 7. September 2013), The U.S. Department of the Treasury (*The Financial Crisis Response in Charts*, April 2012—estimates $19.2 trillion in lost household wealth, or $160,000 per household based upon 120 million households), and the United States Government Accounting Office (*Report to Congressional Requesters, Financial Regulatory Reform—Financial Crisis Losses and Potential Impacts of the Dodd Frank Act*, January 2013, citing at p. 20, The Federal Reserve's Survey of Consumer Finances' estimate of damage in the form of lost median household net worth of $49,000 per household, between 2007 and 2010) have all calculated loss, cost or damage by reference to American households. In addition, Better Markets in its reports on the cost of the crisis, dated, September 15, 2012 and July 2014, estimate, loss, cost or damage by house hold and on a gross basis, more than $12.8 trillion ($106,667 per household) in 2012, and more than $20 trillion ($166,667, per household) in 2015, respectively. Accordingly, the government would find it convenient to face a class composed of approximately 120 million American households, suffering damages of $83,334 per household, identified and calculated by the criteria set forth above.

Washington's and Wall Street's money debasement is realized by dilution and diminishment the value of the dollar as it used in all its capacities, and specifically by the ordinary people and households of America.

Americans have looked to the powerful, privileged governmental, economic and financial institutions of America to protect their interests in accordance with the law of the land, but who instead combined as a corrupt racketeering enterprise to loot the value of the dollar through the weapon of fraudulent debasement, to profit and benefit the enterprise from that fraud and to beat the accompanying losses and damages onto unsuspecting ordinary working American households. A beating with an economic and financial cudgel money debasement leaving losses and damages as the wounds, broken bones, cuts bruises and ruined lives of the ordinary working American households—the fruits of their labor appropriated by the Washington Wall Street corrupt criminal racketeering enterprise.

American money debasement and the entirely predictable damages it causes is in fact is fairly traceable to the conduct of the Washington Wall Street corrupt criminal racketeering enterprise and can be redressed in an adversary legal context capable of judicial resolution.

Americans have been devastated by the financial crisis. Each American individual household member has sufficient personal stake in the outcome of the case to ensure the court that each is a "proper party to present the claim in a legally adversary context and in a form historically viewed as capable of judicial resolution." Personal stake is established when the damaged party or parties allege having suffered a "discrete," "palpable," "injury-in-fact" fairly traceable to the conduct of the Washington Wall Street enterprise and likely to be redressed by the requested relief. Ordinary Americans as a class have suffered and been damaged, "injured in fact," in a myriad of individual ways and to a greater or lesser degree, by the financial crisis. American's damages from the Washington and Wall Street created financial crisis are real injuries in fact.

Earlier in this work I described the damages suffered by the Great Financial Crisis. That description warrants repetition in the context of the remedies available to ordinary Americans for legal redress. According to the Federal Reserve Bank of Dallas, *Staff Report No. 20,* July 2013, the *General Accounting Office Report to Congressional Requesters,* GAO - 13 - 180, January 2013, and other official sources, the symptoms of the injury in fact suffered by each American household in fact are the following, appearing in different varieties and to greater of lesser degrees. Each and all of the injuries are a manifestation, or symptom, of the injury in fact suffered and constituting for each them as a household and as aggregated, caused by Washington's and Wall Street's commission of the torts of abuse of trust and power and of intentional misrepresentation of the value of their money and assets through money debasement.

The scourge of money debasement includes demonstrable higher rates of incidence of crime and violence. The bloodstained headlines of the news have not appeared from nowhere, *sua sponte,* so to speak. They are part and parcel of the injuries in fact complained of in this case.

Increasing violence and crime is a caused and exacerbated by and is a direct response to dramatic increases and distortions of unjustified economic inequality which are inherent in the intentional fraudulent debasement of money perpetrated by the Washington Wall Street corrupt racketeering enterprise as confirmed by the evidence in this case.[794]

The foregoing described symptoms or manifestations of Americans' injuries in fact of which they complain and for which they can seek redress under the American rule of law. These injuries bear the same relationship to the injury in fact, by comparison, as the relationship of the bloody wounds, broken bones, bruises and trauma that are the proof of the tort of assault committed on unwitting victims, bears on a physical brutal beating.

The well documented phenomenon of today's increasing levels of violence and crime is caused and exacerbated by and is a direct response to dramatic increases and distortions of unjustified economic inequality which are inherent in the intentional fraudulent debasement of money perpetrated by the Washington Wall Street corrupt racketeering enterprise. This is not a new phenomenon. It has occurred regularly throughout history. The cause is always the same. The response can be conducted in accordance with the rule of law, or it will eventually out in crime and violence to the point of increasing repression, violent and bloody war, revolution and the upheaval and chaotic transformation of society; wiping the slate clean, so to speak and forcing a leveling of the economic playing field.

The monetary damages exceed the total assets of the Wall Street banks and is approximate to the national debt.

Pursuant to 18 U.S.C. § 1964(c), and 12 U.S.C. § 1975 the ordinary Americans in this case would also be entitled to recover threefold the damages they have sustained and the cost of the suit, including reasonable attorneys' fees and costs.

[D] The False Dread Specter of a Wall Street Financial Death Sentence

A judgment in this in this case in favor of ordinary Americans against Washington and Wall Street would be tantamount to a financial death sentence, which would be historically appropriate considering the severity of their wrongful conduct (and considering the likely result of predictable public extrajudicial violent remedies if the judicial system fails the American public in their hour of need). However just and appropriate that judgment may be, the demand on the FDIC insurance fund and predictable disruption and economic chaos inflicted on the nation's, and the world's economies, dictates that damages in this case be determined by the court in an amount sufficient to provide meaningful compensation to ordinary Americans for their losses, punish Wall Street and Washington for their conduct and be sufficient to prevent them from the ongoing continuation of their illegal conduct.

The damages imposed by the court must also be sufficient to break the criminal, corrupt racketeering enterprise and induce Washington and Wall Street to respect, obey and comply with the American rule of law and establish that the American judicial system will now and always protect the peoples' rights and interests under the common law, the *Constitution* and federal statutory law. Relief may include the nationalization of the Wall Street banks, their break-up into a series of smaller regional banks, the interests of which are to serve the public as opposed to the perpetuation of

Washington's and Wall Street's closed enterprise of illegal profiteering posing as the "American Financial System." It is undisputed that the American economy can be well-served by a banking and monetary system that does not include an illegal corrupt, criminal racketeering enterprise at its center.

§10.09 RESTORATIVE JUSTICE

This case presents a unique opportunity to reach justice in a judicial forum that extends beyond retribution and punishment. In 2007, Lawrence W Sherman and Heather Strang, of The Smith Institute produced an instructive work entitled *Restorative Justice: The Evidence*[795] providing references and history for the use of the principles of restorative justice to reach the best resolution for all parties in the wake of wrongdoing that demands more a more effective remedy than the mechanics of retributive justice can offer. The authors characterize restorative justice as "... a process whereby all the parties with a stake in a particular offence come together to resolve collectively how to deal with the aftermath of the offence and its implications for the future."

Dr. Carolyn Boyes-Watson at Suffolk University's Center for Restorative Justice defines restorative justice as a peaceful, not necessarily adversary, approach to harm, problem-solving and violations of legal and human civil rights. The objective is to engage those who are harmed, the wrongdoers and their affected communities in search of solutions that promote repair, reconciliation and the rebuilding of open honest relationships. Restorative justice seeks to build consensus to reestablish mutual responsibility for constructive responses to wrongdoing. Restorative approaches seek a balanced approach to the needs of the victim, wrongdoer and community through processes that preserve the safety and dignity of all constituents.[796]

A purely consensual resolution of the claims and demands of the American people is impossible without the imprimatur of a judicial mandate, including in the mix, the courts imposition of damages and penalties on the Wall Street banks.

§10.10 THIS CASE IS A CIVIL RIGHTS CASE

The United Stated Supreme Court is not uninformed with the necessity of flexibility in granting justice in cases of national significance involving our most basic civil rights, due process and equal protection under the rule of law. In Brown v. Board of Education of Topeka, 349 U.S. 294 (May 31, 1955) (often referred to as "Brown II"), the Supreme Court directions for restorative justice in the landmark racial desegregation civil rights case are not dissimilar to possible holdings the Court might ultimately reach in a decision on the case to be made in the civil rights aspects of the case to be made by ordinary Americans against Washington and Wall Street. The Syllabus of the Court's opinion published in Brown II, serves as a template that the Court might determine to be applicable to the present case:

- Debasement of the United States dollar is unconstitutional and all provisions of federal, state or local law requiring or permitting such discrimination must yield to this principle.
- The judgments below (when issued, if conflicting these holdings) are reversed and the cases are remanded to the District Courts to take such proceedings and enter such orders and decrees consistent with this opinion as are necessary and proper to the performance of the letter and spirit of Article I, § 8, Clause 5 of the *Constitution*, Congress' power and duty: "To coin Money, regulate the Value thereof, and of foreign Coin, and fix the Standard of Weights and Measures," to thereby provide an honest, safe and sound American sovereign money and monetary system.
- The Department of the Treasury and the Federal Reserve System shall have the primary responsibility for elucidating, assessing and solving the varied monetary issues which conflict with this ruling and which may require solution in fully implementing the governing constitutional principles.
- Courts will have to consider whether the action of the Department of the Treasury and the Federal Reserve System constitutes good faith implementation of the governing constitutional principles.
- In fashioning and effectuating the decrees, the courts will be guided by equitable principles—characterized by a practical flexibility in shaping remedies and a facility for adjusting and reconciling public and private needs.
- At stake is the personal interest of the plaintiffs in relief from the ongoing harm caused by money debasement and the failure of congress and the executive to provide and maintain an honest, safe and sound sovereign money, the value of which is regulated by Congress in reference to a sound, stable and immutable standard as soon as practicable.
- Courts of equity may properly take into account the public interest in the elimination in a systematic and effective manner of a variety of obstacles in making the transition to a system of sovereign money and accompanying monetary system operated in accordance with the constitutional principles enunciated in this case; but the vitality of these constitutional principles cannot be allowed to yield simply because of disagreement with them.
- While giving weight to these public and private considerations, the courts will require that the defendants make a prompt and reasonable start toward full compliance with the ruling of the Court.
- Once such a start has been made, the courts may find that additional time is necessary to carry out the ruling in an effective manner.
- The burden rests on the defendants to establish that additional time is necessary in the public interest and is consistent with good faith compliance at the earliest practicable date.
- The courts may consider problems related to administration, arising from the monetary system, personnel, revision of statutory law and rules, regulations and other orders and directions pertaining to the United States sovereign money and monetary system, and revision of local laws and regulations which may be necessary in solving the foregoing problems.

- The courts will also consider the adequacy of any plans the defendants may propose to meet these problems and to effectuate a transition to an honest, safe and sound sovereign money and monetary system.
- During the period of transition, the courts will retain jurisdiction of these cases.

§10.11 STRUCTURE PAYMENT OF MONETARY DAMAGES AND RESTORATIVE JUSTICE

The plaintiffs might urge the court to consider the structure of payment of damages by Wall Street to the ordinary American households in this case through a judgment entailing the payment of substantial monetary damages currently with the balance payable over time through an independently managed fund of damages, established for the benefit of ordinary Americans, to be disbursed in conjunction with the affirmative action program mandated by the Court with respect to Washington institutions and agencies, in an amount sufficient to maximize the payment of damages at the time of judgment and over a reasonable period of time thereafter without precipitation of a global financial crisis.

§10.12 PRACTICAL RECOMMENDATIONS FOR ORDINARY AMERICANS TO INITIATE LEGAL ACTION FOR FINANCIAL CRISES

Ordinary Americans must urge the court to mandate that the Congress, through the United States Department of the Treasury and the existing Federal Reserve Board of Governors, provide for their education, the education of the Washington institutions and agencies, and Wall Street, and for the education of the American people, about the causes of systemic financial crises historically and the great financial crisis specifically. The occurrence of institutional abuse of trust and power to enable lying to, cheating and stealing from the people by the rich and powerful is not unheralded. Washington and Wall Street must learn from the people and document the extent and specific circumstances of the damage individual American households have suffered as a part of the crisis; they must explore with the public its desire to determine with particularity the specific identities and respective roles of the persons and individuals responsible for the great financial crisis and their will and determination to enforce justice and accountability. Washington and Wall Street must explore with the public the range of alternative actions for legal enforcement of ordinary Americans' right to financial accountability and justice under the American rule of law with respect to the nation's banking, finance and economic system.

Ordinary Americans must urge the court to establish a center for public education and action to force Congress, through the power of current collective action and consolidated legal proceedings, to fund a public interest foundation to continue constant pressure on Washington and Wall Street for redress in this crisis as it continues and through ongoing honest, transparent action to deliberately, openly and honestly establish a legitimate standard of value and liquidity of American money, including both sovereign money and transferable credit, however structured. This action should include establishment of clear definitions of American money and the types of money, including credit denominated in dollars that function as money and to exclude those that do not keeping them from infecting the American and global money supply. They must clearly and transparently explicate constitutional American money in all respects to establish limits that control money debasement by the Congress, the Treasury, the Fed or by banks or other financial institutions through excess levels of public and private debt that are monetized.

§10.13 CONCLUDING THOUGHTS AND RECOMMENDATIONS

The America government, specifically Congress, the Executive Branch and its financial regulatory agencies, the DOJ and related government sponsored entities, including the Federal Reserve System, Fannie Mae and Freddie Mac and their respective federal regulators, the SEC, other securities regulatory agencies and securities rating agencies caused the financial crisis causing approximately $20 trillion in financial damages to the American public.

Commentators on the financial crisis have uniformly reached common agreement on the facts of the case. None have heretofore made a realistic case for justice under the rule of law and for the enforcement of the existing rule of American law.

The seemingly intractable, persistent situation the American public is now experiencing as the effects of the great financial crisis requires a great realignment of American interests based on self-interest. So long as Washington and Wall Street have no incentive to change their behavior, they will not admit the necessity of change or engage in any meaningful effort to change.

The American public cannot continue to pretend that today's incarnation of the American dream is real when it is largely financed by insupportable credit. Credit driven excesses temporarily provide a phantom dream for some of the American public until they are forced to realize the damages they have suffered, albeit not uniformly. The dream now remains a phantom for a very large proportion of the American public. This state of affairs will not change until Washington and Wall Street have experienced the incentive to act honestly within the existing rule of law in their pursuit of the American dream. All American will have to work hard, be smart and productive to realize their experience of the American dream.

Without discipline under rule of law, the ongoing burden of money debasement sets the stage for eventual civil strife. It may sound improbable to most American who are inclined to inquire into the conditions and conduct giving rise to this most recent crisis, but history tells us otherwise. When America's founding fathers formed this country under the *Constitution* and the rule of law, this amazing, wise and competent group consisted of small group of public spirited but powerful individuals. America no longer can boast of such credit to our country's leadership. Powerful public figures might act differently if systemic economic, financial, monetary, and market abuse is punished, and all Americans can see benefits of a transparent, honest, safe and sound, fair economy grounded in the American rule of law.

Basing our financial and economic system on a monetary foundation that is inherently dishonest sets a precedent and standard for financial success to be achieved through deception and dishonesty. That approach is fundamentally wrong and un-American.

The objectives of the action advocated here do not include the complete eradication of the American banking system, despite the insidious manner in which Washington and Wall Street have repeatedly and continuously expanded and consolidated their control, power and wealth over it. Washington's and Wall Street's concentration of income, wealth and power has been based on the conduct of a banking industry prepared, sponsored and controlled through reactive legislation and rulemaking on short notice in the interest of meeting what are posed as existential emergencies. The so existential emergencies following financial crises have been largely self-inflicted. Washington and Wall Street react with political expediency and with Congress scarcely taking time or interest to even read proposed legislation or the depth, breadth of rules of their own device. The results are riddled with possibilities for abuse of discretion, created and granted with expedited approval "to serve the public interest," with virtually no debate and no evidence of service of the interest of the American pubic apart from a strengthening the banking monopoly that protects the "banking monopoly," allowing it to continue its growth and profitability unabated. Repeated commissions and reports conducted and prepared in the wake of successive financial crises detail the same rhetoric chronicling pubic concerns, while at the same time moving policy and legislation that fail to address or meet the reported concerns of public interest, but serve rather increasing Wall Street and Washington concentration of power, wealth, and income and expanding discretionary authority. Although consistently portrayed and admittedly proved to be the dominant partner in the Washington Wall Street partnership and an admitted monopoly monetary and credit cabal, Wall Street accountability to the public for its strangle hold over the American public and individual civil right to an open economic opportunity and a competitive level playing field in the work-a-day world has drawn a strangle hold on the American dream. The rule of law must provide relief and redress to the American public lest our country follow the footsteps of failed societies that have succumbed to unrestrained economic and political power, debasing the society's wellbeing until the weight of income and wealth inequality and crushed expectations from a crippled society brings civil society to its knees.

The specter is intolerable, un-American and the power of the American public must be brought to bear under the rule of law to overcome congressional concentrations of political power through self-serving internal rules and representative gerrymandering to frustrate the will of the electorate, perpetuating bureaucratic entrenchment through a mutually rewarding, revolving door of political favoritism for Wall Street, rewarded by the amassing of wealth and power in the private sector as a reward for maintaining the iniquitous Washington Wall Street enterprise partnership that brings us to the low point that we occupy today.

The accountability demanded by the American public in Washington and on Wall Street is not the same as the separate but related demands for American fiscal transparency, responsibility and accountability in a system that now consistently misrepresents the true nature, scope and cost of congressional and executive transfer payments. Government tax exemptions, preferences, credits deductions and other benefits are not reported in an accurate and transparent manner understandable to the American public. Electoral gerrymandering and mutual back scratching make any broad-based understanding of and accountability for American fiscal policy virtually impossible.

The accountability demanded in a case for financial crisis accountability is directed to money; its debasement and the structural legitimacy of monetary policy under the existing Federal Reserve System. It is a precondition to pursuit of accountability in tax policy and the priorities, burden and distribution of benefits and burdens of fiscal and discretionary administrative policies that pervade the federal government. Fiscal and monetary policy can become understandable and effective if the language of its existence is honest, transparent and consistent, and if the costs and benefits of government action are not distorted by the hidden con-man's touch of money debasement and legal and accounting chicanery perpetrated by Washington and Wall Street. The fight for accountability and justice outlined in this work pits the ordinary American people, the makers, against Washington and Wall Street, the takers. The people of America are the only "makers" in America.

Enforcing accountability and justice through the political electoral process has been a failure. Electoral efforts and the lobbying of Congress and Executive agencies for pro-forma accountability and justice has been a failure. Financial and regulatory reform has been a failure. The varied efforts to educate the public by countless foundations, non-profits and other groups with politically partisan agendas have stated missions to promote political change, accountability and justice but they have made little discernable progress in protecting the public interest. Their interests, rather, seem overwhelmingly to be self-preservation.

Limited action by the DOJ, FDIC, SEC and other law enforcement authorities have been settled with fines paid by Wall Street, funded with open as well as hidden government subsidies, the costs of which are ultimately borne by the American people. Civil legal action to force accountability has been largely limited to investor claims for securities laws violations. The billions of dollars extracted from the public simply move from one pocket of the wealthy and powerful in America to another. Ordinary American people and the public interest have been abandoned.

The people who formed this country and those who have long fought for the principles upon which this great nation is founded, have all been left out in the cold. The people desperately need leadership and advocacy to break the Washington Wall Street enterprise financial gridlock—a gridlock that locks the vast majority of Americans out of the prospect for protection of American ideals and hope to realize the American Dream.

America is founded upon the rule of law. The common law, the foundation for the American *Constitution*, the "law of the land," as well as state and federal statutory law, all emanating from the will and life of the people. The DOJ once proudly proclaimed that "The common law is the will of mankind issuing from the life of the people" "Lying cheating and stealing. That's white-collar crime in a nutshell." The term "white-collar crime was reportedly coined in 1939, but is now synonymous with the full range of frauds committed by *banking*, big *business and government* professionals." ... "It's not a victimless crime. A single scam can destroy a company, devastate families by wiping out their life savings, or cost investors billions of dollars (or even all three, as in the Enron case). Today's fraud schemes are more sophisticated than ever, and we are dedicated to using our skills to track down the culprits and stop scams before they start." The costs of financial crises are measured in trillions of dollars. The DOJ's promised dedication is nowhere to be found.

The American people can band together and take the enforcement of financial crisis accountability and justice under the American rule of law in their own hands. Not as victims, but as a sovereign people taking command of their own fate, fortune and future. Given a viable opportunity to act together in a powerful, cohesive and focused effort can harness the collective power of the American people in active lawful opposition to those people and institutions in Washington and on Wall Street that have abused the trust and confidence reposed in them by the people and used that abuse of power to deceive, disarm, lie to, cheat and steal from the people, crushing them under the heel of concentrated wealth and power with impunity.

With appropriate leadership and guidance, most Americans are ready, willing and able to take informed, intelligent and meaningful action: to protect themselves and their own; to redress their damages; to deter the ongoing predation of the people; to free ordinary Americans from and be no longer beholden to the powerful people and institutions that have abused the power, trust and confidence granted to them. The vast damages the Washington Wall Street enterprise has inflicted on ordinary American people have been wrought with an unbridled and firm belief in the Washington Wall Street enterprise's own self-righteous sense of entitlement, hubris, and arrogance and that comes with their "taking from the people" through the intentional exercise of their concentrated wealth and power; through their ability to lie with impunity, accompanied by the vacuous absence of any hint of acknowledgment of legal accountability for their actions under the rule of law.

A well-informed effort driven by an assembly of professionals who understand that formal imposition of legal and financial accountability and justice for ordinary Americans as well as the rich and powerful is the only way for a civil society to force change in Washington and on Wall Street. The same American laws that forbid the people from lying, cheating and stealing also apply to Washington and Wall Street. The legal rights of the individual people have no less dignity than the legal rights of their oppressors, to the faithful execution of due process of law in the enforcement of their equal rights under the law.

The collective mission of Washington and Wall Street, as the cornerstones of the American financial and economic system, must be to act transparently, honestly and fairly so as to preserve the public's interest in the "world's greatest economy" in a trustworthy and functional financial and economic system.

Humanity, civility, decency, honesty and trust are on trial in the case for financial crisis accountability. These virtues—these fundamental principles that define our country—have been trampled under the feet of the nation's wealthy, powerful and greedy. The integrity and continuity of America's traditional rewards for individual hard work and entrepreneurial zeal have been subverted by the ancient crime of exploitation of the public interest and well-being through the debasement of the public's money. The fruit of the public's labor has been fed upon by Washington and Wall Street; devouring the public interest though the inhumane, uncivilized, indecent, dishonest, and depraved blood lust of the rich and powerful. The grasping by these elites of wealth and power has risen to heights heretofore unimagined; to levels eclipsing those preceding historical civil upheavals caused by money debasement, as such evil has been repeatedly chronicled throughout our world's history. America can overcome this tragedy, balance the public interest with presently unchallenged avarice and moral collapse of its political, bureaucratic and financial leadership under the existing American rule of law and the principles of humanity, civility, decency, honesty, truth, honor and justice that Americans hold dear and must assert today. The case for American financial crisis accountability is the ultimate test of the viability of the American dream and the values upon which our republic is founded.

End Notes

1. *Black's Law Dictionary*.
2. Coinage Act of 1792, 1 Stat. 246 (April 2, 1792).
3. Nicholas Fitz, Scientific American, "Economic Inequality: It's Far Worse than You Think, The great divide between our beliefs, our ideals, and reality," March 31, 2015.
4. *Id.*
5. Subprime Meltdown—It's All About Money, G N Olson (2008) pp 180-182 and from Banks in Distress, G N Olson (2000) pp 215-218.
6. (Online Book Review and interview - Timothy Geithner vs. Elizabeth Warren in new book 'Stress Test' 05/14/14 11:37 AM—UPDATED 05/14/14 03:48 PM, By Suzy Khimm.
7. Felix Martin, Money: The Unauthorized Biography (2013) ("Martin")
8. Martin, p. 26
9. *Id.*
10. Holy See Press Office, Papal Bulletin N. 180517a "'Oeconomicae et pecuniariae quaestiones'. Considerations for an ethical discernment regarding some aspects of the present economic-financial system" of the Congregation for the Doctrine of the Faith and the Dicastery for Promoting Integral Human Development, (May 17, 2018)
11. Henry A. Kissinger, The Atlantic, "How the Enlightenment Ends, Philosophically, intellectually—in every way—human society is unprepared for the rise of artificial intelligence", (June 2018 Issue)
12. *Id.*
13. *Id.*
14. *Id.*
15. Brown v. Board of Education of Topeka, 347 U.S. 483 (S. Ct., 1954).
16. Brown v. Board of Education (II,) 349 U.S. 294, 75 S. Ct. 753, 99 L. Ed. 1083, (S. Ct. 1955).
17. Purple Mountain Trust, et al., vs Wells Fargo & Company, et al., Wells Fargo & Company's Notice of Motion and Motion to Dismiss the Consolidated Complaint for Violation of the Federal Securities Laws; Memorandum of Law in Support Thereof, Case No. 3: 18-cv-03948-JD, in the United States District Court, Northern District of California, filed November 2, 2018.
18. See, e.g., The Fed Just Acknowledged Its Too Big to Jail Policy, Zach Carter, Senior Political Economy Reporter, Shahien Nasiripour, Chief Financial and Regulatory Correspondent, Huff-post, http://www.huffingtonpost.com/2014/11/21/fed-too-big-to-jail_n_6201476.html; Prosecute Now: The Justice Department Can Still Act Against Bad Bankers, Nov. 26, 2014, updated Jan 26, 2015, Richard (RJ) Eskow, Writer/Editor http://www.huffingtonpost.com/rj-eskow/prosecute-now-the-justice_b_6225686.html; Eric Holder Admits Some Banks Are Just Too Big To Prosecute Mark Gongloff, Managing Editor, Business and Tech, The Huffington Post, http://www.huffingtonpost.com/2013/03/06/eric-holder-banks-too-big_n_2821741.htmlEric Holder, Wall Street Double Agent, Comes in From the Cold, Barack Obama's former top cop cashes in after six years of letting banks run wild, Matt Taibbi, Rolling Stone, July 8, 2015, http://www.rollingstone.com/politics/news/eric-holder-wall-street-double-agent-comes-in-from-the-cold-20150708#ixzz42WaBveNq, Testimony on Improving Financial Institution Supervision: Examining and Addressing Regulatory Capture, William C. Dudley, President and Chief Executive Officer, Federal Reserve Bank of New York, November 21, 2014,Testimony before the Senate Committee on Banking, Housing, and Urban Affairs Financial Institutions and Consumer Protection Subcommittee, January 27, 2009. (Dudley, among other capacities, serves as the vice chairman and a permanent member of the Federal Open Market Committee (FOMC), the group responsible for formulating the nation's monetary policy), Attorney General Holder Remarks on Financial Fraud Prosecutions at NYU School of Law, Wednesday, September 17, 2014, Eric Holder Gives Prosecutors 90 Days to File Wall Street Collapse Charges, Thursday, 19 February http://www.reuters.com/article/us-usa-mortgages-holder-idUSKBN0LL1X920150217 2015 00: 00, By Sam Knight, The District Sentinel News Analysis https://www.districtsentinel.com/in-last-gasp-attempt-to-shake-corrupt-reputation-holder-gives-prosecutors-90-days-to-file-wall-street-collapse-charges/U.S. identifying people to target for role in mortgage crisis, Julia Edwards and Karen Freifels, Reuters, Tue Feb 17, 2011, http://www.reuters.com/article/us-usa-mortgages-holder-idUSKBN0LL1X920150217, and finally, Letter of Phil Angelides, Chairman of

the National Commission on the Causes of the Financial and Economic Crisis in the United States, to the Attorney General of the United States, February 1, 2016.

19. Jim Tankersley, Washington Post Wonkblog "The wealthy have nearly healed from recession. The poor haven't even started" (August 18, 2016).
20. Michael Snyder, "Zero Hedge, More Than 101 Million Working Age Americans Do Not Have A Job, April 8th, 2013.
21. See CBO, http://www.census.gov/quickfacts/table/HSD410214/00 estimates total U.S.
22. Federal Reserve Bank of Dallas, Staff Paper No. 20, July 2013 and Economic Letter Vol 8, No. 7. September 2013.
23. US Department of the Treasury, The Financial Crisis Response in Charts, April 2012. See also, United States Government Accounting Office Report to Congressional Requesters, Financial Regulatory Reform – Financial Crisis Losses and Potential Impacts of the Dodd Frank Act, January 2013, at p. 20.
24. See, e.g., "Jealous of the Joneses: conspicuous consumption, inequality, and crime," Oxf. Econ. Pap. (2014) 66 (4): 1090-1120 first published online June 20, 2014; Pablo Fajnzylber, University of Minas Gerais Daniel Lederman, World Bank and Norman Loayza, World Bank Inequality and Violent Crime*, Journal of Law and Economics, vol. XLV (April 2002), The University of Chicago; and Walter Scheidel, "The Great Leveler: Violence and the Global History of Inequality from the Stone Age to the Present", Princeton University Press (2014, 2015); and see Mark Buchanan and Mark Whitehouse, "Want to Fight Crime? Address Economic Inequality," Bloomberg, January 6, 2013. http://www.bloombergview.com/articles/2013-01-06/want-to-fight-crime-address-economic-inequality.
25. Reeves, A., McKee, M., & Stuckler, D. (2014). Economic suicides in the Great Recession in Europe and North America. British Journal of Psychiatry, 205(3), 246-247. doi:10.1192/bjp.bp.114.144766.
26. Hans Christian Anderson, "The Emperor's New Clothes" was first published with "The Little Mermaid" on 7 April 1837 by C.A. Reitzel in Copenhagen as the third and final installment of the first collection of Andersen's Fairy Tales Told for Children. The first two booklets of the collection were published in May and December 1835. Andersen waited a year before publishing the third installment of the collection.
27. See Wells Fargo & Company's Notice of Motion to Dismiss the Consolidated Complaint for Violation of the Federal Securities; Memorandum of Law in Support Thereof, filed in Case No. 3:18-CV-03948-JD, on 2.11.18, in the United States District Court, Northern District of California.
28. Daniel Kahneman, Amos Tversky, and Paul Slovic, eds., Judgment under Uncertainty: Heuristics & Biases, (Cambridge, UK, Cambridge University Press 1982).
29. Gramm–Leach–Bliley Act (GLBA), also known as the Financial Services Modernization Act of 1999, (Pub.L. 106–102, 113 Stat. 1338, enacted November 12, 1999) is an act of the 106th United States Congress (1999–2001).
30. Amos Tversky; Daniel Kahneman, Judgment under Uncertainty: Heuristics and Biases, Science, New Series, Vol. 185, No. 4157. (Sep. 27, 1974), (pp. 1124-1131).
31. G. N. Olson, Banks in Distress – Lessons from the American Experience of the 1980s (Kluwer Law International, 2000) (Banks in Distress).
32. H.R.4173—*Dodd-Frank Wall Street Reform and Consumer Protection Act*, 111th Congress (2009-210) (Dodd Frank).
33. See, *infra*.
34. G. N. Olson, *Subprime Meltdown: It's All About Money* (BookSurge Press/Amazon 2008) (Subprime Meltdown).
35. Carmen M. Reinhart and Kenneth S. Rogoff, *This Time is Different – Eight Centuries of Financial Folly* (Princeton University Press, 2009) (Reinhart and Rogoff).
36. Barry Eichengreen, *Exorbitant Privilege – The Rise and Fall of the Dollar and the Future of the International Monetary System* (Oxford University Press, 2011) (Eichengreen 2011).
37. Barry Eichengreen, *Hall of Mirrors – The Great Depression, The Great Recession and the Uses and Misuses of History* (Oxford University Press 2015) (Eichengreen 2015).
38. R. Christopher Whalen, *Inflated – How Money and Debt Built the American Dream* (John Wiley & Sons, Inc., 2011) (Whalen).
39. Frederick L. Feldkamp and R. Christopher Whalen, *Financial Stability – Fraud, Confidence and the Wealth of Nations* (John Wiley & Sons, Inc. 2014) (Feldkamp and Whalen).
40. Peter Conti Brown, The Power and Independence of the Federal Reserve, (Princeton University Press 2016).

41. Adair Turner, Between Debt and the Devil, Money, Credit and Fixing Global Finance, (Princeton University Press 2016).
42. James Rickards, Currency Wars - The Making of the Next Global Crisis (Portfolio / Penguin 2012) (Rickards, 2012), The Death of Money - The Coming Collapse of the International Monetary System (Portfolio / Penguin 2014) (Rickards 2015), and The new Case for Gold, (Portfolio / Penguin 2016) (Rickards (2016).
43. Neal Barofsky Bailout, (Free Press 2012) (Barofsky).
44. Mervin King, The End of Alchemy - Money, Banking, and the Global Economy, (W.W. Norton & Company 2016).
45. Niall Ferguson, The Ascent of Money - A Financial History of the World, (The Penguin Press 2008).
46. Charles Kindleberger Manias, Panics, and Crashes; a History of Financial Crises, (John Wiley & Sons, Inc., 2000).
47. F. A. Mann, The Legal Aspect of Money, 4th Ed.,(Clarendon Press 1982) (Mann).
48. Felix Martin, Money - the Unauthorized Biography, (The Bodley Head 2013) (Martin).
49. Paul Kennedy, The Rise and Fall of the Great Powers,—Economic Change and Military Conflict from 1500 to 2000 (Random House 1987).
50. Federal Reserve Act (Ch. 6, 38 Stat. 251, enacted December 23, 1913, 12 U.S.C. Ch. 3) (FRA).
51. Lawrence Kotlikoff, (The Fiscal Times, November 8, 2011).
52. *Id.*
53. Federal Deposit Insurance Corporation, History of the Eighties - Lessons for the Future (1997).
54. James Madison, The Federalist No. 48, These Departments Should Not Be So Far Separated as to Have No Constitutional Control Over Each Other, New York Packet (February 1, 1788).
55. Phil Gramm, Washington Times, (July 9, 2008).
56. Eichengreen 2011.
57. See, generally, Bank for International Settlements, 86th Annual Report, 2015/16, (June 26, 2016), and related publications of The Basel Committee on Banking Supervision.
58. A U.S. government "bailout" program, the Troubled Asset Relief Program, implemented under the Emergency Economic Stabilization Act of 2008 (Division A, of Pub. L. 110-343, 122 Stat. 3765, enacted October 3, 2008).
59. John M. Mason, Seeking Alpha, "Federal Reserve Watch: Might Fed Stop Reduction in Securities Portfolio? (January 27, 2019).
60. See, Note 28, *supra*.
61. The Financial Crisis Inquiry Commission, The Financial Crisis Inquiry Report - Final Report of the National Commission on the Causes of the Financial and Economic Crisis in the United States, (Public Affairs, Authorized Edition 2011) (Crisis Report).
62. Edwin Vieira, Jr., Pieces of Eight, The Monetary Powers and Disabilities of the United States Constitution, 2nd Ed., (RR Donnelley & Sons, Inc. 2002) (Vieira).
63. (Martin, p. 13).
64. Walter Bagehot, "The General Aspect of the Banking Question." No. 1, a letter to the editor of *The Economist*, February 7, 1857, in *The Collected Works of Walter Bagehot*, ed. Norman St. John-Stevas (London, *The Economist*, 1978), vol. 9, p. 319. See also, Kindleberger, pp, 51—55.
65. Keynes 1937, p. 213.
66. See generally, Ludwig Von Mises, *The Theory of Money and Credit*, (Liberty Fund 1981), pp. 41, *et. seq.*
67. *Id.*
68. *Id.*
69. *Id.*, p. 73, *et. seq.*
70. See, generally, Feldkamp and Whalen, pp. 39, *et. seq.*, and 159, *et. seq.*
71. United Nations Monetary and Financial Conference, Bretton Woods, New Hampshire, July 1-22,1944 Final Act and Related Documents, Department of State publication 2187, Conference Series 55; also, Department of State publication 2511, Treaties and Other International Acts Series 1502. Agreement signed at Washington December 27, 1945; effective December 27, 1945. Public Law 171, 79th Cong., lst sess., H. R. 3314: An Act ("Bretton Woods Accord") to provide for participation of the United States in the International Monetary Fund and the International Bank for Reconstruction and Development was approved July 31, 1945. Agreement establishing official relationship between the Bank and the United Nations was approved by the General Assembly November 15,1947.
72. Mann, pp. 30—48.

73. Mann, p. 36.
74. Von Mises, p. 453, *et. seq.*
75. *Id.*
76. Martin, p.12.
77. *Id.*
78. *Id.*
79. *Id.*, p. 13.
80. *Id.*, p. 42.
81. *Id.*, p. 43.
82. *Id.*
83. *Id.*, p. 26.
84. *Id.*
85. *Id.*
86. *Id.*, p. 27.
87. *Id.*
88. *Id.*, p.26.
89. *Id.*, p. 36.
90. *Id.*, pp. 36, 37.
91. *Id.*, p.43.
92. *Id.*, pp. 43, 44.
93. *Id.*, p. 45.
94. *Id.*, p. 51.
95. *Id.*
96. *Id.*, p. 52.
97. *Id.*, p. 53. See generally, Chapter 4, Morality and Law, *infra.*
98. *Id.*, pp. 58, 59.
99. *Id.*
100. *Id.*, pp. 59, 60.
101. *Id.*, p. 60.
102. *Id.*
103. *Id.*, p. 61.
104. *Id.*
105. *Id.*
106. *Id.*, p. 62.
107. *Id.*, p. 63.
108. *Id.*
109. *Id.*, p. 65.
110. *Id.*, p. 71.
111. *Id.*, pp. 70, 71.
112. Mann, *p. 38, et. seq.*
113. See, George Friedrich Knapp, *The State Theory of Money*, English translation of 4th ed. (Macmillan & Company Limited, 1924), p. 21.
114. Mann, p.45.
115. Martin, p. 72.
116. *Id.*, p. 73.
117. *Id.*, p. 74.
118. *Id.*, pp. 74, 75.
119. *Id.*, p. 77.
120. *Id.*
121. *Id.*, pp. 77, 78.
122. *Id.*, p.78.
123. *Id.*, p. 81.
124. *Id.*, p.83.
125. *Id.*
126. *Id.*
127. *Id.*, p. 85.
128. *Id.*, p. 86.
129. *Id.*, pp, 87, 88.
130. *Id.*, p. 88.

131. *Id.*
132. *Id.*, p. 89.
133. *Id.*, p. 90.
134. *Id.*, pp. 90, 91.
135. *Id.*
136. *Id.*
137. *Id.*
138. *Id.*, p 92.
139. *Id.*, p. 93.
140. *Id.*
141. *Id.*, p. 94.
142. *Id.*, p. 96.
143. *Id.*, p.97.
144. *Id.*
145. *Id.*, p. 98.
146. *Id.*
147. *Id.*
148. *Id.*, p. 100.
149. *Id.*
150. *Id.*, p. 101.
151. *Id.*, pp. 101, 102.
152. *Id.*, p. 102.
153. *Id.*
154. *Id.*, p. 104.
155. *Id.*
156. *Id.*
157. *Id.*, p. 105.
158. *Id.*, p. 107.
159. *Id.*, pp.109, 110.
160. *Id.*, 110.
161. *Id.*
162. *Id.*, 111.
163. *Id.*
164. *Id.*
165. *Id.*, 112.
166. *Id.*
167. *Id.*
168. *Id.*, p. 113.
169. *Id.*, p. 115.
170. *Id.*, 116.
171. *Id.*, p. 117.
172. *Id.*, pp. 117, 118.
173. *Id.*
174. *Id.*, p. 119.
175. *Id.*, p. 120).
176. *Id.*, p. 121.
177. *Id.*
178. *Id.*, p.122.
179. *Id.*, p.123.
180. *Id.*, p.124.
181. *Id.*
182. *Id.*, p. 125.
183. *Id.*
184. *Id.*, p. 127.
185. *Id.*
186. *Id.*
187. *Id.*, p. 128.
188. *Id.*, pp. 128, 129.
189. *Id.*, p. 129.

190. *Id.*, p. 129, 130.
191. *Id.*, p. 130.
192. *Id.*
193. *Id.*, p. 131.
194. *Id.*, pp. 131, 132.
195. *Id.*, p. 132.
196. *Id.*
197. *Id.*, p. 133.
198. *Id.*
199. *Id.*, p.139.
200. *Id.*, p. 140.
201. *Id.*
202. *Id.*, p. 141.
203. *Id.*, p. 142.
204. *Id.*, pp. 142, 143.
205. *Id.*, p. 145.
206. *Id.*, pp. 144, 145.
207. *Id.*, p.145.
208. *Id.*
209. *Id.*
210. *Id.*
211. *Id.*, p. 146.
212. *Id.*
213. *Id.*, pp. 154, 155.
214. *Id.*, 155, 156.
215. *Id.*, pp. 156, 157.
216. *Id.*, p.179, 180.
217. *Id.*, p. 180.
218. *Id.*
219. *Id.*, p. 182.
220. *Id.*, p. 183.
221. *Id.*
222. Id.
223. Id.
224. *Id.*, p. 184.
225. *Id.*, p. 186.
226. *Id.*
227. *Id.*, pp. 186, 187.
228. First Epistle to Timothy in the *New Testament* (1 Timothy 6:10, KJV): "For the love of money is the root of all kinds of evil."
229. Jun Luo, *Bloomberg*, "Shadow Banking" (September 24, 2018).
230. Carolyn Sissoko, *Shadow Banking: Why Modern Money Markets are Less Stable Than 19th c. Money Markets But Shouldn't Be Stabilized by a "Dealer of Last Resort"* Center for Law and Social Science, Research Papers Series No. CLASS14-20 Legal Studies Research Papers Series No. 14-21, April 25, 2014 (Sissoko).
231. Perry Mehrling, Zoltan Pozsar, James Sweeney, Dan Neilson, members of the Shadow Banking Colloquium, a project of the Financial Stability Research Program of the Institute for New Economic Thinking, *Bagehot was a Shadow Banker: Shadow Banking, Central Banking, and the Future of Global Finance,* August 15, 2012 (Mehrling, *et. al.*, 2012), Revised December 6, 2013 (Mehrling, *et al.*, 2013). See also, Tyler Durden,*"Bagehot Was A Shadow Banker"—A Monetary System That Is Only As Good As Its First Broken Promise*, TwitterFacebookReddit, July 27, 2013 7:02 PM.
232. Mehrling, *et.al.*, 2012, p. 1.
233. *Id.*
234. *Id.*, p.2.
235. Bagehot, Walter. 1857. "The General Aspect of the Banking Question." no. 1 a letter to the editor of The Economist, February 7. In The Collected Works of Walter Bagehot, ed. Norman St. John-Stevas (London: *The Economist*, 1978, vol. 9, p. 319). (Bagehot).

236. John Maynard Keynes, *The Quarterly Journal of Economics*, "The General Theory of Employment." February 1937.[Pagination from *The Collected Writings of John Maynard Keynes*, vol. XIV, pp. 109-123] [Page 109].
237. Mann, p. 43. George Canning was a British statesman and Tory politician who served in various senior cabinet positions under numerous Prime Ministers, before himself serving as Prime Minister for the final four months of his life. Canning's feud with Castlereagh was notorious, the two having fought a duel on 21 September 1809 on Putney Heath.
238. *Id.*
239. *Id.*, p. 42.
240. *Id.*, p. 36.
241. *Id.*, p. 37, at note 44, and pp. *38, et. seq.*
242. *Id.*, at p. 14, note 68, citing the Uniform Commercial Code, § 1—201 and the comment to § 3—107.
243. Uniform Commercial Code § 1—201 (24) (2001). The Comment to § 1—201 (24): "Money." "Unchanged from former Section 1-201. The test is that of sanction of government, whether by authorization before issue or adoption afterward, which recognizes the circulating medium as a part of the official currency of that government. The narrow view that money is limited to legal tender is rejected."
244. Bagehot, p. 319.
245. Mann, Chapters IV and V.
246. See Michael V. White and Kurt Schuler, "Retrospectives: Who Said "Debauch the Currency": Keynes or Lenin?" *Journal of Economic Perspectives*—Volume 23, Number 2 (Spring 2009), pp. 213–222, at pp. 213 and 214, for a discussion of money debauchery and debasement.
247. Carolyn Sissoko, "Shadow Banking: Why Modern Money Markets are Less Stable Than 19th c. Money Markets But Shouldn't Be Stabilized by a 'Dealer of Last Resort,'" *Center for Law and Social Science Research Papers Series* No. CLASS14-20, *Legal Studies Research Papers Series* No. 14-21 (April 25, 2014) (Sissoko).
248. Sissoko, pp. 2 and 3.
249. *Id.*, p.3.
250. *Id.*, pp. 13 and 14.
251. *Id.*, pp. 14 and 15.
252. *Id.*, pp. 15 and 16.
253. *Id.*, pp. 16 and 17.
254. *Id.*, p. 17.
255. *Id.*
256. *Id.*
257. *Id.*
258. *Id.*, p. 18.
259. *Id.*
260. *Id.*, pp. 18 and 19.
261. *Id.*, p. 20.
262. *Id.*
263. *Id.*, p. 21.
264. *Id.*
265. *Id.*
266. *Id.*, p. 22.
267. Uniform Commercial Code § 1—201 (19) (2001).
268. Uniform Commercial Code § 1—204 (2001).
269. Uniform Commercial Code § 1—302 (2001).
270. Bernie Sanders, *The Speech* [United States Senate, December 10, 2010], p. 16).
271. Hall Scott, 2009.
272. See, Reutershttp://www.reuters.com/article/2015/12/03/us-markets-mortgages-fed-idUSKBN0TM2K420151203#drqQafSYsBABEdzX.99).
273. John M. Mason, *Seeking Alpha*, "Federal Reserve Watch: Might Fed Stop Reduction In Securities Portfolio? (January 27, 2019).
274. Reinhart & Rogoff, p. 241.
275. *Id.*, p. 281.
276. *Id.*, pp. 281, 282.
277. *Id.*, p. 292.

278. See, Reutershttp://www.reuters.com/article/2015/12/03/us-ecb-policy-qe-idUSKBN0TM1P420151203#mebOUKRVR9ex3Yjy.99.
279. See, Reutershttp://www.reuters.com/article/2015/12/03/us-ecb-nowotny idUSKBN0TM2W720151203#1KlYSgOhdjEYv54H.99.
280. Minsky, 1996.
281. Roche & McKee, p. 32, Figure 26.
282. Committee Report, pp. 45, 46.
283. Roche & McKee, P. 82, Figure 62).
284. Actions taken by a country's central bank to counter the effects on the money supply caused by a balance of payments surplus or deficit. Sloman, John (2004). *Economics*. Penguin. p. 969. ISBN 0-7450-1333-3. This can involve open market operations undertaken by the central bank whose aim is to neutralize the impact of associated foreign exchange operations. Paul Krugman and Maurice Obstfeld, "International Economics, Theory and Policy", Addison Wesley, 2003, 6th Edition, pgs. 488–489).
285. Roche & McKee, p. 90, figure 72).
286. *Id.*, pp. 31-33.
287. *Id.*
288. *Id.*
289. *Id.*
290. *Id.*
291. *Id.*
292. *Id.*
293. *Id.*
294. *Id.*
295. *Id.*
296. *Id.*
297. *Id.*
298. Eichengreen, p.100.
299. *Id.*
300. Eichengreen, p. 101.
301. *Id.*
302. *Id.*
303. Eichengreen, p. 2, quoting *The Wall Street Journal*, "In the black market, the dollar still rules."
304. Eichengreen, p. 4.
305. Department of the Treasury, Federal Reserve Bank of New York, Board of Governors of the Federal Reserve System, *Foreign Portfolio Holdings of U.S. Securities as of June 30, 2017* (April 2018), p. 3.
306. Eichengreen, p. 5.
307. *The Uniform Agreement on the Classification and Appraisal of Securities Held by Depository Institutions* attached to FDIC Financial Institution Letter FIL-51-2013 (October 29, 2013).
308. *Id.*
309. *Id.*
310. *RepoWatch*,April 7, 2011, updated January 3, 2013).
311. (John Mauldin, Matt Nesto, *Fed Has a Secret Third Mandate*, Breakout—Yahoo Finance, Tuesday, (Oct 29, 2013).
312. *Id.*
313. *Derivatives: The Unregulated Global Casino for Banks*, Demon.ocracy.info, citing *Zero Hedge* (undated, © 2012).
314. Tyler Durden, *Zerohedge, "Financial Weapons of Mass Destruction: Top 25 US Banks Have 222 Trillion Dollars Derivatives Exposure," May 17, 2017.*
315. Vieira, p. 1427, Citing Reuss v. Balles, 584 F. 2d 461, 468-69 (D.C. Cir. 1978) and Committee for Monetary Reform v. Board of Governors of the Federal Reserve System, 766F. 2d 538, 542-43 (D.C.Cir. 1985).
316. The Gramm–Leach–Bliley Act (GLBA), also known as the Financial Services Modernization Act of 1999, (Pub.L. 106–102, 113 Stat. 1338, enacted November 12, 1999) is an act of the 106th United States Congress (1999–2001). It repealed part of the Glass–Steagall Act of 1933, removing barriers in the market among banking companies, securities companies and insurance companies that prohibited any one institution from acting as any combination of an investment bank, a commercial bank, and an insurance company. With the bipartisan

passage of the Gramm–Leach–Bliley Act, commercial banks, investment banks, securities firms, and insurance companies were allowed to consolidate. Furthermore, it failed to give to the SEC or any other financial regulatory agency the authority to regulate large investment bank holding companies.

317. Vieira, p. 774.
318. *Id.*, pp. 774, 775.
319. *Id.*, pp. 784, 785.
320. Excerpted from the July 2014 edition of A. Gary Shilling's *INSIGHT)* illustrates the current exposure of the Wall Street banks to derivative risks.
321. Federal Reserve Act (ch. 6, 38 Stat. 251, enacted December 23, 1913, 12 U.S.C. ch. 3). Part 2.
322. 12 USC 225a. As added by act of November 16, 1977 (91 Stat. 1387) and amended by acts of October 27, 1978 (92 Stat. 1897); Aug. 23, 1988 (102 Stat. 1375); and Dec. 27, 2000 (114 Stat. 3028).
323. *The Report of the Monetary Commission of the Indianapolis Convention, Hollenbeck Press, Indianapolis* (1900).
324. Whalen, p. 79.
325. Vieira, p. 728.
326. *Id.*
327. Vieira, p. 730.
328. Vieira, pp. 738, *et. seq.*
329. See, e.g., Michael Greenberger, *Institute for New Economic Thinking*, "Working Paper No. 74, Too Big to Fail U.S. Banks' Regulatory Alchemy: Converting an Obscure Agency Footnote into an "At Will' Nullification of Dodd-Frank's Regulation of the Multi-Trillion Dollar Financial Swaps Market" (June 2018).
330. Reinhart & Rogoff, p. 88, Box 6.1.
331. Dylan Grice, *Short History of Currency Debasement* (republished as Memo to Central Banks: *You're debasing more than our currency*, in the John Mauldin *Newsletter*, October 26, 2012.
332. See Kindleberger, *Outline of Financial Crises*; Reinhart & Rogoff, Appendix A.4, Table A.4.1 *Historical Summaries of Banking Crises*, pp. 348 through 392; and see generally, Paul Kennedy *The Rise and Fall of the Great Powers*, (1987).
333. Vieira, p.126.
334. *Id.*, p. 128.
335. *Id.*, p. 158.
336. *Id.*, pp. 159-161.
337. *Id.*, p. 161.
338. *Id.*, p. 161.
339. Reinhart & Rogoff, p. 88. Box 6.1.
340. Vieira, p. 614.
341. *Id.*, p. 77.
342. *Id.*, p. 192.
343. See Reinhart & Rogoff, pp. 174—179.
344. See, *Understanding the Risks Inherent in Shadow Banking—A Primer and Practical Lessons Learned, Dallas Fed Staff Paper No. 18*, November 2012. See also, Chapter 2, *supra.*
345. *The Coinage Act of April 2, 1792*, (1 Stat. 246).
346. John Mauldin *Big Banks Shift to Lower Gear*, July 30, 2014 (Excerpted from the July 2014 edition of A. Gary Shilling's *INSIGHT* (Mauldin Shilling).
347. *Mauldin Shilling*, Chart 8.
348. *Id.*, Chart 9. Authors note: counterparty risk = liquidity risk and therefore value risk due to illiquidity.
349. See Mauldin and Shilling, generally.
350. Sarah N. Lynch, *Reuters—Business News*, "Goldman Sachs fined over trade rule violations in dark pool" (July 1, 2014).
351. Jillian Berman, *Any Hope of American Equality Died In The 1980s (And Here's Proof) The Huffington Post*, 12/20/2013 2:10 pm EST.
352. Eamon Javers, "Inside Obama's bank CEOs meeting", 04/03/09 01:00 PM EDT. See also: http://www.politico.com/story/2009/04/inside-obamas-bank-ceos-meeting-020871#ixzz4LNrWmwd1.
353. See, *Gallup News, Congress and the Public*, for historical and current congressional approval ratings, http://news.gallup.com.

354. Ariel Edwards-Levy, *The Huffington Post, Politics,* "Americans Find Congress Slightly More Honest Than Car Salesmen: Poll." (December 3, 2012).
355. Dr. Lawrence M. Parks, Executive Director, the Foundation for the Advancement of Monetary Education paper *Currency Debasement: How it harms the World Economy* (undated).
356. *Legal Tender Cases,* 110 U.S. 421 (S. Ct. 1884). See Chapter 9, *infra.*
357. *Gold Clause Cases, Norman v. Baltimore & Ohio Railroad Co., United States v. Bankers Trust Co.*, 294 U.S. 240 (1935), *Nortz v. United States*, 294 U.S. 317 (1935), and *Perry v. United States*, 294 U.S. 330 (1935) See Chapter 9, *infra.*
358. See generally, 14 *Fed. Prac. & Proc. Juris.* § 3658.2 (4th Ed.).
359. United States v. Lee, 106 U.S. 196, 220 (S. Ct., 1882). See also, Vieira, p. 1643, *et seq.*
360. A Temporary Court of Appeals decision in 1978, 573 F. 2d 1268, at 1278.
361. See Vieira, p. 1643, *et seq.*
362. Vieira, p. 1648.
363. Attorney General Holder Remarks on Financial Fraud Prosecutions at NYU School of Law, New York City, NY, United States, Wednesday, September 17, 2014.
364. Sam Knight, *Eric Holder Gives Prosecutors 90 Days to File Wall Street Collapse Charges* The District Sentinel, (February 19, 2015).
365. *US Identifying People to Target for Role in Mortgage Crisis*, Thomson/Reuters 17 February 17, 2015.
366. The federal statutory foundation for these claims has also been briefly noted by Frederick Feldkamp and Christorher Whalen, without further analysis, in their book *Financial Stability* (Feldkamp and Whaley, 2014, p. 159).
367. Suzy Khimm, *Timothy Geithner vs. Elizabeth Warren in new book 'Stress Test'*, MSNBC (May 14, 2014).
368. Tim Graham Executive Editor of *NewsBusters* and Media Research Center's Director of Media Analysis, May 20, 2014—See more at: http://newsbusters.org/blogs/tim-graham/2014/05/20/no-game-hardball-time-asks-tim-geithner-why-everyone-so-unhappy-about-gr#sthash.tcfCwKVh.dpuf).
369. Marilyn Geewax, *It's Geithner vs. Warren In Battle Of The Bailout,* NPR (May 25, 2014).
370. See, e.g., Daniel Griswold, *America's Record Trade Deficit: A Symbol of Strength,* Cato Institute (February 21, 2001).
371. See generally, James Rickards, *The New Case for Gold* (2016); see particularly, pp. 29-33.
372. Whalen, p. 321.
373. *Id.*, p. 322.
374. *Id.*, p. 328.
375. *Id.*, p. 329.
376. *Id.*, p. 330.
377. Samuel Gregg, *Beyond Sovereignty: Money and its Future,* (March 5, 2010), p. 1.
378. *Id.*, p.7.
379. *Id.*, pp. 4, 5.
380. *Id.*, p. 5.
381. Quoting the *Wall Street Journal, "In the black market, the dollar still rules."* Eichengreen, p. 2.
382. (Eichengreen, p.4).
383. *Id.*
384. See Reinhart & Rogoff, pp. 174—179.
385. *Id.*
386. Whalen, pp. 280, 281.
387. Reinhart & Rogoff, p. 180.
388. This chapter is based in part on a paper presented at Innovations in Financial Laws and Systems Colloquium (Part II), A Tribute to Professor Joseph J. Norton Southern Methodist University Dedman School of Law, Dallas, Texas, entitled, *Honesty, Money, Natural Law • Moral Law* and *The American Rule of Law* May 5, 2017.
389. Ovid, *Heroides*, 5th century BC., giving rise to the normative ethical theory of consequentialism and utilitarianism, expressed by Jeremy Bentham, Max Weber and John Stuart Mill, among others.
390. This image appears in the work of Sima Dave, *The Canned Historian,* powered by Blogger, "The Storming of the Bastille, posted July 14, 2014. It has been digitally edited by G. N. Olson, Jr., © G N Olson & Company, LLC.

391. See, e.g., Rebecca L. Spang, *Stuff and Money in the Time of the French Revolution*, January 2015.
392. It's one of the most famous quotes in history. At some point around 1789, when being told that her French subjects had no bread, Marie-Antoinette (bride of France's King Louis XVI) supposedly sniffed, "Qu'ils mangent de la brioche"—"Let them eat cake." With that callous remark, the queen became a hated symbol of the decadent monarchy and fueled the revolution that would cause her to (literally) lose her head several years later. But did Marie-Antoinette really say those infuriating words? Not according to historians. Lady Antonia Fraser, author of a biography of the French queen, believes the quote would have been highly uncharacteristic of Marie-Antoinette, an intelligent woman who donated generously to charitable causes and, despite her own undeniably lavish lifestyle, displayed sensitivity towards the poor population of France. History.com Staff, "Did Marie-Antoinette really say 'Let them eat cake'?" October 24, 2012.
393. In September 2014, Fox Business commentator Todd Wilemon told Daily Show correspondent Aasif Mandvi that poor people should "stop being poor" in order to afford healthcare.
394. *Online Etymology Dictionary*.
395. See, William Simpson, *The Structure of Complex Words (1951)*.
396. Seth Lobis, *"Honesty"—A frank look at the word,"* The John Templeton Foundation http://incharacter.org/ (April 1, 2007) ("Lobis").
397. See, generally, Satoshi Nakamoto, Bitcoin: A Peer-to-Peer Electronic Cash System, Satoshi Nakamoto Institute, October 31, 2008.
398. According to *Wikapedia*, the term "gas lighting" is described as "a form of manipulation that seeks to sow seeds of doubt in a targeted individual or members of a group, hoping to make targets question their own memory, perception, and sanity. Using persistent denial, misdirection, contradiction, and lying, it attempts to destabilize the target and delegitimize the target's belief. Instances may range from the denial by an abuser that previous abusive incidents ever occurred up to the staging of bizarre events by the abuser with the intention of disorienting the victim. The term owes its origin to a 1938 play *Gas Light* and its 1944 film adaptation. The term has been used in clinical and research literature, as well as in political commentary." Gas lighting is at the heart of the false narratives regarding money emanating from Washington and Wall Street leading to and following the financial crisis.
399. See Lobis.
400. See *Online Etymology Dictionary* under entry "Spin (propaganda)."
401. Curtis W. Copeland, Congressional Research Service, *Rulemaking Requirements and Authorities in the Dodd-Frank Wall Street Reform and Consumer Protection Act* (November 3, 2010).
402. Richard (RJ) Eskow, *Huffpost*, "Prosecute Now: The Justice Department Can Still Act Against Bad Bankers," January 26, 2015.
403. Jörg Guido Hülsmann, *The Ethics of Money Production*, 2008 ("Hülsmann"), pp. 187, 188.
404. Jessica Bennett," The Truth Is, We're All Liars," *Newsweek* (August 25 2009) (Bennett).
405. Robert Feldman, *The Liar in your Life* (August 13, 2009).
406. See Bennett.
407. As detailed in the preceding chapters of this work, the phenomenon of structured finance consisting of securitization of illiquid assets employing rigged securities ratings and layers of derivatives, and the representation of those securities and derivatives as current liquid money substitutes, and accounting for them as such, is a perversion of the bankers' special responsibility to provide money through disciplined credit while managing the risk and uncertainty inherent in making illiquid asset appear to be liquid at market value, without discount for the underlying risk and uncertainty of value in the future posed by risk and uncertainty manifest in financial crises. See, *e.g.*, an announcement in the *Wall Street Journal*, April 16, 2014 where Madison International Realty states explicitly that its securities offering is intended to "monetize" [...] "partial ownership interests [...] embedded equity and recapitalizations of Class A properties [commercial real estate; notoriously illiquid in times of financial crisis] and portfolios in the United States, United Kingdom, and Western Europe."
408. Stephanie Blankenburg and Jose' Gabriel Palma, "Introduction: the global financial crisis," *Cambridge Journal of Economics* 2009, 33, 531–538, at p.532.doi:10.1093/cje/bep038.
409. National Commission on the Causes of the Financial and Economic Crisis in the United States, *The Financial Crisis Inquiry Report*, January 2011.
410. Suzy Khimm, "Timothy Geithner vs. Elizabeth Warren in new book 'Stress Test,' msnbc, May 14, 2014.

411. David Dayen, "Obama on Bank Prosecutions: They did Nothing Illegal, Only Found Loopholes that We Worked to Close", *Shadow Proof*, October 6, 2011.
412. President Barack Obama, Office of the Press Secretary, The White House, Press Release *Remarks by the President in State of the Union Address*, January 24, 2012.
413. See, e.g., Hülsmann, at Chapters 7—12, pp. 103-175.
414. The Dallas Federal Reserve Bank (Staff Paper NO. 20. July 2013 and *Economic Letter* Vol 8, NO. 7. September 2013), The U.S. Department of the Treasury (*The Financial Crisis Response in Charts*, April 2012—estimates $19.2 trillion in lost household wealth, or $160,000 per household based upon 120 million households), and the United States Government Accounting Office (*Report to Congressional Requesters, Financial Regulatory Reform—Financial Crisis Losses and Potential Impacts of the Dodd Frank Act*, January 2013, citing at page 20, The Federal Reserve's Survey of Consumer Finances' estimate of damage in the form of lost median household net worth of $49,000 per household, between 2007 and 2010) have all calculated loss, cost or damage by reference to American households. In addition, Better Markets in its reports on the cost of the crisis, dated, September 15, 2012 and July 2014, estimate, loss, cost or damage by house hold and on a gross basis, more than $12.8 trillion ($106,667 per household) in 2012, and more than $20 trillion ($166,667, per household) in 2015, respectively. Accordingly, the government would find it convenient to face a plaintiff's class composed of approximately 120 million American households, suffering damages of $83,334 per household, identified and calculated by the criteria set forth above.
415. The illegality of American money debasement is detailed in this book, *Money Morality and Law*.
416. Oliver Scott Curry, Daniel Austin Mullins and Henry Whitehouse, *Journal of Anthropology Vol. 60, No.1*, "Is It Good to Cooperate? Testing the Theory of Morality-as-Cooperation in 60 Societies (February 2019).
417. *Id.*, (Non-paginated online version).
418. *Id.*
419. + Luis F. Ladaria, S.I., Peter Card. Turkson, X. Giacomo Morandi and Bruno Marie Duffé, Bulletin, N. 180517a, issued Thursday, 17.05.2018, entitled "'Oeconomicae et pecuniariae quaestiones' (Papal Bulletin, Considerations for an ethical discernment regarding some aspects of the present economic-financial system" of the Congregation for the Doctrine of the Faith and the Dicastery for Promoting Integral Human Development, Rome, (January 6, 2018), pp. 1, 2.
420. *Id.*, p. 5.
421. *Id.*
422. *Id.*, p. 5, 6.
423. *Id.*, p. 7.
424. *Id.*, p. 7.
425. *Id.*, p. 9.
426. *Id.*
427. *Money Law, The Coinage Act of April 2, 1792* (1 Stat. 246).
428. The literature relating to financial crises is crowded with excellent works tracing and documenting histories of wars and financial crises. What they uniformly fail to address is the legal foundation for public enforcement of government and banking, without the tragedy of social collapse to force a return to honest money, government and bankers.
429. De La Démocratie en Amérique (published in two volumes, the first in 1835 and the second in 1840) de Tocqueville, Alexis (1835). De la démocratie en Amérique. I (1 ed.). Paris: Librairie de Charles Gosselin. Retrieved 24 June2015. via Gallica; de Tocqueville, Alexis (1835). De la démocratie en Amérique. II (1 ed.). Paris: Librairie de Charles Gosselin. Retrieved 24 June 2015. via Gallica de Tocqueville, Alexis (1840). De la démocratie en Amérique. III (1 ed.). Paris: Librairie de Charles Gosselin. Retrieved 24 June2015. via Gallica; de Tocqueville, Alexis (1840). De la démocratie en Amérique. IV (1 ed.). Paris: Librairie de Charles Gosselin. Its title translates as *On Democracy in America*, but English translations are usually simply entitled *Democracy in America*.
430. The Federal Reserve System Chart, *Money Creation in the U.S. Federal Reserve System*.
431. See *infra*, regarding the false narratives drawn from the *Legal Tender Cases* and the *Gold Contract Cases*.
432. In a telephone conference in May, 2016 with Dr. Lawrence M. Parks, Executive Director of the New York-based Foundation for the Advancement of Monetary Education, we discussed my

approach to enforcement of the accountability of Washington and Wall Street for damages caused by the 2008 financial crisis, based on the case described in this work. Dr. Parks made two specific points that illustrate the difficulty experts' encounter in the necessary shift they must make in their attitude and assessment of the law of money, the judicial process and the nature of accountability for wrongdoing. Dr. Parks is of the opinion that (i) as the landmark United States Supreme Court constitutional cases involving monetary matters, the *Legal Tender* cases and the *Gold Clause* cases addressed in some detail, *infra.*, arose out of contract disputes, and that therefore, for some inexplicable reason, for some inexplicable reason, any subsequent case involving monetary issues must, be made in contract law and not in tort law, and (ii) having canvased the members of the United States Supreme Court, naming specifically Justice Ginsberg, and based upon the respective Justices specific comments to Dr. Park, the present Court would decline to hear any case involving constitutional sovereign money matters as a political question. The premises of this work, including the Appendix, are in direct conflict with both of Dr. Park's opinions.

433. Alex Scott, H.L.A. Hart's *The Concept of Law* (2004), (Scott), p.1.
434. Ronald Dworkin, *Law's Empire* (1988).
435. Harvard University Press' website description of *Law's Empire.*
436. *Id.*, pp. 2,3.
437. William C. Starr, *Law and Morality in H.L.A. Hart's Legal Philosophy*, 67 MARQ. L. REV. 673 (1984). Available at: http://scholarship.law.marquette.edu/mulr/vol67/iss4/8 (Starr), p. 673.
438. Id., pp. 673, 674.
439. *Id.*, p.4.
440. *Id.*
441. The history of American financial crises and the progressive, systematic perversion of banking laws and regulations to falsely represent conformity to moral and natural law principles expressed in moral philosophy as well as in the *Constitution*, common law and federal statutory law, is detailed my forthcoming book, currently in manuscript, entitled *Money, Morality and Law; The Case for Financial Crisis Accountability.*
442. Scott, p. 679.
443. *Id.*
444. *Id.*, p. 683.
445. *The Gallup Poll, Politics*, December 16, 2013.
446. *The Huffington Post*, December 3, 2012.
447. Danielle Douglas, *The Washington Post*, March 6, 2013.
448. Zach Carter, Shahien Nasiripour, *Huffpost*, "The Fed Just Acknowledged Its Too Big To Jail Policy," November 22, 2014.
449. *Id.*
450. Richard (RJ) Eskow, *Huffpost*, "Prosecute Now: The Justice Department Can Still Act Against Bad Bankers," January 26, 2015.
451. Vince Lanci, *Zero Hedge* "Trump Has 6 Goldman Appointees- Swamp Drains You," January 14, 2017.
452. See, e.g., "Four Stories of Quantitative Easing," *Federal Reserve Bank of St. Louis Review*, January/February 2013, 95(1), pp. 51-88. The effects of these policies are uncertain at best. See, e.g., *The Economist*," QE, or not QE? An assessment of the most controversial weapon in the central banker's armoury." July 14th 2012. Incredibly, the fact that these policies intentionally misrepresent the liquidity and values of assets (effectively, intentionally lying, cheating and stealing) appears to be generally accepted as a valid lawful monetary policy option.
453. See, Emily Flitter, *Feds Weighing New Strategy To Criminally Charge Wall St. Bankers Tied To Housing Bust*, Reuters, Posted: 07/17/2013 2:42 pm EDT.
454. Reinhart & Rogoff, p. 88, Box 6.1.
455. "To Regulate The Value Of Money—An Analysis Of The Power Of Government To Create And Set A Value On Money" By Edwin Vieira, Jr., (undated), available online at http://www.fame.org/HTM/Vieira_Edwin_To_Regulate_the_Value_of_Money_EV-006.HTM.
456. *Id.*
457. Vieira and Becraft, not paginated.
458. Vieira and Becraft, not paginated.
459. Whalen, p. 31.

460. Vieira, p. 689.
461. *Id.*, p. 693.
462. *Id.*
463. *Id.*, p. 695.
464. *Id.*, p. 700.
465. *Id.*, p. 661.
466. *Id.*, pp. 717, 718.
467. Elbridge Gerry Spaulding, *History of the Legal Tender Money*, including as an Appendix, Mr. Spaulding's Speech on the National Currency Bank Bill, February 19, 1863.
468. *Id.* (Emphasis added in italics)
469. *Id.*
470. *Legal Tender Cases*, 110 U.S. 421 (1884).
471. *Legal Tender Cases*, 79 U.S. 457 (1870) (Legal Tender Cases), p. 553.
472. *Id.*, p. 560 (J. Bradley, concurring).
473. R Christopher Whalen, *Inflated: How Money and Debt Built the American Dream*, (Whalen), 2011, p. 34.
474. Ellis Paxson Oberholtzer, *A History of the United States Since the Civil War* (1926) 3:79–122; see also Murry N. Rothbard, *A History of Money and Banking in the United States* (2002) (Rothbard History), pp. 147-159.
475. Richard H. Timberlake, Jr., (1997). Panic of 1893. In David Glasner, David; Thomas F Cooley, Business Cycles and Depressions: an Encyclopedia, (1997) pp. 516–18. See also, Rothbard History, pp.154—159.
476. Gerald Parshall, "The Great Panic Of '93." U.S. News & World Report 113.17 (1992).
477. Rothbard History, p. 154.
478. John J. Klein, *Money and the Economy* (1986), pp. 145—146.
479. Jon R. Moen and Ellis W. Tallman, "The Panic of 1907", *Federal Reserve History*, (2015).
480. *Id.*
481. Rothbard History, p. 240.
482. *Id.*, pp. 240—259.
483. *Id.*, pp. 258 and 259.
484. *Money Trust Investigation—Investigation of Financial and Monetary Conditions of the United States under House Resolutions Nos. 429 and 504 before a Subcommittee of the Committee on Banking and Currency* (1913). (the *Pujo Report*)
485. Eustace Mullins, *The story of the Aldrich Plan and the Modern History Project Secrets of the Federal Reserve and The history, organization and controlling interests behind the Federal Reserve* (1983).
486. This article originally appeared in *Quarterly Journal of Austrian Economics*, Vol. 2, No. 3 (Fall 1999), pp. 3–51. It is also reprinted in Rothbard History, *A History of Money and Banking in the United States* and as a monograph.
487. *Id.*
488. Michael Snyder, "The Federal Reserve Is Holding A Conference On Jekyll Island To Celebrate 100 Years Of Dominating America", *The Economic Collapse*, (November 3, 2010).
489. Charles Erwin Wilson, President Eisenhower's nominee for defense secretary, faced the Senate Armed Services Committee in 1953, the General Motors CEO reluctantly agreed to sell his GM stockholdings to avoid a conflict of interest. The folksy, outspoken executive explained that he honestly hadn't foreseen any problem "because for years I thought what was good for our country was good for General Motors, and vice versa." http://www.nationalreview.com/article/352429.
490. See attached Appendix describing these purported missions, directly quoting agency public representations.
491. See the "Villarreal Shuffle," Vieira, pp. 827—829.
492. Eric deCarbonnel, *Banks Operating without Reserve Requirements*, March 29, 2009.
493. Vieira, p. 1427, citing Reuss v. Balles, 584 F. 2d 461, 468-69 (D.C. Cir. 1978) and Committee for Monetary Reform v. Board of Governors of the Federal Reserve System, 766F. 2d 538, 542-43 (D.C. Cir. 1985).
494. *Id.*, 766 F.2d at 542.
495. Vieira, p. 1427.
496. Vieira, p. 774.
497. Vieira, pp. 774, 775.

498. Vieira, pp. 784, 785.
499. The Pecora Commission Report, *Stock Exchange Practices. Hearings before the Committee on Banking and Currency Pursuant to S.Res. 84 and S.Res. 56 and S.Res. 97,* Report No. 1455 (1934) (Pecora Report).
500. Pecora Report, pp. 393 and 394.
501. Whalen, p. 190.
502. *Id.*
503. *Id.*, p. 194.
504. *Id.*, p. 206.
505. *Id.*, p. 207.
506. US Congress: House Joint Resolution 192 of June 5, 1933.
507. Whalen, pp. 229, 230.
508. *Id.*, pp. 161,162,163).
509. *Id.*, p. 246.
510. *Id.*, p. 254.
511. Jim Grant, *A Piece of My Mind, included in Thoughts from the Frontline, A Gold Standard,* by John Mauldin, April 28, 2012.
512. Whalen, pp. 229, 230.
513. See, Neil Fligstein, Jonah Stuart Brundage and Michael Schultz, "Why the Federal Reserve Failed to See the Financial Crisis of 2008: The Role of "Macroeconomics" as Sense-Making and Cultural Frame, Department of Sociology, University of California at Berkeley, September 2014; and see Matthew Yglesias, "Ben Bernanke's Biggest Mistake," *Money Box,* February 24, 2014.
514. Norman v. Baltimore & Ohio Railroad Co., 294 U.S. 240 (1935) ("Norman"); Nortz v. United States, 294 U.S. 317 (1935); and Perry v. United States 294 U.S. 330 (1935).
515. *Veazie Bank v. Fenno,* 8 Wall. 533, 75 U. S. 549.
516. Norman v. Baltimore & Ohio Railroad Co., 294 U.S. 240 (1935), at p. 304.
517. *Id.*, at p. 316.
518. Richard H Timberlake, "From Constitution to Fiat Money: The American Experience," *Cato Journal,* Vol. 32, No. 2 (Spring/Summer 2012), at pp.356-358.
519. Richard H. Timberlake, *Constitutional Money—A Review of the Supreme Court's Monetary Decisions* (2013) (Timberlake 2013).
520. Bray Hammond, *Banks and Politics in America* (1957); Gerald Dunn, *Monetary Decisions of the Supreme Court* (1960); James Willard, *A Legal History of Money in the United States 1774-1970* (1973); Edwin Vieria. Jr., *Pieces of Eight* (1983); and Henry Mark Holzer, *The Gold Clause* (1934) (limited to a discussion of the Gold Cases, see *infra.*)
521. Timberlake 2013, p. x.
522. *Id.*
523. *Id.*, p. 2.
524. *Id.*, p. 3.
525. *Id.*, p. 232. Timberlake quotes James Buchanan, who suggests that what is needed is, "[c]learly, some defined process and institutional structure [that] must be established, with genuine constitutional authority, over and beyond that of democratic majoritarian politics, Something analogous to the independent judiciary, under the Supreme Court seems required – a monetary authority that is independent of politics, but which remains itself bound by the parameters set out in the constitution... The constitution remains the ultimate sovereign authority Rather than the government as such." See, Timberlake 2013, at p. 232, note 19.
526. See *supra*, Note 48.
527. See, Owen Humpage, Federal Reserve Bank of Cleveland, *Federal Reserve History,* "The Smithsonian Agreement," (November 22, 2013); and Douglas A. Irwin, *World Trade Review,* "The Nixon shock after 40 years: the import surcharge revisited," (2012), 12:1, pp. 29-56.
528. Whalen, p. 268.
529. Id., at Note 22.
530. Whalen, p. 275.
531. Whalen, p. 277, at Note 33.
532. Whalen, p. 279.
533. Whalen, pp. 268, 269.
534. Whalen pp. 269, 270.

535. Henry Hazlet, *From Bretton Woods to World Inflation: A Study of Causes and Consequences*, (2009).
536. Whalen p. 275.
537. Whalen p. 279.
538. Vieira, p. 1520, at note 6117.
539. Vieira, pp. 1520, 1521.
540. Vieira, pp. 1521-1523.
541. Vieira, p. 1523, citing 12 U.S.C. § 411.
542. *Id.*
543. Eichengreen, p. 62.
544. Reinhart & Rogoff, pp. 213, 214.
545. Id., p. 221.
546. Shahien Nasiripour and Ryan Grim, *Huffpost*, Posted: 01/02/2014 7:50 pm EST, Updated: 01/03/2014 11:58 am EST.
547. Commission Report, p. xviii.
548. *Id.*
549. *Id.*
550. Id., pp. xv-xxv.
551. Eichengreen p.19.
552. "No Budget, No Pay Act of 2013". Pub.L. 113–3; H.R. 325, February 4, 2013.
553. Nicholas Wapshott, *Keynes Hayek, The Clash That Defined Modern Economics*, (2011).
554. Matthew Yglesias, *Vox*, "Donald Trump just threatened to cause an unprecedented global financial crisis. There's a big difference between government debt and private debt." (May 6, 2016).
555. Asawin Suebsaeng, Lachlan Markey, CNBC, "Trump on Coming Debt Crisis: 'I Won't Be Here' When It Blows Up—The president thinks the balancing of the nation's books is going to, ultimately, be a future president's problem." (December 5, 2018).
556. Thomas J. Sargent and Neil Wallace, *The Real Bills Doctrine Vs. The Quantity Theory: A Reconsideration, Staff Report #64*, January 1981 (FRBM Staff Report).
557. FRBM Staff Report, p. 1.
558. *Id.*, pp. 1, 2.
559. *Id.*, pp. 2, 3.
560. *Id.*, p. 4.
561. Thomas M. Humphrey Federal Reserve Bank of Richmond, *The Real Bills Doctrine, Economic Review*, September/October 1982 (FRBR Humphrey) (FRBR Staff Paper).
562. *Id.*, p. 1.
563. *Id.*
564. *Id.*
565. Per Hortlund, *In Defense of the Real Bills Doctrine, Econ Journal Watch*, Volume 3, Number 1, (January 2006, pp. 73-87) (Hortlund).
566. Hortlund, pp. 75, 76.
567. *Id.*, pp. 76, 77.
568. *Id.*
569. *Id.*, p. 82.
570. *Id.*, pp. 82, 83.
571. *Id.*, pp. 83, 84.
572. *Id.*, p. 84.
573. Vieira p 749, at note 2977 and 2978, Board of Governors of the Federal Reserve *System: Purposes and Functions of The Federal Reserve System* (8th Ed. 1994 at pp. 3 and 5).
574. See Vieira, pp.1430, et seq. and pp. 1461, et seq.
575. On August 15, 1971, Nixon unilaterally imposed 90-day wage and price controls, a 10% import surcharge, and most importantly "closed the gold window," making the dollar inconvertible to gold directly, except on the open market. This was the "Nixon shock." Unusually, this decision was made without consulting members of Congress, the international monetary system or even his own State Department. As the crisis generated by the Nixon shock progressed, President Nixon met with Treasury Secretary Connally and Office of Management and Budget Director George Shultz on August 2 to map out next steps. Tapes of their conversations on August 2 reveal Connally as the primary architect of the essential elements in the New Economic Policy (NEP) the President would announce on August 15. The

State Department and the National Security Council were not represented at Camp David where, according to Kissinger, "a decision of major foreign policy importance had been taken about which neither the Secretary of State nor the national security adviser had been consulted." At no time was Congress or the Fed involved, nor did either respond directly to this policy statement that drove directly to the heart of Congress' constitutional responsibility to "to coin money" and "regulate the value thereof".

576. Vieira, p. 1461.
577. Vieira, p. 1427, citing Reuss v. Balles, 584 F. 2d 461, 468-69 (D.C. Cir. 1978) and Committee for Monetary Reform v. Board of Governors of the Federal Reserve System, 766 F. 2d 538, 542-43 (D.C.Cir. 1985).
578. 766 F.2d at 542.
579. Reuss v. Balles, 584 F. 2d 461 (D.C. Cir. 1978).
580. *Id.*, p.542.
581. Thomas Hart Benton was the author of a 16-volume *Abridgement of the Debates of Congress* through 1850, and served as a United States Senator from Missouri for 30 years.
582. Thomas Hart Benton, *Abridgment of the Debates of Congress, from 1789 to 1856: Nov. 7, 1808-March 3, 1813,* (1857), published January 1, 1857 by D. Appleton noted at page 270.
583. George Rothwell Brown, *The Leadership of Congress*, (1922), p. 29.
584. David Schoenbrod, "Delegation and Democracy: A Reply to My Critics," published in the *Cardozo Law Review* [Vol. 20:731 1999], at p. 731.
585. *Id.*, p. 732 at note 7.
586. *Id.*, at note 8.
587. *Id.*, at note 9.
588. *Id.*, p. 732.
589. *Id.*
590. *Id.*, p.733.
591. *Id.*
592. *Id.*, p.734.
593. *Id.*, p. 734, at note 19.
594. *Id.*
595. *Id.*, p. 736.
596. *Id.*, p. 737.
597. *Id.*
598. *Id.*, p. 739, at note 49.
599. *Id.*, p. 740.
600. *Id.*, p. 741.
601. *Id.*, p. 747.
602. *Id.*
603. *Id.*, 748.
604. Id., p. 752.
605. *Id.*, p. 761.
606. *Id.*, p. 764.
607. *Justia US Law* http://law.justia.com/constitution/us/article-1/03-delegation-of-legislative-power.html (Justia).
608. *Id.*
609. *Id.*
610. *Id.*
611. *Id.*
612. Felix Martin, *Money—The Unauthorized Biography* (2013) (Martin).
613. Martin, p. 26.
614. *Id.*, p. 27 at note 41.
615. Martin, p.27.
616. Justia, at note 74.
617. *Id.*
618. Scott Lanman and Steve Matthews, *Bloomberg.* "Greenspan Urges Tighter Regulation After 'Breakdown'" (Update1)—October 23, 2008 01:00 EDT.
619. Jon Hilsenrath, Wall Street Journal, based on remarks of Alan Greenspan at the Economic Club of New York February 17, 2009, Embargoed until 8pm EST 02/17/09.
620. As recorded on C-Span: UPDATE: 11:50 AM Updated: 05/25/11.

621. UPDATE C-Span: 10:45 AM Greenspan Says Financial World Too Complex For Regulators—Shahien Nasiripour.
622. David Paul, *Huff Post*, "Congress Can No Longer Take Wall Street Money and Ignore the Damage It Does", Posted: 08/26/2013 2:35 am).
623. *Id.*
624. Michael Flaherty and Howard Schneider, Reuters Washington, *Yellen drives wedge between monetary policy, financial bubbles*, Wednesday, July 2, 2014, 4:02 pm EDT.
625. Remarks of Governor Jeremy C. Stein: International Research Forum on Monetary Policy, Washington, D.C. Governor Stein presented identical remarks at the International Monetary Fund 2014 Spring Meetings on April 13, 2014, and at the 2014 Financial Markets Conference on April 16, 2014.
626. Greg Robb, Market Watch "Powell says Fed 'will remain alert' to any financial stability risks" (February 13, 2018).
627. *Id.*
628. Felix Martin, *Money—the Unauthorized Biography* (2013) (Martin), p. 74.
629. Martin p. 126.
630. Martin, pp. 127—137.
631. Christine Idzelis and Craig Torres, "Risky Loans Shunned by Banks Are Booming in Wall Street's Shadow," *Bloomberg*, May 21, 2015, Updated on May 22, 2015.
632. *The Uniform Agreement on the Classification and Appraisal of Securities Held by Depository Institutions* attached to FDIC Financial Institution Letter FIL-51-2013, October 29, 2013.
633. *Id.*
634. *Id.*
635. Id.
636. Quoted in *RepoWatch*, dated April 7, 2011, updated January 3, 2013.
637. Matt Nesto, *Breakout—Yahoo Finance*, "Fed Has a Secret Third Mandate, Mauldin," Tuesday, Oct 29, 2013.
638. *Id.*
639. The Report, p. xi.
640. *Id.*, pp. xi and xii.
641. *Id.*, p. xii.
642. *Id.*, p. xxii.
643. *Id.*
644. *Id.*, p. xxiii.
645. *Id.*
646. *Id.*, pp. xxvii and xxviii.
647. Michael Simkovic, *The Evolution of Valuation in Bankruptcy* (July 16, 2016). Financial analyses such as valuation, solvency and capital adequacy play a crucial role in bankruptcy. They are central to allowance of claims, adequate protection, avoidance actions such as fraudulent transfer and preference, rejection of collective bargaining agreements, plan confirmation, and 363 sales. Today, established methods of analysis accepted by most bankruptcy courts include discounted cash flow (DCF), comparable companies and comparable transactions. However, newer methods based on market prices for equity, debt, or options and derivatives are supplementing, and in some cases supplanting more established approaches.
648. "H.R. 4173 — 111th Congress: Dodd-Frank Wall Street Reform and Consumer Protection Act." www.GovTrack.us. 2009. October 26, 2016, https://www.govtrack.us/congress/bills/111/hr4173.
649. See Web Site for Davis Polk Law Firm, *Doss Frank Progress Report.*
650. See, however, Starr Int'l Co. v. United States, 121 Fed. Cl. 428, 430-431 (2015). Discussion of the implications of the Starr case and related litigation is beyond the scope of this short paper. See also with respect to the safe harbor of derivatives in bankruptcy: The Bankruptcy-Law Safe Harbor for Derivatives: A Path-Dependence Analysis Posted by June Rhee, Co-editor, HLS Forum on Corporate Governance and Financial Regulation, on Monday, December 9, 2013, Bankruptcy, Commodities, Derivatives, Financial crisis, Safe harbor, Securities Regulation, Swaps, Systemic Risk and accompanying post by Steven L. Schwarcz, Stanley A. Star Professor of Law & Business at Duke University School of Law based on a paper co-authored

by Professor Schwarcz and Ori Sharon of Duke University School of Law. See also, Ryan Tracy and Katy Burne, *New Fed Bailout-Prevention Rule to Reach Beyond Banks, WSJ*—Update 05/03/2016 | 02:07pm EDT.

651. Martin, pp. 221, 222.
652. James Rickards, *The Death of Money—The Coming Collapse of the International Monetary System* (2014) (Rickards 2014).
653. See, Rickards 2014, generally, for his views on the possible future relevance of the Bretton Woods institutions in the establishment of a new global system of regulation of the value of money—a new global financial architecture.
654. The acronym for Brazil, Russia, India and China, which are all deemed to be at a similar stage of newly advanced economic development. It is typically rendered as "the BRICs" or "the BRIC countries" or "the BRIC economies" or alternatively as the "Big Four". A related acronym, BRICS, adds South Africa. There are arguments that Indonesia should be included into grouping, effectively turning it into BRIIC or BRIICS.
655. See, *e.g.*, BRICS set up bank to counter Western hold on global finances (Reuters Wednesday, July 16, 2014).
656. Eichengreen, p. 89.
657. *The Maastricht Treaty* (a/k/a the "Treaty of Maastricht" or the "Treaty on Economic Union") created the Euro as Europe's single currency. The treaty was signed Feb. 1, 1992 and came into force Nov. 1, 1993, although the Euro didn't come into use until 1999.
658. Eichengreen, p. 98.
659. *Id.*, pp.101, 102.
660. *Id.*, p.109.
661. *Id.*, p.110.
662. *Id.*
663. *Id.*
664. *Id.*, p. 122.
665. *Riegle-Neal Interstate Banking And Branching Efficiency Act of 1994,* Pub. Law 103-328, 108 STAT. 2338, enacted September 29, 1994.
666. *Home Ownership and Equity Protection Act of 1994*, Pub. Law 103-325, title I, subtitle B (Sec. 151 et seq.), 108 Stat. 2190, enacted September 23, 1994.
667. *Economic Growth and Regulatory Paperwork Reduction Act of 1996*, Pub. Law 104-208, div. A, title II, 110 Stat. 3009-394, enacted September 30, 1996.
668. The specific Article I, Section 8, Clause 5 Constitutional Congressional mandate to create and regulate the value of money could be lawfully delegated by Congress to the Fed. Congress has not done so.
669. 12 U.S.C Chapter 34, § 3301 *et seq.*
670. See, e.g., *GAO Report 13-180*, January 2013: Losses in output from $10 trillion (p 15) to $13 trillion (p 17); plus loss of home equity of $9.1 trillion (p 21); and potential losses from government bailout programs, including QE, due to interest rate manipulation and corresponding manipulation of asset market values, plus effect of Fed control of MBS and Treasury Bond Markets through (non-market value purchases with values temporarily inflated by interest rate suppression) and (excluding increased costs of regulation and supervision under *Dodd Frank*); and *Federal Reserve Bank of Dallas Staff Paper No. 20*, July 2013: Losses conservatively estimated at 40% to 90% of one year's output equal to $6 trillion to $14, trillion. (pp. 1and 2) Better Markets, Inc. (2012) estimated $12.8 trillion (p. 3) and Boyd and Heitz (2012) lowest conceivable crisis cost of $7.3 trillion. (p. 3) (See also updated Better Markets Report dated July 2015, losses at $20 trillion and counting).
671. See *Forbes, The Little Black Book of Billionaire Secrets*, "Q1 2014 Banking Review: Basel III Common Equity Tier 1 Capital Ratio," June 2, 2014. The common equity Tier I (CET1) capital ratios are most often used as a quick reference to gauge a bank's capital strength. As calculated by *Forbes*, the top 10 U.S. banks' average approximately 10% in 2014.
672. See, e. g. *Forbes*, "The Little Black Book of Billionaire Secrets," "Largest U.S. Banks Captured Over 36% Of Global Equity Capital Market In Q3.", October 5, 2017. Notably, the five largest U.S. investment banks have captured the top five ranks in the global equity underwriting league table for almost every quarter over recent years. The five largest U.S. banks from increased their market share to over 36% in Q3 [2017]—the highest in ten quarters. Notably, the average market share for these banks over the first nine months of 2017 (35.7%) is well above the figure of below 32% for full-year 2016.

673. Carnell Macey Miller, p. 216.
674. See, Holzman, Thomas L. Counsel, Legal Division FDIC, 19 *Ann. Rev. Banking L.* 425 (2000).
675. Gerald Olson, *Subprime Meltdown: It's All About Money* (2008), p. 173.
676. *Wall Street Journal,* December 29, 2009.
677. See *Wall Street Journal,* August 11, 2010 regarding SEC inquiry into CVB Financial reporting practices.
678. *Third Quarter 2017 NCREIF Indices Review,* Fall Conference November 7, 2017.
679. *Sec. 39, FDI Act, 12 U.S.C. 1831 p-1; Appendix A, Clauses G. Asset Quality and H. Earnings.*
680. Ray Ball, Sudarshan Jayaraman and Lakshmanan Shivakumar, *Mark-to-Market Accounting and Information Asymmetry in Banks,* August 12, 2012. See also, Michelle Clark Neely, Federal Reserve Bank of St. Louis, *Making Sense of Mark to Market,* January 1994.
681. FDIC Financial Institution Letter (FIL--87--92) dated December 3, 1992. See, footnote 1, specifically referencing, among other sources of pertinent guidance meeting applicable officer and director standards and duties, The Directors Book (OCC, 1987).
682. See Alan S. Blinder, Publication of the Federal Reserve Bank of Minneapolis, *The Strategy of Monetary Policy,* September 1, 1995, September 1995 issue. Mr. Blinder, then Vice Chairman, Federal Reserve Board, states the obvious about the legislative goals of the Fed: The Federal Reserve Act tells us to pursue both "maximum employment" and "stable prices." Pursuit of these goals necessarily involves manipulation of asset liquidity and values. As it happens, that is inherently unsafe and unsound. Although the Fed generally purports to have as a goal the assurance of banking and monetary safety, soundness and systemic financial stability, Mr. Blinder does not mention these as goals of Fed monetary policy.
683. The Bretton Woods system was the first example of a fully negotiated monetary order intended to govern monetary relations among independent nation-states. Each country was required to adopt a monetary policy that maintained the exchange rate (± 1 percent) by tying its currency to gold and the ability of the IMF to bridge temporary imbalances of payments. 730 delegates from all 44 Allied nations gathered at the Mount Washington Hotel in Bretton Woods, New Hampshire, United States, for the United Nations Monetary and Financial Conference, also known as the Bretton Woods Conference. The delegates deliberated during July 1-22, 1944, and signed the Bretton Woods agreement on its final day. These accords established the International Monetary Fund (IMF) and the International Bank for Reconstruction and Development (IBRD), which today is part of the World Bank Group. The United States, which controlled two thirds of the world's gold, insisted that the Bretton Woods system rest on both gold and the US dollar. These organizations became operational in 1945 after a sufficient number of countries had ratified the agreement. On August 15, 1971, the United States unilaterally terminated convertibility of the US dollar to gold, effectively bringing the Bretton Woods system to an end and rendering the dollar a fiat currency. This action, referred to as the Nixon shock, created the situation in which the US dollar became a reserve currency used by many states. At the same time, many fixed currencies (such as the pound sterling, for example) also became free-floating. The value of the US dollar then ceased to be regulated. Thus began the modern day phenomenon progressively more severe financial crises and the collapse of boundaries between banking and private shadow banking creation of money through credit, unrestrained by either banking law and regulation, or by the commercial law relating to negotiable credit instruments.
684. F.A. Mann, *The Legal Aspects of Money, Fourth Edition* (1982) (Mann), p. 36.
685. *Id.*
686. *Id.*
687. *Id.,* p. 38.
688. *Id.,* p. 41.
689. *Law of Financial Institutions, Fifth Edition,* Professors Richard Scott Carnell of Fordham University, Jonathan R. Macey of Yale, and Geoffrey P. Miller of New York University (2013) (Carnell Macey Miller), pp. 58-60.
690. *The Works and Life of Walter Bagehot,* Mrs. Russell Barrington, Ed., "Lombard Street," "The Banknote and the Fiduciary Issue", Vol. VI, pp. 3,4 (1915).
691. Wulf A. Kaal, Associate Professor at the University of St. Thomas School of Law, and Dale A. Oesterle, the J. Gilbert Reese Chair in Contract Law at the Moritz College of Law at The Ohio State University. The quoted material is based on the co-authored article: Wulf A. Kaal & Dale Oesterle, "The History of Hedge Fund Regulation in the United States," *Handbook on Hedge Funds,* Oxford University Press (2016).

692. Shadow banks referred to here as hedge funds and private equity, investments banks or affiliates whether or not regulated by the SEC or CFTC and other entities acting as financial institutions although not directly regulated by federal financial regulators.
693. *Id.*
694. *Id.*
695. *Id.*
696. *Id.*
697. *Id.*
698. *Id.*
699. *Id.*
700. Value Walk Staff, "Leverage Concentrated in a Small Number of Large Hedge Funds—Financial Stability Oversight Council", June 22, 2016 3:40 pm in *Business.*
701. *Id.*
702. Securities and Exchange Commission, 17 CFR Parts 230, 239, 270, 274 and 279, Effective October 14, 2014, Release No. 33-9616, IA-3879; IC-31166; FR-84; File No. S7-03-13, RIN 3235-AK61, Money Market Fund Reform; Amendments to Form PF.
703. Tami Luhby, CNNMoney.com senior writer, *Run ends on money market funds. Investors are no longer yanking billions of dollars out of money market funds, thanks to a new federal government insurance program.* September 29, 2008.
704. The Volker Alliance, *Unfinished Business—Banking in the Shadows* (2016), p. 14.
705. *Id.*, p. 21.
706. Shahien Nasiripour, *Huffpost* Blog First Posted: 06/07/10, Updated: 05/25/11.
707. *Id.* Greenspan: "Banks Have Been Undercapitalized For Past 40 to 50 Years."
708. *Id.*, UPDATE: 10:45 AM Greenspan Says Financial World Too Complex For Regulators.
709. *Id.*, Neil Irwin and Amit R. Paley, Greenspan Says He Was Wrong On Regulation, October 24, 2008.
710. Lauren Tara LaCapra and Douwe Miedema Filed July 21, 2013. See also *How the Bank Lobby Loosened U.S. Reins on Derivatives*, Silla Brush in Washington at sbrush@bloomberg.net; Robert Schmidt in Washington at rschmidt5@bloomberg.net.
711. See, Ryan Grim and Shahien Nasiripour, *Huffington Post*, October 30, 2013, "Democrats Claim Barney Frank, Sheila Bair, Maxine Waters, Back Deregulation Bill. That's Not True."
712. *Derivatives: Is Your Member of Congress Owned By Wall Street?* Posted: November 5, 2013.
713. *How Washington Caved to Wall Street How Washington Caved to Wall Street*, by Joseph Stiglitz TIME.com http://ideas.time.com/2013/09/23/how-washington-caved-to-wall-street /#ixzz2lWHbQjcD.
714. Solesbee v. Balkcom, 339 U.S. 9, 16 (1950) (Justice Frankfurter dissenting).
715. Snyder v. Massachusetts, 291 U.S. 97,105 (1934)] (*CRS Annotated Constitution*).
716. See, W. McKechnie, *Magna Carta—A Commentary on the Great Charter of King John* 375-395 (Glasgow, 2d rev. ed. 1914). The chapter became chapter 29 in the Third Reissue of Henry III in 1225.
717. *Id.* at 504, and see 139-159. See also J. Holt, *Magna Carta* 226-229 (Cambridge: 1965).
718. Quoted by P.A. Madison, *Historical Meaning Behind Equal Protection of the Laws*, published by the Cato Institute, February 6, 2009.
719. *Id.*
720. Federal Reserve Bank of Kansas City, "Understanding Antitrust Considerations in Banking Proposals" (undated).
721. Bob Moon, *Marketplace*, "Can antitrust laws break up big banks?" Interview with Professor Zepher Teachout, Duke University Law School (podcast transcript, undated).
722. (See Timothy D. Naegele, *The Bank Holding Company Act's Anti-Tying Provision: 35 Years Later, The Banking Law Journal*, March 2005, Page 212).
723. See more at: http://rico.uslegal.com/civil-remedies/#sthash.CKJs04hW.dpuf.
724. (See, *Feds Weighing New Strategy To Criminally Charge Wall St. Bankers Tied To Housing Bust*, Reuters By Emily Flitter, Posted: 07/17/2013 2:42 pm EDT) (Note: the author provided an initial outline of the case presented in this work to the Dallas office of the FBI at the direction of the United States Attorney's office for the Northern District of Texas on December 15, 2011).
725. *Restatement (Second) of Torts* § 874A (1979), updated October 2013, Division 11. Miscellaneous Rules, Chapter 43. Rules Applicable to Certain Types of Conduct § 874A Tort Liability

for Violation of Legislative (Constitutional) Provision. The comments to § 874A are dealt with in detail in the Annex to *Money, Morality and the Law.*

726. James Rickards, *The New Case for Gold* (2016) (Rickards 2016).
727. *Id.*, pp. 4-18, See also for example, James Rickards, *Currency Wars, The Making of the Next Global Financial Crisis* (2011 and 2012); *The Death of Money, The Coming Collapse of the International Monetary System* (2014); and Jörg Guido Hülsman, *The Ethics of Money Production* (2008) (Hülsman).
728. Hülsman.
729. *Id.*, pp. 44 and 45.
730. *Id.*, pp. 48 and 49.
731. Solesbee v. Balkcom, 339 U.S. 9, 16 (1950) (Justice Frankfurter dissenting).
732. Snyder v. Massachusetts, 291 U.S. 97,105 (1934)] (*CRS Annotated Constitution*).
733. See also J. Holt, *Magna Carta* 226-229 (Cambridge: 1965).
734. Quoted by P.A. Madison, *Historical Meaning Behind Equal Protection of the Laws*, published by the Cato Institute, February 6, 2009.
735. *Id.*
736. Patten, 51 S.E.C. at 572, citing Mawod, 46 S.E.C. 865, 871-872.
737. *Securities Act of 1933* (the 1933 Act, the Securities Act, the Truth in Securities Act, the Federal Securities Act, or the '33 Act, Title I of Pub. Law. 73-22, 48 Stat. 74, enacted May 27, 1933, *codified at* 15 U.S.C. § 77a *et seq.*).
738. The Securities Exchange Act of 1934 (also called the Exchange Act, '34 Act, or 1934 Act) (Pub.Law. 73–291, 48 Stat. 881, enacted June 6, 1934, codified at 15 U.S.C. § 78a et seq.).
739. Jean Braucher *Arizona Legal Studies, Discussion Paper No. 06-43 Deception, Economic Loss and Mass-Market Customers: Consumer Protection Statutes as Persuasive Authority in the Common Law of Fraud*, The University of Arizona, James E. Rogers College of Law, November 2006 (Braucher).
740. Braucher, Note 8.
741. *Id.*, Note 9.
742. *Id.*, Note 10.
743. *Id.*, Note 12.
744. Braucher, p. 3.
745. Braucher, Note 21.
746. *Id.*, Note 22.
747. *Id.*, p. 5.
748. *Id.*, Note 46.
749. *Id.*, Note 49.
750. See 15 U.S. Code § 15c—Actions by State Attorneys General (Oct. 15, 1914, ch. 323, § 4C, as added Pub. L. 94–435, title III, § 301, Sept. 30, 1976, 90 Stat. 1394; amended Pub. L. 96–349, § 4 (a)(3), Sept. 12, 1980, 94 Stat. 1157).
751. See, the U.S. *Class Action Fairness Act of 2005*, 28 U.S.C. Sections 1332(d), 1453, and 1711-1715, (enacted February 18, 2005); National Association of Attorneys General, National *Class Action Fairness Act and State Attorney General Suits: Recent Developments*, NAAG NAAGazette ArchiveVolume 6, Number 3-4 (April 13, 2012); and William B. Rubenstein, UCLA Program on Class Actions, "Understanding the Class Action Act of 2005"); and see also H.R.985—Fairness in Class Action Litigation and Furthering Asbestos Claim Transparency Act of 2017, 115th Congress (2017-2018), pending.
752. See, US Attorneys, Resources, US Attorneys' Manual, Criminal Resource Manual, CRM 500-999, Criminal Resource Manual 901-999, 968, Defenses—Statute of Limitations.
753. (Justia › US Law › US Codes and Statutes › US Constitution › Article III. Judicial Department › *Standing to Challenge Lawfulness of Governmental Action, Standing to Challenge Lawfulness of Governmental Action Substantial Interest: Standing* http://law.justia.com/constitution/us/article-3/ ("Justia," reference notes in original are omitted here) (p.1).
754. *Id.*
755. *Id.*, p. 2.
756. James Keenley, "How Many Injuries Does It Take—Article III Standing in the Class Action Context," Vol. 95, Issue 3, Article 4, *California Law Review*, June 30, 2007 ("Keenley") p. 2.
757. Justia, p. 3.
758. See Keenley, generally.

759. See, e.g., *The Fed Just Acknowledged Its Too Big to Jail Policy,* Zach Carter, Senior Political Economy Reporter, Shahien Nasiripour, Chief Financial and Regulatory Correspondent, Huffpost, http://www.huffingtonpost.com/2014/11/21/fed-too-big-to-jail_n_6201476.html; *Prosecute Now: The Justice Department Can Still Act Against Bad Bankers,* Nov. 26, 2014, updated Jan 26, 2015, Richard (RJ) Eskow, Writer/Editor http://www.huffingtonpost.com/rj-eskow/prosecute-now-the-justice_b_6225686.html; *Eric Holder Admits Some Banks Are Just Too Big To Prosecute* Mark Gongloff, Managing Editor, Business and Tech, The Huffington Post, *http://www.huffingtonpost.com/2013/03/06/eric-holder-banks-too-big_n_2821741.html* Eric Holder, *Wall Street Double Agent, Comes in From the Cold, Barack Obama's former top cop cashes in after six years of letting banks run wild,* Matt Taibbi, Rolling Stone, July 8, 2015, http://www.rollingstone.com/politics/news/eric-holder-wall-street-double-agent-comes-in-from-the-cold-20150708#ixzz42WaBveNq, *Testimony on Improving Financial Institution Supervision: Examining and Addressing Regulatory Capture,* William C. Dudley, President and Chief Executive Officer, Federal Reserve Bank of New York, November 21, 2014,*Testimony before the Senate Committee on Banking, Housing, and Urban Affairs Financial Institutions and Consumer Protection Subcommittee,* January 27, 2009. (Dudley, among other capacities, serves as the vice chairman and a permanent member of the Federal Open Market Committee (FOMC), the group responsible for formulating the nation's monetary policy), *Attorney General Holder Remarks on Financial Fraud Prosecutions at NYU School of Law,* Wednesday, September 17, 2014, *Eric Holder Gives Prosecutors 90 Days to File Wall Street Collapse Charges,* Thursday, February 19, http://www.reuters.com/article/us-usa-mortgages-holder-idUSKBN0LL1X920150217 2015 00:00, *By Sam Knight, The District Sentinel News Analysis* https://www.districtsentinel.com/in-last-gasp-attempt-to-shake-corrupt-reputation-holder-gives-prosecutors-90-days-to-file-wall-street-collapse-charges/ *U.S. identifying people to target for role in mortgage crisis,* Julia Edwards and Karen Freifels, Reuters, Tue Feb 17, 2011, http://www.reuters.com/article/us-usa-mortgages-holder-idUSKBN0LL1X920150217, and finally, Letter of Phil Angelides, Chairman of the National Commission on the Causes of the Financial and Economic Crisis in the United States, to the Attorney General of the United States, February 1, 2016.
760. Justia, pp. 6-8.
761. Justia, p. 10.
762. Justia at p. 11, note 371.
763. Justia, p. 13.
764. *Id.*, p. 13, at note 381.
765. *Id.*, at note 383.
766. Justia, p. 14.
767. Justia, p. 24.
768. *Id.*
769. Justia, p. 26.
770. Justia, p. 2.
771. *Id.*
772. See Baker, 369 U.S. 186, 210, 82 S. Ct. 691, 706, 7 L. Ed. 2d 663 (1962).
773. Baker, at 217, 82 S. Ct. at 710.
774. See also Baker, at p. 707.
775. Baker, 369 U.S. at 217, 82 S. Ct. at 710.
776. *Id.*
777. Aktepe, at p. 1404.
778. Baker, at p. 710.
779. *Id.*
780. *Id.*
781. See generally, Perry Mehrling, *The Inherent Hierarchy of Money,* January 25, 2012.
782. See, *Value Walk,* Guest Post on June 27, 2016 2:50 pm in Politics, *The Never-Ending Fiasco Of Fiat Money by Thorsten Polleit,* Foundation For Economic Education [This speech was delivered to the Commodity Club, Zurich, June 15, 2016]: "Ladies and gentleman, we live in a world ruled by fiat money. That means investors have no choice but to grin and bear both booms and busts. American economist Murray Rothbard had a refreshingly vivid simile for the juice that keeps this tired old nag in the running: *'Like the repeated doping of a horse, the boom is kept on its way and ahead of its inevitable comeuppance by repeated and accelerating doses of the stimulant of bank credit. It is only when bank credit expansion must finally stop*

or sharply slow down ... that retribution finally catches up with the boom. ... [T]he longer the boom is kept going, the greater the malinvestments that must be liquidated, and the more harrowing the readjustments that must be made'" Gold is not only the ultimate means of payment. It is also a line of defence against the evils of fiat money. As Mr. Greenspan so pointedly put it a couple of years ago: "Gold still represents the ultimate form of payment in the world. Fiat money in extremis is accepted by nobody. Gold is always accepted."

783. Whalen, p. 83.
784. Other divisions of the DOJ who should have an active interest in the issues addressed in this book, include the Civil and Criminal Divisions, the Anti-Trust Division, the Civil Rights Division and the National Security Division.
785. To his credit, President Roosevelt did seek to save ordinary Americans, not just bankers. The DOJ prosecuted individual bankers for criminal and civil violations of law and President Roosevelt urged the Senate to continue its investigation of depression era bank fraud, conducted by Ferdinand Pecora, producing *The Pecora Report* referred to earlier in this work.
786. Former Fed chair Yellen has recently, in testimony before the House Financial Services Committee on September 28, 2016, at a speech in Jackson Hole Wyoming and at a Brookings Institution Conference, that with policy rates near zero, in the event of another crisis the Fed might have to maintain low rates in order to create another bubble to rescue us from the last bubble and the then current bubble and to keep that bubble going indefinitely, shunning financial stability risks. Yellen also stated that although the Fed does not now have the power to purchase corporate stocks and bonds, the next financial crisis might leave no effective alternative for economic stimulus other than to purchase corporate stocks and bonds. The self-evident effect of the asset purchases under Quantitative Easing programs or under any future plan to purchase corporate stocks and bonds is asset value and liquidity manipulation that benefits the sellers. There is no evidence that the economy in general, or that ordinary Americans benefit from such purchases. In fact, the evidence is to the contrary. See, *Reuters,* September 29, 2016; Tyler Durdan, *Zero Hedge,* September 28, 2016; and Tyler Durdan, *Zero Hedge,* September 14, 2018.
787. See: http://execgate.tumblr.com/post/58326515816/a-bad-day-for-jamie-dimon-just-got-a-lot-worse#sthash.rOVDFJcp.dpuf. August 15, 2013.
788. See generally, Roche and McKee.
789. See generally, Roche and McKee.
790. Peter Schroeder, *Reuters, Politics,* "Banks spent record amounts on lobbying in recent election" (March 8, 2017).
791. Gouge, pp. 5 and 6.
792. Paul Mason, The Guardian, The Great Leveler by Walter Scheidel review—an end to inequality (March 29, 2017).
793. *Id.*
794. See, e.g., "Jealous of the Joneses: conspicuous consumption, inequality, and crime," Oxf. Econ. Pap. (2014) 66 (4): 1090-1120 first published online June 20, 2014; Pablo Fajnzylber, University of Minas Gerais Daniel Lederman, World Bank and Norman Loayza, World Bank Inequality and Violent Crime*, *Journal of Law and Economics*, vol. XLV (April 2002), The University of Chicago; and Walter Scheidel, "The Great Leveler: Violence and the Global History of Inequality from the Stone Age to the Present", Princeton University Press (2014, 2015); and see Mark Buchanan and Mark Whitehouse, "Want to Fight Crime? Address Economic Inequality," Bloomberg, January 6, 2013. http://www.bloombergview.com/articles/2013-01-06/want-to-fight-crime-address-economic-inequality.
795. Lawrence W Sherman and Heather Strang, *Restorative Justice: The Evidence,* Section 3.1, p. 32 (2007).
796. Boyes-Watson, C. (2014). Suffolk University, College of Arts & Sciences, Center for Restorative Justice.

INTERNATIONAL BANKING AND FINANCE LAW SERIES

1. Jan Job de Vries Robbe, *Innovations in Securitisation. Yearbook 2006,* 2006 (ISBN 90-11-2533-7).
2. Jim Bartos, *United States Securities Law: A Practical Guide,* Third edition, 2006 (ISBN 90-411-2362-8).
3. Hui Huang, *International Securities Markets: Insider Trading Law in China,* 2006 (ISBN 90-411-2557-4).
4. Barth et al., *Financial Restructuring and Reform in Post-WTO China,* 2007 (ISBN 90-411-2573-6).
5. Zhongfei Zhou, *Banking Laws in China,* 2007 (ISBN 978-90-411-2519-4).
6. Jan Job de Vries Robbe & Paul Ali, *Expansion and Diversification in Securitization Yearbook 2007,* 2007 (ISBN 978-90-411-2661-0).
7. Ross Buckley, *International Financial System. Policy and Regulation,* 2008 (ISBN 978-90-411-2746-4).
8. Jan Job de Vries Robbe, *Securitization Law and Practice: In the Face of the Credit Crunch,* 2008 (ISBN 978-90-411-2715-0).
9. Phoebus Athanassiou, *Hedge Fund Regulation in the European Union: Current Trends and Future Prospects,* 2009 (ISBN 978-90-411-2856-0).
10. Jan Job de Vries Robbe, *Structured Finance: On from the Credit Crunch: The Road to Recovery,* 2009 (ISBN 978-90-411-2787-7).
11. Gaetane Schaeken Willemaers, *The EU Issuer-Disclosure Regime: Objectives and Proposals for Reform,* 2011 (ISBN 978-90-411-3394-6).
12. Panagiotis Delimatsis & Nils Herger (eds), *Financial Regulation at the Crossroads: Implications for Supervision, Institutional Design and Trade,* 2011 (ISBN 978-90-411-3355-7).
13. Raffaele Scalcione, *The Derivatives Revolution: A Trapped Innovation and a Blueprint for Regulatory Reform,* 2011 (ISBN 978-90-411-3430-1).
14. Douglas Arner & Ross Buckley, *From Crisis to Crisis: The Global Financial System and Regulatory Failure,* 2011 (ISBN 978-90-411-3354-0).
15. Anton P. Trichardt, *Letters of Comfort: A Trans-Systemic Analysis,* 2012 (ISBN 978-90-411-3600-8).
16. Eddy Wymeersch, *Alternative Investment Fund Regulation,* 2012 (ISBN 978-90-411-3690-9).
17. Asif H. Qureshi & Xuan Gao (eds), *International Economic Organizations and Law: The Perspective and Role of the Legal Counsel,* 2012 (ISBN 97890-411-3427-1).
18. Rhys Bollen, *The Law and Regulation of Payment Services: A Comparative Study,* 2012 (ISBN 978-90-411-3818-7).
19. Ramandeep Kaur Chhina, *Standby Letters of Credit in International Trade,* 2012 (ISBN 978-90-411-4560-4).

20. Dirk A. Zetzsche (ed.), *The Alternative Investment Fund Managers Directive: European Regulation of Alternative Investment Funds*, 2012 (ISBN 978-90-411-4044-9).
21. Lorenzo Sasso, *Capital Structure and Corporate Governance: The Role of Hybrid Financial Instruments*, 2013 (ISBN 978-90-411-4843-8).
22. Pablo Iglesias-Rodríguez, *The Accountability of Financial Regulators: A European and International Perspective*, 2013 (ISBN 978-90-411-3874-3).
23. Seraina Neva Grünewald, *The Resolution of Cross-Border Banking Crises in the European Union: A Legal Study from the Perspective of Burden Sharing*, 2014 (ISBN 978-90-411-4909-1).
24. Megan Bowman, *Banking on Climate Change: How Finance Actors and Transnational Regulatory Regimes are Responding*, 2015 (ISBN 978-90-411-5223-7).
25. Jin Sheng, *China's Listed Companies: Conflicts, Governance and Regulation*, 2015 (ISBN 978-90-411-5925-0).
26. Sven Schelo, *Bank Recovery and Resolution*, 2015 (ISBN 978-90-411-4959-6).
27. Luis M. Hinojosa–Martínez & José María Beneyto (eds), *European Banking Union: The New Regime*, 2015 (ISBN 978-90-411-5263-3).
28. Gill North, *Effective Company Disclosure in the Digital Age*, 2015 (ISBN 978-90-411-3815-6).
29. Hanneke Wegman, *Investor Protection: Towards Additional EU Regulation of Investment Funds?*, 2016 (ISBN 978-90-411-5252-7).
30. Ruth Plato-Shinar, *Banking Regulation in Israel: Prudential Regulation versus Consumer Protection*, 2016 (ISBN 978-90-411-6791-0).
31. Bader Alkhaldi, *Saudi Capital Market: Developments and Challenges*, 2017 (ISBN 978-90-411-8351-4).
32. Yves Mauchle, *Bail-In and Total Loss-Absorbing Capacity (TLAC): Legal and Economic Perspectives on Bank Resolution with Functional Comparisons of Swiss and EU Law*, 2017 (ISBN 978-90-411-8998-1).
33. Uzma Ashraf Barton, *Rethinking Regulation of International Finance: Law, Policy and Institutions*, 2018 (ISBN 978-90-411-8838-0).
34. Phoebus L. Athanassiou, *Digital Innovation in Financial Services: Legal Challenges and Regulatory Policy Issues*, 2018 (ISBN 978-90-411-8781-9).
35. Gu Bin, *The Law and Governance of the Asian Infrastructure Investment Bank*, 2019 (ISBN 978-94-035-0631-9).
36. Gerald Nels Olson, *Money, Morality and Law: A Case for Financial Crisis Accountability*, 2019 (ISBN 978-94-035-0941-9).